Notes and Emendations to the Text of Shakespeare's Plays

The Textual Controversy

JOHN PAYNE COLLIER
N.E.S.A. HAMILTON
THOMAS DUFFUS HARDY

CAMBRIDGE
UNIVERSITY PRESS

CAMBRIDGE UNIVERSITY PRESS

Cambridge, New York, Melbourne, Madrid, Cape Town,
Singapore, São Paolo, Delhi, Mexico City

Published in the United States of America by Cambridge University Press, New York

www.cambridge.org
Information on this title: www.cambridge.org/9781108059459

© in this compilation Cambridge University Press 2013

This edition first published 1852–60
This digitally printed version 2013

ISBN 978-1-108-05945-9 Paperback

CAMBRIDGE LIBRARY COLLECTION

Books of enduring scholarly value

Literary Studies

This series provides a high-quality selection of early printings of literary works, textual editions, anthologies and literary criticism which are of lasting scholarly interest. Ranging from Old English to Shakespeare to early twentieth-century work from around the world, these books offer a valuable resource for scholars in reception history, textual editing, and literary studies.

Notes and Emendations to the Text of Shakespeare's Plays

The editor and forger John Payne Collier (1789–1883) claimed to have discovered a Second Folio of Shakespeare which had been 'corrected' in a mid-seventeenth-century hand. He published this catalogue of the emendations, including his commentary on them, in 1852. Collier then presented the so-called 'Perkins Folio' to the Duke of Devonshire, whose successor allowed it to be loaned in 1859 to the British Museum, where a thorough examination exposed it as a forgery. A storm of controversy followed and three of the key documents in the debate, all published in 1860, are also reissued here: 'An Inquiry into the Genuineness of the Manuscript Corrections in Mr. J. Payne Collier's Annotated Shakspere Folio, 1632' by Nicholas Hamilton (d.1915), assistant keeper of manuscripts at the British Museum; Collier's attempt to refute Hamilton's findings; and 'A Review of the Present State of the Shakespearian Controversy' by Thomas Duffus Hardy (1804–78).

NOTES AND EMENDATIONS

TO THE TEXT OF

SHAKESPEARE'S PLAYS,

FROM

EARLY MANUSCRIPT CORRECTIONS IN A
COPY OF THE FOLIO, 1632,

IN THE POSSESSION OF

J. PAYNE COLLIER, ESQ. F.S.A.

FORMING

A SUPPLEMENTAL VOLUME TO THE WORKS OF SHAKESPEARE

BY THE SAME EDITOR,

IN EIGHT VOLUMES, OCTAVO.

LONDON:
PRINTED FOR THE SHAKESPEARE SOCIETY.
1852.

COUNCIL

OF

THE SHAKESPEARE SOCIETY.

President.

THE EARL OF ELLESMERE.

Vice-Presidents.

THE RT. HON. THE EARL OF CLARENDON.

THE RT. HON. THE EARL OF GLENGALL.

THE RT. HON. THE EARL HOWE.

THE RT. HON. LORD BRAYBROOKE.

THE RT. HON. THE LORD JUSTICE SIR JAMES KNIGHT BRUCE.

Council.

WILLIAM AYRTON, ESQ., F.R.S., F.S.A.

BAYLE BERNARD, ESQ.

J. PAYNE COLLIER, ESQ., V.P.S.A., Director.

W. DURRANT COOPER, ESQ., F.S.A.

BOLTON CORNEY, ESQ., M.R.S.L.

PETER CUNNINGHAM, ESQ., F.S.A., Treasurer.

JOHN FORSTER, ESQ.

J. O. HALLIWELL, ESQ., F.R.S., F.S.A.

THE REV. WILLIAM HARNESS.

SWYNFEN JERVIS, ESQ.

CHARLES KNIGHT, ESQ.

DAVID LAING, ESQ.

MARK LEMON, ESQ.

THE HON. GEORGE O'CALLAGHAN.

FREDERIC OUVRY, ESQ., F.S.A.

T. J. PETTIGREW, ESQ., F.R.S., F.S.A.

GEORGE SMITH, ESQ.

WILLIAM JOHN THOMS, ESQ., F.S.A.

BENJAMIN WEBSTER, ESQ.

HIS EXCELLENCY M. SILVAIN VAN DE WEYER.

F. GUEST TOMLINS, ESQ., Secretary.

INTRODUCTION.

In preparing the following sheets it has been a main object with me to give an impartial notion of the singular and interesting volume from which the materials have been derived. It is a copy of the folio of " Mr. William Shakespeare's Comedies, Histories, and Tragedies," which was published in 1632: we need hardly say, that that edition was a reprint of a previous impression in the same form in 1623 ; and that it was again reprinted (with additional plays) in 1664, and for the fourth time in 1685. The reprint of 1632 has, therefore, been usually known as the second folio of the collected plays of Shakespeare.

The singularity and interest of the volume arise out of the fact, that, from the first page to the last, it contains notes and emendations in a hand-writing not much later than the time when it came from the press. Unfortunately it is not perfect: it begins, indeed, with " The Tempest," the earliest drama, but it wants four leaves at the end of " Cymbeline," the latest drama, and there are several deficiencies in the body of the book[1], while all the preliminary matter, consisting of dedication, address, commendatory verses, &c., may be said to be wanting, in as much as it has been

---

[1] It deserves remark that all the defects in the body of the book are in the division of " Histories," the plays forming which have been especially thumbed and maltreated.

supplied by a comparatively recent possessor, from another copy of the second folio, and loosely fastened within the cover.

Without adverting to sundry known mistakes of pagination, it may be stated that the entire volume consists of nearly 900 pages, divided between thirty-six plays; and, besides the correction of literal and verbal errors, as well as lapses of a graver and more extensive kind, the punctuation has been carefully set right throughout. As there is no page without from ten to thirty of these minor emendations, they do not, in the whole, fall short of 20,000: most of them have, of course, been introduced in modern editions, since the plain meaning of a passage often contradicts the old careless and absurd pointing; but it will be seen hereafter, that in not a few instances the sense of the poet has thus been elucidated in a way that has not been anticipated[2]. With regard to changes of a different and more important character, where letters are added or expunged, where words are supplied or struck out, or where lines and sentences, omitted by the early printer, have been inserted, together with all other emendations of a similar kind, it is difficult to form any correct estimate of their number. The volume in the hands of the reader includes considerably more than a thousand of such alterations; but to have inserted all would have swelled its bulk to unreasonable dimensions, and would have wearied the patience of most persons, not merely by the sameness of the information, but by the monotony of the language in which it was necessarily conveyed.

Nothing that was deemed essential has been left out: no striking or valuable emendation has been passed over, and many changes have been mentioned, upon which the writer of the notes seems to have insisted, but in which, in

---

[2] As it is not easy to put the explanation of this apparently trifling matter in a short compass, the reader is referred particularly to pp. 111, 117, 325, 399, and 507.

some cases, concurrence must either be withheld, or doubt expressed. Whenever I have seen ground for dissenting from a proposed amendment, or for giving it only a qualified approbation, I have plainly stated my reasons, more particularly in the later portion of the work : I pursued, indeed, the same method, to a certain extent, in the earlier portion ; but while I have there, perhaps, more sparingly questioned the fitness of adopting some changes, I have also noticed others, which, as I proceeded, and as the matter accumulated, might possibly have been omitted³. If subsequent reflection or information appeared to warrant a modification of opinion, such modification will be found in the notes appended to the volume. I can only expect that each suggested alteration should be judged upon its own merits; and though I can, in no respect, be answerable for more than submitting them to critical decision, I have thought myself called upon, where they appeared to deserve support or elucidation, to offer the facts, arguments, or observations that occurred to me in their favour.

In the history of the volume to which I have been thus indebted, I can offer little that may serve to give it authenticity⁴. It is very certain that the manuscript notes in

³ The old corrector of the folio, 1632, has himself allowed some apparent mistakes to escape him : thus, in " All's Well that Ends Well," Act III. Scene I., we might have expected that he would alter "the younger of our nature" into " the younger of our *nation.*" Again, in " Henry IV. Part II.," Act IV. Scene II., it may seem that " success of mischief " ought to be " *successive* mischief;" but neither of these variations from the old text is absolutely necessary.

⁴ I am by no means convinced that this copy of the folio, 1632, is an entire novelty in the book-world ; but it is quite certain that its curiosity and importance were never till now understood, nor estimated. Sir Thomas Phillipps, Bart., of Middle Hill (the discoverer of the marriage-bond of Shakespeare, who has most readily aided me in my inquiries), recollects to have seen, many years ago, an annotated copy of the folio, 1632, which he has always regretted that he did not purchase ; and since the general contents of my volume became known, several gentlemen appear to be in possession of folios with manuscript emendations. I more than suspect, however, that one of these is the edition of 1685,

its margins were made before it was subjected to all the ill-usage it experienced. When it first came into my hands, and indeed for some time afterwards, I imagined that the binding was the original rough calf in which many books of about the same date were clothed ; but more recent examination has convinced me, that this was at least the second coat it had worn. It is, nevertheless, in a very shabby condition, quite consistent with the state of the interior, where, besides the loss of some leaves, as already mentioned, and the loosening of others, many stains of wine, beer, and other liquids are observable : here and there, holes have been burned in the paper, either by the falling of the lighted snuff of a candle, or by the ashes of tobacco. In several places it is torn and disfigured by blots and dirt, and every margin bears evidence to frequent and careless perusal. In short, to a choice collector, no book could well present a more forbidding appearance.

I was tempted only by its cheapness to buy it, under the following circumstances :—In the spring of 1849 I happened to be in the shop of the late Mr. Rodd, of Great Newport-street, at the time when a package of books arrived from the country : my impression is that it came from Bedford-shire, but I am not at all certain upon a point which I looked upon as a matter of no importance. He opened the parcel in my presence, as he had often done before in the course of my thirty or forty years' acquaintance with him, and looking at the backs and title-pages of several volumes, I saw that they were chiefly works of little interest to me. Two folios, however, attracted my attention, one of them gilt on the sides, and the other in rough calf: the first was an excellent copy of Florio's " New World of Words," 1611, with the name of Henry Osborn (whom I mistook at the moment

formerly the property of the poet Southerne, with his autograph upon the title-page: of the notes it contains I was able, by the kindness of the then proprietor, to avail myself, when formerly editing the Shakespeare to which the present work is a Supplement.

for his celebrated namesake, Francis) upon the first leaf; and the other a copy of the second folio of Shakespeare's Plays, much cropped, the covers old and greasy, and, as I saw at a glance on opening them, imperfect at the beginning and end. Concluding hastily that the latter would complete another poor copy of the second folio, which I had bought of the same bookseller, and which I had had for some years in my possession, and wanting the former for my use, I bought them both, the Florio for twelve, and the Shakespeare for thirty shillings[5].

As it turned out, I at first repented my bargain as regarded the Shakespeare, because, when I took it home, it appeared that two leaves which I wanted were unfit for my purpose, not merely by being too short, but damaged and defaced: thus disappointed, I threw it by, and did not see it again, until I made a selection of books I would take with me on quitting London. In the mean time, finding that I could not readily remedy the deficiencies in my other copy of the folio, 1632, I had parted with it; and when I removed into the country, with my family, in the spring of 1850, in order that I might not be without some copy of the second folio for the purpose of reference, I took with me that which is the foundation of the present work.

It was while putting my books together for removal, that I first observed some marks in the margin of this folio; but it was subsequently placed upon an upper shelf, and I did

[5] I paid the money for them at the time. Mr. Wilkinson, of Wellington-street, one of Mr. Rodd's executors, has several times obligingly afforded me the opportunity of inspecting Mr. Rodd's account-books, in order, if possible, to trace from whence the package came, but without success. Mr. Rodd does not appear to have kept any stock-book, showing how and when volumes came into his hands, and the entries in his day-book and ledger are not regular nor particular: his latest memorandum, on 19th April, only a short time before his sudden death, records the sale of "three books," without specifying their titles, or giving the name of the purchaser. His memory was very faithful, and to that, doubtless, he often trusted. I am confident that the parcel was from the country; but any inquiries, regarding sales there, could hardly be expected to be satisfactorily answered.

not take it down until I had occasion to consult it. It then struck me that Thomas Perkins, whose name, with the addition of "his Booke," was upon the cover, might be the old actor who had performed in Marlowe's "Jew of Malta," on its revival shortly before 1633. At this time I fancied that the binding was of about that date, and that the volume might have been his; but in the first place, I found that his name was Richard Perkins, and in the next I became satisfied that the rough calf was not the original binding. Still, Thomas Perkins might have been a descendant of Richard; and this circumstance and others induced me to examine the volume more particularly: I then discovered, to my surprise, that there was hardly a page which did not present, in a handwriting of the time, some emendations in the pointing or in the text, while on most of them they were frequent, and on many numerous.

Of course I now submitted the folio to a most careful scrutiny; and as it occupied a considerable time to complete the inspection, how much more must it have consumed to make the alterations? The ink was of various shades, differing sometimes on the same page, and I was once disposed to think that two distinct hands had been employed upon them: this notion I have since abandoned; and I am now decidedly of opinion that the same writing prevails from beginning to end, but that the amendments must have been introduced from time to time, during, perhaps, the course of several years. The changes in punctuation alone, always made with nicety and patience, must have required a long period, considering their number; the other alterations, sometimes most minute, extending even to turned letters and typographical trifles of that kind, from their very nature could not have been introduced with rapidity, while many of the errata must have severely tasked the industry of the old corrector[6].

[6] It ought to be mentioned, in reference to the question of the authority of the emendations, that some of them are upon erasures, as if the cor-

Then comes the question, why any of them were made, and why such extraordinary pains were bestowed on this particular copy of the folio, 1632 ? To this inquiry no complete reply, that I am aware of, can be given ; but some circumstances can be stated, which may tend to a partial solution of the difficulty.

Corrections only have been hitherto spoken of ; but there are at least two other very peculiar features in the volume. Many passages, in nearly all the plays, are struck out with a pen, as if for the purpose of shortening the performance[7] ; and we need not feel much hesitation in coming to the conclusion, that these omissions had reference to the representation of the plays by some company about the date of the folio, 1632. To this fact we may add, that hundreds of stage-directions have been inserted in manuscript, as if for the guidance and instruction of actors, in order that no mistake might be made in what is usually denominated stage-business[8]. It is known that in this respect the old printed copies are very deficient[9]; and sometimes the written additions of this kind seem even more frequent, and more

rector had either altered his mind as to particular changes, or had obliterated something that had been written before—possibly, by some person not so well informed as himself.

[7] "Antony and Cleopatra" is the only drama that is entirely exempt from this treatment : possibly, the old corrector never witnessed the performance of it. In all the other plays, more or less is "cut out," generally, it should seem, in proportion to popularity.

[8] In a few cases these manuscript stage-directions are of the highest importance in illustrating the wonderful judgment and skill of Shakespeare in conducting the business of his scenes. This matter cannot well be explained in the compass of a note; but if the reader will turn to p. 5, it will be seen of what consequence the mere words, *Put on robe again*, are to understanding in what way the sudden somnolency of Miranda, which has always excited remark, had been produced, and was to be accounted for. It would be easy to point out other instances, but they will occur in the course of the volume.

[9] There is, I think, but one printed note of *aside* in the whole of the six-and-thirty plays; but in manuscript the utmost care is taken so to mark all speeches intended to be heard by the audience, but not by the characters engaged in the scene.

explicit, than might be thought necessary. The erasures of passages and scenes are quite inconsistent with the notion that a new edition of the folio, 1632, was contemplated; and how are they, and the new stage-directions, and "asides," to be accounted for, excepting on the supposition that the volume once belonged to a person interested in, or connected with, one of our early theatres? The continuation of the corrections and emendations, in spite of, and through the erasures, may show that they were done at a different time, and by a different person; but who shall say which was done first, or whether both were not, in fact, the work of the same hand[1]?

Passing by these matters, upon which we can arrive at no certain result, we must briefly advert to another point upon which, however, we are quite as much in the dark :—we mean the authority upon which these changes, of greater or of less importance, were introduced. How are we warranted in giving credit to any of them?

The first and best answer seems to be that which one of the most acute of the commentators applied to an avowedly conjectural emendation—that it required no authority—that it carried conviction on the very face of it[2]. Many of the most valuable corrections of Shakespeare's text are, in truth, self-evident; and so apparent, when once suggested, that it seems wonderful how the plays could have passed through the hands of men of such learning and critical acumen, during the last century and a half (to say nothing of the period occupied by the publication of the four folios), without the detection of such indisputable blunders. Let us take an instance from "The Taming of the Shrew," Act I. Scene I., where Lucentio, arriving in Padua, to read

[1] Some expressions and lines of an irreligious or indelicate character are also struck out, evincing, perhaps, the advance of a better, or purer, taste about the period when the emendator went over the volume.

[2] Monk Mason, in a note upon "Troilus and Cressida," Act III. Scene III.; which, however, was there singularly inapt.

at the university, Tranio, his man, entreats his master not to
apply himself too severely to study :—

> "Only, good master, while we do admire
> This virtue, and this moral discipline,
> Let's be no stoics, nor no stocks, I pray,
> Or so devote to Aristotle's checks,
> As Ovid be an outcast quite abjur'd."

Such has been the invariable text from the first publication
of the comedy, in 1623, until our own day; yet it is unquestionably wrong, and wrong in the most important word
in the quotation, as the old corrector shows, and as the
reader will be sure to acknowledge the moment the emendation is proposed :—

> "Let's be no stoics, nor no stocks, I pray,
> Or so devote to Aristotle's *Ethics,*
> As Ovid be an outcast quite abjur'd."

In the manuscript, from which the old printer worked, *Ethics*
was, no doubt, written with a small letter, and with *ke* near
the end of the word, as was then the custom, and the careless compositor mistook *ethickes* for "checkes," and so printed
it: "checkes" is converted into *ethickes* in the hand-writing
of the emendator of the folio, 1632; and it is hardly too
much to say that this misprint can never be repeated.

Another proof of the same kind, but perhaps even stronger,
may be taken from "Coriolanus," Act II. Scene III. It
relates to a word which has puzzled all editors, and yet
ought not to have delayed them for a moment, the corruption, when pointed out by an emendation in the folio, 1632,
being so glaring. The hero, disdainfully soliciting the "sweet
voices" of the plebeians, asks himself,—

> "Why in this woolvish toge should I stand here,
> To beg of Hob and Dick?"

Johnson says that "woolvish" is *rough, hirsute;* and Malone,
Steevens, Ritson, Douce, &c., have all notes regarding wolves
(as if wild beasts had any thing to do with the matter), and

all erroneous, but Johnson's the most unfortunate, because it has been previously stated that the "toge" (or gown) was not *hirsute*, but absolutely "napless." It seems astonishing, on this very account, that the right word was never guessed, as it is found in the margin of my volume:—

> " Why in this *woolless* toge should I stand here,
>   To beg of Hob and Dick?"

Can there be an instant's hesitation about it ? The printer, or the scribe who wrote the copy used by the printer, mistook the termination of the word, and "woolvish" has been eternally reiterated as the real language of the poet. It seems impossible that "woolvish" should ever hereafter find a single supporter.

Other verbal amendments are restorations of words that were becoming somewhat obsolete in the time of Shakespeare, such as *bisson*, blind, *blead*, fruit, &c; but there is one instance of the sort so remarkable, that I cannot refuse to notice it here. It regards the expression " a woollen bagpipe," in " The Merchant of ˜enice," Act IV. Scene I. ; and it must appear strange that "woolless" in one play, and " woollen" in another, should have formed such hard and insuperable stumbling-blocks to all the commentators. When Shylock observes,

> " As there is no firm reason to be render'd,
>   Why he cannot abide a gaping pig,
>   Why he a harmless necessary cat,
>   Why he a woollen bagpipe," &c.

ingenuity has been exhausted to explain, or to explain away, the epithet " woollen," as applied to a bagpipe. Some would have it *wooden*, others *swollen*, and a third party (myself among the number) were for adhering, in a case of such difficulty, to the text of the old editions. What turns out to be the fact ? that every body was in error, and that our great dramatist employed an old word, which he had already used in his " Lucrece," 1594, and which means swollen, viz.

bollen : it is the participle of the verb *bolne,* "to become puffed up or swollen," as Sir F. Madden states, in his excellent "Glossary to the Wycliffite Versions of the Bible." *Bollen* is spelt in various ways by old and modern lexicographers ; but we may be confident that we shall never again see "woollen bagpipe" in any edition of the text of Shakespeare, unless it be reproduced by some one, who, having no right to use the emendation of our folio, 1632, adheres of necessity to the antiquated blunder, and pertinaciously attempts to justify it.

By the mention of the scribe, or copyist, who wrote the manuscript from which the printer composed, we are brought to the consideration of another class of errors, for which, probably, the typographer was not responsible. If there be one point more clear than another, in connexion with the text of Shakespeare as it has come down to us, it is that the person, or persons, who prepared the transcripts of the plays for the printer, wrote by the ear, and not by the eye : they heard the dialogue, and wrote it down as it struck them. This position has been completely established by Malone[3]; and only in this way can we explain many of the whimsical mistakes in the quartos and folios. It is very well known that associations of actors, who bought dramas of their authors, were at all times extremely averse to the publication of them, partly under the persuasion that the number of readers would diminish the number of auditors[4]. The managers and sharers did their utmost to prevent the appearance of plays in print ; and it is the surreptitious manner in which pieces got out to the public that will account for the especial imperfectness, in respect to typography, of this department of our early literature. About half the productions of Shakespeare remained in manuscript until seven years after his death : not a few of

---

[3] See Malone's Shakespeare, by Boswell, vii. p. 36 ; xi. p. 422 ; xii. pp. 268, 287, 313 ; xiv. p. 26 ; xix. p. 472, &c.

[4] Another reason, of course, was the apprehension lest rival companies, then under very lax control, might act the piece.

those which were printed in his life-time were shamefully
disfigured, and not one can be pointed out to the publication
of which he in any way contributed. When he finally retired to Stratford-upon-Avon, we cannot find that he took the
slightest interest in works which had delighted living thousands, and were destined to be the admiration of unborn
millions: he considered them the property of the theatre
for which they had been written, and doubtless conceived
that they were beyond his control.

If, therefore, popular dramas did make their way to the
press, it was generally accomplished either by the employment of shorthand writers, who imperfectly took down the
words as they indistinctly heard them, or by theconniv-
ance and aid of inferior performers, who, being "hirelings" at
weekly wages, had no direct interest in the receipts at the
doors. They may have furnished the booksellers with such
parts as they sustained, or could in any way procure from the
theatre; and it is not unlikely that, listening, as they must
have daily done, to the repetitions of the principal actors, they
would be able to recite, with more or less accuracy, whole
speeches, and even scenes, which a little ingenuity could com-
bine into a drama. We may readily imagine, that what these
inferior performers had thus got by heart, they might dictate
to some mechanical copyist, and thus many words, and even
sentences, which sounded like something else, would be misrepresented in the printed editions, and nobody take the
pains to correct the blunders. Of course, those who were
sharers in theatres would be the last to remedy defects;
and in this way oral representations on our early stages,
by the chief actors, might easily be more correct than the
published copies of performances.

Upon this supposition we must account for not a few of the
remarkable manuscript emendations in my folio, 1632: the
annotator of that volume may have been connected with one
of our old play-houses; he may have been a manager, or a
member of a company, and as an admirer of Shakespeare, as

well as for his own theatrical purposes, he may have taken the trouble, from time to time, to set right errors in the printed text by the more faithful delivery of their parts by the principal actors. This might have been accomplished by him as a mere spectator, and he may have employed the edition nearest his own day as the receptacle of his notes; he may, however, have been aided by the prompt-books; and the whole appearance of our volume seems to afford evidence that the work of correction was not done speedily, nor continuously, but as the misprints became apparent, and the means of correcting them occurred. Thus a long interval may have elapsed before this copy of the second folio was brought to the state in which it has reached us.

An example or two will suffice to make what is meant intelligible; and here, as in former instances, I take them from many, almost at random, for the real difficulty is selection. When Henry VIII. (Act III. Scene II.) tells Wolsey,—

> " You have scarce time
> To steal from spiritual leisure a brief span,
> To keep your earthly audit;"

he cannot mean that the Cardinal has scarcely time to steal from "leisure," but from *labour:* the word was misheard by the scribe; and while " leisure" makes nonsense of the sentence, *labour* is exactly adapted to the place:—

> " You have scarce time
> To steal from spiritual *labour* a brief span."

The substituted word is found in the margin of the folio, 1632. This instance seems indisputable; but we meet with a more striking proof of the same kind in " King Lear" (Act IV. Scene VII.), where, after he has read Goneril's letter of love to Edmund and hate to her husband, Edgar exclaims, as the poet's language has been represented,

> " O, undistinguish'd space of woman's will!
> A plot upon her virtuous husband's life."

The commentators have striven hard to extract sense from the first line, but not one of them satisfied another, nor indeed themselves. Edgar, in truth, is shocked at the profligate and uncontrollable licentiousness of Goneril:—

" O *unextinguish'd blaze* of woman's will!' "

in other words, desire (*i. e.* "will" or lust) in the female sex bursts forth in a flame that cannot be subdued. The scribe did not understand what he put upon paper, misheard *unextinguish'd blaze*, and wrote "undistinguish'd space." Such was, probably, the origin of the hitherto received nonsense.

Another brief and laughable proof may be adduced from "Coriolanus:" it is where Menenius, in Act II. Scene I., is talking of himself to the Tribunes:—"I am known" (he says in all editions, ancient and modern) "to be a humorous patrician, and one that loves a cup of hot wine, with not a drop of allaying Tyber in it; said to be something imperfect in favouring the first complaint." Nobody has offered a note explanatory of "the first complaint," and it has always passed current as the language of Shakespeare. Is it so? Assuredly not; for what has "a cup of hot wine" to do with "the first complaint?" The old corrector calls upon us to read "a cup of hot wine, with not a drop of allaying Tyber in it; said to be something imperfect in favouring the *thirst* complaint," and the utterly lost humour of the passage is at once restored. The scribe misheard *thirst*, and wrote "first;" and the blunder has already lasted between two and three centuries, and might have lasted two or three centuries longer, but for the discovery of this corrected folio.

It is to be observed that these last emendations apply to plays which were printed for the first time in the folio, 1623. This fact tends to prove that the manuscript, put into the hands of the printer by Heminge and Condell, in spite of what they say, was not in a much better condition than the manuscript used by stationers for the separate plays which they had previously contrived to publish. The effect of the ensuing pages must be considerably to lessen our confidence in the text furnished by the player-editors, for the integrity of which I, among others, have always strenuously contended. Consequently, I ought to be among the last to admit the validity of objections to it; and it was not until after long examination of the proposed alterations, that I was compelled to allow their general accuracy and importance. There are some that I can yet by no means persuade myself to adopt; others to which I can only give a qualified approbation; but still a large remainder from which I am utterly unable to dissent[5].

It was, as may be inferred, very little, if at all, the habit of dramatic authors, in the time of Shakespeare, to correct the proofs of their productions; and as we know that, in respect to the plays which had been published in quarto before 1623, all that Heminge and Condell did, was to put the latest edition into the hands of their printer, so, possibly, in respect to the plays which for the first time appeared in the folio, 1623, all that they did might be to put the manuscript, such as it was, into the hands of their printer, and to leave to him the whole process of typography. It is not at all unlikely that they borrowed playhouse copies to aid them; but these might consist, sometimes at least, of the separate parts allotted to the different actors, and, for the sake of speed in so long a work, scribes might be employed, to whom the manuscript was read

---

[5] Some of the most interesting, if not the most curious emendations, apply not only to the songs by Shakespeare, introduced into various plays, but to the scraps of ballads and popular rhymes put into the mouths of many of his characters. Nearly all these, especially the latter, are corrected, and in some places completed; for it is not difficult to imagine that, even if originally accurately quoted, corruptions in the course of time, by the licence of comic performers and other causes, crept into them. These manuscript restorations are so frequent, that it is out of the question to enumerate them, but they apply to nearly every play; and in addition it may be noticed, that whenever the poet borrows any thing, it is invariably underscored by the old corrector: thus several quotations, not hitherto suspected to be such, are clearly indicated; and, as a singular specimen, we may point to the conclusion of "Troilus and Cressida," where Pandarus cites four lines, not hitherto suspected to have been written by any other author.

as they proceeded with their transcripts. This supposition, and the fraudulent manner in which plays in general found their way into print, may account for many of the blunders they unquestionably contain in the folios, and especially for the strange confusion of verse and prose which they sometimes exhibit. The not unfrequent errors in prefixes, by which words or lines are assigned to one character, which certainly belong to another, may thus also be explained: the reader of the drama to the scribe did not at all times accurately distinguish the persons engaged in the dialogue; and if he had only the separate parts, and what are technically called the *cues*, to guide him, we need not be surprised at the circumstance. The following is a single proof, the first that occurs to memory: it is from "Romeo and Juliet," Act III. Scene V., where the heroine declares to her mother that, if she must marry, her husband shall be Romeo:—

> " And when I do, I swear,
> It shall be Romeo, whom you know I hate,
> Rather than Paris.—These are news indeed!"

This is the universal regulation; but, as we may very well believe, the closing words, "These are news, indeed!" do not belong to Juliet, but to Lady Capulet, who thus expresses her astonishment at her daughter's resolution: therefore, her speech ought to begin earlier than it appears in any extant copy. Juliet ends,—

> " And when I do, I swear,
> It shall be Romeo, whom you know I hate,
> Rather than Paris.
> *La. Cap.*   These are news, indeed!
> Here comes your father; tell him so yourself,
> And see how he will take it at your hands."

There cannot surely be any dispute that this is the mode in which the poet distributed the lines, and in which the old corrector of the folio, 1632, had heard the dialogue divided on the stage in his time.

It has been stated that he did not pass over minute

changes, sometimes of most trifling consequence; but it is obvious that alterations, very insignificant in appearance, may be of the utmost importance in effect. A single letter, wrongly inserted, may strangely pervert or obscure the meaning; and it may never have been suspected that the early editions were in fault. We meet with a remarkable instance of it in "Macbeth," Act I. Scene VII., where the Lady is reproaching her irresolute husband for not being ready to murder Duncan when time and opportunity offered, although he had previously vaunted his determination to do it: she asks him,—

> " What beast was't, then,
> That made you break this enterprise to me?
> When you durst do it, then you were a man."

Such is the text as it has always been recited on modern stages, and printed in every copy of the tragedy from the year 1623 to the year 1853; yet that there is a most singular misprint in it will be manifest, when the small, but most valuable, manuscript emendation of the folio, 1632, is mentioned. In truth, Lady Macbeth does not ask her husband the absurd question, "what beast" made him communicate the enterprise to her? but, what induced him to vaunt that he would kill Duncan, and then, like a coward, shrink from his own resolution?—

> " What *boast* was't, then,
> That made you break this enterprise to me?
> When you durst do it, then you were a man."

She taunts him with the braggart spirit he had at first displayed, and the cowardice he had afterwards evinced. It cannot be denied by the most scrupulous stickler for the purity of the text of the folio, 1623 (copied into the folio, 1632), that this mere substitution of the letter *o* for the letter *e*, as it were, magically conjures into palpable existence the long-buried meaning of the poet

In another place, and in another play, the accidental

a 2

omission of a single letter has occasioned much doubt and
discussion. In Act III. Scene I. of "The Tempest," Ferdinand, while engaged in carrying logs, rejoices in his toil,
because his burdens are lightened by thoughts of Miranda :—

> " This my mean task
> Would be as heavy to me, as odious ; but
> The mistress which I serve quickens what's dead,
> And makes my labours pleasures ; "

and he afterwards adds, as the passage is given in the folio,
1623 :—

> " But these sweet thoughts do even refresh my labours,
> Most busy lest when I do it."

The folio, 1632, altered the hemistich to "Most busy *least*
when I do it," and Theobald read " Most *busiless* when I do
it," not understanding how Ferdinand, at the same moment,
could be most busy, and least busy. The corrector of the
folio, 1632, however, removes the whole difficulty by showing
that in the folio, 1623, a letter had dropped out in the press,
the addition of which makes the sense clear and consistent,
and concludes the speech by a most felicitous compression of
the sentiment of the whole in seven words :—

> " But these sweet thoughts do even refresh my labours ;
> Most busy,—*blest* when I do it :"

that is to say, he was most laboriously employed, but *blest* in
that very toil by the sweet thoughts of his mistress. The
old corrector converted "least," of the folio, 1632, into *blest*,
by striking out *a*, and by inserting *b* with a caret.

The constantly recurring question in all these cases is,
from whence the information was derived, which enabled a
person, so frequently and so effectually, to give us what, by
implication, he asserts to be the real language of the greatest
poet of mankind ? Was he in a condition to resort to other
and better manuscripts ? Had he the use of printed copies
which do not now remain to us ? Was he instructed by more
accurate recitation at a theatre ? Was he indebted to his

own sagacity and ingenuity, and did he merely guess at arbitrary emendations? I am inclined to think that the last must have been the fact as regards some of his changes; and, so far, his suggestions are only to be taken as those of an individual, who lived, we may suppose, not very long after the period when the dramas he elucidates were written, and who might have had intercourse with some of the actors of Shakespeare's day. As to this, and other sources of his knowledge, all we can do is to speculate[6].

There is a class of emendations, not yet adverted to, even more convincing, than the happiest alterations we have already noticed, that the old corrector must have had recourse to some not now extant authority. Malone contended that lines, in the old editions, were more frequently omitted than ordinary readers were disposed to believe; and he might well so argue, seeing that in his own text, as we last receive it in the Variorum Edition of 1821[7], no fewer than three entire lines are left out in three separate plays; while those who have been content to reprint that text have not discovered the deficiencies[8]. No wonder, then, if

[6] We have not spoken of another circumstance which ought to be taken into account. About one-fifth of the plays in the folios are not divided into acts and scenes; but in this corrected folio, 1632, the omissions are supplied. In many instances the divisions there made do not accord with those in modern impressions: and in some the old printed divisions are struck out, and others substituted—perhaps, such as prevailed about the time when the second folio was published. This fact may tend farther to show, that the early possessor of the volume was in some way concerned in dramatic representations.

[7] As it comprises the notes of all editors and commentators, from Rowe to Malone, it may be as well to state that it is the impression used hereafter, when speaking of their remarks and suggestions. If, in any instance, I have not stated that a proposed emendation has been previously suggested, it has arisen from my ignorance of the fact, or from pure inadvertence. In many cases the older conjectures of Theobald, Warburton, Pope, Hanmer, &c., are remarkably confirmed.

[8] See Malone's Shakespeare, by Boswell, v. 479, xiii. 91, xxi. 272. The imperfections may be supplied by referring to the corresponding portions of the plays in the edition published by Messrs. Whittaker and Co. in 1844, 8 vols. 8vo.

the old editors and printers, who made no professions of peculiar care and accuracy, were guilty of similar mistakes, and that several of them should have remained undetected to our own day. They are indicated in the folio, 1632, and are written in the margin for insertion in the proper places.

To say nothing of words, sometimes two, three, and four together, which are wanting in the folios, and are supplied in manuscript, to the improvement both of meaning and measure, there are at least nine different places where lines appear to have been left out. From what source could these have been derived, if not from some more perfect copies, or from more faithful recitation? However we may be willing to depreciate other emendations, and to maintain that they were only the results of bold, but happy speculation—the *feliciter audentia* of conjecture—how can we account for the recovery of nine distinct lines, most exactly adapted to the situations where they are inserted, excepting upon the supposition that they proceeded from the pen of the poet, and have been preserved by the curious accuracy of an individual, almost a contemporary, who, in some way, possessed the means of supplying them[9]?

In certain cases the absence of a corresponding line, in a rhyming speech, affords evidence that words terminating with the required jingle have been lost. Are we prepared to say that the old corrector, noting the want, has, of his own head, and out of his own head, forged and furnished it, making it also entirely consistent with what precedes and follows? When, in "Henry VI. Part II." Act II. Scene III., Queen Margaret calls upon Gloster to relinquish his staff of

---

[9] A few words, occurring in certain of the emendations, may be thought to be of rather a more modern stamp than the time of Shakespeare—such as "struggling," "wheedling," "generous," "exhibit," &c. It is not impossible, however, that they were in earlier use than our lexicographers represent; nor is it unlikely that in some cases the old corrector's merely conjectural emendations (supposing them to deserve that character) were coloured by the language of his own later day. Our tongue had then undergone some material changes.

office to her son, the Protector, addressing the young king, exclaims,—

> "My staff? here, noble Henry, is my staff:
> *To think I fain would keep it makes me laugh;*
> As willingly I do the same resign,
> As e'er thy father Henry made it mine."

The line in Italic type is met with in no old copy, but when we find it in a hand-writing of about the time ; when we see that something has so evidently been lost, and that what is offered is so nicely dovetailed into the place assigned to it, can we take upon ourselves to assert that it was foisted in without necessity or authority ? On the contrary, ought we not to welcome it with thankfulness, as a fortunate recovery, and a valuable restoration ?

In several instances, it is easy, on other grounds, to understand how the blunders were occasioned. In more than one of those places, where Malone was himself guilty of omissions of the sort, two consecutive lines ended with the same word, and the modern printer missed one of them, thinking that he had already composed it. Such was, doubtless, the predicament of the ancient printer ; and we may quote a remarkable proof of the fact from " Coriolanus," that worst specimen of typography in the whole folio. In Act III. Scene II., Volumnia thus entreats her indignant and impetuous son to be patient :—

> " Pray be counsell'd.
> I have a heart as little apt as yours,
> But yet a brain, that leads my use of anger
> To better vantage."

To what is Volumnia's heart as little apt as that of Coriolanus ? She does not tell us, and the sense is undeniably incomplete; but it is thus completed in the folio, 1632, by the addition of a lost line :—

> " Pray be counsell'd.
> I have a heart as little apt as yours

To brook control without the use of anger,
But yet a brain, that leads my use of anger
To better vantage."

It seems impossible to doubt the genuineness of this insertion, unless we go the length of pronouncing it not only an
invention, but an invention of the utmost ingenuity; for
while it renders perfect the deficient sense, it shows at once
what caused the error: the recurrence of the same words,
"use of anger," at the end of two following lines, deceived
the old compositor, and induced him to fancy that he had
already printed a line, which he had excluded.

Are we not entitled, then, to consider this copy of the
folio, 1632, an addition to our scanty means of restoring and
amending the text of Shakespeare, as important as it is unexpected? If it had contained no more than the comparatively few points to which we have adverted in this Introduction, would it not have rendered an almost inappreciable
service to our literature, and to Shakespeare as the great
example of every species of dramatic excellence? It strikes
me as an impossible supposition, that such as these were
purely conjectural and arbitrary changes; and it follows
as a question, upon which I shall not now enlarge, how far
such indisputable emendations and apposite additions warrant us in imputing to a higher authority, than we might
otherwise be inclined to acknowledge, some of the more
doubtful alterations recorded in the ensuing pages.

In order to give the reader an exact notion of the handwriting of the old corrector, and of his businesslike method
of annotation, a facsimile has been prefixed, which faithfully
represents the original. In this place the ink seems uniform,
but our choice has been influenced, not so much by the
worth of the play, or by the value of the emendations, as by
the circumstance that it includes, in the compass of an
octavo page, examples of the manner in which corrections of
nearly all kinds are made, from the insertion of a single

letter to the addition of a line, omitted in all the folios, together with the striking out of a passage not considered necessary for the performance[1].

It will be remarked, from the title-page, that the present volume is supplemental to the edition of Shakespeare's Works I formerly superintended. It was there my leading principle to adhere to the old quartos and folios, wherever sense could be made out of the words they furnished: that they were wrong, in many more places than I suspected, will now be evident; but I allowed myself no room for speculative emendation, even where it seemed most called for. Had the copy of the folio, 1632, the authority for nearly all that follows, devolved into my hands anterior to the commencement of that undertaking, the result would have been in many important respects different: as it is, those volumes will remain an authentic representation of the text of our great dramatist, as it is contained in the early editions; and all who wish to ascertain the new readings proposed in the present work, will have the means of doing so without disturbing the ancient, and hitherto generally received, language of Shakespeare.

It will, I hope, be clear from what precedes, that I have been anxious rather to underrate, than to overstate the claims of this annotated copy of the folio, 1632. I ought not, however, to hesitate in avowing my conviction, that we

---

[1] It also explains the mode in which the corrector proceeded, when the division of a new scene had been improperly introduced in the old copy; for the erasure of *Actus Quintus, Scœna Prima*, and the insertion of *same* in manuscript mean, that what follows is merely a continuation of a preceding scene. The word *briefely*, lower down in the margin, exactly illustrates the way in which, by the non-crossing of the letter *f*, it was frequently mistaken for the long *s*: of course in this case no such blunder could be made. Those who were present on any of the four occasions, last year, when this volume was exhibited before the Shakespeare Society and the Society of Antiquaries, had an opportunity of observing all these peculiarities on other pages. It has been separately shown to many who wished to see the character of the alterations.

are bound to admit by far the greater body of the substitutions it contains, as the restored language of Shakespeare. As he was especially the poet of common life, so he was emphatically the poet of common sense; and to the verdict of common sense I am willing to submit all the more material alterations recommended on the authority before me. If they will not bear that test, as distinguished from mere verbal accuracy in following old printed copies, I, for one, am content to relinquish them. Hitherto the quartos and folios have been our best and safest guides; but it is notorious that in many instances they must be wrong; and while, in various places, the old corrector does not attempt to set them right, probably from not possessing the means of doing so, the very fact, that he has here refrained from purely arbitrary changes, ought to give us additional confidence in those emendations he felt authorized to introduce.

I shall probably be told, in the usual terms, by some whose prejudices or interests may be affected by the ensuing volume, that the old corrector knew little about the spirit or language of Shakespeare; and that, in the remarks I have ventured on his emendations, I prove myself to be in a similar predicament. The last accusation is probably true: I have read and studied our great dramatist for nearly half a century, and if I could read and study him for half a century more, I should yet be far from arriving at an accurate knowledge of his works, or an adequate appreciation of his worth. He is an author whom no man can read enough, nor study enough; and as my ambition always has been to understand him properly, and to estimate him sufficiently, I shall accept, in whatever terms reproof may be conveyed, any just correction thankfully.

J. P. C.

CONTENTS.

Enter Charles, Alanson, Burgundie, Baſtard,
and Pucell.

Char. Had Yorke and Somerſet brought reſcue in,
We ſhould have found a bloody day of this.
Baſt. How the yong whelpe of _Talbots_ raging wood,
Did fleſh his puny-ſword in Frenchmens blood.
Puc. Once I encountred him, and thus I ſaid:
Thou Maiden youth, be vanquiſht by a Maide.
But with a provd Majeſticall high ſcorne _So maſhing in_
He anſwer'd thus: Yong _Talbot_ was not borne _igottow lt_
To be the pillage of a Giglot Wench, _of the horning_
He left me proudly, as unworthy fight.
Bur. Doubtleſſe he would have made a noble Knight:
See where he lyes inherced in the armes
Of the ~~moſt bloody~~ Nurſſer of his harmes. _ſtill blooding_
Baſt. Hew them to peeces, hack their bones aſſunder,
Whoſe life was Englands glory, Gallia's wonder.
Char. Oh no forbeare: For that which we have fled
During the life, let us not Wrong it dead.
Enter Lucy. ~~and heraunt~~
_Lu._ Herald, conduct me to the Dolphins Tent,
To know who hath ~~obtain'd~~ the glory of the day.
Char. On what ſubmiſſive meſſage art thou ſent?
Lucy. Submiſſion Dolphin? Tis a meere French word:
We Engliſh Warriours wot not what it meanes.
I come to know what Priſoners thou haſt tane,
And to ſurvey the bodies of the dead.
Char. For priſoners askſt thou? Hell our priſon is.
But tell me whom thou ſeek'ſt? _e now_
Luc. But where's the great Alcides of the field,
Valiant Lord _Talbot_ Earle of Shrewsbury?
Created for his rare ſucceſſe in Armes,
~~Great Earle of Waſhford, Waterford, and Valence,~~
Lord _Talbot_ of _Goodrig_ and _Vrchinfield_,
Lord _Strange_ of _Blackmere_, Lord _Verdon_ of _Alton_,
Lord _Cromwell_ of _Wingefield_, Lord _Furnivall_ of _Sheffeild_,
~~The thrice victorious Lord of Falconbridge,~~
Knight of the Noble Order of S. _George_,
Worthy S. _Michael_, and the _Golden Fleece_,
Great Marſhall to our King _Henry_ the ſixt,
Of all his Warres within the Realme of France.

briefly

THE TEMPEST.

ACT I. SCENE I.

P. 9. THE introductory stage-direction in the old folios, especially with the manuscript addition in that of 1632 (which we have marked in Italics), is striking and picturesque :—

"A tempestuous noise of thunder and lightning heard : Enter a Ship-master, and a Boatswain, *as on shipboard, shaking off wet.*"

In Malone's Shakespeare, by Boswell, (vol. xv. p. 19), it stands only,—"A storm with thunder and lightning. Enter a Ship-master and Boatswain;" but, from the corrected folio, 1632, it appears that the two actors who began the play entered as if on deck, shaking the rain and spray from their garments as they spoke, and thus giving an additional appearance of reality to the scene. "Enter Mariners, wet," occurs soon afterwards, and we are left to conclude that they showed the state of their dress in the same way, but we are not told so, either in print or in manuscript. Alonso, Sebastian, Antonio, Ferdinand, Gonzalo, and the rest, come up *From the cabin,* (a part of the direction also supplied in manuscript, in the folio, 1632,) meaning, no doubt, that they ascended from under the stage, and are consequently supposed not to be in the same dripping condition.

P. 9.

"*Alon.* Good boatswain, have care."

It may be just worth remark, that the colloquial expression is, "Have *a* care;" and *a* is inserted in the margin of the corrected folio, 1632, to indicate, probably, that the poet so wrote it, or, at all events, that the actor so delivered it.

B

SCENE II.

P. 12. The reading of all editions has been this :—

> "The sky, it seems, would pour down stinking pitch,
> But that the sea, mounting to the welkin's cheek,
> Dashes the fire out."

The manuscript corrector of the folio, 1632, has substituted *heat* for "cheek," which is not an unlikely corruption by a person writing only by the ear. The welkin's *heat* was occasioned by the flaming pitch, but the fire was dashed out by the fury of the waves. The firing of the "welkin's cheek" seems a forced image ; but, nevertheless, we meet elsewhere with "heaven's face," and even the "welkin's face."

P. 12. Miranda exclaims :—

> "A brave vessel,
> Who had, no doubt, some noble creature in her,
> Dash'd all to pieces !"

Creatures, for "creature," was the reading of Theobald, and he was right, though it varies from all the old copies. The corrector of the folio, 1632, added the necessary letter in the margin. Miranda speaks also of "those she saw suffer," and calls them "poor souls."

P. 13. The emendation in the subsequent lines, assigned to Prospero, is important. The reading, since the publication of the folio, 1623 (with one exception to be noticed immediately), has invariably been as follows :—

> "The direful spectacle of the wreck, which touch'd
> The very virtue of compassion in thee,
> I have with such provision in mine art
> So safely order'd, that there is no soul—
> No, not so much perdition as an hair
> Betid to any creature in the vessel."

The only exception to the above text was a corruption which found its way into the folio, 1632, where "compassion" of the second line was repeated in the third :—

> "I have with such *compassion* in mine art," &c.

the printer having caught the word from the preceding line.

> "I have with such *provision* in mine art,"

the word in the folio, 1623, has always been followed ; but that it was an error may be said to be proved by the manuscript-corrector of the folio, 1632, who altered " compassion " (as it stood there) not to "provision" (as it stood in the folio, 1623), but to *prævision*, in reference to Prospero's power of foreseeing what would be the result of the tempest he had raised :—

> " I have with such *prevision* in mine art
> So safely order'd, that there is no soul," &c.

"Provision" would answer the purpose of giving a meaning, because Prospero might have provided that no soul should suffer ; but *prevision* supplies a higher and finer sense, showing that the great magician had by his art foreseen that there should not be "so much perdition as an hair" among the whole crew. The alteration of a single letter makes the whole difference.

P. 14. There is certainly some misprint in the following conclusion of a speech by Prospero :—

> " And thy father
> Was Duke of Milan, and his only heir
> And princess no worse issued."

The sense is intelligible, but the expression obscure. Malone and Steevens read,—

> " And his only heir
> *A* princess, no worse issued ; "

but the corruption, according to the corrector of the folio, 1632, is in the preceding line ; for he alters the passage thus :—

> " And thy father
> Was Duke of Milan, *thou* his only heir
> And princess, no worse issued."

which removes the difficulty. The compositor, perhaps, caught " and" from the line above.

P. 15. A very trifling change, the transference of a preposition from one word to another, clears up one of the most celebrated passages in this drama. Prospero, speaking of his false brother, Antonio, who, having been entrusted with unlimited power, had turned it against the rightful Duke, observes :—

> " He being thus lorded,
> Not only with what my revenue yielded,
> But what my power might else exact,—like one
> Who having, unto truth, by telling of it,
> Made such a sinner of his memory
> To credit his own lie,—he did believe
> He was indeed the duke."

Various modes of improving this unquestionably corrupt sentence have been suggested by Warburton (who changed *into* of the folios to "unto"), Monk Mason, Steevens, Malone, and Boswell; but not one of them hit upon the right emendation, which is indicated by the corrector of the folio, 1632, in the shortest and simplest manner, by erasing the preposition in one place, and by adding it to the word immediately adjoining: he also substitutes *loaded* for "lorded" in the first line,—perhaps, a questionable change. He puts the whole in this form :—

> " He being thus *loaded*,
> Not only with what my revenue yielded,
> But what my power might else exact,—like one
> Who having, *to untruth*, by telling of it,
> Made such a sinner of his memory
> To credit his own lie,—he did believe
> He was indeed the duke."

There cannot be a doubt that this, as regards "untruth," is the true language of Shakespeare; and, by an insignificant transposition, what has always been a stumbling-block to commentators is now satisfactorily removed.

P. 16. The ordinary reading has been this :—

> " Whereon,
> A treacherous army levied, one midnight
> Fated to the purpose, did Antonio open
> The gates of Milan ; and i' the dead of darkness,
> The ministers for the purpose hurried thence
> Me, and thy crying self."

Here we see the word "purpose" awkwardly and needlessly repeated with only an intervening line. The manuscript-corrector of the folio, 1632, supplants "purpose," in the first instance, by *practise :* he was, most likely, supported by some good authority ; and Shakespeare constantly uses the word *practise* to denote contrivance, artifice, or conspiracy, and therefore, we may presume, wrote,—

> " One midnight
> Fated to the *practise*, did Antonio open
> The gates of Milan," &c.

P. 17. In all the old copies the following reading has been preserved :—

> " Where they prepar'd
> A rotten carcass of a butt, not rigg'd,
> Nor tackle, sail, nor mast; the very rats
> Instinctively have quit it."

Rowe altered " butt" to *boat*, and " have quit it," to *had quit it :* in both changes he is supported by the corrector of the folio, 1632. Modern editors, who were naturally anxious to adhere to the folios, as the best existing authority, finding that sense could be made out of the reading of the old copies, followed them, as above, in what appear to be two errors.

P. 18. An important and curious point is settled by a manuscript stage-direction opposite the words used by Prospero in the commencement of his third speech on this page,—

> "Now I arise."

What is written in the margin of the corrected folio, 1632, is, *Put on robe again ;* and the full force of this addition may not at first be obvious. It refers back to an earlier part of the same scene (p. 12), where Prospero says to Miranda,—

> " Lend thy hand
> And pluck my magic garment from me.—So :
> Lie there my art."

The words *Lay it down* are written against this passage, as *Put on robe again* are written against " Now I arise." The fact is that Prospero, having put off his " magic garment," never put it on again, according to all existing copies of the drama ; and it was this singular omission that the manuscript-corrector of the folio, 1632, supplied. The great propriety of Prospero's removal of his robe of power, during his narration to his daughter, is evident : he did not then require its aid ; but just before he concluded, and just before he was to produce somnolency in Miranda by the exercise of preternatural influence, he resumed it, a circumstance by which the judgment and skill of the poet are remarkably illustrated. Annotators have endeavoured to account for the sudden disposition of Miranda to sleep, in spite of her interest in her father's story, in various ways, but the effect upon her, by the resumption of his "magic garment" by Prospero, has escaped observation, because every editor, from the first to the last, seems to have forgotten that Prospero, having laid aside his outer dress near the beginning of the scene, ought to put it on again, at all events, before the end of it. When, therefore, he says, "Now I arise," he does not mean, as Steevens absurdly supposed, "Now my story heightens," because the very reverse is the fact ; but that he rose from the seat he had taken, in order to invest himself again in his "magic garment," having occasion to use it now in producing sudden drowsiness on Miranda. The manuscript-corrector of the folio, 1632, has previously pointed out what nobody else ever noted, viz., the precise moment when, of old, the actor of the part of Prospero took his seat, by writing *Sit down* opposite the following lines (p. 13) with which the magician commences his narrative :—

> "The hour 's now come,
> The very minute bids thee ope thine ear ;
> Obey, and be attentive." [*Sit down.*

Having here taken his seat, we may conclude that he continued to occupy it until he uttered "Now I arise." Miranda, who had stood eagerly listening by his side, then sat down in her turn : her father, clothed again in his "magic garment," enjoins her to "sit still ;" and not long afterwards we come to the manuscript stage direction, *She sleeps,*— an effect wrought upon her senses, not by any physical weariness, but by the agency of Prospero, empowered by that robe with which he had only recently re-invested himself for the purpose. Thus we see the value of apparently trifling stage directions in explaining so singular an incident as the sudden and deep slumber of Miranda, at the moment when Prospero had concluded his surprising and exciting story.

P. 20. Ariel, giving Prospero an account of the fate of the rest of the dispersed fleet, tells him,—

> "They all have met again,
> And are upon the Mediterranean flote,
> Bound sadly home for Naples."

In order to make the sentence grammatical, it has been necessary to consider "flote" a substantive, from the Fr.

flot, a wave. The misprint of "are" for *all* near the beginning of the second line has led to this imaginary introduction
of a foreign and affected word into our language, when it was
never contemplated by Shakespeare. The reading, as given
in manuscript in the corrected folio, 1632, is,

> "They all have met again,
> And *all* upon the Mediterranean float,
> Bound sadly back to Naples."

"Float," in fact, is a verb, used by every body, and not a
substantive, used by no other English writer.

P. 23. In no printed copy of this drama is inserted any
stage direction to show when Miranda awakes out of her
slumber, although we are told when she goes to sleep. According to the manuscript-corrected folio, 1632, she wakes
with the excuse to her father,—

> "The strangeness of your story put
> Heaviness in me."   [*Waking.*

Johnson, not knowing that what Prospero calls "a good
dullness" (because it was what he wished) in Miranda had
been magically superinduced, maintains that "experience
proves that any violent agitation of the mind easily subsides
in slumber." This explanation is altogether needless, for the
audience had seen Prospero resume his art with his magic
garment, and was aware that Miranda's "heaviness" was the
effect of preternatural influence.

P. 25. The speech beginning,—

> "Abhorred slave,
> Which any print of goodness will not take," &c.

was first assigned to Prospero, instead of Miranda (to whom
it is given in all the folios), by Dryden and Davenant in their
alteration of this drama. Theobald and others have followed
this arrangement, and the fitness of it is confirmed by the
corrected folio, 1632, where the prefix *Mir.* is changed to
Pro. in the margin.

P. 26. There is no dispute that in Ariel's song, "Come
unto these yellow sands," a line is misprinted in all the old
copies, where it appears exactly thus :—

> "*Foot it featly here and there, and sweet sprites bear
> the burthen.*"

It ought to run thus :—

> " Foot it featly here and there,
> And sweet sprites the burthen bear."

In this form it has been ordinarily printed, and so it stands in manuscript in the corrected folio, 1632. It seems manifest that the words, in a new line, " the burthen,"—were meant as the indication of the commencement of that burthen, and as a sort of heading or title to what immediately follows.

P. 27. The manuscript stage direction in the corrected folio, 1632, *Music above,* in the middle of Ferdinand's speech,

> "The ditty does remember," &c.

proves, we may infer, that when the play was formerly acted, the air was continued while the performer was speaking.

P. 28. The stage-direction, *Kneels,* in manuscript, opposite the speech of Ferdinand,

> " Most sure a goddess," &c.

shows that the performer of the part assumed a posture of wonder and adoration, which he kept till Miranda had finished her reply, when *Rising* is also inserted in the margin of the corrected folio, 1632. *Aside* is there noted when Prospero says, a few lines afterwards,—

> " The Duke of Milan," &c.

It is the earliest direction of the kind that occurs in the volume, and we need only mention that it is repeated several times afterwards in this scene.

ACT II. SCENE I.

P. 32. The portion of the scene from

> " He receives comfort like cold porridge," &c.

down to

> " Aye and a subtle, as he most learnedly delivered,"

is crossed out with a pen in the corrected folio, 1632, probably with the object of shortening the performance.

P. 35. Modern editors have concurred with Malone in the following reading:—

> " And the fair soul herself
> Weigh'd, between lothness and obedience, at
> Which end o' the beam she'd bow."

It deviates from the old copies by converting *should* into " she'd," which is unnecessary (and to the detriment of the sense) if we correct, as is done in manuscript in the folio, 1632, a single literal error, and read,—

> "And the fair soul herself
> Weigh'd between lothness and obedience, *as*
> Which end o' the beam should bow."

P. 36. From the speech of Sebastian, " Foul weather," down to the entrance of Ariel, p. 38, is struck through with a pen, but several literal errors are nevertheless corrected in the folio, 1632. The erased portion includes the celebrated passage, copied almost verbatim from Florio's translation of " Montaigne's Essays," fol. 1603, B. I. ch. 30. p. 102.

P. 38. The old stage direction on the entrance of Ariel is,—

Enter Ariel playing solemn music,

to which the manuscript-corrector of the folio, 1632, has added, *above, invisible.* The spirit was therefore supposed to be in the air, listening to what passed below. In all modern editions, *Exit Ariel,* as soon as Alonso falls asleep ; but from the words in the margin, *Come down,* added in manuscript to the printed direction, *Enter Ariel, with music and song,* on p. 42, we may, probably, be warranted in inferring that the spirit hovered in the air unseen all the time Sebastian and Antonio were plotting against the life of Alonso, and then descended to sing in Gonzalo's ear, and give him warning of the danger. Ariel remains present, but invisible, to the end of the scene ; and that there was some contrivance for suspending performers in the air, we know from several authorities, and among them, from the last scene of Act III., where Prospero remains, as it is stated, *on the top, invisible,* until near its conclusion.

P. 40. There is a comparatively trifling change in Antonio's speech,—

> " She that is queen of Tunis," &c.

The old folios all read, in the fifth line of it, "she that from whom ;" but Rowe (who has been here followed by later editors) omitted "that," and printed, "she from whom." The true reading seems to be "she *for* whom," or on account of whom ; and this correction is made in the margin of the folio, 1632. In the third line of the next speech by Antonio, "Measure us back to Naples," ought, on the same authority, to be, "Measure *it* back to Naples." Nevertheless, the former seems preferable.

P. 42. When Alonso starts out of his sleep and finds Sebastian and Antonio with their swords drawn, about to slay him, he asks, according to all modern editions,—

> " Why are you drawn ?
> Wherefore this ghastly looking ?"

" This" was misprinted for *thus* (a common error), and *u* for *i* was therefore inserted in the margin of the corrected folio, 1632,—

> " Wherefore *thus* ghastly looking ?"

The change is minute, and may be said to be not absolutely necessary. In the fifth line of Gonzalo's speech, on the next page (43), another literal error occurs, where the old courtier says, "That's verily," instead of "That's *verity*." The old corrector of the folio, 1632, did not allow the mistake to escape him.

SCENE II.

P. 45. Trinculo, sheltering himself under the gabardine of Caliban, says,—

> " I will here shroud, till the dregs of the storm be past ; "

but a manuscript correction in the folio, 1632, informs us that " dregs" is a misprint for *drench ;* and certainly Trinculo was much more likely to be anxious to avoid the *drench*, or extreme violence of the storm, than the mere " dregs," or conclusion of it.

P. 49. Caliban's song has this line :—

> " Nor scrape trenchering, nor wash dish;"

but the manuscript-corrector of the folio, 1632, has obli-

terated the last syllable of "trenchering," so that the passage
there stands more correctly,

> "Nor scrape *trencher*, nor wash dish."

ACT III. SCENE I.

P. 50. The hemistich, at the conclusion of Ferdinand's
speech, has occasioned much doubt and controversy. It seems
set at rest by the manuscript correction in the folio, 1632.
The following is the usual reading of the whole passage : —

> "But these sweet thoughts do even refresh my labours :
> Most busy, least when I do it."

Such, in fact, are the words in the folio, 1632; but in the
earlier folio, 1623, the last line stands thus :—

> "Most busy lest, when I do it."

The editor of the folio, 1632, not understanding "lest," in
that connexion, altered it to *least*. It appears (as was not an
uncommon occurrence), that a letter had dropped out in the
press, and that the real language of the poet was as beautiful
as it was brief. We are indebted for it to the manuscript of
the corrector of the folio, 1632, who has merely inserted the
missing letter. Earlier in his speech, Ferdinand, exclaiming
against his laborious employment, adds that the thought of
Miranda rendered delightful what would otherwise be in-
tolerable :—

> "This my mean task
> Would be as heavy to me as odious; but
> The mistress which I serve quickens what's dead,
> And makes my labours pleasures;"

and, at the close of what he says, he repeats the same sentiment, but in a shorter form :—

> "But these sweet thoughts do even refresh my labours :
> Most busy—*blest*, when I do it."

That is to say, he deems himself *blest* even by heavy toils,
when they are made light by the thoughts of Miranda ; he
was "most busy," but still *blest*, when so employed. The
accidental dropping out of the letter *b* has been the cause of
all the doubt that, for nearly two centuries and a half, has

involved this passage. It is right to add that this emendation is, like a few others, upon an erasure, as if something
had been written there before: perhaps the page had been
blotted.

ACT IV. SCENE I.

P. 63. Prospero, commending his daughter to Ferdinand,
remarks,—

> "For I
> Have given you a third of mine own life."

Such is the reading of all the folios, and there seems no
especial reason why Prospero should divide his life into three,
and call Miranda "a third" of it. The text has been much
disputed, and for "third" of the old printed copy, the corrector of the folio, 1632, has written *thrid* (i. e. thread)
in the margin. This fact may possibly be decisive of the
question.

P. 66. In the subsequent passage, from the speech of Iris,
two manuscript corrections are made in the folio, 1632. We
first give the lines, as ordinarily printed:—

> " Thy banks with pioned and twilled brims,
> Which spongy April at thy hest betrims,
> To make cold nymphs chaste crowns ; and thy broom groves
> Whose shadow the dismissed bachelor loves,
> Being lass-lorn."

In the corrected folio, 1632, they stand thus :—

> " Thy banks with pioned and *tilled* brims,
> Which spongy April at thy hest betrims,
> To make cold nymphs chaste crowns ; and thy *brown* groves
> Whose shadow the dismissed bachelor loves,
> Being lass-lorn."

Tilled of course refers to cultivation by "pioning," or
digging ; but *brown groves*, in allusion to their deep shade, is
a more important emendation. There seems no reason why
a "dismissed bachelor" should love the covert of "broom
groves," especially recollecting that broom trees are seldom
found in "groves." It may be added that the word *slowly*

is subjoined to the printed stage-direction, *Juno descends*,— to show, perhaps, that the goddess was gradually descending all the time Ceres and Iris delivered their speeches.

P. 68. An important change is made in the song given to Juno (and not divided, in the corrected folio, 1632, between her and Ceres, as has been usual) in the couplet,—

> " Spring come to you, at the farthest,
> In the very end of harvest."

The first line is altered to,—

> "*Rain* come to you, at the farthest," &c.

It may be asked why Juno should wish spring to be so long deferred? On the other hand, *rain* before " the very end of harvest," would be a misfortune, and the singer is deprecating such disasters.

P. 68. The following would seem to be mistakenly printed as a couplet :—

> " So rare a wond'red father and a wise
> Makes this place Paradise."

The unequal length of the lines, and the fact that the last is a hemistich, completed by the opening of Prospero's next speech, militates against this notion : Malone and others therefore printed *wife* for " wise," supposing that the compositor had mistaken the long *s* for *f*. Under the circumstances, perhaps, the decision of the corrector of the folio, 1632, may be held final, and he adopts *wife* :—

> " So rare a wond'red father, and a *wife*
> Makes this place Paradise."

In the next speech of Iris, " windring" has been treated as a misprint for *winding*, and " sedg'd crowns," is altered in the margin to " sedge-crowns," regarding the fitness of which we can hardly doubt.

P. 71. To the old stage-direction, *Enter Ariel, loaden with glistering apparel*, the manuscript-corrector of the folio, 1632, has added the explanatory words, *Hang it on the line ;* but whether we are to understand a *line tree* (as has been suggested by Mr. Hunter, in his learned Essay on the Tempest, 8vo. 1839), or a mere rope, is not stated.

When Stephano and Trinculo discover it, *Seeing the apparel* is written opposite the speech of the latter, beginning, "O, king Stephano! O peer! O, worthy Stephano! look, what a wardrobe here is for thee!" p. 72.

ACT V. SCENE I.

P. 75. Only one manuscript emendation is made in Prospero's great speech, abjuring his magic; but it is worth attention. The passage has invariably run:—

> " You demy puppets, that
> By moonshine do the green-sour ringlets make,
> Whereof the ewe not bites."

For "sour" the corrector substitutes *sward*—"the *green-sward* ringlets," or ringlets on the green-sward, which sheep avoid, and to which the unusual compound epithet "green-sour" may properly be applied. Here we may not see the necessity of this alteration, though it may have been warranted by some manuscript to which the corrector of the folio, 1632, was able to resort.

P. 76. We meet with changes of the received text in two consecutive lines of the continuation of the speech of Prospero, after Alonso, Gonzalo, Sebastian, Antonio, &c., have become "spell-stopped" in the magic circle. The reading of all the editions has been,—

> " Holy Gonzalo, honourable man,
> Mine eyes, even sociable to the show of thine,
> Fall fellowly drops."

The epithet "holy" is inapplicable to Gonzalo, while *noble* (substituted by the corrector of the folio, 1632) is on all accounts appropriate. In the "Winter's Tale" (Act V. Scene I.) Leontes tells Florizel, "You have a *holy* father," where the word seems equally out of place, and where the corrector has, as in "the Tempest," erased it and written *noble* in its stead. In both these cases the copyist must have misheard; but the second error in the same passage, "show" for *flow*, most probably arose out of the common mistake between the long *s* and the *f.* The manuscript-corrector gives the whole in these terms:—

> " *Noble* Gonzalo, honourable man,
> Mine eyes, even sociable to the *flow* of thine,
> Fall fellowly drops."

The eyes of Gonzalo were flowing with tears, and those of Prospero wept in fellowship with them.

P. 77. In the same speech Prospero again addresses Gonzalo as—

> " O, good Gonzalo,
> My true preserver, and a loyal sir
> To him thou follow'st."

This is an uncommon, though not unprecedented, use of the word " sir ;" and the fact is (according to the corrector of the folio, 1632), that it was a misprint for *servant*. In the manuscript used by the printer the word *servant* was probably abbreviated, and thus the error produced, the true reading being,—

> " My true preserver and a loyal *servant*
> To him thou follow'st."

P. 78. Prospero, in the words of the manuscript stage-direction, being *Attired as duke* of Milan, presents himself before his astonished brother, after Gonzalo has prayed some heavenly power to guide them out of the " fearful country." Antonio, in the first instance, believes that the whole is a diabolical delusion, and, according to all editions, exclaims,

> " Whe'r thou beest he, or no,
> Or some enchanted trifle to abuse me,
> As late I have been, I not know."

The word " trifle" seems a most strange one to be employed in such a situation, and it reads like a misprint : the manuscript-corrector of the folio, 1632, informs us that it undoubtedly is so, and that the line in which it occurs ought to run,

> " Or some enchanted *devil* to abuse me."

Sebastian just afterwards declares of Prospero, that " the devil speaks in him."

P. 80. To the printed stage-direction, *Here Prospero discovers Ferdinand and Miranda playing at chess*, the manuscript-corrector of the folio, 1632, adds a note, showing in what way, according to the simplicity of our early theatres, the lovers were disclosed to the audience : his words are,

Draw curtain; so that Prospero drew a traverse at the back of the stage, and showed Ferdinand and Miranda at their game.

P. 84. Prospero describing Sycorax, in the presence of Caliban, tells Antonio,—

> " His mother was a witch ; and one so strong,
> That could control the moon, make flows and ebbs,
> And deal in her command, without her power."

The words "without her power" have naturally occasioned considerable discussion, in which Malone hinted that Sycorax might act by a sort of " power of attorney" from the moon, while Steevens strangely supposed that "without her power" meant "with less general power." All difficulty, however, is at an end, when we find the manuscript-corrector of the folio, 1632, marking "without" as a misprint, and telling us that it ought to have been *with all ;*—

> "That could control the moon, make flows and ebbs,
> And deal in her command *with all* her power :"

that is, Sycorax could " make flows and ebbs" matters in the command of the moon, with *all* the power exercised over the tides by the moon. The error of the press here is, we think, transparent.

THE TWO GENTLEMEN

OF

VERONA.

ACT I. SCENE I.

P. 92. The reading of the subsequent line has hitherto been,—

> " 'Tis true; for you are over boots in love;"

but the manuscript-corrector of the folio, 1632, has changed it to

> " 'Tis true; *but* you are over boots in love;"

which seems more consistent with the course of the dialogue; for Proteus, remarking that Leander had been " more than over shoes in love" with Hero, Valentine answers, that Proteus was even more deeply in love than Leander: Proteus observes of the fable of Hero and Leander,—

> " That's a deep story of a deeper love,
> For he was more than over shoes in love."

Valentine retorts:—

> " 'Tis true; *but* you are over boots in love."

" For," instead of *but*, was perhaps caught by the compositor from the preceding line.

The following change, lower in the page, seems hardly necessary, but it is not the only instance in which the manuscript-corrector of the folio, 1632, has converted the active into the passive participle: he altered

> " Even so by love the young and tender wit
> Is turn'd to folly; blasting in the bud,"

C

to "*blasted* in the bud;" for the bud does not blast, but is itself *blasted :* the "young and tender wit" is a "bud" *blasted* by love.

P. 96. Steevens and Malone differed about Speed's observation to Proteus, as it stands in the folio, 1623 :—"And being so hard to me that brought your mind, I fear she'll prove as hard to you in telling your mind." Steevens adopted the words from the folio, 1632 —"And being so hard to me that brought your mind, I fear she'll prove as hard to you in telling her mind." Probably neither old reading is quite right, and the manuscript-corrector of the folio, 1632, has made it intelligible by his emendation,— "And being so hard to me that brought *to her* your mind, I fear she'll prove as hard to you in telling *you* her mind." The words *to her* and *you* are added in the margin. The fact is, that the whole speech was intended for irregular familiar verse, and the manuscript-corrector has added the word *better* at the end of the first line, which had apparently dropped out : the whole will therefore run as follows :—

> " Sir, I could perceive nothing at all from her *better*,
> No, not so much as a ducat for delivering your letter ;
> And being so hard to me that brought *to her* your mind,
> I fear she'll prove as hard to you in telling *you* her mind."

As a slight confirmation of the opinion that rhyming verse was intended, it may be mentioned, that in the folios the lines begin with capital letters as they are above printed. Still the same circumstance belongs to other places, where it is clear that prose only was to be spoken.

SCENE II.

P. 97. Rhyme is also restored in the next scene between Julia and Lucetta, where they are discussing the merits and claims of various amorous gentlemen. An apparent misprint of another kind, "lovely" for *loving*, is also corrected in manuscript in the folio, 1632. Julia has asked her maid what she thinks of Proteus, and Lucetta's answer provokes the following, as we find it in all editions :—

> " *Jul.* How now ! what means this passion at his name ?
> *Luc.* Pardon, dear madam : 'tis a passing shame,

> That I, unworthy body as I am,
> Should censure thus on lovely gentlemen.
> *Jul.* Why not on Proteus, as of all the rest?
> *Luc.* Then thus,—of many good I think him best."

It seems clear that the two middle lines should rhyme as well as all the others; and the manuscript-corrector not only cures this defect, but gives Lucetta's answer a particular application to the very person of whom both she and her mistress are speaking. The emendation is this:—

> "That I, unworthy body, as I *can*,
> Should censure thus *a loving* gentleman."

Lucetta, knowing that Proteus is a " *loving* gentleman" to her mistress, wishes to be excused from giving her opinion, as well " as she can" form one, upon him, until Julia compels her to do so. The above is by no means the only part of the scene that is in rhyme, and in two subsequent places the corrector restores what we may presume to have been the original jingle, thus (p. 100):—

> " She makes it strange, but she would be pleas'd *better*
> To be so anger'd with another letter."

Here for " pleas'd *better*," the ordinary reading has been " best pleas'd." Again (p. 101):—

> " Ay, madam, you may *see* what sights you *think;*
> I see things too, although you judge I wink."

Hitherto the first of these lines has been,

> " Ay, madam, you may say what sights you see."

It is not improbable, that in this comedy, confessedly one of its author's earliest works, rhymes originally abounded more frequently than at the time it was printed in 1623, the fashion. in the interval having so changed, that they were considered not only unnecessary, but possibly had become distasteful to audiences. When " The Two Gentlemen of Verona" was, according to our best conjectures, first produced, blank verse had only recently been adopted on the stage. We shall see this point more fully illustrated hereafter, when we come to speak of " Titus Andronicus," in which several passages have been restored by the corrector of the folio, 1632, apparently to the form in which they were recited when the tragedy was acted quite in the beginning of Shakespeare's career.

ACT II. SCENE I.

P. 106. There can be no doubt that the small word we have printed below in italics, and which was inserted by the manuscript-corrector of the folio, 1632, is necessary in the following ridicule by Speed of his master, for having been changed by his love for Silvia:—

" You were wont, when you laughed, to crow like a cock; when you walked, to walk like one of the lions; when you fasted, it was presently after dinner; when you looked sadly, it was for want of money; and now you are *so* metamorphosed with a mistress, that, when I look on you, I can hardly think you my master."

Nevertheless, *so* has been always omitted.

SCENE IV.

P. 116. The following passage, as it stands in all impressions, is unquestionably a piece of tautology. The Duke asks Valentine if he knows Don Antonio?

" *Val.* Ay, my good lord; I know the gentleman
    To be of worth, and worthy estimation,
    And not without desert so well reputed."

The manuscript-corrector of the folio, 1632, substitutes a word in the second line, easily misprinted, and which being restored, is certainly an improvement:—

" To be of *wealth* and worthy estimation."

Wealth would be an additional recommendation to the Duke, and it entirely avoids the objectionable repetition: if Antonio were of "worth" and "worthy estimation," he could not well be so reputed "without desert."

P. 119. The line

" Disdain to root the summer-swelling flower,"

has been disputed, the epithet "summer-smelling" having been preferred by some critics; but the old copies having "summer-swelling," that reading has generally prevailed. The corrector of the folio, 1632, has however altered the compound, probably on good authority, with which we are not now acquainted, to "summer-*smelling*."

SCENE VI.

P. 124. Johnson tells us, that

> " O sweet suggesting love! if thou hast sinn'd,
>   Teach me, thy tempted subject, to excuse it,"

means, " Oh, tempting love! if thou hast influenced me to
sin ;" but, when Proteus is lamenting the breach of his vows
to Julia, it seems much more natural for him to say, " if
I have sinn'd," and so it is given by the corrector of the
folio, 1632. Further on, in the same soliloquy, he reads,
" precious *to* itself" for " precious in itself," which is quite
consistent with the context,—

> " I to myself am dearer than a friend,
>   For love is still most precious *to* itself."

SCENE VII.

P. 126. The epithet *wide* substituted by the corrector of
the folio, 1632, seems more appropriate in the following
lines, but it has been uniformly printed " wild:" Julia is
speaking of a current that "with gentle murmur glides" between its banks,—

> " And so by many winding nooks he strays
>   With willing sport to the *wide* ocean."

This is, of course, one of the cases in which either reading
may be right : if we prefer *wide*, it is mainly because the
old corrector had some ground for adopting it.

P. 128. There is a misprint in the following line, as pointed
out by the corrector of the folio, 1632 ;—

> " To furnish me upon my longing journey."

Julia is about to travel in male attire in search of the object
of her devoted regard, Proteus, and desires her maid to provide her with all the apparel necessary, and to come with her
to her chamber—

> " To take a note of what I stand in need of
>   To furnish me upon my *loving* journey."

" *Loving* journey," in reference to the purpose of it, seems
to recommend itself.

ACT III. SCENE I.

P. 131. There are several oversights as to the place of action in this comedy. For instance, in Act II. Scene V. (p. 122), Speed welcomes Launce to Padua instead of Milan ; and here we find the Duke telling Valentine

"There is a lady in *Verona* here,"

when it ought also to be Milan. Again, in Act V. Scene IV. (p. 168), Valentine is made to speak of Verona, when he means Milan. In the two last places three syllables are necessary for the verse ; and Pope and Theobald resorted to different contrivances to obviate the difficulty: in one case Pope interpolated "Sir," and in the other Theobald read *behold* for "hold." The manuscript-corrector of the folio, 1632, has shown how both these changes may be avoided, by only supposing that Shakespeare, instead of speaking of Milan, as it is called in our language, inserted *Milano*, the Italian name of the city. Milano suits the measure just as well as Verona, and it is more likely that the printer or copyist were in fault, than the poet.

SCENE II.

P. 141. On the same authority, "some" ought to be printed *sure* in the following line, where the Duke is about to employ Proteus most confidentially :—

"For thou hast shown some sign of good desert."

Sure is written in the margin, and "some" struck out, because Proteus had already given undoubted proofs of fidelity to the Duke, and of treachery to Valentine. In the next page, "weed," as it stands in the folios, and in subsequent editions, reads like an error of the press, and doubtless it was so, since "weed" was displaced by the corrector of the folio, 1632, and *wean*, a word much better adapted to the situation, inserted :—

"But say, this *wean* her love from Valentine,
It follows not that she will love Sir Thurio."

A third mistake of the same kind is pointed out on p. 146,

in the first scene between Valentine and the Outlaws, where the whole body having chosen him captain, the third Outlaw exclaims,—

> " Come, go with us : we'll bring thee to our crews,
>   And show thee all the treasure we have got."

For " crews" we ought to read *cave*, in which the treasure was deposited : *cave* is therefore written in the margin, and *crews* erased : the " crews" (so to call them) were present on the stage, and Valentine needed not to be brought to them.

ACT IV. SCENE II.

P. 148. In the song, " Who is Silvia?" &c., there is a repetition of " she" in the third line, as the rhyme to " she" in the first line ; and although such a licence was by no means unprecedented, still it was usual for writers not to avail themselves of it. If the corrector of the folio, 1632, give the song as it was written by Shakespeare, the inelegance to which we refer was avoided by the adoption of an epithet which our great dramatist has elsewhere employed with reference to female simplicity and innocence (" Twelfth Night," Act II. Scene IV.). The first stanza of the song, as corrected in the folio, 1632, is this :—

> " Who is Silvia? what is she,
>   That all our swains commend her?
> Holy, fair, and wise *as free ;*
>   The heaven such grace did lend her,
>   That she might admired be."

SCENE III.

P. 153. We have here a very important emendation, supplying a whole line, evidently deficient, and yet never missed by any of the commentators. It is in one of the speeches of Sir Eglamour, wherein he consents to aid Silvia in her escape. Until now, it has run :—

> " Madam, I pity much your grievances ;
>   Which since I know they virtuously are plac'd,
>   I give consent to go along with you."

Here there is no connexion between the first and the second lines, because Sir Eglamour could not mean that the "grievances," but that the *affections* of Silvia were "virtuously placed." Shakespeare must, therefore, have written what we find in an adjoining blank space of the folio, 1632, which makes the sense complete :—

> "Madam, I pity much your grievances,
> *And the most true affections that you bear ;*
> Which since I know they virtuously are plac'd,
> I give consent to go along with you."

We shall hereafter see that other passages, more or less valuable, are supplied by the corrector of the folio, 1632. These were, probably, obtained from some better manuscript than that used by the old printer.

SCENE IV.

P. 155. Proteus having sent a little dog as a present to Silvia, meets Launce, and learns that the latter, having lost the little dog, had offered to the lady his own huge cur. Proteus asks him,—

> "What! didst thou offer her this *cur* from me ?"

The word *cur* being derived from the manuscript of the corrector, and necessary to the completion of the line. Besides this novelty, there is an emendation of Launce's reply, which explains a point never yet properly understood. The folio, 1623, reads :—

> "Ay, sir: the other squirrel was stolen from me by the hangman's boys in the market-place," &c.

The folio, 1632, gives the hangman only one boy,—"by the hangman's boy in the market-place ;" but the true reading seems to be that of the corrected folio, 1632, where "a hangman boy" is used just in the same way that Shakespeare elsewhere speaks of a gallows boy,—"Ay, sir: the other squirrel was stolen from me by *a hangman boy* in the market-place ;"—that is, by a rascally boy.

P. 157. We give the following to show how Shakespeare's verse has probably been corrupted. Julia, presenting Silvia with a paper, says,—

> "Madam, please you peruse this letter :"

a line which requires two additional syllables, naturally, and most likely truly, furnished by the corrector of the folio, 1632:—

"Madam, *so* please you *to* peruse this letter."

Two little words, not absolutely necessary to the sense, but absolutely necessary to the measure, were omitted by the copyist, or by the old printer.

P. 159. It is worth notice that Julia, descanting on Silvia's picture, says, in the first folio, that "her eyes are grey as glass," which may be right; but which the second folio alters to "her eyes are grey as grass," which must be wrong. The manuscript-corrector of the folio, 1632, converts "grey" into *green*—"her eyes are *green* as grass;" and such we have good reason to suppose was the true reading.

ACT V.—SCENE II.

P. 162. The sudden entrance of the Duke is not marked in the old copies, and is supplied in manuscript in the folio, 1632, *Enter Duke, angerly;* and his first speech is there thus corrected:—

"How now, Sir Proteus! How now, Thurio! Which of you saw Sir Eglamour of late?"

The folio, 1623, gives the last line,—

"Which of you saw Eglamour of late?"

And the folio, 1632, before it was corrected in manuscript,—

"Which of you, *say*, saw Sir Eglamour of late?"

There is no note when the Duke goes out, but *Exit in haste*, is written in the margin. The additional stage-directions in the corrected folio, 1632, are very numerous throughout this play; but they are, in general, merely explanatory of what may be gathered from the text, so that it is seldom necessary to remark upon them. They must have been intended to make what is technically termed the stage-business quite intelligible.

P. 164. Two passages in the speech of Valentine, as they

appear in all the printed copies, and as they stand in the manuscript of the corrector of the folio, 1632, require notice, on account of valuable emendations.

The usual opening is in these lines :—

> " How use doth breed a habit in a man!
> This shadowy desert, unfrequented woods,
> I better brook than flourishing peopled towns."

The manuscript-corrector renders the second line,—

> " *These* shadowy, desert, unfrequented woods," &c.

Lower down we are informed, in an unprinted stage-direction, that *shouts* are heard, and then follow these lines :—

> " These my *rude* mates, that make their wills their law,
> Have some unhappy passenger in chace ;"

which is certainly better than the common mode of printing the passage, which leaves the verb "have" without any antecedent :—

> " These are my mates, that make their wills their law,
> Have some unhappy passenger in chace."

The first speech of Proteus to Silvia, on entering, is also altered by reading "have" *having*, and by making the sentence continuous, as in the old copies, and not, as in modern editions, terminating it by a period at the end of the fourth line. The corrector of the folio, 1632, puts it in this amended form :—

> " Madam, this service *having* done for you,
> (Though you respect not aught your servant doth)
> To hazard life, and rescue you from him,
> That would have forc'd your honour and your love,
> Vouchsafe me, for my meed, but one fair look." &c.

SCENE IV.

P. 166. It is admitted by the commentators that the measure in the following extract is defective: they have tried to amend it in various ways, but they have not been so fortunate as to hit upon the right changes. We first quote the passage as Malone regulates it, and follow it by the alteration recommended by the corrector of the folio, 1632. Valentine says :—

> " The private wound is deepest: O time most accurst!
> 'Mongst all foes, that a friend should be the worst!
> *Prot.* My shame and guilt confounds me !"

Malone, in justification, observes that Shakespeare sometimes employs lines of twelve syllables; but here, in three lines, we have three varieties: the first line is of twelve syllables, the second of ten, and the third of only seven. We are far from wishing to reduce the language of Shakespeare to a finger-counting standard, but the subsequent emendation shows, at all events, that at an early date the passage was deemed corrupt, and that it ought to run as follows:—

> " The private wound is deep'st.   O time accurst,
> 'Mongst all *my* foes, a friend should be the worst!
> *Prot.* My shame and *desperate* guilt *at once* confound me!"

It seems more than likely that we have here recovered the language of Shakespeare; and it is to be remarked that the lines of the poet are regular, both before and after the preceding quotation.

P. 170. The following manuscript emendation in the corrected folio, 1632, tends to establish that *conclude* was the right word, and that "include," adopted by editors from the folios, was a misprint:—

> " Come; let us go : we will *conclude* all jars
> With triumphs, mirth, and rare solemnity."

The epithet "rare," in the folio, 1623, is *all* in the folio, 1632; but restored to "rare" by the manuscript-corrector, perhaps from the prior edition, or possibly on some other authority. In all impressions the word *stripling*, in the next line but two, is omitted in the following speech by Valentine, introducing Julia to the Duke,—

> " What think you of this *stripling* page, my lord?"

Stripling is written in the margin of the corrected folio, 1632, as well as *Valentine* at the end of the next line but one, where it must have been accidentally left out:—

> " What mean you by that saying, *Valentine?*"

The two lines which close the play are in rhyme, according to the same authority. In the folio, 1623, they do not rhyme, and there stand,—

> " That done, our day of marriage shall be yours;
> One feast, one house, one mutual happiness."

The manuscript-corrector of the folio, 1632, tells us that the lines ought to run as follows: —

> " Our day of marriage shall be yours *no less*,—
> One feast, one house, one mutual happiness."

We have no doubt that this is an accurate representation of the fact: no fewer than twenty-nine of the thirty-six plays in the folio terminate with couplets; and considering, as already observed, that " The Two Gentlemen of Verona" was written at so early a date, when rhyme was popular, it would be strange if it, of all others, had been an exception.

THE MERRY WIVES

OF

WINDSOR.

ACT I. SCENE I.

P. 177. All the characters who take part at any time
during the scene are mentioned at the commencement of the
scenes in this play, but the manuscript-corrector of the folio,
1632, has struck out all the names but those of Justice Shallow, Slender, and Sir Hugh Evans, who, in fact, begin the
comedy. The entrances of the others are afterwards noted in
the margin, precisely at the places where they come upon the
stage. Thus, when Evans, on p. 179, knocks at Page's door,
the master of the house does not enter at first, but looks out
at a window (*above*, as the manuscript-corrector states) and
asks, "Who's there?" but does not join the rest outside
his house, until the end of Evans's answer, when *Enter Page*
is marked. This old mode of commencing the comedy may
seem to give the scene additional vivacity and reality.
Falstaff, Bardolph, Nym, and Pistol, of course, enter, when
Page says, "Here comes Sir John," &c., p. 180.

P. 184. Opposite Slender's ejaculation, "O heaven! this is
Mistress Anne Page!" the corrector of the folio, 1632, has
written this stage-direction, *Following her;* from which we
may gather that Slender, struck by Anne's appearance,
follows her a few steps towards the door of the house, when
she quits the stage. Such, probably, was the practice of some
old comedian who had the part of Slender, and it is a curious
relic of stage-business.

P. 185. It was not meant that Sir Hugh Evans should, like Slender, grossly misapply words : therefore, in the following observation, the corrector of the folio, 1632, has properly altered "command" to *demand*. "But can you affection the 'oman ? Let us command to know that of your mouth, or of your lips ; " &c.

P. 186. According to the manuscript-correction of the folio, 1632, the commentators have been right in altering the old reading of the sentence, "I hope, upon familiarity will grow more content," into "I hope, upon familiarity will grow more *contempt ;*" for Slender could hardly misquote a proverb he found in his copy-book. Besides, the humour of the passage depends upon the use of the word "contempt."

P. 187. When Slender asks Anne Page, "Why do your dogs bark so ?—Be there bears i' the town ?" the insertion of a manuscript stage-direction in the folio, 1632, *Dogs bark*, affords evidence that there was formerly an imitation of the barking of dogs out of sight of the audience, in order to give greater verisimilitude.

SCENE III.

P. 189. A rigid adherence to the old copies has here misled editors, who have given Nym's speech as, "The good humour is to steal at a minute's rest," instead of "a *minim's* rest," which the sense seems to require, in allusion to what has just been said of "an unskilful singer" not keeping time. The manuscript-corrector of the folio, 1632, has converted "minute's" into *minim's*.

P. 190. A misprint in the old editions of "carves" for *craves*, has occasioned some difficulty in the passage where Falstaff, speaking of the expected result of his enterprise against Mrs. Ford, observes, as the words have been invariably given, "I spy entertainment in her ; she discourses, she carves, she gives the leer of invitation." A note in the margin of the corrected folio, 1632, shows that we ought to read "she *craves*, she gives the leer of invitation." There seems no sufficient reason for supposing that "carves" ought to be taken in the figurative sense of *wooes ;* and although ladies might now and then " carve" to guests, in the literal meaning of the word (as in the passage quoted by Boswell from Webster's " Vittoria Corombona," Shakesp. by Malone, VIII. 38), yet carving was undoubtedly an accomplishment peculiarly belonging to men.   Falstaff evidently, from the context, intends to say that Mrs. Ford has a *craving* for him, and therefore gave "the leer of invitation."   The misprint was a very easy one, occasioned merely by the transposition of a letter, and any forced construction is needless.

P. 190. The word " legend," in the sentence, " He hath a legend of angels," is altered to *legion* in the corrected folio, 1632 ; but still the passage does not conform to the old 4to, 1602, where it is said "*she* hath *legions* of angels."   That, however, is evidently an edition of no accuracy.

P. 191. The reading of all the printed authorities, speaking of Mrs. Page, is, "She is a region in Guiana,—all gold and bounty," which might be accepted, had we no warrant for improving the text to, " She is a region in Guiana,—all gold and *beauty*," such being the manuscript emendation in the folio, 1632.   Guiana was famous for its beauty, as well as for its gold, and thus the parallel between it and Mrs. Page was more exact.   The 4to, 1602, lays particular emphasis on her *beauty ;* and "bounty" and *beauty* were easily mistaken.

P. 191. The corrector of the folio, 1632, like modern editors and the 4to, 1602, reads : —

> "Falstaff will learn the humour of this age,"

and not " *honour* of this age," as in all the folios.

P. 192. Pistol's exclamation, " By welkin, and her star !" is, " By welkin, and her *stars !*" in the corrected folio, 1632, and as far as we can judge, rightly, since the welkin has not one, but innumerable stars.

SCENE IV.

P. 197. Mrs. Quickly's speech, at the bottom of this page, begins, in the corrected folio, 1632, " Will I ?   I'faith, that *I* will !" and not " that *we* will," as in the printed copies.

ACT II. SCENE I.

P. 198. Dr. Farmer conjectured that "Though love use reason for his precisian" ought to be, "Though love use reason for his *physician*." The word "precisian" is so altered in the margin of the manuscript-corrected folio, 1632 ; and of the fitness of it there can now be no doubt.

P. 202. Dr. Johnson's conjecture that the words "Believe it, Page ; he speaks sense," belong to Nym, and are not a continuation of Pistol's speech, is fully confirmed by a correction in the folio, 1632, where *Nym* is written as the prefix in the margin opposite.

P. 204. In all editions, where the entrance is marked at all, the Host and Shallow are made to come upon the stage together ; but it is clear that they did not, for when the Host, having entered, calls out, "Cavaliero-justice, I say !" Shallow, coming after him, answers, "I follow, mine host, I follow." Their entrances are separately noted in the corrected folio, 1632, and this fact shows that the emendator paid great attention to these little points.

P. 205. It is necessary here to quote the whole of the Host's short speech, as it is ordinarily printed, for the sake of observations arising out of two parts of it :—

"*Host.* My hand, bully : thou shalt have egress and regress ; said I well ? and thy name shall be Brook. It is a merry knight.—Will you go, An-heires ?"

With regard, first, to the name assumed by Ford : in the 4to, 1602, it is Brooke, and in all the folios, 1623, 1632, 1664, and 1685, it is *Broome ;* but from the pun upon the name made by Falstaff, in a subsequent scene (p. 211), "Such *Brooks* are welcome to me, that o'erflow such liquor," it has always been considered a misprint in the folios. That the name was misprinted there we cannot doubt, but we may doubt whether *Broome* was a misprint for "Brooke," or for *Bourne* (the latter being decidedly the more probable), and whether, in fact, the name was not originally *Bourne*, which the manufacturer of the surreptitious 4to, 1602 (for there never was an authentic impression of "The Merry Wives" until the folio, 1623), altered to "Brooke," not understanding, perhaps, how the joke about "o'erflowing such liquor" could, at all events, so well apply to *Bourne*. The truth is, that as *Brooke* and *Bourne* mean the same thing, viz., a small stream, the joke would apply to the one as to the other; and the manuscript-corrector of the folio, 1632, invariably strikes out *Broome*, and substitutes *Bourne*. Hence we may not unreasonably infer, that the true *alias* of Ford was not Brooke (which originated in the 4to, 1602), but Bourne; and that when the comedy was acted, in the time of the corrector, he always heard it pronounced *Bourne*, and not "Brooke." In the manuscript used for the folio, 1623 (followed in all the other editions in that form), we have little hesitation in believing, that the name was written *Bourne*, which the compositor misprinted *Broome*.

There is certainly another error of the press, which we may allow the corrector of the folio, 1632, to set right upon his better knowledge of the true reading. We allude to the last clause, "Will you go, An-heires?" out of which no sense can be made. Warburton suggested "*heris*, the old Scotch word for master;" Steevens, *hearts*; Malone, *hear us*; Boaden, *cavaliers*, &c. The manuscript-corrector of the folio, 1632, merely changes one letter, and omits two, and leaves the passage, "Will you go *on, here*?" The Host urging them forward, as he does again just afterwards, nearly in the same words, differently placed, "Here, boys, here, here!—shall we wag?" He is anxious that no time should be lost. How so ordinary an expression as "Will you go on, here?" came to be misprinted, "Will you go, An-heires?" we are at a loss to imagine: perhaps the writing before the printer was very illegible, and he could not believe that any thing so simple and intelligible could be intended. It is singular that nobody seems ever to have conjectured that *on here* might be concealed under "An-heires."

P. 205. Page observes, of the duellists, "I had rather hear them scold than fight." This may have been an elliptical sentence, but it is more likely that two words were accidentally omitted, and that the true reading is that furnished by the corrector of the folio, 1632, "I had rather hear them scold, than *see them* fight."

SCENE II.

P. 206. In Falstaff's reply to Pistol, the compound epithet, according to the manuscript-corrector of the folio, 1632, is not, "Coach-fellow, Nym," but "*Couch*-fellow, Nym," as, indeed, it was printed by some of the earlier editors, as equivalent to "bed-fellow." Nevertheless, "coach-fellow" may be, and has been, reconciled to sense.

P. 208. It seems improbable that Mrs. Quickly should have had "twenty angels" given to her "*this* morning" by a person who wished to be in the good graces of Mrs. Ford ; and in the folio, 1632, the sentence is thus altered in manuscript, "I had myself twenty angels given *of a* morning."

P. 212. Ford, pressing his "bag of money" upon Falstaff, says, "If you will help to bear it, take all, or half, for easing me of the carriage." It seems more likely that Ford would say, "take half, or all." Falstaff would draw back at first, and Ford would then endeavour to induce him to take all, if half did not make the impression he expected. The manuscript-corrector has changed the places of "all" and "half,"—"Take *half, or all,* for easing me of the carriage." The difference is not material either way. Throughout the whole of this scene Ford is called *Bourne,* and the old corrector has, therefore, erased Broome, in favour of the other name, in ten separate instances.

P. 213. The propriety of the following emendation can hardly be questioned. Ford, adverting to the hopelessness of proceeding in his intended suit to Mrs. Ford, as the passage has always hitherto been given, speaks thus to Falstaff :—"She dwells so securely on the excellency of her honour, that the folly of my soul dares not present itself." The manuscript-corrector of the folio, 1632, reads *suit* for "soul"—"that the folly of my *suit* dares not present itself."

SCENE III.

P. 216. In the beginning of the scene between Caius and Jack Rugby, the former wishes to practise his fencing on his

man, and, offering to lunge at him with his rapier, Jack
Rugby exclaims, "Alas, sir! I cannot fence." The corrector
of the folio, 1632, has added, as a descriptive marginal direction, the words, *A feard, runs back ;* which amusingly shows the
manner in which the old actor of Jack Rugby received, or
rather shunned, the advances of his master.

P. 218. We meet here with a singular blunder by the
printer, which has occasioned much puzzle and conjecture,
but which is at once set right by the manuscript-corrector
of the folio, 1632. It occurs at the end of one of the
Host's speeches to Dr. Caius :—

"I will bring thee where Mistress Anne Page is, at a farm-house a feasting, and thou shalt woo her. Cried game, said I well?"

The difficulty has been how to make any sense out of
" Cried game ;" and various suggestions, such as *tried game,*
cry aim, &c., have been made ; but the truth seems to be,
that the Host, having said that Anne Page was feasting at a
farm-house, in order still more to incite Dr. Caius to go
there, mentioned the most ordinary objects of feasting at
farm-houses at that time, viz. *curds and cream :* "curds and
cream" in the hands of the old compositor became strangely
metamorphosed into *cried game*—at least this is the marginal explanation in the corrected folio, 1632. The Host,
therefore, ends his speech about Anne Page's feasting at the
farm-house by the exclamation, " Curds and cream! said I
well ?"

ACT III.   SCENE I.

P. 219. The passage is not one of any great importance,
but for " the pitty-ward, the park-ward, every way ; Old
Windsor way, and every way but the town way," the corrected folio, 1632, has, certainly with the advantage of intelligibility, " the pit-way, the park-way, Old Windsor way, and
every way but the town way," the words or letters not wanted,
and probably not understood, have been struck through with
a pen.

P. 222. The folios are evidently deficient in that part of

the Host's speech, where he is endeavouring to make recon-
cilement between Evans and Caius. The folio, 1623, reads,
" Give me thy hand (celestial), so. Boys of art, I have deceived you both." Malone's text has been, " Give me thy
hand, terrestrial ; so :—Give me thy hand, celestial ; so.—
Boys of art, I have deceived you both." The reading of the
corrected folio, 1632, has " and terrestrial" added in manuscript, giving the following as the language of the poet, and
still preserving the antithesis in about half the number of
words :—" Give me thy hands, celestial *and terrestrial :* so.
Boys of art, I have deceived you both."

SCENE II.

P. 223. The pronoun *your* seems clearly necessary in the
following answer by Ford to Mrs. Page, who asks, whether
his wife is at home ?—" Ay, and as idle as she may hang
together for want of *your* company. I think, if your husbands were dead, you two would marry." The word is in the
margin of the corrected folio, 1632.

P. 224. *Where* for " there" is doubtless the true mode of
printing Ford's observation—" The clock gives me my cue,
and my assurance bids me search ; there I shall find Falstaff "
—" and my assurance bids me search *where* I shall find Falstaff " is the corrected and more natural reading of the folio,
1632. The stage-direction, *Clock strikes ten*, is written in the
margin : and Falstaff had already told Ford that he was to
visit Mrs. Ford " between ten and eleven."

SCENE III.

P. 230. We have a glimpse of the comic business of the
scene in the manuscript stage-direction (there is no printed
one in the folios), when Falstaff, in great alarm, hides himself among the foul linen in the buck-basket. The words
are, *Gets in the basket and falls over ;* meaning, probably,
that in the eagerness of his haste he " fell over" on the other
side of the basket, and occasioned still greater ludicrous confusion.

ACT IV. SCENE I.

P.'243. The change of a letter makes an improvement in the speech of Evans: "No; Master Slender is let the boys leave to play." For "let" the corrector of the folio writes "get;" that is to say, "Master Slender is *get* (or has obtained) the boys leave to play." "To let the boys leave to play" is not a phrase that even the Welsh parson would have used. On the next page the corrected reading is, "Hast thou no understandings for thy cases, and the numbers, *and* the genders," instead of "of the genders," but the difference is trifling.

SCENE II.

P. 249. There is no stage-direction in the old copies when Ford meets the servants with the buck-basket in the second instance, and, in the words of modern editions, *Pulls the clothes out of the basket.* The old manuscript stage-direction in the folio, 1632, affords a much more striking picture of Ford's anger and its consequences, when it informs us that he *Throws about the clothes all over the stage,* and adds, lower down, that they are *All thrown out.* Such is consistent with the modern practice, and Ford's suspicions would hardly let him leave a rag unexamined.

SCENE IV.

P. 253. In the doubted passage, "I rather will suspect the sun with gold," whether the last word should not be *cold,* the corrected folio, 1632, shows that Rowe was justified in adopting the latter: the *g* in "gold" is struck through, and doubtless, if the margin had not there been torn away, we should have seen *c* inserted in its stead. On the next page Evans is made by the old corrector to remark, "You *see,* he has been thrown into the rivers," instead of "You *say,*" &c. The fact is, that the other persons engaged in the scene had *said* nothing of the kind, and Evans referred merely to the known sufferings of Falstaff, as a reason why he would not again be entrapped.

SCENE V.

P. 258. Modern editors have needlessly changed the prefixes of the folios in this part of the scene: the corrector of
that of 1632 has altered two small words, and made the dialogue run quite consistently. Simple tells Falstaff and the
Host that he had other things to have spoken on behalf of
his master to "the wise woman of Brentford :"

> "*Fal.* What are they? let us know.
> *Host.* Ay, come; quick.
> *Fal.* *You* may not conceal them, sir.
> *Host.* Conceal them, *and* thou diest."

The common method has been to put "I may not conceal
them, sir," into the mouth of Simple, followed by a mark
of interrogation; and the Host's next speech has been invariably printed "Conceal them, *or* thou diest." The
Host was desirous that Simple should reveal, and would
not, therefore, threaten death if he disclosed them. Dr.
Farmer wished *reveal* to be substituted for "conceal,"
but the only alteration here required is *and* for "or,"—
"Conceal them *and* thou diest." Such is the emendation
of the corrector of the folio, 1632.

P. 258. Bardolph, rushing in, complains of cozenage, and
the Host inquires what has become of his horses? Bardolph, in all editions, replies,—

> "Run away with the cozeners;"

as if the horses had run away with the cozeners against their
will. The manuscript-corrector of the folio, 1632, inserts *by*
in the margin,—

> "Run away with *by* the cozeners,"

and the rest of Bardolph's speech confirms this interpretation: as soon as they had thrown him off into the mire, the
cozeners "set spurs and away" with the Host's horses.

ACT V. SCENE III.

P. 265. The text of the folios, " Where is Nan now, and
her troop of fairies ? and the Welsh devil, Herne," is certainly
wrong. Theobald altered " Herne" to *Hugh*, and he was, of
course, right as to the person intended ; but the manuscript-
corrector of the folio, 1632, erases " Herne," and inserts
Evans, as the proper reading. Had "Hugh" been the word, it
seems probable that Mrs. Ford might have paid him the respect of calling him Sir Hugh.

SCENE V.

P. 267. We have the evidence of the corrected folio, 1632,
in favour of " *bribe*-buck," instead of " brib'd-buck" of the
early printed copies. This was Theobald's emendation.

P. 267. In several preceding scenes we are informed that
Anne Page was to represent the Fairy Queen in the attack
upon Falstaff in Windsor Park. Nevertheless, Malone and
others assigned all her speeches to Mrs. Quickly, the only
excuse being that the first of the prefixes is "Qui." The manuscript-corrector of the folio, 1632, changed it to *Que*, and
made it *Que.* (for Queen) in all other places ; and after the
printed stage-direction, " Enter Fairies," he added, *with the
Queen, Anne.* It does not, indeed, appear that Mrs. Quickly
took any part at all in the scene, although she most likely
in some way lent her assistance, in order that she might be
on the stage at the conclusion of the performance.

P. 268. The whole of what is delivered by the Queen and
the rest of the Fairies is in verse, with the exception of two
lines, which have constantly been misprinted thus :—

> " Cricket, to Windsor chimneys shalt thou leap :
> Where fires thou find'st unrak'd, and hearths unswept," &c.

There is no doubt that this was originally a couplet, until
a corruption crept in, which no editor felt himself competent to set right. Tyrwhitt, indeed, does not seem to have
been aware of the defect ; but it struck the corrector of the
folio, 1632, who, by manuscript changes in the margin, in-

forms us that the lines ought to run as follows, by which the
rhyme is preserved :—

> " Cricket, to Windsor chimneys *when thou'st leap't,*
> Where fires thou find'st unrak'd, and hearths unswept,
> There pinch the maids as blue as bilberry," &c.

This must have been the way in which the passage originally
stood. Lower down in the same page, for

> " Raise up the organs of her fantasy,"

the same authority reads, " *Rouse* up the organs," &c.　He
removes the vulgarism, in the next line but one, by reading,
" But those *that* sleep," &c., instead of " But those as sleep,"
&c., which, however, was sometimes in the language of the
day.

P. 274. Fenton, vindicating his conduct in marrying Anne
Page against the will of both her parents, says, in all impressions of the play,—

> " And this deceit loses the name of craft,
> Of disobedience, or unduteous title," &c.

" Title" sounds like a misprint, and so it appears to be ; the
true word, which entirely corresponds with the preceding
line, having perhaps been misheard by the copyist.　The corrector of the folio, 1632, inserts what he tells us is the
proper reading in the margin :—

> " Of disobedience or unduteous *guile.*"

MEASURE FOR MEASURE.

ACT I. SCENE I.

Vol. II. p. 7. The Duke, in all editions of this play, observes to Escalus, after calling him to his side,—

> " Of government the properties to unfold,
>   Would seem in me t' affect speech and discourse;
>   Since I am put to know, that your own science
>   Exceeds, in that, the lists of all advice
>   My strength can give you : then, no more remains,
>   But that, to your sufficiency, as your worth is able,
>   And let them work."

This reading has been derived from the four folios; but, according to the corrected folio, 1632, it is erroneous in three particulars: the first is not of any great consequence, inasmuch as "Since I am *put* to know" is as intelligible and forcible as " Since I am *apt* to know ;" but the great improvement is in the sixth line quoted above, in which "that" is a misprint for *add*, and into which the conjunction *as*, and the two words at the end have, accidentally perhaps, been foisted. The correct reading, with the aid of the manuscript in the margin of the folio, 1632, is as follows :—

> " Since I am *apt* to know, that your own science
>   Exceeds, in that, the lists of all advice
>   My strength can give you : then, no more remains,
>   But *add* to your sufficiency your worth,
>   And let them work."

These small changes remove what has always been a difficulty on the very threshold of this play.

P. 9. It has been made a question between Johnson, Steevens, and Tyrwhitt, whether, when the Duke says,—

" Hold, therefore, Angelo,"

he offered to his intended deputy the commission which had
been prepared for him. Now, the manuscript stage-directions
in the folio, 1632, make it certain that at the words " Hold,
therefore, Angelo," the Duke *Tendered the commission* to
Angelo, but did not actually place it in his hands until he
finished his speech with " Take thy commission." The point
would scarcely be worth notice, if it had not been dwelt upon
by the commentators.

SCENE II.

P. 12. Near the end of Mrs. Overdone's speech, " is " is required before the words " to be chopped off "—" and within
three days his head *is* to be chopped off." It is deficient in
all printed copies, and is inserted in manuscript in the margin of the corrected folio, 1632. In the same way, the word
" bawdy " is omitted in the Clown's speech (p. 13) : " All
bawdy houses in the suburbs of Vienna must be plucked
down." The proclamation was against " bawdy houses in
the suburbs," and not against other houses there. The word
wanting is supplied in manuscript, which accords with Tyrwhitt's suggestion.

SCENE III.

P. 14. The division *Scena tertia* is struck through, and
properly, because there is clearly no change of place, the
Provost, Claudio, and Officers walking in, as the Clown,
Bawd, &c. make their *exit.* Juliet is mentioned as one of
the characters entering, but her name is erased by the corrector of the folio, 1632, for it does not appear that she took
any part in the scene, and in fact is spoken of by Claudio as
absent. Nevertheless, in all editions the scene is erroneously
marked as a new one, and Juliet is stated to have come on
the stage with Claudio, and to have listened patiently to the
description of her offence. It was, therefore, not the practice
of our stage, when the folio of 1632 was corrected, to place

her in a situation so painful and indelicate, and Shakespeare could hardly have intended it.

P. 15. Two rather important words are altered in the corrected folio, 1632, in Claudio's speech. The usual reading is,—

> " She is fast my wife,
> Save that we do the denunciation lack
> Of outward order : this we came not to,
> Only for propagation of a dower."

" Denunciation " is changed to *pronunciation*, and " propagation " to *procuration*, meaning, of course, the procuring of the dower.

SCENE IV.

P. 18. In the following line, as it stands in all the folios,—

> " The needful bits and curbs to headstrong weeds,"

Theobald rightly altered " weeds " to *steeds*, as it stands corrected in manuscript in the folio, 1632. Lower down, in the same speech, Pope added the word " becomes " in the passage,—

> " In time the rod
> Becomes more mock'd, than fear'd ; so our decrees," &c.

But the true language of the poet, as far as the evidence of the corrected folio, 1632, enables us to judge of it, was this :—

> " In time the *rod's*
> More mock'd than fear'd ; so our *most just* decrees,
> Dead to infliction," &c.

It is evident that two syllables were deficient in the second line ; and it seems likely that the Duke would dwell emphatically upon the justice of the decrees neglected to be enforced, rather than use so tame an expression as " *Becomes* more mock'd than fear'd."

P. 19. It was proposed by Pope, Hanmer, Johnson, Steevens, &c., to alter the following passage in the folio, 1623, in various ways,—

> " And yet my nature never in the fight,
> To do in slander."

Without adverting to the discordant proposals of the commentators, we may quote the satisfactory words, and their
context, as they are exhibited in the manuscript correction
of the folio, 1632 :—

> " I have on Angelo impos'd the office,
> Who may, in th' ambush of my name, strike home,
> And yet my nature never in the *sight*
> To *draw on* slander."

That is to say, "I have imposed the duty upon Angelo of
punishing severely, while I draw no slander on myself, being
out of sight." The use of the long *s* will easily explain how
the error of "fight" for *sight* arose ; but it is not so easy to
understand how *drawe*, as it is spelt in the manuscript note,
came to be misprinted "doe," as it is spelt in the folio, 1632.

SCENE V.

P. 20. Malone took a great liberty with the text, when he
printed

> " Sir, make me not your storie "

of the first folio, " Sir, mock me not—your story." The fact
is that Sir W. Davenant gave the true word in his alteration
of " Measure for Measure,"—

> " Sir, make me not your *scorn*."

The manuscript-corrector of the folio, 1632, has also *scorn*
for " storie," as might be expected.

ACT II. SCENE I.

P. 27. In Froth's sentence, " I have so ; because it is an open
room, and good for winter," some difficulty has arisen, because
it could not well be understood how " an open room " could
be "good for winter." Froth, in truth, did not speak of
" winter " at all, but rather of summer, since reading *windows*
for " winter," as is done by the manuscript-corrector of the
folio, 1632, the matter is set right and an error of the press
removed—" I have so ; because it is an open room, and good
for *windows* "—that is, good on account of the windows.

P. 30. The Clown, adverting to the ruin that would be brought on Vienna by enforcing the law against bawdy houses, is made to employ a word which is not easily understood in the place where it is found: he says, "If this law hold in Vienna ten year, I'll rent the fairest house in it after three pence a bay." The commentators have explained it by reference to "bays of building," "bay windows," "bays of barns," &c. It is a mere error of the press—"bay" for *day;* "after three pence a *day*" is the word in the corrected folio, 1632. Three pence a day would be only 4*l.* 11*s.* 3*d.* a year for the "fairest house in Vienna."

SCENE II.

P. 35. We meet with a bold and striking emendation in one of Isabella's noble appeals to Angelo. The common text has been,—

> " How would you be,
> If he, which is the top of judgment, should
> But judge you as you are ?"

The amended folio, 1632, has it,—

> " How would you be,
> If he, which is the *God* of judgment, should
> But judge you as you are ?"

This is not to be considered at all in the light of a profane use of the name of the Creator, as in oaths and exclamations ; and while *top* may easily have been misheard by the scribe for "God," the latter word, though the meaning is of course the same, adds to the power and grandeur of the passage.

P. 35. Sir Thomas Hanmer's proposal to read " But *ere* they live to end" is fully supported by the corrected folio, 1632. The first folio has " But *here* they live to end," which Malone, with remarkable infelicity, altered to "But *where* they live to end."

P. 37. Angelo starting at the offer of Isabella to bribe him, she interposes, in the words of all modern editions, that she will do it,

> " Not with fond shekels of the tested gold," &c.

It is spelt *sickles* in the old copies, but the true word may be *circles ;* and the manuscript-corrector of the folio, 1632, has altered " sickles " to *sirkles,* paying no other attention to the spelling of the word.   Nevertheless " shekels " may be right, and it is used, exactly with the same spelling, by Lodge in his " Catharos," 1591, sign. C, where we read, " Here in Athens the father hath suffred his sonne to bee hanged for forty *sickles,* and hee worth four hundred talents."

SCENE III.

P. 40. The manuscript-corrector of the folio, 1632, makes an important change in a line of the Duke's speech which has been doubted, while he passes over some preceding lines, regarding which needless disputes have arisen.   The amended line is,—

> " Showing, we would not *serve* heaven, as we love it."

The common reading is " spare heaven," which some editors would print " *seek* heaven ;" but " *serve* heaven," which seems unquestionably right, did not occur to any of them.   The whole passage will therefore stand thus :—

> " 'Tis meet so, daughter : but least you do repent,
> As that the sin hath brought you to this shame ;
> Which sorrow is always toward ourselves, not heaven,
> Showing, we would not *serve* heaven, as we love it,
> But as we stand in fear."

The old corrupt reading of " spare heaven " seems little better than nonsense—the emendation indisputable.

SCENE IV.

P. 44. Tyrwhitt is authorized by the corrected folio, 1632, in reading *in-shell'd,* for " enshield " of the old copies, in the following passage :—

> " As these black masks
> Proclaim an enshield beauty ten times louder
> Than beauty could displayed."

Lower down on the same page Angelo says,—

> " As I subscribe not that, nor any other,
> But in the loss of question ;"

which occasioned discussion between Johnson, Steevens, and Malone as to the meaning of the phrase " in the loss of question." The corrector of the folio, 1632, writes, in the margin, "but in the *force* of question"—that is to say in the compulsion of question, or for the sake of question, a sense the word will very well bear, the copyist having misheard *force* "loss." Four lines lower we have in manuscript "the manacles of the all-*binding* law," instead of "all-building law," which was the mistaken epithet in the old copies. Dr. Johnson first substituted all-*binding*.

ACT III. SCENE I.

P. 49. The sentence in the Duke's homily on death, ending,—

> " For all thy blessed youth
> Becomes as aged, and doth beg the alms
> Of palsied eld :"

is altered in manuscript in the corrected folio, 1632, to

> " For all thy *boasted* youth," &c.

which, looking at the context, appears to be a decided improvement upon the old text.

P. 51. We are glad to obtain an authority, which we may consider to a certain extent decisive, upon a much doubted portion of the scene between Isabella and her brother. She tells him of Angelo's design upon her virtue, and he exclaims in astonishment, according to the first folio,—

> " The prenzie Angelo ?"

The second folio, not being able to find any sense in *prenzie*, gives it " princely :"—

> " The princely Angelo ?"

and the editors of Shakespeare have not at all known what to make of the epithet, which is repeated in Isabella's reply. Warburton proposed *priestly*, and that now appears to be the word of the poet, but another corruption found its way into the text, which nobody pointed out, and which is thus set right in manuscript in the corrected folio, 1632 :—

> *Claud.*   " The *priestly* Angelo?
> *Isab.* O, 'tis the cunning livery of hell,
>   The damned'st body to invest and cover
>   In *priestly garb*."

For "priestly garb" the first folio has "prenzie guards," and the second "princely guards;" but *priestly garb* is unquestionably the true language of Shakespeare, which has reference to the sanctimonious appearance and carriage of Angelo. Warburton is to have the credit of "priestly," but all the commentators have been under a mistake as to "guards."

P. 54. After Claudio has withdrawn, the Duke tells Isabella, "The hand that hath made you fair hath made you good;" and then follows what, in the ordinary text, is not easily understood—"the goodness that is cheap in beauty makes beauty brief in goodness." The manuscript-corrector of the folio, 1632, proposes to read, "the goodness that is *chief* in beauty makes beauty brief in goodness;" from which we may deduce this meaning—that when goodness consists chiefly in beauty, beauty is rendered brief in the possession of that goodness.

SCENE II.

P. 57. A play upon the double meaning of the word *usances* has been hitherto lost by printing it "usuries," where the Clown, in allusion to the suppression of bawdy houses, and to the allowed interest of money observes, in the received text, "'Twas never merry world, since, of two usuries, the merriest was put down, and the worser allowed by order of law," &c. The word *usances* is substituted for *usuries* in the margin of the corrected folio, 1632, *usance* being to be taken as usage or custom, as well as interest of money.

P. 58. In the line of the Duke's speech,

" I drink, I eat, array myself, and live,"

the old copies misprint "array" *away;* but the true word is restored by a correction in the folio, 1632. Theobald saw that the change was necessary.

P. 59. The pronoun *it* was omitted in the old editions before "clutched" in Lucio's speech, but is inserted in the margin in the corrected folio, 1632. Near the end of the same speech occurs the question,—"What say'st thou, Trot?" and several notes have been written upon "Trot," which turns out on the same authority to be a misprint for *troth*, one of the most common expletives—"What say'st thou, *troth ?*"

P. 65. Three small, but not unimportant, words—"the due of"—appear to have dropped out in the press, or to have been left out in the manuscript used by the compositor in the beginning of the speech of Escalus, which, according to the corrected folio, 1632, ought to run, "You have paid the heavens *the due of* your function, and the prisoner the very debt of your calling." The invariable reading has been, "You have paid the heavens your function," &c.

P. 66. Two portions of the Duke's twenty-two short verses, concluding this Act, are amended in manuscript in the corrected folio, 1632. The first is,—

> " Grace to stand, virtue *to* go,"

instead of

> " Grace to stand *and* virtue go :"

which exactly accords with Coleridge's suggested emendation in his Lit. Rem. ii. 124. The other change marked in the folio, 1632, applies to those difficult lines,—

> " How may likeness, made in crimes,
> Making practice on the times,
> To draw with idle spiders' strings
> Most pond'rous and substantial things !"

The proposed alteration does not clear away the whole difficulty, but, notwithstanding, it is valuable,—

> " How may likeness, made in crimes,
> *Masking* practice on the times,
> Draw with idle spiders' strings
> Most ponderous and substantial things !"

Warburton boldly asserts "Shakespeare wrote it thus," and then gives his own notion ; while Steevens recommended another method, and Malone that generally received, viz. "*Mocking*, practise on the times." By "*masking* practice on the times" is to be understood *concealing* methods of deception, and then the whole passage may mean—"How many persons, alike in criminality, conceal their deceptions so successfully as to draw ponderous and substantial advantages, even with spiders' webs !"

E

ACT IV. SCENE I.

P. 69. In the Duke's soliloquy on "place and greatness," this passage occurs,—

> " Volumes of report
> Run with these false and most contrarious quests
> Upon thy doings."

But "these" can hardly be right, since no "false and contrarious quests" have been previously mentioned. The reading of the line appears from the corrected folio, 1632, to be,—

> "Run with *base*, false, and most contrarious quests."

In the next line, "dream" is converted into *dreams*, which seems fit, since "fancies," in the next line, is also in the plural.

SCENE II.

P. 73. The line in the old folios,—

> " Wounds th' unsisting postern with these strokes,"

has produced discussion, Blackstone contending that "unsisting" was to be taken as *never resting ;* but the corrector of the folio, 1632, marks "unsisting" as an error of the press, and very naturally substitutes *resisting :* the postern resisted the entrance of the messenger, who, therefore, wounded it with strokes. When he enters, the Duke observes, " It is his *lordship's* man," and not " his lord's man," as it stands printed in the folios.

SCENE III.

P. 80. After the Duke's interview with Barnardine, he is made to exclaim, in all editions, and nobody has found fault with the expression,—

> " Unfit to live or die. O, gravel heart !"

The words " gravel heart " having been considered equivalent to *stony* heart ; but the fact seems to be, that it is a misprint. And that the Duke's real exclamation is much more appropriate,—

> " Unfit to live or die. O, *grovelling beast !*"

the character of Barnardine having been reduced by idleness

and intoxication to that of a mere prone brute.　Such is the manuscript correction in the folio, 1632.

P. 81.　For the disputed epithet of the folios, Hanmer, Heath, and Monk Mason recommend *well*-balanced in the line,—

> " By cold gradation and weal-balanced form ;"

and that they were judicious in this opinion, the corrector of the folio, 1632, furnishes evidence in his margin.

P. 82.　The manuscript stage-direction in the folio, 1632, *Catches her*, shows that the performer of the part of Isabella fell into the Duke's arms at the unexpected tidings that Angelo, in spite of his promise, had taken the life of her brother.　In her exclamation just afterwards,—

> " Injurious world !　Most damned Angelo !"

the epithet "injurious" reads tamely and out of place ; and the word substituted by the corrector of the folio, 1632, is certainly more adapted to the occasion, though but rarely used,—

> " *Perjurious* world !　Most damned Angelo !"

Two syllables are wanting in the third line of the Duke's speech, lower down,—

> " Mark what I say, which you shall find," &c.

The omission was, doubtless, accidental, and the required words are found in the margin of the folio, 1632,—

> " Mark what I say *to you*, which you shall find," &c.

In the Duke's next speech, the usual text of the eighth line has been,—

> " I am combined by a sacred vow ;"

but "combined" for *confined* was an easy misprint, and the latter a more natural word, which has been supplied by the manuscript-corrector of the folio, 1632.

SCENE IV.

P. 85.　A passage, the subject of comment, is found in Angelo's soliloquy, which is not entirely explained, but still is rendered more comprehensible by a slight alteration of the received reading, proposed by the corrector of the folio, 1632.

We will quote the whole, with his amended punctuation
also :—

> " But that her tender shame
> Will not proclaim against her maiden loss,
> How might she tongue me ! yet reason dares her; no ;
> For my authority bears *such* a credent bulk,
> That no particular scandal once can touch,
> But it confounds the breather."

The folios have " of a credent bulk," and Steevens suspected
" of " to be a blunder, as it appears in fact to have been.
Malone read " *off* a credent bulk," which hardly affords sense,
whereas " bears *such* a credent bulk" is, at least, intelligible.
Still, though the poet's meaning may be collected from his
language, it is obscure.

SCENE VI.

P. 87. Theobald's happy emendation of the last line of
Isabella's first speech is borne out by the corrector of the
folio, 1632. Before correction it stood thus :—

> " I am advis'd to do it,
> He says, to vail full purpose ;"

that is, as Theobald suggests, " t'availful purpose," which
Malone objected to, and, at the recommendation of Johnson,
read, " to *veil* full purpose." In the folio, 1632, as amended
in manuscript, it stands precisely in this form :—

> " He says, to 'vail-full purpose ;"

that is, to a purpose that is *availful* or beneficial, and seems
the true reading ; for in the next line, Isabella, disliking du-
plicity, says the same thing by a figure,—

> " 'tis a physic
> That's bitter to sweet end."

ACT V. SCENE I.

P. 89. To show how easily words, even of importance, sometimes drop out in the press, we may mention that in the line
of the first folio,—

> " And she will speak most bitterly and strange,"

the second folio has it imperfectly,—

> " And she will speak most bitterly."

The manuscript-corrector of the folio, 1632, therefore added *and strangely* at the end of the line, and he slightly altered the next line, which commences the retort of Isabella, thus:—

> " Most strangely, yet most truly will I speak."

It is a decided improvement, and was most probably the form in which Shakespeare left the line, the old and less elegant reading being,—

> " Most strange, but yet most truly will I speak."

P. 90. We have here a misprint that can only have arisen from the carelessness of the copyist or the printer. The invariable text of Isabella's passionate appeal has been,—

> " O, gracious duke !
> Harp not on that ; nor do not banish reason
> For inequality ; but let your reason serve
> To make the truth appear."

" Inequality " could not be right : and what does the manuscript-corrector of the folio tell us is the real word that ought to be put in its place ?—

> " O, gracious duke !
> Harp not on that ; nor do not banish reason
> For *incredulity ;*"

i.e. do not refuse to give your reason fair play, on account of the incredulity with which you listen to my complaint.

P. 93. Another word is more than plausibly substituted in the speech of the Friar, where he is giving a character of the Duke, who, he pretends, was a brother of his order. The way in which the passage is usually printed is this, and it does not seem liable to much objection ; but nevertheless we may feel confident that there has been an error of the press in it :—

> " And, on my trust, a man that never yet
> Did, as he vouches, misreport your grace."

Now, " on my trust," that is to say, on my belief or credit, is infinitely less forcible than what is placed in the margin as the poet's word,—

> " And, on my *truth*, a man that never yet," &c.

The Friar was of course anxious in the most emphatic way to bear testimony to the good conduct of the disguised Duke.

P. 98. This is an instance of a similar kind ; but not so strong as the preceding, because the word, which the manuscript-corrector of the folio, 1632, would induce us to throw out of the text, is not very ill adapted to the place, though not so well adapted as that which he has written in the margin. The Duke, returning to the scene in his friar's disguise, declares that the suppliants, Isabella and Mariana, have been unfairly treated by the Duke, when he referred the decision on their case to the party who was himself accused :—

> " The Duke's unjust,
> Thus to retort your manifest appeal,
> And put your trial in the villain's mouth,
> Which here you come to accuse."

The manuscript-corrector informs us that " retort," in the second line, is a misprint for *reject*, a mistake not unlikely to be made. Isabella had appealed to the Duke, and he had rejected that appeal, and left the trial to Angelo : therefore, the reading ought to be,—

> " The Duke's unjust,
> Thus to *reject* your manifest appeal," &c.

P. 100. The manuscript stage-directions in this scene are minute and numerous, the more so as the printed ones are few and unsatisfactory—by no means sufficient to regulate the acting and business of the play. Thus, whenever Isabella or Mariana are to *kneel*, or *rise*, or *unveil*, it is duly noted in the margin ; and, when the Duke is to be discovered, Lucio is told to *seize on him* and to *pull off his disguise*, at which, it is added in another place, *all start and stand*, gazing upon the Duke. It is remarkable that there is no *Exeunt* at the end of the play, but the words " Curtain drawn " are appended in manuscript, perhaps the first time they were ever applied in that way. They may be taken as proving that, in this instance, at least, the characters did not go out, but that a "curtain" was "drawn" before them, in order to separate them from the audience, in the same way that in more modern times a cur-

tain (formerly of green baize) is let down from the top of
the proscenium at the conclusion of the performance. It is
possible that this mode of denoting that the drama was at an
end was not very uncommon at the period when the folio,
1632, was corrected ; but we are not aware of the existence
of any other distinct proof of the prevalence of it on our
stage anterior to the Restoration.

COMEDY OF ERRORS.

ACT I. SCENE I.

P. 114. The life of Ægeon being forfeit to the laws of Ephesus, by his accidental arrival there in search of his son, he relates his story to the Duke (who has just passed sentence upon him), observing, as the passage has hitherto stood,—

> " Yet that the world may witness, that my end
> Was wrought by nature, not by vile offence,
> I'll utter what my sorrow gives me leave."

The manuscript-corrector of the folio, 1632, states that " nature," in the second line, ought to be *fortune*, since Ægeon was not about to lose his life in the course of " nature," but by having been so unlucky as to arrive in a town by the laws of which it was sacrificed: his end, therefore,—

> " Was wrought by *fortune*, not by vile offence."

Possibly, by " nature" we might understand the natural course of events.

P. 115. Ægeon, overtaken by a storm at sea, which threatened death to himself, his wife, and two children, says,—

> " Which though myself would gladly have embrac'd,
> Yet the incessant weeping of my wife," &c.

There seems no reason why Ægeon should " gladly have embraced" death, if he could have escaped it; and a marginal correction in the folio, 1632, shows that the word *gently* (*i. e.* patiently and submissively) was Shakespeare's word,—

> " Which though myself would *gently* have embrac'd."

Six lines lower, in the same speech, " And this it was" is altered to "And *thus* it was," not necessarily, but certainly judiciously.

P. 117. The expression "of all love," indicating strength of impulse, is not unusual in Shakespeare and in other writers of his time. Ægeon consents that the twin-son and twin-servant, preserved with him, should go in search of their brothers; and in the following lines, as they appear in all copies of the play, there are on the authority of the manuscript-corrector of the folio, 1632, two errors :—

> " Whom whilst I labour'd of a love to see,
> I hazarded the loss of whom I lov'd."

They ought to run,—

> " Whom whilst *he* labour'd of *all* love to see,
> I hazarded the loss of whom I lov'd."

It was the son who was to undertake the task of seeking his brother, although the father, having in this way " hazarded the loss of whom he loved," afterwards went in quest of his " youngest boy."

P. 118. The line, near the end of the Duke's last speech, as it appears in the folios,—

> " To seek thy help by beneficial help,"

has produced several conjectures for its emendation, and among them one by the editor of the present volume, who suggested that the true reading might be,—

> " To seek thy *hope* by beneficial help ;"

and such is precisely the change proposed by the corrector of the folio, 1632 : Ægeon was to seek what he hoped to obtain (viz. money to purchase his life), by the " beneficial help" of some persons in Ephesus. Four lines lower, the verse is deficient of a syllable ; and, to supply it, *now* is inserted in manuscript in the margin :—

> " Jailor, *now* take him to thy custody."

P. 121. Pope's emendation of " clock" for *cook* is supported by the manuscript-corrector of the folio, 1632, in the following passage :—

> " Methinks, your maw, like mine, should be your *clock ;*
> And strike you home without a messenger :"

nevertheless, obvious as the error seems, *cook* was, we believe, printed in all editions until Pope's time, and has even been restored in our own.

ACT II. SCENE I.

P. 124. By the misprint of " doubtfully" for *doubly* in two places, as pointed out by the corrector of the folio, 1632, the humour of one of Dromio's replies has been entirely lost. He has been beaten by a person he took for his master, when sent to bring him home to dinner. Luciana asks, according to the usual text, " Spake he so doubtfully, thou couldst not feel his meaning ?" Here " doubtfully" ought to be *doubly*, as well as in Dromio's reply, " Nay, he struck so plainly, I could too well feel his blows ; and withal so doubtfully, that I could scarce understand them." We ought here also to read, " and withal so *doubly* that I could scarce understand them ;" *i. e.* the blows were so *doubly* powerful that Dromio could hardly stand under them.

P. 126. It is worth while to mention that the line,—

" I see, the jewel best enameled,"

and the two next lines (the folio, 1632, omits two others in the folio, 1623) are struck out, perhaps, as unintelligible to the manuscript corrector, he having no means of setting the corrupt passage right.

SCENE II.

P. 130. It has been thought rather a happy conjectural emendation by Pope, when he converted " trying" of the old copies into *tiring* in the following sentence, yet he was certainly mistaken :—" The one to save the money that he spends in 'tiring ; the other that at dinner they should not drop in his porridge." Antipholus and Dromio of Syracuse are talking of hair, and on the advantages of baldness, and the word *trimming* was quite technical in reference to cutting and dressing the hair : it is misprinted *trying* in the old copies, and it is clear that the letter *m* had dropped out, *tryming*, or trimming, being the word intended—"to save the money that he spends in *trimming*," not in "'tiring" or attiring, which has relation not to the hair merely, but to the whole apparel, whereas the hair only was under discussion. The manuscript-corrector of the folio, 1632, has done no more than place the missing letter in the margin.

P. 131. A doubt is removed by the corrector of the folio, 1632, regarding the last line of Adriana's speech,—

"I live disstain'd, thou undishonoured."

The use of the word "disstained" in this way has no example, and Theobald recommended *unstain'd*, but did not insert it in his text. It is found in manuscript, and we cannot doubt that it was the word of the poet.

P. 133. Antipholus of Syracuse, wonder-struck at the advances of Adriana, who invites him home, exclaims, according to the usual text,—

"To me she speaks; she moves me for her theme!"

"Moves" here is a misprint for *means*, and so it is marked by the corrector of the folio, 1632: "She *means* me for her theme." Three lines lower we have another mistake of the same kind, where Antipholus asks,—

"What error drives our eyes and ears amiss?"

"Drives" ought incontestably to be *draws*, as we learn on the same authority; and we may perhaps accept the old corrector's emendation of the next line but one with as little hesitation,—

"I'll entertain the *proffered* fallacy,"

for "I'll entertain the *free'd* fallacy" of the old copies. The last has generally been printed "the offer'd fallacy," without much objection. For "elvish sprites," four lines below (the folio, 1623, has no word corresponding with "elvish"), the corrector reads "elves *and* sprites," and he makes no change in "owls," for which Theobald needlessly, though not without plausibility, substituted *ouphes*.

ACT III. SCENE I.

P. 135. Two words, omitted in a line in a speech by Dromio of Ephesus, were supplied by the manuscript-corrector of the folio, 1632: a word is also changed for the better in the preceding line.   We give the couplet as it stands with the marginal emendation:—

> " If *my* skin were parchment, and the blows you gave were ink,
> Your own hand-writing would tell you *for certain* what I think."

P. 136. Another change for the better, both as regards the rhyme and the sense, is made in a speech by the same character, farther on in the scene.   The common reading is,—

> " If thou hadst been Dromio to-day in my place,
> Thou wouldst have chang'd thy face for a name, or thy name for an
>   ass."

" Or thy name for *a face*" are the words inserted by the corrector of the folio, 1632, which seem more accurately to preserve the antithesis and the rhyme.

SCENE II.

P. 140. The first four lines of this scene are thus given in the folios:—

> " And may it be that you have quite forgot
> A husband's office? shall, Antipholus,
> Even in the spring of love thy love-springs rot?
> Shall love in buildings grow so ruinate?"

Malone, for the rhyme's sake, changed " ruinate" to *ruinous;* but it appears by the manuscript-correction in the folio, 1632, that the lines ought to run as follows, and that Malone altered the wrong word:—

> " And may it be, that you have quite forgot
> A husband's office ? *Shall unkind debate,*
> Even in the spring of love, thy love-spring rot?
> Shall love in building grow so ruinate?"

P. 142. The line,—

> " Far more, far more to you do I decline,"

may be reconciled to sense ; but the reading of the corrector

of the folio, 1632, which makes a very trifling change, seems
preferable :—

> " Far more, far more to you do I *in*cline."

P. 144. All that intervenes between the question of Antipholus, " What complexion is she of?" and Dromio's observation, on the next page, " O ! sir, I did not look so low," is
struck out in the corrected folio, 1632.

<hr>

ACT IV   SCENE I.

P. 148. " Among my wife and *their* confederates " of the
folio, 1632 (as well as that of 1623), is altered by the manuscript-corrector to " Among my wife and *these* confederates."
The common reading is " her confederates," which may be
right.   In the next speech of Antipholus the corrector of the
folio has added *me* in the second line, " I promis'd *me* your
presence, and the chain."   In the second line of Angelo's
reply *raccat* of the folio, 1632 ("chareect," folio, 1623), is
properly corrected to " carrat."

P. 149. The change of " send *by me* some token " for " send
me by some token " seems scarcely required ; but it was
necessary to insert *more* in Angelo's speech lower down,
" You wrong me more, sir, in denying it," the word having
been omitted in the folio, 1632.

P. 150. Angelo demanding his money for the chain of
Antipholus of Ephesus, is answered in the folio, 1623, " Consent to pay thee that I never had ?" *Thee* having been
omitted in the folio, 1632, the corrector caused the line to
run thus :—

> " Consent to pay *for* that I never had ? "

which is certainly more to the purpose.

SCENE II.

P. 152.   Dromio arrives in great haste to obtain from his
mistress and her sister the purse to pay his master's supposed

debt, and when he enters, out of breath, he exclaims, as the passage has always been printed,—

"Here, go: the desk! the purse! sweet, now make haste."

But he would hardly address the ladies so familiarly as to call them *sweet;* and the corrector of the folio, 1632, tells us that he did not, "sweet" having been misprinted for *swift:* Dromio wishes them to use the utmost dispatch—"*swift* now, make haste."

P. 153. A line is evidently wanting in Dromio's speech, which, but for that omission, and a small word which has dropped out, is entirely in rhyme: the line ending with *steel* has no corresponding verse; but the deficiency, though apparent, has never been remarked upon. In all editions the passage has stood thus:—

"No, he's in Tartar limbo, worse than hell:
A devil in an everlasting garment hath him,
One whose hard heart is button'd up with steel,
A fiend, a fairy, pitiless and rough;
A wolf, nay, worse, a fellow all in buff."

It is thus given by the manuscript-corrector of the folio, 1632:—

"No, he's in Tartar limbo, worse than hell:
A devil in an everlasting garment hath him, *fell;*
One whose hard heart is button'd up with steel,
Who has no touch of mercy, cannot feel;
A fiend, a *fury*, pitiless, and rough;
A wolfe, nay worse, a fellow all in buff," &c.

Theobald suggested *fury* for "fairy;" but he entertained no notion that a whole line had been lost, to say nothing of the word *fell* as the triplet-rhyme in the second line. It is not likely that any objection will be felt on account of irregularity in the measure, coming as it does from Dromio, a sort of *ad libitum* versifier.

SCENE III.

P. 157. Antipholus of Syracuse fancies himself surrounded by witches and sorcerers, and when the Courtezan asks him to go home with her, he exclaims, "Avoid then, fiend!" The manuscript-corrector of the folio, 1632, has it, "Avoid, *thou* fiend!" which is probably accurate, but the change is trifling.

P. 161. Two small variations are made, both in speeches by Dromio, one where, alluding to the beating he had received, he says his "bones bear witness,"—

> "That since have felt the vigour of his rage."

The manuscript-corrector of the folio, 1632, here reads *rigour* for "vigour;" and lower down he makes Dromio exclaim,—

> "God and the rope-maker *now* bear me witness,"

instead of merely "bear me witness," which is not in the regular measure which Dromio just here employs.

ACT V. SCENE I.

P. 167. For the line,—

> "In company I often glanced it,"

the manuscript-corrector reads, with apparent fitness,—

> "In company I often glanc'd *at* it."

In the speech of the Abbess the epithet "moody" is applied to "melancholy" in the folio, 1623, which is altered to *muddy* in the folio, 1632. The manuscript-corrector most properly restored "moody."

P. 168. The line in the Merchant's speech, as it is given in the folios,—

> "The place of depth and sorry execution,"

is amended in manuscript in the folio, 1632, to

> "The place of *death* and *solemn* execution;"

both words, as we may suppose, having been misheard by the copyist.

P. 169. Adriana, speaking of her husband, who had been seized as a madman, says,—

> "Anon, I wot not by what strong escape,
> He broke from those that had the guard of him."

"Strong" the corrector of the folio, 1632, converts into "strange," perhaps because all were astonished at the escape.

P. 172. Antipholus of Ephesus, describing the manner in which he had been seized, bound, and confined, observes,—

> " They fell upon me, bound me, bore me thence,
> And in a dark and dankish vault at home
> There left me," &c.

The corrector of the folio, 1632, alters it to " *They* left me," which is clearly right.

P. 174. Ægeon, astonished at not being recognized by Antipholus of Ephesus, exclaims, in the reading of the first and other folios,—

> " O, time's extremity !
> Hast thou so crack'd and splitted my poor tongue?" &c.

but we learn from the manuscript-corrector of the folio, 1632, that the last line ought to be, as seems natural,—

> " Hast thou so crack'd *my voice, split* my poor tongue?"

P. 177. All copies agree in what appears to be a decided though a small error in reading,—

> " And thereupon these errors are arose."

" These errors *all* arose " has been suggested as the poet's words ; and we find *all* in the margin of the corrected folio, 1632, while " are " is erased in the text.

P. 178. The following lines, as they are printed in the folio, 1623, have been the source of considerable cavil :

> " Thirty-three years have I but gone in travail
> Of you, my sons, and till this present hour
> My heavy burden are delivered."

That the above is corrupt there can be no question ; and in the folio, 1632, the printer attempted thus to amend the passage :—

> " Thirty-three years have I been gone in travail
> Of you, my sons, and till this present hour
> My heavy burdens are delivered."

Malone gave it thus :—

> " Twenty-five years have I but gone in travail
> Of you, my sons; until this present hour
> My heavy burden not delivered."

The manuscript-corrector of the folio, 1632, makes the

slightest possible change in the second line, and at once removes the whole difficulty : he puts it,—

> " Thirty-three years have I been gone in travail
> Of you, my sons, and *at* this present hour
> My heavy burdens are delivered."

The Abbess means, of course, that she was, as it were, delivered of the double burden of her twin sons *at* the hour of this discovery of them. With such an easy and clear solution of what has produced many conjectural emendations, it is needless to notice the various proposals of Theobald and others, which are all nearly equally wide of the mark.

F

MUCH ADO ABOUT NOTHING.

ACT I. SCENE I.

P. 188. In the stage-direction at the opening of the scene the manuscript-corrector of the folio, 1632, has expunged the words *Innogen, his wife,* as if the practice had not then been for her to appear before the audience in this or in any other portion of the comedy ; and it is certain that no word ever escapes from her in the dialogue. It has been supposed by some that, though merely a mute, she was seen by the spectators, but in what way she was to be known to them to be the mother of Hero and the wife of Leonato is not stated. Another change in the same stage-direction merits notice : it is that the word "Messenger" is converted into *Gentleman,* and the manner in which he joins in the conversation shows, that he must have been a person superior in rank to what we now understand by a messenger. Consistently with this notion all the prefixes to what he says are altered from *Mes.* to *Gent.* In other dramas Shakespeare gives important parts to persons whom he only calls Messengers ; and it requires no proof that in the reign of Elizabeth the Messengers who conveyed news to the Court from abroad were frequently officers whose services were in part rewarded by this distinction. It was in this capacity that Raleigh seems first to have attracted the favour of the Queen.

P. 195. For "he that hits me," the corrector of the folio, 1632, gives "he that *first* hits me," which supports the notion that the successful marksman was to be called Adam, as *the first man.* The allusion can hardly be to Adam Bell, because it is William of Cloudesley who, in the ballad, is the principal archer, and who cleaves the apple on his son's head.

P. 197. There is certainly a misprint in the second line of Don Pedro's speech, where he is adverting to Claudio's reason for loving Hero :—

> " What need the bridge much broader than the flood ?
> The fairest grant is the necessity."

Here " grant" has little or no meaning, for Hero has not yet been even sounded upon the point, and the line ought to run in the manner in which the corrector of the folio, 1632, has left it,

> " The fairest *ground* is the necessity."

The fairest *ground* for Claudio's love was the necessity of the case, which rendered needless any " treatise."

SCENE III.

P. 199. John the Bastard, telling Conrade of his melancholy, says " There is no measure in the occasion that breeds," the pronoun *it* being wanting after the verb, which is found in the margin of the corrected folio, 1632. Lower, on the same page, Conrade remarks " You have of late stood out against your brother ;" but they had been reconciled, and the expression ought to be, as we find it in the same authority, " You have *till* of late stood out against your brother."

ACT II.   SCENE I.

P. 202. The speech of Beatrice requires *father* in the first clause as well as in the second, but all the folios are without it : it is thus added in manuscript in the folio, 1632, " Yes faith ; it is my cousin's duty to make courtesy, and say, *Father*, as it please you," &c.

P. 203. The drollery of Beatrice's description of the difference between " wooing, wedding, and repenting" is much injured by the omission of a pun just at the conclusion—

" The first suit (she says) is hot and hasty, like a Scotch jig, and full as fantastical ; the wedding, mannerly, modest, as a measure, full of state and ancientry ; and then comes repentance, and with his bad legs falls into the cinque-pace faster and faster, 'till he sink *a pace* into his grave.' The words in Italics are left out in the printed copy, but are added in manuscript in the margin of the folio, 1632.

P. 204. It is just worth observation that the corrector of the folio, 1632, altered *love* of the folios to "Jove" of the quarto.

P. 206. The last line of Claudio's soliloquy is redundant in measure, by the use of " therefore" instead of *then :* the corrected folio, 1632, has the line

"Which I mistrusted not.   Farewell, *then,* Hero."

P. 207. In the folio, 1632, there are two decided errors of the press in Benedick's soliloquy, where " fowl" is misprinted *soul,* and "yea" *you :* both are remedied in manuscript. They do not exist in the folio, 1623.

P. 208. It was proposed by Johnson, in Benedick's long speech to the Prince against Beatrice, to read *importable,* for "impossible" (of all the printed editions) in the sense of unbearable, insupportable ; and "impossible" is converted into *importable* by the corrector of the folio, 1632. Three lines lower *her* is properly inserted before "terminations ;" but the change made in the next sentence of *lent* for "left" is of more consequence and quite as evidently right :—" I would not marry her (he exclaims) though she were endowed with all that Adam had *lent* him before he transgressed." Adam was endowed with every thing "*before* he transgressed" and Benedick is referring to his state of perfection. The folio, 1623, has also the blunder of " left" for *lent.*

P. 209. The folios give the latter part of the speech of Beatrice thus—" But civil, Count, civil as an orange, and something of a jealous complexion." The 4to, 1600, has " of *that* jealous complexion ;" but the corrector of the folio, 1632, reads "something of *as* jealous *a* complexion," which affords exactly the same point, and seems to prove that he was not guided by the old 4to.

SCENE II.

P. 213. In Borachio's statement of the mode in which he would proceed in tainting the character of Hero, he tells John the Bastard, that if he will bring the Prince and Claudio at night, they shall hear Margaret, disguised as Hero, "term me Claudio," which must be an error, as Claudio was to be one of the spectators. For "Claudio" Theobald wished to substitute *Borachio*, in order to remove the difficulty, and the abridgment of the name of *Borachio* is inserted in the margin of the corrected folio, 1632, proving that Theobald was not mistaken.

P. 214. The word "truths" of the folios ought to be *proofs*, where Borachio says, "There shall appear such seeming *truths* of Hero's disloyalty." The corrector of the folio, 1632, has it, "There shall appear such seeming *proofs* of Hero's disloyalty," which is unquestionably what is meant.

SCENE III.

P. 215. For "orthography" of the folios, modern editors have "orthographer," and in this change they are supported by the manuscript-corrector of the folio, 1632.

Stage-directions in this scene, so necessary to the intelligibility of it, are omitted in the old printed copies. When Benedick enters, we are told in manuscript in the folio, 1632, that he has his *Boy following*; and when at the end of his speech, with the words "I will hide me in the arbour," he *withdraws*, as Malone expresses it, the corrector of the folio, 1632, has added *Retires behind the trees*. The name of "Jack Wilson" (who did not sing the song when the folio, 1632, was corrected) is struck out, and Balthazar's entrance is marked in the proper place. When Benedick afterwards comes from his ambush, nothing is said in the printed folios to indicate the fact ; but *Forward*, meaning that he advanced to the front of the stage, is written in the margin of the folio, 1632. Against his speeches to himself, while he is concealed, is written *Behind;* so that we here see exactly the mode in which the rather complicated business of the scene was anciently conducted.

P. 217. The second verse of Balthazar's song is thus altered in manuscript in the folio, 1632.

" Sing no more ditties, sing no mo,
        Or dumps so dull and heavy ;
    The *frauds* of men were ever so
        Since summer first was leafy."

It seems right thus to distinguish between *ditties* and *dumps*, apparently two distinct species of composition ; and the third line is evidently improved by putting " frauds," like the verb it governs, in the plural: the usual mode of printing it has been,

" The *fraud* of men *was* ever so."

P. 219. The difference is not very material, but the meaning is heightened by the addition of the word *full* at the close of the speech of Leonato, " there will she set in her smock, till she have writ a sheet of paper full." The sentence ends at " paper," excepting in the manuscript of the corrector of the folio, 1632. Lower down Claudio has been made to say, " Then, down upon her knees she falls, weeps, sobs, beats her heart, tears her hair, prays, curses ;—O sweet Benedick! God give me patience." For " curses" the corrector of the folio, 1632, substitutes *cries;* and we are hardly to suppose that Beatrice utters "curses" at all, but especially at the very moment when she exclaims, " O, sweet Benedick !" and when she " prays" that God would " give her patience." For " It were an alms to hang him," put into the mouth of Don Pedro, the corrected folio has, " It were an alms *deed* to hang him," such being the usual expression.

P. 222. The force of Beatrice's speech is considerably increased by the insertion of a negative. Benedick asks Beatrice whether she takes pleasure in the message to him ? and she answers, as the passage has always been printed, " Yea, just so much as you may take upon a knife's point, and choke a daw withal." The corrected folio, 1632, tells us that the pleasure to which Beatrice acknowledged was so little that it might be taken on a knife's point " and *not* choke a daw withal:" it was not enough even to choke a daw.

ACT III.   SCENE I.

P. 223. "Enter Beatrice *stealing in behind*" is the expressive stage-direction in the corrected folio, 1632, and the scene is conducted much in the same way as the preceding, in which the same trick is played upon Benedick. When Hero and Ursula are to talk *loud* in praise of Benedick, in order that Beatrice may overhear them, that word is inserted in the margin.

P. 225. Ursula asks Hero, when she is to be married, and the unintelligible answer is, "Why, every day ;—to-morrow :" the correction of the folio, 1632, has made it quite clear by setting right a misprint : there Hero replies, "Why, *in a* day, —to-morrow."

P. 226. There is a curious misrepresentation of the poet's language in Beatrice's soliloquy, on coming *forward* after lying concealed in the "woodbine coverture." It begins,

> "What fire is in mine ears ? Can this be true ?
> Stand I condemn'd for pride and scorn so much ?
> Contempt, farewell ! and, maiden pride, adieu !
> No glory lives behind the back of such."

Nobody has explained what is meant by the words "behind the back of such," nor need we inquire into it, since they are merely one of the perversions arising out of the mishearing of the scribe of the copy of the play used by the printer : the real words of the fourth line appear to be

> "No glory lives *but in the lack* of such;"

that is to say, no maiden can expect to triumph or glory in any love enterprise, who is afflicted with pride, scorn, and contempt : let her want, or *lack* them, and she may attain the object of her wishes. The sound of "behind the back," and of "but in the lack" is not so dissimilar, that we cannot account for the blunder, on the supposition that the copyist wrote from what was read, or possibly recited to him.

ACT IV. SCENE I.

P. 243. Pope altered Claudio's exclamation as it stands in the old copies, "Out on thee seeming!" to "Out on *thy* seeming!" The corrector of the folio, 1632, supports the change by converting "thee" into *thy*. For

> "That rage in savage sensuality,"

he substitutes,

> "That *range* in savage sensuality;"

which does not seem a necessary emendation, any more than his change of *wild* into "wide" in the next line.

P. 246. Two important mistakes are made in Leonato's speech on the supposed detection of Hero: the father wishes her to die, rather than survive the imputation cast upon her, and tells her, according to the folio, 1623,

> "For did I think thou would'st not quickly die,
> Thought I thy spirits were stronger than thy shames,
> Myself would on the reward of reproaches
> Strike at thy life.   Griev'd I, I had but one?
> Chid I for that at frugal nature's frame?"

The folio, 1632, has *rearward* for "reward," and makes no other change; but what appears to be the true reading? We have it among the manuscript-corrections of the second folio,

> "Myself would, on the *hazard* of reproaches,
> Strike at thy life;"

or at the risk of the reproaches that would follow such a deed: and afterwards

> "Griev'd I, I had but one?
> Chid I for that at frugal nature's *frown?*"

that is to say, Did I complain of the *frown* of frugal nature, which forbade my having more than one daughter?

> "Chid I for that a frugal nature's frame,"

puzzled the commentators, and they endeavour to reconcile us to the word "frame" in various ways; but they never seem to have supposed, as now appears to be the case, that "frame" had been misprinted for *frowne*.

There is a still more injurious representation of Shakespeare's language in the last line of the same speech :—

> "O! she is fallen
> Into a pit of ink, that the wide sea
> Hath drops too few to wash her clean again,
> And salt too little, which may season give
> To her foul tainted flesh!"

This has been the universal reading, upon which Steevens remarks that "the same metaphor from the kitchen" occurs in "Twelfth Night." This "metaphor from the kitchen" has entirely arisen out of the ordinary error of mistaking the *f* and the long *s*; for the correction in the margin of the folio, 1632, shows that Shakespeare had no notion of the kind, and instead of using such commonplace epithets as "foul" and "tainted," that he employed one of his noblest compounds,—*soul-tainted*,—

> "And salt too little, which may season give
> To her *soul-tainted* flesh."

Hero's flesh was tainted to the soul by the accusation just made against her.

P. 247. The old printer was peculiarly unfortunate in this great scene: in the third line of the Friar's speech

> "And given way unto this course of fortune,"

ought to be, in allusion to the unexpected charge against Hero, which had altered Claudio's purpose,

> "And given way unto this *cross* of fortune."

But the last line is still worse, where the Friar, after maintaining from circumstances that Hero had been unjustly accused, says,

> "Trust not my age,
> My reverence, calling, nor divinity,
> If this sweet lady lie not guiltless here
> Under some biting error."

The corrector of the folio, 1632, informs us that this passage should certainly run thus :—

> "Trust not my age,
> My *reverend* calling, nor divinity,
> If this sweet lady lie not guiltless here
> Under some *blighting* error."

To show in what a brief, but still intelligible, way the corrector of the folio, 1632, made his alterations, we may notice that, *blighting* being mis-printed "biting" in the old copies, he did nothing more than add the letter *l* after the letter *b*, leaving the rest of the letters to be understood.

P. 248. Further on we meet with two other blunders of the same kind, though perhaps not of so much importance—one of them in a line which has been quoted by Steevens to justify the use of "frame" in a former passage:—

> " Whose spirits toil in frame of villainies."

The manuscript-corrector of the folio, 1732, changes "frame of" to *fraud and*—

> " Whose spirits toil in *fraud* and villainies,"

which seems a much more easy and natural expression than "frame of villainies;" but in this way the commentators have sometimes vindicated one corruption by another. At the same time, it must be admitted that "in frame of villainies," may mean in the fabrication of villainies.

More doubt may be entertained as to the next, real or supposed, error of the press: it is in Leonato's indignant speech, where this couplet occurs:

> " But they shall find, awak'd in such a kind,
> Both strength of limb and policy of mind."

Now, independently of the consideration, which perhaps deserves little weight, that a grieved and infuriated father would not be disposed to rhyme under such circumstances, it will be observed that "find," also rhyming to "kind" and "mind," is met with in the first of the two lines: —neither is "kind" very well fitted to the place where it occurs. On the whole, we may feel willing to adopt the emendation of the corrector of the folio, 1632, when he reads,

> " But they shall find, awak'd in such a *cause*,
> Both strength of limb and policy of mind."

The "cause" in which his strength, and policy, were to be awaked, was, of course, that of his daughter, should it turn out that she had been traduced. The taste of the corrector may here have come in aid of such a change.

P. 249. To show the minuteness of the criticism of the manuscript-corrector we may advert to a mere transposition (but still triflingly affecting the sense), which he makes in the Friar's speech, where he remarks,

> "That what we have we prize not to the worth
> Whiles we enjoy it, but being lack'd and lost,
> Why, then we rack the value."

Now, as a thing would probably not be "lacked" till after it had been "lost," the corrector changed the position of the words and read "lost and lack'd," which might be the order in which the words came from Shakespeare's pen.

SCENE II.

P. 252. In this comic scene, in the old copies, great confusion prevails in the prefixes of the various speeches. The names of the actors, such as Kemp, Cowley, and Andrew, are put instead of those of the characters they sustained, and the manuscript-corrector of the folio, 1632, perhaps did not think it necessary to set them right. Dispute has arisen as to the mode of dividing a part of the dialogue, obviously misprinted in other respects: in the folios it stands as follows :—

> "*Const.* Come, let them be opinioned.
> *Sex.* Let them be in the hands of Coxscomb.
> *Kem.* Gods my life, where's the Sexton?" &c.

This has been distributed in different ways, into which it is not necessary to enter, but we will subjoin the manner in which it is corrected in manuscript in the folio, 1632 :—

> "*Const.* Come, let them be opinioned.
> *Sexton.* Let them be *bound*.
> *Borachio.* Hands off, coxcomb."

P. 255. When Dogberry, to show his importance, says that he is "a rich fellow enough, go to ; and a fellow that hath had losses," it has naturally puzzled some persons to see how his losses could tend to establish that he was rich. Here, in truth, we have another misprint: *leases* was often spelt of old —*leasses*, and this is the origin of the blunder; for, according to the corrector of the folio, 1632, we ought to read, "a rich fellow enough, go to ; and a fellow that hath had *leases*." To have been the owner of leases might very well prove that Dogberry was "a rich fellow enough."

ACT V. SCENE I.

P. 256. The defective line,

> " And bid him speak of patience,"

Ritson, who had no very good ear, but who was nevertheless right in this instance, recommends should be thus printed:—

> " And bid him speak *to me* of patience."

The addition is obvious enough, and it is made by the corrector of the folio, 1632.

Few passages have produced more contention and doubt than this line, as it is given in the first and other folios,

> " And sorrow, wag ! cry hem, when he should groan."

Leonato is telling his brother, that his grief is beyond all example, and that he can never be comforted, until he shall meet with a man, suffering under equal calamities, who can defy his misfortunes,

> " If such a one will smile, and stroke his beard ;
> And sorrow, wag ! cry hem, when he should groan," &c.

The corrector of the folio, 1632, shows that, "And sorrow wag," was a misprint for " Call sorrow joy," so that he reads,—

> " If such a one will smile, and stroke his beard ;
> *Call* sorrow *joy ;* cry hem, when he should groan ;
> Patch grief with proverbs ; make misfortune drunk
> With candle-wasters ; bring him *you* to me,
> And I of him will gather patience."

This seems to be as good a solution as we are likely to obtain : the difficulty is to account for the misprint.

P. 261. Boiled calf's head and capers was formerly not an unusual dish ; and when Claudio tells Don Pedro, that Benedick hath " bid him to a calf's head and a capon," the corrector of the folio, 1632, marks it as an error of the press, and alters it to " calf's head and capers." Claudio means to joke upon the challenge that he had received.

P. 262. For the scriptural allusion, in the words " God saw him, when he was hid in the garden," the corrector puts it as

a question, "Who saw him, when he was hid in the garden ?"
It seems likely that the speech was so amended, in consequence of the increased prevalence of puritanism soon after
the date when the folio, 1632, was published.   We shall have
to notice other changes of the same kind and, perhaps, for
the same reason hereafter.

P. 265. According to the folio, 1623, Leonato says to
Claudio,—

> " I cannot bid you bid my daughter live."

The folio, 1632, in its uncorrected state, gives it,—

> " I cannot bid you daughter live ; "

and the manuscript-corrector of that impression tells us that
the line should be,—

> " I cannot bid you *cause my* daughter live."

It is impossible now to know from what source this eupho-
nious emendation was derived.

SCENE III.

P. 271. The following is the " Song" as it is found corrected in the folio, 1632 :—

> " Pardon, goddess of the night,
>   Those that slew thy virgin *bright*,
>   For the which, with songs of woe,
>   Round about her tomb *we go*.
> Midnight, assist our moan ; help us to sigh and groan
>   Heavily, heavily,
>   Graves yawn and yield your dead
>   Till death be uttered,
>   *Heavily, heavily*."

Thus we see *virgin bright* for " virgin knight ;" *we go* for ' 'they
go ;" and *Heavily, heavily*, in the last instance, for " Heavenly,
heavenly."   There was a well-known tune of " Heavily,
heavily," and probably the above was sung to it. (See
British Bibliographer, ii. 560.)   It will be remarked that the
rest of this scene is in rhyme, with the exception of these
two lines :—

> " Thanks to you all, and leave us : fare you well.
>   Good morrow, masters : each his several way."

Probably this couplet also rhymed as the play was originally

written, and the corrector of the folio, 1632, shows how
slight a change was necessary to restore the jingle,—

> " Good morrow, masters : each his way *can tell.*"

SCENE IV.

P. 272. Leonato desires his daughter, his niece, and Ursula to withdraw, and to return to the scene "masked."
Such was, no doubt, the course when this comedy was originally produced, about the year 1599 ; but it should seem
that in the time of the corrector of the folio, 1632, it was the
practice for the ladies to enter *veiled*, when Claudio was
expecting to be married to the niece, and not to the daughter
of Leonato. Therefore, when Antonio enters with the ladies
(p. 274), we are told, in a manuscript stage-direction, that
they are *veiled ;* and when Hero, and subsequently Beatrice,
discover themselves, *unveil* is in both instances written in
the margin. In the interval between the first acting of
" Much Ado about Nothing," and the reprinting of it in the
folio, 1632, the fashion of wearing masks had perhaps declined among ladies, and for that reason *veils* may have been
substituted for masks in the performance.

P. 274. When Hero unveils, Claudio can hardly believe
his eyes, but the lady re-assures him by saying, according to
the folios,—

> " One Hero died, but I do live ;"

which is a defective verse, and the quarto, 1600, has the line
thus :—

> " One Hero died *defil'd*, but I do live."

Now, it is most unlikely that Hero should herself tell Claudio
that she had been " defiled," and the word supplied by the
corrector of the folio, 1632, seems on all accounts much preferable :—

> " One hero died *belied*, but I do live."

Here we see the lady naturally denying her guilt, and attributing her death to the slander thrown upon her. Shakespeare's word must have been *belied*, and the mishearing of it
may have led to the insertion of " defiled" in the 4to, 1600.
The editor of the folio, 1623, perhaps purposely omitted
defiled on account of its unfitness.

P. 275. Sir Thomas Hanmer conjecturally added *for* in the subsequent line to the improvement of the metre,—

> " Have been deceived ; *for* they swore you did."

The corrector of the folio, 1632, takes precisely the same course, and in the few succeeding lines makes changes clearly recommended by the greater accuracy of the verse and language. We transcribe them as they stand in manuscript, but it is not necessary to accompany them by the text as ordinarily represented, and we have printed the added or altered words in italics :—

> " *Bene.* Why then your uncle, and the prince, and Claudio
> Have been deceived ; *for* they swore you did.
> *Beat.* Do not you love me ?
> *Bene.* Troth, no more than reason.
> *Beat.* Why then, my cousin Margaret and Ursula
> Are much deceived, for they *swore* you did.
> *Bene.* They swore *that* you were almost sick for me.
> *Beat.* They swore *that* you were well-nigh dead for me.
> *Bene. It is* no matter.—Then, you do not love me.
> *Beat.* No truly, but in friendly recompence."

Here the halting measure of the lines, as contained in all the folios is set right, and the effect of the retorts much increased by the adoption by each party of precisely the same forms of expression.

P. 276. The old editions assign " Peace ! I will stop your mouth" to Leonato ; but most modern editors, following the example of Theobald, have transferred it to Benedick. So does the corrector of the folio, 1632.

After the word " Dance," at the very conclusion of the play, the manuscript-corrector has added *of all the actors,* to show that every person on the stage joined in it. Perhaps it might have been guessed from what is said, without this information.

LOVE'S LABOUR'S LOST.

ACT I. SCENE I.

P. 285. Theobald judiciously proposed to alter the line,—

> " When I to fast expressly am forbid,"

as follows :—

> " When I to *feast* expressly am forbid."

The same change was made in manuscript by the corrector of the folio, 1632. Lower down, that edition has,—

> " Light, seeking light, doth light beguile ; "

evidently defective in sense and measure, and the corrector, by inserting " of light" in the margin, makes the passage run as in the folio, 1623,—

> " Light, seeking light, doth light *of light* beguile ; "

which of course is the true reading.

P. 287. The folio, 1623, presents us with this passage :—

> " So you to study now it is too late,
> That were to climb o'er the house to unlock the gate."

This text the folio, 1632, adopted, excepting that it has *t'unlock* for " to unlock." The quarto, 1598, had previously printed the couplet thus :—

> " So you to study now it is too late,
> Climb o'er the house to unlock the little gate."

Finally, we present it as it appears in the folio, 1632, corrected in manuscript, which seems preferable to the other authorities :—

> " So you, *by* study now it is too late,
>   Climb o'er the house-*top* to unlock the gate."

Five lines lower we meet in the folio, 1623, with,—

> " Yet, confident, I'll keep what I have sworne ; "

which is exactly copied from the quarto, 1598. The editor of the folio, 1632, seeing that a rhyme was intended, printed the line,—

> " Yet confident I'll keep what I have *swore* ; "

But the manuscript-corrector of that impression gives us what Shakespeare wrote, which preserves the rhyme, and at the same time avoids the vulgarism :—

> " Yet confident I'll keep *to* what I swore."

We come to a more important emendation lower down, where Biron reads the decree " that no woman shall come within a mile" of the court, " on pain of losing her tongue." This Longaville declares, according to all editions, to be

> " A dangerous law against gentility ; "

the corrector of the folio, 1632, tells us to read,—

> " A dangerous law against *garrulity*."

The two words were easily confounded, but the latter certainly affords the clearer, the stronger, and the more humorous meaning.

P. 288. All the folios have,—

> " If I break faith, this word shall break for me ; "

which must be wrong, and *speak* has usually been placed instead of "break" in the second instance ; but the corrector of the folio, 1632, informs us that the true word is *plead* :—

> " If I break faith, this word shall *plead* for me."

P. 289. The King describes Armado as

> " A refined traveller of Spain,
>   A man in all the world's new fashion planted."

The folio, 1632, has it thus :—

> " A man in all the world new fashion planted."

G

Planted yields but a poor sense, and the manuscript-corrector
of that edition reads,—

" A man. in all the *world-new* fashions *flaunted.*"

That is, a man *flaunted,* or decked out, in all the world-
new fashions. Shakespeare elsewhere uses the substantive,
"flaunts," but not the verb.

P. 290. Theobald congratulated himself on the change of
"heaven" to *having* in this passage, "A high hope for a low
heaven : God grant us patience!" He was most likely
wrong. The subject of conversation is "a letter from the
magnificent Armado" just brought in by Costard, upon
which Biron observes, "How low soever the matter, I hope
in God for high words." Longaville's reply has reference to
these "high words," and the corrector of the folio, 1632,
says that we ought to erase "heaven" for *hearing :*—

" A high hope for a low *hearing :* God grant us patience ! "

What Biron adds seems consequent upon it, when he asks
whether the patience prayed for is to be granted, "to hear,
or to forbear *hearing.*" Four lines below, the manuscript-
corrector has altered "clime in the merriness" of the old
copies, to "*chime in* in the merriness," in allusion to the
laughable contents expected in Armado's letter, "in the
merriness" of which the King and his companions hope to
"chime in," or participate.

P. 291. The words of Armado's letter, "that shallow
vassal," appear always to have been misprinted, and the
context, as well as the manuscript-corrector of the folio,
1632, require us to alter it to "that shallow *vessel.*" The
connecting words are "that unlettered small-knowing soul,
that shallow *vessel,* which, as I remember, hight Costard," &c.

P. 293. "Sirrah, come on," has uniformly been assigned
to Biron ; but it seems more properly to belong to the
Constable, who had Costard in custody, and to him they are
given by the corrector of the folio, 1632. He also, five lines
below, inserts *thee* in the proverbial sentence, "Set *thee*
down, sorrow," as it stands in the quarto, 1598, and as it
occurs again, Act IV. Scene III. p. 331, where Biron exclaims, "Well, set *thee* down, sorrow!" The same proverb
was most likely quoted in the same words in both places.

SCENE II.

P. 296. When Moth apostrophises, " My father's wit, and
my mother's tongue, assist me !" Armado, in foolish admiration, breaks out, " Sweet invocation of a child ! most
pretty and most pathetical !" Thus it is given in all editions ;
but the old corrector changes " pathetical" into *poetical*,
in reference to the boy's poetical " invocation." Yet he
allows " pathetical" to remain in the text in Act IV. Scene I.
(p. 324), where Costard terms Moth " a most pathetical
nit." The word occurs in " As you like it," Act IV. Scene II.
(p. 77), where Rosalind tells Orlando that if he " come one
minute behind his hour" she will consider him a " most
pathetical break-promise ;" but there no reason existed for
making any correction.

P. 299. When Armado, relinquishing arms for love, exclaims, " Adieu, valour ! rust, rapier ! be still, drum ! for
your manager is in love," nobody has made a note upon the
uncouth word " manager" so applied. The corrector of the
folio, 1632, shows it to have been an error of the printer, or of
the scribe, for a much more appropriate and expressive term,
which, perhaps, they did not understand, *armiger*—" Adieu,
valour ! rust, rapier ! be still, drum, for your *armiger* is in
love." This emendation is followed by another, two lines lower,
where the old copies have " Assist me some extemporal god
of rhyme, for, I am sure, I shall turn sonnet." For *sonnet*,
which, so used, is little better than nonsense, the proposed
reading is *sonnet-maker*, as ballad-maker, song-maker, &c.,
" for, I am sure, I shall turn *sonnet-maker*." The usual word
has been *sonnetteer*, which would answer the purpose, if it
were in use at the time. The form of the word at that date
and earlier would rather have been *sonnetter*, like *enginer*,
mutiner, &c.

ACT II.   SCENE I.

P. 300. Steevens has appended a note to the line,—

" Now, madam, summon up your dearest spirits,"

in which he observes, that " *Dear*, in our author's language, has many shades of meaning : in the present instance and the next, it appears to signify, best, most powerful." The fact is (if we may trust the corrector of the folio, 1632) that "dearest" was a misprint for *clearest ;* and it is easy to see how *cl* might be mistaken for *d.* He gives the line :—

> " Now, madam, summon up your *clearest* spirits ; "

that is, her brightest and purest spirits, that the Princess might adequately discharge the important embassy entrusted to her by her father.

P. 306. All the folios have a decided corruption in the line,—

> " Though so denied farther harbour in my house,"

which has commonly been printed with *fair* for "farther." This may be right, but the manuscript-corrector inserts perhaps a better word in his margin :—

> " Though so denied *free* harbour in my house : "

alluding to the refusal to the Princess of the unrestrained rights of hospitality in the King's palace.

P. 306. In the short snip-snap dialogue between Rosaline and Biron, the prefixes to the speeches of the latter are always wrong, as if Boyet had been engaged with the lady in the wit-contest. The corrector of the folio, 1632, puts them right, in consistency with the quarto, 1598.

ACT III. SCENE I.

P. 309. In the folios this Act commences thus :—

> " *Enter Braggart and Boy.*
> SONG.
> *Brag.* Warble, child : make passionate my sense of hearing.
> *Boy.* Concolinel.
> *Brag.* Sweet air ! Go, tenderness of years," &c.

Hence we may gather that the scene opens while the Boy is singing, and that Armado (called *Braggart*), delighted with the music, requires more, upon which the boy commences an Italian song, the first words of which are *Con Colinel.* The manuscript-corrector of the folio, 1632, inserts the first words both of the English and of the Italian song, *See my love,* being the first, and *Amato* (which he spells *armato*) *bene,* the second. This circumstance may lead to the detection of them in some of our ancient collections of musical airs. Possibly, if not probably, *Con Colinel* was not the same as what in manuscript is called *Amato bene,* and it may, in the time of the corrector, have been substituted, the air of *Con Colinel* having gone out of fashion. Any scrap of information regarding the songs written or introduced by Shakespeare is highly interesting.

P. 310. After the Page's dissertation on the mode of "betraying nice wenches," Armado asks,—

> " How hast thou purchas'd this experience ? "

and the answer is, as it stands printed in the old copies,—

> "By my penne of observation."

Sir Thomas Hanmer altered "penne" to *penny,* and Farmer and Ritson say that it alludes to a tract called " The Pennyworth of Wit." The manuscript-corrector entertained an entirely different notion : he tells us, as seems not at all unlikely, that *paine* (so spelt of old) was misprinted "penne ;" and this is the more probable, because the letter *y* at the end of *penny* would hardly have been converted into *e.* The true answer would therefore be, when Armado inquires how the Boy had procured his knowledge ?—

> " By my *pain* of observation,"

or by the pains he had taken in observing the characters of men and women. What most militates against this alteration is the figurative use of the word " purchased," for obtained, by Armado.

P. 311. For " a message well sympathised" we ought unquestionably to substitute "a *messenger* well sympathised." Costard was to be the *messenger,* not the message. "Message" is altered to " messenger" in the margin of the corrected folio, 1632.

P. 312. There are two emendations in Armado's soliloquy, after his Page has gone out to fetch Costard, one of them denoting a strange corruption which has crept into the text from the earliest date, and in all impressions. The lines have been universally printed as follows :—

> " A most acute juvenal; voluble and free of grace!
> By thy favour, sweet welkin, I must sigh in thy face :
> Most rude melancholy, valour gives thee place."

In the corrected folio, 1632, they are made to run :—

> " A most acute juvenal; voluble and *fair* of grace!
> By thy favour, sweet welkin, I must sigh in thy face :
> *Moist-eyed* melancholy, valour gives thee place."

"Fair of grace" is good-looking, whereas "*free* of grace" means little more than had been already said by the epithet voluble. "Most rude melancholy" has no particular appropriateness, whereas " *moist-eyed* melancholy" is peculiarly accordant with the sighs Armado breathes, with due apology, in the face of the welkin.

It may be enough to say with reference to Costard's speech, a few lines below, that the manuscript-corrector completely justifies Tyrwhitt's emendation " no salve in *them all.*"

P. 313. The last line of the Page's *Lenvoy* is this in the manuscript-corrected folio, 1632 :—

> " Staying the odds by *making* four,"

instead of " adding four :" to add four would not have " stayed the odds." The next line is thus divided between Armado and the Page in the corrected folio, whereas in all editions it is made to belong to the Page only :—

> " *Arm.* A good Lenvoy !
> *Page.* Ending in goose, would you desire more ?"

This change gives greater pungency to the dialogue, and makes Armado's position more ridiculous.

P. 314. A point has been wholly lost by the omission of a word supplied by the manuscript-corrector. The ordinary, indeed the only, text has been this :—

> " *Armado.* Sirrah Costard, I will enfranchise thee.
> *Costard.* O ! marry me to one Frances ?" &c.

This is unintelligible, for how could Costard imagine that Armado meant " to marry him to one Frances" or to any

body else by merely saying to him, " I will enfranchise thee ?"
What Armado says is,—

> " Sirrah Costard, *marry*, I will enfranchise thee ; "

to which Costard's blundering answer applies naturally enough,
" O! marry me to one Frances ?" &c. Just afterwards, for the
incomplete expression of Armado, "I will give thee thy liberty,
set thee from durance," the manuscript-corrector gives " set
thee *free* from durance," the omission by the printer having
been caused, no doubt, by the words " thee" and " free" following each other immediately.

P. 317. What has usually been printed,—

> " A whitely wanton with a velvet brow,"

the manuscript-corrector of the folio, 1632, converts into " a
witty wanton," the true word, in reference to Rosaline's
talents, and certainly not to her complexion, which we are
over and over again told is dark. The word is *whitly* in the
old copies, and is a mere error of the press. We must therefore certainly read,—

> " A *witty* wanton with a velvet brow."

ACT IV.　SCENE I.

P. 319. The Princess good-humouredly rebukes the Fo-
rester for flattering her, and exclaims,—

> " O, heresy in fair, fit for these days !
> A giving hand, though foul, shall have fair praise."

The corrector of the folio, 1632, has it,—

> " O, heresy in *faith*, fit for these days ! "

which is probably right, although Shakespeare, like many
other poets of his time, uses " fair" for *fairness* or *beauty*.

P. 324. Costard speaks a soliloquy in rhyme at the close
of this scene, one line in which is wanting, as is evident from
the corresponding line, and from the insertion of the addition,
though in a wrong place, by the corrector of the folio, 1632.
He perhaps intended to write it in the blank space nearest

to where it ought to come in, but he has written it in another
blank space above it, and has drawn a mark with his pen to
the spot where it is wanted. The whole passage is this, and
the line in manuscript we have printed in italics:—

> " Armado o' the one side,—O, a most dainty man !
> To see him walk before a lady, and to bear her fan !
> To see him kiss his hand ! and how most sweetly a' will swear !
> *Looking babies in her eyes, his passion to declare ;*
> And his page o' t' other side, that handful of *small* wit !
> Ah heavens, it is a most pathetical nit !"

Besides the entire line, which escaped the printer or the
copyist of the drama, the word *small* was also left out.

SCENE II.

P. 324. The manuscript-corrector of the folio, 1632, has
made Act IV. commence with this scene ; but improperly, because Holofernes, Sir Nathaniel, and Dull enter on the *exit*
of Costard, so that there is, in fact, no change of place, which
usually constitutes the division.

P. 325. Part of Sir Nathaniel's speech is in rhyme, and
part in prose, and there can be little doubt that the whole of
it was originally in irregular jingling verse : the corrector of
the folio, 1632, shows that some words, necessary to it, had
been lost, though he evidently does not supply all that is
wanting. Sir Nathaniel's first line rhymes to what Holofernes had said,—

> " O, thou monster ignorance, how deformed dost thou look !"
> *Nath.* Sir, he hath never fed of the dainties that are bred in a book.
> He hath not eat paper, as it were, he hath not drunk ink :
> His intellect is not replenished ; he is only an animal, *not to*
> *think ;*
> Only sensible in the duller parts, and such barren plants
> Are set before us that we thankful should be,
> Which we, *having* taste and feeling, are for those parts that do
> fructify in us more than he :
> For as it would ill become me to be vain, indiscreet, or a fool,
> So were a patch set on learning, to *set* him in a school," &c.

It is not possible to put the whole right, but the old corrector's contributions towards the original text are printed
above in italics : how it happened that he could add so

much, and not be able to furnish the rest, is a point we do not pretend to explain. The sense is a little obscure ; and as far as jingle is concerned, the line ending with "plants" has nothing to rhyme with it.

P. 329. The characters of Holofernes (usually called the *Pedant* in the old prefixes) and of Sir Nathaniel are much confused in this scene ; it may be sufficient to state that the speech " Here are only numbers ratified," &c., is given to Holofernes ; but Theobald's apparently excellent emendation of *imitari* for " imitary" of the old copies is not countenanced by the corrector of the folio, 1632, who, instead of " imitary is nothing," reads, " *imitating* is nothing," meaning that there is no merit in mere imitation. For " tired horse" he reads " *trained* horse," which affords a clearer and less dubitable meaning.

SCENE III.

P. 331. The manuscript stage-directions in this scene, inserted in manuscript in the folio, 1632, are extremely minute, and the King cannot enter with " Ay me !" but we are informed in the margin that *he sighs*. When, at this juncture, Biron conceals himself, the printed stage-direction is only *He stands aside*, but that is obliterated, and *He gets him in a tree* is put in its place in manuscript. When, too, Biron interposes some remark to himself, it is added that he is *in the tree*, and when he descends to detect his companions, *Come down* is inscribed in the margin. As each character retires or advances on the stage, information of it is duly given, so that the whole business and conduct of the scene are clearly explained.

P. 332. Two transpositions, one of them of some moment, are pointed out by the manuscript-corrector: the first occurs in the fourth line, where " night of dew" (strangely justified by Steevens) is altered to *dew of night :* the second instance is only *thou dost* for " dost thou," in the fifteenth line of the King's sonnet.

P. 333. A question has been agitated, whether, when Biron says, *aside,* in the old copies,—

> " O, rhymes are guards on wanton Cupid's hose ;
>   Disfigure not his shop,"

we ought to read *shape* or *slop*. Theobald was in favour of *slop*, and his conjecture is confirmed by the corrector of the folio, 1632, who erases the *h* in the text, and inserts *l*.

P. 334. The old reading of quarto and folios,—

> " By earth, she is not corporal : there you lie,"

has also created dispute. Malone and other modern editors have usually adopted Theobald's alteration, " By earth, she is *but* corporal." The corrector of the folio, 1632, substitutes *most* for *not*, " By earth she is *most* corporal," which affords a still stronger contradiction to Dumaine.

P. 336. Steevens contended that the line in Dumaine's " Sonnet,"—

> " Thou for whom Jove would swear,"

was defective, and wished to read, with Pope,—

> " Thou for whom *ev'n* Jove would swear ; "

while Malone absurdly insisted that " swear" was to be read as a dissyllable. The corrector of the folio, 1632, treats the line as if it wanted a syllable, and gives it,—

> " Thou for whom *great* Jove would swear,"

the word *great* having dropped out in the press. After Dumaine has read his poem, he says, in all editions,—

> " This will I send, and something else more plain,
>   That shall express my true love's fasting pain."

Here we see nearly the same error pointed out by the old corrector which we also find set right in " Hamlet" (Vol. vii. p. 222), " fasting" for *lasting*, although Johnson thought that " fasting" might here be taken as longing, hungry.

P. 338. When Jaquenetta and the Clown enter with Biron's letter, the King, according to all copies of the play, asks them,—

> " What present hast thou there ?"

when he had no reason whatever to think that they had

brought any "present." The mistake has been the printing of " present" for *peasant,*

> " What, *peasant,* hast thou there ? "

Costard was a clown or *peasant,* and is so addressed by the King. The manuscript-corrector of the folio, 1632, points out the blunder.

P. 341. Biron having pronounced a eulogium upon the dark complexion of Rosaline, is laughed at by the King and his other companions :—

> " O, paradox !   Black is the badge of hell,
> The hue of dungeons and the school of night,"

This, the reading of the old copies, is evidently nonsense, and the corrected folio, 1632, contains the last line in this form :—

> " The hue of dungeons and the *shade* of night,"

which is possibly the true reading, and not " *scowl* of night," which has been generally adopted.

P. 342. Nobody has suspected a misprint where one certainly occurs : it is in the passage,—

> " For where is any author in the world
> Teaches such beauty as a woman's eye ? "

The misprint is in the word " beauty," which incontestably should be *learning,*

> " Teaches such *learning* as a woman's eye ? "

and it stands thus corrected in the folio, 1632. The whole tenor of Biron's argument proves that the change is necessary, for he proceeds :—

> " Learning is but an adjunct to ourself,
> And where we are our learning likewise is :
> Then, when ourselves we see in ladies' eyes,
> Do we not likewise see our learning there ? "

The hemistich, " With ourselves," which in the quarto, 1598, and in the folio, 1623, precedes the last line, is omitted in the folio, 1632, and is not restored in manuscript, so that we are better warranted in treating it as an accidental and unnecessary interpolation.

P. 344. The line, as it has always stood,—

> " And plant in tyrants mild humility,"

according to the evidence of the old corrector should be,—

> " And plant in tyrants mild *humanity* ; "

an evident improvement, since tyrants are void rather of *humanity* than of "humility," and the preceding line shows that the correction must be right. The next five lines are crossed out in the folio, 1632, three of them being nearly a repetition of what Biron had said in a previous part of his harangue to prove that oath-breach was lawful.

ACT V.   SCENE I.

P. 346. Theobald's conjecture that "infamie" of the old copies, near the close of the speech of Holofernes, ought to be *insanie*, is warranted by the corrector of the folio, 1632, excepting that he gives it in Latin, *insania ;* but he adds to it a farther emendation, which clears the passage still more : he gives it—" This is abhominable, which we would call abominable : it insinuateth *one* of *insania.*" Thus *one* is substituted for *me*, which Farmer wished to change to *men ;* while the blunder of "infamie" for *insania* was the result of the common mistake of reading *f* for the long *s*.

P. 348. Armado asks Holofernes, "Do you not educate youth at the charge-house on the top of the mountain ?" Steevens tells us that he "supposes the 'charge-house' means the free-school ;" but neither he nor any other person has adduced a single instance to show that "charge-house" and *free-school* were synonymous. It appears that it was only a misprint for "*large* house," for so the corrector of the folio, 1632, treats it.

SCENE II.

P. 350. To the stage-direction, "Enter Princess and Ladies," the corrector of the folio, 1632, has added, *with presents*, in order to show that the performers displayed to the audience the various gifts they had accepted from the King and his companions.

P. 351. When Rosaline says that she also has received laudatory verses, she is laughed at, and Katharine taunts her with being

" Fair as a text B in a copy-book ;"

but there seems no reason to choosing the letter B ; and the corrector, in reference to the first letter in Rosaline's name, alters it to,—

" Fair as a text *R* in a copy-book."

The next four lines are erased, probably because they were not intelligible, or were inapplicable.

P. 352. The commentators have been puzzled by the following line in the folio, 1623, which is repeated in the other folios :—

" So pertaunt like would I o'ersway his state."

They at length agreed that it should be read " portent-like," excepting Douce, who, somewhat at random, suggests *scoffingly*. It turns out that the disputed word (obviously not understood by any old editor or printer) is purely an error of the press. Rosaline thus alludes to the absolute power she would exercise over Biron, were she sure that he was unalterably attached to her :—

" How would I make him fawn, and beg, and seek,
　And wait the season, and observe the times,
　And spend his prodigal wits in bootless rhymes,
　And shape his service wholly to my behests,
　And make him proud to make me proud with jests !
　So *potently* would I o'ersway his state,
　That he should be my fool, and I his fate."

The use of *potently* here can require no explanation ; and it seems scarcely possible to doubt that it was the word of the poet, and for this reason it is placed in the margin of the corrected folio, 1632.

P. 353. Boyet brings word of the intended attack upon the Princess and her Ladies by the King and his Lords :—

" Arm, wenches, arm ! encounters mounted are."

But it is not " encounters," but *encounterers* that are

"mounted," and so the old corrector notes. Again, six lines lower, the Princess, in all ordinary editions, is made to ask,—

> " What are they
> That charge their breath against us?''

"To charge their breath" is nonsense, and the corrector alters it, most naturally, to,—

> " What are they
> That charge *the breach* against us ?''

The Princess carrying on the joke of supposing that she and her Ladies are in a state of siege.

P. 354. We do not feel so confident respecting the next emendation, at the end of Boyet's long account of the project he had overheard, the concoction of which had given such delight to the King and his merry companions : in fact they had laughed at it until they cried ;—

> " That in this spleen ridiculous appears,
> To check their folly, passion's solemn tears.''

"Solemn tears" may possibly be right ; but we do not think it is, because the corrector of the folio, 1632, erases the word, and substitutes another in the margin, which certainly better answers the purpose :—

> " To check their folly, passion's *sudden* tears.''

That is to say, they laughed until they suddenly burst out crying, and thus checked their folly. We are to recollect that, as the old spelling of "sudden" was usually *sodaine*, the mistake would be easily made.

Five lines lower we arrive at a change which cannot be doubted, and again rendered necessary by the blunder of *f* for long *s*. Boyet says that the King and his Lords will come to court the Ladies as Muscovites, and the invariable text has been,—

> " And every one his love-feat will advance
> Unto his several mistress.''

"Love-feat" could hardly be Shakespeare's word, and as amended by the corrector of the folio, 1632, the line reads thus unobjectionably :—

> " And every one his love-*suit* will advance
> Unto his several mistress.''

The fitness of the alteration seems self-evident.

P. 360. The King and his Lords are so derided, jeered, and flouted by the Princess and her Ladies, that they are compelled to make a precipitate retreat, Biron having admitted that they had all been "dry-beaten with pure scoff." As soon as they are gone, the triumphant party burst out in expressions of joy and ridicule, and, among others, the Princess exclaims, as the line has always been printed,—

"O, poverty in wit, kingly poor flout!"

Of which readers have been left to make what sense they could. The old corrector clearly saw no sense in it, and has furnished us with other words so well qualified for the place that we cannot hesitate to approve of them. The enemy had been utterly routed and destroyed, and the Princess, in the excess of her delight, breaks out,—

"O, poverty in wit! *kill'd by pure* flout!"

meaning, of course, in consistency with what Biron had said of "pure scoff," that the King and his companions, disguised as Muscovites, had been driven from the field by the mere mockery of the Ladies.

P. 375. In the old editions, Costard makes his *exit* after the speech of the King, "Stand aside, good Pompey," and, according to the corrector of the folio, 1632, he enters again after Armado has delivered the words, "This Hector far surmounted Hannibal," the manuscript stage-direction being, *Enter Costard in haste and unarmed :* he is suddenly to bring word to Armado respecting the pregnancy of Jaquenetta, and afterwards to engage in his shirt in a conflict with the Spaniard, who turns out to be shirtless. Such was, doubtless, the manner in which this portion of the comedy was originally conducted, notwithstanding modern editors have needlessly and clumsily inserted a stage-direction, *Biron whispers Costard,* as if the latter had never left the scene. He had quitted it to disarm from his part of Pompey, and to convey the alarming tidings regarding Jaquenetta.

P. 377. The emendation proposed by Theobald,—

"A heavy heart bears not a *nimble* tongue,"

instead of "an humble tongue" of the old impressions, is warranted by good sense, and by the change introduced by the corrector of the folio, 1632; but three lines lower, we come to a passage hitherto passed over, but which evidently requires the emendation which it has received from the same authority. The lines are commonly printed,—

> " The extreme parts of time extremely form
> All causes to the purpose of his speed."

The passage is corrupt, and the manuscript alteration made in the folio, 1632, thus sets it right, and renders the sense distinct : the Princess is on the point of hastily quitting Navarre, on the news of the death of her father, and the King observes,—

> " The extreme *parting* time *expressly* forms
> All causes to the purpose of his speed."

Another error occurs in the answer of the Princess to the request of the King, that she would not forget his love-suit : the reading has been,—

> " I understand you not : my griefs are double."

She did not understand him, because her sorrows had deadened her faculties, and the line, as we find from the manuscript-correction in the folio, 1632, ought to be,—

> " I understand you not : my griefs are *dull*,"

the copyist mishearing "double" for *dull*. Biron then takes up the subject, and when, among other things, he says,—

> " As love is full of unbefitting strains,
> As wanton as a child,"

we ought to read *strangeness* for " strains," which is quite consistent with what he adds just afterwards when he tells us that love is

> " Full of *strange* shapes, of habits, and of forms ;"

instead of " straying shapes," as it is misprinted in the folios. Both these words are altered by the old corrector.

P. 378. It seems clear that Biron meant to conclude his address in rhyme, but it closes thus in all editions of the play :—

> " We to ourselves prove false,
> By being once false for ever to be true
> To those that make us both,—fair ladies, you :
> And even that falsehood, in itself a sin,
> Thus purifies itself, and turns to grace."

Read, with the corrector of the folio, 1632, and the sense is precisely the same, while the rhyme is restored,—

> " And even that falsehood, in itself *so base,*
> Thus purifies itself, and turns to grace."

P. 379. The six lines in all the old copies, which read only like an abridgment of the penance imposed afterwards by Rosaline on Biron, are expunged by the corrector of the folio, 1632, as a needless and injurious reduplication.

P. 380. Rosaline tells Biron that he is

> " Full of comparisons and wounding flouts,
> Which you on all estates will execute."

"Will *exercise*" is the plausible manuscript-correction in the folio, 1632.

P. 381. There can, we apprehend, be no doubt that, instead of the following,—

> " Then, if sickly ears,
> Deaf'd with the clamours of their own dear groans,
> Will hear your idle scorns, continue then,
> And I will have you and that fault withal,"

we ought, with the old corrector, to read,—

> " Then, if sickly ears,
> Deaf'd with the clamours of their own *dire* groans,
> Will hear your idle scorns, continue *them,*
> And I will have you and that fault withal ;
> But if they will not, throw away that spirit," &c.

Dire for " dear" and *them* for " then" are slight changes, but editors have hitherto been unwilling to make them in the face of the old impressions.

H

A

MIDSUMMER NIGHT'S DREAM.

ACT I. SCENE I.

P. 391. Rowe was the first editor who changed the old reading,—

> " And then the moon, like to a silver bow,
>   Now bent in heaven,"

to "*new* bent in heaven ;" but the corrector of the folio, 1632, was of the same opinion as Rowe, although it is in vain to inquire whence he derived his knowledge.

P. 392. By a very trifling emendation he makes Theseus end his speech with a couplet, which seems so naturally led to, that it is a wonder the alteration should never before have suggested itself :—

> " But I will wed thee in another key,
>   With pomp, with triumph, and with revelry,"

the common reading being " with revelling."

The old corrector also renders it quite clear that " Stand forth, Demetrius," and " Stand forth, Lysander," lower down in the same page, are parts of the speech of Egeus, and not mere stage-directions, as they are printed in the ancient editions in quarto and folio. The corrector placed *carets* where the words ought to come in, and drew a line from the *carets* to the words, adding in the margin directions for the performers to step *forward*. Still lower, he reads "stubborn *hardness*" for "stubborn harshness," which is more in accordance with the rest of the sentence.

P. 394. Capel's emendation,—

> "But *earthly happier* is the rose distilled,"

which has been generally adopted since his time, is supported by a similar correction in the folio, 1632. The old reading is, "But earthlier happy," &c.

P. 396. We here meet with a confirmation of Theobald's change of "love" to *low*, in—

> "O cross! too high to be enthrall'd to low."

The line in the old copies, three lines farther down,—

> "Or else it stood upon the choice of merit,"

is evidently misprinted, and *friends* has ordinarily been substituted for "merit;" but *men*, inserted in the margin by the corrector of the folio, 1632, is more likely to have been the real word misheard by the copyist :—

> "Or else it stood upon the choice of *men*."

P. 398. The corrector of the folio, 1632, gives the subsequent line differently from any other early authority, *viz.*—

> "His *fault, fair* Helena, is none of mine."

Fisher's quarto has it,—

> "His folly, Helena, is no fault of mine;"

and Roberts' quarto and the folios,—

> "His folly, Helena, is none of mine."

P. 399. Near the end of Helena's speech occurs this couplet, where she is stating her determination to inform Demetrius of the intended flight of Lysander and Hermia :—

> "and for this intelligence,
> If I have thanks, it is a dear expense;"

which is only just intelligible, but the old corrector singularly improves the passage by the word he substitutes :—

> "and for this intelligence,
> If I have thanks, it is dear *recompense*."

It cannot be doubted that the original reading is thus restored, although here, as in many other places, it is difficult to understand how the corruption crept into the text.

P. 400. In the first scene of the actors of the burlesque tragedy of Pyramus and Thisbe, a question has arisen out of the words of the old copies, at the end of Bottom's second speech, "and so grow on to a point." The expression has not been well understood, and it appears that, when the corrections in the folio, 1632, were made, it was deemed a misprint, and that the words ought to be, "and so *go* on to *appoint;*" that is, to appoint the different actors to their parts, which, in fact, is done immediately afterwards.

P. 401. Bottom's declaration that if he play Pyramus, "let the audience look to their eyes; I will move storms," is amended in manuscript in the folio, 1632, to "I will move *stones;*" and when the word was written "stormes," it was not an unlikely blunder for a printer or scribe to make: either word will do.

ACT II. SCENE I.

P. 403. The words, "Take pains; be perfect; adieu," are given to Quince by the old corrector, as well as "At the Duke's oak we meet," and they seem to belong to him, as the manager of the play, rather than to Bottom.

P. 404. The Fairy, soon after meeting Puck, says, speaking of Titania,—

> " The cowslips tall her pensioners be ;
> In their gold coats spots you see :
> Those be rubies, fairy favours,
> In those freckles live their savours."

There seem several objections to this passage as it has stood in all editions. First, cowslips are never " tall," and, next, the crimson spots are not in their " coats," or on the petals, but at the bottom of the calix, as Shakespeare has himself told us in " Cymbeline," Act II. Scene II.,

> " Like the crimson drops
> I' th' bottom of a cowslip."

The alteration authorised in manuscript in the folio, 1632, is, therefore, as follows :—

> "The cowslips *all* her pensioners be ;
> In their gold *cups* spots you see :
> Those be rubies, fairy favours,
> In those freckles live their savours."

Rubies would be singular decorations for a " coat," but were common ornaments to golden chalices.

P. 405. Johnson and others saw that the line commenced by the Fairy's question,—

> " Are you not he ? "

was not completed by Puck's answer,—

> " Thou speak'st aright ; "

and it was proposed to fill up the vacancy by " *I am ;* thou speak'st aright ;" but the true word seems to be that given by the corrector of the folio, 1632,—

> " *Fairy,* thou speak'st aright."

P. 408. It is a mere trifle, but still, in relation to the integrity of Shakespeare's text, worth notice, that in the corrected folio, 1632, Titania tells Oberon,—

> " *Thy* fairy land buys not the child of me."

It is "The fairy land" in the old editions ; but Titania afterwards repeats nearly the same words when she again refuses the boy to Oberon, "Not for *thy* fairy kingdom." We may, therefore, conclude, that *thy* is the original.

In a later part of the same speech the expression occurs, "her womb then rich with my young squire," which is altered in manuscript in the folio, 1632, to "her womb then *ripe* with my young squire ;" the word "*rich*" had perhaps been caught from a line just below.

P. 410. There is a defect in the construction of the subsequent extract :—

> " The juice of it, on sleeping eye-lids laid,
> Will make a man or woman madly dote
> Upon the next live creature that it sees ; "

accordingly we find the old corrector altering the last line
thus, which is probably what the poet wrote:—

> " Upon the next live creature that *is seen.*"

Puck's answer to Oberon has constantly been printed,—

> " I'll put a girdle round about the earth
> In forty minutes ; "

but Oberon had not required any such task of him, but
merely to fetch a plant of " Love in idleness." What Puck
means is to show his readiness to obey, even if he had been
commanded to do much more, and therefore the manuscript-
corrector has it,—

> " *I'd* put a girdle round about the earth
> In forty minutes."

The word " round," which is also inserted by him as necessary to the measure, is only met with in the quarto published by Fisher.

P. 412. The change recommended, from " flowers" (which
is the old reading) to *bowers*, in the following passage, may
admit of doubt : but *bowers* certainly appears best adapted to
the place ; and if best adapted, we may feel well assured
that it was the word Shakespeare employed :—

> "Quite over-canopied with *lush* woodbine,
> With sweet musk-roses and with eglantine :
> There sleeps Titania, some time of the night,
> Lull'd in these *bowers* with dances and delight."

It is certain that the " *lush* woodbine," musk-roses, and
eglantine, which " quite over-canopied" the bank, converted
it into *bowers*. *Lush* (also supplied by the manuscript-
corrector of the folio, 1632) is a decided improvement upon
" luscious," which is too much for the verse. Theobald had
proposed to read *lush*, and we have already met with it in
" The Tempest," Act II. Scene I.

SCENE II.

P. 415. Hermia and Lysander, wearied by wandering in
the wood, are about to lie down, when Hermia, in maiden
modesty, asks her lover to rest farther from her, but he

urges her to repose her trust in him. The usual text has
been :—

> " O, take the sense, sweet, of my innocence ;
> Love takes the meaning in love's conference."

But the passage, as amended by the corrector of the folio,
1632, is clearly much more to the purpose :—

> " O, take the sense, sweet, of my innocence ;
> Love takes the meaning in love's *confidence*.

ACT III. SCENE I.

P. 421. In the rehearsal scene of the mock-play by the
Athenian artisans, the corrector of the folio, 1632, gives
Bottom's speech, as to the contrivance of a wall, thus:
" And let him have some plaster, or some *lime*, or some
roughcast about him, *and* let him hold his fingers thus," &c.
The ordinary reading is "loam" and " or"; but the sentence
is clearly not in the alternative. Theseus afterwards speaks
of the wall as made of " *lime* and hair." In the play
itself, the first line delivered by Pyramus ought to run,—

> " Thisby, the flowers *have* odious savours sweet,"

and not " of odious savours sweet ;" because the next line
is,—

> " So hath thy breath, my dearest Thisby, dear."

Pope, to meet the difficulty, altered " hath" to *doth ;* but the
error was, as the corrector of the folio, 1632, shows, in the
word " of" in the previous line ; properly, therefore, the
passage ought to be printed hereafter,—

> " Thisby, the flowers *have* odious savours sweet,
> So *hath* thy breath," &c.

P. 422. The manuscript stage-directions in this scene,
and indeed in others, are as precise and full as can possibly
be required, and supply all deficiencies of the kind in the
printed copies. Thus, when the " hempen home-spuns" are
in the utmost dismay and confusion, just previous to the

return of Bottom after his transformation, we are told that *Robin* is *among them,* that the *Clownes all exeunt in confusion,* and that Snout afterwards *Exit frighted,* having seen the Weaver with the *Ass head on his own.* It may be here mentioned that when the eyes of Titania and the others are to be touched with the magic herbs, there is no information in the printed copies as to the exact moment ; but in manuscript we have *annoint her eyes* and *annoint his eyes* in the precise place in the margin, in the hand-writing of the corrector. In the same way, though the printed copies state when the characters *sleep,* we are told only in manuscript when they *wake,* which is quite as material.

P. 424. The five lines in Titania's speech, declaring her love for Bottom, are strangely confused in the folio editions, and in Roberts' quarto ; but the corrector of that of 1632, by inserting a figure opposite each line, shows that they are to be read in the order in which they stand in Fisher's quarto, and such has properly been the modern arrangement.

SCENE II.

P. 428. Hermia, imagining that Demetrius has killed Lysander, vents her rage upon him in a speech of some length and great violence ; upon which, as the passage has hitherto been given, Demetrius coolly remarks,—

> " You spend your passion on a mispris'd mood :
> I am not guilty of Lysander's blood ;"

but the corrector of the folio, 1632, says that we ought to read,—

> " You spend your passion *in* a mispris'd *flood ;*"

that is, in a mistaken torrent, which appears to give additional force and greater intelligibility.

P. 431. The conjecture hazarded in note 6, that "princess of pure white" ought to be read "*impress* of pure white," is confirmed by the manuscript-corrector of the folio, 1632, and the quotation ought in future to stand,—

> " O, let me kiss
> This *impress* of pure white, this seal of bliss."

In fact, the use of the word "impress" in the beginning of the line naturally led to the word "seal" at the end of it.

P. 432. The old corrector, in accordance with Fisher's quarto, inserts *Helen* before "It is not so," in Lysander's speech, in order to complete the verse.

P. 433. In Helen's speech occurs the same misprint as that pointed out in "The Two Gentlemen of Verona," Act I. Scene II. p. 18.

> " So we grew together
> Like to a double cherry, seeming parted,
> But yet an union in partition ;
> Two lovely berries moulded on one stem."

It is not at all likely that Helena would call herself one of the "lovely berries," whatever she might say of Hermia; but the fact is that the whole speech turns upon their mutual employment and mutual affection, and as the old corrector of the folio, 1632, informs us, we ought to displace "lovely" for *loving :*—

> "Two *loving* berries moulded on one stem."

The heraldic couplet which follows is struck out by the same hand, probably because, like most other readers, he did not understand it.

P. 436. In Hermia's first speech, on this page, a ludicrous error of the press has been eternally repeated. She is wonder-struck and bewildered by Lysander's infidelity,—

> " What! can you do me greater harm than hate ?
> Hate me ! wherefore ? O, me !"

and then what follows ? this strange question,—

> " What news, my love ?"

It is astonishing that the blunder did not long ago expose itself; but it is easily accounted for: "news" was formerly spelt *newes,* and so it stands in the folios, and the printer or copyist misread *meanes* "newes." Hermia's question ought, indisputably, to be,—

> " What *means* my love ?"

which is a natural inquiry for an explanation why Lysander had abandoned her. The manuscript-corrector obliterates *newes*, and inserts *meanes*.

ACT IV.—SCENE I.

P. 444. The expression of Titania,—

> " Fairies, be gone, and be all ways away,"

has occasioned some controversy, the word being "always" in the old copies: Theobald made the suggestion of "all ways ;" Upton, Steevens, and Malone stating their concurrence or dissent. It seems to be an error of the press, for Titania does not wish her attendants to be permanently, but only temporarily absent—not "always," but *a while*—and such is the manuscript-correction in the folio, 1632. Titania could not mean to dismiss the Fairies entirely and for ever, and therefore says,—

> " Fairies, be gone, and be *a while* away."

The error arose from the compositor confounding the words *a while* and " away," which come next each other.

P. 450. A blunder from a somewhat similar cause has been committed in Lysander's speech, which in the folios and in one of the quartos is thus given :—

> " And he bid us follow to the temple,"

instead of

> " And he *did* bid us follow to the temple."

The words "did" and "bid" being in juxta-position, the printer omitted the first of them (which is found in Fisher's quarto only), and thus ruined the verse. The manuscript-corrector places *did* in the margin.

P. 450. Bottom concludes his speech in these terms in all the old copies: he is speaking of the ballad of " Bottom's Dream,"—" I will sing it in the latter end of a play, before the Duke : peradventure, to make it the more gracious, I

shall sing it at her death." Now, no particular play is here
mentioned, and "at her death" seems to have no personal
application. Nevertheless it is evident that *the* play of Pyramus and Thisbe was in the Clown's mind; and what he
proposed to do was to sing "Bottom's Dream" at the death
of Thisbe. Such is the statement of the manuscript-corrector
of the folio, 1632, who, to make the matter quite clear, has
ended the speech thus : "And I will sing it at the latter end
of *the* play before the Duke : peradventure, to make it the
more gracious, I shall sing it at *Thisbe's* death."

SCENE II.

P. 451. In this scene Flute, the bellows-mender, is throughout introduced as a speaker by the name of the part he performs in the mock-tragedy ; but the manuscript-corrector has
been careful, in every instance, to alter the prefix from
"Thisbe" to *Flute*.

ACT V.   SCENE I.

P. 453. There is a remarkable discrepancy between the old
folio, and the old quarto editions in respect to an important
passage, which we give as it appears in the latter, which
have been almost universally followed :—

> " And, as imagination bodies forth
> The forms of things unknown, the poet's pen
> Turns them to shapes, and gives to airy nothing
> A local habitation and a name."

The quartos, therefore, have "gives to *airy* nothing," and
the folios, without any point after *aire*, "gives to *aire*
nothing." With some editors it has been a question, which
reading ought to be adopted ; but, as the manuscript-corrector
of the folio, 1632, by placing the letter *i* in the margin,
indicates that the word was *airie*, and as the line is incomplete without the additional syllable, we need not entertain
much hesitation upon the point.

P. 454. The doubling of the parts of Egeus and Philostrate,

that is, one actor filling both, perhaps led to the confusion between the prefixes of those characters in this scene. Theseus, in the quarto editions, says, " Call Philostrate," and in the folios, "Call Egeus." The folio, 1623, adopted the quarto, by Roberts, as its foundation ; but at some time subsequent to the publication of that quarto, the part of Philostrate, having been given, in the economy of our old stage, also to the actor of Egeus, the name of Egeus became substituted for that of Philostrate in the folio, 1623. This is probably the cause of the variation, which the corrector of the folio, 1632, only in part sets right ; for while Egeus produces the " brief " of the "sports " that are " rife," Lysander reads it, and then Philostrate takes up the dialogue, by giving a description of the play, the players, and the rehearsal. It seems likely that the poet meant the whole of this to have been said by one man, Philostrate, who in the very opening of the drama is sent out by Theseus to " stir up the Athenian youth to merriments," and who acted as a sort of Master of the Revels on this occasion.

P. 455. Theseus, referring to the ridiculous contradiction in " the tragical mirth " of the title of the play about to be represented before him, observes

> " That is, hot ice and wondrous strange snow."

Now, unless we read " wondrous " as a trisyllable the measure is defective : the sense too is much in the same predicament ; for " wondrous *strange* snow," does not necessarily imply opposition, like " hot ice." The truth is that Shakespeare meant *boiling* snow, only the compositor, or copyist, mistook *seething* for " strange," the true word having been supplied by the old corrector,—

> " That is, hot ice and wond'rous *seething* snow ;"

which is exactly what was intended to be expressed. Theseus, in the fourth line of the scene, has already used the word " seething," which renders the misprint here less pardonable.

P. 457. After the Prologue by a speaker who, as Theseus remarks, did not " stand upon his points," we come to the introduction of the mock-actors, and the old stage-direction in the folios is " Tawyer with a trumpet before them." It has been thought that " Tawyer " was the name of the trumpeter ;

but a manuscript-correction in the folio, 1632, calls him *Presenter*, and it places *Pres.* as a prefix to the argument of the main incidents of the burlesque. In it, it was necessary to observe punctuation for the sake of intelligibility, and not to derange it, as in the case of the Prologue, for the sake of laughter. This argument was, therefore, not delivered by the Prologue speaker, as has been invariably stated, but by the *Presenter*, whose name was in all probability Tawyer.

P. 460. On the *exit* of Wall, Theseus observes, in the quartos, "Now is the *moon used* between the neighbours." The folios read, with even less intelligibility, "Now is the *moral* down between the neighbours." Theobald altered "moral" to "mural," but no instance has been adduced of the employment of *mural* as a substantive; and the manuscript-corrector erases "moral" and inserts *wall*, which, at least, is the word wanted. Lower down in the Lion's speech we ought, on the same authority, to read,—

> "Then know, that I, one Snug the joiner, am
> A *lion's* fell, nor else no lion's dam."

By "lion's fell" we are to understand lion's skin, and Snug was to assure the ladies, that he was no more than a man in a lion's hide. This correction was conjecturally proposed some years ago by the late Mr. Barron Field, who never imagined that he had been anticipated in the emendation by full two centuries.

P. 462. The manuscript-corrector of the folio, 1632, converts "mouz'd" of the old copies into *mouthed*, in the exclamation of Theseus, "Well moused, lion." Steevens was in favour of the same change; but, nevertheless, the old reading may perhaps stand, from *museau*, French, muzzle, and the Italian *muso*.

P. 463. The lamentation of Pyramus on the supposed death of Thisbe produces an observation from Theseus, which has been always thus printed:—"This passion, and the death of a dear friend, would go near to make a man look sad;" but it has particular reference to the "passion" of Pyramus on the fate of Thisbe, and therefore the corrector of the folio, 1632, properly changes "and" to *on*, and reads, "This passion *on* the death of a dear friend," &c. When Pyramus kills himself with the words,—

> "Thus die I, thus, thus, thus!"

there is this singular manuscript stage-direction in the opposite margin, *Stab himself as often;* that is, as often as he exclaims, "thus, thus, thus!" *Exit Moonshine* is inserted just before *Pyramus dies.* These instructions to the players are not in any of the old impressions.

P. 464. In part of Thisbe's dying rhapsody, as it appeared before Theobald's time, he saw that the rhymes did not correspond, as they ought :—

> "These lily lips,
>   This cherry nose,
> These yellow cowslip cheeks," &c.

He therefore proposed *brows* instead of "lips ;" but he missed the alteration of the right word : the manuscript-corrector of the folio, 1632, gives it, and, no doubt, accurately,—

> "*This* lily *lip*,
>   This cherry *tip*,"

in allusion to the *tip* of the nose of Pyramus, to which, we may imagine, Thisbe pointed at the moment.

P. 465. The early editions do not inform us where the "Bergomask Dance" was introduced ; but the old corrector tells us, that it came in just before Theseus recommences his speech, with "The iron tongue of midnight," &c. The words written in a blank space are *Dance : then, the Duke speaks.* It is a singular addition to the old stage-direction of "Enter Puck," to be told that he came in *with his broom on his shoulder*, doubtless in the very way in which he is represented on the title-page of the old tract of "Robin Goodfellow, his Mad Pranks," &c., in the library of Lord Ellesmere, and in the chap-book in verse upon his history : that Puck was so furnished we have his own evidence, when he tells the audience,—

> "I am sent with broom before,
>   To sweep the dust behind the door."

P. 467. In "the Song," just preceding Puck's last speech, there are two small, but not trifling emendations, made by

the corrector of the folio, 1632. The one is by a change in
the punctuation to carry on the sentence about "the blots
of nature's hand" for another line, thus :—

> " And the blots of nature's hand
> Shall not in their issue stand :
> Never mole, hare-lip, nor scar,
> Nor mark prodigious, such as are
> Despised in nativity
> Shall upon their children be,
> With this field-dew consecrate."

That is, none of these disfigurements shall be seen on the
children consecrated with the field-dew. Then begins a new
sentence, which is judiciously altered in two words by the
corrector, and reads as follows :—

> " Every fairy take this gait,
> And each several chamber bless,
> Through this palace, with sweet peace :
> Ever shall *it safely* rest
> And the owner of it blest.
> Trip away ; make no stay ;
> Meet me all by break of day."

The question is whether the fairies, or the issue of the different couples are to be " consecrate" with the " field-dew ;"
and there seems no reason why such delicate and immortal
beings should require it, while children might need it, to secure
them from "marks prodigious." Reading the line, as in old
as well as modern editions,—

> " Ever shall in safety rest,"

there is a want of an antecedent ; whereas, the manuscript
emendation in the folio, 1632, renders the whole "song"
consecutive, grammatical, and intelligible.

MERCHANT OF VENICE.

ACT I. SCENE I.

P. 478. In the following quotation Rowe changed "when" of all the old copies, quarto and folio, into *who*,—

> " When, I am very sure,
> If they should speak, would almost damn those ears,
> Which, hearing them, would call their brothers fools."

Rowe was followed in this change by Pope, Theobald, Warburton, Malone, and others; but the emendation recommended on the authority of the corrector of the folio, 1632, is much slighter, simpler, and more effectual—merely " would" to *'twould* :—

> " When, I am very sure,
> If they should speak, *'twould* almost damn those ears,
> Which, hearing them, would call their brothers fools."

P. 479. Only one of the two quartos printed in 1600 gives this line as it ought to stand, *viz.*—

> " Farewell: I'll grow a talker for this gear."

The other quarto of the same date, and all the folios read, to the injury of the verse,—

> " Fare *you* well: I'll grow a talker for this gear."

The manuscript-corrector of the folio, 1632, who seems to have had an accurate and a sensitive ear, properly strikes out *you*.

P. 480. Bassanio tells Antonio, in all editions,—

> "I owe you much, and, like a wilful youth,
> That which I owe is lost."

The folio, 1632, as corrected, substitutes a more appropriate word in reference to Bassanio's extravagance,—

> "I owe you much, and, like a *wasteful* youth,
> That which I owe is lost."

It is not easy to account for some of these blunders, either by the copyist or by the compositor; and "wilful" may possibly have been the poet's word; but he does not elsewhere represent Bassanio as "wilful," while Bassanio admits and deplores his own wastefulness.

SCENE II.

P. 482. The corrector of the folio, 1632, seems here to have inserted another alteration from one of the early quartos: in the folios Portia observes, "But this reason is not in the fashion," &c.; but in the quartos "reason" is *reasoning*. In her next speech but one Portia observes of the Neapolitan Prince and his horse, that "he makes it a great appropriation to his own good parts that he can shoe him himself." "Appropriation to" is altered by the manuscript-corrector of the folio, 1632, to *approbation of*, in the sense of proof—a great *proof of* his own good parts, &c. *Approbation* is not unfrequently used by Shakespeare in this way; whereas, if "appropriation" were his word, this is the only place where he has employed it.

P. 483. In order not to offend James I., the word "Scottish" of the quartos, published more than two years before he came to the throne, was altered in the folio, 1623, to *other*, in Nerissa's question, "What think you of the Scottish lord, his neighbour?" In the folio, 1632, the word *other* is struck through with a pen, and *Irish* placed in the margin, as if it had not been considered objectionable, in the time of the corrector, so to stigmatise Irish lords.

SCENE III.

P. 486. There is here a transposition in all printed copies of this play, by which Shylock is made to call "*land*-thieves,"

I

instead of "*water*-thieves," pirates. He tells Bassanio,
"There be land-rats and water-rats, water-thieves and land-
thieves ; I mean, pirates." Shylock could not mean that
land-thieves were pirates, and therefore the corrector of the
folio, 1632, reverses the words, and makes them follow
the order of "land-rats and water-rats,"—"there be land-
thieves and water-thieves ; I mean, pirates." The change is
not very important, but as it shows that comparative trifles
did not escape.

P. 487. The corrector of the folio, 1632, again adopts the
text of both the quarto editions in reading " well-won thrift,"
for " well-*worn* thrift," as the epithet stands in the folios.

P. 488. The whole passage regarding Jacob and Laban
down to Antonio's reflection,—

> " O, what a goodly outside falsehood hath ! "

is erased ; but nevertheless an emendation is made in Antonio's answer to Shylock, as hitherto printed,—

> " Was this inserted to make interest good?"

which is changed by the corrector of the folio, 1632, to,—

> " Was this *inferred* to make interest good?"

There is no doubt that Shakespeare frequently uses the
verb to *infer* in the sense of to *bring in;* and Antonio inquires whether Shylock *brought in* the story of Laban to
justify the taking of interest.

ACT II. SCENE I.

P. 492. In the second line of the speech of the Prince of
Morocco we meet with a change of epithet which deserves
notice : the reading has been :—

> " The shadow'd livery of the burnish'd sun ;"

but the corrector has written,—

> " The shadow'd livery of the *burning* sun,"

which seems much more proper, when the African Prince is
speaking of his black complexion as the effect of the sun's

rays. To speak of the sun as artificially "burnish'd" is very unworthy. Lower down the reading of the corrector is, "I would *out*-stare" of one of the quartos, instead of "o'er-stare" of the other quarto, and of the folios.

P. 493. The almost inevitable conjecture of Theobald,—

> " So is Alcides beaten by his page,"

instead of "beaten by his *rage*" of all the early impressions, is borne out by the corrector of the folio, 1632.

SCENE II.

P. 494. Launcelot in the old copies calls the devil "a courageous fiend," a word certainly very ill applied, when he is advising the boy to run away ; and in the margin of the folio, 1632, the word is made *contagious*, as appropriate as "courageous" is inappropriate, unless we suppose Launcelot, to speak ironically. At the end of what he says, he is about to make his escape with all speed, and this manuscript stage-direction is added, *As he is going out in haste*, when he is met by his father. As the dialogue between them proceeds, we are told when Launcelot *kneels* to receive his father's blessing, and when he *rises*, after the old man has compared his son's hair to Dobbin's tail.

SCENE V.

P. 504. The manuscript-corrector again introduces the reading of the quarto editions where Shylock is speaking of Launcelot : the folio, 1623, has it,—

> " Snail-slow in profit, but he sleeps by day
> More than the wild-cat."

The folio, 1632, omits "he ;" but the quartos have, " *and he* sleeps by day," &c. Both words are inserted in the margin of the folio, 1632. The proverb with which the speech ends is given differently both from quartos and folios ; for instead of "Fast bind, fast find," we have "*Safe* bind, *safe* find." The lines from,—

> "O ! ten times faster Venus' pigeons fly,"

down to the entrance of Lorenzo, are crossed out ; but the

gross error of the folios, "to *steal* love's bonds," instead of "to seal love's bonds," is duly corrected. The two quartos have "seal."

SCENE VII.

P. 507. When the Prince of Morocco enters to his choice of the caskets, we are informed by a manuscript stage-direction in the folio, 1632, that a *curtain is drawn* or rather withdrawn in front of them, as, indeed, is the case afterwards when the Prince of Arragon and Bassanio go through the same ceremony. This fact is easily to be collected from what is said by the characters, but the object was to take care that the caskets should be exposed to the view of the audience at the proper moment. The inscription upon the golden casket, in the second line of the speech of the Prince of Morocco, is different in the folios from the subsequent repetitions of it, by the omission of the word "many,"—

> " Who chooseth me shall gain what men desire,"

instead of "what *many* men desire." In the quarto impressions "many" is found, and the corrector of the folio, 1632, has placed it in the margin : thus all three inscriptions were rendered of the same length, and are in the same measure.

SCENE IX.

P. 512. There is a material emendation in the speech of the Prince of Arragon, when commenting on the caskets. The reading has always been,—

> " What many men desire : that many may be meant
> By the fool multitude, that choose by show,
> Not learning more than the fond eye doth teach ;
> Which pries not to th' interior, but, like the martlet,
> Builds in the weather," &c.

This is certainly intelligible, but the verse is redundant in the first line by "many," which is erased, and the corrector of the folio, 1632, farther informs us that the words of the poet, in the fourth line, were,—

> " Which *prize* not th' interior, but, like the martlet,
> Builds in the weather," &c.

That is to say, the fool multitude do not prize, or value the interior, but judge only by externals. It will be observed also, that this new reading restores in some degree the regularity of the verse.

ACT III. SCENE I.

P. 516. Where Shylock calls Antonio "A beggar that used to come so smug upon the mart," the manuscript-corrector of the folio, 1632, reads " A beggar that *was wont* to come," &c. ; and as in the subsequent part of the same short speech Shylock repeats the expression, " he *was wont* to call me usurer," and " he *was wont* to lend money," it seems probable that in the different clauses of the same sentence the same words would be employed.

SCENE II.

P. 520. The expression "to peize the time" in Portia's introduction of Bassanio to the caskets has not been well understood: to "peize" is to weigh, to poise; but the sense wanted is to delay, and that sense we have in the corrector's manuscript, who writes *pause* for "peize" in the following extract :—

> " I speak too long : but 'tis to *pause* the time,
>   To eke it, and to draw it out at length,
>   To stay you from election."

Portia wished to postpone Bassanio's choice, lest he should select the wrong casket, and thus necessarily and suddenly terminate their intercourse.

P. 522. Much controversy has been produced by these lines, where Bassanio is moralizing upon the deceitfulness of external appearance :—

> " Thus ornament is but the guiled shore
>   To a most dangerous sea, the beauteous scarf
>   Veiling an Indian beauty ; in a word,
>   The seeming truth which cunning times put on
>   To entrap the wisest."

As to the first line, the folio, 1623, has " guiled shore," as above, which the editor of the folio, 1632, not understanding, he altered it to *guilded, i. e.* gilded ; so that when Steevens asserts that "all the ancient copies" have "guiled," he was mistaken. The manuscript-corrector of the folio, 1632, not approving *guilded*, and seeing that the participle ought to be active and not passive, a point to which Shakespeare did not much attend (as indeed it was not the habit of his age), changed *guilded* to *guiling*. This however is not by any means the most important emendation in the passage, since a remarkable alteration for the better is wrought by the mere change of punctuation. No editor has been satisfied with "Veiling an Indian beauty," because "beauty" was obviously the very converse of what the poet intended : Sir Thomas Hanmer therefore proposed "Indian dowdy ;" but no other variation from the old text is necessary than to observe the stops which the corrector of the folio, 1632, introduced, and to read the lines as follows :—

> "Thus ornament is but the *guiling* shore
> To a most dangerous sea, the beauteous scarf
> Veiling an Indian : beauty, in a word,
> The seeming truth which cunning times put on
> To entrap the wisest."

Here every thing is clear and consistent ; but it is most likely that had the introducer of this emendation written in the time of the author he illustrates, he would not have thought it necessary to change "guiled" to *guiling*. It was perhaps recited *guiling* on the stage in his day.

P. 523. Bassanio, descanting on the portrait of Portia, thus expresses his admiration of the eyes :—

> "How could he see to do them? having made one,
> Methinks, it should have power to steal both his,
> And leave itself unfurnish'd."

The corrector has it, "And leave itself *unfinish'd*," which reads extremely well, if we suppose that the word applies to the portrait, and not to the eye alone. "Unfurnish'd," if it refer to the fellow eye, reads awkwardly, and Shakespeare would scarcely have left the expression of what he intended so imperfect. Steevens hesitated about *unfinish'd*.

P. 524. Portia, stating the sources of her happiness after the successful choice by Bassanio, thus sums them up :—

> "Happiest of all is, that her gentle spirit
> Commits itself to yours to be directed."

The correction of *in* for "is" appears a trifle, but it makes a great difference in the grace of the expression :—

> "Happiest of all, *in* that her gentle spirit
> Commits itself to yours to be directed."

The use of *in that* for *inasmuch as* was common.

P. 526. Gratiano, speaking of his eager courtship of Nerissa, observes :—

> "For wooing here, until I sweat again,
> And swearing till my very *roof* was dry," &c.

The manuscript-corrector of the folio tells us that "roof" ought to be *tongue* : the old spelling is "rough," and as *r* was often misprinted for *t*, and *u* for *n*, *tongue* seems at least as probable an error, especially as "roof" was never, even of old, spelt *rough* :—

> "And swearing till my very *tongue* was dry"

is more natural, though not necessary.

P. 529. Bassanio tells Portia that Antonio is,—

> "The best condition'd and unwearied spirit
> In doing courtesies ;"

but the corrector has put "unwearied" also in the superlative, "*unwearied'st* spirit," which is quite in the manner of Shakespeare, and quite consistent with Bassanio's opinion of his friend.

P. 535. What passes between Lorenzo and Launcelot, regarding the negro with child by him, is erased in the corrected folio, 1632.

ACT IV. SCENE I.

P. 539. We here meet with an emendation which must, in all probability, have been derived from some good authority ; certainly better than any resorted to for all the printed editions, judging from the result. The commentators have been at fault respecting an epithet applied by Shylock to a bagpipe :—

" As there is no firm reason to be render'd
Why he cannot abide a gaping pig,
Why he, a harmless necessary cat,
Why he a woollen bagpipe," &c.

The question at issue was, why a bagpipe should be called
"woollen," and some have argued that it was because the bag
was covered with cloth, while Johnson was for changing the
word to *wooden*, and Hawkins and Steevens, more plausibly, to
swollen. As to the meaning, they were right, though wrong
as to the word. Shakespeare's word unquestionably was
bollen, from the Anglo-Saxon, which means swollen. It was
spelled in various ways, as boln, bolne, boll'n, and bollen, and
it is used by several authors of Shakespeare's time, which it
is needless to refer to, because he avails himself of it in his
own "Lucrece," vol. viii. p. 455 :—

" Here one, being throng'd, bears back, all boll'n and red."

It was, therefore, a word with which he was well acquainted,
and there can be no doubt that in future the passage above
quoted from this drama ought to be printed as follows :—

" As there is no firm reason to be render'd,
Why he cannot abide a gaping pig,
Why he, a harmless necessary cat,
Why he, a *bollen* bagpipe," &c.

P. 540. All appeals failing to move Shylock, Antonio
entreats for judgment, observing, as the lines are printed in
the folio, 1632,—

" Or even as well use question with the wolf,
The ewe bleat for the lamb : when you behold."

Such are the words, and such the punctuation ; but the earlier
folio, of 1623, gives the sentence even more imperfectly :—

" Or even as well use question with the wolf,
The ewe bleat for the lamb ; "

the rest of the line being wanting. How, then, is the defect
remedied by the corrector of the folio, 1632 ? Simply by a
transposition and the removal of a colon, which accomplishes
all that is wanted by making the meaning indisputable : he
reads,—

" Or even as well use question with the wolf,
When you behold the ewe bleat for the lamb."

This is nearly the text of the quarto published by Heyes, in the copy belonging to the Earl of Ellesmere.

P. 542. Malone was disposed to preserve the misprint in the following :—

> " O, be thou damn'd, inexecrable dog : "

at all events he thought it doubtful whether "inexecrable" were not the true word, in preference to *inexorable*, which it did not become in print till 1664. "Inexorable" is in the margin of the corrected folio, 1632, and there can surely be no doubt that it is what Shakespeare really wrote.

P. 546. When Portia asks,—

> " Are there balance here to weigh
> The flesh ? "

Shylock answers instantly,—

> " I have them ready ; "

but neither in ancient nor modern printed editions is there any stage-direction, showing that at this point it was the duty of the actor to display his scales to the audience. The deficiency is supplied in manuscript by the corrector of the folio, 1632, by the words, *Produce them*, in the margin. Afterwards (p. 547), when Shylock exclaims,—

> " Most learned judge ! a sentence ! come, prepare ! "

there is another note, which proves that the scales were again effectively paraded by the Jew as ready for use, *Show scales again ;* while we are previously told that he *whets his knife.* These particulars are not necessarily to be inferred from what is said, and we may conclude that they represent the practice of our elder stage.

P. 548. The change of a word in the subsequent passage, seems, if not required, probable :—

> " If thou tak'st more
> Or less than a just pound,—be it so much
> As makes it light or heavy in the *balance*," &c.

The usual reading has been " in the substance ; " but the addition by the heroine,—

> " Nay, if the scale do turn
> But in the estimation of a hair,"

renders it likely that *balance* was the right text, and "sub-stance" is altered to *balance* in manuscript in the margin of the folio, 1632.

———

ACT V. SCENE I.

P. 555. There could hardly be a doubt on the point whether "Sweet soul," at the commencement of Lorenzo's speech, belong to him, or to Launcelot, to whom the words are assigned in all the old copies. In the folio, 1632, the expression is "Sweet *love*," which the manuscript-corrector has not thought it necessary to change to "Sweet soul" (the reading of the earlier folio and of the quartos), but he has transferred it to Lorenzo.

P. 556. In the folio, 1632, there is a singular misprint upon which modern editors have not remarked, and which it is only necessary to notice here, in order to state that the manuscript-corrector of that impression detected and remedied the blunder. It stands, as printed,—

> " Therefore the poet
> Did feign that Orpheus drew *tears*, stones, floods," &c.

For *tears*, we should of course read "trees," in accordance with the folio, 1623, and with the two early editions in quarto. The corrector's first emendation was to *beasts*, but he struck it out subsequently, and properly inserted "trees" in its stead. This may look like speculative emendation.

P. 557. At the end of Portia's speech we have this passage, as it is found in all the old copies :—

> " Peace ! how the moon sleeps with Endymion,
> And would not be awak'd."

Malone changed it to " Peace, hoa ! the moon," &c. ; but the manuscript-corrector of the folio, 1632, tells us that the error was not *how* for "hoa," but *how* for "now :" this is the more likely, because when the folios came from the press it was not usual to spell the interjection "hoa," but *ho ;* and we know that it was a very common mistake to

print " how" for *now,* and *vice versâ ;* therefore we ought to
read,—

> " Peace ! *now* the moon sleeps with Endymion,
> And would not be awak'd."

P. 558. The corrector of the folio, 1632, has taken pains
to set right even the most minute errors.   Thus, in the
fifth line, he has erased "from," and properly substituted
for.   Lower down, he has shown us how the versification
of a defective line ought to be amended : it is where
Gratiano says, that he had already had a quarrel with
Nerissa

> " About a hoop of gold, a paltry ring,
> That she did give me ; whose poesy was,
> For all the world, like cutlers' poetry."

Here we must read, for the sake of the measure, "That she
did give *to* me," &c.   That "poesy" ought not to be read as
three syllables we have evidence within three lines, where
Nerissa uses it as two syllables only :—

> " What talk you of the poesy, or the value ?"

The carelessness of the printer, or of the transcriber, omitted
"to," and spoiled the harmony : the old corrector inserted it.

P. 560. To the same cause we may probably attribute the
employment of " contain," in Portia's accusation of Bassanio,
instead of *retain,* although the words, of old, were sometimes
used nearly synonymously :—

> " Or your own honour to contain the ring."

Shakespeare often has to *retain* in the sense of to *keep ;* but
the change here made may show only the customary mode
of delivering the line in the time of the corrector.

P. 561. Antonio, pleading to Portia for Bassanio, says, in
the folio impressions,—

> " I once did lend my body for thy wealth ; "

but it ought to be " for *his* wealth," and so it stands in the
quarto editions, and so it has been made to stand in the
folio, 1632, by the corrector of it.

P. 562. An adverb of place instead of an adverb of time

has been misprinted in all the editions of this play, where
Gratiano remarks,—

> " Why, this is like the mending of highways
> In summer, where the ways are fair enough."

We ought certainly to substitute *when* for " where" in this
passage, because the question is not as to where the roads
are to be repaired, but when ; the speaker means to point
out the absurdity of doing a particular act at the period
when it is least wanted. The manuscript-corrector places
when in the margin, and expunges " where." It is a misprint of frequent occurrence.

AS YOU LIKE IT.

***

ACT I. SCENE I.

Vol. iii. P. 7. The corrector of the folio, 1632, has made an emendation at the very outset of this play, which is nearly in accordance with Malone's proposal, to insert a period after "fashion," and to commence a new sentence with *he*, in reference to the bequest of Orlando's father. The corrector's reading is this :—"As I remember, Adam, it was upon this fashion : *he* bequeathed me by will but a poor thousand crowns," &c. Orlando and Adam enter talking on the subject of the will of Sir Roland de Bois. When Oliver comes in shortly afterwards (p. 8), a manuscript stage-direction informs us that, while the two brothers are conversing, *Adam goes apart*, and comes *forward* again, when Orlando has taken Oliver by the throat, and, in the words written in the margin, *shakes him.*

P. 10. To remove ambiguity regarding the " old " and the " new" Duke, both spoken of by Charles, the wrestler, the manuscript-corrector inserts the words *old* and *new*, where they are not found in the early copies, but where they seem required, and were, probably, originally found :—

" *Oliver.* Can you tell if Rosalind, the *old* duke's daughter, he banished with her father?
Charles. O! no ; for the *new* duke's daughter, her cousin, so loves her," &c.

The meaning is more complete with the added words, though intelligible without them.

P. 11. The two last portions of the two speeches of Charles

and Oliver, after the word "withal" in the first, and after the word "living" in the second instance, are struck out in the corrected folio, 1632. The object seems to have been to shorten the colloquy.

SCENE II.

P. 16. A trifling change, the omission of a letter, shows that Shakespeare intended to make Le Beau talk in an affected manner. He enters to give Rosalind and Celia tidings regarding the wrestling, and the common reading has been,—

> "*Le Beau.* Fair princess, you have lost much good sport.
> *Celia.* Sport? Of what colour,
> *Le Beau.* What colour, madam? How shall I answer that?"

The point, such as it is, is thus entirely lost: Celia ought to say,—

> "*Spot?* Of what colour,"

viz. of what colour is the *spot*, for Le Beau must have pronounced the word "sport," as if it were *spot*, or Celia's question "Of what colour?" is as unintelligible to others as it was to Le Beau. The corrector of the folio, 1632, has put his pen through the letter *r* in "sport."

P. 18. Sir Thomas Hanmer was right in altering, "there is such odds in the man," to "there is such odds in the *men*," *viz.* the two men, Orlando and Charles, the wrestler. "Man" answers the purpose; but as the old corrector puts it in the plural, we may perhaps be satisfied that it ought to be so. Lower down the sentence is thus changed, and evidently for the better, "If you saw yourself with *our* eyes, or knew yourself with *our* judgment, the fear of your adventure would counsel you to a more equal enterprise:" the folios have "your" in both places.

P. 19. In the old copies there is no stage-direction that Charles is *thrown* by Orlando, and *carried out;* nor, on the next page (20) that Rosalind puts *a chain round the neck* of Orlando. These are supplied in manuscript by the corrector of the folio, 1632.

P. 21. The old copies represent Le Beau as telling Orlando

that "the *taller*" is daughter to the Duke—an oversight
in the author, or an error in the printer.   Malone substituted
"smaller," but the manuscript-corrector informs us that the
word was *shorter*, and he therefore displaced " taller."

SCENE III.

P. 22.   We are rejoiced to find Coleridge's delicate conjecture fortified, or rather entirely justified, by the folio, 1632,
as amended in manuscript : Celia asks,—

> " But is all this for your father ? "

and Rosalind replies, as her answer has always been printed,—

> " No, some of it is for my child's father,"

which turns out to be an unnecessary piece of coarseness.
The passage, as it stands with the change in manuscript, is
merely this :—

> " No, some of it is for my *father's child*,"

Rosalind meaning herself as her father's child, and not
Orlando as the father of a child to be born of her.

P. 23.   When the Duke suddenly banishes Rosalind from
the Court, he tells her,—

> " Mistress, dispatch you with your safest haste ; "

but, if we may trust the old corrector, supported by obvious
plausibility, we ought in future to give the line thus :—

> " Mistress, dispatch you with your *fastest* haste,"

or with your greatest speed.   In "The Merchant of Venice"
(p. 115), we have seen *safe* misprinted "fast," in two instances close together : here we have *fastest* misprinted
" safest."

P. 24.   The line in Celia's speech,—

> " Still we went coupled and inseparable,"

is altered in the folio, 1632, to,—

> " Still we went coupled and *inseparate*,"

Shakespeare uses *inseparate* in "Troilus and Cressida," Act
V. Scene II., but he also has "inseparable" in "King John,"
Act III. Scene IV.   "Inseparate" is in the poet's manner,

and the old corrector states that such was the word in "As you like it." But for the sake of accuracy, it would hardly have seemed necessary for him to have pointed out the difference: one word was as good as the other, excepting as one must have been the text of Shakespeare.

P. 26. The line in the folio, 1632,—

> " Maids as we are, to travel so far,"

clearly wants a word which had dropped out, and is found in the folio, 1623,—

> " Maids as we are, to travel *forth* so far."

The corrector puts "forth" in the margin, and perhaps he derived it from the earlier edition. On the same page the line,—

> " I'll have no worse a name than Jove's own page,"

is corrected to

> " I'll have no *worser* name than Jove's own page,"

which is a form of the comparative of perpetual occurrence in Shakespeare and in authors of his time.

ACT II. SCENE I.

P. 27. The banished Duke remarks,—

> " Here feel we not the penalty of Adam,
> The seasons' difference ; as, the icy fang
> And churlish chiding of the winter's wind," &c. ;

but the sentence is improved by a very small restoration by the corrector of the folio, 1632, who reads,—

> " The seasons' difference, *or* the icy fang," &c.

In the 1st Lord's speech also (p. 28), *hath* for "had" is decidedly for the better :—

> " Giving thy sum of more
> To that which *hath* too much."

It is clearly of the essence of the thing, that the stream should have too much at the moment when the "hairy fool" is weeping into it; otherwise the satire of Jaques is almost meaningless.

SCENE III.

P. 31. The folio, 1632, erroneously reads,—

> " O, unhappy youth,
> Come not with these doors : within this roof
> The enemy of all your graces lives."

The folio, 1623, has, properly enough, "within these doors;" but it has also "within this roof," which can hardly be right, and the manuscript-corrector gives what is doubtless the true text, the printer having carelessly repeated "within:"—

> "Come not *within* these doors : *beneath* this roof
> The enemy of all your graces lives."

A misprint is also pointed out in a line below the preceding, which runs, to say the least of it, rather uncouthly :—

> " Of a diverted blood and bloody brother."

The commentators dwell upon the meaning of "diverted," which cannot well be doubted, but the word in fault is that which follows it, and the manuscript-corrector of the folio, 1632, puts it thus:—

> " Of a diverted, *proud*, and bloody brother."

When "blood," as in this very line in the old copies, was spelt *bloud*, the error of the press which converted *proud* into *bloud* might easily be committed.

P. 32. Orlando, addressing Adam, says,—

> " O, good old man ! how well in thee appears
> The constant service of the antique world,
> When service sweat for duty, not for meed ! "

The word "service" thus occurring in two consecutive lines may nevertheless be right, but the manuscript-corrector of the folio, 1632, changes the second line to

> " The constant *favour* of the antique world."

The " *seventy* years" of the old copies, occurring afterwards, is properly altered to " seventeen years," though it, somewhat unaccountably, remained " *seventy* years" until the time of Rowe.

SCENE IV.

P. 33. The old editions begin this scene with Rosalind's exclamation,—

> "O, Jupiter! how merry are my spirits!"

a decided misprint for "how *weary* are my spirits," to which it is changed in manuscript by the old corrector. Theobald has "weary," and was the first to adopt it in print.

P. 34. All known impressions represent Silvius as *sitting* in the presence of Rosalind, Celia, and Corin, by printing his speech thus:—

> "Or if thou hast not sat, as I do now,
> Wearying thy hearer in thy mistress praise," &c.

It is *sate* in the folios; but the language of the poet was undoubtedly, as the context shows, as well as the correction in the folio, 1632,—

> "Or if thou hast not *spake*, as I do now," &c.

The scribe, probably, misheard "sate" for *spake*.

P. 35. Rosalind's observation in short rhyme,—

> "Jove! Jove! this shepherd's passion
> Is much upon my fashion,"

reads like a quotation from an old ballad, as well as Touchstone's reply; and not only does the old corrector underscore the lines, as if to mark the fact, but he slightly alters them, and makes an important addition of a line in what is said by the Clown: the whole, therefore, runs thus, according to his statement; and it is to be remarked that he does not represent Rosalind as calling upon "Jove! Jove!" but upon "*Love! Love!*" which, under such circumstances, was much more in keeping:—

> "*Ros. Love! Love!* this shepherd's passion
> Is *too* much on my fashion.
> *Clo.* And mine; but
> It grows something stale with me,
> *And begins to fail with me.*"

The Italic type marks what is only found in the hand-

writing of the corrector. We take it that the addition by
the Clown was a farther portion of the same popular production.

P. 36. The whole of Scene V., with the song of Amiens
and the parody by Jaques, is struck out; possibly, when this
play was revived, at some date subsequent to the appearance
of the folio, 1632, no performer who could sing well enough
belonged to the company. The omissions may, however, have
been made merely for the sake of compression.

SCENE VI.

P. 38. Orlando tells old Adam to cheer up, and says to
him, "For my sake be comfortable." There seems no particular reason for any change, excepting that what is printed
was perhaps not the true reading: there is a correction in
the folio, 1632, which may restore it, in the words, "For my
sake be *comforted*." Shakespeare in many other places uses
both "comfortable" and *comforted*.

SCENE VII.

P. 41. There is an evident defect in every old copy in the
following lines by Jaques :—

> " He, that a fool doth very wisely hit,
> Doth very foolishly, although he smart,
> Seem senseless of the bob : if not," &c.

Theobald inserted "Not to" before "seem senseless," and he
was nearly right, though not entirely so, for the better correction in the folio, 1632, is,—

> " Doth very foolishly, although he smart,
> *But to* seem senseless of the bob : if not
> The wise man's folly is anatomiz'd," &c.

Lower in the same page occurs another line, which has
caused dispute. The printed words in the folio, 1623, are
these :—

> " Till that the weary very means do ebb."

This is indisputably corrupt; and Pope, and nearly all editors
after him, altered it as follows :—

"Till that the very very means do ebb."

This repetition is poor and unlike Shakespeare, and the corrector gives us, we may believe, the poet's words,—

"Till that the very means *of wear* do ebb:"

"of wear" in some way got transposed, and the printer or transcriber, not knowing how to restore it to its right place, mutilated the meaning, which, however, is now quite intelligible: we are to take "the very means of wear" to be the money which buys the apparel.

P. 45. Amiens' song is struck out, and the Duke ends by calling for music, which, we may presume, was played while he talked with Orlando regarding his parentage. There is a manuscript stage-direction, wanting in every printed copy, *Duke confer with Orlando*. The object must have been here, as elsewhere, to make the stage-business clear.

ACT III. SCENE I.

P. 46. The Duke enters talking with Oliver about the absence of his brother, Oliver having previously told him that he has not seen him,

"Not *seen* him, Sir?"

exclaims the incredulous Duke, according to the corrector of the folio, 1632, and not, "Not see him, Sir?" as it has always been printed and reprinted.

SCENE II.

P. 48. Orlando after *hanging a paper on a tree*, in the words of a manuscript stage-direction, makes his *exit* and Touchstone and Corin enter; but the latter half of what they say, after the words "mockable at court," down to "I cannot see else how thou should'st 'scape," is crossed out. Still, several literal errors are set right.

P. 50. In Touchstone's verses the line,—

"Wintred garments must be lin'd,"

is corrected to

" *Winter* garments must be lin'd,"

which may be the true reading, although the folios all have
wintred. The variation from the old copies by modern
editors ought, at least, to have been noted.

P. 51. The first line of Orlando's Poem has the indefinite
article supplied by the corrector, in conformity with Pope's
emendation,—

" Why should this *a* desert be ? "

Tyrwhitt and Malone took a needless liberty with the text
when they thrust *silent* into the line.

P. 57. Rosalind offers to tell Orlando the different paces of
time with different people, and afterwards " whom he stands
still withal ;" and when she comes to the last, Orlando,
according to all editions, asks " Whom *stays it* still withal?"
For " stays it " the manuscript-corrector inserts *stands he*
which is consistent with what has gone before, and assuredly
the language of the poet.

SCENE III.

P. 62. A misprint is met with in the middle of Touchstone's speech upon horns, which, we think, has hitherto not
been suspected, but the correction of which makes an obscure
passage quite clear. It is given in the four folios in these
terms:—

" Many a man has good horns and knows no end of them. Well, that
is the dowry of his wife: 'tis none of his own getting ; horns even so
poor men alone : No, no, the noblest deer hath them as huge as the
rascal."

Malone and others printed, " Horns ? even so :—Poor men
alone ?" and what follows these words is an answer to the
obscure question, which explains what was the import of that
question. It appears that *are* had accidentally dropped out,
and that for " even so " we ought to read *given to,* and then
Touchstone's question will be perfectly intelligible : " *Are*
horns *given to* poor men alone ?" " No, no (replies Touchstone
to his own interrogatory) ; the noblest deer hath them as
huge as the rascal." This emendation may have been obtained
from some good authority.

P. 63. All printed editions have missed the rhyme in the last line of the fragment of the ballad, " O, sweet Oliver." Perhaps it was only the extemporal invention of Touchstone, but it is thus given by the manuscript-corrector of the folio, 1632.

> " O sweet Oliver, O brave Oliver!
> Leave me not behind thee :
> But *wend* away ; begone I say,
> I will not to wedding *bind* thee."

"I will not to wedding *with* thee," has hitherto been the conclusion. " *Wend* away " was Johnson's suggestion.

SCENE IV.

P. 66. Perhaps "dies," in the following passage, is to be taken in the sense of causes to die; but the corrector of the folio, 1632, removes all doubt, if we may take his representation of the original text, by substituting *kills*. Silvius is asking Phebe whether she will be more cruel than the common executioner :—

> " Will you sterner be
> Than he that dies and lives by bloody drops? "

If we may read *kills* for "dies," the difficulty upon which Warburton, Johnson, Steevens, Tollet, and others have dwelt is at an end. Can *dines* have been the true word ?

P. 67. The commentators differ as to the precise meaning of " capable " in this passage :—

> " Lean but on a rush,
> The cicatrice and capable impressure
> Thy palm some moment keeps;"

but "capable" appears not to have been the poet's word, and the manuscript-corrector has it "*palpable* impressure,"— an indentation that may be felt.

P. 69. It is worth a note that Marlowe's celebrated line, quoted in this play,—

> " Who ever lov'd that lov'd not at first sight? "

was underscored by the corrector because it was a quotation.

P. 70. From " But what care I for words ?" down to " For

what had he to do to chide at me?" is crossed out in the folio, 1632, apparently for brevity's sake.

P. 73. There is a remarkable misprint of Rosalind's speech, which has been every where repeated, because not till now made apparent. She and Orlando are talking of kissing, as a resource if a lover be "gravell'd for lack of matter." The dialogue has always been this :—

> " *Orl.* How if the kiss be denied?
> *Ros.* Then she puts you to entreaty, and there begins new matter.
> *Orl.* Who could be out, being before his beloved mistress?
> *Ros.* Marry, that should you, if I were your mistress, or I should think my honesty ranker than my wit."

The blunder pointed out by the corrector of the folio, 1632, is in the last speech ; and when the genuine text is given it will be seen in an instant how the errors, for there are more than one, occurred. Rosalind ought to say, in answer to Orlando's question, "Who could be out, being before his beloved mistress ?"

> "Marry, that should you, if I were your mistress, or I should *thank* my honesty *rather* than my wit."

This is a singular restoration of Shakespeare's text, which could scarcely have arisen from any ingenious guess at the author's meaning.

P. 74. The folio, 1632, is very ill-printed in this scene, and it makes Orlando say, *I do*, instead of "I die," and lower down converts Coroners into *Chroniclers.* These mistakes are corrected in the margin.

P. 76. Sir Thomas Hanmer made a tolerable guess, when he altered "occasion," in the following sentence, to *accusation*,—"O, that woman that cannot make her fault her husband's occasion, let her never nurse her child herself, for she will breed it like a fool." It is *accusing* in the corrected folio, 1632 ; no doubt, Shakespeare's word.

P. 77. The manuscript-corrector adds a small word to the sentence with which Rosalind parts with Orlando in this scene, "Well, time is the old justice that examines all such offenders, and let time try *you*." The sentence is incomplete without *you*, which is found in the margin.

ACT IV. SCENE II.

P. 78. This short scene is erased, perhaps on account of the song ; but if nothing of the kind were given on the stage it would bring the two interviews of Rosalind and Orlando in juxta-position, and allow no interval. Although the song is struck out with the rest, that which is only a prose direction, but is printed as part of the song, "Then sing him home : the rest shall bear this burden," is underlined by the corrector to indicate the mistake.

SCENE III.

P. 78. It has struck nobody that what Celia says in the commencement of this scene must be a quotation, and it is underscored as such by the corrector of the folio, 1632. Rosalind, impatient at Orlando's apparent want of punctuality, observes,—

> " How say you now ? Is it not past two o'clock?
> And here much Orlando ! "

To which Celia answers jestingly by two lines taken, we may suppose, from some now unknown production,—

> " I warrant you, with pure love and troubled brain,
> He hath ta'en his bow and arrows, and gone forth—
> To sleep."

We hear nothing before, nor afterwards, about bows and arrows, and Celia terminates her quotation by two words of her own, jeering Rosalind upon the inattention of her lover. The two lines before " To sleep," read like a quotation ; and if they were not, there seems no reason why the corrector should have drawn his pen under them : he erases the redundant word *is*, "and *is* gone forth," as injurious to the measure, and most likely not in the original from which Shakespeare took the lines.

P. 83. Malone believed that a line had been lost after

> " As, how I came into that desert place ; "

but if there be any such deficiency, which we do not suspect, it must apply to what precedes, and not to what follows the above. The corrector of the folio, 1632, does not give the slightest hint that any thing is missing, which he has done in other places, and, if properly read, the sense is carried on, in spite of erroneous punctuation, through the whole passage. When Rosalind just afterwards *swoons*, and is *raised* by Oliver, the circumstance is noted in the margin, in the absence of printed stage-directions.

ACT V. SCENE II.

P. 89. Silvius, describing love, says, among other things, that it is to be made of

> " All adoration, duty, and observance ;
> All humbleness, all patience, and impatience ;
> All purity, all trial, all observance."

Malone suggested that "observance" in the second instance ought to be *obedience;* but the fact is that the misprint is in the first "observance," for the corrector of the folio, 1632, makes the line,—

> "All adoration, duty, and *obedience*,"

obedience more properly following "duty" than "trial."

SCENE III.

P. 91. Considering the difference among the commentators upon the point, it may be fit to mention that in the burden of the song, "It was a lover and his lass," the line runs, in the corrected folio,—

> " In the spring time, the only pretty *ring* time,"

and not "*rang* time," as in the old copies, nor "*rank* time," as Johnson recommended. Steevens was for "*ring* time," and Pope for a repetition of "*spring* time." Figures against the separate stanzas show that the order in which they are printed is wrong, and that the song ought to be as represented in the manuscript in the Advocates' Library, Edinburgh. Probably the company for which this comedy was prepared could manage this three-part song, and therefore it was not erased, like others for only one voice. The word, in Touchstone's comment upon the singing, is not "untuneable," as in the folios, but *untimeable*, as corrected in that of 1632. This has been a disputed point.

SCENE IV.

P. 92. A misprinted line in Orlando's first speech has produced much doubt, and many proposals for emendation. It stands as follows in all the old copies :—

> " As those that fear they hope, and know they fear."

It seems strange that nobody should yet have suggested the right change ; for the mere substitution of *to* for " they," in the first instance, gives a very intelligible and consistent meaning. The Duke asks if Orlando believes Rosalind can do what she has promised, and Orlando replies :—

> " I sometimes do believe, and sometimes do not,
> As those that fear *to* hope, and know they fear."

He was afraid to hope that she could be as good as her word, and knew that he was afraid.

In the next line but one Rosalind observes,—

> " Patience once more, whiles our compact is urg'd."

" Urg'd" seems a word not well adapted to the place, and the manuscript-corrector of the folio, 1632, informs us that it is another error of the press, and that we ought to read,—

> " Patience once more, whiles our compact is *heard ;* "

and then she proceeds, orderly and audibly, to recapitulate to the party the several articles of the compact.

P. 93. Rosalind makes her *exit* with an imperfect line, as it stands printed in all editions : she addresses Silvius,—

> " Keep your word, Silvius, that you'll marry her,
> If she refuse me :—and from hence I go,
> To make these doubts all even. [*Exeunt* ROSALIND *and* CELIA."

It appears that the dropping out of two small words after "To make these doubts all even," rendered the line defective, and spoiled the intended rhyme, which gives point to the termination of the speech. According to the manuscript-corrector of the folio, 1632, the couplet ran thus in its complete state :—

> " If she refuse me :—and from hence I go,
> To make these doubts all even—*even so.*"

The words thus recovered are of little value, in themselves, but we can hardly doubt that they came from Shakespeare's pen.

P. 96. A stage-direction (wanting in the old printed copies) informs us that when Rosalind returns, ushered by Hymen, she is apparelled *as a woman ;* and from this part of the scene to the end of the play the old corrector has been very particular, by writing in the initials and otherwise, to "bar confusion" as to the various persons addressed, and to make every thing so clear that the actors could commit no mistake.

P. 97. Hymen's address ends thus, as always printed :—

> " That reason wonder may diminish,
> How thus we met, and these things finish."

But it is put much more tersely in the manuscript of the corrector of the folio, 1632 :—

> " That reason wonder may diminish,
> How thus we met, and *thus we* finish."

We can readily believe that such was the authentic conclusion of the speech.

P. 98. The line in Hymen's song,—

> " To Hymen, god of every town,"

is slightly altered by the old corrector, and with apparent fitness,—

> " To Hymen, god *in* every town."

He also introduces an emendation into the last line but two
of the Second Brother's speech :—

> " His crown bequeathing to his banish'd brother,
> And all their lands restor'd to *them* again
> That were with him exil'd."

The old text is " him" for *them,* which may by ingenuity be
reconciled to propriety ; but *them* makes the passage more
easily understood, which here, at least, in the winding up of
the plot, must have been a main object with the poet.

TAMING OF THE SHREW.

INDUCTION. SCENE I.

P. 107. The stage-direction at the commencement of this comedy in the old folios is confused and redundant: *Enter Beggar and Hostess, Christophero Sly;* but the "Beggar" and Christophero Sly are the same person: therefore, the corrector of the folio, 1632, has made the stage-direction run merely as follows: *Enter Hostess and Christophero Sly.* The prefixes to what Sly says are always printed *Beg.,* for "Beggar," but they are in every instance changed in manuscript to *Sly.*

Sly's exclamation from "The Spanish Tragedy," "Go by S. Jeronimy," has given commentators some trouble, in consequence of the capital S. before "Jeronimy." It seems to be merely a printer's blunder (who might fancy that St. Jerome was alluded to), and so the old corrector treated it, by unceremoniously putting his pen through it.

P. 110. The folios have this line in the Lord's speech of instructions to his servants :—

> " And when he says he is, say that he dreams : "

later editors have printed it thus :—

> " And when he says he is—, say, that he dreams : "

leaving it to be supposed that the Lord left his sentence incomplete. Such does not appear to be the fact, for the

manuscript-corrector of the folio, 1632, makes the line run
naturally enough,—

> " When he says *what* he is, say that he dreams."

In modern editions, by the separate printing of insignificant words, such as *is it* for "is't" and *an it* for "an't"
of the old copies, syllables have been multiplied in preceding lines, so as to conceal an evident defect in one near
the bottom of the page,—

> " That offer service to your lordship."

Here two syllables are wanting, and the corrector of the
second folio credibly informs us that we should complete the
measure thus :—

> "That offer *humble* service to your lordship."

Adopting this word, it will be necessary to put the Lord's
question in this very usual form :—

> " How now! who *is't* ?
> *Serv.* An't please your honour, Players,
>   That offer humble service to your lordship."

The Players then enter, and after the words, *Enter Players*,
" 5 or 6" are added in parentheses, to show that there ought
not to be fewer in the company offering their services.

SCENE II.

P. 113. The Lord (dressed like a servant), wishing to
persuade Sly that he has been insane, begins his speech, as
commonly printed, with this line :—

> " Heaven cease this idle humour in your honour ! "

and the manuscript-corrector strikes out "idle," and inserts
evil, which is probably right, as is proved by the context,
where the Lord adds that Sly had been possessed by a
"foul spirit." "Idle humour" was, therefore, by no means
so proper as " *evil* humour," and was most likely an error of
the press.

P. 114. Shakespeare has mentioned his native county in a
place where hitherto it has not been at all suspected. Sly,
according to all editions, says,—

" Ask Marian Hacket, the fat alewife of Wincot, if she know me not :
if she say I am not fourteen pence on the score for sheer ale, score me up
for the lyingest knave in Christendom."

Malone did not know what to make of "sheer ale," but
supposed that it meant *shearing* or reaping ale, for so reaping
is called in Warwickshire.   What does it mean ?   It is spelt
sheere in the old copies, and that word begins one line,
Warwick having undoubtedly dropped out at the end of the
preceding line.   The corrector of the folio, 1632, inserted the
missing word in manuscript, and made the last part of the
sentence run,—

" If she say I am not fourteen pence on the score for *Warwickshire* ale,
score me up for the lyingest knave in Christendom."

Wincot, where Marian Hacket lived, is some miles from
Stratford-upon-Avon.   It was formerly not at all unusual
to spell " shire" *sheere ;* and Sly's " sheer ale" thus turns
out to have been *Warwickshire ale,* which Shakespeare celebrated, and of which he had doubtless often partaken at
Mrs. Hacket's.   We almost wonder that, in his local particularity, he did not mention the sign of her house.   This
emendation, like many others, must have been obtained from
some better manuscript than that in the hands of the old
printer.

P. 117. Sly thus addresses his supposed wife :—

" Madam wife, they say that I have dream'd,
And slept above some fifteen year, and more."

The sense tells us that we ought to read,—

" And slept *about* some fifteen year, or more ; "

and "above" is altered to *about* by the corrector of the
folio, 1632.

P. 118. A misprint of a different kind, and an awkward
transposition, destroyed the rhyming couplet with which the
Induction ought to end.   It has been always printed as
follows : Sly is speaking of the play about to be exhibited
before him :—

" Well, we'll see't.   Come, madam wife, sit by my side,
And let the world slip : we shall ne'er be younger."

We are to bear in mind that Sly's expression, used in the
very opening, is " Let the world *slide.*"   How, then, does

the manuscript-corrector of the folio, 1632, state that the above lines should run ?—

> " Well, we'll see't.   Come, madam wife, sit by my side ;
> We shall ne'er be younger, and let the world *slide*."

The comedy then begins ; and, according to the ancient arrangements of our theatres, the supposed spectators, *viz.* Sly, his Lady, the Lord, &c., occupy the balcony at the back of the stage, and facing the real audience: the manuscript stage-direction, therefore, in this place is, *They sit above, and look on below ;* that is, look on at what is acted on the stage below them.

ACT I. SCENE I.

P. 119. Recollecting how many learned hands our great dramatist's works have passed through; it is wonderful that such a blunder as that we are enabled now to point out, should not have been detected and mentioned in print at least a century ago.   Lucentio, attended by Tranio, having arrived at Padua to study in the university there, the servant thus addresses his master, and our quotation is the same in all impressions, ancient and modern :—

> " Let's be no stoics nor no stocks, I pray ;
> Or so devote to Aristotle's checks,
> As Ovid be an outcast quite abjur'd."

What are " Aristotle's checks?"   Undoubtedly a misprint for Aristotle's *Ethics*, formerly spelt *ethicks*, and hence the absurd blunder.

> " Or so devote to Aristotle's *ethics*"

is the line as it stands authoritatively corrected in the margin of the folio, 1632.

In the last line of this page, Lucentio is represented as apostrophising his absent boy, Biondello,—

> " If, Biondello, thou wert come ashore," &c.

The real words being merely in the form of an observation,—

> " If Biondello *now were* come ashore," &c.

This is one of the mistakes that must have arisen from mis-hearing on the part of the copyist of the play. The manu-script-corrector of the folio, 1632, sets the matter right.

P. 120. Two errors, one of omission and the other of com-mission, occur in a question by Katherine and an answer by Hortensio. The first is leaving out the word *gracious*, which is wanting for the completeness of the line, and the other the misprint of "mould" for *mood ;* both are thus corrected in the margin of the folio, 1632:—

> " *Kath.* I pray you, sir, is it your *gracious* will
>   To make a stale of me among these mates?
>   *Hort.* Mates, maid! how mean you that? no mates for you,
>   Unless you were of gentler, milder *mood.*"

P. 123. Lucentio breaks out into a speech in rhyme in ad-miration of Bianca's beauty, but it is injured by the mis-printing of so poor a word as "had" for *race :* —

> " O, yes, I saw sweet beauty in her face,
>   Such as the daughter of Agenor's *race,*
>   That made great Jove to humble him to her hand,
>   When with his knees he kiss'd the Cretan strand."

The above is the greatly improved reading of the corrector of the folio, 1632.

P. 125. The old copies present us with this corrupt and imperfect line, where Tranio is urging his master to speed in exchanging clothes with him:—

> " In brief, sir, sith it your pleasure is,"

which is thus altered by the old corrector :—

> " Be brief *then*, sir, sith it your pleasure is."

Malone, without any authority, had guessed at the insertion of *then*, but allowed "In brief" to remain. Lower down, for "wounded eye" the correction is "*wond'ring* eye," which may or may not be right, but the presumption is much in its favour.

SCENE II.

P. 134. Gremio, referring to Petruchio's enterprise against Katherine, tells Hortensio,—

> " This gentleman is happily arriv'd,
> My mind presumes, for his own good, and yours ; "

but it was for Gremio's good, as well as for that of Hortensio, both being suitors to Bianca ; and there is little doubt that the corrector of the folio, 1632, was justified in changing "yours" to *ours.*

ACT II. SCENE I.

P. 137. In the line of Bianca's speech,—

> "That I disdain ; but for these other goods,"

Theobald read *gauds* for "goods," but the manuscript-corrector tells us that *gards* or guards, in the sense of ornaments, was our great poet's word. It may be so.

P. 139. Petruchio says, when ironically praising Katherine to her father,—

> "That, hearing of her beauty, and her wit,
> Her affability, and bashful modesty,
> Her wondrous qualities, and mild behaviour,"

he had come to woo her. The word "wondrous" seems out of place, and in the corrected folio the line in which it occurs thus stands, with evident improvement,—

> " Her *woman's* qualities, and mild behaviour ; "

for the hero was dwelling upon the heroine's female recommendations and attributes.

P. 144. The point of Katherine's retort to Petruchio has been lost by an error either of the copyist or of the printer. Petruchio tells her,—

> " Women are made to bear, and so are you ; "

to which she replies, as the line has been given since the publication of the second folio,—

> "No such jade, sir, as you, if me you mean ; "

thus calling Petruchio a jade ; but the point of her reply is, that although a woman and made to bear, she was not such a jade as to bear Petruchio :—

> "No such jade *to bear* you, if me you mean."

The folio, 1623, gives the line even less perfectly than that of 1632, and it is evident that the corrector of the second folio has supplied words which had in some way escaped from the text. The coarse joke about the wasp's sting, near the bottom of the page, is struck out by him.

P. 147. Petruchio, giving Baptista an account of his interview with Katherine, remarks,—

> "She is not froward, but modest as the dove ;
> She is not hot, but temperate as the morn ; "

to which ordinary text no objection would perhaps present itself, did not the corrector inform us, by a marginal note, that the last line ought to be,—

> "She is not hot, but temperate as the *moon* ; "

which, in reference to the chaste coldness of the moon, was doubtless the true word.

P. 151. Steevens thought a couplet was intended at the close of this Act, and proposed to read *doing* for "cunning." He wished to alter the wrong word, for the manuscript-corrector makes it appear that, for the purpose of the rhyme, "wooing" ought to be *winning* :—

> "but in this case of *winning*,
> A child shall get a sire, if I fail not of my cunning."

ACT III. SCENE I.

P. 151. Lucentio and Hortensio, disguised as a language-master and a musician, quarrel as to precedence in the instruction of Bianca. All editions represent Hortensio's speech as beginning thus defectively :—

> "But, wrangling pedant, this is
> The patroness of heavenly harmony."

The corrector of the folio, 1632, gives "But" as a misprint for the interjection *Tut !* (of frequent occurrence in this and other plays) and furnishes two missing words in the following manner :—

> " *Tut !* wrangling pedant, *I avouch* this is
> The patroness of heavenly harmony," &c.

which is somewhat better than the insignificant mode adopted by Ritson, who only wanted to fill up the line, " But, wrangling pedant, *know* this *lady* is," &c. There must have existed some original for *I avouch.*

SCENE II.

P. 156. Biondello's exclamation, as it is given with obvious defectiveness in the early impressions, " Master, master ! news, and such news as you never heard of," has been amended in various ways ; but the manuscript correction in the folio, 1632, differs from all others, and is doubtless what the poet intended, *viz.* " Master, master ! news, and such *old* news as you never heard of." That *old* is wanted appears from Baptista's question, " Is it old and new too ?" which immediately follows. *Old* is often used as a superlative.

P. 157. If the manuscript-corrector of the folio, 1632, be accurate in one of his emendations, it appears to throw a new and singular light upon an incident in Shakespeare's life,—a difference with Michael Drayton, and why the latter, having praised our greatest dramatist and his " Lucrece " in " Matilda," first published in 1594, withdrew the stanza in 1596, and never afterwards reprinted it. It is not easy to account for this change on any other ground than that some offence had been taken by Drayton at Shakespeare, and the point is adverted to in Vol. viii., p. 411. We have, perhaps, a clue to the origin of the difference in one of the manuscript changes made in the play under consideration, which would show that it arose out of a particular allusion by Shakespeare to one of Drayton's poems, and not out of any competition between them as dramatic authors. Biondello, bringing an account of the arrival of Petruchio and his man Grumio, and of their strange caparisons and appearance, says of the latter, that he wore " an old hat, and the humour of forty fancies prick'd in't for a feather." This is precisely as the passage is given in all editions of all periods; and Warburton and Steevens speculated that "the humour of forty fancies" was a collection of short popular poems, which Grumio had stuck in his hat by way of ornament. The notion that such was the case is strengthened by the corrector of the folio, 1632; but he gives us more than a hint what was the publication in question, by altering the text as follows :—

"An old hat, and the *Amours, or* Forty Fancies, prick'd in't for a feather."

The commentators could find no work at all corresponding in title to "the humour of forty fancies;" but here it is stated by the old corrector, that the title was erroneously quoted, or in other words that the compositor had printed "Humour" for *Amours*, and "of" for *or*. Now, there is a small production, by Drayton, consisting of love poems, the title of which, though not identical, approaches sufficiently nearly to what is found in the amended text, to warrant a suspicion that it might be the work alluded to by our great dramatist, and that Drayton had been so annoyed by the reference that he expunged from the later editions of his "Matilda," the praise he had given to Shakespeare in the first impression in 1594. This notion may be a little supported by the fact, that the ridicule, if intended, was effectual, for Drayton never afterwards reprinted the poetical tract in question, although he inserted some of the sonnets it contains in others of his republications. The tract came out in 1594, under the subsequent brief title :—

"Ideas Mirrour. Amours in Quatorzains."

The word "Amours" is in such large type, compared with "Ideas Mirrour," that, popularly, it might be called Drayton's "Amours," and although not in "forty," it is in fifty "fancies," or short love poems; but "forty fancies," with the introductory word "Amours," was probably enough for Shakespeare's purpose, and he might not wish to be more exact. It is, of course, merely conjecture that he meant to produce a harmless laugh against his contemporary by an allusion to this collection of his small poems; and, if well-founded, it would carry back the composition and first representation of "The Taming of the Shrew" to about the period assigned by

Malone, *viz.* 1595 or 1596. It is to be observed that Shakespeare's " Lucrece," Drayton's " Amours," and " Matilda," and the old " Taming of *a* Shrew," were all published with the date of 1594. Upon the last, Shakespeare, as is well known, founded his comedy, and his attention might be directed to the subject by the appearance of " The Taming of *a* Shrew," in 1594. We give the whole of this merely as a speculation ; and it is nearly twenty years since we saw the sole existing copy of Drayton's " Amours in Quatorzains."

P. 158. If any confirmation were needed that the scrap of a ballad repeated by Biondello, and printed as prose in all previous editions, was in verse, and a quotation, it is afforded by the corrector of the folio, 1632, who as usual underscores it on that account. When Petruchio and Grumio enter, instantly afterwards, a manuscript stage-direction is inserted to tell us that they are *strangely clad,* and something else seems to have been added, which was erased, and is therefore not legible. The first line spoken by Petruchio, alluding to his apparel, is deficient of a syllable,—

" Were it better, I should rush in thus."

The word wanting is supplied by the corrector,—

" Were it *much* better, I should rush in thus."

P. 159. Having inquired after Katherine, and talked for some time, Petruchio suddenly reproves himself,—

" But what a fool am I to chat with you,
When I should wish good-morrow to my bride,
And seal the title with a lovely kiss ? "

" Lovely " is here misprinted, as in various other places, for *loving,* and that word is found, therefore, in the margin of the folio, 1632. Five lines lower in the folio, 1632,—

" But, sir, love concerneth us to add,"

is amended in manuscript to

" But *to our* love concerneth us to add,"

which while it preserves the verse, makes the meaning apparent. Theobald has " our " for *to our,* and Tyrwhitt recommended, " But, sir, to her," which, however, renders the measure redundant.

ACT IV. SCENE I.

P. 168. The manuscript stage-directions in this part of the play are descriptive and particular: thus we are informed that when Petruchio and his wife enter, *all the servants, frightened,* run away—that he *sings* the two fragments of ballads—that the *meat is served in*—that *both sit* down to it, and that he *throws it all about.* Modern editions have only some of these instructions for the due performance of the piece, and the old folios none of them.

SCENE II.

P. 172. The evident misprint at the end of Hortensio's speech "them" for *her,* which the second folio caught from the first, is duly set right by the manuscript-corrector. Tranio, immediately afterwards, says,—

> " And here I take the like unfeigned oath
> Never to marry with her, though she would entreat."

The words "with" and "would" are both redundant, and are struck through by the old corrector, leaving the line, thus perfect ;—

> " Never to marry her, though she entreat."

In the first line of Hortensio's reply the necessary pronoun *her* is omitted ;—

> " Would all the world, but he, had quite forsworn *her.*"

It is written in the margin, and had probably dropped out at the end of the line.

P. 173. The word "Angel" in the following line,—

> " An ancient Angel coming down the hill,"

has produced various conjectural emendations, the one usually adopted being that of Theobald, who proposed to read "ancient *engle ;*" but we are to recollect that the person spoken of was on foot, and we have no doubt that the word wanting is *ambler,* which we meet with in the margin of the corrected folio, 1632. As to *engle* or *ingle,* which means a person of weak understanding, how was Biondello to know that "the Pedant" was so, by merely seeing him walk down the hill? he could see at once that he was an *ambler*. How *ambler* came to be misprinted "angel" is a difficulty of perpetual recurrence.

SCENE IV.

P. 183. Baptista, conferring with the false Vincentio, consents to the marriage of Bianca on the passing of a sufficient dower: if so, he adds,—

> "The match is made, and all is done."

This is clearly a defective line, out of which the word *happily* has escaped, as we learn from the corrector of the folio, 1632,—

> "The match is made and all is *happily* done."

In the next line but one, we have "know" misprinted for *hold*, "Where, then, do you know best," instead of "Where, then, do you *hold* best."

P. 185. Lucentio, receiving from Biondello instructions how he should proceed, the latter says in the folio, 1623, which has been commonly followed by modern editors, "The old priest at St. Luke's Church is at your command at all hours:"

> "*Luc.* And what of all this?
> *Bion.* I cannot tell; expect; they are busied about a counterfeit assurance, take you assurance of her," &c.

The folio, 1632, properly prints *except* for "expect," but does not go quite far enough in the emendation, which is thus finished by the old corrector,—

> "*Bion.* I cannot tell; except, *while* they are busied about a counterfeit assurance, take you assurance of her," &c.

This addition of *while* cannot be wrong, for Lucentio was to make off with Bianca to St. Luke's during the time that the old folks were "busied" about the pretended deed for the lady's dower.

P. 186. When Petruchio cannot make his wife say that the sun is the moon, he resolves, as a punishment to her, not to proceed on his journey to Baptista's, and tells one of his servants to fetch the horses back that he had sent forward : the invariable text has been,—

> " Go on, and fetch our horses back again."

But *one* was of old often spelt " on," and such was the case here, for a marginal note informs us that we ought to read,—

> " Go *one*, and fetch our horses back again."

It is a mere trifle ; and lower down, in the same page, Katherine admitting that the sun is the moon, says,—

> " And so it shall be so for Katherine."

The manuscript-corrector very properly makes the last " so " *still :*—

> " And so it shall be *still* for Katherine."

ACT V. SCENE I.

P. 192. The real father of Lucentio, having been roughly treated by the pretended father and Tranio, exclaims in old and modern editions,—

> " Thus strangers may be haled and abus'd,"

which is hardly verse, but the addition of two omitted letters makes it indisputably so,—

> " Thus strangers may be *handled* and abus'd."

Handled, which was misprinted " haled," is supplied in manuscript in the corrected folio, 1632.

SCENE II.

P. 194. Petruchio remarks, in all the folios,—

> " And time it is, when raging war is come,
>   To smile at 'scapes and perils overblown."

Rowe altered " come " to " done," some emendation of the kind being necessary ; but, according to the correction in the folio, 1632, the proper word was not " done " but *gone*, as conjectured in note 2, at the foot of this page.

P. 196. The corrector of the folio, 1632, informs us, as we may readily believe, that the word *several* has strangely escaped from the subsequent line by Petruchio :

> " Let's each one send unto his wife,"

instead of

> " Let's each one send unto his *several* wife,"

which makes the sense and measure complete. Words would scarcely have been inserted in this way without some adequate warrant in the possession of the corrector.

P. 198. Lucentio's wife, Bianca, not obeying his directions to come to him, he tells her that her refusal,—

> " Hath cost me five hundred crowns since supper time."

We need have no scruple in amending a line so manifestly corrupt both in substance and form, for the wager was not *five* hundred, but "one hundred crowns," and the verse is also redundant, though easily reduced to its proper length without any loss, excepting of a useless word that, in some unexplained manner, found its way into it. In the corrected folio, 1632, the passage appears thus :—

> " The wisdom of your duty, fair Bianca,
> Cost me *one hundred* crowns since supper time."

Pope was the first to set right the numerical blunder in print ; but until now, when we have this new authority before us, no editor has thought himself at liberty to reject the needless auxiliary.

ALL'S WELL THAT ENDS WELL.

ACT I. SCENE I.

P. 208. The Countess, speaking of Gerard de Narbon, says, as the passage has been invariably printed, "Whose skill was almost as great as his honesty; had it stretched so far, would have made nature immortal," &c. The auxiliary verb "was" is struck out in the corrected folio, 1632, and the sentence is made to run less elliptically, "Whose skill, almost as great as his honesty, had it stretched so far, would have made nature immortal," &c.

P. 210. In the passage of Helena's speech,—

"My imagination
Carries no favour in't but Bertram's,"

the last line is clearly defective, the word *only* having been accidentally omitted:

"Carries no favour in't but *only* Bertram's,"

is doubtless the true reading from the corrected folio, 1632.

P. 212. In the dissertation on virginity by Parolles, "ten" is altered to *two*, which has not been the usual mode of printing the sentence, "Within *two* years it will make itself two, which is a goodly increase." This was Steevens' mode of curing the misprint, and, on the whole, it seems preferable to Sir Thomas Hanmer's change of "two," in the second instance, to *ten*, "Within ten years it will make itself *ten*," Parolles would hardly look forward to so distant a period. This speech, and indeed all the rest of the scene

until the entrance of the Page, is crossed out in the folio,
1632. Nevertheless several emendations are made in the
margin : thus Parolles at the end of his harangue asks
Helena, "Will you *do* any thing with it," which connects
her reply, "Not *with* my virginity yet," and the question :
do and *with* are both added by the old corrector of the
folio, 1632. The whole of this part of the scene is a very
blundering specimen of typography.

P. 214. A difficulty which has arisen respecting the
couplet,—

> " The mightiest space in fortune nature brings
> To join like likes, and kiss like native things,"

is in a great degree, if not entirely, removed by the transposition of the words "fortune" and "nature :" the manuscript-corrector instructs us to read thus :—

> " The mightiest space in *nature fortune* brings
> To join like likes, and kiss like native things."

The meaning is then evident, *viz.*, that fortune occasions
things that are like each other to join, notwithstanding the
mightiest space in nature may intervene between them.

SCENE III.

P. 220. It has been stated that it was the practice of the
corrector of the folio, 1632, to mark under every passage
quoted, whether from a ballad or a book ; and by amending
the Clown's repetition of an old song he has supplied a
deficiency, which Warburton perceived and would have set
right, but not in the right way. We may feel satisfied that
it ran thus, and the necessary words, *Good sooth it was*, are
written in an adjoining blank space :—

> " Was this fair face, quoth she, the cause
> Why Grecians sacked Troy ?
> Fond done, done fond, *good sooth it was ;*
> Was this King Priam's joy ?"

The rest is the same as in the old folios. The Countess
complains that the Clown "corrupts the song," which he
denies ; and his answer contains another addition to the
text of some importance, besides the correction of a
printer's error, which has always been amended in a way to
injure, instead of improving, the sense. The Clown says, in

reply to the charge that he "corrupts the song" by allowing only one good woman in ten,—

> "One good woman in ten, madam, which is a purifying o' the song *and mending o' the sex*. Would God would serve the world so all the year! we'd find no fault with the tithe-woman, if I were the parson. One in ten, quotha! An we might have a good woman born—but *one*— every blazing star, or at an earthquake, 'twould mend the lottery well."

Thus, besides the restoration to the original text of the words "and mending o' the sex," the meaning is strengthened by "but *one*" instead of "but ere," or "but *ore*" as it stands in the old impressions. Steevens left it out because he did not know what to make of it, and Malone suggested "but *or*." The emendation of "ore" to *one* adds point to the satire intended by the Clown.

P. 221. The Clown's ridicule of the puritans and the Steward's remark about the "queen of virgins" are both erased—the last, probably, because it was unintelligible to the corrector.

P. 222. The Countess has received information from her Steward of Helena's secret love for Bertram, and in a soliloquy (for according to the manuscript-corrector of the folio, 1632, the heroine enters too early in all editions) makes excuses for the young lady's passion, ending with this couplet, as it has always been printed:—

> "By our remembrances of days foregone,
> Such were our faults; or then we thought them none."

Here there is a misprint, arising no doubt out of the mishearing of the scribe, the correction of which is of importance, because it makes the meaning of the Countess quite evident, whereas, in the ordinary state of the text, it is obscure. The lines ought to run, as we learn from the old corrector's manuscript,—

> "By our remembrances of days foregone
> *Search we out* faults—*for* then we thought them none."

i. e. let us measure faults in others by the recollection of our own, when we thought them none. Helena enters at the moment, and the suspicions of the Countess are confirmed by her appearance, "Her eye is sick on't," &c.

P. 225. In Helena's speech, describing her father's pre-scriptions, she says, in all copies of the play, that they are

> " such as his reading
> And manifest experience had collected."

For "manifest," the corrector of the folio, 1632, places *mani-fold* in the margin, in allusion to the old physician's great practice. We may safely admit the emendation.

ACT II. SCENE I.

P. 229. The corrector of the folio, 1632, not being able to make any thing out of the words, "there do muster true gate," has struck them out, and left the sentence to run thus : "For they wear themselves in the cap of the time, eat, speak, and *move* under the influence of the most re-ceived star." For *move*, the second folio has the misprint of *more*.

P. 230. Some of the commentators fancied that a line had been lost at the close of Lafeu's speech, in praise of the won-derful prescription he had seen, which was able to do much more than cure the King, for it could raise Pepin from his grave, and enable Charlemaine to write a love letter to the owner of the medicine. The passage has hitherto been given as follows :—

> " whose simple touch
> Is powerful to araise King Pepin, nay,
> To give great Charlemaine a pen in's hand
> And write to her a love-line."

Of the word "araise," we have no other example, and the old corrector writes it *upraise*, for which it was most likely misprinted—while to alter "and" to "to," at the beginning of the next line but one, makes the whole meaning clear, without supposing any thing to have been lost :—

> " whose simple touch
> Is powerful to *upraise* King Pepin, nay,
> To give great Charlemaine a pen in's hand
> *To* write to her a love-line."

P. 233. The manuscript-corrector reads, " despair most

fits," for "shifts" in the last line of Helena's speech ; and, supported as the change is by other authorities, there can be no dispute that it is the right word, in preference to "despair most sits" of Pope.

P. 234. In the King's speech, accepting the services of Helena, occurs a line of only eight syllables, to which Warburton added the word "virtue" to complete the measure. It has been supposed by some that it might have been left by the author purposely defective ; but, on the other hand, we now find that the corrector of the folio, 1632, introduced an emendation of it, and we cannot but conclude that he had some warrant for doing so, especially as the change he recommends is free from the objection to which the suggestion of Warburton was liable : he also proposes a slight change in the next line, which appears to be a decided improvement. The couplet stands thus in all the folios :—

> " Youth, beauty, wisdom, courage, all
>   That happiness and prime can happy call."

As amended by the old corrector, it runs,—

> " Youth, beauty, wisdom, courage, *honour*, all
>   That happiness *in* prime can happy call."

"Happiness in prime" is of course happiness in youth, the spring of life, as Johnson explains the word "prime."

SCENE III.

P. 240. The King, after his cure, calls forth the young lords under his wardship, that Helena may make her choice from them, telling her that "they stand at his bestowing :"—

> " O'er whom both sovereign power and father's voice
>   I have to use."

The manuscript-corrector of the folio, 1632, puts "sovereign" as well as "father" in the genitive :—

> " O'er whom both *sovereign's* power and father's voice
>   I am to use."

The King was to use his power as a sovereign, as well as his voice as a father, with his youthful nobility. In Lafeu's speech, just below, "And writ as little beard" is changed to "And *with* as little beard," with obvious fitness in this place, although elsewhere Shakespeare may use "writ" and "write" with some peculiarity.

P. 242. When Helena makes her choice of Bertram with the words, "This is the man," a stage-direction is added in manuscript, *He draws back*, to show in what way the hero on the instant indicated his astonishment and reluctance. The notifications of the kind throughout this play are comparatively few and of little moment.

P. 243. Regarding the sentence,—

> " My honour's at the stake, which to defeat
> I must produce my power,"

the commentators differ, some being for *defend* and others for preserving "defeat." There can be no doubt that *defend* is the word naturally required by the sense, and we find "defeat" altered to *defend* in the margin of the corrected folio, 1632. It seems a mere error of the press.

P. 247. Another misprint occurs in Lafeu's attack upon Parolles, where he says, according to all old copies of the play, "You are more saucy with lords and honourable personages, than the commission of your birth and virtue gives you heraldry." Malone altered the places of "commission" and "heraldry" without any improvement, and without being aware that "commission" was merely a blunder for *condition*: "than the *condition* of your birth and virtue gives you heraldry," is the true reading, supplied by the corrector of the folio, 1632.

P. 248. Rowe was the first in print to change "detected" to *detested* in the following passage,—

> " War is no strife
> To the dark house, and the detested wife."

It is "detected" in the old editions; but in the folio, 1632, it is corrected in manuscript to *detested*—thus setting right an indisputable error.

SCENE IV.

P. 250. In modern editions (in some without notice) two speeches by the Clown are made only one; and in the old folios he is represented as speaking twice running. The fact is (as conjectured in note 6), that an answer by Parolles to the Clown's first speech has been accidentally omitted in the printed copies, but is supplied in manuscript in the folio, 1632. The dialogue, therefore, ought to run,—

" *Par.* Go to, thou art a witty fool : I have found thee.
Clo. Did you find me in yourself, sir, or were you taught to find me ?
Par. Go to, I say : I have found thee : no more ; I have found thee, a witty fool.
Clo. The search, sir, was profitable," &c.

What we have printed in Italics is written in the lower margin of the folio, 1632, with a line drawn to the place in the page where it ought to come in. The omission was not of great value in itself; but we are, of course, glad to preserve any lost words (if such they be) of our great dramatist.

SCENE V.

P. 252. As might be expected, the mistake, in Bertram's speech, of, " And ere I do begin," for " *End* ere I do begin," did not escape the corrector of the folio, 1632, who marked the emendation in the margin. Another instance of misprinting " end " *and*, occurs in " Henry the Fifth."

ACT III.   SCENE II.

P. 258. The commencement of the speech of the Countess to Helena, on the return of the latter to Rousillon, has always been given as follows :—

" I pr'ythee, lady, have a better cheer ;
If thou engrossest all the griefs are thine,
Thou robb'st me of a moiety."

The old corrector tells us, and we may readily believe him, that there is a small, but important, error in the second line,—

> " If thou engrossest all the griefs *as* thine,
> Thou robb'st me of a moiety."

P. 259. A decided corruption is pointed out in one of the French Envoy's remarks upon Parolles : the words, as commonly printed, are,—

> " Indeed, good lady,
> The fellow has a deal of that too much,
> Which holds him much to have."

If two errors in the last line had not been committed, the commentators would have been spared much useless conjecture ; for the passage ought, as we learn from a manuscript note in the folio, 1632, to stand as follows :—

> " Indeed, good lady,
> The fellow has a deal of that too much
> Which 'hoves him much to *leave*."

What was unintelligible, without the exercise of peculiar and misplaced ingenuity, is thus rendered clear and palpable.

P. 260. In the same way, and upon the same evidence, we are able to set right a quotation which has given infinite trouble and occasioned many notes. It occurs in Helena's speech, where she is reflecting on the danger to which Bertram will be exposed in the wars : she says, according to the folio, 1623,

> " O ! you leaden messengers,
> That ride upon the violent speed of fire,
> Fly with false aim ; move the still-peering air,
> That sings with piercing, do not touch my lord ! " &c.

The folio, 1632, has " still-piercing air " and " that stings with piercing." Malone printed " still-piecing air," and so far was right ; but the old corrector substitutes *volant* for " violent " and *wound* for " move," and gives the whole passage thus distinctly :—

> " O ! you leaden messengers,
> That ride upon the *volant* speed of fire,
> Fly with false aim ; *wound* the still-piecing air,
> That sings with piercing, do not touch my lord ! " &c.

The mistake of " violent " for *volant* was almost to be expected ; and the copyist, having misheard the word, wrote " move" instead of *wound*. This is an emendation that might possibly have been made without the assistance of a better

manuscript than that used for the folio in which the error
first appeared.   Malone truly states that in the line,—

> " I met the ravin lion when he roar'd,"

" ravin " means *ravening*: the old corrector states that
" ravin " was a misprint for *ravening*.

SCENE IV.

P. 263. In the passage,
> " Which of them both
> Is dearest to me, I have no skill in sense
> To make distinction,"

" skill *or* sense" seems preferable, and " in " is altered to
or by the corrector of the folio, 1632.

SCENE VI.

P. 269. For " let him fetch his drum," the correction in
the folio, 1632, is " let him fetch *off* his drum," which is the
very phrase used in the next speech.   Theobald speculated
that " lump of ours," of the old copies, should be " lump of
ore," but " lump of *ores*" is proposed in the margin of the
folio, 1632.

ACT IV.   SCENE II.

P. 278. We here meet with an easy misprint and a happy
emendation of the text.   Bertram, endeavouring to melt and
mould the virtuous Diana to his wishes, tells her,—

> " If the quick fire of youth light not your mind,
> You are no maiden, but a monument:
> When you are dead, you should be such a one
> As you are now, for you are cold and stern."

Steevens seems to have had a notion that " stern " was not
the right word, but he did not know what to put instead
of it.   Bertram complains that Diana is not a " maiden, but
a monument," and the old corrector explains how she was
a monument,—

> " For you are cold and *stone*."

P. 279. The seven lines in Diana's speech, which begin "What is not holy," and end "That I will work against him," are erased in the corrected folio, perhaps as difficult to be understood, and Johnson and others have admitted themselves to be "at a loss" for the meaning.

P. 280. The following passage, as it is printed in all the old editions, has caused much vexation: Diana is speaking to Bertram, who is doing his utmost to make his suit acceptable to her,—

> " I see, that men make ropes in such a scarre,
> That we'll forsake ourselves."

The reading of Rowe, the earliest editor after the appearance of the last of the four folios in 1685, was,—

> " I see that men make *hopes* in such *affairs*,
> That we'll forsake ourselves."

Other emendations have been proposed; but it may be sufficient to state that Malone adopted *hopes* from Rowe, and substituted " in such a *scene*," for " in such a scarre." The corrector of the folio, 1632, appears to have detected the real misprint, and the correction of it makes it evident that Diana intends to say, that when men endeavour to seduce women from virtue, they indulge hopes that the weaker sex, thus assailed, will abandon themselves " in such a suit," and submit to importunity:—

> " I see, that men make *hopes* in such a *suit*,
> That we'll forsake ourselves."

Thus we find that *hopes* (as Rowe supposed), had been misprinted "ropes," and that *suit* (often spelt *suite* of old), had been misprinted " scarre." With these two errors set right the meaning of the poet seems ascertained.

P. 281. Diana, having assented to Helena's wish that she should be her substitute, exclaims, just before Bertram makes his *exit*,—

> " You have won
> A wife of me, although my hope be done."

The manuscript-corrector erases " done," and inserts *none*: she had gained a wife for Bertram, although her hope in the transaction was nothing. We may take it for granted, perhaps, that the original word was *none*; but here, as in some former cases, it may be thought, on any other account, a matter almost of indifference.

SCENE III.

P. 282. Those who have desired to adhere closely to the folio, 1623, have sometimes been induced to refuse to correct even decided errors of the press ; as in the following instance, where the French Gentleman is made to ask, "Is it not meant damnable in us, to be trumpeters of our unlawful intents ?" "Is it not *most* damnable," &c., is required by the sense, as well as warranted by the corrector of the folio, 1632. In the next speech of the same character we ought, on the same warranty, to change "company" into *companion*, although sense may certainly be made out of "company" of the old impressions.

P. 283. There are three mistakes of the same description in another short speech by the French Gentleman on this page : we first quote it as printed in the folio, 1632 :—

" The stronger part of it by her own letters ; which make her story true, even to the point of her death : her death is self, which could not be her office to say, is come, was faithfully confirmed by the rector of the place."

The corrector of the folio, 1632, and common sense, tell us for "stronger," to read *stranger;* for "is self," to read *itself* (as has of course been done by all modern editors) ; and for "was," to read *and.*

P. 286. After Parolles has offered to take the sacrament, in order to testify the truth of what he says, the following words, "All's one to him," are absurdly made part of his own speech in the old copies. It has been usual, with Malone and others, to assign them to Bertram, but Ritson contended that they rather belonged to Dumain. A manuscript-correction shows that it was an observation made aside by the person who pretended to act as Interpreter, the prefix *Int.* having been inserted in the margin of the folio, 1632.

SCENE IV.

P. 293. The passage in Helena's speech, beginning, "But O, strange men," and ending, "But more of this hereafter," is struck through with a pen. We may here mention that such is the case with a part of the next scene, from Lafeu's question, "Whether dost thou profess thyself," &c., down to the Clown's speech ending with the words, "the great fire." The reason for the last omission we can readily understand.

P. 294. When Helena is in haste to take her departure from Florence, with Diana and the Widow, she is represented in the folios as saying to them,—

> " We must away ;
> Our waggon is prepar'd, and time revives us."

Nearly all the commentators agree that "revives" must be a misprint, and Johnson suggests *invites* as the proper word ; but the corrector of the folio, 1632, informs us that "revives" is an error for *reviles :* the time found fault with Helena and her companions for delay. In the earlier part of the same speech he converts "word" into *world :*—

> " But with the *world* the time will bring on summer."

Helena wishes Diana to wait with patience the issue of events, which would produce as happy a result, as in the natural world, where the beauty of summer followed the dreariness of winter. This trifling change seems to render unnecessary any speculation.

SCENE V.

P. 295. For "*salad*-herbs" (which Rowe inserted, the word being only "herbs" in the folios), we ought, according to the old corrector, to read *pot*-herbs, the printer, or scribe, as in some other cases already pointed out, having blundered, because two words came together with nearly the same letters and sound :—"They are *not pot*-herbs, you knave ; they are nose-herbs." Lower down, we have properly *name* for " maine" of the old impressions.

P. 296. The Countess, describing the Clown, says that " he has no pace, but runs where he will." A letter has merely been omitted, as we learn from a manuscript-correction, and we ought to read *place* for " pace," the Countess meaning that the Clown had no fixed duties, although allowed the run of the house. This slight change, which accords with Tyrwhitt's notion, renders it needless to suppose, with Johnson, that the Countess makes a far-fetched allusion to the pace of a horse.

ACT V. SCENE I.

P. 298. Steevens originally fancied that "Astringer" was an error of the press for *a stranger;* but he afterwards introduced a long note to show that "a gentle Astringer" of the folio, 1623, was "a gentleman falconer." In the folio, 1632, the word is printed *A stranger,* and the manuscript-corrector has altered the stage-direction to this form, *Enter a gent. a stranger;* that is, *Enter a gentleman, a stranger,*—a person not known to Helena and her companions. We may feel confident that it was a mistake, first made in the folio, 1623, and that this *gentleman, a stranger,* had no necessary connexion with falconry. In confirmation it may be added, that when he afterwards appears again before the King at Rousillon, he is only called in the old copies *a gentleman,* without any hint that he is what Steevens terms "an astringer;" and the manuscript-corrector of the folio, 1632, has altered the stage-direction in that place to *Enter the gentleman stranger,* in order to identify him with the *Gent. a stranger,* in the former scene.

SCENE II.

P. 299. To the words, "Enter Clown and Parolles," the old corrector has subjoined *ill-favoured,* to show that the apparel of Parolles was very different, in this scene, to the gay attire he had worn before his exposure and dismissal.

SCENE III.

P. 302. The alteration of *blaze* for "blade" in the line,—

"Natural rebellion, done in the blade of youth,"

of the old copies, is confirmed by a manuscript marginal

note in the folio, 1632. Theobald was the first judiciously to substitute *blaze*.

P. 304. In the King's speech, beginning "Well excus'd," the epithet "sour," before "offence," is altered to *sore* with apparent fitness, while the two strange lines,—

> "Our own love, waking, cries to see what's done,
> While shameful hate sleeps out the afternoon,"

are erased, giving some countenance to Johnson's "hope" that they were "an interpolation of a player," though we believe it to be an inexplicable corruption. It has been the practice of all modern editors to assign the couplet,—

> "Which better than the first, O, dear heaven bless!
> Or, ere they meet, in me, O nature, cease,"

to the Countess instead of the King, to whom they are certainly wrongly given in all the folios. The manuscript-corrector of the folio, 1632, places the prefix of *Lafeu* before them, making his speech begin there, and not at "Come on, my son," &c. No material objection to this arrangement seems to present itself. The conclusion of the speech, as it stands in the old impressions,—

> "Such a ring as this,
> The last that ere I took her leave at court,
> I saw upon her finger,"

runs much more intelligibly as follows :—

> "Such a ring as this,
> The last *time* ere *she* took her leave at court,
> I saw upon her finger."

Rowe proposed *she;* but the alteration of "that" to *time* seems equally necessary, and it is justified in the handwriting of the old corrector.

P. 307. A good deal of contrariety of opinion has prevailed respecting Lafeu's speech, rejecting Bertram. In the folio, 1623, it is this, with the observance of the old punctuation, which is here material :—

> "I will buy me a son in law in a fair, and toll for this. I'll none of him."

The folio, 1632, furnishes the text thus varied :—

> "I will buy me a son in law in a *fear* and toll *him* for this. I'll none of him."

The old corrector of that edition merely alters the stops (setting right the mis-spelling of the word "fair"), and renders the sentence quite perspicuous:—

> " I will buy me a son in law in a fair, and toll him : for this, I'll none of him."

i. e. pay toll, as usual in fairs, on the transaction, but have nothing more to do with Bertram.

P. 308. An improvement in the versification is produced by the addition of a single letter in one of the King's speeches, where he says,—

> " Come hither, count.   Do you know these women?"

The manuscript-correction is,—

> " Come hither, *county.*   Do you know these women?"

County, for " count," is of constant occurrence.

P. 309. The line in Bertram's explanation how Diana obtained the ring from him,—

> " Her insuit coming with her modern grace,"

has been supposed to refer to her *solicitation* for the ring ; but the words, " insuite comming," as they are spelt in the folio, 1623 (the folio, 1632, omits the final *e*), are merely misprinted ; and on the evidence of the manuscript-corrector, as well as common sense, we must print the passage hereafter,—

> " Her *infinite cunning,* with her modern grace,
> Subdued me to her rate."

This appears to be one of the instances in which a gross blunder was occasioned, in part by the mishearing of the old scribe, and in part by the carelessness of the old printer. The sagacity of the late Mr. Walker hit upon this excellent emendation. See Athenæum, 17 April, 1852.

P. 310. The word " have" is struck out in the following line ; and as it is injurious to the measure, as well as needless to the meaning, we may feel assured that it accidentally found its way into the text of the folios :—

> " You that have turn'd off a first so noble wife."

It must have originally stood,—

> " You that turn'd off a first so noble wife."

Malone felt the objection to "have" so strongly that he omitted it, but inexcusably without notice.

P. 313. When Bertram, just after the entrance of Helena, exclaims, "Both, both! O, pardon!" he flung himself upon his knees, when this play was anciently acted, and *Kneels* is therefore inserted as a marginal stage-direction. We might gather from the first words of the "Epilogue" (not so called in the old copies, the six lines having no heading), that it was spoken by the King; but it is so stated in manuscript by the corrector of the folio, 1632, *Epilogue by the King.*

TWELFTH NIGHT;

OR,

WHAT YOU WILL.

ACT I. SCENE I.

P. 325. From the manuscript stage-direction in the corrected folio, 1632, inserted before the Duke speaks,—*Music behind*—we may infer that the comedy opened by the performance of some instrumental strains at the back of the stage. When the Duke exclaims " Enough! no more," *Cease* is written in the margin ; so that, perhaps, the musicians continued to play, in a subdued manner, while the Duke was delivering his first seven lines.

An authority has been long wanted for the word *south* (in preference to " sound " of all editions until Pope's time), in the passage,—

> " O! it came o'er my ear like the sweet *south*,
> That breathes upon a bank of violets."

The corrector of the folio, 1632, supplies that authority, and has struck out the two last letters of "sound," and replaced them by *th*, in his ordinary brief and business-like manner. We may thus, perhaps, consider "sound," which has had but few advocates in modern times, as in future exploded from the text of Shakespeare.

SCENE III.

P. 332. The old copies, when Maria is going, make Sir Toby say, " An thou let part so, sir Andrew," omitting a

pronoun which seems necessary, and which is supplied by
the manuscript-corrector, "An thou let *her* part so, sir
Andrew." Farther on in the same dialogue the folio, 1632,
left out *me* in the sentence by sir Andrew, "Never in your
life, I think ; unless you see Canary put *me* down." A note
in the margin makes the passage correspond in this particular
with the folio, 1623.

P. 333. Theobald detected a singular printer's error, when,
in all early editions, Sir Toby tells sir Andrew that his hair
"will not cool my nature," instead of "will not *curl by*
nature." The old corrector of the folio, 1632, alters "cool"
to *curl*, and "my" to *by*, as might be expected.

P. 335. Pope was wrong in his change respecting "flame-
colour'd stock:" the old editions have it "*dam'd* colour'd
stock," which the manuscript-corrector informs us ought to
be "*dun*-colour'd stock." When sir Andrew, referring just
before to his dancing, tells Sir Toby, that he has "the back-
trick simply as strong as any man in Illyria," a stage-direction is inserted in the margin, *Dances fantastically*, to show
that the knight exhibited his proficiency to the audience.
At the close of the scene, when Sir Toby observes to Sir
Andrew, "Let me see thee caper," the stage-direction is
Dances again, we may presume as ridiculously as before.
These notes, for the direction of the performer of the part,
are not in any edition ancient or modern, and were very possibly derived in part from the practice of the old actor of the
character of Sir Andrew.

SCENE IV.

P. 337. The Duke having directed Viola to make love on
his behalf to Olivia, the latter replies,—

"I'll do my best
To woo your lady,"

and then adds, *aside*,—

"Yet, a barful strife ;
Whoe'er I woo, myself would be his wife."

The force of the last passage is much augmented by making
the first hemistich an exclamation,—

"Yet, O barful strife!"

which is the judicious reading afforded by the corrector of the
folio, 1632.

SCENE V.

P. 342. It is clear that the following ought to be in the alternative; Malvolio speaks: " He says, he'll stand at your door like a sheriff's post, and be the supporter of a bench, but he'll speak to you." Viola could not suppose herself "a sheriff's post," and " the supporter of a bench " at the same time; therefore the manuscript-correction is " *or* be the supporter of a bench." Such emendations are minute, but they are generally important, as far as the sense of the poet is concerned; and, at all events, they show the attention the corrector paid even to what might be considered trifles, did they relate to any other author than Shakespeare.

P. 345. The expression, "Such a one I was this present," has excited much comment, editors not exactly knowing what to make of it. The manuscript-corrector says that we ought to read, "Such a one I *am at* this present," which, bearing in mind that Olivia unveils at the instant, is reasonable; but, nevertheless, the old reading might stand.

ACT II.　SCENE I.

P. 349. It is not easy to determine with whom the responsibility rests of the strange, but decided, blunder here pointed out by the corrector of the folio, 1632. Sebastian is speaking of his reputed likeness to his sister :—

" A lady, sir, though it was said she much resembled me, was yet of many accounted beautiful : but, though I could not with such estimable wonder overfar believe that, yet thus far I will boldly publish her," &c.

It is not surprising that the commentators should have been at strife regarding the meaning of this passage; and Warburton was so gravelled by it, that he felt obliged to omit the words, "with such estimable wonder," as "a player's interpolation." This is a very ready way of overcoming any obstacle. It certainly is difficult to account for the gross misprints in the above short sentence; but they are most distinctly pointed out by the corrector of the folio, 1632, in his own clear and accurate manner; and when we read the words he has substituted for those of the received text, we see at once that he could not be mistaken.

Sebastian modestly denies that he much resembled his beautiful lost sister, observing,—

> "A lady, sir, though it was said she much resembled me, was yet of many accounted beautiful; but, though I could not with *self-estimation wander so far to* believe that, yet thus far I will boldly publish her," &c.

May we conclude, that this new and self-evident improvement of the absurd old reading was derived from some original source, perhaps from some better manuscript than that employed by the old printer of the folio, 1623, which was exactly followed in the folio, 1632? Such an emendation could hardly be the result of mere guess-work.

P. 351. The ambiguity, to say the least of it, belonging to Viola's words, " She took the ring of me," is entirely avoided by reading, " She took *no* ring of me ;" and this, no doubt, was the language of the poet. The corrector of the folio, 1632, strikes out " the" in the body of the text, and places *no* in the margin. This alteration renders what the heroine afterwards says quite consistent, " I left *no* ring with her," and " Why, he sent her *none.*"

SCENE III.

P. 353. We meet here with a welcome addition to the text where it cannot be doubted that something is wanting. One of the speeches of Sir Andrew has hitherto only terminated with a hyphen, showing that even the conclusion of a word has been carelessly omitted in the old copies: in modern editions the hyphen has been elongated, as if the knight had been interrupted by the Clown, and not allowed to finish his sentence. In the first and other folios, this part of the dialogue stands exactly as follows :—

> " *Sir To.* Come on : there is sixpence for you; let's have a song.
> *Sir An.* There's a testril of me, too : if one knight give a-
> *Clo.* Would you have a love-song, or a song of good life ?"

The elongation of the hyphen in modern editions, has made Sir Andrew's speech of course appear thus, but it is a misrepresentation of the originals :—

> " *Sir And.* There's a testril of me too : if one knight give a——"

Now, what ought to be the text, according to the addition made to it by interlineation in the corrected copy of the folio, 1632? It will be seen that the continuation of the sentence, thus cut short by a hyphen in the early impressions, completes the word, of which the two syllables had been separated: we give the speech, to the minutest particular, in the form in which it appears, partly in print, and partly in the hand-writing of the old corrector, marking the latter by Italic type :—

" *Sir An.* There's a testrill of me too: if one knight give a- *way sixe pence so will 1 give an other : go to, a song.*"

The first line ends with *a-*, and the next begins with *way :* unless, therefore, the corrector of the folio, 1632, invented this termination of an unfinished sentence, he must have obtained it from some accurate and authentic source. In this instance, we apprehend that the manuscript used by the old printer was not defective, but that a line, consisting of what is above inserted in Italics, was accidentally left out by the compositor of the folio, 1623, and the defect never discovered. In all the copies of the folios, 1623 and 1632, which we have had an opportunity of examining, the same deficiency is to be noted.

P. 354. An alteration is made in the Clown's song, which gives a different, if not an improved, meaning to the second line of it :—

> " O, mistress mine ! where are you roaming ?
> O ! stay, *for here* your true love's coming," &c.

The ordinary words are " O ! stay and hear," &c.

The stage-directions regarding the singing of the scraps of ballads, catches, &c., in this scene, are numerous and precise: but there is one manuscript note opposite the line of the ballad,—

> " O ! the twelfth day of December,"

which is not easily understood: it merely consists of " 17 *Nov.*" Why the 12th December was especially mentioned in the ballad quoted, we know not ; but the 17th November was the day on which Queen Elizabeth ascended the throne, and it was usual to compose and publish loyal songs to celebrate it. When this comedy was first produced, it seems probable that Elizabeth was still reigning, and a song on the 17th

November may possibly have been originally introduced in
her honour, which might be altered to some other, beginning, " O ! the twelfth day of December," after her
demise. This curious fact may have been within the knowledge of the corrector of the folio, 1632, and he may have
thus briefly recorded it.

SCENE IV.

P. 363. Just before the *exit* of the Clown the Duke is made
to say, in the old copies as well as in modern editions, " Give
me now leave to leave thee," which can hardly be right,
seeing that it is the Clown who is going to leave the Duke, not
the Duke the Clown : the old corrector therefore makes these
necessary changes : " *I* give *thee* leave to leave *me.*" *Thee*
and *me* got transposed, and *I* was omitted.

SCENE V.

P. 367. In Malvolio's speech beginning, " And then to
have the humour of state," we meet with the common misprint of " humour " for *honour.* There can be little doubt
that the corrector of the folio, 1632, has furnished the true
word, although the false one has been argued upon by various
commentators, " And then to have the *honour* of state."
Malvolio is fancying himself married to the Countess, and
assuming dignity in consequence among his menials.

The suggestion in note 10, that " cars " has been misprinted,
gives a hint at the explanation of a speech by Fabian,
which we find in the hand-writing of the corrector. Fabian
is enforcing silence in order that Malvolio, while they are
watching him, may not discover them, and says in the
folio, 1623, " Though our silence be drawn from us with
cars, yet peace ! " The folio, 1632, prints " cars " *cares,*
and many proposals have been made to alter " cars " to
cables, carts, &c. ; but " with cars " turns out to be an error
of the press for *by th' ears,* or *by the ears,* and the meaning
is perfectly clear when we read, " Though our silence be
drawn from us *by th' ears,* yet peace ! "

This scene is very carelessly printed in the old copies, and
subsequently we have " stallion " for *stannyel* (the corrector
of the folio, 1632, gives the word *falcon,* which means nearly
the same thing), " become " for *born,* &c. The folio, 1632,

renders the matter worse by additional errors, besides those in the earlier impression of 1623 ; but they are all set right in manuscript.

ACT III. SCENE I.

P. 374. Viola, disserting upon the qualifications of a professed jester, remarks :—

> " He must observe their mood on whom he jests,
> The quality of persons, and the time,
> And, like the haggard, check at every feather
> That comes before his eye."

The haggard was a wild hawk that flew at all birds ; and what Viola is therefore made to say is the contrary of what she must mean. The old corrector renders her speech consistent by reading,—

> " *Not*, like the haggard, check at every feather
> That comes before his eye."

P. 377. Olivia, in her apology to Viola for sending the ring after her, says, in all printed copies of this comedy,—

> " Under your hard construction must I sit,
> To force that on you, in a shameful cunning," &c.

The manuscript-corrector tells us to substitute *shame-fac'd* for " shameful," as the poet's original language. The fitness of this emendation seems disputable.

SCENE III.

P. 382. The folio, 1632, omits two lines, contained in the folio, 1623, from which it was printed, and they are written in the margin by the corrector of the later of these impressions, but not in the defective terms in which they are found in the earlier : in 1623 they were thus given :—

> " And thanks : and ever oft good turns
> Are shuffled off with such incurrent pay."

Two syllables are clearly wanting in the first line, and

N

editors have resorted to various expedients for supplying them ; but certainly none so good as the following,—

> "And thanks, *still thanks ;* and *very* oft good turns
> Are shuffled off with such incurrent pay,"

which the old corrector inserts as the passage in his time. We have no doubt that he was right ; but it is to be re-marked that "still thanks" is interlined, in the same hand-writing, but in different ink.

SCENE IV.

P. 384. The manuscript stage-directions in this scene are remarkable for the minute manner in which they describe the conduct of Viola and Sir Andrew, when Sir Toby and Fabian are inciting them to a desperate encounter. When Sir Andrew enters we are told that he *hangs back ;* and of Viola it is said that she is *unwilling ;* while they afterwards, at the instance of Sir Toby and Fabian, both *draw,* but in-stead of advancing, *go back.* It would not be easy to act such a scene without these or other similar instructions, which are not in the old printed copies.

P. 396. The moment the following misprint is pointed out it will probably be admitted. Antonio, seized by the officers, appeals to Viola, thinking her Sebastian, and to his grief and disappointment is repelled as a stranger. He then re-proaches the supposed Sebastian with the services he had rendered to him, and with the affection he had borne him, adding these lines,—

> "And to his image, which, methought, did promise
> Most venerable worth, did I devotion."

The corrector of the folio, 1632, places the letters in the margin, which convert "venerable" (an epithet hardly appli-cable to persons like Viola or Sebastian) to *veritable.* He found the worth not *veritable,* because he fancied himself deceived in his friend when most he needed his aid. At the same time it must be allowed that "venerable," in a certain sense, answers the author's purpose, though his own word must have been *veritable.*

ACT IV. SCENE I.

P. 398. For the Clown's declaration, "I am afraid this great lubber, the world, will prove a cockney," the manuscript-corrector has "*lubberly* world."

SCENE II.

P. 405. An alteration in the margin of the corrected folio, 1632, proves that Farmer and Steevens were right in supposing that for "Adieu, goodman devil," in the last line of the Clown's introduced ballad, the reading ought to be,—

"Adieu, goodman *drivel.*"

In a preceding line,—"Like to the old Vice,"—the corrector erases "to ;" and has "*with* a trice" for "in a trice," the former being the older expression, and probably the true word of the ancient ballad cited.

ACT V. SCENE I.

P. 408. For "The triplex, sir, is a good tripping measure," said by the Clown when he wishes the Duke to give him a third piece of money, the manuscript-corrector gives "the *triplet,*" the allusion apparently being to the *triplet,* or triple mode of rhyming in poetry.

P. 412. Olivia commands the Priest, on his entrance, to relate what had passed between herself and Sebastian, when he married them: he replies,—

"A contract of eternal bond of love,"

instead of "A contract *and* eternal bond of love," which is most likely right, the printer having by mistake inserted "of" for *and.* The change is marked in the margin of the folio, 1632. Lower down, the second folio has "*How* little faith," for "Hold little faith," of the first folio ; and the right word is restored by the same authority, thus making the second folio accord with the first.

N 2

P. 414. On the entrance of Sebastian, the corrector of the folio, 1632, has added, as a stage-direction, *All start*, to indicate, no doubt, the surprise which ought to be expressed by the performers at the evident and remarkable similarity between him and Viola.

P. 415. The resemblance in sound between *true* and "drew" may have misled the copyist of this play in the second of the following lines :—

> " So comes it, lady, you have been mistook ;
> But nature to her bias drew in that."

The old corrector converts "drew" into *true*, by merely striking out *d*, and inserting *t* in the margin : nature was *true* to her bias, although Olivia had been mistaken in supposing herself contracted to Viola.

P. 416. The Duke, sending for Malvolio, checks himself,—

> "And yet, alas, now I remember me,
> They say, poor gentleman, he is distract.
> A most extracting frenzy of my own
> From my remembrance clearly banish'd his."

The printer of the folio, 1632, converted " extracting," of the folio, 1623, which could hardly be right, into *exacting*, which is more wrong ; for the corrector of that edition informs us that *exacting* ought to be *distracting*, inasmuch as the Duke is representing himself as in the same condition with Malvolio. Malone persuaded himself that "extracting" was Shakespeare's word, but here we have strong evidence to the contrary.

P. 417. Olivia, speaking of the joint celebration of her own and of the Duke's nuptials, says,—

> " One day shall crown the alliance on't, so please you,
> Here at my house, and at my proper cost."

The corrector of the folio, 1632, puts it thus :—

> " One day shall crown the alliance, *and*, so please you,
> Here at my house," &c.

P. 418. When Malvolio is brought upon the scene by Fabian, we meet with a very particular stage-direction, obedience to which must have been intended to produce a ludicrous effect upon the audience : *Enter Malvolio, as from prison, with straw about him ;* in order to show the nature of the confinement to which the poor conceited victim had been subjected.

P. 418. In the speech of the Countess there appear to be two errors of the press in these lines, as they are contained in all editions :—

> " It was she
> First told me thou wast mad ; then cam'st in smiling,
> And in such forms which here were presuppos'd
> Upon thee in the letter."

According to corrections in the margin of the folio, 1632, the passage should be printed thus :—

> " It was she
> First told me thou wast mad : *thou* cam'st in smiling,
> And in such forms, which here were *preimpos'd*
> Upon thee in the letter."

Both emendations seem required : *thou* was easily misprinted "then," and " presuppos'd upon thee" is little better than nonsense.

P. 419. Olivia adds insult to injury when she thus laments Malvolio's ill-treatment :—

> " Alas, poor fool, how have they baffled thee ! "

What Shakespeare made her say was merely compassionate, if we may believe the old corrector :—

> " Alas, poor *soul*, how have they baffled thee ! "

Soul being written with a long *s* was very likely to be confounded with " fool." Lower in the page, the Clown is made to repeat Maria's letter correctly, " Some have greatness *thrust* upon them," not " *thrown* upon them," as it erroneously stands in all the folios.

P. 420. The Clown sings his song at the end *to pipe and tabor*, the usual musical instruments of such personages ; and in the first scene of Act III. he enters, *playing on his pipe and tabor*, two stage-directions only found in the manuscript additions to the folio, 1632. There can be no doubt that he was furnished on both occasions with these accessories. The fourth stanza of his " song" is thus altered by the manuscript-corrector :—

> " But when I came unto my *bed,*
>> With hey, ho, the wind and the rain,
>> With toss-pots still *I* had drunken *head,*
>> For the rain it raineth every day."

Modern editors have rightly put " bed" and " head" in the singular, instead of the plural as in the old impressions ; but the insertion of the pronoun in the third line is new, and necessary, unless we can suppose it to be understood. We may presume, perhaps, that it was not understood in the original manuscript.

THE WINTER'S TALE.

ACT I. SCENE I.

P. 430. The word *so* seems to have been accidentally omitted where Camillo is speaking of the friendly intercourse kept up between Leontes and Polixenes, while at a distance in their separate dominions: he says: "Their encounters, though not personal, have been *so* royally attorney'd, with interchange of gifts, letters, loving embassies, that they have seemed to be together, though absent," &c. The manuscript-corrector of the folio, 1632, adds *so* in the margin, and puts *gifts* in the plural, which is in the singular in that edition.

SCENE II.

P. 431. The subsequent passage in the speech of Polixenes has given trouble to the commentators:—

> "That may blow
> No sneaping winds at home, to make us say,
> 'This is put forth too truly.'"

The allusion seems unquestionably to be to the putting forth of buds or blooms in spring, when they may be cut off by "sneaping," or nipping winds; and the alteration of "truly" to *early*, as we find it in the corrected folio, 1632, seems to remove great part of the difficulty; there is also an emendation at the commencement, which renders the whole intelligible; we there read as follows:—

> " *May there* blow
> No sneaping winds at home, to make us say,
> 'This is put forth too *early.*' "

At all events, the above is not " nonsense," which Warburton calls the original, as first printed in the folio, 1623.

P. 432. We learn from a manuscript stage-direction, that Leontes *walked apart,* as if not paying particular attention, while Hermione was using arguments to prevail upon Polixenes to stay.

P. 433. There is no doubt that we ought to amend the words of the old copies, "What lady she her lord," to " What lady *should* her lord," not merely because it so stands corrected in the folio in Lord Ellesmere's library, but because precisely the same alteration is made in the margin of the folio, 1632, in our hands. Two concurrent and independent authorities must be decisive.

P. 435. The line given to Hermione,—

> " With spur we heat an acre.   But to the goal,"

is to be read, as in no edition it has been yet given ; the context, as always printed, is,—

> " You may ride's
> With one soft kiss a thousand furlongs, ere
> With spur we heat an acre.   But to the goal :—
> My last good deed was to entreat his stay :
> What was my first ? "

The Queen first speaks of the facility with which women may be won by kindness to do any thing ; and from thence she proceeds to advert to the two " good deeds" which Leontes admitted she had done.   The changes recommended by the corrector of the folio, 1632, are singularly to the purpose :—

> " With spur *we clear* an acre.   But to the *good:* "

that is, women may be made to go a thousand furlongs for a kiss, while by spurring they can hardly be made to clear an acre.   In the first part of the line, *clear* was misprinted " heat ;" and in the last, *good* was misprinted " goal."   Hermione is reverting to the *good* her husband had admitted she had twice done, and calls upon him to name her first good deed as well as her last. "But to the *good*," is as much as to say, "But come to the good deeds which you admit I have done."

P. 436. Malone was well warranted by the old corrector in supposing that in the following line we ought to substitute "*bounty's* fertile bosom" for

> " From heartiness, from bounty, fertile bosom ; "

from which, however, sense may be extracted.

P. 437. An expression used by Leontes, usually printed, "As o'er-dyed blacks," is shown on the same authority to be an error of the press : it occurs where the King is speaking of the falsehood of women, which he likens to the false show of mourning often put on at funerals, and then technically called "blacks :"—

> " But they were false
> As o'er-dyed blacks, as wind, as waters."

The commentators fancied that the allusion was to the want of permanence in *over-dyed* blacks, or blacks that were dyed too much ; some of them properly took " blacks" to mean funeral mourning, but they stumbled at " o'er-dyed." The corrector, by a slight change, shows the precise meaning of the poet :—

> " But they are false
> As *our dead* blacks, as winds, as waters."

"*Our dead* blacks," were blacks worn at the deaths of persons whose loss was not at all lamented. This emendation may have been derived from a better manuscript, or, perhaps, from a better recitation ; but, nevertheless, the obscure conclusion of this speech, from "Affection ? thy intention," &c., is crossed out in the folio, 1632.

P. 438. A stage-direction, *Holding his forehead*, proves that Hermione's observation,—

> " You look,
> As if you held a brow of much distraction,"

is to be taken literally.

P. 444. The dispute whether to read " her medal" or "*his* medal," is set at rest by the assurance of the old corrector that neither is right, but that "*a* medal" was the poet's language.

P. 448. It may be enough to mention that the punctuation of the passage, beginning, "As you are certainly a gentleman," &c., is exactly that introduced by the corrector of the folio, 1632, and is opposed to the regulation of the passage in this respect adopted by Malone (Shaksp., by Boswell, xiv. p. 269). Lower down, the corrector represents Camillo as saying, "I *am* appointed him to murder you," which agrees with the reading of the folio, 1623.

P. 450. Much discussion has been produced by a passage near the end of this scene where Polixenes says,—

> " Good expedition be my friend, and comfort
> The gracious queen, part of his theme, but nothing
> Of his ill-ta'en suspicion."

Warburton reasonably asks, how could "good expedition" comfort the queen ? and Johnson, Steevens, and Malone have each disserted upon the question at large. If we may confide in the manuscript-correction we meet with in the folio, 1632, there are two errors of the press, the removal of which, at he same time removes all doubt : for one of them, "and" for *heaven*, we are not well able to account; the other, "theme" for *dream*, has clearly arisen from mishearing :—

> " Good expedition be my friend : *heaven* comfort
> The gracious queen, part of his *dream*, but nothing
> Of his ill-ta'en suspicion."

While Polixenes was befriended by expedition, he prayed heaven to comfort Hermione, part of the jealous dream of Leontes, but no part of his unfounded suspicion.

ACT II. SCENE I.

P. 452. In the following, there appears to be a decided misprint :—

> " There may be in the cup
> A spider steep'd, and one may drink, depart,
> And yet partake no venom."

The emendation in the folio, 1632, is,—

> " and one may drink *a part*,
> And yet partake no venom ; "

i. e. drink a part of the contents of the cup, and yet take no portion of the venom supposed to be communicated by the spider.

P. 456. The conjecture in note 7 respecting the word " stables," in the ensuing observation by Antigonus, is in some degree confirmed by the manuscript-corrector :—

> " If it prove
> She's otherwise, I'll keep my stables where
> I lodge my wife."

We ought to read " stables" in the singular, and to substitute *me* for " my ;" and the meaning then is, that Antigonus would keep himself stable where he lodged his wife, lest she should offend in the same way as Hermione : —

> " If it prove
> She's otherwise, I'll keep *me stable* where
> I lodge my wife."

He would never allow her to be out of his sight : he would keep his *stabulum*, or abode, always near her. In the next note, more than a doubt is expressed that " land-damn," of the old copies, was not a misprint for *lambáck*, a word of not unfrequent occurrence ; but the corrector of the folio, 1632, erases " land-damn" in the text, and places *lamback* in the margin. At all events, this fact will put an end to the conjectures respecting *lant*, by Sir T. Hanmer, and *laudanum*, by Steevens. Johnson was well founded in thinking the word, for which " land-damn" was intended, " one of those which caprice brought into fashion."

SCENE II.

P. 460. When Paulina, in the subsequent exclamation, speaks of the " dangerous unsafe lunes i' the king," it is mere tautology, for what is " dangerous," is evidently " unsafe." By " lunes," Shakespeare means fits of distraction, and when the old corrector directs us to read, instead of " unsafe," *unsane,*—

"These dangerous *unsane* lunes i' the King, beshrew them,"—
we must at once admit the value of the emendation.

SCENE III.

P. 462. The manuscript stage-directions in this scene, clearly required for the government of the actors, are frequent and explanatory. Paulina first enters *at the back* of the stage, *with the babe*, and after a struggle with the attendants, *lays it down before Leontes*. When she is pushed out, she *leaves the child* behind her : when the Lords *kneel*, we are told so ; and information is similarly given when the King *draws his sword* to swear Antigonus upon it, who *takes up the infant*, and departs with it. None of these needful instructions are found in the old printed copies, and they show the precise manner in which the business was conducted when, we may suppose, the corrector of the folio, 1632, saw the drama performed at one of our early theatres.

ACT III. SCENE I.

P. 470. This whole scene is crossed out with a pen, as capable of being dispensed with ; but it seems to have been inserted by the author for the purpose of giving more time for the preparation of the trial-scene of Hermione. If it were not acted, the interval between the second and third acts must have been proportionally extended.

SCENE II.

P. 471. To the old brief stage-direction, *Silence. Enter*, is added, in manuscript, *Hermione attended to her trial*, just before the indictment against her is read.

P. 473. Few passages in this play have occasioned more notes than this, in Hermione's address :—

" Since he came,
With what encounter so uncurrent I
Have strain'd, t' appear thus : " &c.

She is alluding to the visit of Polixenes, out of which, by some "uncurrent encounter," or unjustifiable meeting, the present accusation had grown. The difficulty has chiefly arisen out of the word "strain'd," for which the corrector writes *stray'd;* and it seems to clear away much of the difficulty. Hermione was charged with having *strayed* from her duty by an "uncurrent encounter" with Polixenes, and she inquires where and how it had happened, in order to justify her appearance before the court :—

> " Since he came,
> With what encounter so uncurrent I
> Have *stray'd* t' appear thus : " &c.

Perhaps the meaning would be still clearer, had the whole been put interrogatively, " Have I *stray'd*," &c.

P. 479. When Paulina brings word of the sudden death of the Queen, we are told, in manuscript, that Leontes *falls back* in his seat, and Paulina begins to repent the cruel recapitulation she has previously made of the consequences of the King's conduct to his dead wife, son, &c. As this part of the scene has always been printed, she thus expresses her regret :—

> " What's gone, and what's past help,
> Should be past grief : do not receive affliction
> At my petition, I beseech you ; rather,
> Let me be punish'd, that have minded you
> Of what you should forget."

Now, what can here be the meaning of the words, "at my petition ?" It is merely an error of the press, or of the copyist. Paulina has repeated in most bitter terms all the evils that have been occasioned by the jealousy and obstinacy of Leontes ; and the corrector of the folio, 1632, striking out " my," and inserting *re* before " petition," makes the sentence stand thus :—

> " Do not receive affliction
> At *repetition*, I beseech you,"—

in other words, " Do not allow my repetition of the fatal results of your jealousy to afflict you." Nothing can surely be plainer, or more pertinent.

SCENE III.

P. 481. Antigonus, in the relation of his dream, in which he imagined he saw the weeping Hermione, says,—

> " I never saw a vessel of like sorrow,
> So fill'd, and so becoming."

"So becoming," can scarcely be right; and we learn from the manuscript-corrector that there was a natural connexion between the words, "so fill'd," and what follows them, which was entirely lost, as we must imagine, by the mishearing of the person who wrote the copy of the play used by the printer. The true reading appears to be:—

> " I never saw a vessel of like sorrow,
> So fill'd, and so *o'er-running*."

The sorrow with which Hermione was so fillcd, was *o'er-running* at her eyes. Lower down on the same page another error occurs in the dream, where Hermione directs Antigonus to proceed with the babe to Bohemia, and adds,—

> " There weep, and leave it crying,"

instead of

> " There *wend*, and leave it crying."

"There *wend*" is, of course, thither proceed; and whether this blunder, constantly repeated by all editors, originated with the scribe, or was introduced by the printer, we are not in a condition to determine. That it was a blunder, appears almost indubitable.

ACT IV. SCENE I.

P. 487. In ancient and modern editions, Camillo informs Polixenes that he has "missingly noted" the absence of his son Florizel from court; the corrector of the folio, 1632, marks "missingly," as an error, and inserts *musingly* instead of it—a somewhat questionable change.

SCENE II.

P. 488. The manuscript-corrector notes, with great particularity, that the fragments of ballads, with which Auto-

licus commences this scene, were sung by him to three
several tunes, putting " 1 *Tune*," " 2 *Tune*," and " 3 *Tune*,"
against each of them.   The three stanzas beginning,—

> " When daffodils begin to peer,"

were sung to the first tune, whatever it may have been ; the
one stanza, commencing,—

> " But shall I go mourn for that, my dear?"

was sung to the second tune ; and the last fragment,—

> " If tinkers may have leave to live,"

to the third tune.   This information is followed by the words
in the margin, *And more if need be,* by which we are probably to understand, that it was left to the comic performer
to decide whether he would not amuse the audience by other
snatches, if he could furnish them.   It may also be remarked
that, for " pugging tooth," of the old copies, the emendator
substitutes "*prigging* tooth ;" and " pugging" may have been
a misprint for the more familiar cant term for stealing.

P. 490. All the necessary (some, perhaps, more than are
absolutely necessary) stage-directions are provided in the
margin : for instance, we are told that Autolicus, pretending
to have been robbed and beaten, *rolls about on the ground,*
and that the Clown *helps him on his legs,* after which he has
his *purse cut* by the party he had assisted.

P. 492. According to the corrector of the folio, 1632, there
has been a singular misconception in the last sentence given
to Autolicus at the close of this scene.   It is where, according to the invariable misrepresentation of Shakespeare's
text, the Pedlar wishes that his name may " be unrolled,"
and "put in the book of virtue ;" the word should be *enrolled,* as is clear from what follows : he wishes his name to
be *enrolled,* and placed in the book of virtue.

SCENE III.

P. 493. Two mistakes are pointed out in Perdita's speech,
one of them in the first line : for

> " Sir, my gracious lord," &c.,

the manuscript-corrector has

> " *Sure*, my gracious lord,
> To chide at your extremes it not becomes me."

The change is at least plausible, but the difference is not important. The other error is near the close of the speech in which Perdita contrasts her own gay apparel with the " swain's wearing," in which the Prince was clad : she remarks :—

> " But that our feasts
> In every mess have folly, and the feeders
> Digest it with a custom, I should blush
> To see you so attir'd, sworn, I think,
> To show myself a glass."

In what way was Florizel " sworn " to show Perdita a glass? Besides the line wants a syllable, which is supplied by the correction in the margin of the folio, 1632, while the sense is also improved :—

> " I should blush
> To see you so attir'd, *so worn*, I think,
> To show myself a glass."

The meaning, therefore, is that Florizel's plain attire was " so worn " to show Perdita, as in a glass, how simply she ought to have been dressed.

P. 494. Ritson was right in recommending that, " Nor in a way so chaste," should be printed, " Nor *any* way so chaste." Such is the emendation in the corrected folio. Lower down, the unusual expression of Florizel, " Be merry, gentle," is altered to " Be merry, *girl*," a mistake not very unlikely when the word was spelt, as of old, with a final *e*, *girle*.

P. 498. Another error of the press is pointed out in the speech of Polixenes, where he is praising Perdita :—

> " Nothing she does, or seems,
> But smacks of something greater than herself."

The proposed alteration is by no means necessary, but it makes the observation more natural :—

> " Nothing she does, or *says*," &c.

Formerly *says* was often written *saies*, which may in some degree account for the misprint. Just afterwards, Camillo remarks to Polixenes, of Florizel,—

> " He tells her something
> That makes her blood look on't."

This is the old text of the folios, but Theobald, for " on't," in spite of the apostrophe, printed *out*, and missed the correction of the true error, *viz.* " makes," instead of *wakes* : —

> " He tells her something
> That *wakes* her blood—look on't."

Such is precisely the mode in which the passage stands corrected in the folio, 1632, " look on't" being addressed emphatically to Polixenes, to direct his attention to the blush of Perdita, thus poetically described as *waking* her blood.

P. 499. The old word *jape*, a jest (generally used in an indelicate sense), according to the corrector of the folio, 1632, has been misprinted " gap" in the following part of the clown's speech regarding the licence of ballad-singers : " And where some stretch-mouthed rascal would, as it were, mean mischief, and break a foul gap into the matter, he makes the maid to answer, ' Whoop, do me no harm, good man.' " For " gap," we are to read *jape*.

Some controversy has arisen respecting the words, " unbraided wares," where the Clown, just below, asks whether Autolicus has any such to sell. Johnson, Steevens, Tollet, Malone, Monk Mason, and Boswell, have each endeavoured to explain what turns out to be a mere misprint for " *embroided* wares," as embroidered commodities were then frequently spelt. This point has, therefore, been set at rest by the corrected folio.

P. 501. For " whistle off those secrets," the folio, 1632, as corrected, has, perhaps needlessly, " *whisper* off those secrets." In the same speech and on the same authority, " Clamour your tongues," ought indisputably to be " *Charm* your tongues," as Grey originally suggested, and as Gifford (Ben Jonson, iv. 405) maintained. In fact, the expression, " Charm your tongue," occurs in " The London Prodigal." See Malone's Supplement, ii. 466, though he never thought of illustrating by it " clamour your tongues" in " The Winter's Tale." The editors of Shakespeare have not hitherto felt themselves warranted in altering his text on the mere suspicion of a misprint, or "charm your tongues" would long ago have been adopted ; and note 2, on this page, affords evidence that the error has been stated, though not always acknowledged, ever since the time of Grey.

P. 506. Florizel, making his protestation of love before his disguised father and Camillo, exclaims, as all editions establish,—

> " Were I the fairest youth
> That ever made eye swerve ; had force and knowledge,
> More than was ever man's," &c.

For " force and knowledge," the corrector of the folio, 1632, writes " *sense* and knowledge ;" and the error of the press is again to be imputed to the compositor's confusion between the long *s* and *f*.

P. 507. We can hardly doubt that another misprint is pointed out, on the same authority, in a subsequent speech by Polixenes, where he is endeavouring (still disguised) to persuade the young prince to consult his father, and asks, whether he refrains because his father is imbecile ?—

> " Can he speak ? hear ?
> Know man from man ? dispute his own estate?
> Lies he not bed-rid ?"

" Dispute his own estate," may be reconciled to sense, but " *dispose* his own estate" seems a much more likely expression, and the manuscript-corrector informs us that it was employed in this place.

P. 514. A very trifling omission in all the early folios, and in subsequent editions, has made Florizel leave off speaking with a broken sentence, when, in fact, the period is complete: he tells Camillo, who urges him to proceed as his father's ambassador to Leontes,—

> " How shall we do?
> We are not furnish'd as Bohemia's son,
> Nor shall appear in Sicily "—

Such is the mode in which the quotation has been hitherto given ; but the slightest possible change, urged by the corrector of the folio, 1632, is thus made with the best possible effect :—

> " We are not furnish'd as Bohemia's son,
>   Nor shall *appear't* in Sicily."

i. e. nor shall appear as Bohemia's son in Sicily. There is an unquestionable error in the answer of Camillo, which is of more importance: he assures Florizel that he will take care to furnish him like Bohemia's son, and adds,—

> " It shall be so my care
> To have you royally appointed, as if
> The scene you play were mine."

To make the scene appear as if it were Camillo's could be of no service to the young prince, and the old corrector supplies what we may conclude was the true word of the poet, although we may not be able well to account for the blunder thus exposed:—

> " It shall be so my care
> To have you royally appointed, as if
> The scene you play were *true :*"

as if he were really the ambassador from his father, which he pretended to be

P. 522. After the departure of the old Shepherd and his son, Autolicus is left to soliloquize, and, among other reflections, he observes, as the words have from the first been printed :—

" I am courted now with a double occasion—gold and a means to do the prince my master good ; which, who knows how that may turn back to my advancement?"

What can be the meaning here of turning " back to his advancement?" What is "to turn back to his advancement?" The corrector of the folio, 1632, may be said to answer the question by pointing out its needlessness, if we only read what was actually written,—" which, who knows how that may turn *luck* to my advancement." Autolicus hopes that the " double occasion" by which he was "courted," would turn *luck* in his favour.

ACT V. SCENE I.

P. 526. The old stage-direction is, *Enter a Servant*, but from what he says, and is said of him, we learn that he had written an elegy upon Hermione. Modern editors have, therefore, called him "a gentleman." He was evidently a retainer in the Court of Leontes, and the manuscript-corrector has added *poet* to his description of servant, *Enter a Servant-poet*, in order, probably, to distinguish him from the ordinary hirelings of the palace. We may notice here the peculiar fulness and explicitness of the stage-directions towards the close of this play, although it has not been thought necessary to particularize them.

P. 529. Polixenes tells Florizel,—

> " You have a holy father,
> A graceful gentleman," &c.

For "holy," which seems quite out of place, the corrector of the folio, 1632, writes *noble* in the margin, the right word having been misheard by the scribe. Precisely the same mistake was made in "The Tempest" (see p. 14), and from the same cause.

SCENE II.

P. 531. Much of this scene is struck out for the purpose, as we may infer, of abridging the performance, because no part that is erased is absolutely necessary to the intelligibility of the plot. The corrections of the text are continued notwithstanding with the same patience and perspicuity. Thus, on p. 533, we have "weather-*beaten* conduit," for "weather-bitten conduit." Again, immediately afterwards, the third Gentleman observes, "I never heard of such another encounter, which lames report to follow it, and undoes description to do it," instead of "undoes description to *show* it," which must surely be right. This part of the drama is even worse printed than the rest; and on p. 534, the third Gentleman tells Autolicus and the rest, in reference to the death of Hermione, that Leontes "bravely confessed and lamented" it, instead of "*heavily* confessed and lamented" it. Minor errors, some of them merely typographical, it is not necessary to point out, as they are not transferred to modern editions, and do not materially affect the text. It may be stated, that when the Shepherd and Clown enter, towards the close of the scene, an addition is made to the stage-direction, to inform us that they are *in new apparel.*

SCENE III.

P. 539. One of those highly-important completions of the old, and imperfect, text of Shakespeare, consisting of a whole line, where the sense is left unfinished without it, here occurs. Warburton saw that something was wanting, but in note 3 it is suggested that Leontes in his ecstasy might have left his sentence unfinished: such does not appear to have been the case. The passage has hitherto been printed as follows :—

> " Let be, let be !
> Would I were dead, but that, methinks, already—
> What was he that did make it?" &c.

" Let be, let be !" is addressed to Paulina, who *offers to draw the curtain* before the statue of Hermione, as we find from a manuscript stage-direction, and the writer of it, in a vacant space adjoining, thus supplies a missing line, which we have printed in Italic type :—

> " Let be, let be!
> Would I were dead, but that, methinks, already
> *I am but dead, stone looking upon stone.*
> What was he that did make it?" &c.

But for this piece of evidence, that so important an omission had been made by the old printer, or by the copyist of the manuscript for the printer's use, it might have been urged, that, supposing our great dramatist to have written here no more elliptically than in many other places, his sense might be complete at "already:" "Would I were dead!" exclaims Leontes, "but that, methinks, *I am* already;" in other words, it was needless for him to wish himself dead, since, looking upon the image of his lost queen, he was, as it were, dead already. However, we see above, that a line was wanting, and we may be thankful that it has been furnished, since it adds much to the force and clearness of the speech of Leontes.

P. 541. When Hermione descends from the pedestal, and advances towards her husband, a manuscript stage-direction informs us that she *comes down slowly*, and that *hautboys and viols* play. There is not a single printed instruction of the

kind in any part of the scene, where they appear to be so requisite for the information of the performers; but that deficiency is abundantly supplied by the old corrector of the
folio, 1632, who has taken great pains that nothing should
go wrong during the representation.   When Paulina first
draws the curtain from before the supposed statue of the
Queen, the *hautboys* are told to play: she several times *offers
to draw* the curtain again, in order to conceal the figure,
when the King becomes too much moved; and she *stays him*
when he declares that he will kiss the statue: she had done
the same, when Perdita had previously wished to kiss the
hand of the supposed representation of her mother.   We are
also told, after Hermione has come down, that she and her
husband *embrace,* and that the daughter *kneels* to receive
her mother's blessing.   Strictly speaking, these last were
needless.

P. 542. The last emendation, of any importance, is in the
last speech of the play, where Leontes is choosing Camillo
as a husband for Paulina.   The prosaic line in which it
occurs is this :—

" And take her by the hand whose worth and honesty ; "

which is redundant by two syllables: these are erased by
the corrector of the folio, 1632, without the slightest detriment to the sense, and with great improvement to the
measure :—

" Come, Camillo,
And take her hand, whose worth and honesty
Is richly noted and here justified."

We may feel well assured that the expletives, " by the," obtained insertion without the participation of the pen of the
author.

KING JOHN.

ACT I. SCENE I.

Vol. iv. P. 8. We cannot but approve of a change made in an important epithet in the reply of King John, where he despatches Chatillon with all haste, and tells him that the English forces will be in France before the ambassador can even report their intention to come. The reading has always been :—

> " Be thou the trumpet of our wrath,
> And sullen presage of your own decay."

In the first place, the sound of a trumpet could not, with any fitness, be called a " sullen presage ;" and, secondly, as Chatillon was instantly to proceed on his return, it is much more probable that Shakespeare wrote,—

> " Be thou the trumpet of our wrath,
> And *sudden* presage of your own decay."

The old corrector says that *sudden* was the word of our great dramatist, and a scribe or a printer might easily mistake *sudden* and " sullen."

P. 9. The folio, 1632, omits " Robert " before Faulconbridge, in the Bastard's first speech, but the corrector restored it in the margin. It is found in the folio, 1623, and must have accidentally dropped out of that of 1632.

P. 14. Besides a misprint, there appears to be an error in punctuation in this part of the Bastard's soliloquy, as given in modern editions :—

> " For new-made honour doth forget men's names :
> 'Tis too respective, and too sociable,
> For your conversion.   Now your traveller,
> He and his tooth-pick at my worship's mess," &c.

The corrector of the folio, 1632, informs us that we should point and read as follows :—

> " For new-made honour doth forget men's names :
> 'Tis too respective, and too sociable.
> For your *diversion*, now, your traveller,
> He and his tooth-pick at my worship's mess," &c.

It was common to entertain " picked men of countries," for the *diversion* of the company at the tables of the higher orders, and this is what the Bastard is referring to in the last two lines, while the sense of the first two is complete at " sociable."

P. 16. In the first and second folios, these lines, thus printed, occur :—

> " Sir Robert could do well, marry to confess
> Could get me Sir Robert could not do it."

This is clearly wrong, and the question is how the passage can be amended.   Modern editors have introduced " he" and a mark of interrogation in the second line,—

> " Could *he* get me ? "

On the other hand, the corrector of the second folio merely inserts a negative ; and if, in the manuscript used by the printer, a mark of interrogation had been found in this place, it would hardly have been omitted : as amended, the couplet stands,—

> " Sir Robert could do well ; marry, to confess,
> Could *not* get me ; Sir Robert could not do it."

ACT II. SCENE I.

P. 18. A single letter makes an important improvement in the following, where young Arthur expresses his acknowledgments to Austria :—

> " I give you welcome with a powerless hand,
> But with a heart full of unstained love."

The love of such a child would, of course, be "unstained:" what he meant to say, according to a correction in the folio, 1632, was, that he bade Austria welcome with a heart full of love, which, without effort, spontaneously flowed from it :—

> " But with a heart full of *unstrained* love."

P. 19. We may presume that the change made in the subsequent passage conformed to some better manuscript than that used by the printer, or that the compositor committed an error:—

> " And then we shall repent each drop of blood,
> That hot rash haste so indirectly shed."

The manuscript-corrector says that we ought to read,—

> " That hot rash haste so *indiscreetly* shed."

Nevertheless, our great poet sometimes uses "indirectly" in a peculiar manner.

P. 20. The old corrector does not read, with modern editors,—

> " An Até stirring him to blood and strife ; "

but instead of " An Ace," of all the folios, he has,—

> " With him along is come the mother-queen,
> *As Até*, stirring him to blood and strife."

P. 23. In the following line there are, according to the ordinary rules of dramatic blank-verse, two redundant syllables, and the punctuation is wrong, according to a correction in the folio, 1632 :—

> " Of this oppressed boy.   This is thy eldest son's son," &c.

The proposed alteration, with the context, stands thus :—

> " Thou and thine usurp
> The dominations, royalties, and rights
> Of this oppressed boy, thy eld'st son's son,
> Infortunate in nothing but in thee."

The above may well be as the poet wrote the passage, "this is" being detrimental, as well as unnecessary.

P. 25. In his speech to the citizens of Angiers, John says, as all the old copies represent it,—

> " All preparation for a bloody siege,
> And merciless proceeding by these French,
> Comfort your city's eyes."

It has been urged by those who wished to adhere to the text of the folios, as long as it was unimpugned by any old authority, that " comfort" was here used ironically : Rowe did not think so, when he printed *confront ;* but the corrector of the folio, 1632, with less violence, has,—

> " *Come 'fore* your city s eyes," &c.

P. 33. We here meet with the converse of the misprint in " The Two Gentlemen of Verona" (Act IV. Scene I.), *niece,* for " neere." The Citizen, from the walls, recommends a marriage between the Dauphin and the lady Blanch, observing,—

> " That daughter there of Spain, the lady Blanch,
> Is near to England."

Such has been the universal reading, " near" being spelt *neere* in the folios ; but she was niece to King John, as indeed she is afterwards called, and the manuscript-corrector of the folio, 1632, tells us, naturally enough, to read,—

> " That daughter there of Spain, the lady Blanch,
> Is *niece* to England."

This is unquestionably right, and the mistake was readily made : we only wonder that it was not till now corrected, because, as Steevens states, Blanch was daughter to Alphonso IX., and niece to King John, by his sister Eleanor.

Three lines lower, the folio, 1632, omits " should," in—

> " If zealous love should go in search of virtue ; "

but the old corrector inserts it, thus making the line tally with the folio, 1623.

P. 38. Monck Mason desired us to read *aim* for " aid," in this line, as given in the folios,—

> " Hath drawn him from his own determin'd aid."

He was right, as appears by a correction in the folio, 1632, but the necessity for the change is not very evident.   Lower down,

> " Not that I have the power to clutch my hand,"

is amended to, "Not that I have *no* power," &c., which comes very near one of the suggestions in note 3, at the foot of the page.

ACT III. SCENE I.

P. 40. Constance says, that she could be content with her grievous disappointment, if Arthur had been

> " Full of unpleasing blots, and sightless stains."

For " and sightless," the manuscript-corrector substitutes *unsightly*, which was most likely the author's word, the scribe having misheard what was read or recited to him.

P. 42. The same circumstance has produced the next blunder pointed out by the old corrector. All impressions have this line,

> " Is cold in amity, and painted peace."

Why should the epithet " painted" be applied to peace? What propriety is there in it, unless we can suppose it used to indicate hollowness and falsehood? The correction in the margin of the folio, 1632, shows that the ear of the scribe misled him : Constance is referring to the friendship just established between France and England, to the ruin of her hopes, and remarks :—

> " The grappling vigour, and rough frown of war,
> Is cold in amity, and *faint in* peace,
> And our oppression hath made up this league."

P. 44. The word " heaven" is repeated with great additional force in the subsequent passage, which we copy as it is given in the corrected folio, 1632. King John speaks :—

> " But as we under heaven are supreme head,
> So, under *heaven*, that great supremacy,
> Where we do reign, we will alone uphold."

For *heaven*, the invariable reading has been " him." Nevertheless, satisfactory as this emendation may appear, it is possible that the original reading (before the passing of the statute of James I., against the use of the name of the Creator on the stage) was *God*, for "heaven," in the first instance, and then "him," in the second instance, might be proper enough. When "heaven" was substituted for *God*, the repetition of "heaven," in the next line, became necessary.

P. 48. The error of "cased," for *caged*, in the following,—

"A cased lion by the mortal paw,"

is so evident, as pointed out by the old corrector, that it is surprising the emendation was never conjecturally adopted; especially when Malone's quotation from Rowley's "When you see me you know me," regarding "a lion in his *cage*," so inevitably led to it.

SCENE II.

P. 51. Precisely the same remark grows out of a passage cited by Percy, in reference to the subsequent speech by the Bastard, when he rushes in with Austria's head, as it has been uniformly printed :—

"Now, by my life, this day grows wondrous hot;
Some airy devil hovers in the sky,
And pours down mischief."

The word is spelt *ayery* in the folio, 1632, and the corrector of that edition has changed the word to *fyery*, which, we may feel confident, was that of the poet, and which is so consistent with the context :—

"Now, by my life, this day grows wondrous hot;
Some *fiery* devil hovers in the sky
And pours down mischief."

Percy quotes Burton's "Anatomy of Melancholy," where, among other things, it is said, "*Fiery* spirits or devils are such as commonly work by blazing stars," &c.

SCENE III.

P. 52. In the subsequent passage *their*, which seems required both by meaning and metre, is inserted in the handwriting of the corrector of the folio, 1632 :—

> " See thou shake the bags
> Of hoarding abbots; *their* imprison'd angels
> Set at liberty."

Malone, as is stated in note 9, transposed "imprisoned angels;" and Hanmer read, "Set *thou* at liberty," both without the slightest authority, and merely as matters of taste.

P. 53. The old corrector supports Pope (if support were here needed), in "some better time," instead of "some better *tune*," as it had been commonly misprinted. In the last line but one of this page, the folio, 1632, as amended, has,—

> " Sound on into the drowsy *ear* of night,"

instead of "race of night," as it stands in the folios: when "ear" was spelt *eare*, as was most frequently the case, the mistake was easy, and we may now be pretty sure that "race" was a mistake.

P. 54. Instead of representing the blood as running "tickling up and down the veins," the manuscript-corrector tells us to read *tingling*; and a few lines lower, for,—

> " Then in despite of broaded watchful day,"

he has "*the broad* watchful day," as if Pope's *broad-eyed* were merely fanciful. We own a preference for *broad-eyed*.

SCENE IV.

P. 55. The same editor was nearly right when he proposed "*collected* sail" for "convicted sail" in what follows:—

> " A whole armado of convicted sail
> Is scattered, and disjoin'd from fellowship."

The true word, given in the margin of the folio, 1632, has the same meaning as *collected*, but is nearer in form and letters to the misprint in the ordinary text, *viz*:—

> " A whole armado of *convented* sail," &c.

i. e., a fleet that had been convened at some port to bring aid to the Dauphin. There is no need, therefore, to strain after a meaning for "convicted," if, as we are assured, it was not the word of the poet.

P. 56. Upon the passage in the speech of Constance, where she is speaking of death,

> " Which cannot hear a lady's feeble voice,
> Which scorns a modern invocation,"

Johnson remarks that "it is hard to say what Shakespeare means by *modern.*" Now, we know that our great dramatist often uses " modern," for common, or ordinary ; but " modern," as used above, is one of the strange errors of the press which found their way into the text ; and a marginal note in the corrected folio, 1632, proves that we ought to substitute for it a word exactly applicable to the condition of Constance :—

> " Which cannot hear a lady's feeble voice,
> Which scorns a *widow's* invocation."

When we bear in mind that *m* and *w* were often mistaken by the old compositors in this volume, the misprint will not be thought so extraordinary. Such an emendation could hardly have had its source in the fancy, or even in the ingenuity, of the old corrector. Four lines above, he reads,—

> " Then with *what* passion I would shake the world ;"

an obvious, though comparatively trifling, improvement of the old text, " Then with a passion," &c. He gives the beginning of the next speech of Constance, " Thou are *not* holy," a change made in the fourth folio, and never disputed. This part of the scene was badly printed in 1623, and not made better in 1632.

ACT IV. SCENE I.

P. 61. The manuscript stage-directions in this play are not so frequent as in some others, but they seem to have been added in all situations where they were necessary. The *asides* are also marked, particularly in this scene, where Hubert speaks not to be heard by Arthur. The *exit* and re-entrance of the Executioners are omitted in the printed copy, but are duly supplied by the old corrector, and when the heated iron is to be brought to Hubert the proper place is noted in the margin.

SCENE II.

P. 68. John has been assigning some reasons to Salisbury, Pembroke, &c., for the repetition of his coronation, princi-

pally founded upon apprehensions arising out of his defective title: at length he tells them, as the folio, 1623,
represents his language :—

> " Some reasons for this double coronation
> I have possessed you with, and think them strong.
> And more, more strong, then lesser is my fear
> I shall indue'you with."

A good deal of controversy has been excited by the hemistich, "then lesser is my fear," which the folio, 1632, prints,
"then less is my fear." Theobald dropped a letter, and read,
in parentheses ("*the* lesser is my fear") ; and Steevens and
Malone ("*when* lesser is my fear"), but they omitted to show
why John should defer the statement of his stronger reasons
till his fear was less, or why he should fancy that his fear
would be less at any time than just after his second coronation, which was to confirm him on the throne. The manuscript-corrector of the folio, 1632, makes it clear that the
King referred to his strong reasons as having diminished
his own apprehensions, which reasons he was ready hereafter
to communicate to his peers: he puts it thus :—

> " And more, more strong, *thus lessening* my fear,
> I shall indue you with."

The strength of his reasons had lessened his own fear, and
he imagined that, when stated, they would produce a good
effect upon others. The misprint was, "then lesser is," for
thus lessening, not a very violent change, and rendering the
meaning apparent.

Lower in the same page, the words "then" and "should"
seem injuriously to have changed places: the old text is,—

> " Why then your fears, which, as they say, attend
> The steps of wrong, should move you to mew up
> Your tender kinsman ? "

instead of

> " Why *should* your fears, which, as they say, attend
> The steps of wrong, *then* move you to mew up
> Your tender kinsman ? "

P. 74. It may be sufficient to mention that the words
"deeds ill," in John's reproach of Hubert, are transposed by
the corrector of the folio, 1632, so as to make the passage
read more naturally, " Makes *ill deeds* done."

P. 75. In John's next speech of the same kind, he says, as the text has always stood,—

> " But thou didst understand me by my signs,
> And didst in signs again parley with sin."

The last word is spelt *sinne* in the old copies, and ought undoubtedly, as we are instructed in manuscript, to be *sign*, formerly spelt *signe :*

> " But thou didst understand me by my signs,
> And didst in signs again parley with *sign.*"

SCENE III.

P. 76. We here meet with an error of the press, which shows how the letters *m* and *w* were again mistaken by the old printer. Pembroke asks,—

> " Who brought that letter from the cardinal ? "

and Salisbury's answer relates to a private communication he had received at the same time. The words of the folios have here always been taken as the true text, *viz.* :—

> " The count Melun, a noble lord of France,
> Whose private with me of the Dauphin's love,
> Is much more general than these lines import."

The notes upon this passage have all referred to the word "private," when the blunder lies in "with me :"

> " Whose private *missive* of the Dauphin's love,"

is the way in which the corrector of the folio, 1632, says that line should have been printed : the Count Melun had, at the same time that he conveyed the Cardinal's letter, brought to Salisbury a "private missive," or communication, containing assurances of the Dauphin's regard. This correction seems to imply resort to some original, such as that which the printer of the folio, 1623, had misread.

Just afterwards, on the next page, the old corrector points out an egregious error, which ought not to have escaped detection, even without such aid: it occurs in Salisbury's reply to the Bastard :—

> " The King hath dispossess'd himself of us :
> We will not line his thin bestained cloak."

The folios place a hyphen between " thin " and " bestained,"

as if to lead us to the discovery of the error, which is thus
set right in manuscript, and at once challenges admission
into the genuine text of our author :—

> " We will not line his *sin-bestained* cloak : "

a fine compound, the use of which is amply justified by the
crimes of which the revolted lords consider John guilty.

P. 78. Nobody suspected the above misprint, but the next
we are to notice was more than hinted at by Farmer, *viz.*
head for "hand" in the first of the ensuing lines, where Salisbury vows never to be "conversant with ease and idleness,"
until he has revenged the death of Arthur,—

> " Till I have set a glory to this hand
>   By giving it the worship of revenge."

A manuscript-correction in the folio, 1632, shows, as Farmer
supposed, and as Malone opposed, that the true language of
Shakespeare was,—

> " Till I have set a glory to this *head*,"

meaning the head of Arthur, whose dead body had just been
discovered on the ground.

ACT V. SCENE I.

P. 83. The preceding emendations may be thought to justify, two others on this page, which occur close together, and
which, though improvements of the usual reading, are not
forced upon our adoption by any thing like necessity. The
Bastard is endeavouring to cheer the spirits of the disheartened King ; and we here give the passage as it has
been handed down to us corrected :—

> " Let not the world see fear, and *blank* distrust,
>   Govern the motion of a kingly eye :
>   Be stirring as the time ; *meet* fire with fire,
>   Threaten the threatener," &c.

For *blank*, old and modern editions tamely read "sad," and
for *meet*, merely "be ;" both words were, perhaps, misheard.
At the end of this speech we have, in all editions,—

> " Forage, and run
> To meet displeasure further from the doors ;"

which ought, on the same credible authority, to be, "*Cou-rage!* and run to meet displeasure," &c. There is, then, no necessity for hunting after what Johnson calls, "the original sense" of "forage." On the next page, for "Send fair-play order," we ought, probably, to read, "Send fair-play *offers*," the last word being written in the margin of the folio, 1632. This portion of the play is abundant in errors of the press of more or less importance.

SCENE II.

P. 85. Salisbury, in anguish at the compulsion he was under to draw his sword against his country, interposes this parenthesis :—

> " I must withdraw, and weep
> Upon the spot of this enforced cause."

"Spot" reads like a misprint, and it appears to be so, although not hitherto suspected ; the corrector of the folio, 1632, in-forms us that "spot" was misheard for a word sounding something like it :—

> " I must withdraw, and weep
> Upon the *thought* of this enforced cause."

That is, the reflection upon the cause, which compelled him to bear arms against his country, drew tears.

P. 89. The manuscript-corrector gives no countenance to Theobald's proposal to read *unhair'd* for "unheard ;" and that his attention was directed to the line, is evident from the fact that he makes an emendation, though not of much importance, in it ; he reads :—

> " This unheard sauciness *of* boyish troops ;"

of instead of "and," referring to the unparalleled insolence of the youthful invaders from France.

Lower down, in the same page and speech, the Bastard ridicules the cowardice of the French when assailed in their own territories ; and here we encounter a very remarkable mistake, either by the old compositor or copyist, most likely the latter, for which we cannot account on the ground of

mishearing. The passage is where Faulconbridge is addressing the French, and charging them with having been made

> " To thrill, and shake,
> Even at the crying of your nation's crow."

What is the French nation's crow? Malone strangely thought
that the allusion was to the "caw of the French crow;"
but Douce's suspicion, that the crowing of the cock might be
meant, is fully confirmed by the emendation which we find
in manuscript in the folio, 1632, where the passage is thus
given,—

> " To thrill, and shake,
> Even at the *crowing* of your nation's *cock*,
> Thinking this voice an armed Englishman."

There can, we apprehend, be no dispute that this must be
the true text.

SCENE IV.

P. 92. Discussion has arisen respecting a line in which
the dying Melun advises Salisbury and Pembroke to return
to their duty to their Sovereign, and to

> "Unthread the rude eye of rebellion,"

as the line stands in the ancient, and in most modern,
editions. Theobald was not far wrong when he changed
"Unthread" to *untread*, and "eye" to *way;* but he missed
the emendation of another word, which, with the others, is
thus altered by the corrector of the folio, 1632 :—

> " *Untread the road-way* of rebellion,"

i. e. return by the road you took when you rebelled against
King John. In confirmation, we may notice, that, very soon
afterwards, Salisbury himself repeats nearly the same terms :—

> " We will untread the steps of damned flight."

To misprint *untread the road-way,* "unthread the rude eye,"
seems an excess of carelessness, which we cannot in any way
explain. The fault must, in this instance, lie with the compositor.

P. 93. Salisbury tells the expiring Melun,—

> " For I do see the cruel pangs of death
> Right in thine eye;"

and some commentators, would for "right" read *fright*, or *pight*, and others *fight : bright* appears, from the old corrector's insertion of the necessary letter in the margin, to be the word, in reference to the remarkable brilliancy of the eyes of many persons just before death :—

> " For I do see the cruel pangs of death
> *Bright* in thine eye."

Editors guessed at almost every word but the right one.

SCENE V.

P. 94. For the line, as it stands in the folios,—

> " And wound our tott'ring colours clearly up,"

the old corrector has,—

> " And wound our *tott'red* colours *closely* up."

Tattered was then usually spelt "tottered," and he preferred the passive to the active participle, though we may doubt if Shakespeare exercised any such discretion. Neither are we prepared to say that we like *closely* better than "clearly," the latter, perhaps, indicating the winding up of the colours without obstruction from the enemy.

SCENE VII.

P. 97. Much contention has arisen upon a question, which the amended folio, 1632, will set at rest, founded upon this passage, where Prince Henry refers to the King's fatal illness :—

> " Death, having prey'd upon the outward parts,
> Leaves them, invisible ; and his siege is now
> Against the mind."

In the old copies, "mind" is misprinted *wind ;* and besides setting right this obvious blunder, the old corrector remedies another defect of greater importance. It has been suggested by different annotators that "invisible," ought to be *insensible, invincible,* &c. There is no doubt that "invisible" is wrong, and the corrector converts it into *unvisited,* which may, we think, be adopted without hesitation—death has abandoned the King's external form, and has laid siege to his understanding :—

> " Death, having prey'd upon the outward parts,
> Leaves them *unvisited ;* and his siege is now
> Against the mind."

P. 98. It appears that the practice of the theatre in the time of the corrector of the folio, 1632, was to bring the dying King in, sitting *in a chair,* and the manuscript stage-direction is in those terms, which are added to the printed stage-direction, "John brought in." We are not told, in any of the old copies, when *he dies,* but those words are written in the margin, just after the Bastard has concluded his statement of the loss of "the best part of his power" in the washes of Lincolnshire. This accords with the modern re-presentation of the fact.

KING RICHARD II.

ACT I. SCENE I.

P. 112. At the very beginning of Bolingbroke's first speech, a word has dropped out, the absence of which spoils the metre: it is found in a manuscript-correction of the folio, 1632, and we have printed it in Italic type:—

> " *Full* many years of happy days befal
> My gracious sovereign," &c.

P. 113. In Bolingbroke's next speech, an error of the press of some consequence is noticed : it is where he denies that he is actuated by any private malice against Mowbray:—

> " In the devotion of a subject's love,
> Tendering the precious safety of my prince,
> And free from other misbegotten hate,
> Come I appellant," &c.

What "*other* misbegotten hate" does he refer to ? The corrector of the folio, 1632, tells us to read the third line,—

> " And free from *wrath or* misbegotten hate,
> Come 1 appellant," &c.

Bolingbroke appeals his antagonist, not out of anger or hatred, but out of loyal affection to his King. We may question the necessity for this change. Lower down, "reins and spurs" are in the singular, but this is a matter of less moment.

P. 116. Mowbray answers the pecuniary part of the charge against him, by asserting that the King was in debt to him—

> " Upon remainder of a dear account,
>   Since last I went to France."

For " dear account," the old corrector has " *clear* account," which has a distinct meaning—the account was clear—while the epithet " dear" seems ill applied to "account," in any of the senses which that word bears in Shakespeare.

SCENE II.

P. 121. We may feel assured that the word "farewell" was repeated in the following line, and we find it in manuscript in the margin of the folio, 1632, though not in any extant printed copy of the play :—

> "Why then, I will.   Farewell, *farewell*, old Gaunt."

The repetition of the word led to the accidental omission of it by the old scribe or compositor.   In the preceding line, the first and second folios have "the widow's champion to defence," instead of " *and* defence."

P. 122. The repetition of the word " desolate," in the subsequent couplet, which ends the Duchess of Gloucester's speech, is unlike Shakespeare :—

> " Desolate, desolate, will I hence and die :
>   The last leave of thee takes my weeping eye."

The carelessness of the printer, or of the copyist, occasioned the blunder, for in the corrected folio, 1632, the first line stands thus :—

> " Desolate, *desperate*, will I hence and die."

She was " desolate" because a helpless widow, and *desperate* because she could not move Gaunt to revenge the death of her husband.

P. 125. It deserves remark that, whereas in the line,—

> " And furbish new the name of John of Gaunt,"

the folios have " *furnish* new ;" the manuscript corrector restores the older and better reading of the earlier quarto impressions. A few lines farther on, the second folio has *captain* for " captive," which did not pass unnoticed.

ACT II. SCENE I.

P. 135. The simplicity of our early stage seldom allowing changes of scene, various contrivances were resorted to in order to render them needless, but at the same time to preserve sufficient verisimilitude. Gaunt was here to be represented ill in bed, and the printed stage-direction is only, *Enter Gaunt sick, with York,* and modern editors have represented Gaunt as *on a couch;* but a manuscript note in the folio, 1632, shows precisely the way in which the matter was managed in the time of the old corrector, and no doubt earlier, the words being, *Bed drawn forth,* so that the dying Gaunt was pulled forward on the boards, in his bed. When it was necessary for him to make his *exit* (the only printed note in that place), the words, added in manuscript, are *Drawn out in bed;* and just afterwards, Northumberland arrives with the news of the death of the old Duke.

P. 138. On the entrance of the King, Queen, &c., York says to Gaunt, as the passage has always stood :—

> "The King is come : deal mildly with his youth ;
> For young hot colts, being rag'd, do rage the more ; "

which is nothing better than a truism, that young hot colts rage the more by being raged. This defect has arisen from a misprint, which seems very obvious as soon as it is pointed out by the corrector of the folio, 1632, who alters the second line as follows :—

> " For young hot colts, being *urg'd,* do rage the more."

This is beyond controversy an improvement.

P. 144. Another easily explained error of the press occurs on this page. Northumberland complains that the King is basely led—

> " By flatterers ; and what they will inform,
> Merely in hate, 'gainst any of us all,
> That will the King severely prosecute,
> 'Gainst us, our lives, our children, and our heirs."

Here " 'Gainst us, our lives," is tautologous ; for, of course, what the King prosecuted against the "lives" of his nobility, must be against them. The correction in the folio, 1632, makes the passage so far unobjectionable :—

> " 'Gainst us, our *wives*, our children, and our heirs."

The copyist, in this case, misheard *wives*, "lives."

P. 145. Northumberland, Ross, and Willoughby are plotting against the King, and Northumberland tells the two others that he fears to let them know how near good tidings are. Ross replies, in all editions :—

> " Be confident to speak, Northumberland :
> We three are but thyself; and, speaking so,
> Thy words are but as thoughts : therefore, be bold."

There was evidently no reason why Northumberland should be bold, merely because " his words were but as thoughts ;" and a very slight change, proposed by the old corrector, brings out most clearly the meaning of the poet :—

> " We three are but thyself; and, speaking so,
> Thy words are but *our* thoughts : therefore, be bold."

His words only conveyed the thoughts of the other two conspirators, who were but himself; and he might, therefore, be bold to utter his tidings.

SCENE II.

P. 148. More than one passage in the scene between the Queen, Bushy, and Bagot, in which she states that she feels that some unknown calamity is hanging over her, has occasioned difficulty. The first place in which the corrector of the folio, 1632, offers us any assistance, stands thus in the folios :—

> " So heavy sad,
> As though on thinking on no thought I think,
> Makes me with heavy nothing faint and shrink."

Here perplexity has been produced by misprinting the word *unthinking* as two words, " on thinking :" the Queen was so sad, that it made her faint and shrink with nothing, although she was so *unthinking*, as not to think. Malone

and others have " in thinking," which seems just the opposite of what was intended.

Bushy assures her that her sadness was merely " conceit,"
to which the Queen replies in five lines, which have still
more puzzled commentators :—

> " 'Tis nothing less : conceit is still deriv'd
> From some forefather grief; mine is not so,
> For nothing hath begot my something grief,
> Or something hath the nothing that I grieve :
> 'Tis in reversion that I do possess," &c.

The old corrector shows that the four last lines ought to be
rhyming couplets, which the scribe seems to have written at
random, and has thus made utterly unintelligible what, at the
best, is difficult.   In the corrected folio the lines are thus
given, we may presume upon some authority :—

> " 'Tis nothing less : conceit is still deriv'd
> From some forefather grief; mine is not so,
> For nothing hath begot my something *woe ;*
> Or something hath the nothing that I *guess :*
> 'Tis in reversion that I do possess," &c.

i. e. the nothing that the Queen *guessed,* had some *woe* in it,
and she possessed it in reversion, before it actually came
upon her.   The scribe blundered from not at all understanding what he was putting upon paper, and the compositor made it worse by knowing nothing of the meaning of
what he was putting in print.

Bushy assures her that her sadness was merely " conceit,"
The proposed changes, *woe* for " grief," and *guess* for
" grieve," besides receiving support from the rhyme, at all
events, supply a meaning to words which some commentators
gave up in despair.

P. 151. The Duke of York enters in dismay at the
troubles that surround him, and a manuscript stage-direction
states that he was only *part armed,* in his haste and confusion : the versification of his speeches was, perhaps, purposely
irregular, but such could hardly be intended where he speaks
of Bolingbroke, and says that, he

> " Is my kinsman, whom the King hath wrong'd :"

a line that is especially uncouth from the want of a syllable,
which the corrector of the folio thus furnishes :—

"Is my *near* kinsman, whom the King hath wrong'd."

P. 156. The epithet used by the Duke of York, in his re-proof of Bolingbroke, when he asks him,—

> "But then, more why, why have they dar'd to march
> So many miles upon her peaceful bosom,
> Frighting her pale-fac'd villages with war,
> And ostentation of despised arms?"

"Despised arms" would not "fright" by their "ostentation;" and Warburton recommended *disposed*, not a very happy sug-gestion; and Sir T. Hanmer, *despightful;* while Monck Mason fancied that York meant that the arms were "despised" by himself. A misprint misled them; for, according to the corrector of the folio, 1632, we ought to read:—

> "With ostentation of *despoiling* arms:"

villages might well be frighted by the "*despoiling* arms" of Bolingbroke. Three lines above, for the awkward phrase, "But then, more why," the change made is, "But more *than that*," exhibiting, if we may believe the old corrector, in four words, a transposition and a blunder, arising, probably, from the repetition of "why" immediately afterwards.

P. 159. This short scene between Salisbury and the Welsh Captain, is struck out, perhaps, as needlessly protracting the performance.

ACT III. SCENE II.

P. 162. On arriving near Berkeley Castle, Richard asks if it be called so, and Aumerle answers by two lines, one with too few, and the other with too many syllables:—

> "Yea, my lord. How brooks your grace the air,
> After your late tossing on the breaking seas?"

The manuscript-corrector amends both:—

> "Yea, my *good* lord. How brooks your grace the air,
> After late tossing on the breaking seas?"

We need hardly doubt that this is as the passage ought to be printed, on the supposition that our great dramatist meant the lines to be regular.

P. 165. The scribe, who wrote the copy used by the printer, must have misheard an epithet of some importance in the following extract:—

> " White-beards have arm'd their thin and hairless scalps
> Against thy majesty; and boys, with women's voices,
> Strive to speak big, and clap their female joints
> In stiff unwieldy arms against thy crown."

Besides the mistake in the epithet, there are two other errors of the press, to the injury of the passage, and the old corrector puts the four lines thus:—

> " White-beards have arm'd their thin and hairless scalps
> Against thy majesty; and boys, with women s voices,
> Strive to speak big, and *clasp* their *feeble* joints
> In stiff unwieldy *armour* 'gainst thy crown."

In the first place, the folios have "white-*bears*" for "white-beards:" this blunder was not derived from the quartos; but they have "clap" for *clasp* (which was Pope's conjectural emendation); and because the poet gave the boys "women's voices," the scribe seems to have thought that they should also have "female joints;" and, lastly, we have "arms," in all the old copies, for *armour:* "arms" more properly signifies weapons, than the "stiff unwieldy" casing, by which the bodies of soldiers were formerly protected.

SCENE III.

P. 172. The old corrector substitutes a very striking for a very poor word, in the fourth of the ensuing lines. York speaks of Richard:—

> " Yet looks he like a king: behold his eye,
> As bright as is the eagle's, lightens forth
> Controlling majesty. Alack, alack, for woe,
> That any harm should stain so fair a show!"

The flat word "harm" presents itself at once as an error, and *storm* is written in the margin instead of it:—

> " Alack, alack, for woe,
> That any *storm* should stain so fair a show!"

In the next line but one, the same authority tells us that "fearful" ought to be *faithful;* and though "fearful" may seem to answer its purpose sufficiently well, the context persuades us in favour of *faithful;* for the King is complaining of Bolingbroke's breach of fidelity.

P. 179. Malone and other modern editors have altered the following passage, as the words are given in the folio, 1623, without due attention there to the regulation of the metre:—

> " They are,
> And Bolingbroke hath seiz'd the wasteful king.
> Oh, what pity is it, that he had not so trimm'd
> And dress'd his land, as we this garden, at time of year,
> And wound the bark the skin of our fruit-trees," &c.

Malone's regulation and changes are these :—

> " They are ; and Bolingbroke
> Hath seiz'd the wasteful king.   Oh ! what pity is it
> That he had not so trimm'd and dress'd his land
> As we this garden !   We at time of year
> Do wound the bark, the skin of our fruit-trees," &c.

The editor of the folio, 1632, seeing that the interjection in the second line overloaded the verse, omitted it, but made no other emendation.   The old corrector of that impression shows that Malone inserted *we* in the wrong place, having omitted "and," and thrust in *do* at the commencement of the next line, to supply the defect of the measure : as amended in the folio, 1632, the passage appears as follows :—

> " They are ; and Bolingbroke
> Hath seiz'd the wasteful king.   What pity is it,
> That he had not so trimm'd, and dress'd his land
> As we this garden !   At *the* time of year
> *We* wound the bark, the skin of our fruit-trees," &c.

This will, perhaps, be allowed to be the most easy and natural mode of giving a passage, which, by the admission of all editors, requires some alteration.

ACT IV. SCENE I.

P. 182. In every edition it is made to appear, at the commencement of this scene, that Bagot entered with the other characters; but the corrector of the folio, 1632, says that such was not the case, and that he did not come in, in custody, until after Bolingbroke had issued the order, "Call forth Bagot." The manuscript stage-direction follows this order, *Enter Bagot, prisoner.* Of course, there would be some pause between the giving and the execution of the order; and the formal introduction of the prisoner afterwards, would communicate additional effect to the opening of the Act. When the various "*gages*" are thrown down, as the scene proceeds, manuscript notice is duly inserted in the margin, but we are not told what Aumerle threw down after the line,—

> " Some honest Christian trust me with a gage,"

when he had no gage of his own left. No passages, here wanting in the folios, are introduced by the old corrector from the earlier quartos.

P. 186. Nevertheless, two emendations are made in Bolingbroke's speech, " Marry, God forbid," &c., which serve to show that the corrector of the folio, 1632, either had recourse to the quarto editions of this play, or to some authority which accorded with them. For instance, for "nobleness," in the line,—

> " Of noble Richard : then, true nobleness would," &c.,

he adopts *nobless* of the quarto, 1597, which was unquestionably Shakespeare's word, since "nobleness" too much burdens the metre. Again, in the line in the folios,—

> " And he himself not present ?   O, forbid it, God,"

he erases "himself," which is unnecessary to the sense, and injurious to the rhythm, and writes *forfend* instead of "forbid." All the quartos have *forfend ;* but, on the other hand, they have "himself." On the preceding page, the corrector has, " As *surely* as I live," of the quarto, 1597, instead of, " As sure as I live," which is the reading of the folios and of some of the quartos.

P. 188. The folio, 1632, misprints the following line,—

> " Give sorrow leave a while to tutor me,"

by absurdly putting *return* for " tutor." This blunder is set right by the old corrector; but it seems as if he had previously substituted some other word, and had erased it. Such may have been the case in several other places, where he himself blundered.

P. 192. To supply the want of printed stage-directions, they are, as usual, added in manuscript in the folio, 1632: thus, when Richard dashes the glass against the ground, we read in the margin, *Throws down the glass;* and when the crown and sceptre are previously brought to him, the proper moment for placing them in the King's hands is noted in the margin.

ACT V. SCENE I.

P. 194. An emendation, giving additional force to an exclamation by the Queen, on hearing her husband's resolution to submit, and improving the defective metre, is met with in the corrected folio, 1632, in reference to these lines, as there copied from the folio, 1623:—

> " What! is my Richard both in shape and mind
> Transform'd and weaken'd?　Hath Bolingbroke
> Depos'd thine intellect? hath he been in thy heart?"

Modern editors, to eke out the measure of the second line, have read "weaken'd," *weakened;* but the glaring redundancy of the third line they did not set right. The old corrector, however, instructs us in future to print thus:—

> " What! is my Richard both in shape and mind
> Transform'd and weaken'd?　Hath *this* Bolingbroke
> Depos'd thine intellect? been in thy heart?"

Much contempt is contained in the expression, "this Bolingbroke," and the repetition of "hath he," in the next line, rather lessens, than increases, the effect of the Queen's despairing interrogatory.

The old corrector again either adopted a word from the quartos, or had recourse to some other authority, when, in the line, as we find it in the folios,—

> "Tell thou the lamentable fall of me,"

he erased "fall," and wrote *tale* in the margin.　Malone

fancied that "fall" for *tale*, was one of Shakespeare's own emendations; but it was much more probably a misprint in the folio, 1623, which, in most respects, slavishly follows the text of the latest quarto before its time, *viz.* that of 1615: the word there is *tale*, as it had been in the earlier editions in the same form, of 1597, 1598, and 1608. It may be more than doubted, whether our great dramatist ever made a single emendation, with his own hand, in any play with a view to its publication.

SCENE II.

P. 200. The word "day," in what follows, may also have been derived from the quartos, for it is in no folio impression; but it is preceded by an improvement in the measure of a line, which has been given corruptly every where :—

> " 'Tis nothing but some bond that he has enter'd into
> For gay apparel against the triumph."

The manuscript-corrector alters both lines thus :—

> " 'Tis nothing but some bond *he's* entered into
> For gay apparel 'gainst the triumph *day*."

Modern editors, of course, insert *day*, but there can be little doubt that Shakespeare also wrote the previous line as it above appears. In the same way we may be sure that the small word, *then*, fell out of the press, or escaped by some other accident, in the Duke of York's speech, a few lines higher on this page :—

> " Yea, look'st thou pale? let me *then* see the writing."

Then is not to be traced in any ancient or modern edition, but it is authorised by the corrector of the folio, 1632, and is necessary to the completeness of the measure. The word "by" shared the same fate as "then," in the subsequent line on the next page :—

> " Now by my honour, *by* my life, my troth."

The second "by" is not in any of the folios, but is in the earlier quartos, though not in that of 1615, from which the first folio was printed: the line is imperfect without *by*, and the corrector of the second folio inserted it. The minute errors and variations in this part of the play are numerous.

SCENE III.

P. 203. When Aumerle arrives in great haste, the quarto editions say that he is *amazed*, but in the folios we have only, *Enter Aumerle :* the corrector of that of 1632, felt that something was wanted to indicate that the performer was to come upon the stage with an appearance of great perturbation, and he added to *Enter Aumerle,* the words *rush in,* to evince the eagerness and impetuosity he ought to display on the occasion. Other manuscript stage-directions apply to other characters. Aumerle *locks the door,* just before the Duke of York arrives and gives the alarm, and the King *draws* to defend himself. Then, the *door is opened* to admit York, and *shut again* that the Duchess, when she reaches the spot and exclaims against her husband, may be on the outside until her son *goes to the door and opens it.* To this follows Aumerle's confession and repentance, and we are duly informed when the different parties *kneel* to the King.

P. 208. The folio, 1632, has the following :—

> " Good uncle, help to order several powers
> To Oxford, or where'er these traitors are :
> They shall not live within this world, I swear,
> But I will have them, once know where.
> Uncle farewell, and cousin adieu."

The corrector of that impression puts it thus :—

> " Good uncle, help to order several powers
> To Oxford, or where *else* the traitors *be*.
> They shall not live within this world, I swear,
> But I will have them, *so* I once know where.
> Uncle farewell, and, cousin *mine*, adieu."

In various particulars, as marked in Italics, this differs from other copies, quarto or folio. Theobald printed "and, cousin *too*, adieu," but " and cousin *mine*, adieu," reads better, and the whole may lead to the conclusion that the corrector was guided by some authority not now known.

SCENE V.

P. 209. In the first line of the King's long speech, we meet with a correction consistent with the earliest, but found in no other old edition of this play. All but the quarto, 1597, read defectively,—

> "I have been studying how to compare,"

instead of

> "I have been studying how *I may* compare,"

which is a perfect line, and which all modern editors have properly adopted. We may feel confident that the allusion just afterwards to Holy Writ, was softened by substituting "faith" for *word* (as it stands in all the quartos), in consequence of the state of religious opinion at the time the folio, 1623, was printed: the manuscript-corrector has left the text, in this respect, as he found it, excepting that he has put his pen through the quotations from the New Testament. On the next page, he struck out the whole of the passage in which the King resembles himself to a clock, which none of the commentators have been able to understand: the erasure begins at "For now hath time," and ends at "Jack o' the clock." It is to be regretted that the old corrector could throw no light upon this obscure question: it deserves remark, however, that he struck out the word "watches," as if it were certainly wrong ; but, as if he did not know what ought to be substituted for it, he has written no corresponding word in the margin.

SCENE VI.

P. 214. The emendations by the corrector of the folio, 1632, in the last scene of this tragedy, only relate to corruptions in the versification. These corruptions begin in the very first line, for whereas Bolingbroke ought to say, as in the folio, 1623,—

> "Kind uncle York, the latest news we hear," &c.,

the word *kind* is supplied in manuscript, because omitted by the printer of the folio, 1632, only. The next is an error of the same sort, on the same page, and applies to all editions, ancient and modern, two small words having apparently dropped out at the end of a line: we have printed them in Italics :—

> "Welcome, my lord. What is the news *with you?*"

A third, and more noticeable instance occurs where Boling-broke, on p. 215, passes sentence on the Bishop of Carlisle :—

> " Carlisle, this is your doom,"

is the whole of the line in all copies ; but the next line, which rhymes with it, proves that some words, perhaps unimportant excepting as they complete the measure, had been lost.　The old corrector informs us what they were :—

> " *Bishop of* Carlisle, this *shall be* your doom :—
> Choose out some secret place, some reverend room," &c.

Several additional stage-directions are inserted, but they are of little consequence, saving for the regulation of the performance : thus, the King *beats the Keeper,* and *kills one* of his assailants, following it up by a blow which *kills another.* He *dies* as Exton pronounces his first line.

THE FIRST PART

OF

KING HENRY IV.

ACT I. SCENE I.

P. 225. The first line of this play presents an alteration, but a questionable improvement, by the corrector of the folio, 1632 : for

> " So shaken as we are, so wan with care,"

he has " *worn* with care," which may be right, although, as far as the sense of the passage is concerned, it may not be necessary to do the violence of changing the received text. No new light is thrown upon the two lines which have produced so many conjectures,—

> " No more the thirsty entrance of this soil
> Shall daub her lips with her own children's blood;"

but that the corrector's attention must have been directed to them, we ascertain from the fact that, as "daub" is misprinted *dambe* in the second folio, that blunder is set right.

P. 227. The manuscript-corrector restores the word "for," of the earlier quartos, instead of *far*, of the quarto, 1613, and the folios, in the following line :—

> " *For* more uneven and unwelcome news
> Came from the north."

We shall see hereafter, that on other occasions he preferred the older text.

P. 228. For the imperfect line,—

> " Of Murray, Angus, and Menteith,"

the old corrector writes,—

> " Of Murray, Angus, and *the bold* Menteith."

How far, and in what manner, he was warranted in this addition, may be a question; but he was doubtless right in transferring (in a shortened form) the words, " In faith, it is," from the end of the King's speech, where they are not wanted, to the beginning of that of Westmoreland, where they are necessary to complete the measure, as well as an improvement to the sense :—

> " *Faith*, '*tis* a conquest for a prince to boast of."

Such also was Pope's judicious mode of giving the speech.

SCENE II.

P. 229. If any doubt were entertained whether the words, " by Phœbus,—he, that wandering knight so fair," were a quotation, it would probably be set at rest by the circumstance that they are underscored, as usual in such cases, by the old corrector.

P. 231. Falstaff's remark, in answer to the Prince, " Yea, and so used it, that were it not here apparent, that thou art heir apparent," has generally been printed with a line after it, as an unfinished sentence ; but the corrector of the folio, 1632, represents it as finished by reading, " Yea, and so used it, that it is here apparent that thou art heir apparent." The negative is omitted in the folios, and was not restored by the corrector from the quartos.

SCENE III.

P. 237. The words, " My Lord," given to Northumberland, do not complete Worcester's hemistich, " Have holp to make so portly," a syllable being wanted: the corrector of the folio, 1632, therefore, represents Northumberland as saying, " My *good* lord ;" and we may feel pretty sure that he did so, not merely because it finishes the line, but because, when he resumes after the interruption, he uses the same expression, " Yea, my *good* lord."

P. 238. Here, again, the old corrector seems to have resorted to the quarto editions of this play, or to some authority that agreed with them, for he not only restores " name," omitted in the folios,—

> "Those prisoners in your highness' name demanded,"

but he sets right a remarkable blunder at the end of the same speech, not in the quartos, but which found its way into the folios : the latter have,—

> " Who either through envy or misprision
> Was guilty of this fault, and not my son ;'

instead of the true text of the quartos :—

> " Either envy, therefore, or misprision
> Is guilty of this fault, and not my son."

P. 240. All impressions, quarto and folio, ancient and modern, have, one after the other, repeated a flagrant error of the press in the earliest edition of this play in 1598 : the mistake has given vast annoyance to each succeeding editor, and the emendation is one of those that must strike the moment it is pointed out. Nobody has been able to explain satisfactorily the use of the word "fears" in the subsequent lines, where the King indignantly asks,—

> " Shall our coffers, then,
> Be emptied to redeem a traitor home?
> Shall we buy treason, and indent with fears,
> When they have lost and forfeited themselves ?"

The corrector tells us to print " fears" *foes ;* and if we do so, nothing can be plainer than the meaning of the poet :—

> "Shall we buy treason, and indent with *foes,*
> When they have lost and forfeited themselves ?"

To "indent," is, of course, to enter into a compact or indenture. Johnson proposed *peers* for " fears :" Steevens contended that "fears" was to be taken as *fearful people,* &c. ; but the question of the King was merely whether it was fit to enter into a bargain with traitors and enemies. It seems strange that, in the course of two hundred and fifty

years, nobody should ever have even guessed at *foes* for
" fears :" if it were merely a guess by the old corrector, it is
a happy one ; and some may be disposed to entertain the
opinion that he had an opportunity of resorting to a better
original than any of the printed copies.

P. 243. The same authority here points out another misprint, not by any means of so much importance, but still, no
doubt, an error, though the word usually received may be
said to answer the purpose.   It is in Hotspur's speech, where
he is entering into the plot of his father and his uncle
against Henry IV., when he breaks out thus :—

> " No ! yet time serves, wherein you may redeem
> Your banish'd honours, and restore yourselves
> Into the good thoughts of the world again."

For " banish'd honours," we are very reasonably instructed
to put " *tarnish'd* honours ;" for Hotspur would hardly say
that the honours of his family were " banished," although
their brightness might for a time be *tarnished.*

P. 247 The old corrector either saw the quarto, 1598, and
corrected the following line by it, or he was indebted to his
own sagacity.   All ancient copies, but the earliest, read,—

> " I'll steal to Glendower, and *to* Mortimer,"

or

> " I'll steal to Glendower, and *loe* Mortimer."

The line in the quarto, 1598, is,—

> " I'll steal to Glendower and Lo : Mortimer ; "

meaning *Lord* Mortimer, which abbreviation " Lo :" was
subsequently strangely misunderstood.   In the text of the
folio, 1632, *loe* is erased, and *Lord* is written in the margin.
There can be no dispute that this is the poet's word, and so,
in fact, it stands in modern editions.

ACT II. SCENE I.

P. 250. Much speculation has been the result of the subsequent speech by Gadshill, where he is talking of the high

rank of the parties with whom, as a highwayman, he was in league :—

> " I am joined with no foot land-rakers, no long-staff, sixpenny strikers : none of these mad, mustachio purple-hued maltworms ; but with nobility and tranquillity : burgomasters, and great oneyers, such as can hold in ; such as will strike sooner than speak," &c.

No question seems to have arisen regarding the word " tranquillity "—" nobility and tranquillity"—although it has no meaning in this place ; but ingenuity has been exhausted upon "great oneyers," which we have been desired to read *moneyers, one-eers, mynheers,* &c., when it is merely, as we learn from the corrector of the folio, 1632, a misprint, the word " tranquillity," which precedes it, being in the same predicament. He sets the whole matter right thus : " I am joined with no foot land-rakers, &c., but with nobility and *sanguinity ;* burgomasters, and great *ones—yes,* such as can hold in," &c. " Tranquillity" was misheard by the scribe for *sanguinity,* in reference to the high blood of the companions of Gadshill ; and " great oneyers" was a lapse for " *great ones—yes,*" the affirmative particle having been added to give more force to the assertion, when, perhaps, the Chamberlain, with whom Gadshill was speaking, intimated his incredulity. The first error seems to have arisen from mishearing, and the last from misprinting.

SCENE III.

P. 259. In the line,—

> " What sayst thou, Kate ? what would'st thou have with me ?"

the folio, 1632, omits the second " what," which the corrector supplies in manuscript. Five lines lower, he furnishes four words, wanting in all editions, where Hotspur asks his wife,—

> " Come ; wilt thou see me ride ?"

The words here carelessly left out are quite consistent with what has passed before, when Hotspur ordered that his horse should be led " forth into the park :"—

> " Come *to the park, Kate :* wilt thou see me ride ?"

They are in themselves of little import, excepting as they

serve to prove that our great dramatist did not leave the line needlessly imperfect.

SCENE IV.

P. 263. The folios, in the following line, omit the negative ; the old corrector inserts it, but whether from the quarto impressions where it is found, or from any independent authority, may be questioned :—

> "Away, you rogue !   Dost thou *not* hear them call ?"

P. 264. The words, "pitiful-hearted Titan that melted at the sweet tale of the sun," are struck out : probably, the old corrector did not understand the allusion. The words, in their corrupted form, appear to be no great loss.

P. 274. Rowe seems to have been right (indeed the emendation hardly admits of doubt) in reading *tristful* for "trustful" in Falstaff's speech, as we learn from the alteration introduced in the folio, 1632 ; and the old corrector, not approving of the use of the name of the Creator, has substituted *heaven* for it in the line,—

> "For *heaven's* sake, lords, convey my *tristful* queen," &c.

In the folio, 1632, a previous speech by Falstaff is erroneously given to the Prince, but the corrector has remedied the defect ; and in Falstaff's long mock-address, he has inserted *own* before "opinion," which is not in any folio. In the same character's next speech, he has changed the common reading to "him keep with *thee*, the rest banish :" this emendation, is, however, disputable, and perhaps scarcely requires notice.

P. 276. The Prince calls Falstaff, according to the old corrector of the folio, 1632, not "that trunk of humours," but "that *hulk* of humours," against all known authorities, but it may very likely be right.

P. 279. The folios, and the quartos of 1608 and afterwards, read, "I know his death will be a match of twelve score ;" but the older text of the quartos, 1598, 1599, and 1604, is "a *march* of twelve score," which is evidently right; and the manuscript-correction in the folio, 1632, is, therefore, from *match* to " march." On the next page, all early editions, with the exception of the quarto, 1598, omit " huge" in the line,—

> " The frame and huge foundation of the earth : "

"huge" is written in the margin of the folio, 1632. This scene is very ill printed in that impression, but the minutest literal error was not neglected.

ACT III. SCENE I.

P. 284. The last line in Worcester's speech, adverting to the course of the Trent,—

> " And then he runs straight and even,"

must have been misprinted in this and in all other editions : the manuscript-corrector gives it thus unobjectionably,—

> " And then he runs *all* straight and *evenly.*"

Hotspur has just before said of the same river,—

> " In a new channel, fair, and evenly."

P. 285. For a similar reason the corrector of the folio, 1632, amends the subsequent lines,—

> " I'll haste the writer, and withal,
> Break with your wives of your departure hence ;"

by giving them thus :—

> " I'll haste the writer, and withal *I'll* break
> With your *young* wives of your departure hence."

Young was, perhaps, omitted by the old printer or scribe, from the similarity of the word *your* just before it. In Act V. (p. 239 of this vol.), we shall see that " your" was left out before " younger."

P. 286. We can readily believe that there must be a misprint in the following :—

> " In faith, my lord, you are too wilful-blame,"

as it stands in the old copies, and has been repeated in all
modern editions : the true reading may very well have been
what the old corrector tells us it was,—

> "In faith, my wilful lord, you are to blame."

The epithet "wilful" in some way became misplaced, and
"too" for *to*, and *vice versâ*, was a very common error.

P. 289. The four last lines in this scene ought to rhyme,
and, no doubt, did so originally, until a misprint prevented
it ; the corrector of the folio, 1632, makes the passage run as
follows :—

> "*Glend.* Come on, lord Mortimer ; you are as slow,
>   As hot lord Percy is on fire to go.
>   By this our book is drawn : we'll seal and *part*
>   To horse immediately.
> *Mort.*   With all my heart."

The text of the two last lines has hitherto been this :—

> "By this our book is drawn : we'll seal and then
>   To horse immediately.
> *Mort.*   With all my heart."

SCENE II.

P. 291. The old printer took more pains than usual with
the great scene between Henry IV. and the Prince, but still,
if we may rely upon the corrector of the folio, 1632, introduced several important blunders. One of them applies to
the last words on this page, "carded his state," which
Warburton, with great sagacity, proposed to read, "*discarded*
state :" such is the emendation proposed in manuscript :
next, the corrector struck out "do," unnecessarily thrust into
a line on page 292 :—

> "As cloudy men use to *do* their adversaries."

Thirdly, in the first line on p. 294,—

> "Thou that art like enough, through vassal fear,"

the printer injuriously omitted "that," which is written in
the margin of the folio, 1632.

P. 295. The line, as it stands in the quartos,—

> " The which, if he be pleas'd, I shall perform,"

is given in the folio, 1623,—

> " The which, if I *perform*, and do *survive*,"

and in the folio, 1632,—

> " The which if I *promise*, and do survive."

The corrector of the last impression erases *promise*, and inserts " perform," making the passage correspond with the first folio, but not with the quarto editions. Lower down, Pope's emendation, " So *is* the business," &c., is supported both by the old corrector, and by the sense of Blunt's reply.

SCENE III.

P. 296. In Falstaff's retort upon Bardolph, he says : " Thou art our admiral, thou bearest the lantern in the poop,—but 'tis in the nose of thee." The correction in the folio, 1632, seems hardly required :—

> " Thou bearest the lantern, *not* in the poop, but 'tis in the nose of thee."

In the preceding line, the common blunder of *thy* for " my" is committed, and set right.

ACT IV.   SCENE I.

P. 303. The corrector of the folio, 1632, restores the oath (if such it is to be considered), " Zounds," from the quartos, in Hotspur's exclamation,—

> " *Zounds !* how has he the leisure to be sick ? "

The folios read, with ridiculous tameness, and most prosaically,—

> " *How !* has he the leisure to be sick *now*."

The printing of this Act in the folios, 1623 and 1632, is full of strange blunders and exhibitions of carelessness, one of which occurs in the last line of this page, where the Messenger is made to say,—

> " His letters bear his mind, not I, his mind,"

instead of "not I, *my lord*;" but this error originated, in fact, with the earlier quartos, where "my mind" was printed for *my lord.* Capel introduced the right word, as we ascertain from a manuscript note in the margin of the folio, 1632. Again, on the next page, we meet with this line, if we may so call it :—

"We may boldly spend upon the hope ;''

whereas, it ought to run,—

"We *now* may boldly spend upon the hope," &c.

P. 305. Worcester observes, in the folios,—

"The quality and *heire* of our attempt
Brooks no division."

In the quartos of 1598 and 1599, "heire" was *haire*, the old mode of spelling *hair ;* and this, the old corrector assures us, was the true word, the meaning of the speaker being (as suggested in note 1), that the power he, and the other revolted lords could produce, was too small to allow of any division of it.

P. 307. As might be expected, he restores from the quartos of 1598 and 1599,—

"Harry to Harry shall, hot horse to horse ;"

which the later quartos and folios misprinted, "*not* horse to horse."

SCENE II.

P. 309. For "old faced ancient," in Falstaff's description of his troops, the corrector of the folio, 1632, substitutes, "old *pieced* ancient," an ensign that, being old, had been patched in order to mend it. Lower down, for "there's not a shirt and a half in all my company," he more naturally reads, "there's *but* a shirt and a half," &c. "Not" and *but* were often confounded by the old printers.

SCENE III.

P. 311. There is a surplusage of two syllables, which certainly weaken the effect of the passage, in a line of Sir

Richard Vernon's answer to Douglas, who had charged him with cowardice.   The invariable reading has been,—

> " I hold as little counsel with weak fear,
>   As you, my lord, or any Scot that this day lives."

"This day" clearly overloads the line, and the manuscript-corrector credibly informs us that those words ought to be struck out as an interpolation :—

> " I hold as little counsel with weak fear,
>   As you, my lord, or any Scot that lives."

On the next page, we are told that the line,—

> " My father, and my uncle, and myself,"

ought to be

> " My father, *with* my uncle, and myself."

The folios omit both "and" and *with*, but the quartos have "and."   On the next page but one, the corrector of the folio, 1632, inserts a word, where a word is certainly wanting, but not the word in the earlier impressions : he gives the line,—

> " Who is, if every owner were *due* plac'd,"

instead of "*well* plac'd" of the quartos : the folios read defectively, "if every owner were plac'd."

ACT V. SCENE I.

P. 317. When Worcester declares to the King that he had "not sought the day of this dislike," the King observes with surprise,—

> " You have not sought it ! how comes it, then ? "

This line is unquestionably deficient of a syllable, and the old corrector supplies it thus :—

> " You have not sought it ! *Say*, how comes it, then ? "

P. 319. The last line of the King's speech is thus given in the folios :—

> " Sworn to us in younger enterprise."

It is altered by the corrector of the folio, 1632, to

> " Sworn to us in *your* younger enterprise,"

which accords with the early quartos. "Your" and "younger," following each other, perhaps caused the omission : see also p. 234 of this vol.

SCENE II.

P. 321. A question has arisen how the subsequent line, as it stands in all old editions, should be corrected :—

> " Supposition, all our lives, shall be stuck full of eyes."

Pope altered "supposition," most properly, to *suspicion*, and the corrector of the folio, 1632, did the same ; but he made no farther change : perhaps it was a line which was meant to be redundant, and, notwithstanding Farmer's proposal, we know not what words could be left out without diminishing its force. The obvious misprint of the folio, 1623, was repeated in the folio, 1632, "Look how *he* can," for "Look how *we* can ;" but it is set right in the margin in manuscript.

P. 324. The last four lines of Percy's address are these, as always hitherto printed :—

> " Sound all the lofty instruments of war,
>   And by that music let us all embrace ;
>   For, heaven to earth, some of us never shall
>   A second time do such a courtesy."

Warburton was of opinion that the poet meant that the odds were so great, that heaven might be wagered against earth, that many present would never embrace again. This is a mistake, according to the manuscript-corrector : Hotspur calls heaven and earth to witness to the improbability that some of those present would ever have an opportunity of re-greeting each other :—

> " *'Fore* heaven *and* earth, some of us never shall
>   A second time do such a courtesy."

P. 326. Hotspur tells Douglas, who has slain Sir Walter Blunt, thinking him the King, because he wore the same armour and insignia,—

> " The King hath many marching in his coats."

This is intelligible, and does not positively require change ; but the old corrector substitutes a word for "marching" (the forces, at this time, were fighting, not marching), which seems much better adapted to the place :—

> " The King hath many *masking* in his coats ;"

i. e. there are many in the field who have disguised themselves like the King, in order, like Sir Walter Blunt, to deceive his enemies.

P. 331. There could be no question as to the corruption here introduced into the text, first by the quarto, 1608, and afterwards into the quarto, 1613, and all the folios,—

> " But that the earth and the cold hand of death."

All the earlier quartos have it as follows, and the old corrector of the second folio restores the reading,—

> " But that the *earthy* and cold hand of death."

It seems not unlikely that here, as in various other places, he resorted to the older impressions, but the sense might be a sufficient guide.   Modern editors of course print *earthy*.

P. 334. The old printed stage-direction, which has been repeated by all subsequent editors, informs us that Falstaff *takes Hotspur on his back*, and it seems, by the same editors, that he kept the body in that position, till (after a considerable interval) he went out, *bearing off the body*. Judging from a manuscript stage-direction in the folio, 1632, this was not the custom of the stage in the time of the old corrector, if not earlier, for opposite the words, " There is Percy," he has written, *Throw him down;* and then the dialogue is continued until the close of Falstaff's soliloquy, ending, " and live cleanly as a nobleman should do."   During this interval, the corpse of Percy must have been lying on the ground, and we can hardly suppose that Falstaff would have been able to sustain the weight, if he had had it on his back all the time he was conversing with the two princes. When the scene, therefore, was at an end, and the body must be removed, Falstaff did not take it up again, but *dragged it out*, and such is the written stage-direction in the margin of the folio, 1632.   He first, with great difficulty, must have got the body on his back ; he then cast it down when he began to talk with the princes, and finally dragged

it off the stage at the end of the scene. Such appears to
have been the way in which the business of this part of the
play was formerly conducted.

P. 335. We meet with a considerable improvement in the
last line of Worcester's last speech; it has always stood
thus :—

> " What I have done my safety urg'd me to,
> And I embrace this fortune patiently,
> Since not to be avoided it falls on me."

The alteration of the manuscript-corrector is trifling, but
effectual, and its fitness can hardly be questioned :—

> " And I embrace this fortune patiently,
> *Which* not to be avoided falls on me."

P. 336. The folios omit the following reply by John of
Lancaster to Prince Henry, when the latter relinquishes to
him the office of setting the Douglas "ransomless and free;"
that reply is found in the earlier, but not in the later
quartos, in these terms :—

> " I thank your grace for this high courtesy,
> Which I will give away immediately."

The corrector of the folio, 1632, inserts two corresponding
lines, but the last differs materially from that quoted above,
and may be thought, in some respects, to read better :—

> " I thank your grace for this high courtesy,
> Which I shall *put in act without delay.*"

This variation may induce the belief that the corrector
had access to some authority independent of any of the
printed copies of this play, whether in quarto or folio;
although not a few of his emendations, as we have seen,
correspond with the earliest and some other quartos, which
had been abandoned by the folios.

R

THE SECOND PART

OF

KING HENRY IV.

INDUCTION.

P. 341. The folios all have,—

> "Stuffing the ears of them with false reports;"

a misprint, probably, from defective hearing, for the text unquestionably ought to be, as commonly given,—

> "Stuffing the ears of *men* with false reports."

The corrector of the folio, 1632, altered "them" to *men*. Lower down, he made "surmise," of the same edition, *surmises*, as required by sense and metre. The first only of these blunders is committed in the folio, 1623.

P. 342. We may doubt the fitness of changing "peasant-towns," as printed with a hyphen in the folios, to "*pleasant* towns;" but it may be right, and it ought, therefore, to be mentioned. In the next line but one, "worm-eaten hole," of all the ancient impressions, is made "worm-eaten *hold*." Theobald was the first to substitute *hold*.

ACT I. SCENE I.

P. 343. The old stage-direction at the opening of the first scene, is, *Enter Lord Bardolph and the Porter*, as if they made their appearance before the audience at the same moment : the modern stage-direction has been, *The Porter before the gate ; enter Lord Bardolph*　It should appear from a stage-direction in manuscript, in the folio, 1632, that the old practice was for Lord Bardolph to enter first, and as soon as he asked, "Who keeps the gate here ? ho !" for the *Warder* (so called) to show himself *above* the castle-gate, and from thence to answer Lord Bardolph. The Warder made his *exit* as soon as Northumberland entered.

P. 345. There can be no question that the printer of the folio, 1623, in the first line of this page, mistakenly repeated "able," as applied to heels, because he had placed the same epithet before "horse," in the preceding line. In the last instance, the word ought to be *armed* instead of "able" :—

> "With that he gave his able horse the head,
> And bending forward, struck his *armed* heels
> Against the panting sides," &c.

It is "*armed* heels" in the quarto, 1600 ; and if the corrector of the folio, 1632, did not obtain that word from thence, he might have heard the passage accurately recited on the stage in his day, or possibly he used some independent, but concurrent authority.

P. 348. Theobald's emendation of "ragged'st hour," of the old copies, to "*rugged'st* hour," which several more recent editors have not admitted, in the line,—

> "The ragged'st hour that time and spite dare bring,"

is warranted by the old corrector, who merely converts *a* into *u* in the margin.

SCENE II.

P. 357. The following manuscript-correction accords with no copy of this play that has come down to us : it is part of Falstaff's speech to the Chief Justice, "Virtue is of so little regard in these costermonger *days*, that true valour is turned bear-herd." It is "costermonger *times*" in the quarto, 1600, while in the folios the necessary word is altogether omitted. Lower down, the old corrector has added, with an asterisk at the proper place, the words, *about three of the afternoon,* which do not precisely agree with the quarto, which reads, "about three *o'clock in* the afternoon:" the folios have no trace of them. On the next page, he leaves out the whole of Falstaff's speech after "well, I cannot last ever," which he makes "last *for* ever." It is only found in the quarto, 1600.

P. 359. Few things can be more evident than the necessity of an emendation in the following passage: "A man can no more separate age and covetousness, than he can part young limbs and lechery; but the gout galls the one, and the pox pinches the other, and so both the degrees prevent my curses." What here are "the degrees?" The poet is referring to two *diseases*, not to two "degrees," and the copyist must have misheard *diseases*, and written "degrees." We must read with the old corrector, "and so both the *diseases* prevent my curses," *i. e.* anticipate my curses.

SCENE III.

P. 361. The first twenty lines of Lord Bardolph's second speech, on this page, are only in the folio impressions, and the corrector of that of 1632 shows that they have been most corruptly printed, probably from defects in the manuscript in the hands of the compositor. Malone and others set right one error in the first line, by converting "if" to *in*, but the second line appears to be even more strangely blundered, for instead of

> "Indeed the instant action, a cause on foot," &c.,

we ought to read the whole passage thus : it is in answer to Northumberland's question, whether it could do harm to hope ?—

> "Yes, *in* this present quality of war:
> Indeed the instant *act and* cause on foot
> Lives so in hope, as in the early spring
> We see appearing buds," &c.

Thus the measure is amended, and the sense cleared. But, farther on, Lord Bardolph draws a parallel between the building of a house and the carrying on a war, which is obscured by the omission of a whole line, fortunately inserted in the margin by the old corrector. Our first extract is as it stands in the folios, and we will follow it by the same quotation as amended. The speaker is supposing that a man

purposes at first to construct a dwelling, which he afterwards
finds beyond his means :—

> " What do we then, but draw anew the model
> In fewer offices ; or at least desist
> To build at all ?   Much more in this great work,
> (Which is almost to pluck a kingdom down
> And set another up) should we survey
> The plot of situation, and the model,
> Consent upon a sure foundation,
> Question surveyors, know our own estate
> How able such a work to undergo
> To weigh against his opposite ; or else
> We fortify in paper and in figures," &c.

As amended by the old corrector, the same passage runs as
follows :—

> " What do we then, but draw anew the model
> In fewer offices ; or at *last* desist
> To build at all?   Much more in this great work,
> (Which is almost to pluck a kingdom down
> And set another up) should we survey
> The plot, *the* situation, and the model,
> *Consult* upon a sure foundation,
> Question surveyors, know our own estate,
> How able such a work to undergo.
> *A careful leader sums what force he brings*
> To weigh against his opposite ; or else
> We fortify *on* paper, and in figures," &c.

That the furnishing of this new connecting line (to say
nothing of verbal emendations, the first of which Steevens
speculated upon) between Lord Bardolph's simile and its application, is an important improvement, although the question still returns upon us, from whence was it derived ?

ACT II.   SCENE I.

P. 365. In the speech of the Hostess we find, " A hundred
mark is a long one for a poor lone woman to bear," altered
to " A hundred mark is a long *score* for a poor lone woman
to bear," with indisputable fitness.

P. 373, The Page, describing Bardolph peeping through
the " red lattice " of an ale-house, observes : " At last I spied

his eyes ; and, methought he had made two holes in the ale-wives' new petticoat, and peeped through." The word *red* is inserted in manuscript before " petticoat," in order to make the resemblance more distinct, but it would scarcely be ne-cessary, if ale-wives usually wore red petticoats at the time.

SCENE II.

P. 374. The prefixes are so arranged by the corrector of the folio, 1632, that the Prince, and not Poins, is made to read Falstaff's letter aloud, which, according to a manuscript stage-direction, *he shows to Poins.* Several literal and trifling verbal corrections are inserted in this part of the scene : the only one it is necessary to notice is the remark of the Prince, " That's *but* to make him eat twenty of his words :" *but* is wanting in all the old copies. Warburton proposed *plenty* for "twenty," but without the slightest necessity, and the manuscript-corrector supports no such change.

SCENE IV.

P. 381. Falstaff enters *singing,* according to a manu-script stage-direction, and it might be gathered from the fragment of the ballad printed. On the same authority, he *sings,* "Your broaches, pearls, and owches," as the frag-ment of another ballad. In his preceding speech, he ad-dresses the words, " Grant that, my poor virtue, grant that," to Doll Tearsheet ; but the old corrector alters "poor" to *pure,* used ironically, which was doubtless the poet's word. The folios, after Falstaff's speech ending, " to venture upon the charged chambers bravely," omit what Doll says, according to the quarto, " Hang yourself, you muddy conger, hang yourself ;" and, excepting the two last words, the manu-script-corrector has duly inserted them with the proper prefix. It is to be remarked, however, that when, on p. 384, Falstaff exclaims, " No more, Pistol," &c., as it stands only in the quarto, that speech is not added by the corrector to the folio, 1632. In this respect his practice was by no means consistent ; and, possibly, whatever authority he may have had was inconsistent also.

ACT III. SCENE I.

P. 394. Two corrections, the second adopted by some commentators, the first not thought of by them, are introduced in the folio, 1632, in the King's soliloquy upon sleep. The first is in the line,—

"Under the canopies of costly state;"

which we are told to read,—

" Under *high* canopies of costly state."

When "high" was spelt *hie*, as was not unfrequent of old, the misprint might easily have been made, and *high* adds considerably to the force of the line. The second correction occurs lower down, where "clouds" is erased with a pen, and *shrowds* written at the side. It has been a much debated point among editors, which was the authentic word, "clouds" or *shrowds*, and this emendation may serve to settle the question.

P. 395. The corrector of the folio, 1632, did not add, from the quarto, the four lines, within brackets, in the middle of King Henry's speech. A leaf, paged respectively 87 and 88, is deficient in the corrected folio of 1632.

ACT IV. SCENE I.

P. 409, The folio, 1632, in the line,—

" Here doth he wish his person, with such powers," &c.,

misprints "here" *how;* but the error (not committed in the folio, 1623) is set right by the old corrector. Lower down, at the end of Mowbray's speech, he points out a curious blunder, arising, in all likelihood, from mishearing on the part of the scribe, which has been the occasion of several notes. In old and modern impressions, the line has thus been printed :—

" Let us sway on, and face them in the field."

Johnson truly says that he had never seen "sway" used in this sense, and Steevens takes the trouble to insert several quotations in which " sway" is found, but always in its ordinary meaning, so that they prove nothing. The plain truth is that the copyist ought to have written different words, that have exactly the same sound, *viz.* :—

> " *Let's away* on, and face them in the field."

We need have no hesitation in at once admitting this change of the received text.

P. 410. This part of the play is extremely ill printed in every old copy, blunders having been continued from one to the other, some of which have never been detected, excepting by the manuscript-corrector of the folio, 1632. Westmoreland says to Scroop :—

> " If that rebellion
> Came like itself in base and abject routs,
> Led on by bloody youth, guarded with rage,
> And countenanc'd by boys and beggary," &c.

For " guarded with rage," we must read " guarded (*i. e.* ornamented, used ironically) with *rags*," which is quite consistent with the rest of the passage. Again, nearer the end of the same speech, *glaves* or *glaives* is misprinted " graves ;" and the last line of what Westmoreland says, is thus given in the folio, 1623 :—

> " To a loud trumpet and a point of war."

Here "point of war" can have no meaning ; but the close of the passage, in which the noble envoy from the King reproaches the Archbishop for abandoning his profession and raising the standard of rebellion, ought to be thus printed in future :—

> "Turning your books to *glaives*, your ink to blood,
> Your pens to lances, and your tongue divine,
> To a loud trumpet and *report* of war."

The folio, 1632, makes the matter worse by putting *low* for " loud" of the folio, 1623. In "Richard III.," Act IV. Scene IV., we have the expression, " the clamorous *report of war*."

P. 412. It may be fit to state that the corrector of the folio, 1632, does not notice the lines from the quarto, which are marked as omitted, nor does he clear up the difficulty regarding the Archbishop's speech, in reply to Westmoreland's question, why he in particular had joined the rebellion.

P. 415. There is an undeniable error in the subsequent lines, at the end of Scroop's speech :—

> " So that this land, like an offensive wife
> That hath enrag'd him on to offer strokes,
> As he is striking, holds his infant up,
> And hangs resolv'd correction in the arm
> That was uprear'd to execution."

To whom does "him" refer ? Indisputably to the husband ; and the line in which it occurs ought to run as follows, as we learn from the manuscript-corrector :—

> "That hath enrag'd *her man* to offer strokes," &c.

Her man, in some way, either by mishearing or misprint, became " him on."

SCENE II.

P. 417. The conclusion of Prince John's reproof to the Archbishop has generally stood thus :—

> " You have taken up
> Under the counterfeited zeal of heaven
> The subjects of heaven's substitute," &c.

The quarto, published before the act of James I., has *God* for " heaven," but the error lies in " zeal" for *seal :*—

> " Under the counterfeited *seal* of heaven"

must be the true reading, and " zeal" is converted into *seal* by the corrector of the folio, 1632. The " seal divine," which Scroop was charged with misapplying, has been before mentioned by Westmoreland on p. 411.

SCENE III.

P. 421. Falstaff's joke, such as it is, upon Sir John Colevile of the Dale, has been lost by a strange misprint of " place" for *dale,* twice in the ensuing quotation : " Colevile shall be your name, a traitor your degree, and the dungeon your place—a place deep enough ; so shall you be still Colevile of the Dale." " Place," in both instances, ought to have been *dale,* "and the dungeon your *dale*—a *dale* deep enough," &c.   The manuscript-corrector has substituted *dale* for both "places."

SCENE IV

P. 429. The manuscript stage-direction after the line,—

"O me! come near me, now I am much ill,"

is not *swoons*, as in modern editions, but *falls back*, we may suppose, into the arms of the Dukes of Gloucester and Clarence : the old printed copies are without any note of the kind ; and, just before, when Westmoreland and Harcourt bring news, and deliver written accounts of it to the King, it is left to be inferred that they did so ; but, lest any mistake should be made by the performers, the old corrector, in both cases, writes in the margin, *Gives a paper*.   Afterwards, when the King desires his nobles to bear him into some other chamber, the audience was left to imagine a change of apartment, for the simple stage-direction is, *Put the King a-bed;* and soon afterwards Prince Henry comes in, and takes away the crown.

P. 431. In note 8 it is conjectured that "rigol" might be a misprint for *ringol*, both here and in "Lucrece," where Shakespeare also uses it.   However this may be, it is certain that the corrector of the folio, 1632, here converts "rigol" into *ringol*, by putting *n* in the margin, and such was, perhaps, the original mode of spelling the word.   Steevens was not aware "that it was used by any other author than Shakespeare," but Middleton, his contemporary, applies the compound "rigol-eyed" to the round eyes of young women, in his "Black Book," 1604, which has been strangely misunderstood *wriggle-eyed*, a word that has no meaning.

P. 436. For "win," in the subsequent line,—

"That thou might'st win the more thy father's love,"

the folios have *joyne*, for which misprint it is easy to account, when we recollect that "win" was of old often spelt *wynne*.   The old corrector strikes out *joyne* in favour of "win," or, as he writes it, *winne*.

P. 437. The expression, "for what in me was purchas'd,"

the manuscript-corrector changes to "for what in me was *purchase*," *i. e.* booty, a meaning constantly given to the word by our poet and his contemporaries ; the verb, to pur-chase, was, we believe, never used in this sense. Lower down, doubts have arisen whether, in the following line, the first "thy" ought not to be *my* : —

"And all thy friends, which thou must make thy friends,"

because afterwards the King observes,—

　　　　　　　　　　　　　"Which to avoid
　　　　　　I cut them off."

The old corrector tells us to read, "And all *my* friends," and "I cut *some* off;" which seems right, inasmuch as Henry adds, that it had been his intention, if his health had per-mitted, to lead others to the Holy Land,

　　　　　"Lest rest and lying still might make them look
　　　　　Too near unto my state."

ACT V.　SCENE I.

P. 441. The folios all have, "and he shall laugh *with in-tervallums*," instead of "without *intervallums*," which is the text of the quarto, and to which the passage is restored by a manuscript-correction.

SCENE III.

P. 452. It was probably intended that Pistol, in his joy at the accession of Henry V., should end this scene with a couplet, but it closes as follows : —

　　　　" ' Where is the life that late I led,' say they ;
　　　　Why here it is : welcome these pleasant days."

The change required is only, "welcome *this* pleasant *day*," to which the old corrector alters the line : he also underscores it as a quotation, and we may feel assured that it was part of the same popular ballad mentioned by Petruchio in "The Taming of the Shrew," Act IV. Scene I. vol. iii. p. 168.

P. 458. In the second paragraph of the "Epilogue" *by one that can dance* (as we are informed in a manuscript parenthesis), the word "forgiven," of the folio, 1623, is *forgotten* in that of 1632, but corrected in manuscript; and after the speaker had knelt down "to pray for the Queen," it is clear that he rose again in order to treat the audience with a dance, for the old corrector adds these words, quite at the close and in a new line, *End with a dance.* The conjecture, therefore, hazarded in note 2, is, so far, not supported.

KING HENRY V.

P. 465. In the folios, the thirty-four introductory lines are headed, "Enter Prologue," but the corrector of the folio, 1632, has altered the title thus, "Enter *Chorus as* Prologue." In the body of the play, the speaker of the interlocutory descriptions is called "Chorus;" and the same at the end, where we have "Chorus" above what was clearly meant as the Epilogue: the corrector, has, therefore, thus amended the heading in the last instance, "Enter Chorus *as Epilogue.*" In the eighteenth line, "imaginary" has the last syllable altered, but a water-stain in the margin of the folio, 1632, prevents our being able to distinguish what was intended: *imaginative* could hardly be Shakespeare's word.

ACT I. SCENE II.

P. 471. In the long speech of the Archbishop, in defence of Henry's title to France, those parts which relate especially to the succession of the Kings of France, in connexion with the salique law, and which were almost *verbatim* derived from Holinshed, are struck out with a pen, as if they would not have been well relished by a popular audience, and might be (and perhaps were) dispensed with in the performance of the play. Nevertheless, the corrections are carried throughout, and near the bottom of p. 472,—

"To find his title with some shows of truth,"

is not altered to "to *fine* his title," as in Malone, &c., but to "to *found* his title," which, on some accounts, may be considered the better reading of the three.

P. 475. The King, speaking of Scotland, says,—

> "Who hath been still a giddy neighbour to us."

The old corrector inserts *greedy* for " giddy :" either word
will suit the place, whether we suppose Henry to mean that
Scotland has been an unsteady neighbour, or a rapacious
one, anxious to seize all opportunities of pillaging England.
Greedy seems rather better adapted to the context, but the
printed copies are uniformly in favour of " giddy."

Lower down, we need have less doubt regarding the alteration of an important word :—

> "The King of Scots, whom she did send to France
> To fill King Edward's fame with prisoner kings." ·

The manuscript-correction here is *train* for " fame."

P. 476. In the subsequent passage,—

> " Playing the mouse in absence of the cat,
> To tear and havoc more than she can eat,"

the folios have *tame*, and the quartos *spoil*, for " tear."
" Tear," which was conjecturally placed in the text, is supported by an emendation in the folio, 1632, where *teare* for
" tame" is written in the margin.

In the next line but one, the old corrector seems to have
taken " crush'd" in the sense of *compelled;* while for " but,"
of the old copies, he has substituted *not*, a misprint of the
most frequent occurrence :—

> " Yet that is *not* a crush'd necessity," &c.

In the last line but one of this page, for " sorts," the plausible
alteration is *state :*—

> " They have a king and officers of *state*."

P. 477. The line, as it has always been printed,—

> " Come to one mark ; as many ways meet in one town,"

is obviously overloaded, and the corrector of the folio, 1632,
gives it, with the context, thus :—

> " As many arrows, loosed several ways,
> Come to one mark ; as many ways *unite ;*
> As many fresh streams meet in one salt sea," &c.

Thus the repetition of the word " meet," in two succeeding
lines, is avoided ; but it may still be a question, whether

Shakespeare might not wish here to vary the regularity of his lines by interposing one of twelve syllables. Two lines lower, "And in one purpose," is amended to "*End* in one purpose," precisely the same literal error that was committed in "All's Well that Ends Well," vol. ii. p. 252. See also Vol. p. 161.

P. 479. From two stage-directions it appears that the tun of tennis balls, sent by the Dauphin, was exhibited and opened by Exeter on the stage, in sight of the audience: *Show it*, and *Open it*, are written in the margin of the folio, 1632.

A striking change is made in some lines where Henry refers to his intended visit to his kingdom of France, which he affects to prefer to that of England:—

> " I will keep my state,
> Be like a king, and show my sail of greatness,
> When I do rouse me in my throne of France."

The word "sail" here has little meaning, and will certainly seem to have less when we mention the word proposed in the place of it :—

> " I will keep my state,
> Be like a king, and show my *soul* of greatness,
> When I do rouse me in my throne of France."

We cannot believe that this emendation will be disputed : it is that of the corrector of the folio, 1632.

P. 480. In the following, as in many other instances, the substitution of a single letter, makes a great improvement. The King is urging the utmost expedition of preparation for the invasion of France, and, as the passage has invariably been printed, he says,—

> " Therefore, let our proportions for these wars
> Be soon collected, and all things thought upon
> That may with reasonable swiftness add
> More feathers to our wings."

Now "reasonable swiftness" was not at all what he wished, but instant dispatch ; and we ought indubitably to read,—

> " That may with *seasonable* swiftness add
> More feathers to our wings."

The greater the speed, the more *seasonable* for the purpose of the speaker.

ACT II.

P. 480. In the third line of the Chorus, we are told to read, not "Now thrive the armourers," &c., but "Now *strive* the armourers," &c., in reference to the vast exertions they were making in preparations for the army about to embark at Southampton. This, we feel convinced, was the poet's word, who was not at all contemplating the profit the armourers would reap from the expedition :—

> " Now *strive* the armourers, and honour's thought
> Reigns solely in the breast of every man."

P. 481. Pope completed a defective line in the Chorus as follows :—

> " Th' abuse of distance, while we force a play."

" While we" is in no ancient copy ; and the old corrector of the folio, 1632, informs us that the words wanting were not those, for he puts it,—

> " Th' abuse of distance, *and so* force a play."

SCENE I.

P. 482. In Nym's speech, the words, "there shall be smiles," are altered to, "there shall be *smites*," *i. e.* blows, which exactly accords with Farmer's suggestion, and *smites*, he adds, is used in this way in the midland counties of England.

In Nym's next speech, at the top of the next page, the old corrector has "tired *jade*," instead of "tired *name*" of the folios. The quartos read "tired *mare*," which is unquestionably to be preferred to *name*, and, probably, to *jade*.

SCENE II.

P. 488. By too earnest an anxiety to follow the old copies, an evident misprint, which could nevertheless be reconciled to fitness by ingenuity, has been preserved. It is in one of the King's speeches at Southampton, ordering the enlargement of a drunkard who had railed on him, and the passage has always been thus printed :—

"It was excess of wine that set him on,
And on his more advice, we pardon him."

Our is substituted for "his," in the folio, 1632 ; it was on the King's "more advice," and not on that of the prisoner, that he was to be set at liberty.　On the same page, the King inquires, as it has always stood,—

"Who are the late commissioners?"

which has been strained by Monk Mason to mean, who are the "lately appointed commissioners?" but the old corrector shows that "late commissioners" was a misprint, or a mishearing, for "*state* commissioners"—the commissioners who were to be in charge of the state during the absence of the King in France.

SCENE III.

P. 493.　We are sorry to be obliged to part with Theobald's fanciful emendation in Mrs. Quickly's description of the death of Falstaff, "for his nose was as sharp as a pen, and a' babbled of green fields," founded upon the following words in the old copies, never understood, and containing two misprints, which we shall point out presently on the authority of the corrector of the folio, 1632—"for his nose was as sharp as a pen and a table of green fields."　The mention of "a pen" and "a table," might have led to the detection of the error: writing-tables were no doubt at that period often covered with green cloth ; and it is to the sharpness of a pen, as seen in strong relief on a table so covered, that Mrs. Quickly likens the nose of the dying wit and philosopher—"for his nose was as sharp as a pen *on* a table of green *frieze.*"　The emendation is merely *on* for "and," and *frieze* for "fields ;" and it is found in the margin of the folio, 1632. Pope's ridiculous suggestion respecting "a table of Greenfields," whom he supposed (there is no extraneous syllable to countenance the notion) to have been the property man of the theatre, has long been exploded ; and such, we apprehend, must now be the fate of other proposals in connexion with this obviously corrupt passage.

SCENE IV.

P. 497.　We cannot hesitate to believe that the line,—

s

" Whiles that his mountain sire, on mountain standing,"

is corrupt ; and a manuscript-correction in the folio, 1632, shows that it ought to be read, in accordance with a previous line, descriptive of the same persons and scene, on p. 474,—

" Whiles that his *mighty* sire, on mountain standing," &c.

The copyist or the printer blundered, and put "mountain" twice over in the same line.

ACT III.

P. 500. In the Chorus, describing the embarkation and sailing of Henry V. from Southampton, we read,—

> " Behold the threaden sails,
> Borne with th' invisible and creeping wind,
> Draw the huge bottoms through the furrow'd sea."

It is true that, in a certain sense, the sails of a ship may be said to be "borne" by the wind ; but the old corrector supplies us with a word which, as it is more picturesque, as well as appropriate, we may confidently attribute to the poet :—

> " Behold the threaden sails,
> *Blown* with th' invisible and creeping wind,
> Draw the huge bottoms through the furrow'd sea."

SCENE II.

P. 503. It is evident, from mere perusal, that the fragments of ballads quoted by Pistol and the Boy, in the beginning of this scene, are imperfectly given. Without thinking it necessary here to quote the ordinary text, we will subjoin the manner in which the dialogue, containing the extracts, ought to be conducted, according to the old corrector of the folio, 1632 :—

> " *Pistol.* The plain song is most just, for humours do abound:
> Knocks go and come
> *To all and some,*
> God's vassals *feel the same,*
> And sword and shield
> In bloody field
> Do win immortal fame.

Boy. Would I were in an alehouse in London! I would give all my fame for a pot of ale and safety.

Pistol. And I

> If wishes would prevail with me,
> My purpose should not fail with me,
> But thither would I *now*.

Boy.   *And* as duly,
> But not as truly,
> As bird doth sing on bough."

It will be easy to compare the above with the words as usually printed, and there can be little doubt that the old corrector had access to some means of information which we do not now possess. We give the words he supplies in Italics, but the whole appears as prose in the folios, and there is no trace of it in the quarto editions.

SCENE III.

P. 507. The second folio absurdly has,—

> " Array'd in *games* like to the prince of friends,"

instead of "array'd in flames" of the first folio ; but the old corrector makes them agree. On the next page he corrects " Desire the locks," as it stands in both folios, to " *Defile* the locks," which was Pope's manifest improvement.

SCENE IV.

P. 509. This entire French scene, between Katharine and her female attendant, is struck out by the corrector of the folio, 1632, who did not venture to offer any changes in the many misprints.

SCENE VI.

P. 516. Gower is speaking of counterfeit and begging soldiers, who pretend to have seen great service, and observes of them, that they study perfectly military phrases, "which they trick up with new-tuned oaths." For "new-tuned oaths," the old corrector assures us, with every appearance of truth, that we should read " new-*coined* oaths."

SCENE VII.

P. 519. The Dauphin, vehement in praise of his horse, exclaims, "He bounds from the earth as if his entrails were hairs," which Warburton explains by an allusion to tennis-balls, which were stuffed with hair; but the misprint in the folios was occasioned by the wrong use of the aspirate, for a marginal note in the folio, 1632, most plausibly substitutes *air* for "hairs," and therefore reads, "He bounds from the earth, as if his entrails were *air*."

ACT IV. SCENE I.

P. 528. A question has arisen whether Fluellen's injunction to Gower ought to be to "speak fewer," as it stands in the old copies, or to "speak *lower*," according to the ordinary phrase. The manuscript-corrector alters "fewer" to *lower*.

P. 533. A line in the King's soliloquy,—

"What is thy soul of adoration?"

has hitherto presented insurmountable difficulties to the commentators. Henry is descanting upon the vanity of regal accompaniments, maintaining that ceremony is all that distinguishes a monarch from a subject, and, apostrophising ceremony, he asks,—

"What are thy rents? what are thy comings in?
O ceremony! show me but thy worth!
What is thy soul of adoration?"

The old corrector points out this last line as having been misprinted; and reading it as follows, the whole dispute between Johnson, Steevens, and Malone, seems at an end :—

"O ceremony! show me but thy worth :
What is thy soul *but adulation?*"

which is strongly supported by the whole context, and especially by two lines that follow almost immediately :—

"Think'st thou the fiery fever will go out
With titles blown from adulation?"

Therefore, the answer, when Henry asks what is the worth of ceremony, is what he himself supplies, that the soul of ceremony is nothing but adulation.

P. 534. We may probably accept the next emendation in the same soliloquy. The King is comparing the happiness and sound slumbers of a slave with the restless nights of a king; the former, according to the universally received text,—

> " Gets him to rest, cramm'd with distressful bread ;"

but if the bread he ate were " distressful," if it were earned with misery and suffering, the simile would not hold ; so that we may infer that " distressful" was not Shakespeare's word. According to a manuscript-correction in the folio, 1632, the epithet was misprinted, and we ought to read,—

> " Gets him to rest, cramm'd with *distasteful* bread ;"

that is to say, bread which was abundant, and well relished by the humble, but which, from its coarseness, would be *distasteful* to kings and princes.

SCENE III.

P. 542. A passage in which the King supposes that the dead bodies of the English, left in France, will putrify and infect the air, and thus pursue their enmity to the inhabitants, has never been properly understood, because never properly worded ; it has been thus given in ancient as well as modern editions :—

> " Mark, then, abounding valour in our English ;
> That, being dead, like to the bullet's grazing,
> Break out into a second course of mischief,
> Killing in relapse of mortality."

The simile of the bullet's grazing from one object, which it destroys, to another, which it also wounds, shows that we ought not to read " abounding," but " *rebounding* valour" of the English ; and that, instead of " relapse," which ill suits the rhythm of the line, we ought to read *reflex*, in allusion to the power of the bullet to injure, when reflected backward from the object first struck. The four lines, therefore, ought to be printed in this manner :—

> " Mark, then, *rebounding* valour in our English,
> That, being dead, like to the bullet's grazing,
> Break out into a second course of mischief,
> Killing in *reflex* of mortality."

Theobald printed " *a bounding* valour," and saw the meaning of the poet, as far as that word is concerned, though he did not give the right emendation ; but Malone poorly imagined that " abounding" was only to be taken as *abundant ;* and neither of them had any notion that " relapse" was a misprint for *reflex.* Both these changes are made by the corrector of the folio, 1632.

SCENE VI.

P. 548. Exeter giving a description of the deaths of York and Suffolk, speaking of the former, says, as the text has been always repeated,—

> " In which array, brave soldier, doth he lie,
> Larding the plain."

Steevens illustrates the word " larding" by a passage in Henry IV. Part I. Act II. Scene 2, where it is humorously said of Falstaff that he " lards the lean earth as he walks along." No quotation could well be less apposite : Falstaff larded the lean earth by the perspiration which fell from his huge carcase ; but it is no where said that the Duke of York was obese, nor have we any reason to suppose that it might be appropriately said of him after death that he " *larded* the plain ;" the true word is thus given in manuscript :—

> " In which array, brave soldier, doth he lie
> *Loading* the plain."

SCENE VII.

P. 551. Montjoy, the herald, after the battle comes to ask leave on behalf of the French to select and bury their dead ; but hitherto the line has been given as if he asked leave to " book" the dead, and as if the French had been in a condition to take and note down a particular account of them. The fact is, that *look*, in the sense of search for, or select, has been misprinted " book :"—

> " I come to thee for charitable licence,
> That we may wander o'er this bloody field,
> To *look* our dead, and then to bury them."

The manuscript-corrector merely altered the first letter of
"book ;" and the use of *look*, as above, is frequent in all our
old writers. It was an English herald who made out a statement of the killed, wounded, and prisoners on both sides,
and afterwards presented it to the King.

ACT V.

P. 559. In the Chorus which opens this Act, the first
words are altered from " Vouchsafe to those," to "Vouchsafe
all those ;" and in the next line, instead of "and of such as
have," we are told to read, "and *for* such as have."   A more
material change was made when the celebrated lines, which
relate to the return of the Earl of Essex from Ireland, were
struck out.   We may easily believe that they would be distasteful at any time after that nobleman's execution, but we
may presume that they were not recited in the time of the
corrector of the folio, 1632, if only because they could then
have no application.   They form, however, one of the least
disputable, as well as one of the most important notes of time,
to be found in any of the plays of our great dramatist.

SCENE II.

P. 565. The Duke of Burgundy, in the course of his long
harangue, asks why peace should not, as formerly, in France,—

> " put up her lovely visage ? "

An awkward phrase arising, no doubt, from the misprint of
one short word for another, and the manuscript-corrector
therefore has,—

> " Should not in this best garden of the world,
> Our fertile France, *lift* up her lovely visage ? "

This change may, nevertheless, have been proposed as a mere
matter of taste.

P. 567. A trifling error of the press has been committed
in the last line of the speech of the French King, in reply
to Henry's request that he would answer, whether he re-

fused or accepted the articles of peace proposed. As always printed, the passage has stood,—

> " We will suddenly
> Pass our accept, and peremptory answer."

"Pass our accept" seems to have been taken for "pass our acceptance," but what the French King intends to say is, that, after further consideration, he will either pass by articles to which he may object, or accept others which seem admissible : he says,—

> " Pleaseth your grace
> To appoint some of your council presently
> To sit with us once more, with better heed
> To re-survey them, we will suddenly
> Pass, *or* accept, and peremptory answer."

The blunder here was merely " our" for *or*, and this use of the word " pass" was common. A few lines lower, we may feel assured that the line,—

> " Shall see advantageable for our dignity,"

was written by the poet,—

> " Shall see advantage for our dignity ;"

and, accordingly, *able* is erased by the corrector of the folio, 1632.

P. 571 The corner of the leaf, containing the interview between Henry V. and Katharine, has been torn away, and there is here only one emendation that demands notice : it occurs not far from the end of the scene, where the King observes, " I dare not swear thou lovest me ; yet my blood begins to flatter me thou dost, notwithstanding the poor and untempering effect of my visage." Warburton's note is " Certainly *untempting ;*" and he was right, for a marginal correction directs us to read *untempting* for " untempering."

P. 573. All the folios have, " girdled with maiden walls, that war hath entered," a negative having been accidentally omitted ; modern editors have invariably inserted " never ;" but, although the difference is not material, the true word was probably *not*, " that war hath *not* entered," because the old corrector places it in the margin.

THE FIRST PART

OF

KING HENRY VI.

ACT I. SCENE I.

Vol. v. p. 9. The subsequent imperfect couplet closes Bed-
ford's speech just before the entrance of the Messenger :—

> "A far more glorious star thy soul will make,
> Than Julius Cæsar on bright ———— "

Johnson proposed to fill the blank with Berenice, which, in
any point of view, could hardly be right. Malone was of
opinion that the blank had been left, because the copyist
could not read the name; it is improbable that the copyist
could not read the name, and still more improbable, that,
even if he could not read it, he would have hesitated in
putting down something, whether right or wrong. The corrector of the folio, 1632, wrote *Cassiopé* in the margin,
which, as far as regards the measure, answers the purpose;
but from whence he derived the information, it is impossible to conjecture: he therefore reads,—

> "Than Julius Cæsar on bright Cassiopé."

P. 10. In the following line, the folio, 1632, omits an important word,—

> "Reignier, duke of Anjou, doth take his part."

The old corrector inserted "take," which, perhaps, he found
in the folio, 1623; at all events, it was not necessary for him
to go to any other authority for it, if even to that.

P. 12. The line has always created a difficulty, where it is said of Sir John Fastolfe,—

> " He being in the vaward, plac'd behind," &c.,

which is a contradiction in terms, unless we suppose, with Monk Mason, that the English army being attacked from behind, the rear became the van. A manuscript-correction makes it evident that "vaward" was a misprint for *rear-ward* :—

> " He being in the *rearward*, plac'd behind
> With purpose to relieve and follow them."

P. 13. The ensuing emendation is one of those which may have been introduced as a mere matter of taste, although it seems more likely that *cause* should have been the poet's word, considering how ill "make" sounds in the place where it occurs :—

> " Ten thousand soldiers with me I will take,
> Whose bloody deeds shall make all Europe quake."

The old corrector erases "make," and substitutes *cause.*

It was Monk Mason's excellent proposal, that the Bishop of Winchester should say, at the end of this scene,—

> "The King from Eltham I intend to *steal*,"
> And sit at chiefest stern of public weal."

The old copies have invariably,—

> " The King from Eltham I intend to send ;"

but there is little doubt that a rhyme was meant, and that the copyist or compositor caught the termination of "send" from the preceding verb. The corrector of the second folio wrote *steal* in the margin, and struck out "send ;" and we shall see hereafter that in several other places he restores rhymes, which had either been obscured by corruption, or, possibly, changed, because audiences in his time did not so well relish the recurrence of same-sounding words.

SCENE II.

P. 14. When the Dauphin observes, in reference to the disastrous state of English affairs in France,—

> " At pleasure here we lie near Orleans,
> Otherwhiles, the famish'd English, like pale ghosts,
> Faintly besiege us one hour in a month ;"

we may be satisfied that the second line, for the sake of measure and meaning, ought to run,—

> " *The whiles* the famish'd English, like pale ghosts," &c.

The correction in the folio, 1632, is precisely this ; and it is surprising that so small, so obvious, and so easy a corruption as "otherwhiles" should have remained till now in the text of this drama.

Lower down in the page occurs another decided blunder, which has never been noticed, nor set right. The French generals have been ridiculing the forbearance of the English in not daring to press the siege, and at last the Dauphin declares his determination to attack the enemy, and compel them to raise it :—

> " Sound, sound alarum ! we will rush on them.
> Now for the honour of the forlorn French."

Why should he call the French "forlorn" at the very moment of their triumph ?   It is an indisputable error:—

> " Now for the honour of the *forborne* French,"

must be the true word, and it is furnished in manuscript. The French had been *forborne* by the English, because the latter were not in a condition to press the siege.   The word is printed "forlorne" in the folios, and the old corrector had nothing more to do than to alter the letter *l* to *b*.   In the last line he puts *flee* for "fly," making it rhyme with "me" in the preceding line.

P. 16. There seems no ground for preserving an evident transposition in

> " Heaven and our Lady gracious hath it pleas'd,"

instead of "our gracious Lady," as it is marked by the corrector of the folio, 1632, unless "gracious" be to be taken as *graciously*.

P. 17. The following seems to have been written originally as a rhyming couplet ; it occurs at the end of the speech where the Dauphin challenges Joan of Arc to the combat :—

> " And, if thou vanquishest, thy words are true,
> Otherwise I renounce all confidence."

The last line is almost ridiculously prosaic, and the change

recommended by a note in the folio, 1632, is small, but a decided improvement :—

> " And, if thou vanquishest, thy words are true,
> *Or* I renounce all confidence *in you.*"

SCENE III.

P. 19. At the heads of some of the scenes in this play, we
are, rather unusually, informed of the place of action. The
corrector of the folio, 1632, tells us that this angry interview between the Duke of Gloucester and Beaufort takes
place *at the Tower;* but it would have been more correct to
have said, near the Tower : *London* is also added, to show
that the scene had been removed from France. The next
scene is supposed to be in *France* again, and that word is
therefore placed in the margin. The second scene of Act III.
is at Rouen, or *Roane,* as it was spelt of old ; and at the
head of the third scene we are told that the stage *still* represents *Roane.* This circumstance may, perhaps, be taken as
indicating that peculiar pains were bestowed upon this play,
and the alterations of different kinds are sometimes even
more minute than elsewhere.

SCENE IV.

P. 25. It has been most strangely made a question by
Steevens, whether when " vile-esteem'd" is misprinted in the
folios, "*pil'd* esteemed" (" vile" being frequently spelt *vild* in
the time of Shakespeare), the poet did not mean that Talbot
complained that he had been *philistined.* There is not the
slightest ground for any such notion : Shakespeare, as Malone
remarked, uses the very word " vile-esteemed" in his sonnets,
and the manuscript-corrector of the folio, 1632, states that he
also used it in the subsequent, which is the disputed line,—

> " Rather than I would be so vile-esteem'd."

P. 26. The eight lines following—

> " In thirteen battles Salisbury o'ercame,"

are struck out, most likely for the purpose of shortening
Talbot's harangue. A leaf is wanting in the corrected copy
of the second folio, between p. 100 and p. 103.

ACT II. SCENE III.

P. 38. Talbot's imperfect line,—

" That will I show you presently,"

is completed by the corrector by the insertion of the word
lady, which, no doubt, in some way escaped from the text :—

"That will I show you, *lady*, presently;"

and then, *winding his horn*, his soldiers appear.

SCENE IV.

P. 41. It is enough to state that the misprint of *fashion*
for "faction," which Warburton pertinaciously refused to
correct, is set right in manuscript in the margin of the
second folio.

P. 42. The line, as constantly printed,—

" He bears him on the place's privilege,"

referring to the Temple, also appears to contain an error of
the press. Plantagenet is speaking of Somerset, and of the
insults he had offered to Suffolk ; and, according to the corrected folio, 1632, we ought to read,—

" He *braves* him on the place's privilege."

Consistently with this emendation, Plantagenet, on the next
page, exclaims,—

" How am I *brav'd*, and must perforce endure it !"

Lower down on the same page, instead of

" A thousand souls to death and deadly night,"

the old corrector has " *Ten* thousand souls," &c. ; and "a
thousand souls" seems a very insignificant number to be pro-
phesied on such an occasion, as likely to fall in the Wars of
the Roses.

SCENE V.

P. 47. Theobald made, and most modern editors have
adopted, a needless change in the text of the old copies, at

the conclusion of Plantagenet's soliloquy after the death of old Mortimer :—

> " And therefore haste I to the Parliament,
> Either to be restored to my blood,
> Or make my will th' advantage of my good."

The word Theobald altered was " will," which he converted to *ill;* but the mistake is in a different word, " advantage," which the corrector states ought to be *advancer;* he leaves " will" as it stands in all old copies, and gives the last line of the quotation thus :—

> " Or make my will th' *advancer* of my good :"

i. e. if he be unable to procure from Parliament the reversal of the attainder of his blood, he resolves to make his own will the advancer of his own interests. The proposed emendation of *ill* for " will," by Theobald, was merely arbitrary and fanciful.

ACT III. SCENE I.

P. 49. Whether such were the case with the ensuing emendation by the old corrector, we can only speculate from probabilities : there are two points in its favour, *viz.* that both the context and the measure of the line call for the alteration. It occurs in Winchester's answer to Gloucester's accusation of covetousness, ambition, and pride :—

> " If I were covetous, ambitious, *proud,*
> As he will have me, how am I so poor ? "

The common reading is, " or perverse," for *proud;* but, in the first place, Gloucester has not charged the prelate so much with perverseness, as with pride,—

> " As very infants prattle of thy pride ;"

and, in the next place, *proud* exactly fits the measure, while " or perverse" overloads it by two syllables. We may, therefore, perhaps conclude that the emendation in the folio, 1632, was in some way authorized.

P. 51. The same may, we think, be said of the next

emendation in the King's appeal to Winchester, which, as ordinarily printed, ends with these lines :—

> " Who should be pitiful, if you are not?
> Or who should study to prefer a peace,
> If holy churchmen take delight in broils?"

For "prefer a peace," the corrector of the folio, 1632, has "*preserve* a peace," peace having been broken by the affray between the adherents of Gloucester and Winchester. "Prefer" is spelt *preferre* in the old copies, and may easily have been mistaken for *preserve*, when written with the long *s*. At the same time, it must be allowed that "prefer a peace" is perfectly intelligible, and well warranted.

When Gloucester, just afterwards, offers Winchester his hand, a manuscript stage-direction informs us that *he scorns it* at first, but subsequently *takes it*.

P. 53. We need not doubt that the word so awkwardly recurring in the two subsequent lines, was a misprint: it is in Plantagenet's speech, thanking the King for restoring him to his blood :—

> " Thy humble servant vows obedience
> And humble service, till the point of death."

The corrector writes *honour'd* in the margin, instead of the first "humble :" and, bearing in mind that Plantagenet had just been raised again to honour by the act of grace of the King, we may willingly accept this representation of the text of our author, and read in future,—

> " Thy *honour'd* servant vows obedience
> And humble service, till the point of death."

Exeter's soliloquy, at the end of the scene, is struck out, as if not wanted.

SCENE II.

P. 57. Talbot, enraged at Joan's success in capturing Rouen, calls her,—

> " Foul fiend of France, and hag of all despite!"

"Hag of all despite," at least, sounds tamely, and a marginal note in the folio, 1632, warrants us in giving the line much increase of energy :—

> " Foul fiend of France, and hag of *hell*'s despite!"

P. 59. Burgundy thus addresses Talbot :—

> " Warlike and martial Talbot, Burgundy
> Enshrines thee in his heart."

To say that Talbot is "warlike and martial," is mere tauto-logy, an offence of which Shakespeare is rarely guilty ; and, as the old corrector assures us that "martial" has been mis-printed, we may gladly welcome his striking improvement of the text :—

> " Warlike and *matchless* Talbot, Burgundy
> Enshrines thee in his heart."

SCENE III.

P. 62. We give the ensuing lines as they are corrected in the folio, 1632; it is the opening of Joan's speech to seduce Burgundy :—

> " Look on thy country, look on fertile France,
> And see *her* cities and *her* towns defac'd
> By wasting ruin of the cruel foe.
> As looks the mother on her *lovely* babe,
> When death doth close his tender dying eyes,
> See, see, the pining malady of France."

The common reading is "the" for *her* in both places, and "lowly" for *lovely :* the last was Warburton's reasonable pro-posal, which ought, we see, to have been adopted, though opposed by Johnson, who treated *lovely* as a needless inno-vation.

SCENE IV.

P. 64. The King, addressing Talbot, observes,—

> " I do remember how my father said,
> A stouter champion never handled sword.
> Long since we were resolved of your truth," &c.

It is clear, as the old corrector instructs us, that the last line ought to be,—

> " Long since we were resolved of *that* truth,"

not merely because Henry is referring to an assertion by his father, which must be universally admitted, but because he follows it up by a statement of the fidelity and merits of Talbot :—

> " Long since we were resolved of your truth,
>   Your faithful service and your toil in war."

To have first applauded Talbot's "truth," and then his "faithful service," would have been repetition, very unlike Shakespeare.

ACT IV. SCENE I.

P. 67. After Talbot has *torn the Garter* (in the words of the manuscript stage-direction) from the leg of Fastolfe, he proceeds to add, that the order had been instituted to reward the deserts of courageous warriors :—

> "Not fearing death, nor shrinking from distress,
>   But always resolute in most extremes."

Such has been the invariable text; but we must feel, when once it is pointed out, that there is an injurious error of the printer in the second line :—

> " But always resolute in *worst* extremes,"

is the word substituted in the margin of the second folio. Lower down, we should hardly hesitate, on the same authority, to change "pretend" to *portend*, when Gloucester asks,—

> " Or doth this churlish superscription
>   Pretend some alteration of good will ?"

" Pretend" answers the purpose ; but *portend* most likely was our great dramatist's word, which he often uses elsewhere.

P. 68. The epithet " envious" in the following line,—

> " This fellow, here, with envious carping tongue,"

is not in the folio, 1632, having, perhaps, accidentally dropped out : the old corrector inserts it ; but whether he obtained it from the folio, 1623, or from some other source, must remain a question. The same remark applies to a line on the next page,—

> " Quiet yourselves, I pray, and be at peace,"

excepting that the corrector of the folio, 1632, inserts " I pray" at the end, instead of in the middle, of the line :

T

perhaps it was so formed in the authority he may have consulted. For

> "Such factious emulations shall arise,"

two lines above, he has "*still* arise," which certainly accords better with the context.

SCENE V.

P. 78. Old Talbot and his son John are contending for the honour of keeping the field, one, by so doing, being certain of destruction, and each is persuading the other to fly. A marginal note in the folio, 1632, instructs us to read *fly* for "bow" in the ensuing lines; and we can hardly doubt that "bow" is a misprint, though we may not be able to account for it: John Talbot speaks :—

> "Flight cannot stain the honour you have won,
> But mine it will, that no exploit have done :
> You fled for vantage, every one will swear,
> But if I bow, they'll say it was for fear.
> There is no hope that ever I will stay,
> If the first hour I shrink, and run away."

There seems no assignable reason why the poet should not have used the word *fly;* and the old corrector informs us that he did use it. When old Talbot returns mortally wounded to the scene (p. 82), it is said, in all modern editions, that he is "supported by a servant ;" the addition to the stage-direction in the folio, 1632, has much greater propriety, for he there is described as entering, *led by a soldier* from the field of battle.

P. 83. The folio, 1632, omits a line in Joan's speech upon this page, *viz.* :—

> "So, rushing in the bowels of the French."

It is supplied by the corrector, perhaps from the folio, 1623 ; but three lines lower he alters,—

> "Of the most bloody nurser of his harms,"

by erasing "most bloody," and writing *still bleeding.* For the evidently imperfect line on the next page,—

> "But tell me whom thou seek'st?"

he gives the following :—

" But tell me *briefly*, whom thou seekest *now ?* "

Just above, he erases " obtain'd," as surplusage, as regards the verse and sense ; but in both the last instances it is by no means clear that Shakespeare intended his verse to be regular.   The list of Talbot's titles is struck out.

Less important variations are frequently noted in this part of the play ; and in one place we have a rhyme restored, which, perhaps, had been lost : it is where Sir W. Lucy demands the bodies of the Talbots, the usual reading being,—

> " Give me their bodies, that I may bear them hence,
> And give them burial, as beseems their worth."

The couplet is thus amended :—

> " Give me their bodies, that I bear them *forth*,
> And give them burial, as beseems their worth."

This change occurs near the close of the Act, where the rhymes are numerous.

ACT V   SCENE I.

P. 86. For " our Christian blood," in Gloster's speech, the corrector of the folio, 1632, has " *much* Christian blood ;" and, lower down, where the Protector recommends the marriage of Henry to the daughter of the Earl of Armagnac, it is said in all the old copies, that that nobleman is " near knit to Charles," instead of " near *kin* to Charles," as we find it in the margin, quite consistently with what Gloster says afterwards, that Armagnac is " near kinsman unto Charles."

SCENE III.

P. 90. The introduction to this scene is erroneous in the early impressions, for they represent Burgundy as fighting with La Pucelle, whereas York ought to contend with her. A correction in the folio, 1632, sets this matter right, and adds, what is wanting in modern, as well as ancient, editions, that *York overcomes Joan.*

Capel was justified in transposing three lines near the bottom of this page, where Suffolk lays his hands " gently on the tender side " of Margaret, and afterwards kisses her fingers. The old corrector always indicates an error of this kind by figures, and 1, 2, 3 in the margin instructs us to read Suffolk's speech thus :—

> " For I will touch thee but with reverent hands,
> And lay them gently on thy tender side.
> I kiss these fingers for eternal peace, &c. [*kissing.*"

P. 91. Much of Suffolk's speech is in rhyme ; and when he exclaims, as Margaret is about to depart,—

> " O, stay !—I have no power to let her pass ;
> My hand would free her, but my heart says—no,"

we might be tolerably certain, even without the correction in the margin of the folio, 1632, that the lines ought to be thus printed :—

> " O, stay !—I have no power to let her *go ;*
> My hand would free her, but my heart says—no."

The two last lines of this speech have given trouble to the commentators, which would have been avoided had they been able to detect the blunder of the printer or of the copyist, which the corrector distinctly points out. The text in the old editions, is this :—

> " Aye ; beauty's princely majesty is such,
> Confounds the tongue and makes the senses rough."

Sir Thomas Hanmer printed *crouch* for " rough ;" and Malone was obliged to pass over the passage by saying that the meaning of " rough" is not " very obvious." Read with the aid of the marginal notes in the folio, 1632, and the obscurity is at an end :—

> " Aye ; beauty's princely majesty is such,
> Confounds the tongue, and *mocks* the sense *of touch.*"

Here, again, who is to determine whether the preceding emendation were derived from some good authority, or whether it was only a lucky guess on the part of the individual through whose hands this copy of the folio, 1632, passed ? Certain it is, that not one of the many editors of Shakespeare were ever so fortunate as to stumble on the meaning, which is thus rendered obvious, while, at the same time, the intended rhyme is preserved : the princely majesty of beauty confounded the power of speech, and mocked all who would attempt to touch it. The printer, not understanding the copy he was composing, seems to have put down words at random, and to have made nonsense of a beautiful and delicate expression.

P. 92. By the same authority we are assured that another portion of this scene between Suffolk and Margaret is especially corrupt. We will first give the text as represented in all editions, and follow it by the text as recommended in manuscript-corrections:—

> "*Marg.* Tush! women have been captivate ere now.
> *Suff.* Lady, wherefore talk you so?
> *Marg.* I cry you mercy, 'tis but *quid pro quo.*
> *Suff.* Say, gentle princess, would you not suppose
> Your bondage happy, to be made a queen?
> *Marg.* To be a queen in bondage is more vile
> Than is a slave in base servility,
> For princes should be free.
> *Suff.*   And so shall you,
> If happy England's royal king be free."

All this appears to have been mangled, both as regards meaning, metre, and rhyme. We now give this part of the dialogue as it stands in a corrected state in the folio, 1632, where the fitness of every thing seems restored:—

> "*Marg.* Tush! women have been captivate ere now.
> *Suff.* Lady, *pray tell me,* wherefore talk you so?
> *Marg.* I cry you mercy, 'tis but *quid pro quo.*
> *Suff.* Say, gentle princess, would you not *then ween*
> Your bondage happy, to be made a queen?
> *Marg.* A queen in bondage is more vile *to me*
> Than is a slave in base servility,
> For princes should be free.
> *Suff.*   And so shall you,
> If happy England's royal king be *true.*"

We have, as usual, marked by Italic type the words written in the margin, which we are willing to think were those of our great poet, his original language having been disfigured by performers, printers, and copyists. Other portions of the same scene are marked by the old corrector as more or less defective.

P. 95. The suggestion thrown out in note 6, that "mad" is to be read *mid* in the following passage,—

> "Bethink thee on the virtues that surmount,
> Mad natural graces that extinguish art,"

is fully borne out by a correction in the folio, 1632, the

meaning being, that the virtues of Margaret (with whom Suffolk is secretly in love) are pre-eminent 'mid the natural graces by which she is adorned.

SCENE IV.

P. 100. The old corrector, by the insertion of *r* for *o*, changed "poison'd" to *prison'd,* in the following passage :—

> "Speak, Winchester; for boiling choler chokes
> The hollow passage of my poison'd voice."

Pope printed *prison'd,* and appears thus to have arrived at the author's meaning, though some more modern editors have adhered to "poison'd."

P. 101. We have here another of the many emendations rendered necessary by the mistake of the person who wrote by his ear the manuscript used by the printer. It is the last of any consequence in this play, and it occurs at the very close of the scene between the English and French commanders, when a peace is negotiated. All parties are agreed upon a league of amity, and York, addressing the Dauphin, says,—

> "Hang up your ensigns, let your drums be still,
> For here we entertain a solemn peace,"

the corrector of the folio, 1632, reads the last line thus :—

> "For here we *interchange* a solemn peace."

The agreement for a peace being mutual: it cannot be said, however, that the change is imperatively called for, though recommended on strong presumptive evidence.

THE SECOND PART

OF

KING HENRY VI.

ACT I. SCENE I.

P. 112. A question has arisen whether to read,—

> " And was his highness in his infancy
> Crowned in Paris, in despite of foes?"

or as follows :—

> " And hath his highness in his infancy
> Been crown'd in Paris, in despite of foes?"

Some editors have given the couplet in one way, and some in another ; but the old corrector of the folio, 1632, informs us that the last is the true reading, *been* having probably dropped out at the commencement of the second line.

P. 116. York introduces a simile of pirates sharing pillage in the presence of the owner of it,—

> " While as the silly owner of the goods
> Weeps over them, and wrings his hapless hands."

A correction in the folio, 1632, instructs us to erase "hapless" in favour of *helpless*, which certainly seems the fitter epithet ; but it is impossible to maintain that "hapless" does not fit the place, and might not be the poet's word. The allusion to Althea's brand, in four lines just below, is for some reason struck out.

SCENE III.

P. 121. Johnson, Steevens, Tollet, and Hawkins have all wasted time and space upon a mere error of the printer, or of the copyist. The first Petitioner says, as has been universally represented,—

> " My masters, let's stand close : my lord protector will come this way by and by, and then we may deliver our supplications in the quill."

The puzzle has been as to the meaning of "in the quill," and each of the commentators had a different notion upon the point. The several Petitioners were to deliver their supplications to Suffolk in succession, one after another, and "the quill" ought, indisputably, to be *sequel*, used ignorantly for sequence,—

> " My lord protector will come this way by and by, and then we may deliver our supplications in *sequel*."

On the next page, the beginning of Peter's second speech is altered to " That my master was," instead of *mistress*, as it stood, absurdly enough, till Tyrwhitt proposed the change, which is fully warranted by a note in the margin of the folio, 1632.

P. 124. According to the old corrector, Suffolk's speech to the Queen, before the entrance of the King, &c., ought to end in a rhyme :—

> "So, one by one, we will weed all *the realm*,
> And you yourself shall steer the happy helm."

This reads easily and naturally enough ; but the folios make the first line end with " at last," very lamely and tamely.

P. 127. Pope was quite right in printing *fast*, for "far" of the old copies, in the following line, where Buckingham is speaking of Eleanor :—

> " She'll gallop far enough to her destruction."

We find *fast* in the margin, and "far" struck out. The adherence to "far" was, of course, occasioned by the desire, in all possible cases, to abide by the early editions.

It may be mentioned, that in the corrected folio, 1632, the Acts and Scenes are noted in manuscript (no such divisions being made in print), and as a new scene (4) is made to commence with the entrance of the King, York, Somerset, &c., on p. 124, another scene, numbered 5, contains the incantations, &c., of Margery Jourdain, Southwell, Bolingbroke, &c., before Eleanor. In all modern editions this is more properly represented as

SCENE IV.

P. 130. For "the silent of the night," the corrector has "the *silence* of the night," which is the very word used in the old drama from which this play was mainly taken. For "break up their graves," he reads, "break *ope* their graves," which was also, most likely, right. Among the manuscript stage-directions is one which shows that while *Bolingbroke questions* the Spirit, raised by the Witch, *Southwell writes the answers.* When the former dismisses the Spirit, called up to ascertain and declare the truth, he exclaims, "*False* fiend, avoid," the impropriety of which is evident, and the manuscript-correction is, "*Foul* fiend, avoid."

ACT II. SCENE I.

P. 133. Gloster, addressing the Cardinal, says,—

> "Churchmen so hot? good uncle, hide such malice ;
> With such holiness can you do it."

The second line, as it stands in all the early copies, is imperfect and prosaic ; the corrector of the folio, 1632, states that two small words have been omitted, and his emendation is better than either of those offered by Warburton and Johnson : he gives the two lines thus :—

> "Churchmen so hot? good uncle, hide such malice ;
> *And* with such holiness you *well* can do it."

SCENE III.

P. 144. The whole of what passes just before Gloster, who has been required to give up his staff of office, quits the scene, is in rhyme ; but there is one line which has nothing to answer to it, and we meet with the corresponding line, as an important addition, in the margin. There are also two emendations deserving notice in the preceding speech by Queen Margaret, and the whole of this part of the play runs as follows in the folio, 1632, the new portions being printed, as usual, in Italic type:—

> " *Q. Mar.* I see no reason why a king of years
>   Should be protected, like a child, by *peers.*
>   God and King Henry govern England's *helm,*
>   Give up your staff, Sir, and the King his realm.
> *Glo.* My staff?—here, noble Henry, is my staff:
>   *To think I fain would keep it makes me laugh.*
>   As willingly I do the same resign,
>   As e'er thy father Henry made it mine," &c.

There appears no sufficient reason for disbelieving that these changes and additions might be made on some independent authority.

Lower down, a striking misprint occurs, and is set right by the old corrector to the great improvement of the passage: the couplet has always thus been given:—

> " Thus droops this lofty pine, and hangs its sprays;
>   Thus Eleanor's pride dies in her youngest days."

Now, as Monk Mason observes, "Eleanor was certainly not a young woman;" and in order to overcome the difficulty, he compelled "her" to refer to "pride," and not to Eleanor; but the printer was in fault for mistaking the poet's word:—

> " Thus Eleanor's pride dies in her *proudest* days,"

is a form of expression peculiarly like Shakespeare, and perfectly consistent with the situation and character of the Duchess of Gloster.

ACT III. SCENE I.

P. 155. Malone, who was generally reluctant to vary from the ancient editions, could not refuse to adopt an emendation proposed by Steevens in the following passage, as it stands in the folios:—

> " My lord of Gloster, 'tis my special hope,
>   That you will clear yourself from all suspense."

Steevens printed *suspects* for "suspense," and the corrector of
the second folio writes *suspect* (not *suspects*) in the margin.
Nevertheless, "suspense" may be strained to a meaning, certainly not adverse to the poet's intention, though we may
feel morally sure that *suspect* must have come from his pen.

P. 162. Regarding the next emendation, recommended in
manuscript in the folio, 1632, we need not doubt, seeing that
both sense and metre call for the alteration. It occurs in
York's soliloquy, where he congratulates himself that his
enemies are playing his game by dispatching him to Ireland
to conduct a large force against the rebels : he says, as the
passage has been amended,—

> "Whiles I in Ireland *march* a mighty band,
> I will stir up in England some black storm," &c.

The ordinary reading has been, "nourish a mighty band,"
which we may conclude was an error of the press,—"nourish"
for *march*. If the former could be accepted, as affording, to a
certain extent, the meaning required, it must be rejected on
the score that it mars the versification, unless we consent to
hurry over "nourish" in the time of a monosyllable.

P. 166. The whole of Margaret's speech, after "Be poisonous too, and kill thy forlorn queen," is crossed out ; but
various emendations are made in it notwithstanding, besides
the necessary correction of "Eleanor" to *Margaret* in three
different places. The change in the line, where she is
speaking of the violent winds which drove her back from
England, must not be passed over, inasmuch as "gentle
gusts," of the old copies, seems properly altered in manuscript to *ungentle* gusts :—

> "What did I then, but curs'd th' *ungentle* gusts,
> And he that loos'd them from their brazen caves."

It was because they were *ungentle* that the winds had been
confined in "brazen caves," and had been set at liberty
in order to drive back the ship that conveyed Margaret
to England. The whole context warrants the alteration. It
ought to be added, that Theobald's substitution near the end,
of *witch* for "watch," however plausible, is not authorised
by the old corrector.

P. 169. Malone observed upon the harsh expression, "to

drain" an "ocean of salt tears" on dead Humphrey's face, and Steevens advocated *rain* for "drain." The letter *d* is struck out in the folio, 1632, showing that Steevens was correct in his suspicion of a misprint. On the next page occurs another error of the press, which only applies to the second folio, where "But both of you were vow'd Duke Humphrey's *death*," should, of course, be "Duke Humphrey's foes:" *death* is erased, and "foes" placed in the margin. On p. 171, the same edition omits "send" in the sentence, "and send thy soul to hell," but it was inserted by the pen of the old corrector.

P. 175. He points out a misprint here which we may accept, although, as the word always printed in the old copies may be said to serve the turn, we may, perhaps, pause before we admit the change into the text. It is where Suffolk is cursing his enemies, "Poison be their drink," &c. :—

> " Their chiefest prospect murdering basilisks,
> Their softest touch, as smart as lizards' stings."

Here we are told to read *sharp* for smart," and, independently of greater propriety, it is unquestionable that a careless copyist might easily miswrite or mishear the word. At the close of the same character's speech to the Queen, on the next page, a trifling error has been committed, introducing a gross inelegance of expression, which Shakespeare would most likely have avoided. The text has always been,—

> " Live thou to joy thy life,
> Myself no joy in nought, but that thou liv'st;"

but as amended it runs,—

> " Live thou to joy thy life,
> Myself *to* joy in nought, but that thou liv'st."

The duplication of negatives was, of course, not at all unusual in the time of Shakespeare, but here it seems as injurious as it is needless.

ACT IV.   SCENE I.

P. 180. Discussion has been produced by the subsequent lines, as they stand in the early impressions:—

> " The lives of those which we have lost in fight
>   Be counterpois'd with such a petty sum."

Malone read, " *Cannot* be counterpois'd," &c., and Steevens, perceiving at once that the last line had thus more than the regular number of syllables, proposed to leave out two small words, but without the slightest warrant, printed or manuscript. Note 1 gives a hint of the proper emendation, such, indeed, as we meet with it, in the shortest possible form, in the margin of the folio, 1632 : there the lines are put thus interrogatively,—

> " *Can* lives of those which we have lost in fight
>   Be counterpois'd with such a petty sum ?"

Surely this slight change is unobjectionable, where some change is absolutely necessary.

P. 181. Suffolk's speech to the Captain, beginning, " Obscure and lowly swain" ("lowly" is altered from *lowsy*, as misprinted in the folios), in which he heaps upon him the bitterest reproaches, contains several errors of the press, but they are not important : in Whitmore's inquiry (p. 182), consequent upon Suffolk's abuse,—

> " Speak, captain, shall I stab the forlorn swain ?"

there is, according to the old corrector, a gross blunder ; and certainly the epithet " forlorn," seems strangely applied : it is much more likely that Whitmore should ask,—

> " Speak, captain, shall I stab the *foul-tongued slave ?* "

and such is actually his question, as represented in a manuscript note in the folio, 1632. We cannot believe that the writer of that note was merely indulging his taste, or exercising his fancy. It is to be remarked that the correction of " forlorn" to *foul-tongued*, is in a different ink to that which was used for the correction of " swain" to *slave*. The whole of the Captain's reply to Suffolk, excepting the first five lines, is crossed out.

P. 184. The prefixes in this scene are confused in the folios, especially as regards Suffolk. The line,—

> " Thy words move rage and not remorse in me,"

is, for some reason, erased ; and Suffolk's last speech is made to begin,—

" Come, soldiers, show what cruelty ye can,"

undoubtedly the right distribution of the dialogue.

SCENE II.

P. 186. When Jack Cade enters, the old printed stage-direction states that he is followed by *infinite numbers*, to which the manuscript-corrector adds, *the more the better, and uproar;* meaning, of course, that the rabble was to be represented on the stage as numerously and as riotously as the means of the old theatre would allow. When Cade subsequently knights himself (p. 189), we are told that he *kneels and rises*, and when the Staffords are killed, that he *puts on the armour* of one of them.

SCENE V

P. 195. In all printed copies this scene terminates very flatly with a speech by Lord Scales :—

" Fight for your king, your country, and your lives !
And so farewell, for I must hence again."

It is given as follows by the corrector of the folio, 1632 :—

" Fight for your king, your country, and your lives !
And so farewell : *rebellion never thrives.*"

This rhyme may, possibly, have been a subsequent introduction, for the sake of giving more spirit to the *exit* of Lord Scales, and of enforcing a loyal maxim.

SCENE VIII.

P. 202. Two blunders of some consequence are detected by marginal notes in the folio, 1632, in the address of Old Clifford to the "rabblement" under Cade: he appeals to them, in all editions, ancient and modern, in these terms :—

" What say ye, countrymen ? will ye relent,
And yield to mercy, whilst 'tis offer'd you,
Or let a rabble lead you to your deaths?"

The speaker was addressing the "rabble," and would hardly ask whether they would allow themselves to lead themselves to

their own deaths: the second misprint is, therefore, "rabble"
for *rebel*, meaning Cade, who was leading the rabble: the
first misprint is less positively wrong, but still the sense (as
well as the old corrector) tells us to read, "relent" *repent:*
the three lines, properly printed, will, therefore, stand thus:—

> " What say ye, countrymen ? will ye *repent*,
> And yield to mercy, whilst 'tis offer'd you,
> Or let a *rebel* lead you to your deaths ? ''

Writers of the time now and then used "relent" for *repent;*
but "rabble" for *rebel* must be wrong.

P. 205. The Duke of York having suddenly returned from
Ireland, a messenger informs the King that he is on his way
to the court,—

> " And with a puissant, and a mighty power
> Of Gallowglasses and stout Kernes
> Is marching hitherward in proud array.''

The first line is tautological, since a "mighty" power would
necessarily be a "puissant" power: the second line is imperfect, owing to the absence of two syllables; but both these
defects are remedied by the corrector of the folio, 1632:—

> " And with a puissant, and *united* power
> Of Gallowglasses and stout *Irish* Kernes,
> Is marching hitherward in proud array.''

Most likely "a mighty" was written for *united*, in consequence of misapprehension by the ear of the scribe : York's
power consisted of Gallowglasses and Kernes in union ; and
as the Kernes were *Irish*, we may be confident that that
word had, in some unexplained way, escaped from the text.

ACT V   SCENE I.

P. 214. York, accused of treason, calls for his sons to bail
him, and afterwards for Salisbury and Warwick, whom he
terms his "two brave bears:"—

> " That with the very shaking of their chains
> They may astonish these fell-lurking curs.''

Steevens thought that "fell-lurking" was, in all probability, a misprint ; and Heath proposed *fell-lurching*, and others *fell-barking* as the fit compound. York has previously spoken of the looks of Clifford and other friends of Henry, and there is every reason to think that this correction in the folio, 1632, is well founded :—

> " That, with the very shaking of their chains
> They may astonish these *fell-looking* curs."

The misprint was easy, but, we believe, no editor ever guessed at the right emendation.   Just below occurs another slight, but decided error, of the same kind, in Richard's simile of " an over-weening cur :"—

> " Who, being suffer'd with the bear's fell paw,
> Hath clapp'd his tail between his legs and cried."

Here one auxiliary was used for another, for we ought clearly to read *having* for " being :"—

> " Who, *having* suffer'd from the bear's fell paw," &c.

It seems strange that Malone should ingeniously strive to vindicate " being," without perceiving that *having* would at once put an end to the difficulty.

SCENE II.

P. 220. We may be pretty sure, if only on account of the disagreeable jingle of " hearts" and " parts" in the same line, that Shakespeare did not write the following, as it has always been handed down to us.   Young Clifford is speaking of the total rout of King Henry's troops :—

> " Uncurable discomfit
> Reigns in the hearts of all our present parts."

Some corruption found its way into the text, and the corrector of the folio, 1632, informs us what it is, but he does not tell us how the word he substitutes became mistaken for that he expunges :—

> " Uncurable discomfit
> Reigns in the hearts of all our present *friends*."

If the transcriber of this play for the press had written as plain a hand as the corrector, such a blunder would not have been committed, and we do not see how any want of clearness could well pervert *friends* into " parts."   That the one

fills the place better than the other, will, probably, not be
denied: neither will it be denied, by those who have examined it, that the latter portion of this play is very incorrectly printed. As a farther proof, we may adduce the first
five lines of York's speech, at the opening of the next scene
on this page :—

> " Of Salisbury, who can report of him ?
> That winter lion, who in rage forgets
> Aged contusions and all brush of time,
> And, like a gallant in the brow of youth,
> Repairs him with occasion."

There appear to be at least three errors in this short passage,
two of which have been guessed at with success by Warburton and Johnson, though Steevens would not allow of
either. The first, but not the most important, has never
been hinted at, but is distinctly shown by a manuscript-
emendation in the folio, 1632, where the extract appears in
this form :—

> " *Old* Salisbury, who can report of him ?
> That winter lion, who in rage forgets
> Aged contusions and all *bruise* of time,
> And, like a gallant in the *bloom* of youth,
> Repairs him with occasion."

As to " *Old* Salisbury," instead of " Of Salisbury," it is to
be observed that not only is the change fully borne out by
the context, but that in the corresponding place of the
drama upon which this play was founded, York inquires,
" But did you see *old* Salisbury ?" *Bruise*, for " brush," was
Warburton's conjecture; and Johnson proposed *blow* for
" brow;" but it turns out, as far as the old corrector may be
trusted, that the poet's word was *bloom; blow* is certainly
nearer the letters, and, in the same sense as *bloom*, might
answer the purpose equally well.

THE THIRD PART

OF

KING HENRY VI.

ACT I. SCENE I.

P. 229. Edward, speaking of the Duke of Buckingham, says that he

> " Is either slain or wounded dangerous."

There are two pieces of evidence to show that we ought to read, "wounded dangerously:" the one is the play from which this drama was in great part taken, and the other a manuscript-correction in the folio, 1632. Either ought, in such a case, to be conclusive.

The old printed copies are without many necessary stage-directions, and when Richard throws down the head of Somerset, *head*, and *throw it*, are written in the margin, as a sufficient instruction to the performer. At the line,—

> " Thus do I hope to shake King Henry's head,"

shake it is placed opposite. York afterwards *takes the throne;* that is to say, places himself in the seat in the Parliament House appropriated to the King. This he is represented in the folio, 1632, as doing earlier than in modern editions, and at the same time that his soldiers retire, or *go up*, as it is expressed in print. This course does not seem to be quite correct according to the dialogue.

P. 235. The folio, 1632, thus blunderingly gives the passage, where Henry consents to reign only during life :—

> " My lord of Warwick, hear but one word.
> Let me for this time reign as king.''

Manuscript-corrections change the lines thus :—

> " My lord of Warwick, hear *me* but one word.
> Let me for this *my life* time reign as king.''

Me, necessary at least to the measure, is found in no known edition of this play; but *my life*, in the second line, makes the passage agree with the folio, 1623 : the insertion of *me*, in the first line, may induce a doubt whether the corrector of the folio, 1632, did not resort to some independent source. This notion is strengthened by an emendation, a few lines above, where, according to all authorities, York exclaims,—

> " Henry of Lancaster, resign thy crown ;''

but York, from the commencement, had demanded the crown as his ; and, in consistency with this assertion of right, and perhaps warranted by some then extant authority, the old corrector makes York say,—

> " Henry of Lancaster, resign *my* crown.''

At all events, such would seem to be the true reading.

A leaf is unfortunately wanting in the folio, 1632, after this part of the scene.

SCENE IV

P. 246. During the speech of Margaret, several stage-directions are inserted, of which there is no trace in any printed copies, ancient or modern. Thus, when she shows York the napkin stained with Rutland's blood, the fit time for producing it is duly marked, and she afterwards, in mockery, *throws it* to him, that he may wipe his eyes upon it. Again, when she and Clifford insultingly place the *paper crown* on York's head, those words are inserted in the margin. Before Clifford and the Queen stab him, York *casts the napkin to her again.*

P. 249. The folio, 1623, has this exclamation by York, in allusion to the death of young Rutland :—

> " That face of his the hungry cannibals
> Would not have touch'd, would not have stain'd with blood ;''

and why the passage should have been altered to the following form in the folio, 1632, it is not very easy to understand, unless, when properly given, it corresponded with some better original than that from which the folio, 1623, was printed :—

> " That face of his
> The hungry cannibals would not have touch'd,
> Would not have stain'd the roses just with blood."

Theobald, to keep, we suppose, as near the letters of the second folio as possible, proposed, somewhat absurdly, to print "*juic'd* with blood ;" but the printer was in fault, by converting *hues* into "just ;" and *hues* is substituted for "just" by the old corrector.

> " Would not have stain'd the rose's *hues* with blood,"

is intelligible enough, and on some accounts superior to the language of the earlier folio, which was derived from the old play Shakespeare altered. We know of no original for the insertion of " the rose's hues" in the folio, 1632.

ACT II. SCENE II.

P. 259. Queen Margaret, endeavouring to animate Henry, thus addresses him, in all editions :—

> " My lord, cheer up your spirits : our foes are nigh,
> And this soft courage makes your followers faint."

What is "soft courage," but a contradiction in terms? Yet the words have always been treated as the genuine text of Shakespeare, when we ought certainly to read, with the old corrector,—

> " And this soft *carriage* makes your followers faint."

The allusion unquestionably is to the mild deportment of the King. The same lapse was committed by the printer in " Coriolanus," Act III. Scene III. ; and what makes it still more evident that, in the instance before us, " soft courage" ought to be " soft *carriage*," is that the corresponding line

in the older play (of which Shakespeare availed himself)
is this :—

> " This harmful pity makes your followers faint."

P. 263. When the Yorkists defy the party of the King and
Queen to battle, this poor couplet is put into Edward's
mouth :—

> " Sound trumpets! let our bloody colours wave,
> And either victory, or else a grave."

The last line is vastly improved in expression and energy by
a manuscript alteration in the folio, 1632 :—

> " Sound trumpets! let our bloody colours wave,
> And either victory, or a *welcome* grave."

It seems hardly possible that a copyist should mishear *welcome*, and write " or else" for it ; but whether *welcome* were
or were not the word of the poet, we may be quite sure that
he never wrote " or else ;" and the great probability seems
to be that he wrote *welcome*.

SCENE V.

P. 270. The folios all have this passage :—

> " And so obsequious will thy father be,
> Men for the loss of thee, having no more," &c.

The word " men" has occasioned discussion among the commentators : Rowe substituted *sad*, and Steevens recommended *man*, which has been sometimes adopted. It is
merely the printer's mistake, who carelessly began the line
with *M* instead of *E* :—

> " And so obsequious will thy father be,
> *E'en* for the loss of thee, having no more,
> As Priam was for all his valiant sons."

"Obsequious" means mournful, as at funeral obsequies : the
father would be as mournful *even* for the loss of this one son,
as Priam had been for the loss of all his sons. There can
be little objection to receive this trifling, but effectual, emendation at the hands of the old corrector.

SCENE VI.

P. 274. We meet with a singular manuscript stage-direction in the folio, 1632, where Edward, Clarence, Richard, and Warwick are exulting over the dead body of Clifford; for we are informed in the margin that *they pull him to and fro*, as each of them in turn insults the corpse by the delivery of a malignant line. We can hardly believe that such an exhibition of brutality would have been generally tolerated even by spectators of that day; but the old corrector, nevertheless, must refer to a practice he had either himself witnessed on the stage, or had heard of as the practice of the theatre before his time.

ACT III. SCENE I.

P. 276. In the introduction to this scene, instead of the names Sinklo and Humphrey, "two Keepers" are substituted; but the prefixes to their several speeches are still abbreviations of the appellations of the performers, *Sin.* and *Hum.* They *stand back* when the King, *disguised as a churchman* (so stated in manuscript), enters; and they come *forward* to carry him away with them.

SCENE III.

P. 286. This scene is numbered 2 in manuscript (for none of the divisions of Acts and Scenes, after the first, are printed in this drama); but it is, in fact, Scene 3, a mistake having been introduced in this respect.

P. 289. A correction, of comparatively little moment, is made in a line of Queen Margaret's speech, which, at least, serves to show the minute accuracy of the person through whose hands this volume once passed :—

> " Look, therefore, Lewis, that by this league and marriage
> Thou draw not on *thee* danger and dishonour."

The above is ordinarily printed "*thy* danger and dishonour," which is only to be questioned, because we here learn that it was not the authentic mode of giving the passage.

P. 294. The regulation of the verse in this part of the dialogue is certainly erroneous as it stands, and the irregularity has arisen from the omission of an important word, which is supplied in the margin of the folio, 1632, and which proves that the lines ought to run thus :—

> " But, Warwick, thou,
> And Oxford, with five thousand *warlike* men,
> Shall cross the seas and bid false Edward battle."

The line, without *warlike*, is clearly defective, and we can hardly suppose that it was inserted in manuscript at random. In the same way, in the last line of the last of King Edward's speeches, on p. 299, the word "have" was carelessly left out in the folio, 1632, and was inserted by the old corrector : *warlike*, however, is not found in any of the old copies.

ACT IV　SCENE II.

P. 301. To the Introduction to this Act, " Enter Warwick and Oxford in England with French soldiers," the words, *and English*, are added, with a caret, after " French ;" for it is not to be supposed that these two noblemen, coming to maintain the right of Henry VI. to the throne, were supported by no English followers. After they have surprised Edward in his tent, and the greatest alarm and dismay prevail, *Shouts, noise, and confusion* is added to the printed stage-direction.

SCENE VII.

P. 312. This scene is wrongly numbered 6 by the corrector; and it is not unlikely that, for the sake of convenience in performance, two scenes, separated in modern editions, were combined. The introduction in the early impressions is, "Enter Edward, Richard, Hastings, and soldiers ;" but *foreign* is placed in manuscript before " soldiers," to show, perhaps, that their forces were chiefly derived from continental aid.

P. 313. We can very readily believe that the small word we have printed in Italics escaped from the following line by Gloster, in ridicule of the complying Mayor of York :—

> " A stout wise captain *he*, and soon persuaded."

It is not met with in any old copy, but it is added in the margin of the folio, 1632. The corresponding passage in " The true Tragedy of Richard Duke of York," is,—

> " By my faith, a wise stout captain, and soon persuaded."

SCENE VIII.

P. 317. The old corrector informs us that *mind* has been misprinted " meed," where King Henry says,—

> " That's not my fear ; my meed hath got me fame ; "

and the context tends to convince us that the alteration was proper, and that the poet did not intend to use " meed" in the sense of merit.   The mild and pious King refers not so much to his own acts, as to the gentle character of his disposition ; and, in conformity with this view, he remarks, just afterwards, as the passage has been uniformly printed,—

> " My mildness hath allay'd their swelling griefs,
> My mercy dried their water-flowing tears."

" Water-flowing" seems a poor and tautologous epithet for " tears ;" and *bitter-flowing* is substituted in the corrected folio, 1632.   " Water-standing eyes" is used afterwards, but under very different circumstances.

ACT V.   SCENE V.

P. 331. The young Prince having been stabbed by Edward, Clarence, and Gloster, Margaret exclaims,—

> " O traitors ! murderers !
> They that stabb'd Cæsar shed no blood at all,
> Did not offend, nor were not worthy blame,
> If this foul deed were by to equal it."

This passage cannot have reached us as Shakespeare wrote it, because one foul deed being present, and only equal to another, also present, would not show either of them off as more heinous. An evident and easy mistake, either by the copyist or by the printer, has represented our great poet as writing what is little better than illogical nonsense ; and the corrector of the folio, 1632, by placing a single letter in the margin, has shown us what, we think, must have come from Shakespeare's pen :—

> " O traitors ! murderers !
> They that stabb'd Cæsar shed no blood at all,
> Did not offend, nor were not worthy blame,
> If this foul deed were by to *sequel* it."

That is, if this foul deed had been by, to follow up the stabbing of Cæsar, the latter act would have appeared no crime in comparison.

SCENE VI.

P. 332. According to all the folios, Richard must have talked with, and subsequently killed Henry VI. *on the walls* of the Tower, for the printed introduction to this scene is, " Enter Henry the Sixth, and Richard, with the Lieutenant, on the walls." This could scarcely have been the case, when the play was originally represented, because in the older drama, upon which it is founded, it is said, at the opening of the corresponding scene, " Enter Gloster to King Henry in the Tower." The corrector of the folio, 1632, enables us to state that, in his time at least, the place of action in this scene was the interior of the Tower, for he erases " on the walls," and writes *in the Tower* instead of them. He also informs us that Henry is *reading*, when Gloster unceremoniously breaks in upon him.

P. 334. Henry, referring to the birth of Richard, tells him,—

> " The owl shriek'd at thy birth, an evil sign ;
> The night-crow cried, aboding luckless time."

For " aboding," as one word, the corrector writes *a boding*, as two words ; and for " time," he writes *tune*,—

> "The night-crow cried, *a boding* luckless *tune*."

This appears to be the right reading, for in the older play, which is here followed more exactly than usual, the words are the same ; but it is, nevertheless, to be admitted that in " Henry VIII." Shakespeare uses " aboded" for *foreboded*, and that " time" was often misprinted *tune*.   There is the same double reason for altering " indigested" to *indigest*, just below ; it stands so in the older play, and it is changed so in the margin of the folio, 1632 ; the line, too, consists only of the regular number of syllables in the old play, the additions being, in all probability, corruptions.   This circumstance is, therefore, adverse to the opinion expressed in note 3 on this page.

SCENE VII.

P. 336.   The folios, where King Edward adverts to the losses sustained during the civil war, have two lines thus printed :—

> " Three dukes of Somerset, threefold renown,
> For hardy and undoubted champions."

The corrector of the folio, 1632, instructs us to read,—

> " Three dukes of Somerset, threefold *renown'd*
> For hardy and *redoubted* champions."

Modern editors have " renown'd," and it is the word in the older play ; but, like the folios, it has " undoubted" for *redoubted*.

The introduction to this scene in the folios speaks of a " Nurse" being present (*with a child*, adds the manuscript-correction), who is altogether omitted in modern editions. The King and his brothers *kiss* the infant, and the proper places for doing so are noted in the margin of the folio, 1632. It deserves remark that, although Gloster's name is introduced in the printed play, as coming in with the King, Queen, Clarence, Hastings, Nurse, &c., at the opening of the scene, according to the old corrector it was the practice for him not to enter until afterwards, while Edward IV. was speaking, and *Enter Richard behind* is there found in the margin. This course appears to be in keeping with Richard's character; and the whole of his first speech is noted as muttered to himself, after which he comes *forward* and joins in the general congratulations. Still he several times delivers passages *aside*, and these are carefully so marked. Some of the manuscript notes, intended for the government of the performance, are in a different ink, as if additions had been made to them when it was found that those previously written were not sufficient.

KING RICHARD III.

ACT I. SCENE I.

P. 348. We notice the following, not so much as an emendation, but as a change of the received text, which the old corrector would, perhaps, not have thought it necessary to make, had it not accorded with some other than the usual authorities. All copies of this play, of our own or of former times, give this line,—

> " I, that am curtail'd of this fair proportion ;"

whereas, by a marginal note in the folio, 1632, we are told to read,—

> " I, that am curtail'd *thus* of fair proportion ;"

as if the performer of the part of Richard had referred not so much to what he had already said, regarding his personal appearance, as to what the audience must see of it. In the last line but one of this page, the second folio has *grandfathers* for " godfathers," but it is, of course, set right.

P. 349. There is a considerable increase of contempt, as well as an improvement in the verse, in the following line, where *same* is added in manuscript, not being found in any printed copy :—

> " Was it not she, and that good man of worship,
> Anthony Woodeville, her *same* brother there,
> That made him send lord Hastings to the Tower ?" &c.

If Woodeville could be read as a trisyllable, there is no absolute need of the addition.

P. 352. Richard observes of Edward IV.,—

> " He cannot live, I hope ; and must not die
> Till George be pack'd with posthorse up to heaven."

For "posthorse," the old corrector has *posthaste ;* but the alteration does not seem to require more than to be pointed out, as possibly right.

SCENE II.

P. 360. The folios very imperfectly represent the text in this part of the scene, for Anne is made to give Richard a ring, and the words, "To take is not to give," which, according to the quartos, she interposes, are omitted. The old corrector makes the folio, 1632, correspond with the quartos in this particular, as well as in reading *suppliant* for "servant," in the line,—

> " And if thy poor devoted servant may," &c.

At all events, therefore, we may feel assured that the word *suppliant*, in the older copies, was that of the poet.

SCENE III.

P. 364. We meet with a very characteristic stage-direction, when Richard enters to complain of the imprisonment of Clarence : it is, *Enter Richard, stamping angerly*, which, no doubt, shows the manner of some early actor of the part, perhaps of Burbage himself, the original Richard ; for, supposing the corrector of the folio, 1632, never to have seen him (he died in March, 1619) his peculiarities in the performance would, most probably, be traditionally handed down to his successors. The manuscript-instructions of the same kind are hardly as numerous in this as in some other plays ; but still, on all occasions, they are sufficient for the due conduct of the representation : when, for instance, " old Queen Margaret," as she is called, arrives, on p. 367, she stands back, and a note of *behind* is made against every sentence she utters, until *she comes forth* with the words,—

> " I can no longer hold me patient."

Start all is then added in the margin, to indicate the surprise, if not alarm, her sudden appearance created.

P. 370. One of the most striking and satisfactory emendations in the corrected folio, 1632, occurs in Queen Margaret's denunciation of Richard, where she addresses him, in all editions, in the following terms :—

> " Thou elvish-mark'd, abortive, rooting hog,
> Thou that wast seal'd in thy nativity
> The slave of nature, and the son of hell," &c.

Here " slave of nature," but especially " son of hell," sound so flatly and tamely near the conclusion of the curse, that an impression rises at once in the mind, that Shakespeare must have written something more fierce and vigorous. How, then, does the old corrector inform us that the last line ought to run ? not as the words are spelt in the folio, 1623, and followed in that of 1632,—

> " The slaue of Nature, and the sonne of Hell,"

but with two remarkable changes,—

> " The *stain* of nature, and the *scorn* of hell."

Stain and *scorn* must surely have been the language of our great dramatist ; and when we bear in mind that " stain " was of old spelt *staine*, and " scorn" *scorne*, it is not difficult to discover how the blunders arose.

P. 371. It may be worth a note, that Queen Margaret, according to a marginal note in the folio, 1632, does not here, and afterwards, call Richard a " bottled spider," but a " *bottle*-spider." A considerable portion of the protracted abuse in this scene, *viz.* from the line,—

> " False-boding woman, end thy frantic curse,"

down to the line,

> " And say, poor Margaret was a prophetess,"

is struck out, so that she only adds two more lines before she makes her *exit*, although by a misprint in the folios (corrected in that of 1632) another speech is attributed to her after she has retired.

SCENE IV.

P. 375. In the quartos, Brakenbury, Lieutenant of the Tower, is represented as hearing Clarence narrate his dream ; but in the folios, the dream is told to a " Keeper," who goes

out as Brakenbury enters.   Perhaps, when this play was first
performed, the company could only afford one actor for both
parts, and Brakenbury was, therefore, made to officiate as
Lieutenant and as Keeper; but afterwards, when the company became more numerous, it was thought better to divide
the characters.   In all editions the two Murderers deliver
their warrant to Brakenbury.

P. 380. The second Murderer, who was for saving the life
of Clarence, says, in the quartos, "I hope my holy humour
will change;" in the folios, "I hope this passionate humour
of mine will change;" and in the corrected folio, 1632, "I
hope this *compassionate* humour of mine will change."

P. 385. One of the speeches of Clarence to the two as-
sassins is left imperfect, though not so printed, and is completed by the addition of three words inserted in the margin
of the folio, 1632.   He asks,—

> "Which of you,   *   *   *   *
> If two such murderers as yourselves came to you,
> Would not entreat for life?   As you would beg,
> Were you in my distress, *so pity me*."

The lines are only in the folios, and have been treated in
various ways by different editors, in consequence of the apparent incompleteness of the sense; but the three small
words in Italics render the whole of this portion of the dialogue clear and consistent.   The punctuation also is that of
the corrector.

ACT II. SCENE I.

P. 391. The old corrector has made the text of the folio,
1632, conform to that of the quartos by the insertion of an
important word, where Richard asks,—

> "Mark'd you not,
> How that the *guilty* kindred of the queen
> Look'd pale?"

Just above, an unimportant word is added to complete a
defective line, which is not found in any known impression
of the play,—

"Come, Hastings, *prithee*, help me to my closet."

Modern editors have generally finished this line by adding to it, "Ah! poor Clarence!" a hemistich spoken by the King just before he goes out, which renders the line as redundant as it was before deficient.

SCENE II.

P. 393. The quartos, speaking of the death of Edward IV., represent him as having gone

> "To his new kingdom of perpetual rest,"

while the folios have it,—

> "To his new kingdom of ne'er changing night."

In the corrected folio, 1632, "night" is made *light.* How it happens that the quartos in some places differ so materially from the folios, has never been explained: the blunder in the folios, twice committed at the end of this scene, in having *London* for "Ludlow," is set right in both instances, in manuscript.

SCENE III.

P. 397. This scene between the three Citizens is struck out, but the emendations are, nevertheless, continued: for "Which, in his nonage," we have, "*With,* in his nonage," substituted, perhaps rightly, but the quartos read, "That, in his nonage."

ACT III. SCENE I.

P. 404. Two emendations, for which we have reason to be thankful, are made in the opening of Buckingham's speech, where he is arguing that the Duke of York cannot be entitled to sanctuary on account of his youth and innocence. Cardinal Bourchier maintains that sanctuary ought in no case to be violated :—

> "God in heaven forbid
> We should infringe the holy privilege
> Of blessed sanctuary ! not for all this land,
> Would I be guilty of so great a sin."

The words, " in heaven," are not in the folios, but were inserted by the corrector of the folio, 1632, and they accord
with the text of the quartos ; but in Buckingham's reply we
encounter two changes, which we can hardly hesitate in admitting, since they so importantly contribute to enforce and
explain the meaning of the poet. The first line of what
Buckingham addresses to the Cardinal (as always hitherto
printed), is needlessly offensive and coarse in its terms ; and
the third line contains two misprints which have been the
source of much speculation between Warburton, Johnson,
Malone, &c. The passage, as invariably given, is this :—

> " You are too senseless-obstinate, my lord,
> Too ceremonious and traditional :
> Weigh it but with the grossness of this age,
> You break not sanctuary in seizing him."

For " senseless-obstinate," a strange and unmannerly compound, the corrector of the folio, 1632, states that we must
substitute words quite consistent with the good breeding of
Buckingham, and at the same time quite consistent with the
argument he is employing, *viz.* that the Cardinal is too rigid
and scrupulous in his unwillingness to violate sanctuary, in a
case for which it was never intended :—

> " You are too *strict and abstinent*, my lord,
> Too ceremonious and traditional :
> Weigh it but with the *goodness* of *his* age,
> You break not sanctuary in seizing him."

The point for which Buckingham contends is, that age and
purity, such as belong to little York, did not require " the
holy privilege," and could not claim it ; " the *goodness* of
his age," refers to the youth and innocence of the prince,
and those words have been (in all cases but in one of the
quartos, where *greatness* is found) misprinted " the grossness of this age." Warburton suggested *greenness* as the
true reading ; but the errors were " grossness" for *goodness*,
and " this" for *his*. These mistakes are remedied in the
folio, 1632 ; and nothing but an excess of carelessness could
have been guilty of them.

P. 408. Little York has been taunting his uncle Richard,
upon which Buckingham remarks,—

> " With what a sharp provided wit he reasons."

X

The manuscript-corrector assures us that, although the intention of the dramatist is evident, a decided misprint has crept into the line : he reads,—

> " With what a *sharply pointed* wit he reasons."

Lower down, instead of the language of the quarto, 1597 (all other editions omit " needs "),—

> " My lord protector needs will have it so,"

a correction in the margin makes the young Prince reply,—

> " My lord protector will *e'en* have it so."

The difference scarcely merits notice on any other account, than because it shows a preference for a word not in any of the extant authorities.

P. 410. In the next emendation, the reading of the folios in Richard's answer to Buckingham,—

> " Chop off his head : something we will determine,"

is made in the folio, 1632, to conform precisely to the words of the quarto impressions, *viz.* :—

> " Chop off his head, man : somewhat we will do."

We may, perhaps, conclude that the actor of the part of Richard so recited the line in the time of the old corrector, and not as it stands more tamely in the folios.

SCENE II.

P. 414. What passes between Hastings, the Pursuivant, the Priest, and Buckingham, is erased in the folio, 1632, perhaps as needless to the very protracted performance of this play. When Hastings alludes to it in Scene IV., on his way to execution, the five lines are also struck through with a pen, as well as the Scrivener's observations, in Scene VI. (p. 427), on the indictment of Hastings.

SCENE V.

P. 422. It is not very easy to understand how this scene was acted of old : modern editors say that it took place on "the Tower walls ;" but to the old stage-direction (besides altering "rotten" to *rusty*) the corrector has added these words, *all in haste, in the Tower*, as if Richard and Buckingham were in some confusion, not on the Tower walls, but in some part of the edifice near the drawbridge, which Richard mentions. When Lovell and Ratcliff enter, just afterwards, with the head of Hastings, we are informed in manuscript that it was exhibited *on a spear.*

SCENE VII.

P. 428. Buckingham giving an account to Richard how he had proceeded and succeeded among the Citizens at Guildhall, tells him that he had thus adverted to the bastardy of Edward IV. :—

> " As being got, your father then in France ;
> And his resemblance, being not like the duke."

This last line is only in the folios ; but Buckingham was to enforce, not Edward's likeness, but his want of likeness to his father, not "his resemblance," but *dis-resemblance;* and precisely in this form the corrector of the folio, 1632, has put it :—

> " As being got, your father then in France ;
> And *dis-resemblance*, being not like the duke."

However unusual the word, it exactly suits the poet's meaning, and *dis* may easily have been read "his." At a later date, "dissemblance" seems to have been employed to express want of similarity.

P. 430. A very slight change in another line, spoken by the Duke of Buckingham to the Lord Mayor and Aldermen, makes a considerable difference :—

> " Happy were England, would this virtuous prince
> Take on his grace the sovereignty thereof ;
> But, sure, I fear, we shall not win him to it."

"Sure" is here a mere expletive ; but the old corrector instructs us how to raise it into importance, by reading the line as nobody has hitherto thought of reading it,—

> " But, *sore* I fear, we shall not win him to it."

Buckingham pretended to be much afraid that Richard would

not be brought to consent. This is one of the smaller emendations that may be thought to need no advocacy.

P. 435. The quartos and folios differ materially in one point, in the scene where Buckingham and the Citizens are pressing the Crown upon Richard. In the folios, Buckingham affects to be weary of solicitation, and retires with,—

"Come, citizens, we will entreat no more."

In the quartos the line has more emphasis :—

"Come, citizens: zounds! I'll entreat no more;"

upon which, Richard, who has a prayer-book in his hand, and who has just left the two bishops, affects to be shocked at the impiety of Buckingham in using even so mild an oath as "zounds!" He, therefore, says solemnly to him,—

"O! do not swear, my lord of Buckingham."

All this was probably expunged by the Master of the Revels before the folio, 1623, was printed, and on this account we meet with no trace of it there. The corrector of the folio, 1632, seems to have thought it too striking and characteristic to be omitted ; but he most likely resorted to some other authority than the quartos to supply the deficiency, as the words he inserts in a vacant space are not precisely the same as are there found : possibly, he had the addition from recitation on the stage, at some date when the injunction of the Master of the Revels was not attended to. He gives Buckingham's line thus :—

"*Zounds!* citizens, we will entreat no more;"

and Richard's rebuke in these words :—

"O! do not swear, my *cousin* Buckingham."

Instead of making the Citizens retire with Buckingham, Buckingham alone goes out, an arrangement of apparent propriety, because it is quite clear that the four lines put into the mouth of Richard, while Buckingham was out of the apartment, were intended to be heard by the Lord Mayor, &c. In accordance with this view, "them" is changed to *him* in the folio, 1632 :—

"Call *him* again ; I am not made of stone,
But penetrable to your kind entreaties," &c.

To whose "kind entreaties" could Richard refer, if not to

those of the Citizens, who had remained behind after
Buckingham had flung away in a pretended passion at
Richard's refusal ?

ACT IV. SCENE II.

P. 446. The portion of this scene, near its close, which is
only in the quarto copies, is passed over in silence by the
corrector of the folio, 1632, and we may feel assured that it
was not usually acted.   After the line,—

> " Thou troublest me : I am not in the vein,"

Exit is the brief printed stage-direction ; but to it the word
angrily, or, as it is spelt, *angerly*, is subjoined in manuscript.

SCENE III.

P. 447. Tyrrell, who had suborned the two ruffians,
Dighton and Forrest, to murder the young princes, says of
them, and of the part they had acted, according to all
editions,—

> " Albeit they were flesh'd villains, bloody dogs,
>   Melted with tenderness and mild compassion,
>   Wept like to children in their death s sad story."

The passage is surely much improved by the trifling alterations in the folio, 1632 :—

> " Albeit they were flesh'd villains, *blooded* dogs,
>   Melted with tenderness and mild compassion,
>   Wept like *two* children in their death's sad story."

The two villains had been fleshed, and were like dogs that
had been allowed the taste of human blood ; yet they wept,
like two children, while narrating the particulars of the
murder of the princes.

SCENE IV.

P. 449. The beginning of this long scene between Queen
Margaret, Queen Elizabeth, and the Duchess of York, contains no emendation of any importance, excepting where, on

p. 454, the old corrector, in accordance with the quartos, tells us to read,—

> " Airy succeeders of intestate joys,"

instead of

> " Airy succeeders of *intestine* joys."

P. 456. Two emendations are proposed in speeches of the Duchess of York: first,—

> "Then patiently *bear* my impatience,"

is put for "hear my impatience" of the folios ; and

> " Art thou so hasty ?　I *once* stay'd for thee,"

for "I have stay'd for thee," of the same impressions.　Both these minor changes seem recommended to adoption by their fitness.

P. 462. Richard tells Queen Elizabeth that Dorset, her son,—

> " Leads discontented steps in foreign soil,"

which may be right, but the old corrector furnishes what seems a more natural word,—

> " *Treads* discontented steps in foreign soil."

P. 466. The following lines, in reference to the intercession of Queen Elizabeth with her daughter in favour of Richard's pretensions, conclude the King's speech in the folios :—

> " Urge the necessity and state of times,
> And be not peevish found in great designs."

The quartos have "peevish *fond*," and the old corrector amends the couplet as follows :—

> " Urge the necessity *of* state *and* times,
> And be not peevish *fond* in great designs."

That is to say, she was to enforce the necessity of state and of the times for the marriage.　It may still be a question whether "peevish found," of the folios, be not preferable, as avoiding all appearance of tautology ; on which account it is advocated in note 10 on this page: nevertheless, "peevish *fond*" has, we see, two pieces of evidence in its favour.

SCENE V.

P. 472. Stanley inquires of Sir Christopher Urswick,—

> " What men of name resort to him ?"

meaning Richmond. The line is evidently defective, while in the rest of the scene the verse is regular ; and the corrector of the folio, 1632, restores two words that seem to have dropped out :—

> " What men of name *and mark* resort to him."

This short scene is struck out with a pen.

ACT V. SCENE II.

P. 474. Richmond speaking of Richard, calls him, as the words have always stood in print,—

> " The wretched, bloody, and usurping boar : "

" Wretched" is an epithet that has little comparative appropriateness, while the word recommended in manuscript to supply the place of it, is especially adapted to the character of Richard, and we may readily believe it to have been that of the poet :—

> " The *reckless*, bloody, and usurping boar."

Reckless was of old frequently spelt *wreckless*, and hence, perhaps, the misprint.

SCENE III.

P. 477. If the following line had been printed in other old copies as it stands in that of 1632 only, we should have hesitated to disturb the text, on the ground that the sense was quite intelligible: it is where Richmond requests Blunt, if possible, to communicate with Stanley ; Blunt replies,—

> " Upon my self, my lord, I'll undertake it."

Every other ancient authority has "life" for *self ;* and as there can be no doubt it is an error of the press, the old corrector made the necessary emendation.

The printed stage-direction here is, *They withdraw into the tent*, that is, Richmond's tent; and according to the old theatrical arrangement of this scene, different sides of the same small stage contained the two hostile tents of the King and Richmond. As soon as Richmond and his friends withdraw into the tent on their side of the stage, the King and his adherents come forward and converse, as if the encampment of the enemy were far out of hearing. A manuscript stage-direction (for there is here no printed one beyond *Exit Ratcliff*) informs us that *Richard lies down and sleeps* as soon as he has said,—

> " And help to arm me.—Leave me, I say."

Richmond and Stanley then meet in the tent of the former, and the word *couch* is added to the printed stage-direction, in order that Richmond, after his conversation and prayer, may lie down and sleep also, as the King was already doing in sight of the audience. Thus, in the simplicity of our early theatres, the two leaders were seen reposing in their tents at the same time, and the Ghosts *enter* (whether by means of trap-doors, or otherwise, is not stated), and severally address them.

P. 480. This complicated scene is ill-printed in all impressions, quarto and folio, especially in the latter, and most especially in the folio, 1632 : several important emendations are, therefore, made in manuscript. One of the earliest of these is the insertion of the word " deadly" in the line,—

> " By thee was punched full of *deadly* holes."

The old corrector may have obtained it from the quartos, but it is not in any folio. On the other hand, however, he may have been indebted to some independent authority ; and some of his changes give a text which varies materially from any extant original. Thus the second line of the next page,—

> " Doth comfort thee in sleep : live and flourish,"

evidently wants a syllable, and the quartos have it,—

> " Doth comfort thee in thy sleep : live and flourish ;"

which may be right, but it does not accord with the line as it stands amended in the folio, 1632, where we read,—

> " Doth comfort thee in sleep : live *thou* and flourish."

When, on page 481, the Ghost of Vaughan says to Richard,—

> " Let fall thy lance.   Despair and die,"

the line wants two syllables, not found in any impression ; but in the corrected folio, 1632, we have it,—

> " Let fall thy *pointless* lance.   Despair and die."

When we find *him* inserted in manuscript in the line, just subsequent,—

> " Will conquer *him*.   Awake, and win the day,"

the emendation might be derived from the quartos ; but such was not the case with an important change in what the Ghost of Anne addresses to Richard : in all editions it stands,—

> " And fall thy edgeless sword.   Despair and die."

This is merely the repetition of a previous line given to the Ghost of Clarence, and the poet could hardly have intended two of the spirits to use the very same words.   The corrector of the folio, 1632, induces us to believe that this was one of the corruptions accidentally introduced, and he makes the Ghost of Anne vary the line thus :—

> " And fall thy *powerless arm*.   Despair and die."

There can here be no impropriety : the emendation may have been obtained from some better authority, on or off the stage ; and it avoids the strong objection to making the Ghosts of Clarence and Anne use precisely the same form of imprecation when threatening Richard with his fate in the approaching battle.

P. 483.   The corrector of the folio, 1632, made the text conform to that of the earliest quarto in the line,—

> " The lights burn blue.—It is now dead midnight,"

every old impression but that of 1597, reading, " It is not dead midnight."   It may be urged that the corrector need not have resorted to the earliest quarto, since this blunder corrects itself : the wonder is, that this play should have gone through, at least, four editions in quarto, and as many in folio, before *not* was expunged for " now."   Eleven lines of Richard's soliloquy, from " What do I fear ? myself ?" down to " Fool, do not flatter," are struck through, and were, probably, not recited by the actor about the period when the erasure was made.

P. 484. There is a material difference between the quartos and folios, where Richard exclaims,—

> "Perjury, perjury, in the high'st degree:"

such is the text as given in the quartos; but the folios omit the second "perjury," and the corrector of that of 1632 supplies the word and something more:—

> "Perjury, *foul* perjury, in the high'st degree."

If "perjury" be pronounced as two syllables, *foul* is requisite for the metre; if "perjury" be pronounced as three syllables, the line, even without *foul*, is redundant. The question rather is, from whence *foul* was obtained, than whether it is necessary.

Lower down on this page occurs an instance in which it may seem that the corrector was giving, not the words of any known impression, but the manner in which the play was acted when he wrote. Two short speeches by the King and Ratcliff, found in the quartos, are left out in the folios, where the King says merely, "O, Ratcliff! I fear, I fear," without adding why he feared, so that Ratcliff's reply,—

> "Nay, good my lord, be not afraid of shadows,"

wants application in the folios. This is clearly a defect, and the corrector remedies it by making the speech assigned to the King run thus:—

> "O, Ratcliff, *I have dream'd a fearful dream;*"

to which Ratcliff's answer applies naturally enough. The words, *I have dream'd a fearful dream,* are in the quartos, but not exactly in the place which they are made to occupy in the folio, 1632. This, therefore, looks like one of the emendations made from recitation.

P. 487. The same may be said of a line in the King's directions for ordering his battle. The quarto, 1597, only, has it as follows:—

> "My foreward shall be drawn out all in length;"

while in every subsequent old impression we have it,—

> "My foreward shall be drawn in length."

How does the old corrector tell us to read it ? thus :—

> " My forward *ranks* shall be drawn *out* in length ;"

which, as far as euphony is concerned, seems the best line of
the three, though the first corresponds more with the words
of Holinshed.

P. 488. In the King's address to his army, Steevens proposed to read *ventures* for " adventures," and Warburton
distrain for *restrain :* both these changes are warranted by
manuscript emendations in the folio, 1632.

P. 491. There can be little doubt that a passage of some
moment in Richmond's last speech has been misrepresented
by blundering punctuation, which is thus set right in the
corrected folio, 1632 :—

> " All this divided York and Lancaster,
> Divided in their dire division,
> O, now let Richmond and Elizabeth,
> The true succeeders of each royal house,
> By God's fair ordinance conjoin together."

The sense clearly runs on, and is complete at " together ;"
but it has been the mistaken custom to place a full stop, followed by a line, after division,—

> " Divided in their dire division.—"

This is an error, which the old corrector amends ; and Johnson's opinion is entirely confirmed that " division " ought to
be followed by only a comma.

P. 492. A blunder has prevailed, from the earliest to the
latest times, in this line :—

> " Abate the edge of traitors, gracious Lord ! "

Steevens says, as indeed everybody must know, that to
" abate," is to lower, depress, or subdue ; but what has that
sense to do with " the edge," which immediately follows ? To
lower, depress, or subdue an edge, is scarcely sense ; and undoubtedly we ought to substitute a word, inserted in the
margin of the folio, 1632, which means to blunt, and which
is used exactly in that way by Shakespeare himself :—

> " *Rebate* the edge of traitors, gracious Lord ! "

i.e. blunt the edge of traitors ; and in "Measure for Measure,"
Act I. Scene V. (vol. ii. p. 21), we read,—

> " But doth rebate and blunt the natural edge," &c.,

where our great dramatist explains the meaning of *rebate,* if
it could be doubted, by the word which follows it.

It is hardly necessary to notice the stage-directions towards the close of this play : in the printed copies they are
comparatively few and general ; but the corrector of the
folio, 1632, felt the importance of supplying this deficiency,
with a view, perhaps, to the representation of this drama, in
a portion of it that is especially confused and complicated.

KING HENRY VIII.

ACT I. SCENE I.

P. 502. There is in this place an obvious mistake in the distribution of the dialogue between Norfolk and Buckingham in all the folios. It was divided differently by Theobald, who has since been followed: he made Buckingham's speech begin with, "Who did guide," &c., at the top of p. 503; but the manuscript-corrector of the folio, 1632, informs us that the observation,—

> "The office did
> Distinctly his full function,"

also belongs to Buckingham, who might very properly give this opinion after Norfolk's description of the scene.

P. 504. The last part of Buckingham's speech, from the words, "and his own letter," is struck out in the corrected folio, 1632. Just below, in

> "What did this vanity,
> But minister communication of
> A most poor issue?"

the old corrector alters "communication" to *the consummation*: the meaning is nearly the same according to Johnson's interpretation, but

> "What did this vanity
> But minister *the consummation* of
> A most poor issue,"

seems much more distinctly intelligible, and the two words were probably mistaken by the compositor.

P. 506. The remark of Buckingham,—

> " A beggar's book
> Outworths a noble's blood,"

has required several notes to show that the allusion was to
Wolsey's learning, which, it is admitted, was not very considerable : the change made in the margin of the folio, 1632,
shows that no note would have been necessary, if the true
text had been given ; the antithesis is also stronger :—

> " A beggar's *brood*
> Outworths a noble's blood."

SCENE II.

P. 511. According to the corrector of the folio, 1632, there
are several misprints in this scene which need correction.
The first is in the Queen's speech, where she is remonstrating
against the exacting commissions sent out by the Cardinal,
which had led to the use against the King of "language
unmannerly,"—

> " Yea, such which breaks
> The sides of loyalty," &c.

We are here instructed to read "*ties* of loyalty." The Cardinal answers (p. 512) that he has done no more, and knows
no more than others ; to which the Queen replies :—

> " You know no more than others ; but you frame
> Things, that are known alike, which are not wholesome," &c.

For "alike," the correction is *belike :*—

> " Things that are known, *belike*, which are not wholesome."

Again, at the end of the Queen's next speech, the expression,
"There is no primer baseness," of all the folios, is altered (in
accordance with Southern's suggestion mentioned in note 6)
to "There is no primer *business;*" and such we may hereafter treat as the original word. Farther on (p. 514), the
King, struck at the amount of the exactions under Wolsey's
commissions, exclaims,—

> " Sixth part of each ?
> A trembling contribution ! "

The old corrector here put his pen through the *m* in
"trembling," making the word *trebling*, as if the King
meant to say that the sum was treble what it ought to have

been. When the Duke of Buckingham's Surveyor enters to give evidence against his lord, the Queen says to the King,—

> "I am sorry that the Duke of Buckingham
> Is run in your displeasure;"

which may be quite right, but it ought to be noticed that a marginal emendation makes the last line,—

> "Is *one* in your displeasure."

This last change, like some of the others, may be deemed no necessary emendation.

P. 516. There can be no dispute that "under the commission's seal," of all the old copies, ought to be "under the confession's seal," as Theobald altered the word on the authority of Holinshed: it so stands also in the hand-writing of the corrector of the folio, 1632.

P. 518. This scene in all printed copies concludes with a very lame rhyming couplet, put into the mouth of the King:—

> "Let him not seek't of us.   By day and night
> He's traitor to the height."

Some words were omitted which cured the defectiveness of the last line, and the old corrector tells us that they were these:—

> "He is *a daring* traitor to the height."

To say the least of it, we may be disposed to admit this emendation, without opposing evidence.

SCENE III.

P. 520. The manuscript-corrector leads us to believe that there are two errors of the press in the following, where Lord Sands is speaking of Wolsey:—

> "Men of his way should be most liberal;
> They are set here for examples."

We can readily accord in the first, if not in the second emendation:—

> "Men of his *sway* should be most liberal;
> They are *sent* here for examples."

SCENE IV.

P. 524. The pronoun *me* may have been left out in the folios at the end of the verse, because there was no room for it without turning the line, or because it accidentally escaped in the press:—

> "Because they speak no English, thus they pray'd *me*
> To tell your grace."

The sense is hardly complete without it, and as the old corrector inserted it, we need have little hesitation in adopting an improvement so doubly recommended.

ACT II.   SCENE I.

P. 528. The folio, 1632, gives this imperfect line to Buckingham, on his way to execution:—

> "You that thus have come to pity me."

The folio, 1623, has it:—

> "You that thus far have come to pity me."

The corrector of the folio, 1632, may have obtained *far* from the earlier impression, and he places it in the margin. Notwithstanding this omission, this portion of the play is well printed in both folios. Just before Buckingham makes his *exit* (p. 531), a change is made in the folio, 1632, in an adverb, which is supported by the sense; Henry's victim is speaking of false friends:—

> "When they once perceive
> The least rub in your fortunes, fall away
> Like water from ye, never found again
> But *when* they mean to sink ye."

The ordinary reading is, "But where they mean," &c. The change is not material.

SCENE II.

P. 534. It is evident from the old stage-direction, "the King draws the curtain, and sits reading pensively," that in the early simplicity and poverty of our stage, Henry himself drew a

traverse at the back of the stage, and discovered himself to
Norfolk and Suffolk, "reading pensively." It would appear
that in the time of the corrector of the folio, 1632, the
practice in this respect had been somewhat improved; for
the words stating that "the King draws the curtain," are
struck out, and "Curtain drawn" is inserted in the margin
in parenthesis, showing that Henry was discovered to his
nobles "reading pensively," by some contrivance which rendered it needless for him to rise from his seat, and then
to resume it after he had drawn the curtain. This is a
curious indication of a slight advance made in the scenical
arrangements of our old theatres. When Henry subsequently asks,—

> "Is this an hour for temporal affairs?"

we are told, in a manuscript stage-direction, that he *holds up
a book* (probably of prayer) to the two noblemen who had in-
truded upon his "private meditations."

SCENE III.

P. 538. Anne Bullen, reflecting on the fall of Queen
Katharine, observes of power,—

> "Though it be temporal,
> Yet, if that quarrel, fortune, do divorce
> It from the bearer, 'tis a sufferance panging
> As soul and body's severing."

Warburton, Hanmer, Johnson, and Steevens have all written
notes upon the words, "that quarrel, fortune," some taking
"quarrel" as an arrow, others in the sense of *quarreller*, &c. ;
but, if we may believe the old corrector, it is only a misprint,
for he gives the second line thus :—

> "Yet, if that *cruel* fortune do divorce," &c.,

which certainly removes the difficulty, and applies to "fortune" an epithet, to which its commonness seems the main
objection. When *cruel* was spelt *crewell*, as was sometimes
the case, the mistake was not difficult.

P. 541. The Lord Chamberlain, on retiring, tells Anne
Bullen, who has just been made Marchioness of Pembroke,—

> " I shall not fail to approve the fair conceit
>   The king hath of you."

" To *improve* the fair conceit," &c., seems the more natural word, although " approve" may be said, upon Johnson's construction, sufficiently well to fill the place in the text. The correction of *improve* for " approve," is made in the folio, 1632.

P. 542. At the end of the scene, Anne Bullen declares that her advancement gives her no satisfaction :—

> " Would I had no being,
>   If this salute my blood a jot."

Whatever meaning may be attached to the expression, "salute my blood," the sense of the poet is rendered much more distinct, if we substitute a different word, easily misread or misprinted :—

> " Would I had no being,
>   If this *elate* my blood a jot."

Elate, as an adjective, is in very old use in our language ; and it is doing no great violence to Shakespeare to suppose that here he converted an adjective into a verb. This has been the practice ever since, and we have the authority of the corrector of the folio, 1632, in favour of *elate*.

SCENE IV.

P. 544. The trial scene of the Queen seems to have been taken more than usual pains with, both by copyist and compositor ; but two exceptions to its general accuracy are pointed out in the margin of the corrected folio, 1632 : both are misprints ; the first less obvious, though more important than the last. Katharine desires that if any charge of infidelity can be made out against her,—

> " In God's name
>   Turn me away ; and let the foul'st contempt
>   Shut door upon me, and so give me up
>   To the sharp'st kind of justice."

We can have no hesitation here in substituting another in the place of the very tame word " kind," in the last hemistich, when the substitution adds much to the force of the

passage, and impresses us at once as the language of the
poet :—

> " And let the foul'st contempt
> Shut door upon me, and so give me up
> To the sharp'st *knife* of justice."

We can hardly suppose this striking improvement merely
speculative and conjectural. When, afterwards, Wolsey says,—

> " It shall be therefore bootless,
> That longer you desire the court;"

though "desire" be in the old editions (excepting the folio
of 1685), and though the intended meaning may be gathered from it, yet we cannot refuse, instead of it, to adopt
defer, which suits the place so much better, and which is
warranted by the same authority which, in the preceding
instance, has given us so expressive a word as *knife*, to the
exclusion of so vague a term as "kind."

ACT III.   SCENE II.

P. 559. When Suffolk informs Surrey that the King has
already married Anne Bullen, the latter exclaims, as it has
always been printed,—

> " Now all my joy
> Trace the conjunction !"

but Surrey did not wish his joy in particular, but all joy to
follow the marriage, and we ought certainly to read with
the annotator of the folio, 1632,—

> " Now *may* all joy
> Trace the conjunction !"

And, in consistency with this wish, Suffolk and Norfolk cry
"Amen" to it.

Several stage-directions are added in manuscript in this
scene. When Wolsey and Cromwell enter, the peers *stand
back* to observe him; and when Wolsey has dismissed his
Secretary, he speaks *to himself*, and finally *stands back
musing*. When the King enters reading a schedule, Wolsey
does not at first see him, but wakes *amazedly* from his
reverie as soon as Lovell touches him. Henry afterwards
gives the schedule to Wolsey, who, when the King is gone,

opens and reads it trembling. After he has glanced at his own letter to the Pope, he *sinks in a chair,* from which he rises when the Dukes of Norfolk, Suffolk, &c., enter, and in the King's name demand the Great Seal from him. Such, we may conclude, was the manner of the old actor of the part of Wolsey, and the way in which the business of the scene was formerly conducted.

P. 562. The King, addressing the Cardinal, says,—

> " You have scarce time
> To steal from spiritual leisure a brief span,
> To keep your earthly audit."

If Wolsey enjoyed so much " spiritual leisure," it would seem as if he might have time also for his earthly audit, and the manuscript-corrector of the folio, 1632, inserts *labour* for " leisure" in the text with decided propriety :—

> " To steal from spiritual *labour* a brief span," &c.

This is another of the many cases in which it is very apparent how the two words were confounded by the ear of the scribe.

ACT IV. SCENE I.

P. 573. The corrected copy of the folio, 1632, is deficient of a leaf containing pp. 223 and 224, which was principally occupied by a description of the coronation of Anne Bullen.

SCENE II.

P. 580. In the folio, 1623, Katharine says of Wolsey,—

> "So may he rest : his faults lie gently on him."

In the folio, 1632, the line stands thus imperfectly :—

> " So may he rest : his faults lie on him."

The corrector of this last edition, instead of taking the word "gently" from the earlier folio, inserts *lightly* in the margin :—

> " So may he rest : his faults lie *lightly* on him."

Possibly, this was the form in which he had heard the passage delivered; but Shakespeare's word was doubtless that of the folio, 1623.

P. 581. Although it has been followed in various modern editions, nothing can be more absurd than the old punctuation of the opening of the speech of Griffith, where he gives a character of the deceased Cardinal :—

> " This cardinal,
> Though from an humble stock, undoubtedly
> Was fashion'd to much honour.   From his cradle
> He was a scholar, and a ripe and good one."

The old corrector, in accordance with the obvious sense of the passage, omits the period before " From his cradle," and inserts it after it :—

> " Was fashioned to much honour from his cradle.
> He was a scholar," &c.

It is astonishing that so decided a blunder, as to represent that the Cardinal was a ripe and good scholar "from his cradle," should have been repeated over and over again from the year 1623 to our own day.   Lower down occurs a line that has occasioned discussion, relating to Wolsey's foundations at Ipswich and Oxford :—

> " One of which fell with him,
> Unwilling to outlive the good that did it."

" The good that did it " has been construed " the virtue that raised the edifice ;" but a note in the folio, 1632, has the passage in a form which clears away all difficulty, and is in all probability the true reading :—

> " Unwilling to outlive the good *man* did it;"

i. e. the good man (for such Griffith represented Wolsey) who laid the foundation.

P. 583. All the early editions print thus, when Griffith speaks of Katharine very soon after the vision,—

> " How pale she looks,
> And of an earthy cold?   Mark her eyes."

Steevens, at a venture, inserted *you* to complete the measure, " Mark *you* her eyes ;" but the error lies earlier, and before

the note of interrogation, for the old corrector gives the last
line as follows :—

> " And of an earthy *coldness ?*   Mark her eyes."

Such we may confidently believe was the original reading :
to say that a dying person looks " of an earthy cold," is
at least a peculiar expression, though " cold" is very often
used as a substantive.

ACT V. SCENE I.

P. 590. Instead of " you a brother of us," the corrected
folio has " *to* a brother of us," which hardly seems required ;
and at the bottom of the page, for

> " The good I stand on is my truth and honesty,"

which is certainly sense, the folio, 1632, has,—

> " The *ground* I stand on is my truth and honesty ;"

which reads better, and *ground* might be carelessly mistaken for " good."

SCENE II.

P. 595. The Lord Chancellor tells Cranmer,—

> " But we all are men,
> In our own natures frail, and capable
> Of our flesh."

Malone, for " and capable," put *incapable*, without any warrant, and without extricating the passage from the difficulty
involving it.   Monk Mason saw what was necessary, and
suggested the word which is found written in the folio, 1632,
as the correction of a mere error of the press :—

> " In our own natures frail, and *culpable*
> Of our flesh."

P. 596. Another misprint is pointed out in Cranmer's
speech in answer to the charges against him.   The passage
has always stood as follows :—

> " Nor is there living
> (I speak it with a single heart, my lords)
> A man that more detests, more stirs against,
> Both in his private conscience and his place,
> Defacers of a public peace, than I do."

Now, in the old copies, " stirs" is printed *stirres ;* and *strives*, the word supplied by the old corrector, appears to have been misread *stirres :* we ought, therefore, in future, to give the line thus :—

> "A man that more detests, more *strives* against,
> Defacers of a public peace," &c.

SCENE III.

P. 603. In the two subsequent lines there appear to be as many unaccountable misprints, which are nevertheless set right by the corrector of the second folio :—

> " Let me ne'er hope to see a chine again,
> And that I would not for a cow, God save her."

God save whom? the cow? Certainly not. To do justice to this singular emendation, we must quote more of the speech of the Man who is keeping back the people, in the palace yard at Greenwich, pressing forward to see the procession of the christening : the Porter is finding fault with his Man for not repelling the crowd, and the Man replies :—

> " I am not Samson, nor sir Guy, nor Colbrand,
> To mow em down before me ; but if I spared any
> That had a head to hit, either young or old,
> He or she, cuckold or cuckold-maker,
> Let me ne'er hope to see a chine again,
> And that I would not for a cow, God save her."

Why should he just at such a moment think of "a chine" or " a cow?" He was about to witness the royal procession to the christening of the princess Elizabeth ; and the old corrector informs us that both " chine" and " cow" are blunders of the copyist, of the compositor, or of both : he reads,—

> " Let me ne'er hope to see a *queen* again,
> And that I would not for a *crown*, God save her."

That is, God save the *queen*, the sight of whom again the Porter's Man would not miss for a *crown*. *Queen* (printed

formerly with a final *e*) became " chine," and *crown* " cow."
This emendation does not look like mere guess-work, but it
is out of the question to speculate upon what authority the
corrector of the folio, 1632, may have proceeded.

It is needless to quote the very particular stage-directions
written in the margin towards the termination of this drama.
It will be sufficient to say, that nothing seems omitted that
could conduce to the exact and successful performance of it
by the actors concerned in the representation.

TROILUS AND CRESSIDA.

P. 11. The Prologue of thirty-one lines fills a whole page in the folios, and is not found in the quarto editions: it is merely headed "Prologue;" but the corrector of the folio, 1632, has subjoined the words *in armour* in parenthesis, showing, as indeed we learn from a passage in it, that the speaker was "a Prologue armed." He alters the mis-spelt name of Antenonidus to Antenorides; and, what is more important, he reads, "sparre up the sons of Troy," for "stirre up the sons of Troy," about which there can be no dispute, although, until the time of Theobald, the four folios, Rowe, and Pope had it "*stir* up the sons of Troy." The proper orthography seems to be "sperr up the sons of Troy," which has precisely the same meaning as "*sparre* up the sons of Troy," the word of the old corrector. We may add that in "The Cobbler of Canterbury," first printed in 1590, and again in 1608, the very year before Shakespeare's "Troilus and Cressida" came out, we meet with the following couplet, which occurs just after the mention of Troilus:—

> "Grey and sparkling, like the stars
> When the day her light *up spars*."

Possibly, therefore, our great dramatist was put in mind of the word by seeing it, in connexion with his hero, in the tract above quoted, just before he sat down to write: Shakespeare's use of it, however, is infinitely more proper, since to "sperr up a gate" is a natural expression, but to "sperr up light," a violent metaphor.

ACT I. SCENE I.

P. 14. Rowe and Pope made two excellent emendations in
the line,—

> " So, traitor !—when she comes ! when is she thence ?"

The manuscript-correction in the folio, 1632, only applies to
"when" instead of *then* of the old copies, while it leaves un-
changed "when she is thence," although the transposition,
"when *is she* thence ?" is equally wanted.   Thus, in this instance, the corrector did only half what seems necessary to
render the poet's meaning intelligible.   Six lines lower, he
properly altered *scorn* to "storm," which was also Rowe's
emendation, but sufficiently obvious.

SCENE II.

P. 17. The Acts and Scenes are not distinguished in any
of the old printed editions, but the corrector has introduced
them in manuscript, with more or less accuracy, in the folio
which went through his hands.

P. 23. Pandarus tells Cressida that Antenor is "a proper
man of person," which it may seem needless to change ; but a
manuscript note in the margin of the folio, 1632, tells us
to read, "a proper man of *his* person."   On the next page,
the necessary word "see" is inserted where it is omitted in
the folios,—"you shall *see* Troilus anon."

P. 27. For the evidently misprinted line,—

> " Achievement is command ; ungain'd beseech,"

we are informed that we ought to read,—

> " *Achiev'd men still* command ; ungain'd beseech."

That *achiev'd men* should have been converted by the old
compositor into "achievement," seems not unlikely ; but
how *still* became "is" in his hands, it is not easy to imagine ;
and we may feel some surprise that the emendation of the
line proposed in note 8,—

> " Achiev'd men *us* command ; ungain'd beseech,"

is not supported by the authority of the corrector of the folio, 1632 : *us* for " is," was a most probable mistake.

P. 28. Agamemnon, referring to the disasters that have hitherto attended the siege of Troy by the Greeks, and observing that disappointment constantly accompanies human undertakings, inquires,—

> " Why then, you princes,
> Do you with cheeks abash'd behold our works,
> And call them shames ?"

This is as the passage has been invariably printed ; but the old annotator points out an easy misprint, the correction of which is in exact accordance with the rest of Agamemnon's speech, where he advises the Greeks not to be disheartened by their previous misfortunes :—

> " Why then, you princes,
> Do you with cheeks abash'd behold our *wrecks*,
> And call them shames ?"

The word *wreck* is frequently used by Shakespeare, and by writers of his day, to signify any kind of disaster or ruin, and such is its meaning in this place.

SCENE III.

P. 29. The folio, 1632, is very carelessly printed in this part of the play ; and for " place and sway," of the earlier impressions, it has " place and *may*." The old corrector does not pass over this blunder, nor others : thus, a few lines above, he has " *replies* to chiding fortune," for " retires to chiding fortune ;" and in the beginning of Nestor's speech, "*godlike* seat" for " godly seat." Pope has " returns," and Hanmer " replies," for *retires ;* and all more modern editors, " godlike" for *godly :* the last was an error of the folios only.

P. 33. Such was not the case with a mistake in the second great speech of Ulysses, where he is referring to the mimicry, by Patroclus, of the chiefs of the Grecian army :—

> " And in this fashion,
> All our abilities, gifts, natures, shapes,
> Severals and generals of grace exact,
> Achievements, plots," &c.

fell under the ridicule of Achilles : here the words, " of grace exact," seem wrong, although always so printed, because the complaint was, that they were not " of grace exact," but grossly caricatured. Therefore the corrector of the folio, 1632, thus altered the expression to a form much more in accordance with the context : —

> "Severals and generals, *all* grace *extract ;*"

i. e. deprived of all the grace which really belonged to the persons Patroclus imitated. This appears to be an important improvement of the received text ; but it is certainly one which did not require resort to any independent authority, inasmuch as close attention to what must have been the meaning of the author, may have led to the detection of the error.

P. 35. In a celebrated speech by Æneas, a fine compound epithet appears to have escaped in the hands of the old printer : —

> " The worthiness of praise distains his worth,
> If that the prais'd himself bring the praise forth ;
> But what the repining enemy commends,
> That breath fame blows ; that praise, sole pure, transcends."

The second folio omits *But* at the commencement of the third line, as injurious to the metre ; and a small manuscript-correction in the margin, converts a poor expression in the fourth line into one of great force and beauty : —

> " What the repining enemy commends,
> That breath fame blows ; that praise, *soul*-pure, transcends."

The scribe wrote, or the compositor wrought, only by the sound, and that sound has hitherto satisfied. To show how readily misprints are even now made, we may mention that both Malone and Steevens give the last line, most ruinously to the measure, thus : —

> " That breath fame *follows ;* that praise, sole pure, transcends."

P. 37. All the folio editions have this line : —

> " I'll pawn this truth with my three drops of blood :"

the quartos, more intelligibly, —

> " I'll *prove* this truth with my three drops of blood."

The old corrector of the folio, 1632, erases *pawn*, and places "prove" in the margin ; but, supposing that he obtained the latter word from the quartos, he made no alteration in the next line, which in the folios varies from the quartos in two not unimportant particulars: the folios read,—

> " Now heavens forbid such scarcity of youth ;"

while the quartos give it,—

> " Now heavens *forefend* such scarcity of *men*."

If, therefore, "prove" were derived by the old corrector from the quartos, it is clear that, for some reason, he preferred the next line as it stands in the folios.

ACT II. SCENE I.

P. 41. Considering the difference between the quartos and the folios, the first reading *unsalted*, and the second "whinid'st," we may notice that the old corrector preferred the last, but altered the spelling of the word to *whinewd'st*, meaning *vinewd'st*, or most mouldy. *Vinny*, or *vinnewy*, for mouldy, is still a word in use in the provinces.

SCENE II.

P. 46. There can be no doubt that the line,—

> " And fly like chidden Mercury from Jove,"

is misplaced in the folios, and rightly placed in the quartos : the corrector of the folio, 1632, appears first to have tried to remedy the blunder in his usual method, by figures in his margin, but not finding that effectual, he struck out the line, and inserted it in manuscript in the situation to which it unquestionably belongs. He subsequently set right two misprints in the same speech, *hard* for "hare," and *lovers* for "livers:" the first belongs also to the folio, 1623, and the last only to the folio, 1632.

P. 50. We may, perhaps, receive with thankfulness a change in what Paris says regarding the dangers which had attended his enterprise in securing and retaining Helen,—

> " Yet, I protest,
> Were I alone to pass the difficulties,
> And had as ample power as I have will,
> Paris should ne'er retract what he hath done,
> Nor faint in the pursuit."

Here for "pass the difficulties" (spelt *passe* in the old copies), the old corrector tells us to substitute "*poise* the difficulties," or *weigh* them, which we may believe, if only from the context, to have been Shakespeare's word.

P. 55. The emendation of "We sent our messengers," instead of "*He* sent our messengers," of the folios, and "He *sate* our messengers," of the quartos, is warranted by an emendation of *W* for *H* in the margin. Theobald read, "He *shent* our messengers;" but this change is not required, nor is it supported by the fact, since, as is stated in note 3, Achilles had not *shent*, or rebuked, any messengers from Agamemnon.

SCENE III.

P. 56. The emendation of "lunes" for *lines,* in

> " His pettish lines, his ebbs, his flows, as if," &c.,

as it stands in the folios (the quartos have an entirely different text), is made in a correction in the folio, 1632 ; and "lunes" is certainly the word intended.

ACT III. SCENE I.

P. 64. Much discussion has been occasioned by the words of Paris, in all the early impressions, where he calls Cressida his " disposer," saying that Troilus is going to sup " with my disposer Cressida." The difficulty has been to discover why Paris should call Cressida his " disposer ;" and some commentators have recommended *deposer*, others *despiser*, instead of " disposer," while Steevens wished to deprive Paris of the speech altogether, and to transfer it to Helen. It is surprising that no editor should have guessed at the right word, when speculating that " disposer" was an error of the press : a manuscript note in the folio, 1632, informs us that for "disposer," we should substitute *dispraiser*, Cressida being a person who did not allow the merits of Paris. Pandarus, just after Paris has called Cressida his *dispraiser*, observes that there had been some difference between them— "She'll none of him ; they two are twain"—and though he does not state on what point they had disagreed, it is enough to warrant us in believing that Paris calls Cressida, not his "disposer," but his *dispraiser*. The word recurs twice in this part of the dialogue, and in each instance the old corrector has converted "disposer" into *dispraiser*. It is to be remarked also, that he makes no change in the prefixes, but allows "You must not know where he sups" to remain in Helen's speech, in contradiction to the practice of modern editors, which, it must be allowed, seems founded upon a correct notion of the course of the dialogue. Possibly the mistake in the prefix in this place, did not attract the attention of the writer of the marginal emendations ; but it can make no difference in the apparent fitness of changing "disposer" to *dispraiser*.

SCENE II.

P. 67. It is a very noticeable circumstance that the expression of Troilus, as found in some copies of the quarto of 1609, as stated in note 2,—

> " Love's thrice repured nectar,"

instead of "Love's thrice *reputed* nectar" of the folios and other quartos, is transferred by the corrector of the folio, 1632, to that impression. This fact may show, if no independent authority were resorted to, how the passage was recited before and after the second folio made its appearance, and confirms it, if confirmation were wanted, as the true reading. We often find *t* and *r* misprinted for each other ; and all that it was necessary to do was to put the pen through the first, and to insert the last in the margin. Although this important emendation was made, another emendation of considerable value, near the end of the play, *aims* for "arms" (p. 141, note 5), also found in some copies of the quarto of 1609, was not adopted. This looks as if the corrector had not there been guided by the same authority.

P. 72. In the amorous dialogue between Troilus and Cressida, the latter, affecting coyness, distinguishes between her two selfs, in all the ordinary copies of this play, as follows :—

> " I have a kind of self resides with you,
> But an unkind self, that itself will leave,
> To be another's fool."

The antithesis, undoubtedly intended by the poet, is thus, according to a note in the folio, 1632, sacrificed to an error of the press, and we are instructed, therefore, to read the passage thus :—

> " I have a *kind self, that* resides with you,
> But an unkind self, that itself will leave,
> To be another's fool."

Cressida represents her *kind self* as wishing to remain with Troilus, and her " unkind self " as wishing to separate itself from his company.

SCENE III.

P. 74. All the old editions have the subsequent passage near the commencement of the speech of Calchas, and several pages of notes have been written upon it :—

> " Appear it to your mind,
> That through the sight I bear in things to love
> I have abandon'd Troy."

Some modern editors have given the second line,—

> " That through the sight I bear in things to *come*,"

an amendment that unquestionably clears the sense of the author, and which Monk Mason considered so happy as to require no authority in its favour. Nevertheless, the most usual course has been to print differently, *viz.:*—

> "That through the sight I bear in things, to Jove
> I have abandon'd Troy."

Here it has been reasonably asked, why should Calchas desert and abandon his native city to Jove, who was its protector? Theobald, Warburton, Johnson, Steevens, and Malone, all wasted their time and ingenuity on a mere misprint, which is set right in a moment, and which proves that the old compositor misread *above* " to love:" there is an error also, but of minor importance, in the preceding line, where "appear" is put for *appeal*, in the sense of recall or bring back, and the whole should, therefore, stand thus :—

> "*Appeal* it to your mind,
> That, through the sight I bear in things *above*,
> I have abandon'd Troy;"

i. e. recall to mind that I abandoned Troy by reason of the sight I enjoy in things *above*—foreseeing what would be the issue of the struggle. If Monk Mason thought "things to *come*" an emendation not requiring authority, *à fortiori*, "things *above*" is an emendation even less requiring it, because nearer the misprinted letters in the quartos and folios, while we have the testimony of the old corrector of the folio, 1632, and common sense in its behalf.

P. 78. There is an indisputable, though hitherto undiscovered misprint, in what follows :—

> "For speculation turns not to itself,
> Till it hath travell'd, and is married there
> Where it may see itself."

This is part of the reply of Achilles to Ulysses, who has adverted to the manner in which an individual sees his virtues reflected in another, and thus becomes sensible of them: Achilles answers that this effect is not at all strange, and explains it by reference to the knowledge obtained of personal beauty by sight of it in a looking-glass, adding,—

> "For speculation turns not to itself,
> Till it hath travell'd, and is *mirror'd* there
> Where it may see itself."

To read "married there where it may see itself," seems sheer nonsense, in comparison with the fine and distinctly expressed meaning of the poet, when, with the aid of a marginal emendation in the folio, 1632, we read *mirror'd* for "married."

P. 79. The quartos and folios differ in an important epithet: the first have the hemistich, "And great Troy shrieking," and the last, "And great Troy *shrinking*." There can be no dispute which is right, though Steevens raised the question; and the old corrector put his pen through the letter *n*, and left the word *shriking*, which was all he thought necessary.

z

P. 80. Here again the folios misrepresent the author's words, if not his meaning: that of 1623 has,—

> " Since things in motion begin to catch the eye :"

the printer of the folio, 1632, seeing that the line was redundant, altered " begin" to '*gin;* but the quartos read,—

> " Since things in motion sooner catch the eye,"

which we may, perhaps, admit as the true text ; but, nevertheless, the manuscript-corrector of the folio, 1632, alters "'*gin to*" to *quicklier*, which may have been the word of the poet, and which he employs elsewhere :—

> " Since things in motion *quicklier* catch the eye."

Here, therefore, the writer of the emendation did not follow the quartos, but he may have guessed at the word he inserted in his margin, or obtained it from some authority. In the next line he alters " out" to *once*, which agrees with the quartos and with the sense. It merits observation that the two changes, *quicklier* and *once*, were, most probably, not made at the same time, since the ink used is different.

P. 81. The following is a couplet, in which there appear to be two lapses by the printer :—

> "Keeps place with thought, and almost, like the gods,
> Does thoughts unveil in their dumb cradles."

Hanmer read, "Keeps *pace* with thought," and so did the old corrector: Warburton vindicated " place," though in the next line, properly represented (which it has never yet been), Shakespeare follows up the idea, and tells us that the providence of a watchful state, like the gods, almost anticipates thoughts—not only keeps *pace* with them, but goes beyond them,—

> "Does thoughts unveil in their dumb *crudities ;*"

i. e. unveils them before they even become thoughts. This must have been the poet's language, and we find *crudities* for " cradles" in the margin of the folio, 1632. Hanmer, Malone, Steevens, &c., saw that "cradles" was not, in point of measure, enough for the line, but they never dreamed that the word was a misprint. The whole passage is, therefore, thus cleared :—

> " The providence that's in a watchful state
> Knows almost every grain of Plutus' gold,
> Finds bottom in th' uncomprehensive deeps,
> Keeps *pace* with thought, and almost, like the gods,
> Does thoughts unveil in their dumb *crudities*."

Here meaning and metre are both accomplished ; but in what way the emendation was arrived at, we have no knowledge : it seems something better than a merely speculative suggestion.

P. 82. For "sweet, rouse yourself," addressed by Patroclus to Achilles, when he is endeavouring to excite him to renewed action, we are instructed in manuscript to read, "*Swift,* rouse yourself." We have before had *swift* misprinted "sweet" (p. 62). Three lines lower, the old corrector does not strike out *airy* in the passage, " Be shook to airy air," as it stands in the folios ; but he makes it, " Be shook to *very* air," which is much more emphatic than merely " Be shook to air." Nevertheless, if the poet intended his measure to be regular, *very* is not required.

ACT IV. SCENE I.

P. 85. Diomed tells Æneas, that when the truce is at an end, he will "play the hunter for his life,"—

> " With all my force, pursuit, and policy :"

the line seems to run more properly as it is amended in the folio, 1632,—

> " By Jove, I'll play the hunter for thy life,
> With all my *fierce* pursuit, and policy."

However, the change is by no means unavoidable.

SCENE II.

P. 90. When Troilus tells Æneas to keep his counsel, the latter replies, in the folios,—

> " Good, good, my lord ; the secrets of nature
> Have not more gift in taciturnity."

Now, unless we read " secrets" as a trisyllable, the measure

is faulty: Theobald proposed "the secret *things* of nature;"
and here resort to the quartos affords no aid, for they absurdly have "the secrets of neighbour Pandar." The corrector of the folio, 1632, inserts a word which, most likely,
had dropped out in the press, and which we may, perhaps,
accept upon his evidence, because it is the very word required, in reference to the hidden operations of nature:—

> "Good, good, my lord, the secret *laws* of nature
> Have not more gift in taciturnity."

SCENE IV.

P. 93. We have already seen that various scraps of ballads,
introduced into the dialogue, have been erroneously given,
when neither copyist nor printer was perhaps in fault; for
the author himself may have quoted from memory. Here
we have another instance of the same kind, where Pandarus
cites some well-known popular production : it is thus given
in the early authorities :—

> "O heart! O heart! heavy heart!
> Why sigh'st thou without breaking?
> Because thou canst not ease thy smart
> By friendship, nor by speaking."

Pope inserted an interjection before "heavy heart," for
metre's sake; but it seems probable, from mere perusal,
that the last line has been mis-remembered, mis-written, or
misprinted, since there is no antithesis between "friendship"
and "speaking." The folio, 1632, has *sittest* for "sigh'st," an
error which the old corrector remedies, and represents that
the quatrain should stand as follows :—

> "O heart! O heart! O heavy heart!
> Why sigh'st thou without breaking?
> Because thou can'st not ease thy smart
> By *silence* nor by speaking."

It is underlined as a quotation, though printed as prose in all
the old copies.

P. 96. Troilus, alluding to the danger of too much reliance
on our own supposed constancy, observes,—

> "And sometimes we are devils to ourselves,
> When we will tempt the frailty of our powers,
> Presuming on their changeful potency."

" Changeful potency" seems the very contrary of what was intended: if the verse would allow it, we ought rather to read,—

> " Presuming on their *un*changeful potency :"

or the potency with which they would resist change ; and a manuscript alteration in the folio, 1632, leads us to believe that the scribe misheard the word,—

> " Presuming on their *chainful* potency,"

the potency with which they chain, and fetter us to the particular object of our affections.

SCENE V.

P. 99. There is a remarkable discrepancy between the quartos and folios, when Cressida is introduced by Diomed to the Grecian commanders, and when such as like kiss her in succession. When Menelaus advances for the purpose, Patroclus interposes and kisses for him: Menelaus says,—

> " I had good argument for kissing once,"

alluding, of course, to the time when he was living with Helen ; and Patroclus answers,—

> " But that's no argument for kissing now ;
> For thus popp'd Paris in his hardiment,
> And parted thus you and your argument."

The last line is only in the quartos, and the corrector of the folio, 1632, seeing its importance, writes it in a blank space, but differing in one word,—

> " And parted you, and your *same* argument;"

adding this explanatory stage-direction, *Puts back Menelaus,* who thus allowed himself to be defeated in his design upon the lips of Cressida. Patroclus, having kissed for Menelaus, afterwards kisses on his own behalf, and then a note of *kisses again* is placed in the margin. If the corrector had derived the additional line from the quartos, it seems probable that he would have followed the precise wording of those editions.

P. 100. Few lines in this play have produced more comment than the second of the following, where Ulysses is censuring the wanton spirit of Cressida :—

> "O! these encounterers, so glib of tongue,
> That give a coasting welcome ere it comes," &c.

What is "a coasting welcome?" has been the question ; and we learn from the old corrector that the word, miswritten, we may suppose, in the manuscript used by the printer, was most appropriate to the place,—

> "O! these encounterers, so glib of tongue,
> That give *occasion* welcome ere it comes,
> And wide unclasp the tables of their thoughts,
> To every tickling reader, set them down
> As sluttish spoils of opportunity,
> And daughters of the game."

They became the "spoils of opportunity" by giving welcome to *occasion* even before it arrived.

P. 102. Shakespeare employs the word "utterance" as the extreme result of a personal encounter in "Macbeth," Act III. Scene I., and in "Cymbeline," Act III. Scene I. The manuscript-corrector of the folio, 1632, informs us that he used it also in the following passage, which refers to the conflict between Hector and Ajax, instead of the much less appropriate term "uttermost:" Agamemnon speaks to Diomed,—

> " As you and lord Æneas
> Consent upon the order of their fight,
> So be it; either to the *utterance*,
> Or else a breach."

i. e. at your discretion either let them pursue the conflict to extremity, or else break off before it comes to that: *breach* is a printed emendation in the folios, instead of "breath," of the earlier editions in quarto, which can only be understood as a breathing time.

ACT V. SCENE I.

P. 110. Nobody has attempted to explain why Thersites, when he calls Patroclus the "male varlet" and "masculine whore" of Achilles, ends by wishing a list of loathsome diseases (part of which only are mentioned in the folios) to afflict "such preposterous discoveries." What can be the meaning of "discoveries" so applied ? The old corrector has it "such preposterous *discolourers;*" and perhaps rightly, the allusion being to the painting and discolouring of nature by Patroclus, like a female prostitute.

SCENE II.

P. 113. The quartos and folios vary materially in one of the speeches of Thersites. According to the first, he says of Cressida, "And any man may sing her, if he can take her cliff; she's noted:" on the other hand, the folios, with evident corruption, give the passage thus: "And any man may find her, if he can but take her *life;* she's noted." The allusion is, probably, indelicate; and the old corrector inserts one word in the folio, 1632, that had been omitted, and alters another that had been misprinted—"And any man may find her *key,* if he can take her *clefft;* she's noted." The figure is, of course, borrowed from singing at sight, and this last reading seems preferable to that of the quartos.

P. 115. In the speech of Cressida,—

"In faith, I will, la: never trust me else,"

we have something like a repetition of the blunder committed in "Henry IV.," Part II. Act I. Scene III., where "lo." for *lord,* of the quartos, was subsequently misprinted *lo!* as if it were an interjection, and then *to* as if it were a preposition. In the instance before us, the corruption seems to have originated with the quartos: *la,* there, became *lo!* in the folio, 1623, and *goe* in the folio, 1632. The old corrector of that edition thought, or knew, that the word ought to be *lord,* and he so amended the line:—

"In faith I will, *lord:* never trust me else."

Still, the earliest impressions may be right, and Cressida may merely have used "la" as a feminine expletive, though we have the above evidence to the contrary. It is not a point of importance.

SCENE III.

P. 121. Andromache's speech to Hector only consists of these words in the amended folio, 1632:—

> "O ! be persuaded : do not count it holy
>   To hurt by being just."

The rest is struck through with a pen, as if the person who introduced the manuscript-emendations could make nothing of the passage either by guess or guide. This, therefore, is one of the places in which we are still left in the dark, not, indeed, as to the meaning of the poet, since that is pretty obvious, but as to the precise form in which he expressed that meaning.

SCENE IV.

P. 126. Cressida, having given to Diomed the sleeve she had received from Troilus, the latter hunts the former through the field to recover it. Thersites watches the pursuit, and, when they enter, observes, as all printed copies have it,—

> "Soft! here comes sleeve and th' other."

A point (not indeed of much value) has certainly been lost ; for, upon the authority of an emendation in the folio, 1632, Thersites ought to say,—

> "Soft! here comes sleeve and *sleeveless*."

Troilus being, as it were, upon "a sleeveless errand," in search of the sleeve he had given Cressida, which was still in the possession of his rival : "Here comes sleeve and th' other" reads so poorly, that we may feel sure Shakespeare never wrote it. In the same way, when Troilus and Diomed fight, while Thersites stands behind, he exclaims, as if alternately encouraging each,—

> "Hold thy whore, Grecian ! Now for thy whore, Trojan ! Now the sleeve ! Now the *sleeveless*."

In all editions we find only, "Now the sleeve ! Now the sleeve !"

P. 133. For the line, as it stands in the quartos,—

> " So, Ilion, fall thou next ! now Troy, sink down,"

the folio, 1632, as corrected, has,—

> " So, Ilion, fall thou ! Now, *great* Troy, sink down !"

which shows that the writer of the marginal notes did not here follow the earlier impressions. He saw that the line

required a syllable, but whether he added *great* upon conjecture, or upon authority, we know not. The folios, 1623
and 1632, omitting "next" of the quartos, left the line
imperfect.

P. 135. There can be no doubt that for "broker, lackey,"
in Troilus' dismissal of Pandarus, we ought to substitute
brothel-lackey, *i.e.* the servant of a brothel, not merely from
the occupation Pandarus had taken upon himself, but from
the peculiarities of the old copies: the quartos read, "broker
lackey ;" the folio, 1623, in one place (where the lines were
mistakenly inserted) has "brother lackey," and afterwards,
"broker, lackey ;" the folio, 1632, has, in one place, "brother
lachy," and in the other, "brother lackey." "*Brothel*-
lackey" was one of the few changes for the better in the
folio, 1664 ; but it must have been preceded by the manuscript-emendation in the folio, 1632, where the passage is
made to run as follows :—

> "Hence, brothel-lackey, ignomy and shame
> Pursue thy life."

Two circumstances are to be noted in reference to the conclusion of this play, as it appears in the corrected folio, 1632.
The first is, that the following words are written in a blank
space opposite the speech of Pandarus, after all the other
characters have made their exit—*Left alone, let him say this
by way of Epilogue.* The other circumstance is that the four
lines after Pandarus asks, "What verse for it ? what instance
for it ?—Let me see," are underlined as a quotation ; and we
may infer that they were extracted from some popular, but
now unknown, production of the day, and applied by the
poet to his own purpose. We have repeatedly seen that the
old corrector scored with his pen under every scrap by any
other author, to whom Shakespeare appears to have been in
this manner indebted.

CORIOLANUS.

ACT I. SCENE I.

P. 141. The earliest manuscript-emendation cannot be called a necessary one; but still it seems, taking the context into account, a considerable improvement, and may, perhaps, be admitted on the evidence of the corrector of the folio, 1632. It occurs in the speech of 1 Citizen, where he is referring to the wants of the poor, and to the superfluities of the rich:—

"But they think we are too dear: the leanness that afflicts us, the *abjectness* of our misery, is as an inventory to particularize their abundance; our suffering is a gain to them."

For *abjectness*, the common reading has been "object"—"the object of our misery;" that is to say, the sight of our misery; but the speaker has talked of the "leanness" of the poor citizens of Rome, and he follows it up by the mention of the *abjectness* of their misery. This substitution could hardly have proceeded from the mere taste or discretion of the old corrector, but still it is hardly wanted.

P. 145. We encounter an important change in one part of Menenius' apologue, where the belly admits that it is the general receiver of food, adding, as the passage has always been given,—

"But, if you do remember,
I send it through the rivers of your blood,
Even to the Court, the heart, to the seat o' the brain,
And through the cranks and offices of man."

It is evident that the last line but one is not measure; and we are instructed to read it, and the next, in a way that not only cures this defect, but much improves the sense, by following up the figure of "the court, the heart," and completing the resemblance of the human body to the various parts of a commonwealth :—

> " Even to the Court, the heart, the *Senate*, brain ;
> And through the *ranks* and offices of man."

Tyrwhitt thought "the seat o' the brain" a very "languid expression ;" and Malone agreed with him in taking " seat" to mean royal seat. When " seat" was written *seate*, the mistake for *senate* was easy ; and the change (which never occurred to any commentator) is supported both by what precedes, and by what follows it, going through the various degrees in a state—the court, the senate, persons of different ranks, the holders of offices, &c.

P. 148. Menenius, speaking of the crowd, says,—

> " Nay, these are almost thoroughly persuaded," &c. ;

whereas, according to the old corrector, the line, as properly read, is much more emphatic,—

> " Nay, these are *all most* thoroughly persuaded," &c.

Lower down, at the end of the next speech of Marcius,—

> " Shooting their emulation,"

of the old copies, is altered to "*shouting* their *exultation*." Modern editors have adopted *shouting;* and " emulation," in the sense in which Shakespeare uses it, does not seem to require change : *exultation*, however, better expresses what is intended ; and " shooting," for *shouting*, shows that the compositor was careless. In the next line, we have *tributes* for " tribunes," and just afterwards, *unroost* for " unroof'd."

SCENE III.

P. 154. The reading of the second folio has almost invariably been accepted, where Volumnia says that

> " The breasts of Hecuba,
> When she did suckle Hector, look'd not lovelier
> Than Hector's forehead, when it spit forth blood
> At Grecian swords contending."

This, at least, is sense, but the first folio had absurdly printed "contending" *Contenning*, putting it in Italic type, as if it were a name, exactly thus :—

> "At Grecian sword. *Contenning*, tell *Valeria*
> We are fit to bid her welcome."

In note 6 of this page a suggestion is offered that *contemning* was, perhaps, Shakespeare's word ; and the probability is confirmed by the fact, that the corrector of the folio, 1632, informs us that we ought to print as follows :—

> " Look'd not lovelier
> Than Hector's forehead, when it spit forth blood,
> At Grecian swords *contemning :*"

i. e. contemning at Grecian swords, despising them. " Tell Valeria," &c., of course begins a new sentence.

SCENE IV.

P. 158. When the Romans are beaten back to their trenches, Marcius enters, " cursing" his flying followers ; and we here arrive at a line which has been fertile of discussion. Malone and most modern editors have concurred in supposing that Marcius, in his rage and vexation, commences a sentence which he does not finish, and have represented the passage thus :—

> " All the contagion of the south light on you,
> You shames of Rome ! you herd of——Boils and plagues
> Plaster you o'er ; that you may be abhorr'd
> Further than seen, and one infect another
> Against the wind a mile !"

In the folios, the words, spelling, and punctuation, are—

> " You shames of Rome : you Heard of Byles and Plagues
> Plaister you o're," &c.

This mode of spelling *heard* leads us to the corruption, which was detected (possibly by mere conjecture, but more probably with the aid of some extraneous authority) by the manuscript-annotator of the folio, 1632 ; and when pointed out, it must, we apprehend, be admitted without an instant's controversy :—

> " All the contagion of the south light on you,
> You shames of Rome ! *Unheard* of boils and plagues
> Plaster you o'er," &c.

The whole difficulty seems to have been produced by a strange lapse on the part of the old printer.

The old stage-directions are confused in this part of the drama, for we are told that Marcius *is shut in* before he enters the gates of Corioli. This blunder is set right in manuscript, and when all the Roman soldiers, seeing the gates close, exclaim, "To the pot I warrant him," an expression that nobody has attempted to elucidate, it is explained at once by the corrector of the folio, 1632:—

> "*Sold.* See, they have shut him in.
> "*All.*   To the *port*, I warrant him."

They finish the sentence the soldier has begun, "See, they have shut him in—to the *port*, I warrant him." The enemy had shut Marcius into the *port* or gate; and very shortly afterwards Lartius directs, "Let the *ports* be guarded." All editions, ancient and modern, have "pot" for *port*.

P. 159. It is worth noting that, "Even to Calues wish," of the first folio, and "Even to *Calves* wish," of the second folio, is properly altered to "Even to Cato's wish," in the margin of the latter impression. Such a blunder seems to expose itself; but, nevertheless, it was continued until the time of Theobald, passing not only through the four folios, but through the editions of Rowe and Pope.

SCENE VI.

P. 164. Marcius, by permission of Cominius, and after an animating speech, wishes to select a certain number of soldiers to accompany him in an attack upon Aufidius and his Antiates : he, therefore, tells the troops,—

> "Please you to march ;
> And four shall quickly draw out my command,
> Which men are best inclin'd."

Here a difficulty has arisen, why "four" were to draw out his command, and many notes have been written upon the question. We print the passage, as we find it amended, which shows that the scribe or the compositor (most likely the former in this instance) was to blame :—

" Please you march *before*,
And *I* shall quickly draw out my command,
Which men are best inclin'd."

Whoever made the copy for the printer, must have understood *before* as *by four*, and put it in the wrong place, curing the defect in the metre of the first line by arbitrarily inserting *to*. Nothing could be more natural than for Marcius to direct the soldiers to march in front of him, that he might himself make the selection of such as he was to lead.

SCENE VIII.

P. 165. When Marcius and Aufidius meet, the latter addresses the former, as the text has always been given,—

"Not Afric owns a serpent I abhor
More than thy fame and envy."

This cannot be right, inasmuch as, taking "envy" even in the sense of *hate*, Aufidius could hardly mean that he abhorred the fame and the hate of Marcius : the printer made a slight error by mistaking the pronoun *I* for the contraction of the conjunction ; therefore the old corrector reads,—

"Not Afric owns a serpent I abhor
More than thy fame *I* envy."

SCENE IX.

P. 168. Tyrwhitt's emendation of *coverture* for "overture," in the subsequent lines, is precisely that found in the margin of the folio, 1632 ; but "them" is also there altered to *it*, with obvious fitness :—

" When steel grows soft as the parasite's silk
Let *it* be made a *coverture* for the wars."

If *coverture* were not introduced into the text, it was from the hope that sufficient meaning might be made out of the old printed language of the folios ; but the authority of a manuscript-correction here comes in aid of a speculative emendation, and it appears to us that we need not hesitate upon the point hereafter.

ACT II. SCENE I.

P. 173. Few scenes are worse printed in the early copies than this between Menenius and the two Tribunes : it is full of literal errors, and of some which are important to the author's sense, and are set right in manuscript in the second folio. Thus Menenius says of himself,—

> "I am known to be a humorous patrician, and one that loves a cup of hot wine, with not a drop of allaying Tyber in't : said to be something imperfect in favouring the first complaint."

What is "the first complaint" in connexion with Menenius's love for "a cup of hot wine?" It is merely an error from mishearing on the part of the copyist ; for, undoubtedly, we ought to alter "first" to *thirst*,—"the *thirst* complaint :"—

> "One that loves a cup of hot wine, *without* a drop of allaying Tyber in't: said to be something imperfect in favouring the *thirst* complaint."

The humour is entirely lost in the old misprinted text, "first complaint ;" and although no objection need be raised to "with not," instead of *without*, nothing could be easier than the misprint of one word for the other: seeing that "thirst complaint" must be right, we can readily believe in the less-important change. Lower down in the same speech, a negative and a pronoun are omitted, and "bisson" is misprinted *beesome ;* while, still lower, we have "rejourn" for *adjourn,* though "rejourn" may answer the purpose. Near the top of the next page, "controversy bleeding" is put for "controversy *pleading,*" or controversy that was in a course of discussion before the Tribunes.

P. 175. The word in the old editions, "emperickqutique," has, naturally enough, occasioned a pause among the annotators, who at last concurred with Ritson in thinking it "an adjective evidently formed from empirick." Such is not the case: the sentence in which it occurs is part of a speech by Menenius, who is so rejoiced at having a letter from the hero, that he declares that it will lengthen his life seven years—"the most sovereign prescription in Galen is but *emperickqutique,* and to this preservative of no better report than a horse-drench." "Emperickqutique" was not, if we are to believe the old corrector, formed from "empirick," but was a blunder of the printer for two words, which he absurdly combined in one, namely, "empirick" and "physique," as physic was then often spelt : we ought, therefore, to read, "the most sovereign prescription in Galen is but empiric physic, and to this preservative of no better report than a horse-drench." "Empiric *physic*" is, of course, only quack-medicine.

P. 178. The first part of the subsequent quotation hardly requires a note ; while the awkward expression in the last part of it has attracted no observation :—

> "Your prattling nurse
> Into a rapture lets her baby cry,
> While she chats him."

Brutus is here referring to the triumphant return of Coriolanus (now so called) to Rome ; and "chats him" is certainly intelligible in the sense of talks about him, though "chats of him" would be more proper : but a note in the folio, 1632, induces us to believe that Shakespeare did not use the term "chats" at all, and that the word has been misprinted, the compositor taking double *ee* for *a*, and *t* (the commonest blunder) for *r* :—

> "Your prattling nurse
> Into a rapture lets her baby cry,
> While she *cheers* him."

This change is quite consistent with the context.

P. 180. In the following, Theobald read "teach," *reach*, on the supposition that, here also, *t* had been inserted by the compositor, instead of *r* :—

> "This, as you say, suggested
> At some time when his soaring insolence
> Shall teach the people," &c.

The right word was neither "teach" nor *reach*, but a word much better adapted to the situation than either :—

> "This, as you say, suggested
> At some time when his soaring insolence
> Shall *touch* the people," &c.

i. e. shall gall or irritate them. This use of *touch* is common in Shakespeare and other writers.

SCENE II.

P. 183. When the Senators and Tribunes have assembled
"to thank and to remember" the services of Coriolanus,
Sicinius remarks,—

> " We are convented
> Upon a pleasing treaty."

The corrector of the folio, 1632, directs us to substitute
treatise for "treaty," a change supported by "theme," which
immediately follows; but he recommends a more necessary
emendation in the speech of Brutus, just afterwards, where
the Tribune adverts to the fitness of honouring and advancing the hero for his services: he says,—

> " Which the rather
> We shall be blest to do, if he remember
> A kinder value of the people."

The scribe clearly misheard the word, and wrote "blest" for
prest, i. e. ready—of perpetual occurrence in all writers of
the time :—

> " Which the rather
> We shall be *prest* to do," &c.

Even the grudging Tribunes might declare themselves *ready*
"to honour and advance the theme of their assembly," but
there seems no reason why they should state that they
should be "blest" in doing so.

P. 185. This scene is ill-printed in the folio, 1623, but
much worse in the folio, 1632, where errors of all kinds are
so numerous that the margin is filled with corrections in
manuscript. It may be sufficient to mention that in the
speech of Cominius, recounting the deeds of Coriolanus, the
old corrector alters "trim'd with dying cries," of the folio,
1632 (it is "tim'd with dying cries" in the folio, 1623) to
" *tun'd* with dying cries," which may be right ; and " shunless *defamy*" to " shunless destiny," which was very likely
derived from the earlier impression.

SCENE III.

P. 190. Many notes have been written upon the question
of Coriolanus, thus represented in the folio, 1623 :—

> " Why in this woolvish tongue should I stand here ?"

In the folio, 1632, "tongue" is altered to *gown;* but the poet's word was doubtless "*togue,*" for *toga,* mistaken by the compositor, and printed "tongue." The difficulty has not arisen out of this substantive, but out of the epithet which precedes it, *woolvish;* and Johnson, Steevens, Ritson, Malone, &c., have all tried in vain to explain its meaning in the place where it occurs. It is nothing but a lapse by the printer, who, earlier in the play (p. 179) did not know what to make of "napless," and called it *Naples,*—"the Naples vesture of humility:" here, again, he did not understand what he was putting in type, and therefore committed a singular, and hitherto inexplicable blunder. A manuscript note in the folio, 1632, sets all right, and offers a most acceptable emendation :—

> "Why in this *woolless* togue should I stand here,
> To beg of Hob and Dick?" &c.

As the *toga* was "napless," so it was *woolless,* an alteration for the better, that carries conviction on the very face of it. Are we to impute it merely to the sagacity of the early possessor of the folio, 1632, when nobody since his time has had any notion of the sort? or are we to suppose that he had in this instance, and in some others, a guide by which his speculations were assisted?

P. 195. Pope's line respecting Censorinus, as one of the ancestors of Coriolanus, was not wanted, inasmuch as this portion of the speech of Brutus was struck out by the old corrector, possibly, because he saw the defect, and was not in a condition to remedy it. Nevertheless, something was at one time written in the margin, but it is so erased as not now to be legible.

ACT III. SCENE I.

P. 201. Modern editors, since the time of Theobald, have properly corrected the first line of the speech of Coriolanus,—

> " O, good, but most unwise patricians !"

which stands in the old copies, " O God ! but most unwise,"

&c. ; but there are very important blunders in subsequent lines, which they have allowed to pass without remark. We will first, as usual, insert the text as it stands universally printed, and follow it by the excellent emendations contained in the folio, 1632 :—

> " O, good, but most unwise patricians ! why,
> You grave but reckless senators, have you thus
> Given Hydra here to choose an officer,
> That with his peremptory ' shall,' being but
> The horn and noise o' the monsters, wants not spirit
> To say, he'll turn your current in a ditch,
> And make your channel his ? If he have power,
> Then vail your ignorance : if none, awake
> Your dangerous lenity."

In the above, besides the first,—*God* for " good,"—there are no fewer than five striking errors of the press, or perhaps of the scribe, for some of them are hardly to be imputed to the compositor. Trusting to the corrector of the folio, 1632, we ought hereafter to give the passage as follows :—

> " O, good, but most unwise patricians ! why,
> You grave but reckless senators, have you thus
> Given Hydra *leave* to choose an officer,
> That with his peremptory ' shall ' (being but
> The horn and noise of the *monster*) wants not spirit
> To say, he'll turn your current in a ditch,
> And make your channel his ? If he have power,
> Then vail your *impotence* : if none, *revoke*
> Your dangerous *bounty*."

The meaning of the last portion of the quotation is, that if the Tribune have power, let the *impotence* (not " ignorance," which is not the proper antithesis of power) of the senate submit to it ; but if he have none, let the senate *revoke* the *bounty* by which such a perilous privilege had been conceded to the populace. The " lenity" of the patricians was not to be " awakened·:" Coriolanus calls upon them to *revoke* the *bounty* which had caused them to relinquish a power properly belonging only to themselves. What the hero says afterwards is in entire consistency with this view of the passage :—

> " At once pluck out
> The multitudinous tongue : let them not lick
> The sweet which is their poison."

The corrector of the folio, 1632, therefore, informs us that the whole passage ought, hereafter, to be printed as above ;

A a 2

and the faults of the received text are glaring enough, without supposing, with Johnson, that, farther on in the same speech, we ought to read "most palates" *must palate*, which the corrector does not require, and which he would, no doubt, have required, had it been necessary.

P. 202. The grossness of the blunders just pointed out, will, in some degree, prepare us for others in the next speech by the same character, where he inveighs against those who had yielded to clamour in distributing corn gratis to the populace. The language of Shakespeare has been hitherto stated to be this :—

> " Th' accusation
> Which they have often made against the senate,
> All cause unborn, could never be the native
> Of our so frank donation.   Well, what then ?
> How shall this bosom multiplied digest
> The senate's courtesy ?"

Corrections in the folio, 1632, call upon us to read thus :—

> " Th' accusation
> Which they have often made against the senate,
> All cause unborn, could never be the *motive*
> Of our so frank donation.   Well, what then ?
> How shall this *bisson multitude* digest
> The senate's courtesy ?"

Monk Mason proposed *motive* for "native ;" but " bosom multiplied," a misprint most evident now it is pointed out, has always been retained in the text.   It can never be reprinted ; and is it too much to infer that the old corrector had somewhere seen or heard the above passage, and others, represented with undoubted improvement?   On p. 173, we have had " bisson" printed *besome*, and here it is printed *bosome :* it is very clear that the compositor did not understand the meaning of the word, which, perhaps, was then becoming somewhat obsolete : this consideration can, however, afford him no excuse for converting " multitude" into *multiplied.*

P. 208. It ought to be remarked that in the subsequent extract,—

> " That our renowned Rome, whose gratitude
> Towards her deserved children is enroll'd," &c.,

the passive participle is changed to the active,—" Towards

her *deserving* children." It may have been so recited at the
time the corrections were made in the folio, 1632.

SCENE II.

P. 211. A rather noticeable change is made by the old annotator in the entrance of Volumnia: in print, she is made
to come in just before the Patrician's speech, "You do the
nobler," standing by and saying nothing, while Coriolanus
speaks of her in the third person. A manuscript-emendation fixes her arrival on the scene, more naturally perhaps,
at the words of Coriolanus, addressed expressly to her, "I
talk of you," &c. We may suppose that this arrangement
represents the practice of our old stage in this respect. Her
first speech begins, not "O, sir, sir, sir," but "O, *son, son,
son,*" which seems more proper.

P. 212. On the same evidence, we here recover a line,
which is certainly wanting in the old copies, since they leave
the sense incomplete without it. It is in Volumnia's entreaty to her son,—

> "Pray be counsell'd.
> I have a heart as little apt as yours,
> But yet a brain, that leads my use of anger
> To better vantage."

To what was Volumnia's heart "as little apt" as that of
Coriolanus? The insertion of a missing line (the absence
of which has not hitherto been suspected) enables us to give
the answer:—

> "I have a heart as little apt as yours
> *To brook control without the use of anger,*
> But yet a brain, that leads my use of anger
> To better vantage."

The line in Italics is written in a blank space, and a mark
made to where it ought to come in. The compositor was,
doubtless, misled by the recurrence of the same words at the
ends of the two lines, and carelessly omitted the first. From
whence, if not from some independent authority, whether
heard or read, was this addition to the text derived?

Nevertheless, a previous line in the folio, 1632, unquestionably misprinted, *things* being used for "thwartings" (a
word excellently guessed by Theobald), is left imperfect in

its meaning, as if it had escaped attention, a most unusual circumstance with the manuscript-corrector.

SCENE III.

P. 217. The following must be allowed to be a valuable emendation of a passage, which is thus given in every edition, ancient or recent :—

> " He hath been us'd
> Ever to conquer, and to have his worth
> Of contradiction."

Malone gravely says, that "to have his worth of contradiction," means to have his *pennyworth* of it ; but the whole figure here is taken from horsemanship. When a restive animal obtains his own way, he is said to have his *mouth* given to him : to give a horse his mouth, is to free him from restraint ; therefore Brutus, speaking of Coriolanus and of his irritable spirit, remarks,—

> " He hath been us'd
> Ever to conquer, and to have his *mouth*
> Of contradiction : being once chaf'd, he cannot
> Be rein'd again to temperance."

The old printer again confounded *m* and *w*, and read *mouth* " worth." The necessary letters are written in the margin of the folio, 1632, and struck through in the text.

P. 219. There is certainly no play in the whole volume so badly printed as that before us ; and passing over several strange blunders, such as *through* for " throng," *actions* for "accents" (both corrected by Theobald), we arrive at one which may not be quite as glaring, but still must be pronounced an error of the press : it is where Coriolanus declares his contempt of death, rather than consent to purchase life by submission to the people :—

> " I would not buy
> Their mercy at the price of one fair word,
> Nor check my courage for what they can give,
> To have't with saying, good morrow."

It is most inconsistent with the noble character of the hero to represent him in this way applauding and vaunting his own " courage :" the old corrector writes *carriage* for " courage," an easy mistake, the setting right of which is an evident improvement :—

> " Nor check my *carriage* for what they can give," &c.

The very same misprint has been pointed out, and remedied in the same way, in Henry VI., Part III., p. 292 of this volume.

ACT IV. SCENE I.

P. 222. The commentators have clearly not understood part of Coriolanus' address to his mother :—

> " Nay, mother,
> Where is your ancient courage ? you were us'd
> To say, extremity was the trier of spirits ,
> That common chances common men could bear;
> That, when the sea was calm, all boats alike
> Show'd mastership in floating ; fortune's blows,
> When most struck home, being gentle wounded, craves
> A noble cunning."

Some editors have inserted *warded* for "wounded ;" Johnson, on the other hand, insisted upon the text of the folios ; but a slight change, which presupposes that the printer again mistook *m* and *w*, is vastly for the better. Coriolanus is distinguishing between the modes in which common men, and those of nobler faculties bear misfortunes ; and, when his language is truly given, observes,—

> " Fortune's blows
> When most struck home, being gentle-*minded* craves
> A noble cunning."

That is, it requires a noble cunning for a man to be gentle-minded, when fortune's blows are most struck home.

SCENE III.

P. 226. The suggestion of Steevens that, in the speech of the Volsce, "appeared" should be *approved*, is supported by the testimony of the old corrector, who also warrants the change, by the same commentator, on p. 229, of "my birth-place have I" to "my birth-place *hate* I."   In a previous line of the same speech,—

" Whose hours, whose bed, whose meal, and exercise,"

the old corrector has, "Whose *house*, whose bed," &c., with
some apparent fitness. The literal errors are here super-
abundant in both folios, but they are multiplied in that of
1632.

SCENE V.

P. 236. Perhaps the following may be considered as
belonging to that class: it is where the third Servant is
speaking of the friends of Coriolanus, who do not dare to
show themselves so "whilst he's in directitude." The first
Servant naturally asks, what is the meaning of "directitude?" and receives no answer, excepting by implication, derived from the supposition that Coriolanus will soon be again
in prosperity, and surrounded by his supporters. "Directitude" is clearly a misprint for *dejectitude*,—a rather fine
word, used by the third Servant to denote the disastrous
condition of the affairs of Coriolanus, which might be just
as unintelligible to the first Servant as "directitude." The
blunder must have been produced by the scribe having
written *deiectitude*, with an *i* instead of a *j*. It has remained, however, "directitude," from the earliest times to
the present.

P. 237. The first Servant, stating his preference of war to
peace, says that war is "sprightly, waking (*walking* in the
folios), audible, and full of vent." Johnson tells us that
"full of vent" means "full of rumour, full of materials for
discourse." "Full of *vaunt*," says the old corrector, with
much greater plausibility, full of deeds deserving to be
vaunted.

SCENE VI.

P. 240. On p. 201 we have seen *god* misprinted for
"good;" and, in what follows, a marginal correction in the
folio, 1632, shows that "good" has been misprinted for *god*.
Brutus could hardly intend to call Marcius "good," when adverting to his reported return; but he applies the word
"god" to him in derision, as if Coriolanus were in a manner
worshipped by a certain class of his admirers: Brutus asserts
that the rumour of his return has been

> " Rais'd only, that the weaker sort may wish
> *God* Marcius home again."

Such is the emendation, which adds vastly to the force of
the passage, and is most accordant with the character of
the speaker ; "good Marcius" is comparatively tame and un-
meaning. Cominius soon afterwards, talking of Coriolanus,
says, "He is their *god*," &c.

P. 242. The point of another passage appears, on the authority of the old corrector, to have been sacrificed to an
error, where Menenius says to the Tribunes,—

> " You have made fair hands,
> You and your crafts ; you have crafted fair."

We ought unquestionably to read *handycrafts* for "crafts,"
and to print the lines as follows, both on account of the
meaning and the metre :—

> " You have made fair hands ;
> You and your *handycrafts* have crafted fair."

This change completes the defective line, and shows that
Menenius uses the introductory expression, "You have made
fair hands," in order that he may follow it up by the con-
temptuous mention of *handycrafts*.

P. 245. The conclusion of the speech of Aufidius, where he
is adverting to the manner in which high merits may be obscured, and even extinguished by the character and conduct
of the possessor, has excited much comment. We print it
first as the passage appears in the folio, 1623 :—

> " So our virtue
> Lie in th' interpretation of the time,
> And power, unto itself most commendable,
> Hath not a tomb so evident as a chair
> T' extol what it hath done.
> One fire drives out one fire ; one nail, one nail ;
> Rights by rights fouler, strengths by strengths do fail."

The only difference between the folio, 1623, and that of
1632, is, that the latter corrects a grammatical blunder by
printing "virtue" in the plural ; but, besides this trifle,
there appear to be several other mistakes, of more consequence, and we subjoin the text as amended in manuscript :—

> " So our virtues
> *Live* in the interpretation of the time,

> And power, *in* itself most commendable,
> Hath not a tomb so evident as a *cheer*
> T' extol what it hath done.
> One fire drives out one fire, one nail, one nail ;
> Rights by rights *suffer*, strengths by strengths do fail."

Most editors have seen that " Rights by rights fouler" must be wrong, and have proposed various changes, though none so acceptable as that above given. However, the main difficulty has arisen out of the word " chair," which the old corrector informs us should be *cheer*, in reference to the popular applause which usually follows great actions ; and, by extolling what has been done, confounds the doer. The change of " lie" to *live*, in a preceding line, is countenanced by the word " tomb," afterwards used ; and the whole passage means, that virtues depend upon the construction put upon them by contemporaries, and that power, though praiseworthy, may be buried by the very applause that is heaped upon it, &c. The last couplet requires no elucidation, when *suffer* is substituted for "fouler," an error that may, in part, have been occasioned by the letter *f* having been employed instead of the long *s*. It is difficult to say how far some independent authority may, or may not, have been used in this emendation.

P. 250. In order to induce the guard to admit him to an interview with Coriolanus, Menenius says, as the lines have always been given,—

> " For I have ever verified my friends
> (Of whom he's chief) with all the size that verity
> Would without lapsing suffer."

This surely is little better than nonsense, the compositor having printed "verified" in the first line from his eye having caught "verity" in the second. We are, therefore, told to read thus :—

> " For I have ever *magnified* my friends," &c. ;

and Menenius goes on to say, that he had *magnified* them to the utmost " size" that truth would allow.

P. 254. Another instance in which the annotator of the folio, 1632, preferred the active to the passive participle occurs here, and where the one seems, to our ears, to answer

the purpose quite as well as the other: it is in Volumnia's
speech to her son,—

> "I kneel before thee, and unproperly
> Show duty, as mistaken all this while
> Between the child and parent;"

mistaking is written in the margin for "mistaken," the word
in all impressions, and requiring no alteration.

P. 256. Shakespeare has always been hitherto represented
as guilty of a grammatical blunder, little less than ridiculous :—

> "Making the mother, wife, and child to see
> The son, the husband, and the father tearing
> His country's bowels out. And to poor we,
> Thine enmity's most capital."

Here the punctuation of the old copies leads to the detection
of two typographical errors, "to" for *so*, and "enmities" for
enemies :—

> "And the father tearing
> His country's bowels out; and *so* poor we
> Thine *enemies* most capital."

i. e. and so poor we *are* thy most capital enemies. These
small and natural changes at once remove the solecism.

P. 258. The additions to the stage-directions in this play
are not many, nor of much consequence; but we here encounter one that requires notice, because it serves to show
the manner of the old actor of the part of Coriolanus at this
point of the noblest scene, perhaps, in the whole range of dramatic literature. After Volumnia's grand and touching appeal,
beginning, "Nay, go not from us thus," we are informed in the
ancient editions that Coriolanus *holds her by the hand silent;*
and the following descriptive addition is made in manuscript,
long, and self-struggling. After this protracted strife, which
shook the whole fabric of the hero, he yields, with the exclamation,—

> "O mother, mother!
> What have you done?" &c.

P. 263. An alteration which can hardly be subject to
doubt or dispute, occurs where Aufidius is descanting on
the manner in which he had "served the designments" of
Coriolanus to his own injury: the passage in all editions
has stood as follows :—

> " Serv'd his designments
> In mine own person ; holp to reap the fame
> Which he did end all his."

Rowe printed *make* for "end," and he was followed by several editors, who did not see how sense could be extracted from "end." Shakespeare is here only using a metaphor which he has often employed before, and it is obvious from the context that for "end" we ought to read *ear*, which means, in its derivation as well as in its use, to plough : therefore, when Aufidius says that he had

> " Holp to reap the fame
> Which he did *ear* all his ;"

he means that Coriolanus had ploughed the ground, intending to reap a crop of fame, which Aufidius had assisted him to harvest. The use of the word "reap" proves what was in the mind of the poet. It is needless to enumerate the places where Shakespeare employs the verb, to *ear*, in the sense of to plough.

P. 266. It is a mistake, in note 7 on this page, to state that Malone (Shakspeare, by Boswell, xiv. p. 225) reads *voices :* he prints it *Volces*, which is strictly right, although all the old copies have Volscians. The folio, 1632, like that of 1623, has, " flattered your Volscians in Coriolus ;" but the corrector of the former has altered " flatter'd " to *flutter'd*, by striking out the *a*, and placing *u* in the margin. *Flutter'd* is the word in the folio, 1664, and so it has continued ever since : " Volcians" is altered to *Volces* in no old copy.

Lower down, where *All People* is the prefix to various exclamations by different citizens against Coriolanus, the figures 1, 2, 3, 4, are placed in manuscript in the margin to show that the speeches, "He killed my son—my daughter—he killed my cousin Marcus—he killed my father," were uttered by different people, whose families Coriolanus was charged with having thinned.

P. 267. In the old impressions, when the Conspirators assail Coriolanus and kill him, the stage-direction is, " *Draw both the Conspirators, and kill Martius ;* but we have already seen Aufidius instructing *three* Conspirators. Perhaps, in the economy of our old stage, only two were so employed at the time the hero was actually struck, and that the actor,

who had played the third Conspirator on p. 264, had other
duties to perform in the busy last scene of the drama. We
have before said that the stage-directions are little added to
or altered in this play ; but, at the very close, some words
are subjoined which require notice: the old printed stage-
direction is, *Exeunt bearing the body of Martius. A dead
march sounded ;* to which the following words are appended
in manuscript—*whiles they leave the stage, marching round :*
the dead march was, therefore, continued to be played, until
the whole procession had passed round the stage, in order,
doubtless, to render the ceremonial more distinct and impressive. This, we believe, is a traditional practice, which
has ever since been continued.

TITUS ANDRONICUS.

ACT I. SCENE I.

P. 275. There can be no difficulty in admitting the subsequent emendation of an evident misprint near the opening of this play, where Bassianus says,—

> "Keep then this passage to the Capitol,
> And suffer not dishonour to approach
> Th' imperial seat, to virtue consecrate,
> To justice, continence, and nobility."

There is no reason why the Capitol should be said to be consecrate to "continence," especially when, in the preceding line, it is stated to be consecrate to "virtue:" the corrector of the folio, 1632, therefore, alters the last line thus :—

> "To justice, *conscience*, and nobility."

Besides, "continence," read as a tri-syllable, is too much for the verse.

SCENE II.

P. 279. Rhymes, whether lost by a change in the practice of the stage, by carelessness of recitation, copying, printing, or otherwise, are restored in various parts of this tragedy : the earliest instance of the kind occurs at the end of one of the speeches of Titus, where he tells Tamora that her son must be slain as a sacrifice for his dead sons ; the rhyme seems so inevitable, that we can hardly suppose it relinquished excepting by design :—

> "To this your son is mark'd ; and die he must
> To appease their groaning shadows that are *dust*."

The printed copies poorly read "gone" for *dust*.

P. 282. When the people wish to elect Titus for their Emperor, he declines on account of age and infirmity :—

> " What ! should I don this robe, and trouble you?
> Be chosen with proclamations to-day,
> To-morrow yield up rule, resign my life,
> And set abroad new business for you all."

" Proclamations" may be right, but *acclamations* is the word written in the margin instead of it ; and for " set abroad," the more natural reading is *set abroach*, which is also supplied in the folio, 1632.

P. 288. We have here a proof that the old corrector may have resorted to the quarto copies of this play, where only, and not in the folios, in the following line,—

> " That slew himself, and wise Laertes' son,"

the epithet "wise" is found. It is possible, however, that the necessary word was obtained from recitation, or even from some independent authority, written or printed. Some of the changes in this play could scarcely have been made without some such aid.

ACT II. SCENE I.

P. 297. When Aaron is prompting Chiron and Demetrius to ravish Lavinia, he tells them that they may safely do it in the forest :—

> " The woods are ruthless, dreadful, deaf, and dull."

To say that the woods are " dreadful," seems the very opposite of what is meant : they were pitiless, and discovery or opposition were not to be dreaded ; we are, therefore, told to read,—

> " The woods are ruthless, *dreadless*, deaf, and dull."

SCENE II.

P. 297. In the opening of this scene, we meet with one of those passages to which the rhymes have been elaborately restored, where, from the nature of the description, they seem natural, and to which we may feel confident they at one time belonged. The use of the phrase, "the hunt is up," in the outset, would almost appear to call for them, especially in a drama of the age to which "Titus Andronicus" must be assigned. It is needless to quote the lines as given in all editions, but we subjoin them with the manuscript-emendations, as they occur in the folio, 1632 :—

> " The hunt is up, the morn is bright and *gay*,
>   The fields are fragrant and the woods are *wide*,
> Uncouple here, and let us make a bay,
>   And wake the emperor and his lovely bride,
> And rouse the prince and *sing* a hunter's *round*,
> That all the court may echo with the *sound*.
> Sons, let it be your charge, *and so will I*,
> To attend the emperor's person carefully :
> I have been troubled in my sleep this night,
> But dawning day *brought* comfort *and delight*."

Nothing can well read more easily, naturally, or harmoniously. The first six lines form a stanza, and such were not uncommonly introduced by Shakespeare in his earlier plays, instances being found in "Love's Labour's Lost," &c. To say that "the morn is bright and grey," as in the old copies, reads a little contradictorily, and the word *gay* is, we see, substituted as that of the poet. How far any of these changes were supported by authority, must remain a question ; at least we are not in a condition to answer it.

An addition to the old stage-direction, *wind horns*, informs us that *The hunt is up* was here *sung* by the performers.

SCENE III.

P. 300. A mere misprint, pointed out by the old corrector, has been the occasion of notes by Heath, Steevens, Malone, and Boswell, upon the lines,—

> " Thy temples should be planted presently,
>   With horns, as were Actæons ; and the hounds
>   Should drive upon thy new transformed limbs."

Heath proposed *thrive* for "drive," and Steevens was for preserving the old word, which, nevertheless, all admitted could scarcely be right. Now, as everybody knows that Actæon was devoured by his own dogs, it is singular that

the blunder was never yet guessed at by any commentator:
it is,—

> "Should *dine* upon thy new transformed limbs."

P. 303. Lavinia tells Chiron and Tamora,—

> "The lion, mov'd with pity, did endure
> To have his princely paws par'd all away."

It was not his "paws," but his *claws*, that he endured to be
pared away:—

> "To have his princely *claws* par'd all away."

It is not likely that pity would have allowed the beast to
remain quiet, while his "paws" were "pared all away."

SCENE V.

P. 310. There can hardly be a doubt, unless we suppose
Shakespeare to have left the line purposely incomplete, that
the ensuing addition to an imperfect hemistich was justified
by some authority with which the corrector of the folio,
1632, was acquainted, though now lost. Marcus is referring
to the music Lavinia sang to the lute before her tongue was
cut out:—

> "Or had he heard the heavenly harmony,
> Which that sweet tongue hath made *in minstrelsy*,
> He would have dropp'd his knife," &c.

ACT III. SCENE I.

P. 321. When Titus Andronicus sends his son to Lucius to
raise an army among the Goths, he ends his speech with a
couplet rhyming with the same word :—

> "And, if you love me, as I think you do,
> Let's kiss and part, for we have much to do."

This was probably a corruption, for the old corrector shows
how easy it was to avoid the awkwardness:—

> "And, if you love me, as I think 'tis true,
> Let's kiss and part, for we have much to do."

It does not require any very strong faith to believe that this must have been the original reading.

SCENE II.

P. 323. That part of the scene which relates to the killing of the fly is erased; and the blunder at the end, where seven lines are given to Marcus, is set right by assigning the five last to Andronicus. Copies of the folio, 1623, differ in this respect; in the folio, 1632, the prefix *And*, for Andronicus, is printed only as if it were the conjunction.

ACT IV. SCENE II.

P. 331. When the Nurse brings to Aaron the black child of the empress, she says,—

> " Here is the babe, as loathsome as a toad
> Among the fairest breeders of our clime."

The child was not a "breeder," but a *burden*, and so it stands amended in the folio, 1632 :—

> " Among the fairest *burdens* of our clime."

P. 334. For the line as we find it in all the old copies,—

> " Not far, one Muliteus my countryman,"

the correction is,—

> " Not far *hence* Muli *lives*, my countryman."

Steevens conjectured that "Muli lives" had been corrupted to *Muliteus*, and he was right; but *hence* appears also to have been misprinted *one :* the latter change is, however, by any means required.

Lower down, for the awkward expression,—

> " This done, see that you take no longer days,"

the old corrector tells us to substitute,—

> " This, done, see that you *make* no long *delays*."

This, too, cannot be said to be a necessary change, but it is clearly an advantageous one, and most likely what the author wrote.

SCENE III.

P. 336. This scene is made part of the preceding by the manuscript-corrector; and very possibly it was so, when the play was acted of old, in order to avoid too frequent changes of the kind. It is also much shortened by the erasure of the two long passages, in which Andronicus shows his distraction, and Publius humours it.

SCENE IV.

P. 339. Rowe amended the following line by the awkward insertion of "as do" in the middle of it :—

> " My lords, you know, as do the mightful gods ;"

but the emendation in the folio, 1632, shows that words had not dropped out in the middle of the line, which was not so likely, but at the end of it, and they were, of course, not what Rowe conjectured :—

> " My lords, you know, the mightful gods *no less.*"

———

ACT V. SCENE I.

P. 345. There can be no doubt, on the evidence of the old corrector of the folio, 1632, that the words, " Get me a ladder," belong to Lucius and not to Aaron, whose speech begins with, " Lucius, save the child." A manuscript stage-direction proves that *a ladder* was *brought,* and that the Moor made all his subsequent speeches *standing upon it.* Before he ascends it, he tells the Goths that he will disclose

> " Complots of mischief, treason, villainies,
> Ruthful to hear, yet piteously perform'd :"

" Piteously perform'd " must be the very reverse of what he means, and there can be no hesitation in printing the last line in future, as we are instructed by an emendation,—

> " Ruthful to hear, *despiteously* perform'd."

B b 2

SCENE II.

P. 349. The old introduction to this scene is, *Enter Ta-mora and her two Sons disguised;* and in manuscript we are informed that the characters they assumed were those of *Revenge, Rape, and Murder.* Andronicus, when they call him, *opens his study door above, i. e.* in the balcony over the back of the stage, from whence he *comes down,* and joins them *below,* to converse about vengeance for the sufferings of himself and the rest of the Andronici. Such appears to have been the mode in which the scene was managed in the time of the corrector, and, perhaps, from the first production of the tragedy.

P. 355. When Andronicus *cuts the throats* of Demetrius and Chiron, Lavinia *catcheth the blood* in a basin she had procured: there seems little occasion for this addition to the usual stage-direction, as we are previously told the part she is to play in the transaction; but the writer of the manu-script notes was anxious to be most explicit.

SCENE III.

P. 358. There is a remarkable discordance between the quartos and folios regarding the speech beginning,—

" Lest Rome herself be bane unto herself:"

the quartos strangely assign it to a *Roman Lord;* and the folios, most absurdly, to a *Goth.* It seems evident from what precedes, where Marcus says,—

" O ! let me teach you how to knit again," &c.,

that the whole belongs to him; and the corrector of the folio, 1632, has, therefore, put his pen through the prefix *Goth,* and makes the next twenty-three lines run on as the continuation of what Marcus delivers.

P. 362. According to the old emendator, rhymes were nu-merous towards the close of this play. Lucius, speaking of his father, says to his young son,—

" Shed yet some small drops from thy tender spring,
Because kind nature doth require it so :
Friends should associate friends in grief and woe.

> Bid him farewell; commit him to the grave;
> Do him that kindness, and take leave of him."

"And take leave of him," besides marring the rhyming couplet, sounds very tamely and weakly, and is, in another form, a mere repetition of "Bid him farewell," of the preceding line. We may, therefore, on all accounts, be prepared to acquiesce in the subsequent manuscript-emendation :—

> "Bid him farewell; commit him to the grave;
> Do him that kindness—*all that he can have.*"

It will excite surprise how rhymes like these escaped: they must have been more impressed upon the memory of the actor; and, even if we suppose them to have been abandoned, on account of the advance made by blank-verse on the stage, that advance had hardly occurred when "Titus Andronicus" was first printed. Moreover, in the instance before us, and in others, the original lines (supposing them to have been such) were so much better adapted to the occasion, and to the person who pronounced them.

ROMEO AND JULIET.

ACT I. SCENE I.

P. 375. A manuscript-emendation in the folio, 1632, makes it certain that "civil," in the following portion of Sampson's speech, is a misprint:—"When I have fought with the men, I will be civil with the maids; I will cut off their heads." "Civil" is struck out, and *cruel* inserted instead of it. Malone rightly preferred *cruel*.

P. 378. The corrected folio, 1632, gives one line differently from any other authority: it is a reading which may be right, but which ought not, perhaps, to have weight enough to induce us to alter the received and very intelligible text. It is met with in the Prince's reproof of Montague and Capulet for allowing the quarrels of their followers to disturb the public peace ; the universal reading has been,—

> " Three civil brawls, bred of an airy word," &c.

For "ayery word" (so spelt in the folios) the substitution is " *angry* word."

P. 382. Romeo, describing love, remarks,—

> " Love is a smoke, made with the fume of sighs;
> Being purg'd, a fire sparkling in lovers' eyes."

Johnson, Steevens, Reed, and others, have contended that "purg'd" cannot have been the poet's language ; and they suggest *urg'd*, in the sense of excited. This emendation might answer the purpose, if no better were offered, but in

the margin of the folio, 1632, we are told to substitute a
word that exactly belongs to the place, and that might be
easily misread "purg'd" by the printer :—

> "Being *puff'd,* a fire sparkling in lovers' eyes."

Every body is aware how a fire sometimes sparkles in the
eyes of those who blow it with their breath : the smoke is first
"made" by the gentle "fume of sighs," and then caused to
sparkle by being violently *puffed* by the lover's breath.

If this emendation be capable of dispute, that in a line
at the top of the next page cannot be doubted, since it
accords, almost exactly, with the old copies, and obviously
gives the sense of the author.   Romeo is speaking of
Rosaline,—

> " She hath Dian's wit,
> And in strong proof of chastity well arm'd,
> From love's weak childish bow she lives unharm'd."

Such has always been the reading since the time of Rowe ;
but the quarto, 1597, and the folios have,—

> "From loves weak childish bow she lives *uncharm'd.*"

"Unharm'd" may here again be said to answer the purpose,
by giving a clear meaning ; but the alteration required by
the corrector of the folio, 1632, is only of a single letter, and
a much more poetical turn is given to the thought :—

> "She hath Dian's wit,
> And in strong proof of chastity well arm'd,
> From love's weak childish bow she lives *encharm'd.*"

That is to say, she was magically *encharmed* from love's bow
by chastity.   Nobody will deny that "unharm'd" is comparatively flat, poor, and insignificant.

SCENE II.

P. 384. The line, which in the folios is printed,—

> " And too soon marr'd are those so early made,"

had been given in the quartos,—

> " And too soon marr'd are those so early *married ;*"

and that should seem to be the true proverbial word, for the
old corrector adopts it, and expunges " made."

SCENE IV.

P. 395. He makes three emendations in Mercutio's description of Queen Mab, all deserving notice, if not adoption: the first is the most singular, where, of the Fairy's wagoner, it is said, in the folio, 1623, that he is not half so big as a worm,—

> " Prick'd from the lazy finger of a *man ;*"

and in the folio, 1632,—

> " Prick'd from the lazy finger of a *woman ;*"

while in the quarto, 1597, only, it stands,—

> " *Pick'd* from the lazy finger of a *maid.*"

The modern reading has been compounded of both :—

> " Prick'd from the lazy finger of a maid."

From whence the writer of the manuscript note in the folio, 1632, derived his information we know not, but he presents us with a fifth variety :—

> " *Pick'd* from the lazy finger of a *milk*-maid."

As might be expected, seven lines lower, he alters *countries knees,* of the same edition, to "courtiers' knees," and *cursies* to "courtesies ;" but his emendation of the last line of the page,—

> " Sometime she gallops o'er a courtier's nose,"

merits most attention. It has been properly objected that this is the second time the poet has introduced "courtiers" into the description. To avoid this, Pope read "*lawyer's* nose," adopting in part the "*lawyers lap*" of the quarto, 1597: but while shunning one defect, he introduced another; for though the double mention of "courtiers" is thus remedied, it occasions a double mention of "lawyers." In what way, then, does the old corrector take upon himself to decide the question ? He treats the second "courtiers" as a misprint for a word which, when carelessly written, is not very dissimilar :—

> " Sometime she gallops o'er a *counsellor's* nose,"
> And then he dreams of smelling out a suit."

That *counsellors,* and their interest in suits at court, should thus be ridiculed, cannot be thought unnatural. The third emendation is in the line,—

> " And bakes the elf-locks in foul sluttish hairs,"

which is changed, more questionably and unpoetically, to " And *makes* the elf-locks," &c.

P. 397. The quarto, 1597, when the wind is spoken of, alone has,—

> " Turning his face to the dew-dropping south :"

it is altered in all other old impressions to

> " Turning his *side* to the dew-dropping south ;"

and by the old corrector, more than plausibly, to

> " Turning his *tide* to the dew-dropping south."

The modern reading has been, " Turning his face," &c. ; but as the quarto, 1597, has a decided mistake in the preceding line, we may receive " Turning his *tide*" as Shakespeare's language, though *tide* may more fitly and strictly belong to water than to wind.

ACT II.　SCENE I.

P. 404. The Acts and Scenes (excepting the first) are not marked in any of the old impressions ; and by a manuscript note in the folio, 1632, Act II. is made to begin before, and not after the Chorus. Such was, perhaps, the ancient arrangement, but the point, though requiring notice, is one of comparatively little consequence.

The words in this page, " Nay, I'll conjure too," assigned in all the quartos and folios to Benvolio, clearly belong to Mercutio, and the prefix is, therefore, altered in manuscript in the edition of 1632. The blunder has, we think, never been repeated in modern times.

SCENE II.

P. 406. Romeo, speaking of the moon, and apostrophising Juliet, tells her,—

> " Be not her maid, since she is envious ;
> Her vestal livery is but sick and green,
> And none but fools do wear it."

Here we meet in the folio, 1632, with an emendation that
calls for explanation :—

> " Her vestal livery is but *white* and green,
> And none but fools do wear it."

The compositor perhaps caught " sick" from a line above,
where Romeo describes the moon as "sick and pale ;" "*white
and green*" must be the true reading, as is proved by what
follows, where it is said that it was worn by "none but
fools." " White and green" had been the royal livery in the
reign of Henry VIII., but Elizabeth changed it to scarlet
and black ; and although motley was the ordinary dress of
fools and jesters, it is capable of proof that, earlier than the
time of Shakespeare, the fools and jesters of the court (and
perhaps some others) were still dressed in "white and
green:" thus it became proverbially the livery of fools. Will
Summer (who lived until 1560, and was buried at Shoreditch
on the 15th June in that year) wore "white and green,"
and the circumstance is thus mentioned in " Certain Edicts
of Parliament," at the end of the edition of Sir Thomas
Overbury's " Wife," in 1614 :—"Item, no fellow shall begin
to argue with a woman, &c., unless he wear *white* for William,
and *green* for Summer"—that is, unless he be a fool, like
Will Summer. Again, in Fox's "Acts and Monuments," iii.
114, a story is told of a person, who, noticing the colours in
which St. John had been painted by the Papists in St. Paul's,
said, " I hope ye be but a *Summer's* bird, in that ye be
dressed in *white* and *green*." It appears also that Skelton
(Works by Dyce, I. xii. and 128), who boasts of "the habit
the king gave" him, wore "white and green," because he
was the royal jester, though he also assumed the rank of
laureat. In the time of Shakespeare it may have been discontinued as the dress even of court-fools, but it seems to
have been traditionally so considered ; and on this account it
is stated by him that " none but fools do wear it."

P. 407. For "lazy-pacing clouds," the old corrector (in
conformity with the suggestion in note 8) converts *lazy-
puffing* of the folios into *lazy-passing;* and gives the line,—

> " Thou art thyself though not a Montague,"

in the following manner, though, perhaps, properly punctuated, the change is not necessary :—

> " Thou art thyself, *although* a Montague."

He erases " belonging to a man," not being aware, possibly,
of the omission of the preceding words, " Nor any other
part," which are found in the quarto, 1597. This circumstance looks as if he had not referred to that edition.

P. 410. On the other hand, we here find him inserting one
word from all the quartos, and substituting another, met
with only in the quarto, 1597 : the folios have,—

> " Lady, by yonder moon I vow ;"

obviously incomplete from the omission of " blessed" before
" moon," which is in every quarto ; but the quarto, 1597,
alone gives the whole line as follows :—

> " Lady, by yonder blessed moon I *swear ;*"

" Swear" is in no other impression, yet the old corrector not
merely inserts " blessed," but erases " vow," and puts *swear*
in the place of it : *swear* is clearly right, as we learn from
Juliet's reply. In these cases it appears most probable, that
the writer of the manuscript-emendations was guided by the
manner in which he heard the text repeated on the stage.

P. 414. The last lines of Romeo's last speech in this scene
as given in the folio, 1632, are erased. Four of them, in fact,
belong to Friar Laurence, in the opening of Scene III., but
as the sense is complete without them, they might not be recited, and the old corrector, therefore, takes no farther notice
of them : he makes the speech of the Friar begin with,—

> " Now, ere the sun advance his burning eye."

SCENE III.

P. 415. A single letter makes an important difference in
the following :—

> " But where unbruised youth, with unstuff'd brain,
>   Doth couch his limbs, there golden sleep doth reign."

Friar Laurence is drawing a contrast between the wakeful-
ness of careful age, and the calm sleep of untroubled youth :

the epithet "unbruised" has, therefore, little propriety, and
we are instructed to amend the line thus:—

> "But where *unbusied* youth, with unstuff'd brain," &c.

This comes, we apprehend, within the class of extremely
plausible emendations.

SCENE IV.

P. 424. The Nurse says to Romeo, regarding Juliet, as the
text has always stood:—"And, therefore, if you should deal
double with her, truly, it were an ill thing to be offered to
any gentlewoman, and very weak dealing." We can easily
believe that "weak" is here not the proper epithet, and a
manuscript marginal note warrants in altering it to "and
very *wicked* dealing." The copyist, probably, misheard; and
in a case like this we certainly might venture to alter the
defective text.

SCENE V.

P. 428. The Nurse brings tidings that Romeo is waiting
for Juliet, in order to be married at the cell of Friar Laurence, and says,—

> "Now comes the wanton blood up in your cheeks,
> They'll be in scarlet straight at any news.
> Hie you to church," &c.

It was not "at any news" that Juliet's cheeks would be in
scarlet, but at the particular and joyful tidings brought by
the Nurse, who, according to an emendation in the folio,
1632, tells her,—

> "Now comes the wanton blood up in your cheeks,
> They'll be in scarlet *straightway* at *my* news."

ACT III. SCENE I.

P. 435. It may be sufficient to state that a correction in
the folio, 1632, converts "fire and fury," of the later quartos
and folios, into "fire-eyed fury," of the quarto, 1597. On a
previous page (432), the same course has been taken with

the words, "Romeo, the hate I bear thee," instead of "the *love* I bear thee." Did the corrector derive these emendations from the quarto, 1597, or from more accurate recitation of the text than as it appears in the folios?

P. 437. We may conjecture that such was the case, from an addition to the text which we here meet with, and which is necessary for the completion of a line, but is not contained in any known copy, quarto or folio. It is in Benvolio's narrative of the fatal encounter between Mercutio and Tybalt: of the former, he says,—

> "And with a martial scorn, with one hand beats
> Cold death aside, and with the other sends
> It back to Tybalt, whose dexterity
> Retorts it. Romeo he cries aloud
> ' Hold friends! friends part!' " &c.

Here it is certain that the line,—

> " Retorts it. Romeo he cries aloud,"

is abridged of a syllable, which is supplied in manuscript:—

> "Retorts it *home*. Romeo he cries aloud," &c.

On the next page we have "hate's proceeding," instead of "*heart's* proceeding, although the quarto, 1597, is the only copy of the play which reads "hate's proceeding."

SCENE II.

P. 439. The line of Juliet's speech, as usually printed,—

> "That run-away's eyes may wink," &c.,

has always been a stumbling-block, and perhaps no emendation can be declared perfectly satisfactory. The change proposed by the corrector of the folio, 1632, at all events makes very clear sense out of the passage, although it may still remain a question, whether that sense be the sense of the poet? another subsidiary question will be, how so elaborate a misprint could have been made out of so simple and common a word? He gives the whole passage thus:—

> "Spread thy close curtain, love-performing night,
> That *enemies'* eyes may wink, and Romeo
> Leap to these arms untalk'd of and unseen."

In the margin of the folio, 1632, *enemies* is spelt *enimyes;* but the letters are, perhaps, too few to have been mistaken for *run-awaies*. At the same time it seems extremely natural that Juliet should wish the eyes of *enemies* to be closed, in order that they might not see Romeo leap to her arms, and talk of it afterwards. The Capulets were, of course, the *enemies* to whom she must particularly refer.

SCENE V.

P. 453. We here encounter a comparatively insignificant error, which is injurious to a very beautiful passage ; it is in the parting scene of Romeo and Juliet :—

> " I'll say, yon grey is not the morning's eye,
> 'Tis but the pale reflex of Cynthia's brow."

Cynthia's "brow" would not occasion a "pale reflex," and by the omission of one letter the light is at once cleared :—

> " 'Tis but the pale reflex of Cynthia's *bow*."

P. 457. The old corrector informs us that the words, "These are news indeed!" do not belong to Juliet, but to her Mother, as seems highly probable : it is where Juliet has directly refused to marry Paris, and Lady Capulet exclaims,—

> " These are news indeed !
> Here comes your father; tell him so yourself," &c.

This judicious arrangement is not in accordance with any known authority ; and just above, "I swear" is erased, perhaps, as not adding to the force of Juliet's expression, hardly consistent with the delicacy of her character, and certainly destructive to the measure.

ACT IV. SCENE I.

P. 462. In Henry VIII. (p. 319) we have seen *way* printed for "sway ;" and here we have "sway" printed for *way*. Paris remarks,—

> " Now, sir, her father counts it dangerous,
> That she doth give her sorrow so much sway."

"So much *way*" is the correction in the margin of the folio, 1632 ; but the text may, perhaps, stand without change, although the corruption is a very easy one.

SCENE II.

P. 468. When Juliet says, speaking of Paris, that she had met him,—

> " And gave him what becomed love I might,"

the corrector of the folio, 1632, alters " becomed," the passive, to *becoming*, the active participle : he has, as the reader is aware, pursued the same course in other places.

SCENE V.

P. 479. It is to be noted, that, contrary to his usual practice, the old corrector adds nothing to Peter's quotation from the poem by Edwards, although it is certainly defective, and is shown to be so by the quarto, 1597, where it is more completely given. He, however, underscores it with a pen, as he always does when Shakespeare employs any thing derived from another author. The whole of this part of the scene is struck out, perhaps as needless to the performance ; and it was most likely inserted by Shakespeare to give more importance to the character of Peter, and to afford William Kemp, who played it, an opportunity of exciting the laughter of the audience. When Kemp was gone, it was, perhaps, no longer wanted.

ACT V. SCENE I.

P. 480. The first line of this act has hitherto presented a serious difficulty. Romeo says,—

> " If I may trust the flattering truth of sleep,
> My dreams presage some joyful news at hand."

Nobody has been able at all satisfactorily to explain the expression, " flattering truth," since " truth" cannot flatter ; and Malone, not liking Johnson's interpretation, preferred

what is to the full as unintelligible, the text of the quarto,
1597—"the flattering *eye* of sleep." The real truth (not the
"flattering truth") seems to be, that the old compositor was
confounded between "trust," in the first part of the line, and
death near the end of it, and printed a word which he compounded of the beginning of the one word, and of the end of
the other. Sleep is often resembled to death, and death to
sleep; and when Romeo observes, as the correction in the
folio, 1632, warrants us in giving the passage,—

"If I may trust the flattering *death* of sleep;"

he calls it "the flattering death of sleep" on account of the
dream of joyful news from which he had awaked: during
this "flattering death of sleep," he had dreamed of Juliet,
and of her revival of him by the warmth of her kisses.

Two lines lower, the folio, 1623, has a remarkable corruption,—

"And all thisan day an vccustom'd spirit,"

which the folio, 1632, prints, in order to remedy the defect,—

"And all this winged unaccustom'd spirit."

Whence it obtained *winged* does not appear, but the true
reading has been the common text,—

"And, all this day, an unaccustom'd spirit:"

to which the folio, 1632, is amended in manuscript. On the
next page, "Then, I *deny* you, stars," is also properly altered
to "Then, I defy you, stars."

SCENE III.

P. 485. The corrector makes a change, not authorised
by any extant authority, in the speech of the Page attending Paris, whom his master has told to lie all along
on the ground under some yew-trees: the line, as always
printed, is,—

"I am almost afraid to stand alone;"

but Paris has expressly ordered him to lie down, with his
ear close to the ground, that he might listen: therefore, the
following alteration seems most proper, and is, doubtless, what
the poet wrote :—

> " I am almost afraid to *stay* alone
> Here in the churchyard ; yet I will adventure."

P. 486. Numerous stage-directions are written in the margins of the folio, 1632. In this scene, Romeo's Man (" Peter" is erased) *enters with a torch ;* and we are previously informed that the *Monument of the Capulets*, or some stage-property to represent it, is seen by the audience, and that Paris brings with him a *basket of flowers.* When he and Romeo fight, *Paris falls*, and Romeo *puts him in* the monument. Printed stage-directions are entirely wanting, and no note is even made when Romeo *drinks* the poison, or *dies.* These, and others in subsequent parts of the tragedy, are supplied.

P. 489. The words " Shall I believe," which are mere surplusage, are struck out, as well as the whole passage, obviously foisted in by some strange mistake, beginning, " Come, lie thou in my arms," and ending, " Depart again."

P. 494. The Prince of Verona, in the midst of the confusion and dismay, tells the people,—

> "Seal up the mouth of outrage for a while,
> Till we can clear these ambiguities."

Perhaps "outrage" is to be taken in the general sense of disturbance ; but the manuscript-corrector gives the word differently,—

> " Seal up the mouth of *outcry* for a while."

The necessity for this change is not very apparent ; but, nevertheless, Lady Capulet has exclaimed on entering,—

> "O! the people in the street cry Romeo,
> Some Juliet, and some Paris ; and all run
> With open outcry toward our monument."

P. 497. The last emendation in this play certainly looks as much like the exercise of taste on the part of the old corrector as any alteration hitherto noticed : it is where old Montague declares his intention to raise a statue of Juliet "in pure gold :"—

> " There shall no figure at such rate be set,
> As that of true and faithful Juliet."

The words "true and faithful" are indisputably tautologous,

and it is not unlikely that Shakespeare left the last line as we read it with the change introduced in the margin of the folio, 1632 :—

> " As that of *fair* and faithful Juliet."

We can suppose "true and faithful," a corruption introduced on the frequent repetition of this popular performance, although the alliteration of "fair and faithful" may seem more impressive upon the memory. We are previously told, in manuscript, that the heads of the two hostile houses *shake hands* over the dead bodies of their children.

TIMON OF ATHENS.

ACT I. SCENE I.

P. 506. After giving the obviously corrupt passage,—

> " Our poesy is as a gown, which uses
> From whence 'tis nourished,''

in this manner, as indeed Pope recommended,

> " Our poesy is as a *gum,* which *issues*
> From where 'tis nourished,''

the old corrector of the folio, 1632, puts his pen through the rest of the Poet's speech, excepting the final question, " What have you there ?" This is certainly an easy method of getting over a difficulty ; but, perhaps, the writer of the emendation here had no other. Johnson suggested *oozes* for " uses," which is, perhaps, hardly as good as " issues," with reference to the process of poetical composition ; and Shakespeare no where else employs *ooze* as a verb, and whenever it occurs as a substantive it is spelt, in the old copies, *ooze,* and never *use.*

P. 507. It seems improbable that Shakespeare, who, like other dramatists of his day, cared little about representing correctly the customs of the time or country in which he laid his scene, should make the Poet speak thus of the new work he was about to present to Timon :—

> " My free drift
> Halts not particularly, but moves itself
> In a wide sea of wax.''

Why "in a wide sea of wax ?" Admitting that not only the

ancients, but that the English, at a very early date, wrote upon waxen tablets (and such is the forced explanation of Hanmer, Steevens, and Malone), it would scarcely be understood by popular audiences before whom this drama was originally acted. "Wax," of old, was commonly spelt *waxe* (although it is "wax" in the folios), and confiding, as we are disposed to do, in a representation in the margin of the folio, 1632, the compositor must have read "waxe" for a word not very dissimilar in form, but much more appropriate and intelligible :—

> " My free drift
> Halts not particularly, but moves itself
> In a wide sea of *verse*."

The Poet's work was, of course, in *verse*, and there is no apparent reason why Shakespeare should not have employed that word instead of "wax," which looks something like a sort of pedantry, of which he would certainly be the last to be guilty.

P. 513. The following answer by Apemantus has produced much dispute :—

> " That I had no angry wit to be a lord."

It is introduced as follows : Apemantus exclaims,—

> " Heavens, that I were a lord !
> *Tim.*   What would'st do then, Apemantus ?
> *Apem.* Even as Apemantus does now ; hate a lord with my heart.
> *Tim.*   What, thyself ?
> *Apem.* Ay.
> *Tim.*   Wherefore ?
> *Apem.* That I had no angry wit to be a lord."

Though a meaning, as Johnson says, may be extracted from these last words, yet nearly all editors have agreed that some corruption has crept into the text. Warburton proposed, "That I had *so hungry* a wit to be a lord ;" and Monk Mason, "That I had *an* angry *wish* to be a lord." The restoration offered in the folio, 1632, is the same as parts of both these suggestions, and at once renders the sense evident—"That I had *so hungry a wish* to be a lord." Apemantus would hate himself for having entertained so strong a desire to be a lord. It thus seems that Warburton and Monk Mason were both right, and yet both wrong.

SCENE II.

P. 518. There appears to be a remarkable lapse by the printer in the four lines which precede Apemantus' grace, where, during the feast, he takes a cup of water in his hand, and says,—

> " Here's that, which is too weak to be a sinner,
> Honest water, which ne'er left man i' the mire :
> This and my food are equals, there's no odds ;
> Feasts are too proud to give thanks to the gods."

These lines are introduced by prose, and it can hardly be doubted, on reading them, that they were intended for two rhyming couplets. Apemantus is adverting to the intoxication which follows drinking strong wines and ardent spirits, and contrasting "honest water" with them ; and we may feel assured that the two first lines ought to be printed hereafter as they are made to run by the old corrector :—

> " Here's that, which is too weak to be a *fire*,
> Honest water, which ne'er left man i' the mire."

Water was too weak to possess the fiery and intoxicating property of wine, which often " left man in the mire." How *fire* came to be misprinted "sinner," cannot be easily explained ; but perhaps the long *s* and the *f* had something to do with the blunder.

ACT II. SCENE II.

P. 527. Flavius, Timon's Steward, lamenting over his master's lavish and thoughtless expenditure, as the text has always stood, says of him that he

> " 'Takes no account
> How things go from him, nor resumes no care
> Of what is to continue. Never mind
> Was to be so unwise, to be so kind."

This can hardly be right : " nor resume no care," as it stands in the folios, is a very uncouth, even if an allowable phrase, and the last line reads still more objectionably. Two valuable manuscript changes are made which remove all ground of complaint :—

> " Takes no account
> How things go from him ; *no reserve ;* no care
> Of what is to continue. Never mind
> Was *surely* so unwise, to be so kind."

Perhaps the occurrence of "to be" in the last part of the line, led to the mis-insertion of it in the first part ; and we can see at once how *no reserve* might become "nor resume."

ACT III. SCENE II.

P. 538. The vagueness of the sum, "so many talents," mentioned by Servilius to Lucius, when the former comes to borrow of the latter, on behalf of Timon, has occasioned remark, and Steevens conjectured that no precise amount was stated by Shakespeare, but that it was left to the player. This does not seem probable, and in a note in the folio, 1632, the sum is given as 500 talents, both here and afterwards, where Lucius speaks of "fifty-five hundred talents." We may presume, therefore, that it was the practice of the theatre, in the time of the corrector, to consider that Timon sent to borrow 500 talents, and that that was the amount required by Servilius, and repeated by Lucius. The point is, however, of little importance, because it does not in any way affect the spirit and purport of the scene.

SCENE V.

P. 548. When Alcibiades is pleading before the Senate on behalf of his friend, who had killed an adversary, he observes,—

> " He did behave his anger, ere 'twas spent,
> As if he had but prov'd an argument."

Here the printer was in error ; in the old copies the lines are thus printed :—

> " He did behoove his anger, ere 'twas spent,
> As if he had but prov'd an argument."

Modern editors have consented to suppose *behoove* intended for "behave," and they have taken great pains to justify the expression, "he did behave his anger ;" but the old corrector of the folio, 1632, shows that their labour has been thrown away, since the author did not use the phrase, but wrote as follows :—

> " He did *reprove* his anger, ere 'twas spent,
> As if he had but *mov'd* an argument."

If these small, but more than plausible, emendations be admitted, no explanation is wanted.

P. 549. In the line, as printed by Malone and others,—

> " If there were no foes, that were enough alone,"

Sir Thomas Hanmer received praise from Steevens for adding the word alone, "to complete the measure." In fact, it more than completes it ; it renders it redundant ; and as it is hardly to be disputed that the passage is wrong, as it stands baldly in the folios,—

> " If there were no foes, that were enough
> To overcome him,"

we may be disposed to place confidence in the change recommended in the folio, 1632,—

> " Were there no foes, that were *itself* enough
> To overcome him."

Here, with little violence, the measure is restored, and the sense of the speaker strengthened.

ACT IV.   SCENE II.

P. 557. Old and modern impressions furnish us with this text :—

> " Who would be so mock'd with glory, or to live
> But in a dream of friendship ?
> To have his pomp, and all what state compounds,
> But only painted, like his varnish'd friends."

Much of the speech is in rhyme, and a couplet precedes the above, which, after the interval of a line, is succeeded by four other rhymes. We learn from manuscript-emendations, that what we have just quoted most imperfectly represents the passage ; that the hemistich ought to be completed by two words carelessly omitted, and that an important verb

ought to be altered : the whole passage will then remain as
follows :—

> "Who'd be so mock'd with glory, *as* to live
> But in a dream of friendship, *and revive*
> To have his pomp, and all state *comprehends*,
> But only painted, like his varnish'd friends?"

SCENE III.

P. 558. Timon's speech, when he enters "in the woods," is
very carelessly printed in the folio, 1623 ; and the errors are
multiplied in the second folio, but they are there corrected
in manuscript : thus for

> " Raise me this beggar, and deny't that lord,"

the reading is, "*decline* that lord," *i. e.* reduce him in his
rank and condition, using the word in the same way as in
"Antony and Cleopatra," Act III. Scene II. Again, for
"brother's sides" we have "*rother's* sides" properly substituted ; farther on, Timon, digging for roots, discovers
gold, and asks,—

> " What is here?
> Gold? yellow, glittering, precious gold? No, gods,
> I am no idle votarist. Roots, you clear heavens!"

The word has always been printed "idle;" but it ought as
certainly to be *idol,*—

> " I am no *idol*-votarist,"

no worshipper of gold, which many make their *idol,* but a
searcher for roots ; for which he again exclaims—"Roots,
you clear heavens!" until, glancing at the treasure once
more, he is led to moralise upon it.

P. 563. There are few instances where mishearing on the
part of the scribe has been the origin of a corruption of the
text more striking, than the blunder we are now about to
point out, and set right, on the authority of the annotator of
the folio, 1632. It is where Phrynia and Timandra entreat
Timon to give them some of his gold, and ask if he has
more : he replies,—

> " Enough to make a whore forswear her trade,
> And to make whores, a bawd."

Johnson strives hard to extract sense from this last clause, for of course the meaning of the first is very evident: it is in the hemistich that the error lies, for we ought beyond dispute to read,—

> " Enough to make a whore forswear her trade,
> And to make whores *abhorr'd.*"

Whoever read, or recited, to the copyist dropped the aspirate, and induced him, merely writing mechanically and without attending to the sense, to put " a bawd" for *abhorr'd.*

P. 565. In the same way ingenuity has been exercised by the same commentator to reconcile us to the word " marrows," where Timon is imprecating the earth in future to bring forth nothing but monsters, and to put an end to the race of " ingrateful man:"—

> " Dry up thy marrows, vines, and plough-torn leas."

What connexion is there between " marrows, vines, and plough-torn leas?" We ought surely to read with the corrector of the folio, 1632,—

> " Dry up thy *meadows,* vines, and plough-torn leas."

Parch them up, that they may produce no " liquorish draughts" or " morsels unctuous" for the gratification and sustenance of man.

P. 567. Timon reproaches Apemantus with his base origin, and tells him that he had never known luxury, adding,—

> " Hadst thou, like us, from thy first swath, proceeded
> The sweet degrees that this brief world affords
> To such as may the passive drugs of it
> Freely command, thou wouldst have plung'd thyself
> In general riot."

"The passive drugs" of the world surely cannot be right. Timon is supposing the rich and luxurious to be, as it were, sucking freely at the " passive *dugs*" of the world; and an emendation in manuscript, which merely strikes out the superfluous letter, supports this view of the passage, and renders needless Monk Mason's somewhat wild conjecture in favour of *drudges.*

P. 572. The accidental omission of *him* has induced editors to convert a participle and preposition into a sort of substantive, by a hyphen. One of the Banditti says of Timon,

as the words have been ordinarily printed, "the falling-from
of his friends drove him into this melancholy." May we not
feel satisfied, upon the assurance of the old corrector, that
the sentence ran thus?—"The mere want of gold, and the
falling from *him* of his friends, drove him into this melancholy."

P. 577. The mercenary Poet and Painter visit Timon at
his cave to ascertain the truth of the report, that he has still
abundance of gold. In all editions the latter says to the
former, "It will show honestly in us, and is very likely to
load our purposes with what they travel for." This is very
like nonsense, although no correction of it has ever been recommended: the annotator of the folio, 1632, thus proves
what must have been in the author's mind:—

"It will show honestly in us; and is very likely to load our *purses* with
what *we* travel for:"

referring, of course, to Timon's wealth. This may be said to
be one of the emendations that requires no authority: it
carries conviction on the face of it.

SCENE IV.

P. 586. The old introduction to this scene is, *Enter a
Soldier in the woods, seeking Timon*, to which is added, in
manuscript, the necessary information, *finding his grave.*
Modern editors say, *and a Tomb-stone seen*, but we meet with
nothing of the kind in the early copies: that there must,
however, have been some rude erection, or pile of earth,
visible to the audience, is clear from the soldier's words,—

"Some beast rear'd this; there does not live a man."

The folios have it, "Some beast *read* this;" but it is undoubtedly an error, and the old corrector converts *read* into
"rear'd." Such has always been the word since Warburton's
time.

P. 588. The last emendation requiring notice, although
it may deserve to be so termed, is certainly not one of the
changes that must be adopted, since the ordinary text,
although somewhat uncouth, will serve: it occurs where the
Senators of Athens are pleading to Alcibiades for the lives of
the citizens:—

> " All have not offended ;
> For those that were, it is not square to take
> On those that are, revenge."

The correction in the folio, 1632, puts it as an interrogative appeal, and substitutes another word for the unusual expression, "it is not square :"—

> " All have not offended ;
> For those that were, is't not *severe* to take
> On those who are, revenge ?"

Steevens altered "revenge" to *revenges*, for the sake of the metre, and very justifiably, since the word occurs just above in the plural, but the old corrector leaves it in the singular.

Prol. and Epilogue is written at the end in a blank space, and perhaps it was meant only as a note that they were deficient ; but such has been the case with the tragedy immediately preceding, and with others, to which no such words are appended. The stage-directions, added in manuscript, are not always as complete and precise as would seem to be convenient ; and the division into Acts and Scenes does not, in some instances, accord with modern editions : the old copies are destitute of any such distinctions : Act IV. is made unusually long, while Act III. and Act V. are too short : Act IV. begins, rather injudiciously, with Timon's banquet of hot water, and in the next scene he is outside the walls of Athens, cursing the city.

JULIUS CÆSAR.

ACT I. SCENE I.

Vol. vii. p. 7. The Acts, but not the Scenes, are distinguished in the old copies of this tragedy: the latter are supplied in manuscript in the folio, 1632, but they do not by any means tally with the same divisions as contained in modern editions. The economy of our early stage, and the deficiency of mechanical and other contrivances to denote changes of place, frequently rendered it necessary to continue the same, or nearly the same objects before the eyes of the audience, although by the characters and dialogue it appeared that the scene was altered. As an illustration, it may be mentioned that the fifth Act of "Julius Cæsar" is divided by Malone and others into five Scenes, by representing that what occurs passes on as many different parts of the plains of Philippi; whereas the old annotator of the folio, 1632, makes the Act consist of only two Scenes, the first where the forces under Octavius and Antony march in, and the second where Brutus endeavours, after the battle, to persuade one of his friends to kill him, in order that he may not survive the freedom of his country. According to this arrangement, Cassius dies on the same ground that had been occupied by his enemies.

SCENE II.

P. 14. The two following lines have always been printed thus :—

> "When could they say, till now, that talk'd of Rome,
> That her wide walks encompass'd but one man?"

This reading has never, we believe, been doubted, and, strictly speaking, a change is not necessary ; but who will say that the last line does not run better with the emendation proposed in the folio, 1632 ?—

> "That her wide *walls* encompass'd but one man?"

Cassius is speaking of the walled city of Rome, and not of the Roman empire, although *walks* reads awkwardly in either case: neither does he refer to Cæsar's "walks and private arbours," mentioned on p. 61. Possibly the occurrence of the verb "talk" in the preceding line, led to the intrusion of "walk" in the second line.

P. 15. The manuscript-corrector requires us to make another change, which seems even less necessary, but at the same time is judicious :—

> "Brutus had rather be a villager,
> Than to repute himself a son of Rome
> Under these hard conditions, as this time
> Is like to lay upon us."

"Under *such* hard conditions" sounds better, followed as it is by "as this time ;" but this is, perhaps, a matter of discretion, and we have no means of knowing whether the writer of the notes might not here be indulging his taste.

SCENE III.

P. 20. A note in the margin of the folio, 1632, will, probably, settle a dispute carried on at considerable length, and with some pertinacity, between Johnson, Steevens, and Malone, regarding a word in a couplet thus printed in the folio, 1623 :—

> "Against the Capitol I met a lion
> Who glaz'd upon me, and went surly by."

Pope was the first to read *glar'd* for "glaz'd," and Johnson poorly substituted *gaz'd :* in the folio, 1632, the second line stands,—

> "Who glaz'd upon me, and went *surely* by ;"

there can be no doubt about the last error, and that, as well as the first, is set right by striking out the *e* in *surely,* and by converting "glaz'd" into *glar'd.*

P. 24. A question has arisen respecting another passage in
this scene :—

> " And the complexion of the element
>   In favour's like the work we have in hand."

The old copies have, " Is favours like the work," &c., and
Reed would have it, " Is *fev'rous* like the work," &c. ; but
only change *Is* to " In," and nothing more can be required.
This is done by the old corrector, and such has been the
usual course in modern times.

ACT II. SCENE I.

P. 31. It is proper to notice a small, but not immaterial
change, where Brutus says,—

> " And let our hearts, as subtle masters do,
>   Stir up their servants to an act of rage,
>   And after seem to chide 'em.   This shall *mark*
>   Our purpose necessary, and not envious."

The usual reading, as authorised by the early copies, has
been " This shall make," instead of " This shall *mark*," or
denote our purpose as necessary, and not as proceeding from
malice or hatred.

P. 32. The observation of Metellus, in the folio, 1623,—

> " Caius Ligarius doth bear Cæsar hard,"

was converted in print in the folio, 1632, to

> " Caius Ligarius doth bear Cæsar *hatred*."

The phrase occurs in two other places in this play ; and
the manuscript-corrector makes the folio, 1632, here conform to that of 1623.

P. 33. When Lucius falls asleep, Brutus says, as the passage has always been given,—

> " Fast asleep ?   It is no matter ;
>   Enjoy the honey-heavy dew of slumber."

The compound unquestionably is not " honey-heavy," but
" honey-*dew*," a well-known glutinous deposit upon the leaves

of trees, &c. : the compositor was guilty of a transposition, and ought to have printed the line in this form : —

> " Enjoy the heavy honey-dew of slumber."

Such is the manuscript emendation.

ACT III.　SCENE I.

P. 44. Artemidorus, pressing forward to deliver his warning to Cæsar, observes, —

> " Mine's a suit
> That touches Cæsar nearer."

To which Cæsar replies, as his answer has constantly been represented, —

> " What touches us ourself shall be last serv'd."

The corrector of the folio, 1632, puts it interrogatively, more pointedly, and more naturally, making Cæsar repeat the very words of Artemidorus : —

> " That touches us ?　Ourself shall be last serv'd."

It was Cæsar who was to be " last served," not what touched him nearly.

P. 45. There is a mistake in the distribution of the dialogue shortly before Cæsar is stabbed : " Are we all ready ?" certainly belongs to one of the conspirators, and some commentators would assign the words to Cinna, making them the conclusion of his speech.　Casca, however, was to strike the first blow ; and, according to a note in the margin, he reasonably first inquires, " Are we all ready ?"　The course of the dialogue will, therefore, properly be this : — Brutus, speaking of Metellus Cimber and of his petition, says, —

> " He is address'd : press near and second him.
> *Cin.*　Casca, you are the first that rears your hand.
> *Casc.*　Are we all ready ?
> *Cæs.*　　　　　　　What is now amiss,
> That Cæsar and his Senate must redress ?"

Metellus Cimber then kneels, and offers his petition on behalf of his brother.　In Cæsar's rejection of it, three misprints are indicated, *viz.* "couchings" for *crouchings*, "the lane of children" for "the *law* of children" (so corrected conjecturally by Johnson), and "low crooked courtesies" for "low *crouched* courtesies." No change is proposed in the passage, "Know, Cæsar doth not wrong," &c., so that the speculation upon it, founded upon Ben Jonson's "Discoveries," is so far not supported.

P. 49. A manuscript stage-direction (the printed copy is destitute of notes of the kind) requires Antony, on his entrance with the line,—

> "O mighty Cæsar! dost thou lie so low?"

to *kneel over the body*, and to *rise*, when he says,—

> "I know not, gentlemen, what you intend," &c.

On the next page, after "I doubt not of your wisdom," he takes *one after other* of the conspirators by the hand, and *turns to the body, and bends over it* while he says,—

> "That I did love thee, Cæsar, O! 'tis true," &c.

SCENE III.

P. 62. When Cinna, the poet, enters, he observes,—

> "I dream'd to-night that I did feast with Cæsar,
> And things unluckily charge my fantasy."

Why should he consider it unlucky to dream of feasting with Cæsar? His fancy was charged with things improbable, not unlucky, and the marginal correction in the folio, 1632, is,—

> "And things *unlikely* charge my fantasy."

The word *unlikely* also suits the measure better.

ACT IV. SCENE III.

P. 69. In the folio, 1623, when Brutus observes,—

> "I had rather be a dog, and bay the moon,
> Than such a Roman,"

Cassius replies, in the folio, 1623, as if he had misheard,—

> " Brutus, *bait* not me."

The fitness of this diversity, " bay " in one place, and "bait"
in the other, has been maintained by Malone, and disputed
by Steevens. If the change from "bait" to *bay*, made in
manuscript in the folio, 1632, can be considered at all conclusive, the difference is at an end: it is there printed
"bait" in both instances, and in both instances *bay* is substituted.

P. 69. An emendation of some interest is made in a celebrated passage in the quarrel-scene between Brutus and
Cassius. The latter has said,—

> " I am a soldier, I,
> Older in practice, abler than yourself
> To make conditions."

Brutus afterwards makes this calm remark :—

> " You say, you are a better soldier :
> Let it appear so ; make your vaunting true,
> And it shall please me well. For mine own part,
> I shall be glad to learn of noble men."

Cassius had said nothing about " noble men," and his reply
to the above has reference to what he did actually utter :—

> " You wrong me every way ; you wrong me, Brutus ;
> I said an elder soldier, not a better."

His word had been " abler," not *noble*, nor *nobler;* and in
order to make the retort of Brutus apply to what Cassius
had asserted, Brutus unquestionably ought to say,—

> " For mine own part,
> I shall be glad to learn of *abler* men."

" Noble" is struck through by the old corrector, and *abler* inserted in the place of it ; whether upon any other authority
than apparent fitness must remain doubtful.

P. 75. A question arising in council, whether the forces of
Brutus and Cassius should march towards the enemy, or wait
for him, Brutus urges the former course, and Cassius the
latter. Brutus contends that if they delay, the enemy will
be strengthened and refreshed as he advances :—

> " The enemy, marching along by them,
> By them shall make a fuller number up,
> Come on refresh'd, new-added, and encourag'd."

The corrector of the folio, 1632, implies by his proposed change, that "new-added" is merely a repetition of what is said in the preceding line—" by them shall make a fuller number up"—and he inserts a word instead of " added," which is not only more forcible, but more appropriate, and which we may very fairly suppose had been misheard by the scribe :—

> " By them shall make a fuller number up,
> Come on refresh'd, new-*hearted*, and encourag'd."

This error might be occasioned by the then broad pronunciation of " added" having been mistaken for *hearted*.

P. 77. The printer of the folio, 1632, blunderingly transposed two lines, spoken by Brutus to the drowsy Lucius. The error has not been noticed, that we are aware of, and we only mention it, to state that it is corrected in manuscript: nothing of the kind seems to have escaped attention. When Lucius, after singing, *falls asleep*, and when Brutus *takes his book*, the circumstances are duly noted in the margin.

ACT V. SCENE I.

P. 81. Octavius, in his interview with Brutus and Cassius, declares that he will never sheathe his sword,—

> "till Cæsar's three and thirty wounds
> Be well aveng'd ; or till another Cæsar
> Have added slaughter to the sword of traitors."

Steevens subjoined what he considered a parallel passage from " King John," Act II. Scene II. :—

> " Or add a royal number to the dead,
> With slaughter coupled to the name of kings."

There is certainly some resemblance, but it is stronger when the quotation from " Julius Cæsar" is printed as the old corrector advises :—

> " Or till another Cæsar
> Have added slaughter to the *word* of *traitor*."

Octavius terms Brutus a traitor, and challenges him to add slaughter to the *word*, in the same way that slaughter, in

"King John," was to be coupled "to the name of kings."
This emendation seems plausible, though we may not be disposed to insist upon it.

P. 82. So with the next emendation, where Cassius informs
Messala,—

> "Coming from Sardis, on our former ensign
> Two mighty eagles fell."

For "former ensign," we are told to read "*forward* ensign,"
which is probably right, although "former" need not necessarily be displaced, and may be understood as *foremost*.
The ensign being described as in front, at the head of the
army, the copyist may have misheard, and therefore miswritten "former" for *forward*.

Near the bottom of this page we are told to read *term* for
"time," and *those* for "some:" it is where Brutus declares
against suicide,—

> "But I do find it cowardly and vile,
> For fear of what might fall, so to prevent
> The *term* of life,—arming myself with patience,
> To stay the providence of *those* high powers,
> That govern us below."

The above unquestionably reads better than as the text has
been ordinarily given: to "prevent the term of life" means,
as Malone states, to anticipate the end of life; but still he
strangely persevered in printing "time" for *term*.

P. 89. The folio, 1632, omits "word" in the following:—

> "And see whe'r Brutus be alive or dead,
> And bring us word unto Octavius' tent."

The line stands correctly in the folio, 1623, and perhaps
from thence the emendator derived "word;" but the vacancy seems almost to supply itself. The second folio is
carelessly printed here; and not long afterwards (p. 90)
"in" was omitted, or allowed to drop out. Brutus, just
before he *runs on his own sword*, and after he has *shaken
hands severally* (these stage-directions, like others, are only
in manuscript) with his countrymen, observes,—

> "My heart doth joy that yet, in all my life,
> I found no man but he was true to me."

The folio, 1632, has "that yet all my life:" "in" is necessary

to the metre, though, as far as the absolute meaning is concerned, it might possibly be spared. It is written in the
margin.

P. 91. In Antony's brief character of Brutus, at the close
of the tragedy, we meet with two material variations pointed
out by the old corrector, which merit notice, and perhaps
adoption: the passage has hitherto appeared as follows:—

> " All the conspirators, save only he,
> Did that they did in envy of great Cæsar ;
> He, only, in a general honest thought
> And common good to all, made one of them."

It must, we think, be admitted that the last two lines are
improved if we read them as we are told they ought to be
amended :—

> " He only, in a *generous* honest thought
> *Of* common good to all, made one of them."

"A general honest thought and common good to all," is at
least tautology ; and to say that Brutus was actuated by
" a *generous* thought *of* common good to all" (*i. e.* a thought
worthy of his rank and blood) is consistent with the disinterested nobility of his character, and an admission that
might be expected from his great adversary. It is hardly
requiring too much, in such a case, to suppose that the scribe
misheard *generous*, and wrote *general;* but the propriety of
introducing the change into the text is a matter of discretion.

MACBETH.

ACT I. SCENE I.

P. 101. Although, as is stated in note 5, "quarry" (so printed in the old copies) affords an obvious meaning, we find the old corrector substituting for it a word sounding very like it, for which it might be mistaken, and which, in fact, Johnson proposed. The line is as follows, and it relates to the rebellion of Macdonwald, who, having supplied himself with kerns and gallowglasses from the Western Isles, for a time had been successful :—

> "And fortune on his damned quarry smiling."

While they continued triumphant the rebels could hardly be called a "quarry," unless by anticipation ; and the corrector of the folio, 1632, introduces this alteration :—

> "And fortune on his damned *quarrel* smiling."

Malone, who was well disposed to adopt the language of the early editions, here deserted them (mainly on the ground that at the end of this play, "quarrel" is used in the same way for the cause of quarrel), and this without any confirmatory authority, such as we now possess.

P. 102. When Ross enters suddenly, with tidings of the victory by Macbeth and Banquo over the Norwegians, Lenox observes,—

> "What a haste looks through his eyes !
> So should he look, that seems to speak things strange."

Various commentators have here seen the difficulty of making

Ross "seem to speak things strange" before he had spoken at all: it was, therefore, suggested that *teems* was the word instead of "seems;" but if the objection be not hypercritical, it is entirely removed by the old annotator, who assures us that "seems" (spelt *seemes* in the folios) had been misprinted:—

> "So should he look, that *comes* to speak things strange."

Ross certainly *came* "to speak things strange," and on his entrance looked, no doubt, as if he did.

SCENE III.

P. 104. After the second and third Witches have bestowed winds upon the first, she says,—

> " I myself have all the other;
> And the very ports they blow,
> All the quarters that they know
> I' the shipman's card.
> I will drain him dry as hay," &c.

All is in rhyme, excepting that "I' the shipman's card" has no corresponding line, and is evidently short of the necessary syllables. These are furnished by an emendation in the folio, 1632, which we can scarcely doubt gives the words of the poet, by some carelessness omitted:—

> "All the quarters that they know
> I' the shipman's card *to show*."

Lower down, we meet with a proof that the ordinary confusion between the *f* and the long *s* extended even to capitals: Banquo, in the folios, asks, "How far is't called to *Soris?*" instead of "Fores." In the manuscript used by the printer, "Fores" was most likely not written with a capital letter, and he read it *soris;* but, supposing it the name of a place, he printed it, as he fancied properly, *Soris.* The error is, of course, set right in the margin of the corrected folio, 1632.

P. 106. The old impressions have,—

> " As thick as tale
> Can post with post."

Rowe wished to read *hail* for "tale," but without warrant; but *Can* was unquestionably misprinted for "Came." Near the bottom of the next page, "That trusted home," of the folios, is changed to "That *thrusted* home." In modern times the word has been variously treated.

SCENE IV.

P. 110. Duncan thus speaks of the merits of Macbeth in the folio, 1623 : —

> " Thou art so far before,
> That swiftest wing of recompence is slow
> To overtake thee."

The folio, 1632, misprints the second line,—

> "That swiftest *wine* of recompence is slow ;"

and the corrector of that edition amends the decided defect, not by converting *wine* into "wing," but into *winde*, or *wind*,—

> " That swiftest *wind* of recompence is slow."

This may, or may not, have been the line as it came from the poet's pen : at all events, and for some unexplained reason, a person writing soon after 1632, seems to have preferred *wind* to "wing," when either would answer the purpose. Another emendation, in the passage which immediately succeeds the above quotation, seems warranted by the sense :—

> " Would thou hadst less deserv'd,
> That the proportion both of thanks and payment
> Might have been mine,"

say the folios ; "might have been *more*," says the annotator on the edition of 1632 : Duncan wishes that his thanks and payment could have been *more* in proportion to the deserts of Macbeth. This change is doubtful.

SCENE V.

P. 113. A very acceptable alteration is made, on the same evidence, in Lady Macbeth's speech invoking night, just before the entrance of her husband : it is in a word which has occasioned much speculation :—

> " Come, thick night,
> And pall thee in the dunnest smoke of hell,
> That my keen knife see not the wound it makes,
> Nor heaven peep through the blanket of the dark,
> To cry, ' Hold, hold ! ' "

Steevens, with reference to "blanket," quotes *rug* and *rugs* from Drayton; and Malone seriously supposes that the word was suggested to Shakespeare by the "coarse woollen curtain of the theatre," when, in fact, it is not at all known whether the curtain, separating the audience from the actors, was woollen or linen. What solution of the difficulty does the old corrector offer? As it seems to us, the substitution he recommends cannot be doubted:—

> " Nor heaven peep through the *blankness* of the dark
>   To cry, ' Hold, hold!' "

The scribe misheard the termination of *blankness*, and absurdly wrote "blanket."

SCENE VII.

P. 116. The folio, 1632, omits some important words, consisting of nearly a whole line, where Macbeth is soliloquizing on the "bloody instructions" which "return to plague the inventor." They are added in manuscript in the margin, perhaps from the folio, 1623; but instead of "this even-handed justice," the old corrector writes, " *thus* even-handed justice," the propriety of which change was urged by Monk Mason.

P. 118. It is not easy to imagine a case in which the alteration of a single letter would make so important a difference as in the ensuing portion of the interview between Macbeth and his Lady, where he is irresolute, and she reproaches him with want of courage to execute the murder he once vaunted he was ready to undertake: we give the text as it has appeared in every edition, from the earliest in 1623 to our own day :—

> " *Macb.*   Pr'ythee peace.
>   I dare do all that may become a man ;
>   Who dares do more is none.
> *Lady M.*   What beast was't, then,
>   That made you break this enterprize to me?
>   When you durst do it, then you were a man," &c.

Surely it reads like a gross vulgarism for Lady Macbeth thus to ask, "What beast made him divulge the enterprize to her?" but she means nothing of the kind: she alludes to Macbeth's former vaunt that he was eager for the deed, and yet could not now "screw his courage" to the point, when

time and place had, as it were, "made themselves" for its
execution : this she calls a mere *boast* on his part :—

> " What *boast* was't, then,
> That made you break this enterprise to me ? "

she charges him with being a vain braggart, first to profess
to be ready to murder Duncan, and afterwards, from fear, to
relinquish it. That this emendation might be guessed by
a person who carefully read the text, without attention to
the conventional mode of giving and understanding these
words, we have this proof,—that it was communicated to
the editor of the present volume, six months ago, by an extremely intelligent gentleman, whose name we have no authority to give, but who dated from Aberdeen, and who had
not the slightest knowledge that *boast*, for " beast," was the
manuscript reading in the folio, 1632. It is very possible,
therefore, that the old corrector of the folio, 1632, arrived
at his conclusion upon the point by the same process : on
the other hand, it is impossible to deny that he may have
had some authority, printed, written, or oral, for the proposed
change ; and it is quite certain that people have been in the
habit of reading " Macbeth" for the last 200 years, some of
them for the express purpose of detecting blunders in the
text, and yet, as far as can be ascertained, have never once
hit upon this improvement, so trifling as regards typography,
but so valuable as respects the meaning of Shakespeare.

ACT II. SCENE I.

P. 122. Steevens suggested " curtain'd *sleeper*" for " curtain'd sleep," and that correction is found in the folio, 1632 ;
as well as " sure" for *sowre*, and " which way they walk" for
" which they *may* walk" of the folios ; but no change is made
in " Tarquin's ravishing sides," as if that expression were not
objectionable.

P. 123. A new scene (numbered 3) has been usually made
to begin, on the entrance of Lady Macbeth, with,—

> " That which hath made them drunk hath made me bold ;"

but the individual who took such singular pains with the folio, 1632, strikes out the printed words, *Scœna secunda,* and writes *Same* against them, indicating that it was not a new scene. Macbeth goes out after the dagger-soliloquy, and then Lady Macbeth enters to await his return from the murder. His re-entrance is marked too early in the old copies at the words, "Who's there? what, ho!" for he makes this exclamation *without*, before he comes in and says, " I have done the deed," &c. Opposite " This is a sorry sight," *bloody hands* is added in manuscript, as an explanatory stage-direction.

SCENE III.

P. 126. All that the Porter says respecting the supposed knocking of different persons at hell-gate, down to the words, "the everlasting bonfire," is struck out, perhaps, as offensive to the Puritans ; but the dialogue between the same character and Macduff is abridged, most likely to shorten the performance. When Macbeth arrives, we are told that he comes in *in his night-gown*, and Banquo subsequently enters *unready*. Opposite Macduff's injunction (p. 131), "Look to the Lady," who is affecting to be overcome by the dreadful tidings, *Lady sw.* (perhaps for *Lady swoons*) is blotted in the margin, and just afterwards, we read, in the same situation, *Exit Lady, borne out.*

The earlier part of Scene IV., with the Old Man's account of the falcon killed by an owl, and Ross's description of Duncan's horses, is erased with a pen, but in so careless a manner that it hardly seems to have been done by the same hand which has elsewhere marked particular portions for omission. Emendations, when necessary, are continued in spite of the erasures, as in former instances.

ACT III. SCENE I.

P. 134. Too rigid an adherence to the early copies has led to the perpetuation of an expression which Shakespeare could hardly have used, and which Sir W. Davenant did not introduce into his alteration of this play. It occurs where

Macbeth requests Banquo's presence at supper, and the latter replies,—

> " Let your highness
>   Command upon me."

The old corrector of the folio, 1632, like Davenant (who was followed by Rowe), puts it much more easily and naturally,—

> "*Lay* your highness'
>   Command upon me."

SCENE III.

P. 142. The folio, 1623, makes the 1 Murderer say,—

> " Now spurs the lated traveller apace
>   To gain the timely inn ; *end neere* approaches
>   The subject of our watch."

Of course *end* is an error for " and ;" and the folio, 1632, has *latest* for " lated :" the old corrector restores " lated," and for " neere" puts " here" in his margin : either may be right ; but as the compositor of the first folio printed " and" *end*, he may, very likely (as we are told he did) have blundered with the next word " here."

SCENE IV.

P. 145. The manuscript stage-directions show particularly how Lady Macbeth conducted herself of old during the banquet. Opposite the words, " Are you a man," *Coming to M. aside to him* is inserted in the margin. When, on the next page, she reminds her husband, " My worthy lord, your noble friends do lack you," the direction is, *Go back to her state.* Thus we see that she came forward upon the stage to reprove Macbeth for cowardice and distraction, and retired to her position upon the dais, when she made an effort publicly to direct his attention to his neglected duties as host. There are several instructions of the same kind for the government of the actor of the part of the Ghost of Banquo, but they are to be collected sufficiently from the dialogue.

P. 147. The conclusion of this great scene is not well printed in the folio, 1623, and worse in the folio, 1632, where " sights" is made *signs*, " stept" *spent*, &c. These errors the corrector carefully amends, and then offers a solution of a passage that has hitherto baffled satisfactory explanation. It is where Macbeth dares the Ghost of Banquo to the desert, and adds, as the folios give it,—

> " If trembling I inhabit, then protest me
> The baby of a girl."

Malone was for converting "inhabit then" to *inhibit thee;* but we do not quite approve of the manuscript change in the folio, 1632, not because it is not very intelligible, allowing for a transposition, but because it is too prosaic :—

> " If trembling I *exhibit,* then protest me," &c.

i. e. if you perceive me tremble. We have been so used to attach some indefinite meaning to "if trembling I inhabit," of the old impressions, that the reader is hardly prepared for so simple an explanation as "if trembling I exhibit." Yet, after all, it may be right.

ACT IV. SCENE I.

P. 154. In his interview with the Witches, Macbeth calls upon them to answer him, as the lines have been always printed,—

> "Though bladed corn be lodg'd, and trees blown down ;
> Though castles topple on their warders' heads ;
> Though palaces and pyramids do slope
> Their heads to their foundations," &c.

No particular objection is obvious in the wording of this quotation; but still the writer of the emendations states that three words in it are wrong, and he alters them thus :—

> "Though *bleaded* corn be lodg'd, and trees blown down ;
> Though castles topple *o'er* their warders' heads ;
> Though palaces and pyramids do *stoop*
> Their heads to their foundations," &c.

As to the word *bleaded,* we are to recollect that "bladed corn" is never "lodged" or layed ; but corn which is heavy in the ear is often borne down and flattened by wind and rain. Shakespeare must have been aware that green corn, or corn in the blade, is not liable to be affected by violent weather. Hence we may safely infer that he wrote "*bleaded*

corn," which means, in some of the provinces, and perhaps in Warwickshire, ripe corn, corn ready for the sickle.
Blead is a general name for fruit ; and the *bleading* of corn
means the yielding of it, the quantity of grain obtained
from the *blead*, or ear.   As to the second word, it seems
almost indifferent whether we adopt *o'er*, or leave "on" as it
stands.   The expression, "*stoop* their heads to their foundations," reads more appropriately and naturally than "slope
their heads to their foundations ;" and we may feel strongly
disposed to believe that it was an error of the press, since
not only was the mistake so easy, but the poet uses the
word *stoop* exactly in the same way in "Hamlet," Act II.
Scene II., and in "Cymbeline," Act IV. Scene II.   Whether
it be, or be not, necessary to alter "on" and "slope," there
can be no doubt that for "bladed" we ought in future to
substitute *bleaded* in the text of our author.

P. 156. Theobald saw the necessity of altering

> " Rebellious dead, rise never, till the wood
>   Of Birnam rise,"

by substituting "head" for *dead ;* but the old corrector does
more : he alters "rebellious" to *rebellion's*, as it were, per-
sonifying insurrection : he was surely right :—

> " *Rebellion's head*, rise never, till the wood
>   Of Birnam rise."

P. 158. When Macbeth is about to leave the cave of the
Witches, Lenox enters and informs him that Macduff has
escaped to England.   "Fled to England?" exclaims Macbeth
in astonishment ; and he goes on to declare his resolution in
future to execute instantly whatever he determines, and first
of all to surprise Macduff's castle :—

> " No boasting like a fool ;
> This deed I'll do, before this purpose cool :
> But no more sights."

Some commentators have supposed that "no more sights"
refers to the visions he had just seen conjured up by
the Witches ; but the corrector of the folio, 1632, gives
the words an entirely new aspect, completely borne out
by the context, which relates to the unexpected escape of
Macduff :—

> " This deed I 'll do, before this purpose cool :
>   But no more *flights.*"

That is, he will take care, by the rapidity with which performance shall follow decision, that nobody shall again have
an opportunity of taking flight. The compositor mistook
the *f* for a long *s*, and omitted to notice the *l* which followed it.

SCENE II.

P. 160. Much of what passes between Lady Macduff and
her young son, *viz.* from " As birds do, mother," down to
"and hang up them," is crossed out with a pen. Several
comparatively small changes are made in the scene : thus
Ross says, " And do not *know't* ourselves" for " And do not
know ourselves ;" and a few lines lower, " *'T shall* not be
long" for " Shall not be long." They are hardly necessary,
but still improvements.

SCENE III.

P. 164. Malcolm, speaking of himself, observes,—

> " In whom I know
> All the particulars of vice so grafted,
> That, when they shall be open'd, black Macbeth
> Will seem as pure as snow."

Here, as has been said on many former occasions, " open'd"
affords sense, but so inferior to that given by the correction
in the folio, 1632, that we need not hesitate in concluding
that Shakespeare, carrying on the figure suggested by the
word "grafted," as applied to fruit, must have written,—

> " In whom I know
> All the particulars of vice so grafted,
> That, when they shall be *ripen'd*, black Macbeth
> Will seem as pure as snow."

Lower down, we are instructed to alter the word "convey"
to *enjoy*, where Macduff tells Malcolm,—

> " You may
> Convey your pleasures in a spacious plenty,
> And yet seem cold."

When *enjoy* was written *enioy*, as it usually was of old, the
printer's lapse may at once be explained.

All that subsequently passes between Malcolm, Macduff, and a Doctor, respecting the cure of the evil, is struck out. It has been supposed that it was inserted, in part, to gratify King James, and after his death it was perhaps omitted.

At the conclusion of the scene (p. 170), the old reading of the folios, "This time goes manly," is changed to "This *tune* goes manly," of which, however, there never has been any doubt since the days of Rowe. It is another of the instances in which we have already seen "tune" and "time" confounded.

ACT V. SCENE II.

P. 174. Another word, very liable to the same perversion, occurs in the next emendation. The Scottish insurgent Lords are talking of the unsettled condition of Macbeth's mind, "Some say he's mad," &c., and Cathness adds,—

> " But, for certain,
> He cannot buckle his distemper'd cause
> Within the belt of rule."

The old corrector substitutes, and with apparent reason, *course* for "cause:" it was not Macbeth's "cause," but his *course* of action that was distempered.

SCENE III.

P. 176. In Coriolanus (p. 361) we have met with "cheer" misprinted *chair;* and here, if we may trust the emendation, we have *chair* misprinted "cheer." Macbeth, distracted between his guilt, his fear, and his confidence in preternatural promises, when besieged in Dunsinane Castle, exclaims,—

> " This push
> Will cheer me ever, or disseat me now.
> I have liv'd long enough : my way of life
> Is fall'n into the sear," &c.

These lines we are advised to correct in the following manner ; and with regard to the first word amended, as we are to take " disseat" in the sense of *unseat* (the folio, 1632, misprints it *disease*), there can be little objection to understanding *chair*, as having reference to the royal seat or throne, which Macbeth occupies, and from which he dreads removal :—

> " This push
> Will *chair* me ever, or disseat me now.
> I have liv'd long enough : my *May* of life
> Is fall'n into the sear," &c.

Chair was Bishop Percy's suggestion, and "*May* of life" was proposed by Johnson : both, we see, are confirmed by a much anterior authority.

P. 177. In note 9 it is urged that in the line,—

> " Cleanse the stuff'd bosom of that perilous stuff,"

the error was more likely to be in the repetition, than in the first use of the word "stuff'd." Such turns out to be the case ; and we may presume that the old printer inserted "stuff" at the end of the line, owing to his having it in his mind from the earlier part of the line. From the writer of the manuscript notes in the folio, 1632, we learn that *grief* ought to have been inserted instead of "stuff;" and it is not impossible that the recurrence of the letter *f* had something to do with the blunder : he, therefore, puts the whole passage thus :—

> " Pluck from the memory a rooted sorrow,
> Raze out the written troubles of the brain,
> And with some sweet oblivious antidote
> Cleanse the stuff'd bosom of the perilous *grief*,
> Which weighs upon the heart."

SCENE IV.

P. 178. Malcolm says of Macbeth's power and followers,—

> "For where there is advantage to be given,
> Both more and less have given him the revolt."

Advantage was hardly so much to be " given," as to be procured by revolt ; and as it also seems unlikely that the same verb should have been used in the very next line, we may feel confident that when the old corrector puts it,—

> " For when there is advantage to be *gotten*,"

he was warranted in making the change. In the next

scene Macbeth complains that the ranks of his enemies were
filled by those who ought to have been his friends :—

> "Were they not *farc'd* with those that should be ours,
> We might have met them dareful, beard to beard."

Farc'd is misrepresented "forc'd" in the old copies, and in
all modern editions ; but, as we gather from the substitution
of the letter *a* in the margin of the folio, 1632, the meaning
is that the ranks of the besiegers were *stuffed* or *filled out* by
soldiers who had revolted from Macbeth.

Just afterwards, we encounter another alteration of more
moment, when Macbeth asks the meaning of the "cry of
women" that he has heard within : he says,—

> "The time has been, my senses would have cool'd
> To hear a night-shriek."

The manuscript-correction here is *quailed* for "cooled," a
much more forcible word ; but this is one of the places
where it is possible, that the person recommending the
change may have exercised his taste, rather than stated his
knowledge. It scarcely seems likely that one word should
have been mistaken for the other, but this observation will,
of course, apply to many of the extraordinary errors that have
been from time to time pointed out. How little old compositors attended to the sense is proved on the next page by the
fact that "dusty death," which occurs only a few lines subsequently, and which is rightly printed in the folio, 1623, is
converted into "*study* death" in the folio, 1632. *Study* is
deleted, and "dusty" placed in the margin by the old corrector. Nevertheless, "*study* death" has met with its perverse vindicator in comparatively modern times.

An addition is made to the printed stage-direction (p. 186),
Enter Macduff with Macbeth's head, in these words, which
show the somewhat remarkable manner in which the spectacle was presented to the audience, *on a pike—stick it in the
ground*. This action precisely accords with what Macduff
says on the occasion :—

> "Hail, king! for so thou art. Behold, where stands
> The usurper's cursed head."

HAMLET.

ACT I. SCENE I.

P. 195. When Bernardo comes to relieve Francisco on his guard, the latter observes,—

" You come most carefully upon your hour ;"

to which Bernardo answers, as the text stands in the old copies, " 'Tis now struck twelve." Steevens suspected that Bernardo ought to say, " 'Tis *new* struck twelve ;" and in the folio, 1632, as corrected in manuscript, such is the reading: Bernardo means that he deserves Francisco's praise for his punctuality in coming just as the clock has struck.

P. 197. The printed stage-directions in this tragedy are more numerous than in many others, so that fewer remain to be supplied in manuscript. Sometimes, where they are not new, additions are made to them: thus, when we have *Enter the Ghost*, the word *armed* is written in parenthesis, to show what was his appearance in this scene ; afterwards, we shall find that when the Ghost makes his visit to Hamlet and his mother in the closet scene (p. 289), he is described in manuscript as *unarmed*, though we are not told, as in the quarto, 1603, that he is "in his night gown." Perhaps, in consistency with what Hamlet says, he was there supposed to be "in his habit as he lived ;" and when the drama was represented before the old corrector it may have been the custom of the theatre that the Ghost should come before the audience, not "in his night gown," but in his ordinary apparel. We may presume also that in this first scene a cock was heard to crow, in order to give the Ghost notice of the fit time for his departure, *Cock crows* being placed in the margin opposite the words "Stop it, Marcellus."

P. 199. Whether the old corrector did or did not resort to any of the quartos for assistance, they all have

> " Shark'd up a list of lawless resolutes,"

for "*landless* resolutes" (to which it was changed in the folios), and "lawless" is imported into the folio, 1632. The cock (p. 201) is called there in manuscript "the trumpet of the morn," and not of the *day*, "morn" being the reading of the quartos, and *day* of the folios.

SCENE II.

P. 202. More passages than usual are crossed out in this play, owing to its extreme length ; and wherever the person who abridged it thought that even two or three lines could be dispensed with, they are erased. Thus in Horatio's speech, near the top of this page, the second and third lines, as well as the eighth and ninth, are struck out; and in the King's speech, opening Scene II., the eleventh, twelfth, and thirteenth lines are marked for omission. Several other parts of the scene are treated in the same way ; but if any corrections were required in them, they, as in other places, are made notwithstanding.

P. 205. When the Queen reproaches her son for continuing to wear his mourning, as the line is represented in the quartos, she says,—

> " Good Hamlet, cast thy nighted colour off :"

the folios have *nightly* for "nighted," which the corrector of the folio, 1632, alters to *nightlike*, which is certainly better than *nightly*, but is not countenanced by any known edition. Perhaps such was the word he had heard upon the stage, and therefore inserted it.

P. 210. Horatio, describing the effect of the appearance of the Ghost upon Bernardo and Marcellus, tells Hamlet, as the text of the quartos has it,—

> " Whilst they, distill'd
> Almost to jelly with the act of fear,
> Stand dumb, and speak not to him."

The folios, on the other hand, read,—

> " Whilst they *bestill'd*
> Almost to jelly with the act of fear," &c.

Neither word, " distill'd" or *bestill'd*, can be perfectly satisfactory ; but it is apparent that *bestill'd* was a misprint in
the folio, 1623 (and from thence copied into the folio, 1632),
for a word, very like it in letters, but affording a very clear
and sensible meaning :—

> " Whilst they, *bechill'd*
> Almost to jelly with the act of fear,
> Stand dumb, and speak not to him."

Bernardo and Marcellus were almost chilled to jelly by their
apprehensions, " the cold fit of fear" having come powerfully
upon them. This must be deemed a text superior to that of
any old or modern edition.

SCENE III.

P. 213. The address of Laertes to his sister, instructing
her how to receive and return Hamlet's love, is full of verbal
and literal errors in the folio, 1632 ; and, besides corrections of these in three places, the text is made to tally
with that of the quartos : thus " safety" is substituted for
sanctity, " act and place" for *sect and force*, and " keep you in
the rear" for " keep *within* the rear." These three mistakes
were transplanted from the earlier folio, and the setting of
them right may look as if the authority of the quartos had
been appealed to.

P. 215. Polonius, advising his son on the subject of apparel, thus speaks, as the lines have always stood,—

> " And they in France, of the best rank and station,
> Are of a most select and generous chief in that."

Malone would explain " chief" heraldically ; but it is simply
an error of the press : " chief" was of old spelt " chiefe," and
the compositor misreading the long *s* for *f*, printed " chiefe"
for *choise* or *choice* :—

> " Are of a most select and generous *choice* in that."

The folios print it *cheff*, but Steevens was disposed to think *choice* the word wanted, and he was not mistaken, for that alteration is made in the folio, 1632.

P. 217. Theobald guessed rightly that "sanctified and pious bonds" ought to be "sanctified and pious *bawds;*" but three lines lower occurs an emendation in the folio, 1632, which nobody has speculated upon, but which is at least equally plausible. Polonius says to Ophelia,—

> "I would not, in plain terms, from this time forth,
> Have you to slander any moment leisure,
> As to give words or talk with the lord Hamlet."

For "slander" read *squander*, and for "moment" *moment's*. she was not to waste a moment's leisure upon him. The scribe seems to have misheard both *bawd* and *squander*. At the end of the speech this imperfect line occurs :—

> "Look to't, I charge you ; come your ways."

The old correction is,—

> "Look to't, I charge you ; *so now*, come your ways."

So now may have dropped out, or may possibly have been added merely to complete the measure.

SCENE IV.

P. 220. When the Ghost enters, a manuscript note states that he is *armed as before*. There is a singular marginal instruction to the player of the part of Hamlet, that after he has exclaimed,—

> "Angels and ministers of grace defend us !"

he is to *pause* before he continues. This seems natural, and therefore judicious ; and we may, perhaps, infer that such was the mode in which Richard Burbage (the original representative of the character) delivered the address. From him it may have been handed down to the time of the old corrector through Joseph Taylor, who followed Burbage in this and some other principal parts. During this *pause* we may suppose that the actor was gasping for breath, with his eyes fixed upon the apparition, and unable for some moments to proceed.

SCENE V.

P. 222. This, according to the ancient stage-arrangements, and according to the representations of the old editions, was, probably, not a new scene; for after Hamlet and the Ghost have gone out, as it were to "a more removed ground," Horatio and Marcellus say a few words and retire: Hamlet and the Ghost then return to the scene, and it seems to have been left to the audience to imagine that the ground on which they stood was not, in fact, the same they had before occupied.

It is to be observed that the Acts and Scenes are not divided in the quartos; and in the folios, though *Actus Primus* and *Actus Secundus* are marked (with the distinction of some of the scenes), we are without any printed notes of the kind during the rest of the tragedy. The emendator of the folio, 1632, was, therefore, the first to supply the deficiency: he appears to have done so accurately (with one or two exceptions) according to the practice in his age, but by no means precisely the same as in modern editions.

In the last line on this page we are desired by the old corrector to read "confin'd to *lasting* fires," instead of "confin'd to fast in fires," a change recommended by Heath in his "Revisal." Steevens, Farmer, and Monk Mason contend that no alteration is required.

P. 225. Regarding the subsequent lines, as invariably printed, an advantageous proposal is made in the corrected folio, 1632:—

> " Thus was I, sleeping, by a brother's hand,
>   Of life, of crown, of queen, at once dispatch'd."

"Dispatch'd" cannot be right, and why should Shakespeare employ a wrong word when another, that is unobjectionable, at once presented itself, *viz.*—

> " Of life, of crown, of queen, at once *despoil'd ?*"

Misreading was, most likely, the cause of this blunder; the earliest quarto, 1603, has *depriv'd* for "dispatch'd," of the other quartos and folios; but we may feel confident that the poet's misprinted word was *despoil'd*. It is written upon an erasure, and possibly the old corrector first inserted *depriv'd*, and afterwards saw reason to change it to *despoil'd*, as the true language of the poet.

ACT II.　SCENE II.

P. 236. We have here one more of the many proofs how one word was put for another, because the word misprinted occurred in a different part of the same line: the quartos assign to Polonius,—

> " My news shall be the fruit to that great feast."

In the folio, 1623, it became,—

> " My news shall be the *news* to that great feast;"

which was more absurdly repeated in the folio, 1632; but "fruit" is restored (perhaps from one of the quartos) in the margin of the second folio.

P. 242. Exactly the same lapse occurs here: the quartos make Polonius ask Hamlet,—

> " I mean the matter that you read, my lord?"

In the folios it stands,—

> " I mean the matter that you *mean*, my lord."

A corresponding correction erases *mean,* and inserts "read" in its place.

P. 246. To show how minute and particular the owner of the folio, 1632, who introduced the manuscript notes, was in the stage-directions, it may be stated that before Hamlet says, "Man delights not me; no, nor woman neither," &c., Rosencrantz is directed to *smile,* in order that the actor might not forget to do so. What afterwards passes between Hamlet and Rosencrantz respecting the popularity of companies of young performers, under the titles of Children of the Revels, Children of Paul's, &c., is crossed out with a pen, because, among other reasons, at the time when the play was shortened this portion was inapplicable.

P. 251. Pope's emendation, in opposition to all the ancient authorities, of *salt* for "sallets," is supported by a correction in the folio, 1632.

P. 254. We must attribute to mishearing a corruption, though not of much importance, in the last line of the

Player's probationary speech, referring to the clamorous grief of Hecuba, when she saw Priam's limbs "minced" by the sword of Pyrrhus:—

> " Would have made milch the burning eyes of heaven,
>   And passion in the gods."

" And *passionate* (*i.e.* compassionate) the gods" is the way in which we learn we ought to read the last hemistich: to say that it made " passion in the gods" is certainly sense, but the emendation proposed should probably be the text.

P. 256. The same may be remarked of the next change that occurs in the folio, 1632: it is in Hamlet's soliloquy, where he adverts to his own irresoluteness :—

> " For it cannot be,
> But I am pigeon-liver'd, and lack gall
> To make oppression bitter."

It was not " oppression," but crime, that was to be punished by him ; and to read

> "To make *transgression* bitter"

is so far an improvement: the similarity in the sound of the terminations of both words may have misled the copyist. " Oppression" is, however, quite intelligible.

ACT III. SCENE I.

P. 260. The manuscript-annotator adopts two changes in the quartos in Hamlet's great soliloquy: these are " the proud man's contumely" instead of " the *poor* man's contumely," as it is given in all the folios ; and " the pangs of despis'd love" instead of " the pangs of *dispriz'd* love," as also there misprinted.

P. 263. Hamlet, in old and modern editions, tells Ophelia, " I am very proud, revengeful, ambitious ; with more offences at my beck, than I have thoughts to put them in." Steevens says that " more offences at my beck" means " always ready to come about me:" this may be so, but a manuscript-correction supplies a much more natural word and easy interpretation, *viz.* that Hamlet is loaded with offences—

" with more offences at my *back*, than I have thoughts to put
them in."

P. 266. The several misprints in the folio, 1623, in
Hamlet's directions to the players, are copied, and multiplied in the folio, 1632, but not one of them escapes correction : among them we may mention that "*or Norman*"
is altered to "nor man" by striking out the conjunction,
and dividing the word. This emendation entirely discoun-
tenances Farmer's notion that Mussulman was intended.
To the printed introduction of the scene, *Enter Hamlet and
two or three of the Players*, is added *unready ;* that is to say,
not yet dressed for the parts they were to fill in the play
within a play.

P. 270. It may be considered a somewhat singular feature
in the manuscript-corrections, of this drama in particular,
that all passages of an indecent character are carefully
erased. Such are portions of the dialogue between Hamlet
and Ophelia, prior to and during the representation before
the King and Queen, which Steevens seemed to think "were
peculiar to the young and fashionable of the age of Shakespeare." It appears, however, that not very long after "the
age of Shakespeare," they were struck out, either on account
of their needless indelicacy, or for the sake of abbreviating
the performance ; perhaps both.

P. 275. Johnson, Steevens, Farmer, and Tollet differed
whether, when Ophelia remarks, "Still better and worse,"
Hamlet ought to say, "So you *mistake* your husbands," as it
is given in the quarto, 1604, and in the folios, or "So you
must take your husbands," *viz.* for better for worse. When
these annotators wrote, it was not known that a still earlier
quarto (1603) has it, "So you must take your husband ;"
and, in addition, it now appears that the old corrector of the
folio, 1632, altered the reading there found to "So you *must*
take your husbands." In the same way, it has been doubted
when Hamlet on a subsequent page (277) speaks of "two
Provincial roses on my *rac'd* shoes" (we spell it as in the
folios ; the quartos print it *raz'd*), he means *rayed* shoes,
razed shoes, or *raised*, that is, elevated shoes. The old
corrector spells it "*raised* shoes," and we may presume
that that is what was intended ; namely, shoes which gave

the actor artificial height. This is the more probable, because Richard Burbage, the original Hamlet, was a man, probably, of rather short stature.

P. 277. The two lines delivered by Hamlet after the sudden breaking off of the play,—

> " For if the King like not the comedy,
> Why then, belike, he likes it not perdy,"

are underscored as a quotation ; and such we may reasonably suppose them to be.

SCENE III.

P. 283. When the King, in his soliloquy, says,—

> " Offence's gilded hand may shove by justice,
> And oft 'tis seen, the wicked prize itself
> Buys out the law,"

we need no great persuasion to make us believe that we ought to read, as a manuscript note tells us,—

> " And oft 'tis seen, the wicked *purse* itself
> Buys out the law."

When Hamlet enters *behind*, another stage-direction (printed in no copy) states that he has *his sword drawn* ready to kill the King, if his resolution had held. The old mode of acting the scene appears to have been, that, when Hamlet came in at the back, the King knelt in front of the stage, and did not *retire and kneel*, as stated in modern editions.

SCENE IV.

P. 285. Before Hamlet comes to his mother, in the closet-scene, Polonius hides himself behind the arras, and says, as it has been invariably printed,—

> " I'll silence me e'en here."

That this is a misprint we might guess without any hint from the corrected folio, 1632, which thus gives the words,—

> " I'll *'sconce* me even here."

Johnson felt obliged to explain that "I'll silence me e'en

here" meant "I'll use no more words." In "The Merry Wives," Falstaff says, "I will ensconce me behind the arras," which is exactly what Polonius does. *'Sconce* and *ensconce* are constantly used figuratively for *hide*.

P. 288. When Hamlet is comparing the representations of his father and his uncle, the first folio has "wholesome *breath*" instead of "wholesome brother" of the quartos, and the second folio adds to it various verbal and literal errors; but all editions, modern as well as ancient, contain a reading, the change of which in the folio, 1632, must be admitted to be a considerable improvement : the misprint, with a careless compositor, must have been an easy one : it occurs where the hero says to his mother,—

> " For, at your age
> The hey-day in the blood is tame, it's humble,
> And waits upon the judgment ; and what judgment
> Would step from this to this ?"

i. e. from his father to his uncle : Hamlet is exalting the first, and debasing the last ; and the expression, "Would step from this to this," is feeble and inexpressive, while a slight alteration in one word makes a vast difference :—

> " And what judgment
> Would *stoop* from this to this ?"

P. 290. After the entrance of the Ghost *unarmed*, as has been already mentioned, Hamlet thus addresses it in all copies,—

> " Do you not come your tardy son to chide,
> That, laps'd in time and passion, lets go by
> The important acting of your dread command ?"

The amended reading offered in the folio, 1632, is,—

> " That laps'd in *fume* and passion," &c. ;

but "laps'd in time and passion" may, nevertheless, be right, supposing Hamlet to intend that he has let slip the proper opportunity.

ACT IV. SCENE III.

P. 298. The emendation next to be noticed is well worthy of consideration, and perhaps of adoption. The King asks

Hamlet where Polonius is at supper, and the answer is this in the quartos:—

"Not where he eats, but where he is eaten: a certain convocation of politic worms are e'en at him. Your worm is your only emperor for diet," &c.

The folios omit "politic," probably unintentionally, but possibly because it was not clearly understood why the worms should be called "politic." The old corrector of the folio, 1632, leads us to suppose that "politic" was misprinted, or miswritten, for an epithet, certainly more applicable in the place where it occurs, in reference to the taste of the worms for the rich repast they were enjoying:—

"A certain convocation of *palated* worms are e'en at him. Your worm is your only emperor for diet: we fat all creatures else to fat us, and we fat ourselves for maggots."

It is easy to suppose that "politic," a word with which the scribe was familiar, was misheard by him for the unusual word *palated*. Shakespeare employs to *palate* as a verb in "Coriolanus," Act III. Scene I., and in "Antony and Cleopatra," Act V. Scene II.; and it is doing no great violence to imagine that he here uses the participle of the same verb. If the text had always stood "*palated* worms," and it had been proposed to change it to "politic worms," few readers would for an instant have consented to relinquish an expression so peculiarly Shakespearian.

SCENE V

P. 304. It is worth a brief note, that the second of Ophelia's fragments of ballads,—

"And at his head a grass-green turf,"

is written in the folio, 1632,—

"And at his head a *green grass* turf."

Again, on the next page, the folio, 1632, for the line, as it stands in the folio, 1623,—

"Let in the maid, that out a maid,"

misprints "Let in" twice, instead of "that out" in the second instance. This blunder is set right in the margin. When Ophelia re-enters, "Fare you well, my dove" (p. 310), is

given in all the folios as part of her ballad ; but it is marked
by the old corrector as spoken, and not sung. Again, the
same authority tells us that the lines on p. 311,—

> " No, no, he is dead ;
> Go to thy death-bed,''

ought to run, as we may very well believe,—

> " No, no, he is dead,
> *Gone* to *his* death-bed,
> He never will come again.''

It has always hitherto been printed, "*Go* to *thy* death-bed,"
and we can scarcely think the proposed change merely arbitrary. For

> " His beard was as white as snow,''

the correction in manuscript is,—

> " His beard was white as snow.''

In the folios it is, "His beard as white as snow," and
the variation may be deemed immaterial. When Ophelia
makes her exit, it is stated that she goes out *dancing distracted*, although she had sung such a melancholy ditty just
before, and had taken such a sad farewell. It is the last we
see of her.

P. 321. A very absurd misprint found its way into the
folio, 1623, where the Queen describes the death of Ophelia :
the quartos properly read,—

> " Pull'd the poor wretch from her melodious lay ;''

which in the folio, 1623, stands,—

> " Pull'd the poor wretch from her melodious *buy;*''

and in the folio, 1632,—

> " Pull'd the poor wretch from her melodious *by.*''

Perhaps "lay," substituted in the margin of the folio, 1632,
was obtained from the quartos ; but it is not impossible, if
the emendation were not guessed at, that it was introduced
from accurate recitation of the passage on the stage : nobody
could imagine *buy* or *by* right.

ACT V. SCENE I.

P. 322. Two small portions of the Grave-diggers' Scene are struck through with a pen: the first relates to Adam being a gentleman: and the second to the length of time the First Grave-digger had filled his office, and the motive for sending Hamlet into England. If William Kemp played the part of the First Grave-digger, as has been conjectured (Chalmers's "Apology," p. 457), we need not be surprised at any expedient to keep such a favourite before the audience; but when he was gone, some reduction of the dialogue may have been held desirable, on account of the great length of the play. However, it is more than doubtful whether Kemp belonged to the same company as Shakespeare when Hamlet was produced. (See "Memoirs of the Actors in Shakespeare's Plays," pp. 105. 115.)

P. 329. The four lines in rhyme which follow Hamlet's prose introduction,—

> "Imperial Cæsar, dead, and turn'd to clay," &c.,

are distinguished in the folio, 1632, as a quotation in the usual way: and they seem to have occurred to the speaker, as extremely apposite to what he had himself just said respecting the "dust of Alexander." We have no notion from whence the passage was taken.

P. 332. When Hamlet tells Laertes, as the line is printed every where,—

> "I'll do't.—Dost thou come here to whine?"

the line clearly wants two syllables; and the corrector of the folio, 1632, makes Hamlet emphatically repeat, "I'll do't," which perfects the measure:—

> "I'll do't: *I'll do't.*—Dost thou come here to whine?"

This repetition was probably omitted by the printer accidentally.

The whole speech, beginning, "This is mere madness," is given to the King in the folios; but it is evident that at least part of it could not have been uttered by him: a new prefix, in the margin of the second folio, assigns the three last lines to the Queen, while the two first are continued as

before. In the quartos the Queen delivers all five lines ; but
it seems more likely that the King should interpose to tell
the spectators of the funeral,—

> " This is mere madness ;
> And thus a while the fit will work on him."

In consistency with this view, the King, just afterwards,
desires Horatio to follow Hamlet, who had rushed out.

SCENE II.

P. 336. The compositor of the folio, 1623, was guilty of a
careless blunder when he printed " Sweet lord, if your *friendship* were at leisure," instead of " if your lordship were at
leisure :" it was, notwithstanding, copied into the folio, 1632,
where it is set right in the margin. We need not say that
from all modern editions the corruption has been excluded.
Precisely the same course was pursued with a lapse on
p. 340, where, in all the folios, *tongue* is misprinted for
" turn," and " hurt my *mother*" for " hurt my brother." This
part of the tragedy is extremely ill-represented in both the
earliest folio impressions ; but the most minute inaccuracy
did not elude the attention of the old amender of the
second folio.

P. 343. The printed stage-directions are extremely frequent
in this last scene ; but, nevertheless, the additions to them
in manuscript in the folio, 1632, are many. Thus, no printed
note being given when the Queen *drinks* the poison, the
proper place is duly marked, as well as when *she dies*. When
Horatio *snatches the cup* in order to poison himself, and when
Hamlet *strives and gets it from him*, the necessary information is furnished in the margin. It should seem that the
directions were not all added at the same time, but, perhaps,
as the writer became aware of their importance, for the ink
is not always alike.

P. 344. During the fencing-match, the Queen interposes
that Hamlet may take breath : in the quartos, her words
are,—

> " He's fat and scant of breath.—
> Here, Hamlet, take my napkin, rub thy brows."

In the folios, the passage is merely this :—

> "He's fat and scant of breath.—
> Here's a napkin, rub thy brows."

The second line is obviously defective, and the corrector of the folio, 1632, does not, in this instance, cure it by adopting the text of the quartos, but that of some independent authority : perhaps his emendation here, as in some other places, represents the passage as it was delivered by the player of the part of the Queen :—

> " He's fat and scant of breath.—
> Here *is* a napkin, rub thy brows, *my son.*"

P. 347. The drama, abridged, as far as we can judge, for, or from, representation some time after the appearance of the folio, 1632, concludes with the two lines spoken by Horatio over the dead body of Hamlet : all the rest, including " Why does the drum come hither," is crossed out, so that nothing is seen of Fortinbras, or of the English ambassadors. The lines put into the mouth of Horatio are these, as they stand in every edition, Hamlet having just expired :—

> " Now cracks a noble heart.—Good night, sweet prince,
> And flights of angels sing thee to thy rest."

However, it seems to have been thought, about the time the abbreviations were made, that the tragedy ought to end with a rhyming couplet, and we may infer that the alteration we meet with in the folio, 1632, was made for the purpose :—

> " Now cracks a noble heart.—Good night, *be blest*,
> And flights of angels sing thee to thy rest."

This couplet is followed by the word *Finis*, in manuscript, to show that it was the conclusion of the piece.

Nevertheless, the necessary changes of the text, as we find it in the second folio, are continued, as if what follows the entrance of Fortinbras, &c., had not been erased. The first is merely " This" for *His*, when Fortinbras says,—

> " This quarry cries on havock," &c.

It is " *His* quarry," &c., in the folios, and certainly wrong.

P. 348. Fortinbras, seeing that the throne of Denmark is vacant, puts in his claim to it :—

> " I have some rights of memory in this kingdom,
> Which now to claim my vantage doth invite me."

These are the terms in the quartos ; the folios, 1623 and 1632, nonsensically have " Which *are* to claim," &c. When Horatio replies, according to the correct text,—

> " Of that I shall have also cause to speak,"

the folio, 1623, gives the line thus inaccurately :—

> "Of that I shall have *always* cause to speak ;"

which the folio, 1632, makes still worse :—

> " Of that I shall always cause to speak."

These careless errors are corrected in manuscript in the later folio, where we also find in the margin an emendation which appears to be of considerable value   Horatio, in reference to the funeral of Hamlet, observes, as the line has invariably been printed,—

> " But let this same be presently perform'd."

Same sounds poorly and awkwardly, and the old corrector states that it was not the poet's word, but one that might easily be mistaken for it : he puts it,—

> " But let this *scene* be presently perform'd,"

viz. the scene of the funeral, at which, while Hamlet's body was placed " high on a stage," Horatio was to explain the cause of his death : the mention of " stage," both before and afterwards, and the use of the word " performed," afford confirmation, if needed, that Shakespeare's language was *scene*, and not " same."   This may have been only a guessed at misprint, but nobody else has ever guessed it.

KING LEAR.

ACT I. SCENE I.

P. 357. The first correction in this tragedy in the folio, 1632, is the erasure of "Sir" at the beginning of Goneril's speech, and the addition of a letter to convert *word* into "words." The line is there exactly reprinted from the folio, 1623, where it stands,—

> "Sir, I love you more than word can wield the matter."

Here "Sir" is clearly redundant and needless, and Regan, soon afterwards, commences her speech without it ; *word* also should evidently be "words," even without the authority of the quartos for the change.

P. 358. The folios also contain the following in Regan's answer to her father,—

> "I profess
> Myself an enemy to all other joys
> That the most precious square of sense professes."

The compositor caught *professes*, instead of "possesses," from the line almost immediately above, and there cannot be a moment's hesitation in following the quartos, which are uniform. The question that has arisen has been as to the uncouth expression, "the most precious square of sense." Edwards contended that it is to be taken as "the full complement of all the senses ;" in other words, the whole circle of the senses ; and the old corrector furnishes a word, misprinted "square," that exactly conveys this meaning,—

> "That the most precious *sphere* of sense possesses."

She loved her father, according to her own assertion, beyond all other joys in the round or *sphere* of sense.

P. 359. The quarto editions read thus at the close of Cordelia's self-vindicatory speech :—

> "Sure, I shall never marry like my sisters,
> *To love my father all.*"

The words in Italics are strangely left out in all the folios, and are added in manuscript in that of 1632. The incompleteness of the sentence makes us wonder how the defective text of the folio, 1623, could have been reprinted.

P. 360. It is to be noted that in the following,—

> "As my great patron thought on in my prayers,"

the folio, 1632, omits "great," which word is not supplied in manuscript, but the line is thus amended :—

> "Lov'd as my father, as my master follow'd,
> *And* as my patron thought on in my prayers."

Hence we may see that the old corrector was not constantly guided by older editions, which are all in favour of "great."

P. 362. The folio, 1632, is made, in manuscript, to differ from all earlier copies where Lear banishes Kent :—

> "Five days we do allot thee for provision
> To shield thee from diseases of the world,
> And on the sixth to turn thy hated back
> Upon our kingdom : if on the *seventh* day following
> Thy banish'd trunk be found in our dominions," &c.

The quartos, as stated in note 10, have "four days," and "on the fifth ;" and it may seem unlikely that Kent should be allowed till "the *tenth* day following" (as in the folios) to quit the kingdom. This, however, is a point of little importance, excepting as it may show, either that the passage was usually recited "the *seventh* day following," as amended in the folio, 1632, or that the person who altered the text had some other authority for it. It is not probable that he would arbitrarily make the change.

P. 364. We come to a more important variation from every old copy, where Cordelia entreats her father to

> " make known
> It is no vicious blot, murder, or foulness,
> No unchaste action, or dishonour'd step,
> That hath depriv'd me of your grace and favour."

" Murder" (spelt *murther* in the folios) seems here entirely
out of place : Cordelia could never contemplate that any
body would suspect her of "murder," as the ground of her
father's displeasure : she is referring to " vicious blots," and
"foulness" in respect to virtue, and there cannot, we apprehend, be a doubt that the old corrector has given us
the real language of Shakespeare when he puts the passage
thus :—

> "make known
> It is no vicious blot, *nor other* foulness,
> No unchaste action," &c.

The copyist or the compositor miswrote or misread *nor other*
"murther," and thus occasioned a corruption, which has
eternally been repeated. But there appears, on the same authority, to be another error in the latter portion of what we
have just above quoted :—

> " No unchaste action, or dishonour'd *stoop*,
> That hath depriv'd me of your grace and favour."

In Hamlet (p. 427) we have seen *stoop* misprinted " step," as
here, and Cordelia alludes to some grossly derogatory act,
some base condescension on her part, and not merely to
some dishonourable "step" which she had taken : "step,"
for *stoop*, here reads most insignificantly, and could hardly
have been the poet's language.

SCENE IV.

P. 381. What the Fool sings,—

> " Fools had ne'er less grace in a year," &c.,

is marked as a quotation in the folio, 1632, perhaps from
some satirical ballad of the time ; and the third line is
amended, so that, like the first, it rhymes in the middle :—

> " And *well may fear* their wits to wear," &c.

The scrap that succeeds almost immediately is also underscored ; but it is evident that the Fool alters this fragment

to suit his purpose. The couplet on the next page has the same stage-direction, *Sing*, opposite to it, and it is likewise underscored.

ACT II. SCENE I.

P. 393. After hearing of the flight of Edgar, when he is supposed to have wounded Edmund for not entering into the conspiracy to murder their father, Gloster says, as the passage stands printed and punctuated in the folios,—

> " Let him fly far :
> Not in this land shall he remain uncaught
> And found ; dispatch, the noble duke my master,
> My worthy arch and patron comes to night," &c.

Here misprinting and mispointing have obscured the poet's meaning, and the old corrector of the folio, 1632, amends as follows :—

> " Let him fly far :
> Not in this land shall he remain uncaught,
> And found, *dispatch'd*. The noble duke, my master,
> My worthy arch and patron comes to night," &c.

That is to say, " Let him fly far ; for if caught and found in this land he shall be dispatched." What succeeds in the dialogue entirely supports this view ; for Gloster declares that by the authority of the Duke, who was expected, " the murderous coward" should be proclaimed and brought " to the stake," adding,—

> " All ports I'll bar ; the villain shall not 'scape."

P. 394. Both the folios are here very carelessly printed ; but, as might be supposed, that of 1632 gives the more imperfect notion of Shakespeare's text. Thus, for " strange news," of the quartos, the folios have *strangeness ;* but all the copies, quarto and folio, are wrong in the line,—

> " He whom my father nam'd ? your Edgar ? "

for it obviously halts for want of two syllables : and the correction of the old annotator shows what they are :—

> " He whom my father nam'd ? *your heir*, your Edgar ? "

It was natural that Regan should speak of him as Gloster's

heir in the presence of Edmund, as hinting at the motive
for Edgar's design on his father's life. Just below, there is a
line with a syllable too many :—

> "Was he not companion with the riotous knights."

The negative is erased in the folio, 1632, by which the
measure is restored, and the sense not injured; for Edmund
immediately afterwards replies,—

> "Yes, madam, *yes;* he was of that consort;"

giving additional emphasis by the repetition of the affirmative *yes*, which is not in any ancient copy : the compositor,
having inserted "yes" once, left it out the second time, and
thus rendered the line defective. The folio, 1632, omits
"his" before "revenues," but it is inserted in the margin.

SCENE II.

P. 396. When Kent tells Oswald, "If I had thee in Lipsbury pinfold, I would make thee care for me," the commentators have been puzzled to know where "Lipsbury
pinfold" was situated, and Farmer and Steevens supposed it
"a cant phrase." In the folio, 1632, it is altered to "*Finsbury* pinfold;" and a misprint was, doubtless, the cause of
the difficulty. There was, probably, an old pinfold standing
in Finsbury in the time of Shakespeare, in connexion with
Moorfields, and well known to his audiences; and to this,
without caring for the anachronism, he alluded.

SCENE IV.

P. 406. In the corrected folio, 1632, we encounter a very
material alteration in the Fool's satirical rhymes, showing
that the conclusion, always hitherto printed as prose, was
also in verse : the last part stands thus in type in the folio,
1632 :—

> "But for all this, thou shalt have as many dolours for thy dear
> daughters, as thou canst tell in a year."

The manuscript-corrector makes the whole run thus :—

> "Fathers that wear rags,
>   Do make their children blind;
> But fathers, that bear bags,
>   Shall see their children kind.

> Fortune, that arrant whore,
> Ne'er turns the key to the poor.
> But, for all this, *it follows,*
> Thou shalt have as many dolours
> For thy daughters dear
> As thou canst tell in a year."

The folio, 1632, alone contains the word "dear," but there it was transposed, since it forms the rhyme to "year."

In the Fool's rhymes on the next page, there is a perversion in the two last lines, which have been always thus erroneously printed :—

> "The knave turns fool that runs away,
> The fool no knave perdy."

This is exactly the contrary of what is meant: in the first six lines the Fool says, that a mercenary knave quits his master in a storm, but that a fool remains with him; and he follows it up by observing that the fool turns knave when he abandons his master, although the knave can be considered no fool for doing so, and taking care of himself :—

> "The fool turns knave that runs away,
> The knave no fool, perdy."

The corrector of the folio, 1632, transposes the words, in order to make them run as above.

P. 410. We have here an instance of mishearing on the part of the scribe, which has occasioned an indisputable blunder. Regan tells Lear to admit to Goneril that he has wronged her, and he breaks out in reply,—

> "Ask her forgiveness?
> Do you but mark how this becomes the house :
> 'Dear daughter, I confess that I am old,'" &c.

What has "the house" to do with it? They are talking outside Gloster's castle, and not in, nor referring to, any habitation. What Lear should say is what the old corrector makes him say :—

> "Ask her forgiveness?
> Do you but mark how this becomes the *mouth:*
> 'Dear daughter, I confess that I am old,'" &c.

Between the copyist and the compositor, *mouth* became "house." After *kneeling,* while he says the above, Lear never gets up again in modern editions; but a note in the folio, 1632, directs the actor to *rise* at the beginning of his next passionate speech, "Never, Regan," &c.

The conjecture, in note 9 on the next page, that the epithet "tender-hafted" ought to be *tender-hearted*, is supported by a marginal emendation in the folio, 1632.

P. 412. Regan again advises Lear to submit, and to return to Goneril : he exclaims, as the passage stands in modern editions,—

> " Return to her ? and fifty men dismiss'd ?
> No, rather I abjure all roofs, and choose
> To wage against the enmity of the air ;
> To be a comrade with the wolf and owl.—
> Necessity's sharp pinch !"

From the folio, 1632, and its corrections, we learn that the omission of the aspirate has occasioned a serious error here : "Necessity's sharp pinch!" has always been printed as an exclamation by itself, without connexion ; but it seems that Shakespeare made the verb *howl* transitive, and that in future the lines ought to be printed as follows :—

> " To be a comrade with the wolf, and *howl*
> Necessity's sharp pinch."

i. e. howl like the wolf when he feels the sharp pinch of necessity. The punctuation of the folios, if that can be any guide, warrants this construction of the text.

ACT III. SCENE I.

P. 417. Kent tells the Gentleman, whom he meets, of some disagreement between the Dukes, information of which has been communicated to France by their

> "servants, who seem no less,
> Which are to France the spies and speculations
> Intelligent of our state."

"Speculations," of all the old copies, must be wrong both as regards meaning and measure ; and the old corrector instructs us to read *spectators* instead of it, although the accentuation may be unusual :—

> " Which are to France the spies and *spectators*
> Intelligent of our state."

A few lines lower he puts *flourishings* for "furnishings," with apparent fitness, though Steevens would justify "furnishings" by a quotation from the preface to one of Greene's tracts, no doubt itself a corruption, where he talks of "lending the world a furnish of wit;" "a *flourish* of wit" must have been Greene's expression. Here, again, one corruption is attempted to be supported by another.

SCENE IV.

P. 425. In two several speeches by Edgar, on this page, the quarto editions are followed and deserted by the old corrector: thus in "through the sharp hawthorn blow the cold winds," *cold*, which he inserts, is found in the quartos only ; while, in the next speech of the same character, for "through sword and whirl-pool" he puts "through *swamp* and whirl-pool:" it is "ford and whirl-pool" in the quartos. The first of these is marked as a quotation (both here and on p. 427, where it again occurs), in the usual manner; and it most likely was derived from some then known ballad.

ACT IV. SCENE I.

P. 443. We meet with two comparatively small, but valuable amendments in the first line of Edgar's speech, which opens this Act, one of which was speculated upon by Johnson. The common reading has been :—

> " Yet better thus, and known to be contemn'd,
> Than still contemn'd and flatter'd."

Johnson's suggestion was to read "and known" *unknown ;* and this is what the corrector states is the true text. Edgar says, that it is better to be contemn'd because unknown, as he is in his disguise, than to be contemn'd and flattered when known. There is, however, a further change which deserves notice, *viz. Yes* for "Yet." Edgar enters, moralising with himself, and giving his assent to some propo-

sition that he had stated before he comes upon the stage:
the passage ought, therefore, to stand as follows:—

> " *Yes*, better thus *unknown* to be contemn'd,
>   Than still contemn'd and flatter'd."

At the bottom of this page we have another example of the
manner in which the frequent mistake of *w* for *m* has in part
led to the introduction of a corruption. Blind Gloster says,
in answer to the Old Man,—

> "I have no way, and therefore want no eyes:
> I stumbled when I saw. Full oft 'tis seen
> Our means secure us ; and our mere defects
> Prove our commodities."

In what way do "our means secure us?" The point is not
that our means secure us, but that having no means is advantageous: "our mere defects," or deficiencies, "prove our
commodities." The printer read *wants* "means," and hence
the blunder. Gloster is speaking of the advantage even of
want of sight:—

> " Full oft 'tis seen
> Our *wants* secure us, and our mere defects
> Prove our commodities."

Pope would read *mean* for "means," but it does not support
Gloster's argument ; and it, besides, requires that the verb
should be in the singular instead of the plural, as it is
printed in all the old copies. "Means" is struck out, and
wants substituted in the folio, 1632.

P. 445. Gloster, giving his purse to Edgar, whom he still
supposes a lunatic beggar, says,—

> "Heavens, deal so still!
> Let the superfluous, and lust-dieted man,
> That slaves your ordinance, that will not see," &c.

Discussion has been produced by the expression, "that
slaves your ordinance:" Johnson understood it to mean, that
slights or ridicules it, and Steevens, that makes a slave
of it ; while Malone, because he could suggest nothing, was
in favour of adhering to the quartos—"that *stands* your
ordinance." The setting right of a trifling typographical
error clears the sense of the whole:—

> "Heavens, deal so still!
> Let the superfluous, and lust-dieted man,

> That *braves* your ordinance, that will not see,
> Because he doth not feel, feel your power quickly."

He *braves* the ordinance of heaven by his luxury, selfishness, and want of charity.   This emendation can want no support.

SCENE IV.

P. 454. Whether the old corrector did or did not resort to the quartos, he makes the reading of the folios tally with them, where Cordelia entreats all the " unpublish'd virtues of the earth" to

> " be aidant and remediate
> In the good man's distress."

The word is *desires,* for " distress," in the folio, 1623, and the error was copied into the second folio.

SCENE VI.

P. 460. Lear having entered dressed *with straws and flowers,* according to the manuscript stage-direction (for no printed note of the kind is found, even where it is most wanted), inveighs against lust and hypocrisy :—

> " Behold yond' simpering dame,
> Whose face between her forks presageth snow ;
> Who minces virtue, and does shake the head
> To hear of pleasure's name."

Malone says that " who minces virtue" means " whose virtue consists in appearance ;" but that is the meaning of the poet, rather than of the words imputed to him ; for it does not follow that " a lady who walks mincingly along," as Malone has it, means thereby to affect virtue.   " Minces," in truth, is a lapse by the printer for *mimics*—" a dame that *mimics* virtue ;" that is, who puts on the externals of modesty :—

> " Who *mimics* virtue, and does shake the head
> To hear of pleasure's name."

Unless it can be shown that "minces" means the same as *mimics,* this emendation must surely hereafter form part of the text of Shakespeare.

P. 463. Lear thus incoherently preaches to blind Gloster, in every known copy of the play,—

> " When we are born, we cry that we are come
> To this great stage of fools.—This a good block ?
> It were a delicate stratagem, to shoe
> A troop of horse with felt."

The commentators have been puzzled to explain why Lear starts away with the words, " This a good block ;" and Ritson asks if we ought not to read " *'Tis* a good block." They suppose that Lear pulls off his hat when he begins to preach, and speaks of it, but how does it appear that he has any hat on his head, when he comes in " fantastically dressed up with flowers." He does not advert to his hat as " a good block " at all, but to the excellent stratagem he has in his mind, of shoeing a troop of horse with felt. The emendator of the folio, 1632, gives the text most satisfactorily, and shows that the word of the poet had been misheard :—

> " 'Tis a good *plot :*
> It were a delicate stratagem, to shoe
> A troop of horse with felt."

This was the " good *plot* " uppermost in Lear's thoughts. Lower down, the corrector adds, " And laying Autumn's dust," perhaps from the quartos (where, however, it stands, " Ay, and for laying Autumn's dust "), in order to complete the sense, which is left defective in the folios.

P. 466. After reading Goneril's letter to Edmund, Edgar exclaims, as the words have always been printed after the folios,—

> " O, undistinguish'd space of woman's will !
> A plot upon her virtuous husband's life ;
> And the exchange my brother !"

Editors have speculated differently as to the meaning of the first line ; but they reasoned upon false premises, since it does not by any means represent the poet's language, if we may put faith in the alteration introduced in the folio, 1632, or if we may trust to common sense. Edgar is struck by the uncontrollable licentiousness of the desires of woman :—

> " O, *unextinguish'd blaze* of woman's will !"

" *Blaze* " is to be taken for fire, and " will " for disposition ; and the scribe misheard, or miswrote, *unextinguish'd blaze* as " undistinguish'd space," making nonsense of a passage which, properly printed, is as striking as intelligible. Malone's explanation was particularly unfortunate, *viz.* that there was no distinguishable space between the likings and loathings of women : the meaning clearly is, " Oh, the blaze of woman's licentiousness, which can never be extinguished!"

SCENE VII.

P. 467. Cordelia urges Kent to put off his humble disguise, but he answers,—

> " Pardon me, dear madam ;
> Yet to be known shortens my made intent."

For "made intent," Warburton would substitute "*laid* intent;" but Johnson contends that "made intent" is only another word for formed intent. Both were wrong : "*main* intent" was miswritten "made intent," and hence the doubt. Kent refers to the chief purpose for which he had disguised himself, which would be anticipated and defeated, if he were too soon known :—

> " Yet to be known shortens my *main* intent."

P. 480. The quartos and folios differ when Albany accuses Edmund of treason, and throws down his gauntlet, saying,—

> "I'll prove it on thy heart
> Ere I taste bread, thou art in nothing less
> Than I have here proclaimed thee."

This is the reading of the quartos ; the folios more imperfectly have,—

> " I'll *make* it on thy heart," &c.

The corrector of the folio, 1632, instead of taking "prove" from the quartos, and striking out "make," which was all that was necessary, keeps "make," and puts *good*, instead of " it," after it :—

> " I'll make *good* on thy heart," &c.

This is another instance where the text of the quartos is deserted, although it would have been quite as easy here, as elsewhere, to follow it. Was the word *good* inserted only as a matter of judgment, to cure the evident defect of the folios, or was it derived from any authority ?

P. 481. When Edgar challenges Edmund, he declares,—

> " Maugre thy strength, youth, place, and eminence," &c.,

"thou art a traitor." The folio, 1632 (like that of 1623) transposes "place" and "youth," and in manuscript "place" is superseded by *skill* :—

  " Maugre thy strength, *skill*, youth, and eminence."

Skill has evidently been written in the margin, but part of it having been accidentally torn away, only the three first letters of the word remain. It seems not unlikely that the mention of *skill* would follow " strength ;" and "place" is certainly not wanted, with "eminence" in the same line.

   P. 487. When Lear enters, bearing the dead Cordelia, he asks for a looking-glass :—
     " Lend me a looking-glass ;
   If that her breath will mist or stain the stone,
   Why, then she lives."

The looking-glass was not "stone," and a manuscript-correction substitutes *shine*, as having been misprinted "stone :"—

  " If that her breath will mist or stain the *shine* ;"

i. e. the polish of the looking-glass. "Stain" and "stone" read awkwardly in juxta-position, and the error might easily be committed. Of old mirrors were made of steel, and Gascoigne wrote a well-known satire called by the contradictory title of "The Steel-glass :" hence it would not have surprised us if the poet's word had been *steel* for "stone."

   P. 488. After Kent has spoken, Lear looks at him doubtingly, and observes, in all impressions,—

  " This is a dull sight.—Are you not Kent?"

The words, " This is a dull sight," are not in the quartos ; and Steevens parallels them by " This is a sorry sight," from Macbeth ; while Blakeway contends that Lear only means that his eye-sight is bedimmed. Lear has previously stated that his eyes "are none of the best," and here he means to complain of the badness, not of his " sight," but of the light :—
   " This is a dull *light*"

is the word in the folio, 1632, as amended. Lear would hardly call the sad spectacle before him " a dull sight ;" but his eyes being dim, and the *light* dull, he could not be sure whether the man before him was Kent. It was a mere misprint of "sight" for *light*.

P. 490. The folio, 1632, generally deficient in stage-directions, went out of its course to insert the word *Dies* after Kent's two lines,—

> " I have a journey, sir, shortly to go :
> My master calls me ; I must not say, no."

Hence some editors have imagined that the Speaker died instantly on the stage, before all the characters *exeunt with a dead march*. No other ancient authority supports this notion, which Malone and Steevens disputed ; and that they were well warranted in doing so, is proved by the fact that the old corrector of the folio, 1632, put his pen decisively through the word *Dies*. We may, therefore, certainly conclude that Kent, in what he says, only contemplates the probability of the near approach of the termination of his career, and that the editor or printer of the folio, 1632, had an entirely mistaken notion upon the subject. *Dies* is found in no quarto impression, nor was it derived from the folio, 1623.

OTHELLO.

ACT I. SCENE I.

P. 499. The first striking emendation in this tragedy is one which admits of much doubt: it occurs in the passage of Iago's speech :—

> " Others there are,
> Who, trimm'd in forms and visages of duty,
> Keep yet their hearts attending on themselves."

For this the corrector of the folio, 1632, substitutes,—

> " Who *learn'd* in forms and *usages* of duty," &c.

It is certain that *usages* was formerly spelt *vsages*, and the compositor may have committed an error by printing " visages" for *usages ;* but, on the other hand, " hearts," in the next line, would seem intended as an antithesis to " visages," or outward appearances ; and, in the second place, if the author had meant to employ the words " forms and *usages*," he would, perhaps, have said, not " *learn'd* in forms and *usages*," but " *train'd* in forms and *usages*."   On the whole, therefore, it may be deemed unsafe to alter the received text in this instance, although in " Troilus and Cressida," Act IV. Scene II., we have the word *visage* misprinted for " usage," exactly as in the case before us.   It is to be remarked that the proposed emendation applies to a part of Iago's speech which is erased with a pen, *viz.* from " We cannot all be masters," down to " I would not be Iago."

P. 500. We should feel no hesitation in altering " timorous" to *clamorous* in the following, where Iago tells Roderigo to awake and alarm Brabantio :—

> " Do ; with like timorous accent, and dire yell,
>   As when by night and negligence, the fire
>   Is spied in populous cities."

Here "timorous," even taking it as *frightened*, seems quite out of place, when coupled with "dire yell;" and we may, therefore, fairly conclude that the poet wrote, as the old corrector states,—

> " Do ; with like *clamorous* accent, and dire yell," &c.

P. 502. Roderigo informs Brabantio that his daughter had " made a gross revolt,"—

> "Tying her duty, beauty, wit, and fortunes
>   In an extravagant and wheeling stranger."

Here the commentators have notes upon " extravagant," but pass over "wheeling" without explanation, although very unintelligible where it stands : a manuscript-correction in the folio, 1632, shows that it is a misprint for a most applicable epithet ; and other emendations are proposed, such as *Laying* for "Tying," and *on* for "in," which render the meaning much more obvious than in the ordinary reading :—

> " *Laying* her duty, beauty, wit, and fortunes
>   *On* an extravagant and *wheedling* stranger."

Pope, adopting "Tying," follows it in the next line by the preposition *to* instead of " in ;" neither *Laying* nor *on* are by any means absolutely necessary, but *wheedling* for " wheeling " is an important improvement of the text, and shows that the word was of older employment in our language than some lexicographers have supposed. Nothing can be more natural than that Roderigo should call Othello a "*wheedling* stranger," who had insinuated himself into the good graces of both father and daughter.

P. 503. Nobody has remarked upon a curious variation between the folios, 1623 and 1632, in Iago's line,—

> " Though I do hate him as I do hell pains."

This is the reading of the quartos ; but in the folio, 1623, the letters of the last word are misplaced,—

> " Though I do hate him as I do hell *apines*."

The printer of the folio, 1632, not being able to understand *apines*, omitted the word altogether, making the line end

G g

imperfectly at "hell." The old corrector either saw what was meant in the folio, 1623, or, perhaps, was assisted by the quartos, for he places *paines* (as the word was then commonly spelt) in his margin, with a caret in the text after " hell."

SCENE III.

P. 509. The 2 Senator, referring to the contents of his letters, as different in the particulars, although alike in the main circumstances, observes,—

> " As in these cases, where they aim reports,
> 'Tis oft with difference."

The expression, " where they aim reports" (or " where the aim reports," as Malone gives it from the folios), has occasioned discussion, although Johnson's interpretation has been usually followed. According to a correction in the folio, 1632, the words were misheard and misprinted, and the line is there given in a manner that clears away all obscurity :—

> " As in these cases, *with the same* reports,
> 'Tis oft with difference."

That is, where the " reports" were substantially *the same*, there were frequent minor discrepancies. Such, we may readily believe, was Shakespeare's meaning, and Shakespeare's language.

P. 513. A manuscript change in the text in the folio, 1632, differs from all known editions. The quartos make the Duke say,—

> " To vouch this is no proof :
> Without more certain and more over test,
> Than these thin habits, and poor likelihoods," &c.

The folio, 1623, gives the second line thus :—

> " Without more *wider* and more over test;"

and in the folio, 1632, as corrected, it stands :—

> " Without more *evidence* and overt test."

Modern editors have " *overt* test;" but from whence *evidence* was derived by the old corrector, we cannot guess, unless he so heard the passage recited : the corruption, originating in the first folio, seems to afford some slight clue to the altered reading in the second folio.

P. 516. It ought to be noted that when, in the folios, Othello tells the Senate,—

"She gave me for my pains a world of kisses,"

the last word of the line is deleted in the folio, 1632, and "sighs" substituted in the margin, in accordance with the quarto impressions ; perhaps "sighs" was obtained from them, or from an actor's mouth.

P. 520. Some material changes are made in Othello's speech, after Desdemona has besought the Senate that she may accompany her husband to Cyprus. The text in the folio, 1623, is the following :—

> " I therefore beg it not,
> To please the palate of my appetite,
> Nor to comply with heat the young affects
> In my defunct, and proper satisfaction,
> But to be free and bounteous to her mind :
> And heaven defend your good souls, that you think
> I will your serious and great business scant
> When she is with me. No ; when light-wing'd toys
> Of feather'd Cupid seal with wanton dulness
> My speculative and offic'd instrument," &c.

The only difference between the folios, 1623 and 1632, is that, in the latter, "affects" is printed *effects ;* but various emendations have been proposed by modern editors (into which it is not necessary here to enter) in order to explain or remove the obscurities belonging to nearly the whole passage. We subjoin the representation of the text as made by the corrector of the folio, 1632 :—

> " I therefore beg it not,
> To please the palate of my appetite,
> Nor to comply wi' the *young effects of heat*
> (In *me* defunct) and proper satisfaction,
> But to be free and bounteous to her mind :
> And heaven defend your *counsels*, that you think
> I will your serious and great business scant,
> When she is with me. No ; when light-wing'd toys
> Of feather'd Cupid *foil* with wanton dulness
> My speculative and offic'd *instruments*," &c.

In the third line it seems that "heat" got transposed, while *of* was omitted ; in the fourth line, *me* was misprinted "my ;" and in the sixth line, *counsels* became "good souls," terms Othello would hardly apply to the Duke and Senators of Venice. *Foil*, in the ninth line, agrees with the quartos, where *instruments* is also in the plural. These changes appear to be so effectual, as far as regards the plain sense of the passage, that all that some commentators have said in favour of *disjunct*, instead of "defunct" (the word in every old edition), is thrown away: Othello did not ask for the company of his wife for his own proper satisfaction, or to comply with the young effects of heat, in him defunct at the age at which he had arrived; and he therefore undertook that no amorous trifling should induce him to neglect the great duties entrusted to him.

P. 524. We meet with the change of an important epithet where Iago is encouraging Roderigo to hope that distaste will soon grow up between Othello and Desdemona: it is where he says, as it is commonly printed,—

"If sanctimony and a frail vow, betwixt an erring barbarian and a super-subtle Venetian be not too hard for my wits, and all the tribe of hell, thou shalt enjoy her."

How had Desdemona given proof that she was "super-subtle?" if she were so, she might be too cunning for the artifices of Iago. What he wished was to persuade Roderigo that her love for Othello was not firmly rooted, that "she must have change," and that ere long she would be found, as her countrywomen proverbially were, complying and yielding to her own desires: therefore, for "super-subtle," the correction in the folio, 1632, is *super-supple:* because she was "a *super-supple* Venetian," Roderigo was to hope that she would submit to his importunity. "A frail vow" had passed between "an erring barbarian and a *super-supple* Venetian," which Iago was soon to break.

ACT II. SCENE I.

P. 533. After Iago has delivered his satirical verses against the female sex, Desdemona asks, "How say you Cassio? is he not a most profane and liberal counsellor?" By "counsellor," Johnson was here obliged to understand "one that discourses fearlessly and volubly;" but if we may believe

the author of the emendations in the folio, 1632, "counsellor" was not the poet's word, but *censurer*, used in the
same way as in "Henry VIII.," Act I. Scene II., where
Wolsey speaks of "malicious censurers:" so Desdemona
appeals to Cassio whether Iago, in the character he had
given of women, was not "a most profane and liberal *censurer ?*"

P. 538. The subsequent quotation, as it appears in the
folios, has occasioned discussion : Iago speaks :—

> "Which thing to do,
> If this poor trash of Venice, whom I trace
> For his quick hunting, stand the putting on," &c.

The quartos have *crush* for "trace," which must be wrong,
and Warburton read *brach*, meaning a dog, for "trash." He
was right in his guess, according to a correction in the folio,
1632, where the passage is thus given :—

> "Which thing to do,
> If this poor *brach* of Venice, whom I *trash*
> For his quick hunting, stand the putting on," &c.

To *trash* a dog was to chastise it ; and Iago in this sense
chastised Roderigo for his too eager pursuit of Desdemona.
The compositor blundered between *brach* and *trash*, and
printed *trash* where he ought to have put "brach," and *trace*
where he ought to have put "trash:" these emendations
remove the whole difficulty.

SCENE III.

P. 541. There is a remarkable discrepancy between the
quarto and folios, which deserves the more notice, because
the correction of an error in the folio, 1632, leads to an entirely new reading of an important word: Iago says, in the
quarto,—

> "Three lads of Cyprus, noble swelling spirits ;"

in the folios it is,—

> "Three *else* of Cyprus, noble swelling spirits,"

an undoubted blunder ; and the question is how "lads," in
the quartos, became *else* in the folios ? Simply from mis-

hearing on the part of the scribe: the poet's word was probably not "lads," but, as Iago jocularly calls them,—

> "Three *elfs* of Cyprus, noble swelling spirits;"

and the manuscript-corrector alters "else" to *elfes.* Whether the true text be "lads" or *elfs,* the variation is curious; and it seems probable, as Iago terms them "spirits" in the last part of the line, that he should call them *elfs* in the first part of it.   Our conviction is that Shakespeare wrote *elfes,* which, not being immediately understood, was printed "lads" in the quarto, 1622.

P. 547. We have several times seen words which begin with *q* printed with *c:* thus in Henry VIII. we have had *chine* for "queen" (p. 327), and in Macbeth *cooled* for "quailed" (p. 417). Here we meet with a repetition of the same strange mistake, in regard to a word that has been the source of considerable discussion in the line,—

> "And passion, having my best judgment collied."

The quarto has *cooled* for "collied;" and various explanations of "collied" have been given, but we are not required to state them, in as much as "collied" was, probably, not the poet's word:—

> "And passion, having my best judgment *quelled,*"

is the substitution in the folio, 1632; and Malone says that some "modern editor," whom he does not otherwise distinguish, had proposed *quelled:* Othello's judgment was *quelled,* or subdued, by his passion.   There can hardly be a doubt that this is the proper restoration.

P. 552. It may be enough to say that the old corrector does not accept the contraction of "probal," as it stands in all editions, but alters it to *probable,* which, pronounced in the time of two syllables, may suit the verse sufficiently well.

ACT III.   SCENE I.

P. 554. The dialogue between Cassio, the Clown, and the Musicians is struck out, probably because it was necessary to abridge the performance : several verbal and literal errors are, nevertheless, set right ; thus, "speak through the nose" is amended to "*squeak* through the nose ;" *me* is erased as injurious surplusage where Cassio says, "Dost thou hear *me*, mine honest friend?" for "the gentlewoman that attends the general," we have "the gentlewoman that attends the general's *wife* ;" and for "I shall seem to notify unto her," we are told to read, "I shall seem *so* to notify unto her." All these emendations seem more or less required.

SCENE III.

P. 559. In the parenthesis in Desdemona's appeal to Othello on behalf of Cassio,—

> " (Save that, they say, the wars must make examples
> Out of her best),"

the word "her" is altered naturally, but by no means necessarily, to "Out of *our* best." All this part of the play is so well printed in the folios, that few corrections, excepting of punctuation, are introduced in the margin. It ought not to escape notice, however, that *mock*, of all the early impressions, is converted into "make" in the disputed line (p. 564),—

> " It is the green-ey'd monster, which doth *make*
> The meat it feeds on ;"

while the conclusion of the same speech is thus given :—

> " Who dotes, yet doubts ; suspects, yet *fondly* loves."

It is "*strongly* loves" in the quartos, and "*soundly* loves" in the folios ; but the old corrector changed *soundly* to "fondly," and we are disposed to conclude that such was the received text in his time.

P. 566. The next emendation seems questionable, because the intention of the poet is expressed with sufficient distinctness as the text has hitherto stood : it is where Iago says,—

> " But pardon me ; I do not in position
> Distinctly speak of her."

He may refer merely to the position Desdemona occupies ; but still, what follows the above appears to countenance the recommended alteration :—

> " But, pardon me, I do not in *suspicion*
> Distinctly speak of her, though I may fear,
> Her will, recoiling to her better judgment,
> May fall to match you with her country forms,
> And happily repent."

P. 568. The imperfect and corrupt line in the folios,—

> " If she be false, Heaven mock'd itself,"

appears thus in the quartos :—

> " If she be false, O ! then heaven mocks itself."

The emendator of the folio, 1632, furnishes a reading different from any old copy :—

> " If she be false, O ! heaven *doth* mock itself.—
> I'll not believe it."

Such may have been his mode of completing the line, or it may have been the way in which he had seen it written or heard it recited, though the difference is not very material.

The unprinted stage-directions are not many, but the ancient impressions have very few, even where most required. When Desdemona produces her handkerchief, in order to bind it round Othello's temples, *Offers to bind* is written in the margin ; and when he rejects it, *Throws it away* is inserted in the same manner. Iago subsequently *snatcheth it* from Emilia.

P. 571. Othello's passionate exclamation in the quarto,—

> " What sense had I of her stolen hours of lust ? "

is the same in the folio, 1623, excepting that " of " is made *in :* in the folio, 1632, it is printed,—

> " What *sent* had I *in* her stolen hours of lust ? "

The old corrector here restores the language of the quarto ; and two lines lower he erases " fed well," which found its way into the folios, and is not only utterly needless, but most prejudicial.

P. 574. The grossest portions of Iago's description of what Othello might wish to see for the sake of conviction, and of Cassio's supposed dream, are struck through with a pen, but errors are still carefully amended : " to bring to that prospect " the corrector makes " to bring *it* " (not " them," as in the folio, 1623) "to that prospect;" he supplies "and" before "then kiss me hard," and converts "sigh," "kiss," and "cry," of the folios, to the past tense, as in each case in the quarto.

P. 576. A printer's error has occasioned difficulty in the line, where Othello draws a simile from "the Pontick sea," which, as the folios have it,—

> " Ne'er keeps retiring ebb, but keeps due on," &c.

"Keeps" must be wrong in the first instance, and Pope altered it to "feels," which was, perhaps, derived by him from the quarto, 1630; but the manuscript-emendation in the folio, 1632, is,—

> " Ne'er *knows* retiring ebb, but keeps due on," &c.

This seems the superior reading, and may have been that of the poet: to say that a sea "ne'er feels retiring ebb," is hardly the language of Shakespeare.

SCENE IV.

P. 579. Othello, wishing to see the handkerchief, says to Desdemona, in the quarto,—

> " I have a salt and sullen rheum offends me,"

which may be the correct text ; but the folios read,—

> " I have a salt and *sorry* rheum offends me."

The manuscript-emendator alters "sorry" to *sudden,* as if Othello meant that the rheum had unexpectedly come upon him, and therefore that he needed his wife's handkerchief :—

> " I have a salt and *sudden* rheum offends me."

This seems natural, and in "King John," Act I. Scene I. (p. 199), we have already seen *sudden* misprinted *sullen.*

P. 582. Cassio entreats Desdemona, if she cannot remove Othello's displeasure, to let him know the result, in order that he may at once adopt some other method of life :—

> " So shall I clothe me in a forc'd content,
> And shut myself up in some other course
> To fortune's alms."

This is as the passage has always appeared, but we are directed in the margin of the folio, 1632, to correct the two following lapses by the printer :—

> " So shall I clothe me in a forc'd content,
> And *shift* myself *upon* some other course
> To fortune's alms."

Cassio was not to "shut himself up in," but to "*shift* himself *upon* some other course" to obtain the favours of fortune, perhaps, by changing his profession.

ACT IV. SCENE I.

P. 587. Just before Othello *falls in a trance*, as the old copies describe it, he exclaims, "I tremble at it. Nature would not invest herself in such shadowing passion, without some instruction. It is not words that shake me thus." He means, of course, that his own conviction of the fact of Desdemona's guilt, not Iago's promptings, produced such a trembling and shaking effect upon him. Warburton has a note in favour of reading *induction* for "instruction;" and Johnson calls a speculation respecting the induction of the moon before the sun, so as to overshadow it, "a noble conjecture." It appears, however, that "shadowing" (often of old spelt *shaddowing*) is a misprint for *shuddering*, which is entirely consistent with what precedes, as well as with what follows about trembling and shaking ; the old corrector alters the passage in the following manner :—

> "I tremble at it. Nature would not invest herself in such *shuddering* passion, without some instruction. It is not words that shake me thus," &c.

"Shadowing passion" seems to have no meaning, but that fancifully suggested by Warburton, where he supposes Othello, in the height of his grief and fury, to illustrate his own condition by reference to an eclipse. It was the mistake of an epithet, very naturally applied to "passion," that forced the commentator upon this speculation. The person who abridged the tragedy (probably for representation at some period soon after 1632) struck out the words from "nature" down to "instruction," as well as a few previous expressions, for a different, but obvious reason.

P. 589. The folios introduce a strange corruption where they convert

> " And his unbookish jealousy must construe "

into " And his unbookish jealousy must *conserve* :" a correction of it is found in manuscript in the folio, 1632 ; but in the last line of this page an emendation of a singular kind is met with. Othello overhearing Cassio laugh, when Iago alludes to Bianca, imagines that Cassio is exulting over him in consequence of his success with Desdemona :—

> " Do you triumph, Roman ? do you triumph ? "

are the words put into Othello's mouth, " Roman," in the old copies, being spelt *Romaine*. Why should Othello call Cassio Roman ? Johnson says, because the word " triumph " brought Roman into his thoughts. This may unquestionably be so ; but the manuscript-corrector says that the word Roman (perhaps written without a capital letter in the copy used by the printer) has been entirely mistaken, and that we ought to read,—

> " Do you triumph *o'er me* ? do you triumph ? "

It is not easy to imagine how *romaine* became *o'er me*, either by mishearing or misprinting ; but certainly the allusion to a Roman triumph seems very forced in the mouth of a Moor, and the question, " Do you triumph *o'er me* ?" most fit and natural. Without confirmation, however, it might require considerable courage to insert in the text of our great poet so peculiar an emendation.

SCENE II.

P. 598. The subsequent passage has produced discussion, arising mainly out of discordance of texts in the quarto and folios. In the quarto it is,—

> " But, alas ! to make me
> A fixed figure for the time of scorn
> To point his slow unmoving finger at."

The folios have "*The* fixed figure," and " slow *and* moving," but both quarto and folios " time of scorn," which Rowe properly changed to "*hand* of scorn," as appears by a correction in the folio, 1632. Another emendation in the next line, converts " slow and moving," not into " slow unmoving," of the quarto, but into *"slowly* moving," the text of no old copy, so that the whole is there thus represented, with manifest improvement :—

> " But, alas ! to make me
> *A* fixed figure for the *hand* of scorn
> To point his *slowly* moving finger at."

P. 600. Here we have another variation in the folio, 1632 (as corrected), from any known copy. The quarto reads,—

> " How have I been behav'd, that he might stick
> The small'st opinion on my great'st abuse ?"

The folios have " my *least misuse"* for " great'st abuse ;" both cannot be right, and the old corrector informs us that neither is so, but that we should print,—

> "The small'st opinion on my least *misdeed;"*

i. e. " how can he have formed the smallest ill opinion of me from the least *misdeed* that I have committed ?"

SCENE III.

P. 607. Desdemona's willow-ballad begins in the folios,—

> " The poor soul sat singing by a sycamore tree."

But the original (Percy's Rel. I. 212) has *sighing* for " singing," and such is the written correction ; but it goes farther by making it commence with the indefinite article :—

> "*A* poor soul sat *sighing* by a sycamore tree."

There is no other change in, or addition to it. That part of the dialogue between Desdemona and Emilia, which relates to the infidelity of wives to their husbands, is marked for omission.

ACT V. SCENE I.

P. 609. There is not a single printed stage-direction in this busy and difficult scene, where so many seem necessary ; but they are furnished in the margin, or in vacant spaces of the folio, 1632. When Roderigo draws his sword, to wait for Cassio, he is told to *stand back ;* Iago *wounds Cassio and exit;* and subsequently enters *unready, with a torch and sword drawn.* The entrance of Emilia is not at all marked in the folios, but the corrector duly notes the place, and the whole business of the scene is elsewhere accurately pointed out. This Act, with a few exceptions, is comparatively well printed in the folios.

SCENE II.

P. 616. One of these exceptions is found in Othello's first speech, where the folios print "I'll smell *thee* on the tree" instead of "I'll smell it on the tree." Before he commences he is instructed to *lock the door.* Another exception occurs on p. 619, where "*Did* yawn at alteration" ought to be "Should yawn at alteration." These changes are introduced in the folio, 1632.

P. 621. The folios give the following imperfectly,—

> "Ay, with Cassio. Nay, had she been true,"

by omitting "nay;" but the old corrector states that the line ought to be,—

> "Ay, with Cassio. Had she been *but* true," &c.

The difference is small, and, as a mere matter of taste, we prefer the reading of the quarto.

P. 624. It is difficult to decide, in the subsequent instance, which text ought to be adopted, that of the quarto, 1622, that of the folio, 1623, and quarto, 1630, or that of the corrected folio, 1632, for they all differ:—

> " No, I will speak as liberal as the north."

So it stands in the folio, 1623, and in the quarto, 1630; but the quarto, 1622, has it, " as liberal as the *air*," and the folio, 1632, as amended,—

> " No, I will speak as liberal as the *wind*."

Why, we may ask, should the old corrector make the change, in as much as no reasonable objection can be urged against the use of "north," which he deletes, not in favour of "air," of the quarto, 1622, but in favour of *wind?* We may presume, perhaps, that he altered the word because he had heard the

line repeated in that manner on the stage. Montano's speech,
near the top of the next page, affords another proof to the
same effect :—

> " Which I have here recover'd from the Moor."

The folios omit "here," clearly necessary to the measure;
but instead of inserting it from the quarto, the old corrector
placed *now* in the margin.

P. 628. The same authority is indisputably right when
he supplied another omission in the folios where Lodovico,
after telling Othello that he must "go with us," turns to
Iago, and threatens him with torture : the line there is,—

> " To the Venetian state.—Come ; bring away."

The quarto has, "Come ; bring him away ;" but both
Othello and Iago were to accompany the officers of justice,
and therefore the old corrector properly puts it, "Come ;
bring *them* away." He again varies triflingly from every old
edition in the concluding words of Othello :—

> "And say, besides, that in Aleppo once,
> Where a malignant and a turban'd Turk
> Beat a Venetian, and traduc'd the state," &c.

He alters "where" to *when :* the "where" had been already
stated, *viz.* in Aleppo, and *when* has reference to the time
and cause of Othello's anger, not to the place in which he
gave vent to it.

We are not informed in the folios, as printed, that Othello
stabs himself at the words, "And smote him thus," but
merely, four lines afterwards, that he "dies"—*on the bed,* adds
the corrector. Emilia expires, without any note in the folios,
after she has been wounded by her husband, also without
note. According to the old mode of performing the part, it
seems that Othello threw himself, in an agony, *upon the
ground* just before Emilia said, "Nay, lay thee down and
roar," but *started up* again, exclaiming, "O ! she was foul,"
&c. In modern editions it is stated that at these points he
fell upon the bed, and *rose* from it again. In the time of the
corrector he did not fall upon the bed until the moment
before his death.

Some descriptive additions are made in manuscript, for
the first time in the volume, to the list of "the Actor's
names" appended to the play : thus we are told that Iago is

Ancient to the Moor, Gratiano *Uncle to Desdemona*, &c.   One
of these, and only one, is of importance, and that with reference to the question agitated by Tyrwhitt, Henley, Malone, Steevens, &c., whether Bianca were a courtezan of
Cyprus or of Venice?   The Venetian courtezans were famous
in the time of Shakespeare, and he here exhibited one of
them on the stage; for to " Bianca, a courtezan," in the
enumeration of the characters, is added *of Venice* in the
hand-writing of the annotator on the folio, 1632.   There is
no doubt, therefore, that she is supposed in the tragedy to
have followed Cassio from Venice to Cyprus, and, to a
certain extent, aided in bringing about the catastrophe.   It
may be deemed more than probable, that she was dressed,
at least in the time of the old corrector, in the costume so
strikingly represented as that of Venetian Courtezans in
Coryat's " Crudities," 4to. 1611.

ANTONY AND CLEOPATRA.

ACT I. SCENE I.

Vol. viii. p. 6. The heroine taunts Antony with supposed subjection to Cæsar:—

> " Who knows
> If the scarce-bearded Cæsar have not sent
> His powerful mandate to you, ' Do this, or this ;
> Take in that kingdom, and enfranchise that ;
> Perform't, or else we damn thee.' "

Such has been the universal reading, and there may be no sufficient reason to alter it ; but the word "damn" sounds ill in Cleopatra's mouth, reads like a vulgarism in the place where it occurs, and may easily have been misprinted :

> " Perform't, or else we *doom* thee "

is the emendation of the corrector of the folio, 1632.

P. 7. An adverb, a decided misprint, as it seems to us, has hitherto escaped correction, where Antony tells Cleopatra that every mood becomes her:—

> " Whose every passion fully strives
> To make itself in thee fair and admir'd."

"Fully strives" is a clumsy expression, and a manuscript note points out a word, so much more acceptable and appropriate, that we may be satisfied in future to reject the blunder: the whole passage is,—

> " Fie, wrangling queen !
> Whom every thing becomes, to chide, to laugh,
> To weep ; whose every passion *fitly* strives
> To make itself, in thee, fair and admir'd."

A compositor might carelessly commit such a blunder: the wonder seems to be that it has never been detected.

SCENE II.

P. 9. It only requires a brief note to state that Warburton's emendation of "fertile," for *foretell* of the folios, is not confirmed by the corrector of the folio, 1632: the word in the margin of that impression is *fruitful; fertile* may come nearer the letters, but *fruitful* is certainly better adapted to the sense :—

> "If every of your wishes had a womb,
> And *fruitful* every wish, a million."

P. 12. The subsequent quotation may be (as indeed it has been) construed into a meaning; but when we state the errors of the press it contains, we can scarcely doubt regarding corruption :—

> "The present pleasure,
> By revolution lowering, does become
> The opposite of itself."

Such has always been the text, and Johnson, after admitting it to be obscure, confesses himself "unable to add any thing" to Warburton's explanation, which relates to the "revolutions of the sun in his diurnal course." Tollett and Steevens each made an attempt with about the same success; but can any thing be better than the changes offered by the old annotator ?—

> "The present pleasure,
> By *repetition souring*, does become
> The opposite of itself."

This needs neither illustration nor enforcement : sour and souring were of old spelt *sower* and *sowering*. Two lines farther on, the printer of the folio, 1632, left out the epithet "enchanting" before "queen," but the old corrector inserted it, perhaps from the folio, 1623.

SCENE III.

P. 15. Few things can be clearer than that the punctuation of the line where Cleopatra tells Charmian,—

> "Thou teachest like a fool : the way to lose him,"

H h

is wrong ; yet it has been almost invariably followed.   Malone, and others after him, have given it in that manner, but
the sense unquestionably runs on :—

> "Thou teachest, like a fool, the way to lose him."

The corrector of the folio, 1632, erases the colon.

P. 18. Cleopatra pretends to doubt the affection of Antony,
who observes, in all editions,—

> " My precious queen, forbear ;
> And give true evidence to his love, which stands
> An honourable trial."

"Evidence" is one syllable too long for the verse, unless it
be read *ev'dence ;* but that, if any, is the smallest objection
to it, as will be seen when we quote the passage as corrected, and as it must be given in future :—

> " And give true *credence* to his love, which stands
> An honourable trial."

SCENE IV.

P. 19. For "one great competitor" we must hereafter read
"*our* great competitor," as Johnson conjectured : the old
corrector substitutes *our* for "one."   In the first line of the
next page, the negative at the end dropped out in the
second folio ; and if it were not obtained from the first
folio, the sense would necessarily supply it.   Lower down, it
appears equally proper to read "*Fall* on him for't," and the
C is struck through, and *F* placed in the margin : Johnson's
forced construction of "*Visit* him" for "Call on him," will
not bear examination ; surfeits and dryness of his bones
were to *fall* (not to "call") on Antony for his unrestrained
voluptuousness.

P. 20. A messenger brings intelligence that "Pompey is
strong at sea," and he adds,—

> "To the ports
> The discontents repair, and men's reports
> Give him much wrong'd."

The emendator of the folio, 1632, substitutes, with much
plausibility, *fleets* for "ports ;" and it seems likely that the
compositor blundered in consequence of the word "report"

being found two lines above, and "reports" just below. It is improbable that Shakespeare would have been guilty of the cacophony : nevertheless, it is not to be disputed that, as far as the sense is concerned, "ports" answers the purpose quite as well as *fleets*.

SCENE V.

P. 24. Alexas arrives, not "from Cæsar," as stated in the old copies, but *from Antony*, as an emendation in the folio, 1632, informs us ; and at the end of his third speech he describes the manner of the hero as he delivered his message for Cleopatra, and then mounted his steed. The words have been usually printed in this manner :—

> "So he nodded,
> And soberly did mount an arm-gaunt steed,
> Who neigh'd so high, that what I would have spoke
> Was beastly dumb'd by him."

The first difficulty has arisen out of the epithet "arm-gaunt," and, without noticing other proposed emendations, we may state that Sir Thomas Hanmer's "arm-*girt*" is precisely that of the old corrector, who also makes a very important change in the last hemistich, which, in the folios, stands,—

> "Was beastly dumbe by him."

The commentators have properly taken "dumbe" as a misprint for *dumb'd*, and have referred to "Pericles," where *dumbs* is used as a verb. It seems that "beastly" was not Shakespeare's word, which we can well suppose : in "Macbeth" we have seen "boast" misprinted *beast*, and in Henry V. (Chorus to Act IV.) we meet with the line,—

> "Steed threatens steed in high and boastful neighs."

In the passage before us, Alexas says that the "arm-girt steed" neighed so "high" that he could not address Antony : in what way, then, does the corrector of the folio, 1632, give the whole passage ?—

> "So he nodded,
> And soberly did mount an arm-*girt* steed,
> Who neigh'd so high, that what I would have spoke
> Was *boastfully* dumb'd by him."

One slight objection to this change is that *boastfully* must be read as a dissyllable, and such is the case with various

words, one of them being " evidence," in a preceding quotation, if we could refrain from admitting *credence* instead of it.
Boastfully might be, and probably was, misprinted " beastly ;"
and the *arm-girt* steed, neighing proudly as Antony mounted
him, " *boastfully* dumbed" what Alexas would have spoken to
his master.

ACT II.   SCENE I.

P. 27.   We own that we do not like the first change in
the following, where Pompey expresses his hope that the
beauty and blandishments of Cleopatra will detain Antony
in Egypt :—

> " Salt Cleopatra, soften thy wand lip.
> Let witchcraft join with beauty, lust with both :
> Tie up the libertine in a field of feasts,
> Keep his brain fuming," &c.

For " wand lip" the old corrector, prosaically as it seems to
us, has " *warm* lip ;" but it is very possible that *warm* was
misheard " wand."   However, he goes on to make a double
alteration in the next line but one, where he puts *Lay* for
" Tie," and *flood* for " field."   It reads very unlike Shakespeare to talk of tying up a libertine in a field of feasts.
The proposed emendations, then, are these :—

> " Salt Cleopatra, soften thy *warm* lip.
> Let witchcraft join with beauty, lust with both :
> *Lay* up the libertine in a *flood* of feasts ;
> Keep his brain fuming," &c.

To us the above appears one of the least satisfactory emendations made in this play in the folio, 1632 : it sounds too
much like conjecture ; yet on p. 449 we have seen *tying* misprinted for " laying."

SCENE II.

P. 29.   When Antony says to Cæsar,—

> " Were we before our armies, and to fight,
> I should do thus,"

we are no where told, in ancient or modern editions, what
Antony did, whether he embraced or shook hands with his

competitor.   There is a manuscript note, *Shake hands*, in the folio, 1632, which may be said to settle the doubt, as far as regards the old practice of the stage; and Cæsar, taking the proffered hand of Antony, says, "Welcome to Rome." This is nearly the first additional stage-direction that has occurred in the hand-writing of the corrector, and instructions of the kind are not so frequent as in some other dramas. *Shake hands* is repeated, when the engagement respecting Octavia is concluded between Antony and Cæsar.

P. 33. When Agrippa first recommends this marriage, Cæsar slily and jocosely remarks, as the passage is given in all modern editions,—

> " Say not so, Agrippa:
> If Cleopatra heard you, your reproof
> Were well deserv'd of rashness."

This is intelligible, but hardly as the poet must have left his text; and the sentence is thus most blunderingly printed in the folios :—

> "Say not, say Agrippa, if Cleopater heard you,
> Your proof were well deserved of rashness."

The old corrector shows, that *proof* is to be taken as " reproof," which was Warburton's supposition, not as " approof," which Theobald inserted ; and the folio, 1632, gives the lines in this way :—

> "Say it not, Agrippa:
> If Cleopatra heard you, your *reproof*
> Were well deserv'd *for* rashness."

This is most comprehensible ; and it is easy to see how part of the blunders found their way into the old impressions: the proposal of a marriage between Antony and Octavia might well deserve *reproof* for its rashness, if Cleopatra had been by to hear it.

P. 35. There seems to be a slight error in the description of Cleopatra's pavilion upon the Cydnus :—

> "She did lie
> In her pavilion (cloth of gold of tissue),
> O'er-picturing that Venus," &c.

A manuscript note informs us, as we may reasonably imagine, that cloth of gold was not " of tissue," but that we ought to read,—

> " In her pavilion (cloth of gold *and* tissue)," &c.

It was composed of cloth of gold and tissue: perhaps the cloth of gold was lined with tissue. Lower in the same page, "To *gloue* the delicate cheeks," of the folio, 1623, and "To *glove* the delicate cheeks," of the folio, 1632, are altered to "To glow the delicate cheeks," as in modern impressions.

On the next page (36) it has been invariable to print as follows:—

> "The silken tackle
> Swell with the touches of those flower-soft hands,
> That yarely frame the office."

Why, or how, was the silken tackle to "swell with the touches of flower-soft hands?" The printer again mistook *m* for *w:* the poet is alluding to the perfume derived by the silken cordage from the flower-soft hands through which it passed, and adds,—

> "From the barge
> A strange invisible perfume hits the sense
> Of the adjacent wharfs."

Therefore, we ought undoubtedly, with the old corrector, to amend the text to

> "*Smell* with the touches of those flower-soft hands," &c.

SCENE III.

P. 38. Whether it be or be not "more poetical," it is certain that the old corrector tells us to read,—

> "But near him thy angel
> Becomes *afear'd*,"

and not "Becomes a fear." This emendation is at least consistent with North's Plutarch—"for thy Demon is *afraid* of his"—as well as with Shakespeare himself, who makes the Soothsayer repeat,—

> "I say again, thy spirit
> Is all *afraid* to govern thee near him."

The poet may, however, have here intended to vary the expression.

P. 40. The Messenger who brings intelligence to Cleopatra of Antony's marriage with Octavia, and who appears again in a subsequent scene (p. 60), is called *Elis* in a marginal note in both places in the folio, 1632. Whether Elis,

or Ellis, were the name of the part, or of the performer may
be doubted, but we have no knowledge of any actor of the
time so called.

SCENE VII.

P. 54. When Antony, during the debauch, says to Cæsar,
"Be a child o' the time," Cæsar replies, rather unintel-
ligibly,—

> " Possess it, I'll make answer; but I had rather fast
> From all four days, than drink so much in one."

What does he mean by telling Antony to " possess it ?"
Profess it is the emendation in the folio, 1632 : that is,
profess to be a child of the time ; but Cæsar follows it up
by stating his dislike of drinking to excess. In the first
scene of " King Lear" (p. 434) we have had the converse of
this misprint—*professes* for " possesses."

A question has arisen whether to preserve *beat,* of the old
copies, or to print " bear," where Enobarbus says, in reference to the boy's song,—

> " The holding every man shall beat," &c.

Theobald was in favour of " bear," and he is proved to have
been right, not merely because that change is made in the
folio, 1632, but because the old annotator has placed the
two last lines of the song in a mark of inclusion, and has designated them as *the burthen,* or " holding," which the jovial
company was to *bear* " as loud as their strong sides could
volley." Johnson's notion that " drumming on the sides"
was intended, is out of the question. No printer's error was
more common than *t* for *r,* and *vice versâ.*

* * *

ACT III. SCENE I.

P. 56. Although at the opening of this drama in the
folios, we have *Actus primus, Scena prima,* no such divisions
are elsewhere noted from beginning to end. Malone and
other modern editors have marked Act III. as commencing
with the entrance of Ventidius in triumph in Syria ; but the
corrector of the folio, 1632, makes Act III. begin after this
scene, where the place of action is Rome, and where we read

in the old editions, *Enter Agrippa at one door, Enobarbus at
another.* This should seem to have been the division in the
time of the corrector; and it is certainly more proper and
convenient than that adopted since the days of Rowe, because
it tends somewhat to diminish the extreme length of Act
III., which, even according to the representation in the
amended folio, 1632, comprises eight scenes. In more than
one instance the place was supposed to be changed, although
no actual alteration had occurred.

SCENE IV.

P. 63. The usual reading of the following has been,—

> " When the best hint was given him, he not took't,
> Or did it from his teeth."

The folio, 1623, has "he not look'd," and the folio, 1632,
"he *had* look'd." There appears no sufficient ground for
doing more than amend the frequent error of "not" for *but;*
it avoids an awkwardness when Antony complains of Cæsar,
that,—

> " When the best hint was given him, he *but* look'd,
> Or did it from his teeth."

Such is the emendation in the folio, 1632, the meaning
being, that Cæsar only looked when the best hint was given
him, or merely applauded Antony from his teeth, and not
from his heart. The opinion of Steevens that "from his
teeth" is to be understood "in spite of his teeth," of course,
cannot be sustained for an instant.

SCENE VI.

P. 67. Cæsar finds fault with Antony for sending back
Octavia without due ceremony and attendance :—

> " But you are come
> A market-maid to Rome, and have prevented
> The ostentation of our love, which, left unshown,
> Is often left unlov'd."

"Left unlov'd" is the reading of all editions ; but, nevertheless, it seems to be wrong, and in the folio, 1632, as corrected,
we are told to print the last part of the quotation thus :—

> " Which, left unshown,
> Is often *held* unlov'd ;"

the meaning being, that where the ostentation of love was omitted, it was often held, or considered, that love did not exist. Lower down, the alteration of two letters in the margin, properly converts *abstract* into " obstruct," which Warburton first introduced.

P. 68. We surely need not pause in making a change which only requires the omission of a letter, which must have accidentally become a part of the text, and which is palpably an " obstruct" to the author's sense. Cæsar is still addressing his sister :—

> " Your letters did withhold our breaking forth,
> Till we perceiv'd, both how you were wrong led,
> And we in negligent danger."

The corrector of the folio, 1632, puts *wrongèd* for " wrong led :" the objection was, not that Octavia had been " wrong led," but *wrongèd* by Antony, who had abandoned her, and returned to Cleopatra. Cæsar, when he informs Octavia of this fact, calls her " my most *wronged* sister."

SCENE VIII.

P. 74. After the loss of the battle, Scarus attributes it to the presence and flight of Cleopatra. Enobarbus asks, " How appears the fight ?" and Scarus replies,—

> " On our side like the token'd pestilence,
> Where death is sure.   Yond' ribald-rid nag of Egypt,
> Whom leprosy o'ertake, i' the midst o' the fight,
> When vantage, like a pair of twins, appear'd
> Both as the same, or rather ours the elder ;—
> The brize upon her like a cow in June,
> Hoists sails, and flies."

Here the folio, 1632, omits *take* in " o'ertake," and has " Both *of* the same" for " Both *as* the same," of the folio, 1623 ; but the two folios read, " Yond ribaldred nag of Egypt," an expression that has occasioned much doubt and comment. Tyrwhitt suggested *hag* for " nag," but the prevailing text has been " nag" and " ribald-rid," for *ribaldred.* It is to be remarked, however (a circumstance mentioned in note 7), that the line is overloaded by a syllable: this redundancy the old corrector remedies, but he also instructs us, in conformity with Tyrwhitt's notion, that *hag* has been misprinted "nag," and that the line ought to run thus :—

> "Where death is sure.   Yond' *ribald hag* of Egypt," &c.

Ribald hag is most appropriate to Cleopatra on account of her profligacy, as well as her witchcraft ; and it is just possible that in the manuscript before the compositor the word was miswritten ribaldry, which in his hands became *ribaldred*, and has been the occasion of considerable difficulty. Besides, how was leprosy to afflict a *nag* ?

SCENE XI.

P. 80. We cannot approve of the commencement of Act IV., as marked in the corrected folio, 1632. It is made to begin with this scene between Cleopatra, Enobarbus, Charmian, and Iras, in Alexandria, instead of the scene where Cæsar enters (near Alexandria) reading a letter, and accompanied by Agrippa, Mecænas, and others. This arrangement still farther shortens Act III., but it lengthens Act IV., and is liable to several objections, into which it is not necessary here to enter.

The conjecture in note 9, founded upon Johnson's hint, that "meered" might be a lapse by the printer for *mooted*, in the expression, "he being the meered question," is supported by a manuscript change of the old corrector. In future we may safely print "*mooted* question."

P. 81. Enobarbus ridicules the challenge of Antony to Cæsar to engage with him in single combat, on the ground that Antony, after the defeat of his forces, and his disgraceful flight, has nothing to lose, while Cæsar has nothing to gain : he exclaims, in soliloquy, as the language of the poet has always been represented,—

> "That he should dream,
> Knowing all measures, the full Cæsar will
> Answer his emptiness!"

Nobody has explained what is meant by "Knowing all measures." It might mean that Antony knows how to measure between himself and Cæsar, were it not clear that Antony is quite ignorant upon the point ; and a correction leads us to believe that the printer was again in

fault, and composed "measures" for a word like it, which he
hastily misread :—

> " That he should dream,
> Knowing all *miseries*, that the full Cæsar will
> Answer his emptiness!"

Enobarbus refers to the miserable plight and prospects of
Antony at the time he dared Cæsar to "lay his gay com--
parisons apart," and meet him "sword against sword." Just
above, " quality",is changed to *qualities*, but this is a variation of little importance ; nevertheless, it reads as if it were
right.

P. 82. Thyreus tells Cleopatra that Cæsar would be pleased
to hear that she had left Antony,

> " And put yourself under his shroud,
> The universal landlord."

The first of these lines halts for want of two syllables ;
nevertheless, the text is such in the folio, 1623 ; but in the
folio, 1632, the word " landlord" is strangely separated from
what precedes, and put two lines lower.   The old corrector
sets this matter right, and adds what completes the measure
of the first line, and was in all probability what Shakespeare
wrote :—

> " And put yourself under his shroud, *who is*
> The universal landlord."

Three lines farther on the folios have,—

> " Say to great Cæsar this in disputation."

It is the introduction to a message of submission from
Cleopatra to Cæsar ; and Warburton, very judiciously, as now
appears, put "deputation" for *disputation*, which last had
Malone and others for adherents ; but the correction in the
folio, 1632, goes somewhat farther :—

> " Say to great Cæsar, *that* in *deputation*
> I kiss his conquering hand," &c.

ACT IV. SCENE IV.

P. 92. According to the regulation of such matters in the
folio, 1632, this is the fifth scene of the fourth act ; but, as

we have already stated, we think the old corrector so far
wrong in his division of the play.

Antony enters calling for his armour:—"Mine armour,
Eros!" and when the man brings it, Antony is made to say
in the old copies, "Put thine iron on;" but surely it ought
to be, as a manuscript note renders it, "Put *mine* iron on:"
Eros then begins to arm the hero, while Cleopatra insists
upon lending her aid; and in this place, in the early editions,
three or four speeches are jumbled together, and all assigned
to Cleopatra. The corrector separates them by marginal
notes, but not precisely as has been done by Sir T. Hanmer
and later editors. We give the mode of regulating the dialogue in the amended folio, 1632, and on comparison it will
be seen that it varies:—

> " *Cleo.*   Nay, I'll help too, Antony,
>   What's this for?
> *Ant.*   Ah, let be, let be; thou art
>   The armourer of my heart. False, false: this, this.
> *Cleo.* Sooth, la, I'll help.
> *Ant.*   Thus must it be. Well, well:
>   We shall thrive now."

The chief difference is that "Thus must it be" is given
by the old corrector to Antony, and not to Cleopatra.
Afterwards Antony observes,—

> " He that unbuckles this, till we do please
>   To doff't for our repose, shall hear a storm."

" Shall *bear* a storm," says a marginal note, with much more
fitness, the compositor having taken a wrong letter. An
enemy who should attempt to unbuckle Antony's armour
was not likely to " hear a storm" of words, but "to *bear* a
storm" of blows.

SCENE VIII.

P. 98. Antony, entering for a time victorious, tells his followers, as it has always been printed,—

> " We have beat him to his camp. Run one before
>   And let the queen know of our guests."

Johnson adds a note, stating that by these words Antony
means to say that he will bring his officers to sup with Cleopatra; but near the end of the scene, while Antony laments

that the palace had not "capacity to camp this host," he
says not a word about feasting even the officers. The
truth is that, from the first, the word has been mistaken,
and because it was spelt *guests* in the old copies, it has
always been supposed to mean what we call company. The
amender of the folio, 1632, merely strikes out the letter *u*,
leaving the word *gests*, and it requires no proof that a *gest*,
from the Latin, formerly meant a *deed*, and was synonymous
with it. When, therefore, Antony directs,—

> " Run one before,
> And let the queen know of our *gests*,"

it is as much as to say, " let her know of our deeds," and the
manner in which we have beaten the Romans to their tents.
Gest was unquestionably Shakespeare's word.

SCENE IX.

P. 101. Enobarbus dying of grief and remorse on the
stage, one of the soldiers present says that he sleeps, but
another observes,—

> " Swoons rather ; for so bad a prayer as his
> Was never yet for sleep."

Steevens arbitrarily changed " sleep" to *sleeping ;* but instead
of " for sleep" we ought to read " '*fore* sleep," or before
sleep, and the word is altered in manuscript accordingly : the
sense is, that so bad a prayer, as Enobarbus had ended with,
was never uttered before sleep.

SCENE X.

P. 103. Antony rushes in in despair, with the words " All
is lost !" and afterwards proceeds,—

> " Betray'd I am.
> O, this false soul of Egypt ! this grave charm,—
> Whose eye beck'd forth my wars," &c.

Is it not evident, upon mere perusal, that " soul" must be
wrong, that it could not be the word of the poet ? Almost
the same may be said of " grave," in connexion with
" charm ;" and when Johnson states that " grave charm"

means "majestic beauty," he forgot that "charm" in Shakespeare's time, and indeed our own, was to be taken as
enchantment. The manuscript-corrector alters both words
thus :—

"O, this false *spell* of Egypt! this *great* charm," &c.

Cleopatra, notwithstanding she was a "false spell," was a
grand piece of witchcraft. On her entrance, immediately
afterwards, Antony receives her with the words, "Ah, thou
spell! Avaunt!"

SCENE XII.

P. 110. When Diomed, speaking of Cleopatra, tells Antony,—

"You did suspect
She had dispos'd with Cæsar,"

Steevens subjoins a note stating that "dispose, in this instance, perhaps signifies to make terms, to settle matters;"
but he adds no example of such being its signification any
where else. A correction in the folio, 1632, treats it as a
mere lapse by the printer: such we may confidently deem it,
and that the poet's language was,—

"She had *compos'd* with Cæsar;"

i. e. had entered into a composition or treaty with him. The
printer used the wrong preposition.

SCENE XIII.

P. 111. This scene, numbered the thirteenth in modern
impressions, according to the old corrector, begins Act V.;
and unless the last act be made unusually short, this should
seem to be the proper division.

Cleopatra, on the next page, declaring to Antony that she
will never be led in triumph by Cæsar, adds, as the text has
been constantly repeated,—

"Your wife Octavia, with her modest eyes,
And still conclusion, shall acquire no honour
Demuring upon me."

What signification can we attach to "still conclusion?"
Johnson replies, "sedate determination," a very forced con-

struction, while a manuscript emendation, proposing the
substitution of three letters, seems to put the matter incon-
trovertibly at rest :—

> " Your wife, Octavia, with her modest eyes,
> And still *condition*, shall acquire no honour
> Demuring upon me."

The stillness of the *condition* of Octavia, her gentleness and
tranquillity of deportment, have already been dwelt upon in
various places.

P. 112. A good deal of doubt has been occasioned by Cleopatra's " strange words," as Johnson calls them (and justly,
if they were such as they have always been represented),
when she and her women are endeavouring with all their
strength to raise the dying Antony into the monument :—

> " Here's sport, indeed !"

Steevens calls it " affected levity," and Boswell wishes to
make it "a melancholy contrast with her former sports."
The corrector of the folio, 1632, strikes out the letter *s* in
" sport," and leaves the word merely *port*—" Here's *port*
indeed !"   Milton uses the participle *ported*, and here Shakespeare appears to have employed *port* as a substantive to indicate weight :—

> " Here's *port* indeed !—How heavy weighs my lord !"

The French use *port* for burden, and *navire de grand port* is a
ship of great burden.   Cleopatra speaks of the weight of Antony by the same word ; and though we may not be able to
point out any other instance where *port* signifies in English a
load or weight, we can hardly doubt that such is the fact in
the case before us, and that, when the heroine exclaims,
" Here's *port*, indeed !" she means, here's a load, weight, or
burden, indeed.   It is evident that the person who made the
emendation in the folio, 1632, so understood it ; the printer
probably did not, and hence his blunder.   The alteration is
very trifling, and it overcomes a great difficulty.

ACT V. SCENE I.

P. 115. The first lines of this act have created discussion : they stand thus in the old copies, where Cæsar speaks of Antony :—

> "Go to him, Dollabella, bid him yield.
> Being so frustrate, tell him,
> He mocks the pauses that he makes.
> *Dol.* Cæsar, I shall."

Malone could not comprehend what was meant by "He mocks the pauses that he makes," and printed "He mocks *us by* the pauses that he makes." This is not at all like the change introduced in manuscript in the folio, 1632, which may be considered all that is necessary both to complete the sense and the verse :—

> "Go to him, Dollabella ; bid him yield.
> Being so frustrate, tell him *that* he mocks
> The pauses that he makes.
> *Dol.*   Cæsar, I shall."

By "he mocks the pauses that he makes," we must understand Cæsar to charge Antony with trifling with the pauses he made in finally submitting to his enemies. It is certain that the corrector considered it necessary to supply nothing but the word *that*, and with this addition (whencesoever he procured it) he imagined, no doubt, that he had left the poet's meaning clear.

P. 116. Dercetas brings tidings of Antony's death in these terms, as commonly printed :—

> "But that self hand,
> Which writ his honour in the acts it did,
> Hath, with the courage which the heart did lend it,
> Splitted the heart. This is his sword ;
> I robb'd his wound of it," &c.

Here, in spite of the word *split* being converted into two syllables, the line in which it occurs is left short of two others. In "the Comedy of Errors" (p. 64) we have seen "splitted," of the folios, amended to *split*, and here the same course has been pursued, and two words added, in entire consistency with what has gone before, and at the same time completing the defective measure. We have "self hand" for *self same* hand in the first line, and in the fourth line, as

amended, we have "self noble heart" for *self same* noble
heart :—

> " But that self hand,
> Which writ his honour in the acts it did,
> Hath, with the courage which the heart did lend it,
> *Split that self noble* heart.   This is his sword," &c.

Every old copy has the defective line in a situation where
there seems no reason why a defective line should be found;
and it is perfected in manuscript of the time by words which,
in all probability, had accidentally escaped.

SCENE II.

P. 118. Cleopatra, contemplating suicide, says it is

> " To do that thing that ends all other deeds,
> Which shackles accidents and bolts up change ;
> Which sleeps, and never palates more the dung,
> The beggar's nurse and Cæsar's."

We must here see the impropriety of talking of palating
"dung," and afterwards calling that "dung" "the beggar's
nurse and Cæsar's."   By "dung" has been understood
"gross terrene sustenance," but the sense is much cleared
when we ascertain from a note in the folio, 1632, that the scribe
misheard "dung" for *dug :* the *dug* of sustenance may most
fitly be called "the beggar's nurse and Cæsar's," and it may
reasonably be supposed to be palated by mankind: the corrector, therefore, has it,—

> " Which sleeps, and never palates more the *dug,*
> The beggar's nurse and Cæsar's."

This emendation may, or may not, have been conjectural, but
we may be pretty sure it is right.

P. 120. The following is pointed out most likely as a
printer's error: Cleopatra is on the same theme, declaring
that she will in some way destroy herself:—

> " Sir, I will eat no meat, I'll not drink, sir ;
> If idle talk will once be necessary,
> I'll not sleep neither."

The poet's word was, no doubt, *accessary :* if idle talk would
keep her awake, and thus be accessary to her death, she would
indulge in it, and never sleep :—

> " If idle talk will once be *accessary*,
> I'll not sleep neither."

P. 122. In the subsequent speech by Dolabella, compassionating Cleopatra, the change of a single letter makes sense out of nonsense: the old copies have this text :—

> " But I do feel,
> By the rebound of yours, a grief that *suites*
> My very heart at root."

Malone and others read "shoots" for *suits*, but the poet's word (as speculatively suggested in note 5) was *smites*, and not *shoots* nor *suits* :—

> " A grief that *smites*
> My very heart at root."

The old corrector put his pen through the letter *u* in *suites*, and wrote *m* in the margin instead of it. Not long afterwards (p. 125), Cleopatra herself uses the word *smites* :—

> " *Ye* gods ! it smites me
> Beneath the fall I have."

In all copies, ancient and modern, it stands, "The gods ! it smites me," &c. ; but as *the* was often formerly written *ye*, the article was mistaken for it in this instance. The sentence has relation to the contradiction of Cleopatra by Seleucus, in the presence of Cæsar, as to the jewels, &c., she had reserved ; and when she desires the Steward to quit her presence, we encounter a change of expression which is not of much moment, and which can hardly be said to be necessary ; but as the folio, 1632, has a note upon it, it is perhaps fit to mention it : it is where Cleopatra says to Seleucus :—

> " Prythee, go hence ;
> Or I shall show the cinders of my spirits
> Through th' ashes of my chance."

Such has been the common reading ; but the old corrector tells us, what appears extremely plausible, that two mistakes are here to be set right :—

> " Prythee, go hence ;
> Or I shall show the cinders of my *spirit*
> Through th' ashes of *mischance*."

" My chance " may here, perhaps, be understood in the same sense as *mischance*. There can be little dispute that just

afterwards "are" should be *and*, where the heroine tells
Cæsar,—

> " When we fall,
> We answer other's merits in our name,
> *And* therefore to be pitied.'"

Of course, "merits" here means *deserts*.

P. 127. Iras declares that her nails shall tear out her
eyes rather than see her queen led in triumph; and Cleopatra's observation is this:—

> " Why, that's the way
> To fool their preparation, and to conquer
> Their most absurd intents."

The old corrector gives it thus :—

> " Why, that's the way
> To *foil* their preparation, and to conquer
> Their most *assur'd* intents."

Theobald proposed *assur'd* for "absurd," but the change has
since his time been rejected; and although *foil* may read
better on some accounts, still "fool" is stronger, and the
alteration of the text so far not called for.

P. 130. After the death of Iras, Cleopatra remarks,—

> " This proves me base :
> If she first meet the curled Antony,
> He'll make demand of her," &c.

The folio, 1632, is most carelessly printed in this part of the
play, and instead of " first meet," repeats *proves*, which the
compositor's eye caught from the preceding line,—

> " If she *proves* the curled Antony," &c.

A marginal note restores the text as it appears in the folio,
1623 ; but even a more stupid blunder of a different kind
is made on the last page of the play ; for there the word
"aspick," occurring in two nearly consecutive lines, one of
them is misprinted *aspect*, and the necessary verb *is* omitted :
the passage there stands precisely thus :—

> " This an aspects traile
> And these fig-leaves have slime upon them, such
> As th' aspicke leaves upon the caves of Nile."

These errors are remedied by the old corrector, though he
does not amend the regulation of the lines ; but it may
deserve remark, that he gives no countenance to the propo-
sition (alluded to in note 3) to read "*canes* of Nile" instead
of " caves of Nile." If Shakespeare had intended to refer to
the reeds that grow upon the banks of the Nile, he would
hardly have called them *canes*.

CYMBELINE.

ACT I. SCENE I.

P. 139. The mode in which the person who made the emendations in the folio, 1632, points and corrects the three first lines in this play, is the following, showing Tyrwhitt's sagacity in omitting the *s* after "kings," as it is printed in all the early editions :—

> "You do not meet a man but frowns. Our bloods
> No more obey the heavens, than our courtiers
> Still seem as does the king."

i. e. Our bloods do not more obey the heavens, than our courtiers imitate the king : as the king frowns, so all others look gloomy. There cannot be a doubt that this is the right reading.

P. 140. The second folio is very ill printed in the opening of this scene: it has "*wy* so" for "why so," "*he* like" for "his like," and "*which* himself" for "within himself." These blunders are set right ; but on the same authority we find all the folios wrong in the parenthesis, not there so printed,—

> "(Then old and fond of issue,")

for we are told that it ought to be,—

> "Then old and fond *of's* issue ;"

or "fond of his issue :" the correction is of little importance, since it varies neither sense nor metre.

SCENE II.

P. 144. As the subsequent passage has been ordinarily printed, it ought to have been followed by a mark of interrogation:—

> "Thou took'st a beggar; would'st have made my throne
> A seat for baseness."

Such, however, has not been the punctuation in ancient or modern editions; and the fact appears to be, that it was not intended as a question, for a slight manuscript alteration in the folio, 1632, makes it run,—

> "Thou took'st a beggar would have made my throne
> A seat for baseness :"

that is, "a beggar, *who* would have made my throne," &c., by a very common ellipsis: Imogen's indignant counter-assertion, "No; I rather added a lustre to it," seems to render it probable that a question was not intended.

SCENE V.

P. 150. We here encounter the first manuscript emendation that is of much value. Iachimo observes, that the marriage of Posthumus with his king's daughter, tends to enhance the opinion of his merits, adding,—

> "Ay, and the approbation of those, that weep this lamentable divorce under her colours, are wonderfully to extend him; be it but to fortify her judgment, which else an easy battery might lay flat, for taking a beggar without less quality."

What can be the meaning of the expression, "under her colours?" how was the "lamentable divorce" under the colours of Imogen? Johnson tells us that "under her colours" is to be understood as "by her influence." Surely not: Posthumus was not banished by the influence of Imogen, but in direct opposition to her wishes. How does the annotator of the folio, 1632, explain the matter? By showing that here occurs another of the many gross mistakes of the scribe, or of the printer, which have been from time to time pointed out: "under her colours" ought to have been *and her dolours*, a word not unfrequently used by

Shakespeare, and most applicable to the distresses of Imogen in her separation from her husband.   But besides this error, there are several others in the sentence, together with the omission of the verb *wont*, carelessly excluded, because, perhaps, as the next word begins with *won*, the compositor missed what is almost essential to the intelligibility of the passage : then, near the close, we have "less" for *more*, although Malone, not aware of any of the preceding defects, strives hard to justify "less." Read the whole, therefore, as the corrector says it was written, and nothing can well be plainer :—

"Ay, and the *approbations* of those, that weep this lamentable divorce *and her dolours*, are *wont* wonderfully to extend him ; be it but to fortify her judgment, which else an easy battery might lay flat, for taking a beggar without *more* quality."

P. 154. Another remarkable corruption has been perpetuated near the close of this scene.   Iachimo has vaunted that he will overcome the chastity of Imogen, and Posthumus has accepted his wager : the latter observes, as the text has always stood,—

"Let us have articles betwixt us.—Only, thus far you shall answer : if you make your voyage upon her, and give me directly to understand you have prevailed, I am no farther your enemy," &c.

Now, "if you make your voyage upon her" may be understood as referring to the voyage Iachimo was to make to Britain, in order to endeavour to carry his vaunt into effect ; but still the expression is awkward, and one which a correction in the folio, 1632, informs us the poet did not use : the word "voyage" is a misprint, in part, perhaps, occasioned by the omission of an adjective which ought almost immediately to precede it : Posthumus observes, that if Iachimo make good his boast, then Imogen would not be worth anger : he therefore says,—

"Only, thus far you shall answer : if you make *good* your *vauntage* upon her, and give me directly to understand you have prevailed, I am no farther your enemy."

In other words, "if you succeed and accomplish your boast, she does not merit debate." It seems probable that *good* was left out in the manuscript, and that the compositor mistook *vauntage*, and printed "voyage," knowing that Iachimo must necessarily cross the sea, in order to carry out his project. The sense of the poet appears to have been as different, as it was superior to the ordinary interpretation.

SCENE VII.

P. 159. Two emendations were proposed by Warburton and Theobald in the following: both are found in the margin of the folio, 1632, with a confirmatory addition of some importance. We here give the passage as amended, marking the changes in Italics as usual:—

> "What! are men mad? Hath nature given them eyes
> To see this vaulted arch, and the rich *cope*
> *O'er* sea and land, which can distinguish 'twixt
> The fiery orbs above, and the twinn'd stones
> Upon th' *unnumber'd* beach," &c.

For *cope* the ordinary text has been "crop," for *O'er* "Of," and for *th' unnumber'd* "the number'd." We may in future safely adopt these emendations, which require no explanation. *O'er* is proposed for the first time.

P. 162. There can be no doubt that the old corrector has, by the alteration of a single letter, rendered quite evident what has puzzled all commentators: it is where Iachimo pretends to describe to Imogen the infidelity of Posthumus while in Rome: the folios have what follows:—

> "Slaver with lips as common as the stairs
> That mount the Capitol; join gripes with hands
> Made hard with hourly falsehood (falsehood as
> With labour) then by peeping in an eye
> Base and illustrous as the smoky light
> That's fed with stinking tallow."

Some editors have adhered to this text, while others, Malone and Johnson for instance, have printed "by peeping in an eye" "*lie* peeping in an eye;" but all have been mistaken, and what was meant was merely an allusion to the game of *bo-peep*, which is mentioned by Shakespeare and other authors (among them Lodge, in his "Alarum against Usurers," 1584), and is here again introduced:—

> "Then, *bo-peeping* in an eye
> Base and illustrous," &c.

Posthumus is represented by Iachimo as pressing the hard

hands of the most hacknied prostitutes, and playing at *bo-peep* in their lack-lustre eyes.

On such evidence we can readily believe in another amendment, proposed on the next page, which, however, is not so necessary, but, at the same time, by no means uncalled for: it is part of the same description of the dealings of Posthumus

> " With diseas'd ventures,
> That play with all infirmities for gold
> Which rottenness can lend nature."

The corrector states that they do not " play" with these infirmities for gold, but *pay*, or make a return for gold by the most loathsome diseases :—

> "That *pay* with all infirmities for gold."

P. 163. When Imogen tells Iachimo,—

> " I do condemn mine ears, that have
> So long attended thee,"

a marginal manuscript note directs us again to change a single letter, and much strengthen the old and ordinary reading :—

> " I do *contemn* mine ears, that have
> So long attended thee."

She despised her ears for having listened so long to the slanders of Iachimo. The reader will almost have anticipated this amendment, which, however, has never been made, though adding much to the force of the heroine's indignation.

We may add that in Iachimo's last speech in this scene, the old corrector of the folio, 1632, substitutes *out-stay'd* for *outstood*, at least with plausibility.

ACT II.　SCENE I.

P. 166. It requires notice, in reference to the divisions of this drama, that when, probably, it was represented in the time of the annotator on the folio, 1632 (we know that it was revived and performed at Court, 1st January, 1633), the second Act began with what is made Scene VII. of Act I. in

modern editions. In all the old printed copies also, Act II.
commences with the entrance of Cloten and the two Lords;
but the words *Actus Secundus, Scœna Prima* are struck
through with a pen in the folio, 1632, and transferréd to
what is headed *Scœna Septima* of the preceding act. This
change seems not unadvisable, if only for the sake of
lengthening Act II. Therefore, above *Enter Cloten and the
two Lords*, is written "Scene 2;" and we are informed, also
in manuscript, that the three characters come on the stage
as from the Bowling Alley.

SCENE II.

P. 168. The introduction to this scene in the old copies, is
merely *Enter Imogen in her bed, and a Lady*, while nothing
is said about the place and manner of Iachimo's conceal-
ment: to remedy this omission, *A great trunk* is added in
manuscript in the folio, 1632, to show that this stage-property
was exhibited to the audience. According to additional directions in the margin, Iachimo not merely *takes off Imogen's
bracelet*, but previously *kisses her*, at the words,—

> "That I might touch!
> But kiss; one kiss!"

It is very possible that such was part of the ancient business
of the scene; but it was a perilous undertaking that, at all
events in modern times, has not usually been risked.   Still, if
the Italian could remove the heroine's bracelet, and turn down
the bed-clothes so as to be able to note the "mole cinque-
spotted" on her left breast (supposing it not to have been
accidentally exposed) without waking her, he might, perhaps,
hazard the kissing of her lips.   Opposite the words, "I will
write all down," *Take out tables*, meaning his table-book, is
placed in the margin, and *Exit into the trunk again*, at the
end of the scene.   These notes are altogether wanting in
print in the folios.

P. 170. It is not easy to make sense out of

> "Swift, swift, you dragons of the night, that dawning
> May bare the raven's eye."

Such was Theobald's emendation, and if the meaning be that
light may make bare the raven's eye, the expression is un-

couth for "may *ope* the raven's eye." The old corrector converts *beare*, of the folios, into *dare* :—

> " That dawning
> May *dare* the raven's eye :"

i. e. may dazzle the eye of the raven, in the same way that larks were *dared* by the glitter of a looking-glass. This may be the true explanation of the sentence, but still it is obscure ; and at a guess, supposing the old corrector's change to be nothing more, we might fancy that *beare* was a misprint for *bleare*, in the sense of to dim.

SCENE IV.

P. 178. When Iachimo returns to Italy, Posthumus, in his confidence in Imogen, asks him, referring to their wager,—

> "Sparkles this stone as it was wont? or is't not
> Too dull for your good wearing ?"

To which Iachimo is always made to reply,—

> " If I have lost it,
> I should have lost the worth of it in gold," &c.

But it was Posthumus who had the chance of losing the ring, and Iachimo the value of it, therefore the old corrector makes him answer, with much more apparent propriety,—

> "If I *had* lost,
> I should have lost the worth of it in gold ;"

and from thence he proceeds to show that he had not lost, but, in fact, had won the wager.

P. 179. All impressions represent Iachimo as not completing his sentence when describing the tapestry in Imogen's chamber :—

> " Which, I wonder'd,
> Could be so rarely and exactly wrought,
> Since the true life on't was "————
> *Post.* 　　　　　　　　　　　This is true," &c.

Here, besides the imperfectness of the sense, the measure is at fault, because " This is true" does not finish the line Iachimo had begun. Corrections in the folio, 1632, remedy both defects in a way that seems to carry conviction in their favour :—

" Which, I wonder'd,
Could be so rarely and exactly wrought,
Since the true life on't 'twas.

Post.   This is *most* true," &c.

Iachimo wondered at the excellence of the tapestry "since *'twas* the true life" of the scene it represented. The word *most* was carelessly left out in the answer of Posthumus, as *'twas* in the preceding line was misprinted "was."

Near the bottom of the page, Iachimo thus describes part of the furniture :—

" Her andirons
(I had forgot them) were two winking Cupids
Of silver."

The emendation here is *wingèd* for "winking" Cupids ; and it certainly is not likely that Iachimo should have so nicely observed at night, as to perceive that they were "winking," though he might have easily seen that they were *winged*. At the same time, this may be looked upon as one of the many cases where the fitness of altering the received text is doubtful, in as much as Shakespeare may have intended thus to show the elaborate exactness of the scrutiny of Iachimo.

SCENE V.

P. 182. In all modern editions, this soliloquy by Posthumus is converted into a new scene ; but such was not the case of old, for Iachimo and Philario go out and leave the hero behind them to make his reflections upon what had passed, and to curse womankind. Here we meet with a word which has produced difficulty : Posthumus supposes Iachimo to have easily overcome the scruples of Imogen, and we first give the terms exactly as they appear in the two earliest folios :—

" Perchance he spoke not, but
Like a full Acorn'd Boare, a Iarmen on,
Cry'de oh, and mounted."

Dispute has arisen as to the meaning of the unintelligible words "a Iarmen on ;" and while Pope and Warburton read "a *churning* on," which Malone calls a sophistication, he himself read "a *German one*," surely a greater sophistication, as if Shakespeare could have had no boars in his thoughts but German ones. There is an evident mis-

print, and the emendator of the folio, 1632, points out what
it was :—

> "Like a full acorn'd boar, a *foaming one*,
>   Cried oh ! and mounted."

The manuscript must have been imperfectly written, and
the printer mistook the *f*, with which *foaming* begins, for
a capital *I*, then frequently carried below the line, and did
not attend to the *g* at the end of the word. *One*, as Malone
truly states, was often miswritten and misprinted " on," and
there seems no doubt that the poet meant to express the
furious and *foaming* eagerness of the full-acorn'd boar. Malone weakly supports his notion about a *German* boar, by
stating that boars were never hunted in England ; but Posthumus was speaking in Italy, and we are not to imagine
that Shakespeare's notions regarding boar-hunting were derived solely from German representations, whether in "water-
work" or in tapestry. We feel no hesitation in substituting
so natural a word as *foaming* for such an utterly unintelligible word as *Iarmen*. The mechanical compositor never
thought of the sense of what he was printing.

ACT III.   SCENE I.

P. 185. A line in Cymbeline's address to Lucius stands
precisely thus in the folios :—

> " Ourselves to be, we do.   Say then to Cæsar."

With the immediate context it has been printed as follows
in modern editions : the king is speaking of the Roman
yoke :—

> " Which to shake off
> Becomes a warlike people, whom we reckon
> Ourselves to be.   We do say, then, to Cæsar,
> Our ancestor was that Mulmutius, which
> Ordain'd our laws," &c.

The clumsy contrivance of making Cymbeline use the expression, " We do say, then, to Cæsar," has proceeded (as an
emendation in the folio, 1632, shows) from a blunder on the
part of the compositor or of the copyist, who made one of
Cloten's impertinent interjections a portion of the speech of
Cymbeline. This part of the dialogue is there divided as
follows :—Cymbeline ends,—

> " Which to shake off
> Becomes a warlike people, whom we reckon
> Ourselves to be.
> *Clot.*   We do.
> *Cym.*   Say, then, to Cæsar,
> Our ancestor was that Mulmutius, which
> Ordain'd our laws," &c.

This interruption by Cloten is most consistent with his character and conduct, and we have no doubt that such was the
mode in which the line we have first quoted was distributed,
before the corruption had crept into the early editions.

SCENE II.

P. 189. Warburton justly calls the phrase, "the sands
that run i' the clock's behalf," fantastical ; but it is only so
because "behalf" was misprinted. Imogen is speaking of
horses that run much faster than the sands in clocks, and
she goes on, by a familiar expression, to state how much
faster they run :—

> " I have heard of riding wagers,
> Where horses have been nimbler than the sands
> That run i' the clocks *by half ;*"

adding, "But this is foolery," in reference, perhaps, to her
own simile.

SCENE III.

P. 190. Belarius, contrasting the life he, Guiderius, and
Arviragus lead in the woods and mountains with that at
court, observes, in the ordinary text,—

> " O ! this life
> Is nobler, than attending for a check ;
> Richer, than doing nothing for a bribe ;
> Prouder, than rustling in unpaid-for silk."

The old copies give the third line,—

> " Richer than doing nothing for a *babe*,"

and Hanmer substituted "bribe," though bribes are seldom
given for doing nothing, while Warburton has *bauble*, and
Malone adhered to *babe*. All three are unquestionably
wrong: the second line supposes a courtier to dance attendance, and only to obtain "a check," or reproof, for
his pains ; and the third line follows up the same notion,

that he does nothing, yet is rewarded with a blow : Shakespeare repeatedly uses *bob* (the word in manuscript in the margin of the folio, 1632) in this way ; and *babe*, then pronounced with the broad open *a*, was miswritten for it : therefore, the passage, properly printed, appears to be this :—

> " O ! this life
> Is nobler, than attending for a check,
> Richer, than doing nothing for a *bob*," &c.

P. 193. The copyist made an evident mistake when he wrote the following, where Belarius is soliloquizing on his two boys, and describing the way in which they listen to his account of " warlike feats :" of the elder, he says,—

> " He sweats,
> Strains his young nerves, and puts himself in posture
> That acts my words. The younger brother, Cadwal,
> (Once Arviragus) in as like a figure
> Strikes life into my speech," &c.

Here *vigour* was misheard "figure" (which could only refer to the "posture" of Guiderius), and for this reason the old corrector alters the word in the margin of the folio, 1632 :—

> " The younger brother, Cadwal,
> (Once Arviragus) in as like a *vigour*
> Strikes life into my speech."

That is, with the same energy with which Guiderius had "strained his young nerves."

SCENE IV.

P. 195. We here arrive at a most singular instance of mishearing, which we must impute wholly to the writer of the manuscript used by the compositor. It is in a speech by Imogen, where she supposes that Posthumus has been seduced by some Italian courtezan :—

> " Some jay of Italy,
> Whose mother was her painting, hath betray'd him :
> Poor I am stale, a garment out of fashion ;" &c.

Now, for "whose mother was her painting," of all editions, we are told by the amender of the folio, 1632, to read,—

> " Some jay of Italy,
> *Who smothers her with* painting, hath betray'd him."

We fairly admit it to be possible that the old corrector, not
understanding the expression, "Whose mother was her
painting," as it was recited before him, might mistake it for
" *Who smothers her with* painting ;" but it is much more likely
that in this place, where Imogen was to give vent to her dis-
gust and anger, she would not use a metaphor, especially
so violent a one, as to call the daubing of the face
actually the "mother" of a courtezan. She was describing
a woman of abandoned character, who not merely tinged
her cheeks, but absolutely smothered herself with painting,
and who, though so made up and artificial, had, nevertheless,
seduced Posthumus from the arms of a beautiful and innocent wife. Imogen would, therefore, be disposed to render
the contrast as strong as words could make it, and would
not be content to throw blame upon her debased and profligate rival, merely by a far-fetched figure of speech. Shakespeare, indeed, even in this very play (p. 215), employs such
a figure, but under extremely different circumstances, *viz.*
where Guiderius ridicules Cloten for asking if he did not
know him by his fine clothes ? The answer is,—

> " No, nor thy tailor, rascal,
> Who is thy grandfather : he made those clothes,
> Which, as it seems, make thee."

These lines occur in Act IV., and what Imogen says of the
"jay of Italy," is inserted in the immediately preceding act ;
and if one thing more than another could persuade us that
"*who smothers her with* painting" is the true text, it is that,
if we suppose differently, it makes Shakespeare employ the
very same metaphor in two consecutive acts. Our great dramatist was neither so poverty-stricken as regards language,
nor so injudicious as regards nature, to repeat himself in this
way, and to make Imogen convey her scorn and detestation
of the prostitute, who had betrayed her husband, in so
mild a form as to term painting the "mother" of the se-
ducer. Imogen would not study metaphors at such a
moment, but, in the plainest and strongest language she
could employ, such as charging the "jay of Italy" with
smothering herself with painting, would express her abhor-
rence of the paint-plastered prostitute. It is an axiom
that genuine passion avoids figures of speech, because passion does not reflect, and a figure of speech is the fruit
of reflection : therefore, we feel assured that the scribe

misheard, and wrote "whose mother was her painting" instead of "*who smothers her with* painting." The coincidence of sound seems otherwise almost inexplicable.

P. 196. We can have little difficulty, on the authority of the old corrector, in treating the word "fellows" in these lines as a lapse by the old printer:—

> "And thou, Posthumus, that didst set up
> My disobedience 'gainst the king my father,
> And make me put into contempt the suits
> Of princely fellows, shalt hereafter find
> It is no act of common passage, but
> A strain of rareness."

For "princely fellows," the emendation is "princely *followers*," the noble suitors whom Imogen had rejected in favour of Posthumus.

Near the top of the next page is an expression upon which Hanmer, Johnson, Steevens, and Malone have very unsatisfactory notes. Pisanio informs Imogen that he has not slept since he received command to destroy her :—

> "*Imo.*   Do't, and to bed, then.
> *Pis.* I'll wake mine eye-balls first.
> *Imo.*   Wherefore, then,
> Didst undertake it?"

What does Pisanio mean by "I'll wake mine eye-balls first?" To extract some sense from the declaration, it has been usual to print "I'll wake mine eye-balls *blind* first;" but another printer's error has occasioned all the trouble. The corrector converts "wake" into *cracke*, and doubt vanishes : he also inserts a small word in Imogen's inquiry, and presents the whole thus perfect in measure and meaning :—

> "*Imo.*   Do't, and to bed, then.
> *Pis.* I'll *crack* mine eye-balls first.
> *Imo.*   *And* wherefore, then,
> Did'st undertake it?"

P. 198. Malone considered it vain to seek for the two-syllable epithet, obviously wanting, in a line where Imogen speaks of Cloten,—

> "With that harsh, noble, simple nothing."

Steevens would complete the measure by *Cloten* at the end, forgetting, perhaps, that the name occurs at the very beginning of the next line; but the missing word is found written in the margin of the folio, 1632 :—

> "With that harsh, noble, simple, *empty* nothing."

It had, doubtless, escaped by mere accident, and we may be thankful for the restoration.

Lower down in the page occur the words "Pretty and full of view." What can be the meaning of "pretty" in that place? It is an indisputable blunder, perhaps from defective hearing: Pisanio is showing Imogen how she may remain concealed, and yet have a full view of all that is passing around her: we print the passage here as it is corrected :—

> "Now, if you could wear a mind
> Dark as your fortune is, and but disguise
> That, which, t'appear itself, must not yet be
> But by self-danger, you should tread a course
> *Privy, yet* full of view : yea, haply, near
> The residence of Posthumus."

She was to remain private, and unknown, while she was able to mark all that was done by others.

The alteration of "courage" to *carriage*, near the top of the next page, may be contested ; and in as much as "courage" answers its purpose, perhaps it would be unwise to displace it, though more than once (see pp. 292, 358) the same easy error has been pointed out. Pisanio tells Imogen that when she has disguised herself as a youth, she must change

> "Command into obedience ; fear, and niceness,
> (The handmaids of all women, or more truly,
> Woman it pretty self) into a waggish courage :
> Ready in gibes, quick-answer'd," &c.

Here "waggish *carriage*" seems more appropriate to a youth, though disputable.

SCENE VI.

P. 206. The old introduction to this scene is merely, "Enter Imogen alone," to which the following necessary words are added in manuscript in the folio, 1632, *'tir'd like a boy, i.e.* attired like a boy. She commences her speech thus :—

> "I see, a man's life is a tedious one :
> I have tir'd myself, and for two nights together
> Have made the ground my bed."

It has always been supposed that "I have tir'd myself" is
to be taken in the sense of "I have fatigued myself;" but
the corrector places an apostrophe before tir'd—'tir'd—and
clearly means that "tir'd," in the speech, is to be understood
in the same way as 'tir'd like a boy in what he appended to
the heading of the scene. This is a point upon which we
may or may not take his word; for we may imagine that
Imogen means that she has tired herself with the tedious-
ness of a man's life, and with sleeping two nights following upon the ground. It seems, however, more likely
that she should refer to her dress, and purposely call the
attention of the audience to the change it had undergone.

The entrance of Belarius, Guiderius, and Arviragus is improperly made a new scene in the folios; but *Scœna Septima*
is struck through with a pen, and *Same* written instead of
it, as in several former instances.

ACT IV. SCENE I.

P. 211. The word "imperseverant," as it stands printed in
the folios, has naturally given trouble to the commentators,
who have not known what to do with it. Hanmer altered
it to "*ill*-perseverant," meaning persevering in ill, while
Steevens argued that it was to be understood as *perseverant*.
It appears, on the authority of an emendation in the folio,
1632, that the compositor blundered by combining two words,
one of which had relation to the obstinacy of Imogen, and the
other to the wandering life to which she had taken. It is
Cloten who speaks, and who is complaining of the perverseness of the heroine, who absurdly preferred Posthumus to him,
and ran away from court in order to avoid him. Very probably the manuscript was here confused and illegible, which
led to the printing of "imperseverant" for *perverse errant*,
as it is amended, and as we may be confident it ought hereafter to be printed—"Yet this *perverse, errant* thing loves
him in my despite." Cloten had come to Milford Haven in
search of this "perverse, errant thing," and to destroy
Posthumus.

SCENE II.

P. 217. The question, somewhat hotly argued between Theobald, Warburton, Mason, Malone, &c., whether in the following, as we find it in the old copies,—

> " Though his honour
> Was nothing but mutation,"

"honour" should not be read *humour*, is decided (if, in truth, decision were wanted) by the old corrector, who converts "honour" into *humour* by the change of two letters in the margin. It has been a misreading of frequent occurrence.

P. 221. An emendation in the folio, 1632, changes "the leaf of eglantine," very naturally, but not necessarily, into "the *leafy* eglantine ;" but at the end of the speech we meet with a valuable improvement of the text in the setting right of a misprint, which has occasioned some pages of useless explanation and comment. It applies to this passage, as given in the folios :—

> " The ruddock would
> With charitable bill (O, bill, sore shaming
> Those rich-left heirs, that let their fathers lie
> Without a monument!) bring thee all this ;
> Yea, and furr'd moss besides, when flowers are none,
> To winter-ground thy corse."

The puzzle has been the compound verb "to winter-ground ;" and Warburton insisted upon "winter-*gown*," while Malone and Steevens were for preserving the text unaltered. Warburton was right in treating "winter-ground" as a blunder, but no farther ; and when we show, from the corrected folio, 1632, what must have been the poet's language, it will be seen that the compositor's mistake was an easy one :—

> " Yea, and furr'd moss besides, when flowers are none,
> To winter-*guard* thy corse :"

i.e. the redbreast would bring furred moss to protect Imogen's corse in winter, when there were no flowers.

P. 222. There is a substitution in the song over the body of Imogen which requires notice, and which improves the reading of a line, but by no means forces adoption upon us : the text has always been,—

> " Golden lads and girls all must,
>   As chimney-sweepers, come to dust."

It is altered as follows in the amended folio, 1632 :—

> " Golden lads and *lasses* must,
>   As chimney-sweepers, come to dust."

"Lads and lasses" may be said to follow each other in every song (as well as in every place), and perhaps Shakespeare here purposely avoided the repetition.

Several variations from the received text are marked in this part of the play ; but near the end of the volume the outer margins are so worn, torn, and encroached upon by damp and rough handling, that although words are corrected, or crossed out, what was substituted for them has sometimes disappeared. The subsequent comparatively trifling change on p. 224, has just escaped : it is where Imogen wakes and says,—

> " I hope I dream,
> For so I thought I was a cave-keeper."

The proposed emendation is to convert an adverb into an interjection :—

> " For *lo !* I thought I was a cave-keeper."

This part of the play is carelessly printed in the second folio, and literal errors (all of them corrected by the manuscript-annotator, though his writing is often obscured or obliterated) are very frequent.

ACT V.   SCENE I.

P. 231. Only about one page of this act has been preserved in the corrected folio, 1632, four leaves at the end of the volume being entirely wanting. A manuscript addition to the heading of the first scene has been partly torn away, so that we can only read in print, " Enter Posthumus alone," and *with a* following it in the writing of the old corrector : probably *napkin* or *handkerchief* was the word lost.

P. 232. The last emendation we have to notice (beyond the insertion of some new stage-directions relating to the battle, such as *Drums and trumpets, Alarums on both sides*,

&c.) is in the soliloquy of Posthumus, and it relates to a passage which has been much discussed, but never clearly understood: the old text has been this :—

> " You some permit
> To second ills with ills, each elder worse ;
> And make them dread it, to the doer's thrift."

Here, in the first place, is an admitted inaccuracy, because, as Malone remarked, the last ill deed, which was the "worse," was, in fact, the younger, and not the "elder." For this the corrector provides a remedy, and writes *later* in the margin for "elder," which was, perhaps, a misprint. The line that follows is far from intelligible, for to what does "them" in it apply ?—

> "And make them dread it to the doer's thrift."

The last antecedent was "ills," but "them" cannot refer to the crimes committed. This appears to be another instance where "them" has been misheard for another word, the adoption of which, on the testimony in our hands, makes a clear meaning out of an obscure line. The passage, therefore, stands thus, as amended in the folio, 1632 :—

> " You some permit
> To second ills with ills, each *later* worse,
> And make *men* dread it, to the doer's thrift."

The doer of ill deeds profited by the fears produced in *men* by still-increasing enormities. *Later*, therefore, was misprinted "elder," and *men* misheard "them." The word *men* is only just legible in the margin, in consequence of a stain and the abrasion of the paper.

NOTES.

It should be added that in "Richard II.," vol. iv. p. 172, the poet speaks of "the cloudy cheeks of heaven;" and, on the whole, *heat* in this place seems to be one of those alterations, which, though supported by some probability, it might be inexpedient to insert in the text.

It ought to be noted that opposite the expression, on p. 13, "*Out* three years old," the old corrector of the folio, 1632, has written the word *Quite*, but he has not erased "Out;" and possibly he only meant that "Out three years old" was to be understood as "*Quite* three years old." As he made no change, we may conclude that the text is right.

Perhaps neither of the smaller emendations on p. 40 is necessary: "she, from whom" may mean, she, coming from whom "we were all sea-swallowed."

Nevertheless, it seems proper so to divide the song; and, possibly, it is a point which did not attract the attention of the corrector of the folio, 1632. The emendation of *rain* for "spring," appears somewhat violent, and *springs* for "spring" might have been all that was really necessary.

In reference to the line supplied in manuscript in the folio, 1632, it is very possible that it was obtained from more correct recitation.

At the bottom of this page, "Scene IV." ought to have been marked as preceding the passage quoted from vol. i. p. 164. This division ought, therefore, to be deleted on p. 26.

We may add that it is much more easy to suppose "include" mis-printed for *conclude*, than to accept the very forced construction of Malone, that all jars were to be "included or shut in the bosoms of the parties, and to be prevented from getting out by triumphs, masques," &c.

Page 34.

In "Othello," Act I. Scene III., the folios misprint "couch" *coach*, where the hero is speaking of "the flinty and steel couch of war."

Page 40.

In the sentence "which, however, was sometimes in the language of the day," dele *in*.

Page 44.

This mistake of "winter" for *windows*, ought not here, properly, to have been charged upon the printer, but upon the copyist, who, writing by his ear, mistook the sound of the word.

Page 45.

It is to be observed, however, that Shakespeare uses "top" sometimes in a peculiar manner: thus in "Macbeth," Act IV. Scene I., he speaks of "the round and top of sovereignty;" and in "Coriolanus," Act I. Scene IX., he has "the spire and top of praises."

Page 47.

This emendation of *boasted* for "blessed" may have been adopted as a mere matter of taste.

Page 50.

It ought to have been stated that Pope made the correction of "his lordship's man," which has ever since been considered the text.—In the last line but three of this page, the full point ought to be only a comma, and the sentence should run—"but the fact seems to be that it is a misprint, and that the duke's real exclamation," &c.

Page 51.

Johnson was once, he tells us, in favour of *confined*, in preference to "combined."

Page 52.

The expression, "bears *such* a credent bulk," may look more like an attempt to mend, than an emendation.

Page 54.

On further consideration we may be disposed to prefer an adherence to the old text, since to "retort" and to "reject" etymologically have nearly the same meaning.

Page 60.

Nevertheless, it seems to us that Malone's alteration of *ruinate* to "ruinous," in order to rhyme with Antipholus, is on some accounts preferable: at all events it is shorter.

Page 67.

The word "father," which is left out in the folios, is found in the quarto, 1600—"to make courtesy and say, *Father*, as it please you." Perhaps the old corrector of the second folio obtained it from thence.

Page 78.

It seems not unlikely that the compositor, confusing the two similar terminations, *died* and *belied*, misprinted the latter "defil'd."

PAGE 79.

It should be stated, as mentioned in note 8, that most of these emendations were suggested by Hanmer, and have since been adopted by Malone and some other modern editors.

PAGE 89.

For " the manuscript stage-directions," read " the stage-directions."

PAGE 96.

Malone has " strange shapes" for "*straying* shapes," but he did not detect the previous error of *strangeness* for " strains."

PAGE 100.

The note on " Take pains; be perfect," &c., belongs to Act I. Scene II. : the same remark applies to the two preceding notes on pp. 400, 401; but that division has been accidentally omitted in its right place. The division, Act II. Scene I., ought to precede the note on p. 404.

PAGE 107.

Theobald supposed that Bottom was to sing the ballad of his dream after his death on the stage, and Steevens terms it a happy emendation; but his own notion, that Bottom might mean that he would sing it at Thisbe's death, turns out to be the correct one.

PAGE 120.

" Bollen" occurs in Chaucer, Compl. of the Bl. Knight, and Tyrwhitt derives it from *Bolge*, of which, he says, it is the part. pa. It may be doubted whether Bolstrum, a bolster, which we meet with in Beowulf, had not its origin in the A. S. word signifying to swell.

PAGE 122.

Of this we have proof in Act V. Scene I. of this play, on the entrance of Launcelot; but elsewhere we sometimes find it printed *hoa*.

PAGE 127.

Nevertheless, "safest haste" may allude to the danger Rosalind would incur by remaining.

PAGE 130.

This emendation, and the note upon it, as we discover in a subsequent scene (Act III. Scene IV.), is founded upon a mistake: " sat," or " sate," seems perfectly right.

PAGE 132.

This quotation should have been " Not seen him *since*," both here and immediately afterwards.

PAGE 143.

It does not follow that this emendation, regarding Warwickshire ale, was necessarily obtained from some better manuscript, in as much as the corrector of the folio, 1632, might have heard the old actor of the part of Sly repeat the true text.

PAGE 148.

See also a note in vol. viii. 475, where it is stated that Shakespeare seems to allude to Drayton and his little volume called " Amours," in sonnet xxi., which begins,—

> "So is it not with me, as with that muse
> Stirr'd by a painted beauty to his verse," &c.

This may have formed another ground of difference between Shakespeare and Drayton. The whole collection of sonnets is headed " Amours;" but on the title-page that word only comes second : we quote it exactly, with the imprint, as we copied it many years since :—" Ideas Mirrour. Amovrs in Qvatorzains. Che serve e tace assai domanda. At London, Printed by James Roberts, for Nicholås Linge. Anno. 1594." 4to.

PAGE 153.

It might be doubted whether "haled" is not to be taken as *hauled;* but still the true word may have been *handled.*

PAGE 167.

Yet if Helena were right in what she says, " Sir, I have seen you in the Court of France," he was not an absolute "stranger" to her. Most likely she only means it as a sort of introduction, to warrant her in addressing him.

PAGE 175.

It is easy to see how this remarkable blunder originated : both the speeches of Sir Toby and Sir Andrew (as amended) end with "song," and the eye of the compositor glanced from one to the other, and omitted the last, with its introductory words.

PAGE 180.

On reconsideration we are inclined to think that the old reading, "drew in that," may be right.

PAGE 190.

Unless we suppose Hermione to mean "there, while you weep yourself, leave the infant crying." This, however, seems a very forced construction, to which we are not at all driven.

PAGE 193.

In fact, the expression, " charm your tongues," wants no illustration from any other author than Shakespeare himself, who uses it in " Henry VI. Part III.," Act V. Scene V. : in " The Taming of the Shrew," Act IV. Scene II., he has " charm your chattering tongue," &c.

PAGE 200.

Farther reflection, on the proposed change of " conversion " into " diversion," induces us to give preference to the former, as well as to the ordinary punctuation. It is, however, not to be disputed that the corrector of the folio, 1632, may be right in his construction ; but we do not consider him so decidedly right as to warrant, in this place, the desertion of the usual text. The next emendation is possibly in the same predicament : the introduction of a mark of interrogation certainly makes the passage read with more spirit.

PAGE 202.

A note ought to have been made applicable to a line on p. 30 of " King John :" it has been common to print it thus :—

> " You equal potents, firy-kindled spirits ;"

but the emendator of the folio, 1632, informs us that it ought to run :—

" You equal *potent, fire-ykindled* spirits."

PAGE 203.

Johnson says that "sightless" is here used for *unsightly :* not so the old corrector; nor have the commentators pointed out any other similar application of " sightless."

PAGE 215.

Scene III. ought to have been placed before the emendation in the line, " And furbish new," &c. A note, applicable to a passage on p. 133, should have been added : Aumerle says,—

" Farewell : and for my heart disdained that my tongue
Should counterfeit oppression of such grief," &c.

The measure of the first of these lines is restored by printing *disdain'd*, and omitting *that*. On p. 35, the two hemistichs, " Where lies he ?" and " At Ely house," are completed by *now* added to the King's interrogatory, and by *my liege* subjoined to Bushy's answer. The faintness of the ink in the correction of the folio, 1632, occasioned the omission.

PAGE 217.

The lines as quoted from a manuscript (note 7, p. 143) do not support the change of " as thoughts " to " *our* thoughts," but the last cannot possibly be wrong.

PAGE 219.

Scene III. ought to have preceded the note upon the epithet *despoiling*, for " despised."

PAGE 226.

It should have been mentioned that the old corrector puts *for*, instead of "sir," in the line beginning " Now, sir, the sound," &c.

PAGE 227.

It has been omitted to be stated that there is a change of punctuation on p. 216, which makes it appear that Bolingbroke declares that he will incontinent, or with all speed, visit the Holy Land; and consistently with this emendation we find him, at the opening of " Henry IV. Part II.," ordering immediate preparations. The passage, just before the closing couplet of " Henry IV. Part I.," is made to run thus in the corrected folio, 1632 :—

" Come, mourn with me for that I do lament,
And put on sullen black. Incontinent
I'll make a voyage to the Holy Land,
To wash this blood off from my guilty hand."

PAGE 231.

When it is said, that the old corrector of the folio, 1632, was indebted for the emendation of *Lord* either to the quarto, 1598, or to his own sagacity, it ought to have been added, as in some other places, that he possibly derived it from some source, independent of the quarto, 1598, such, for instance, as having heard the passage properly delivered on the stage.

PAGE 235.

A small, but interesting emendation, on p. 287, escaped notice, which may be mentioned here: it is *welling* for "swelling," when Mortimer tells his weeping wife,

> "That pretty Welsh,
> Which thou pour'st down from these swelling heavens,
> I am too perfect in."

Steevens maintained that "swelling heavens" meant Lady Mortimer's "two prominent lips," while Douce rightly argued that her eyes were intended, and that they were swollen with tears. The poet's word was, doubtless, *welling*, the compositor having preceded it by *s* by mistake. To *well* is to issue as from a spring; and Lady Mortimer's tears *welled* from her blue eyes: we must in future read,—

> "Which thou pour'st down from these *welling* heavens."

PAGE 247.

In vol. vi. p. 312 of "Notes and Queries," an emendation of the closing couplet of Henry's speech on sleep is proposed by Mr. Cornish: for "happy low, lie down," he proposes to read "happy *lowly* clown." The change, we may remark, is needless, the sense being very evident, and the expression not at all improved: the King by "happy low" means all the humble classes of the community, and does not confine himself to mere country clowns. Just before, he has expressly mentioned "the wet sea-boy," and he would hardly fly off, without the slightest introduction, to such a discordant object as a lowly clown. The corrector of the folio, 1632, makes no alteration in the received text.

PAGE 250.

It ought here to have been stated, that in the quarto, 1600, the word is *win*, so spelt.

PAGE 255.

For "see also vol. p. 161," read "see also *this* vol. p. 161."

PAGE 264.

For "Julius-Cæsar on bright Cassiope," read "*or* bright Cassiope."

PAGE 268.

It ought to have been mentioned that the regulation of the verse, near the close of the Master Gunner's second speech, is materially altered in the folio, 1632, by the insertion of the words *on my post* after "I can stay no longer." The lines are thus rendered quite regular. On p. 44, an emendation makes blind Mortimer refer to his long imprisonment "in a *cage* of care," meaning the Tower, instead of "in an age of care," which are the words in the folios.

PAGE 292.

See this vol. p. 358; but, perhaps, it is hardly as certain there as here, that "courage" ought hereafter to be printed *carriage*. A third instance is pointed out in a subsequent play (p. 498), but still it is not decisive.

PAGE 295.

How English and foreign soldiers were distinguished, as regards dress, at that time, on the stage, is not explained any where that we remember. It is not stated that Edward, Richard, and Hastings had any English soldiers with them.

Page 297.

The line, "They that stabb'd Cæsar shed no blood at all," is from the older play which Shakespeare used, but there is no trace in it of the two lines which follow.

Page 298.

Except that "a boding" is printed as one word: it has also *undigest* for "indigest," but they were, in fact, the same.

Page 319.

This blunder of printing *way* for "sway," with the pronoun "his" before it, occurs in a couplet at the end of "Henry IV. Part I.," where, in the folios, we read,—

"Rebellion in this land shall lose his *way*,"

instead of "lose his sway."

Page 326.

The words, "And of an earthy *coldness*," ought not to be followed by a mark of interrogation: it is not a question, but an observation.

Page 332.

It stands "that breath fame *follows*," &c., in Malone's Shakespeare, by Boswell, vol. viii. p. 271. In the quarto, 1609, it is properly printed "fame blows."

Page 334.

At the same time, "pass the difficulties," in the sense of go through the difficulties, is very intelligible, and may be right.

Page 352.

It should have been stated that although physic of old was sometimes spelt physique, the most usual orthography of the word at that time was *physicke*. Even this mode of spelling might account for the corruption, and *emperickqutique* is mere nonsense.

Page 356.

When referring to the misprinting of *bisson* on p. 173, we ought to have added that in the folios it is spelt *beesome* in one place, as it is *bosome* in the other.

Page 361.

The note applicable to p. 245 ought to have been preceded by "Scene VII.," which was accidentally omitted.

Page 370.

In the note on p. 334, for the words, "the latter change is, however, by any means required," read "the latter change is, however, *not* by any means required."

Page 373.

There is a mistake in reference to the date when Titus Andronicus was "printed:" the word "printed" ought to have been *acted*. We know of no impression older than that of 1600, in the library of the Earl of Ellesmere; but Langbaine tells us that it originally came out in 1594, and we find it entered in the Stationers' Register on 6th February, 1593, which looks like a memorandum just anterior to publication. Henslowe inserts a play, which he calls "Titus *and* Andronicus," under the date of 23

Jan., 1593: it was then a new play, and it may very likely have been the piece entered at Stationers' Hall only a fortnight afterwards.

PAGE 379.

Correctly speaking, something more is required than the alteration of a single letter, in as much as to make "unbruised" *unbusied*, not only the *r* is to be struck out, but the place of the *i* is to be changed.

PAGE 380.

The blood had begun to mantle in Juliet's cheeks, and the Nurse anticipated that the moment afterwards they would be scarlet at the news she had just communicated.

PAGE 382.

The letters would scarcely be too few, if we suppose (as was frequently the case, though not here in the margin of the folio, 1632) that *enemies* was spelt *ennemyes*. We can also imagine that the compositor may have been puzzled by the word "eyes," which immediately followed *ennemyes*.

PAGE 383.

It is not unlikely that the corrector of the folio, 1632, did not know Edwards's poem, although he might be sure that the lines he underscored were a quotation.

PAGE 394.

When it is said that "to load our purposes" is very like nonsense, compared with the expression "to load our *purses*," it ought to have been admitted that some meaning may be gathered from the passage by a forced construction, which supposes that the Poet and Painter came to have their designs loaded.

PAGE 411.

But for this emendation of *Lay* for "Let," we should have thought that the alteration might have been only that of a letter, viz.—

> "*Set* your highness'
> Command upon me,"

Set would have answered the purpose nearly as well as *Lay*: it is a mere trifle, but "Let" can hardly be right.

PAGE 413.

With reference to the amended word *bleaded* for "bladed," Spelman, in his *Glossarium*, p. 83, tells us: *Certè apud priscos Saxones (a quibus latè per Europam vox diffunditur)* blada, *seu* blæda, *omnem fructum significat, etiam arborum et vitis:* he also gives *seges* and *frumentum* as other meanings of the word. Jamieson, in his Etym. Dict., under *Bled*, speculates that in the expression, "Of his blude bled," *bled* is to be understood as sprung of his blood, from A. S. *blaed*, fruit.

PAGE 414.

An objection to *ripened*, instead of "opened," may be, that Malcolm is representing these "particulars of vice" in him as already at maturity.

PAGE 416.

The old corrector writes "*may* of life" without a capital, and we feel assured that the blunder was caused by the confusion, common with the old printer, between *m* and *w*. We have had many instances of it.

In the repetition of the line,—
"Cleanse the stuff'd bosom of that perilous *grief,*"
"that" is accidentally misprinted *the.*

PAGE 426.

Still the emendation of *purse* for " prize " is liable to the objection that " prize," or price, in the sense of *purse,* affords a consistent meaning.

PAGE 432.

The word *Finis* marks " the conclusion of the piece;" of course, as it was abridged probably for performance, with the omission of all the portions struck through with a pen.

PAGE 437.

In "Notes and Queries," vol. vi. p. 6, is a suggestion by Mr. Singer for reading the commencement of this quotation as follows :—

" Let him fly far,
Not in this land shall he remain uncaught,
Unfound," &c.

According to this conjectural change, " despatch" would hardly refer to Edgar, so much as to the Duke, whose speedy arrival was expected.

PAGE 438.

We have not been able to find in Stow, or in any other authority, a notice of Finsbury Pinfold, but we need scarcely doubt of its existence in Shakespeare's time.

PAGE 440.

But for the sake of the verse, which would be continued redundant, we might read, with even a smaller alteration of the old text,—

" Which are to France the spies and specula*tors.*"

We are by no means satisfied with " spectators," recommended in the margin of the folio, 1632.

PAGE 441.

As the sentence ends at " flattered," the words " when known," which we have added in our comment, are supposed to be understood.

PAGE 443.

If *delires* had been a word in use in Shakespeare's age, it would on all accounts appear preferable to " distress :" *delires* might easily have been misprinted " desires," and it would most accurately express the state of King Lear's mind.

PAGE 449.

Todd, in his edit. of Johnson's Dict., derives the verb "to wheedle" from the A. S., which he says means *seducere,* " to entice by soft words;" but the earliest instance he cites of its use is from Butler's " Hudibras." Richardson gives *wœdlian,* A. S., to cajole, to coax, as the etymology.

PAGE 462.

It is very possible that Richard Burbadge, the original Othello, cast himself on the ground in the agony of his despair and remorse; but not at all likely that he would be guilty of the needless brutality of dragging Desdemona by the hair, as described in a ballad written, it should seem, shortly before the Civil Wars. Eyllierdt Swanston, as he spelt his own name, was a distinguished actor, who, certainly at one time, between 1619 and 1642, had the part of Othello; and it is not unlikely that he, in order to give greater effect to the scene, before a degenerate audience, introduced more coarseness and violence than was ever displayed by his great predecessor.

PAGE 467.

We might have guessed that *dumbe*, or *dumb'd*, was a misprint for *drown'd;* but the words of Alexas could not have been drowned, unless they had been first spoken : he says that what he " would have spoke " was " *boastfully* dumb'd " by the neighing of the horse.

PAGE 469.

The expression, " well deserv'd of rashness," may, perhaps, be understood in the same sense as " well deserv'd *for* rashness."

PAGE 475.

Still it may be fit to hesitate before *miseries* for " measures " is introduced into the text.

PAGE 487.

Shakespeare does not elsewhere use the word *vauntage*, but " vaunting ;" and on p. 401 we have already seen " make your vaunting true," in the same way as here we have " make good your *vauntage*."

PAGE 489.

At the same time the meaning may certainly be, that they gamble with their infirmities, staking them against the gold that is paid to them.

PAGE 497.

Mr. Halliwell has thought this emendation worthy of a separate and clever tract (London, 1852), in which he has inserted various passages where Shakespeare resorted to a similar mode of expression. The more our great and original poet has done so elsewhere, the less likely is he to have done so here; but if some of Mr. Halliwell's quotations are apposite, which we admit them to be, others are opposite, as most people will perceive them to be. Mrs. Cowden Clarke's admirable " Concordance " will furnish them all, so that it is not necessary to quote them; and we freely acknowledge Mr. Halliwell's ingenuity in sometimes applying to his purpose what in no way makes in his favour: it is one thing to represent a prostitute as the mother of her painting, and another to say that painting is the mother of the prostitute : so it is one thing to represent a young fop as the father of his garments, and another to make the garments the father of the young fop. This is a distinction to which Mr. Halliwell has, perhaps, hardly sufficiently attended.

THE END.

GILBERT & RIVINGTON, Printers, St. John's Square, London.

1.

Enter Talb̃. Bard. Pystoll Nim .

2.

Ey

3.

Going

4.

God

5.

in a

6.

ſtraĩnes, *ngo*

7.

Sing in your ſweet Lullaby, *now*

8.

wall

9.

(aſide)

10.

Exit.
dead bodie

11.

(apart) *ouer*

12.

cxu

13.

Enter Ghoſt. armed as before

14.

And crooke the pregnant Hindges of the knee,
Where thrift may follow faining . Doſt thou heare?[2]

F. G. NETHERCLIFT, FAC-SIMILE LITH: 17, MILL ST., HANOVER SQ.

AN INQUIRY

INTO THE

GENUINENESS OF THE MANUSCRIPT CORRECTIONS

IN

MR. J. PAYNE COLLIER'S

ANNOTATED SHAKSPERE, FOLIO, 1632;

AND OF CERTAIN SHAKSPERIAN DOCUMENTS
LIKEWISE PUBLISHED BY MR. COLLIER.

BY

N. E. S. A. HAMILTON.

LONDON:
RICHARD BENTLEY, NEW BURLINGTON STREET,
Publisher in Ordinary to Her Majesty.
MDCCCLX.

LONDON: PRINTED BY W. CLOWES AND SONS, STAMFORD STREET.

FACSIMILES.

PREFACE.

THE following pages are meant to redeem the pledge given to the public in *The Times* of July 2, 1859, in which a more complete examination was promised into the genuineness of numerous modern alterations in Shakspere's text, than was possible in the columns of a newspaper. The matter, I believe, has a great importance, greater than is even suspected as yet. It is really this—whether we shall retain our National Poet's works in a form approaching perfection, or miserably corrupted.

The last century saw Shakspere's text pretty nearly established. Malone, Steevens, and others, succeeded in presenting it, if not in complete purity, still as accurately as it was read by men who knew Shakspere, lived with, and survived him. The "old folios" and quartos had yielded up their readings, and the doubtful province of

B

conjectural emendation alone remained for the most ambitious editor.

But the year 1849 saw a great change. The entirely new element of *manuscript authority* was introduced; and under cover of this, alterations innumerable were made in the text of the Poet. If these corrections rested on a valid basis, a more signal benefit to literature had seldom been conferred; but if doubtful or spurious, then the wrong done to the cause of letters was at least as great.

The greatness and glory, however, of the discovery were well kept before the public. The few competent Shaksperian critics who dissented and raised doubts, were put to silence as frivolous or envious, and the "Old Corrector" seemed destined to become one of those

> "dead but sceptred sovereigns, who still rule
> Our spirits from their urns."

Unfortunately, those who impugned the genuineness of these alterations did so on grounds which, however scholar-like, could hardly be conclusive; whether, for instance, such and such words were in use, or bore a certain signification,

in Shakspere's time; while others, again, con-
tented themselves with urging the improbability
of the corrections having been copied from the
prompt-books, or in exposing the absurdity
involved in the idea of a man's taking a folio to
the pit of a theatre, and correcting it on his
knee. Such criticism, while it might raise doubts,
could never turn them into certainties against
the corrections. That question could only be
settled by the genuineness or otherwise of the
corrections themselves. Were they really of the
middle of the seventeenth century, or were they
skilful imitations of a *much more recent* date?
And this could only be ascertained by a critical
examination of the handwriting of the annotations,
conducted by those well used to such inquiries.

It needs not be said that no examination of the
kind was undertaken until quite recently. The
"annotated folio," it is true, was *seen* a few times
in public, that is to say, thrice at the evening
meetings of the Society of Antiquaries, and once at
a meeting of the Shakspere Society ;* but, wonder-

---

* See Mr. Collier's Affidavit, p. 15. As early as 1853 Mr. Charles
Knight pointed out, in a temperate but forcible manner, the propriety of having the " Folio " " deposited in the custody of some

ful as it may seem, notwithstanding the fierceness
of controversy to which they gave rise, no one appears to have thought of submitting the marginal
corrections to a strict palæographic examination,
or of postponing the discussion of their *intrinsic
merits* to the more important and preliminary
inquiry as to the *genuineness* of their character.
The book shortly passed into the hands of a
late noble duke, the controversy lost the interest
of novelty, and the general impression of the
public, both at home and abroad, seemed to be
that something very wonderful, after all, had
been made out, and that Shakspere, as well as
everything else now-a-days, had been "improved."

And not only Shakspere. The latter half at least
of the present volume is devoted to the discussion of
the genuineness of certain "documents," bearing
more or less on the history of the Poet and the
literature of his day. The importance of these
documents is even greater than that of the "corrections." They profess to be originals; and both
from the facts they contain themselves, and the

---

public body, who will allow access, under proper regulations,
for a full and free inspection of its contents."—*Old Lamps or
New*, p. lix. Pity it is that such a course was not adopted.

light they throw on others, would be invaluable,
if authentic. Unfortunately, their importance is
much diminished by their undoubtedly spurious
nature. While it is grievous to see lessened the
scanty number of facts referring to Shakspere's
external history, that very circumstance, that we
know so little about him, renders it the more in-
cumbent upon us to be rigorous and accurate in
what we do accept concerning him. The manuscripts and papers I refer to are fully described
further on. The authenticity of several of them
has never even been questioned till now. They
have gradually filtered into our literature, and are
the cause of an ever-spreading dissemination of
error. That this should be arrested, however painful the discovery or process may prove, I think
must be desired by every friend to Letters.

This, therefore, is the ground that I take up. I
do not meddle with the *intrinsic* and purely literary
part of the question at all. I do not discuss the
date or the use of certain words. I merely examine,
on *external* grounds, the authenticity of the handwriting. While this method is a great deal more
conclusive, it is the first time it has been applied

in this discussion. If the following pages be found *dry* and technical, it is inevitable from the very nature of the inquiry. As a sense of its importance kept me up, I hope and believe a similar feeling will animate my reader. It certainly *is* no trifling matter, whether the works of one of the greatest minds that ever adorned humanity be correct or corrupt—entire or mutilated : it *is not* unimportant that in our time, and before our eyes, we should see their grandeur defaced and their purity stained. And not easily forgiven should we be, if, seeing this, we strove not to hinder it.

It merely remains to add, that throughout this self-imposed task, the notion of a personal controversy or dispute has never guided my pen. This disclaimer, while it is superfluous for my friends, I wish pointedly directed to the notice of the public. My aim has been to remove from English literature a discreditable imposition. If one or more are aggrieved by the results I have come to, I regret but cannot help it. While I ask for no favour, I can show no partiality. My inquiries have no recommendation but their honesty and

candour ; and if they receive from competent judges
the verdict of Truth, I shall be amply rewarded,
and feel that my labour has not been in vain.

Before concluding this prefatory statement, I
have one duty left which fills me with unmixed
pleasure—the offer of my grateful thanks to those
to whom I am indebted for the opportunity of
bringing this Inquiry before the public, or who have
assisted me with their aid and counsel in a labour
of no slight difficulty and of grave responsibility.

To his Grace the Duke of Devonshire, for the
courtesy with which he placed the volume under
discussion at my disposal, and permitted me not
only to publish fac-similes of the pen and pencil
corrections on its margins, but also to make
several important physical experiments in regard
to them.

To the Right Hon. the Earl of Ellesmere, for
the liberality with which he gave me access to
his Library, and permitted me to make use of his
unique copy of the first folio edition of Shakspere's
Plays, as well as to examine and have fac-similes
taken of the disputed Shakspere documents at
Bridgewater House.

To the Governors of Dulwich College, for the ready access I obtained to their valuable muniments ; and especially to the Rev. Alfred Carver, the Master of the College, for the friendly aid which converted what might possibly be esteemed an ordinary civility paid to literary men, into a lasting personal obligation to myself.

To my friends and colleagues in the British Museum, whom I gladly avail myself of the opportunity of thanking for the unvarying kindness I have ever received from them in my literary pursuits. Above all to Sir Frederic Madden, the chief of the Department to which I have the honour to belong, and to whom an acknowledgment is due, beyond the mere expression of my thanks for the invaluable assistance of his observations and experience. It is, indeed, a simple act of honesty and justice alike to him and to the world, that I should state the origin of the discovery presumed to be established in the following pages. The ' Annotated Shakspere ' was placed in Sir F. Madden's hands by the Duke of Devonshire. His independent examination of it completely convinced him of the fictitious character of the writing of the marginal corrections; and this conclusion he freely communicated to inquirers interested in knowing it. The correspondence between certain pencil-marks in the margins with corrections in ink, first noticed by myself, led him to a closer examination of the volume, and to the detection of numerous marks of punctuation and entire words in pencil, and in a modern character, in connection with the pretended older writing in ink; instances of which were subsequently found to occur on nearly every page. It was, moreover, owing in a great measure to Sir Frederic Madden's encouragement that I was originally induced to bestow that attention to the subject, which has developed the inquiry to its present results.

To the numerous other friends who have aided and assisted me in my labour, I have to tender the general expression of a gratitude as lively as it is sincere.

N. E. S. A. HAMILTON.

Department of Manuscripts, British Museum,
January, 1860.

C

AN INQUIRY, ETC.

In the year 1852, Mr. John Payne Collier published a volume of "*Notes and Emendations*" of the Plays of Shakspere, derived from a corrected copy of the second edition, in folio, 1632, the history of which he gives in the Introduction to the volume, as follows :—

"In the spring of 1849 I happened to be in the shop of the late Mr. Rodd, of Great Newport Street, at the time when a package of books arrived from the country ; my impression is that it came from Bedfordshire, but I am not at all certain upon a point which I looked upon as a matter of no importance. He opened the parcel in my presence, as he had often done before in the course of my thirty or forty years' acquaintance with him, and looking at the backs and title-pages of several volumes, I saw that they were chiefly works of little interest to me. Two folios, however, attracted my attention, one of them gilt on the sides, and the other in rough calf :

the first was an excellent copy of Florio's " New World
of Words," 1611, with the name of Henry Osborn
(whom I mistook at the moment for his celebrated
namesake, Francis) upon the first leaf ; and the other a
copy of the second folio of Shakespeare's Plays, much
cropped, the covers old and greasy, and, as I saw at a
glance on opening them, imperfect at the beginning and
end. Concluding hastily that the latter would complete
another poor copy of the second folio, which I had
bought of the same bookseller, and which I had had
for some years in my possession, and wanting the former
for my use, I bought them both,—the Florio for twelve,
and the Shakespeare for thirty shillings.*

" As it turned out, I at first repented my bargain as
regarded the Shakespeare, because when I took it home
it appeared that two leaves which I wanted were unfit

---

* " I paid the money for them at the time. Mr. Wilkinson, of
Wellington Street, one of Mr. Rodd's executors, has several
times obligingly afforded me the opportunity of inspecting
Mr. Rodd's account-books, in order, if possible, to trace from
whence the package came, but without success. Mr. Rodd does
not appear to have kept any stock-book, showing how and when
volumes came into his hands, and the entries in his day-book
and ledger are not regular nor particular. His latest memorandum, on 19th April, only a short time before his sudden death,
records the sale of "three books," without specifying their
titles, or giving the name of the purchaser. His memory was
very faithful, and to that, doubtless, he often trusted. I am
confident that the parcel was from the country ; but any inquiries regarding sales there, could hardly be expected to be
satisfactorily answered."—[C.]

for my purpose, not merely by being too short, but damaged and defaced : thus disappointed, I threw it by, and did not see it again until I made a selection of books I would take with me on quitting London. In the mean time, finding that I could not readily remedy the deficiencies in my other copy of the folio 1632, I had parted with it ; and when I removed into the country with my family, in the spring of 1850, in order that I might not be without some copy of the second folio, for the purpose of reference, I took with me that which is the foundation of the present work.

"It was while putting my books together for removal that I first observed some marks in the margin of this folio ; but it was subsequently placed upon an upper shelf, and I did not take it down until I had occasion to consult it. It then struck me that Thomas Perkins, whose name, with the addition of "his Booke," was upon the cover, might be the old actor who had performed in Marlowe's "Jew of Malta," on its revival shortly before 1633. At this time I fancied that the binding was of about that date, and that the volume might have been his ; but in the first place I found that his name was Richard Perkins, and in the next I became satisfied that the rough calf was not the original binding. Still, Thomas Perkins might have been a descendant of Richard ; and this circumstance, and others, induced me to examine the volume more particularly. I then discovered, to my surprise, that there was hardly a page which did not present, in a handwriting of the time, some emendation in the pointing or in the text, while on most of them they were frequent, and on many numerous.

" Of course I now submitted the folio to a most careful scrutiny ; and as it occupied a considerable time to complete the inspection, how much more must it have consumed to make the alterations ? The ink was of various shades, differing sometimes on the same page, and I was once disposed to think that two distinct hands had been employed upon them : this notion I have since abandoned ; and I am now decidedly of opinion that the same writing prevails from beginning to end, but that the amendments must have been introduced from time to time, during perhaps the course of several years. The changes in punctuation alone, always made with nicety and patience, must have required a long period, considering their number : the other alterations, sometimes most minute, extending even to turned letters, and typographical trifles of that kind, from their very nature, could not have been introduced with rapidity, while many of the errata must have severely tasked the industry of the old corrector."*

---

* " It ought to be mentioned, in reference to the question of the authority of the emendations, that some of them are upon erasures, as if the corrector had either altered his mind as to particular changes, or had obliterated something that had been written before—possibly by some person not so well informed as himself."—[C.] I may remark, in reference to this note by Mr. Collier, that the erasures and obliterations are very numerous, and both they and the corrections *are by one and the same hand throughout the volume.* Of those partially obliterated I have given some examples in the collations from Hamlet.—[H.]

The veracity of this account Mr. Collier reiterated in an Affidavit sworn to in the Court of Queen's Bench in 1856.

"AFFIDAVIT.

" IN THE QUEEN'S BENCH.

" I, John Payne Collier, of Maidenhead, in the County of Berks, Esquire, Barrister-at-Law, and one of the Vice-Presidents of the Society of Antiquaries of London, make oath and say :—

" 1. That in the years 1841, 1842, 1843, and 1844, I prepared for the press, and published an edition of the works of Shakespeare : that in the spring of the year 1849 I purchased of the late Mr. Rodd, of Great Newport Street, bookseller, a copy of the second folio of Shakespeare's Plays, bearing the date of, and which I believe was published in the year 1632 ; and which copy contained, when I so purchased it, a great number of manuscript notes, purporting to be corrections, alterations, and emendations of the original text, made, as I believe, by the same person, and at a period nearly contemporaneous with the publication of the said folio itself.

" 2. In order that any person interested in the subject might have an opportunity of inspecting the said book, and examining the said manuscript notes, I exhibited the said book to and before the Shakespeare Society, and three times before the Society of Antiquaries, and it was inspected and examined by a great number of persons. The said folio has, since the publication of the

volume next hereinafter mentioned, become, and is now,
the property of his Grace the Duke of Devonshire.

" 3. In the year 1852 I published a volume containing
some, but not all, of the said manuscript corrections,
alterations, and emendations, and a fac-simile of a part
of one page of the said folio, with the manuscript emendations thereon ; and an 'Introduction,' setting forth
the circumstances under which I became possessed of the
said folio edition, and which induced me to publish the
said volume.

" 4. In the year 1853 I published a second edition of
the said Notes and Emendations, containing, besides the
said ' Introduction,' a statement, in the form of a Preface to the last-mentioned edition, of facts and circumstances which occurred subsequently to the publication of
my first edition of the said ' Notes and Emendations '—
a copy of which second edition is now shown to me and
marked with the letter A.   And I say, that all the statements in the said Preface and Introduction, relative to
the discovery, contents, and authenticity of the said folio
copy, and the manuscript notes, corrections, alterations,
and emendations thereof are true ; and that every note,
correction, alteration, and emendation in each of the said
two editions, and every word, figure, and sign therein,
purporting or professing to be a note, correction, alteration, or emendation of the text, is, to the best of my
knowledge and belief, a true and accurate copy of the
original manuscript in the said folio copy of 1632;
and that I have not, in either of the said editions,
to the best of my knowledge and belief, inserted a single

word, stop, sign, note, correction, alteration, or emendation of the said original text of Shakespeare, which is not a faithful copy of the said original manuscript,* and which I do not believe to have been written, as aforesaid, not long after the publication of the said folio copy of the year 1632," &c.   [The remainder of the affidavit refers to the *Coleridge Lectures*, published by Mr. Collier in 1856.—H.]

"(Signed)   JOHN PAYNE COLLIER."

" Sworn at the Judge's Chambers,
  Rolls Garden, Chancery Lane,
  this 8th day of January, 1856,
  before me, Wm. Clark, Com-
  missioner, &c."

---

* Apparently Mr. Collier has since altered his opinion as to the respect due to the " said original manuscript," to the extent of occasionally *correcting the Corrector*. Of this, I quote the following singular instance from the play of Coriolanus. In his first edition of the MS. corrections, Mr. Collier announced the important and truly interesting fact, that in Act iii. sc. 2, of that drama a whole line had been left out in all preceding editions, and was now restored through the help and accuracy of the invaluable Corrector. Here is the passage—Volumnia says :—

> "Pray be counsailed,
> I have a heart as little apt as yours
> *To brook control without the use of anger,*
> But yet a braine, that leads my use of anger
> To better vantage."

The third line in italics being the new discovery ; and it remained as above accurately copied from the corrected folio for six years, viz. in the *Notes and Emendations*, 1852 and 1853, in

D

On the 2nd and 16th of July, 1859, I laid
before the public, through the medium of *The
Times*, a summary of facts to prove that the *Notes*

---

the privately distributed fac-similes, in the one-volume Shakspere, and in the Complete List, 1856.

Strange as it may seem, in the last edition, of 1858, Mr. Collier
has substituted " reproof " instead of " control " *as the emendation of the " Old Corrector,"* and this, notwithstanding the scrupulous accuracy with which he would lead us to suppose he
invariably followed his venerable and *manuscript* authority.

I contrast Mr. Collier's first version of the line printed in
Notes and Emendations, 1852, with his account of it in his last
edition of Shakspere's Works, 1858.

Notes and Emendations, Coriolanus, Act iii. sc. 2, J. P.
Collier, 1852.

" (P. 212) On the same evidence, we here recover a line,
which is certainly wanting in the old copies, since they leave
the sense incomplete without it. It is in Volumnia's entreaty
to her son —

> " Pray be counsell'd.
> I have a heart as little apt as yours,
> But yet a brain, that leads my use of anger
> To better vantage."

" To what was Volumnia's heart 'as little apt' as that of
Coriolanus? The insertion of a missing line (the absence of
which has not hitherto been suspected) enables us to give the
answer :—

> " I have a heart as little apt as yours
> *To brook control without the use of anger,*
> But yet a brain, that leads my use of anger
> To better vantage."

" The line in italics is written in a blank space, and a mark
made to where it ought to come in. The compositor was,

and Emendations contained in Mr. Collier's annotated copy of Shakspere's Plays, 1632, were
in reality modern fabrications of our own day,
although written in a feigned hand intended to
represent the style of writing common in the
seventeenth century; and that the statement of
Mr. Collier that the volume, "from the first page
to the last, contained notes and emendations in a
handwriting *not much later* than the time when
it came from the press," was incorrect.

Several months have elapsed since these facts
were published, but no satisfactory attempt has
been made by Mr. Collier to refute them, or to

---

doubtless, misled by the recurrence of the same words at the
ends of the two lines, and carelessly omitted the first. From
whence, if not from some independent authority, whether heard
or read, was this addition to the text derived?"

Shakespeare's Works, ed. Collier, 1858.—Coriolanus, Act iii. sc. 2.

"Pray be counsell'd.

I have a heart as little apt as yours
To brook reproof without the use of anger,[1]
But yet a brain," &c.

[1] ("To BROOK REPROOF WITHOUT THE USE OF ANGER.")

"This line is from the corr. fo. 1632, and is clearly wanted,
since the sense is incomplete without it. The eye of the old
compositor was doubtless misled by the words 'use of anger' at
the end of two following lines. Those who are unwilling to
insert the line are obliged to suppose Volumnia to speak elliptically; but until the discovery of the corr. fo. 1632, nobody suspected even an ellipsis. We rejoice in the discovery."

remove the stigma of forgery from his "folio."
I must therefore suppose that he is aware of
the impossibility of doing this, and that he is
now at length convinced of the spurious character
of the corrections ; the more so as he has proffered
no explanation of the circumstances by which he
may have been himself originally deceived, or of
the reasons which induced him to accept and publish as genuine emendations of the seventeenth
century, what in fact it requires no rigorous
examination to discover are worthless counterfeits
of the nineteenth.

As in denouncing the character of the corrections, the only objects I had in view were the
vindication of truth, and the desire to warn the
world of the spurious nature of the "emendations"
by which they had been too readily deceived,
I would gladly have left the more minute features
of the case to be developed by the recognised
guardians of Shaksperian literature.   Above all,
I naturally supposed that Mr. Collier (who alone
has introduced into his editions of Shakspere the
corrections derived from this Folio, and to whom
the discovery of the Folio itself is due,) would have
hastened to lend his aid to sift to the bottom the
particular evidences against the credibility of the
volume, which I had brought so distinctly and

prominently to his notice   In this, however, I was mistaken.   So far from assisting in an inquiry, in the results of which he, more than any living man, must have been deeply interested, he has only broken silence to give utterance to a desire, rather petulantly expressed, and under the circumstances impossible to regard, that he and his Folio might be let alone, and considered privileged from further scrutiny.

I may have regretted this expression of feeling on Mr. Collier's part as an error of judgment ; but I feel less concern in regard to the line of con-duct adopted by some other and later champions of the Folio, who, in their need of argument forgetting the duty of courtesy, seem to have imagined that the civilities of ordinary life do not extend to literary disputants.   However, on all sides, "fuller and further particulars" were called for ; and as, in the course of my inquiries, I had made the extraordinary discovery that not only in reference to the corrected folio of 1632, but in other instances in which Mr. Collier had published "facts" and "documents," relative to Shakspere, these facts and documents turned out on investigation to be likewise spurious, I have resolved to lay before the world all the results of my investigations, leaving any inferences deducible from them to the judgment of the individual reader.

On the 18th of May, 1859, Sir Frederic Madden, Keeper of the MSS. in the British Museum, attaching at that time, as I understand,* no great importance to the various doubts respecting the authenticity of the corrections in the annotated folio 1632, which from time to time had reached him, but having a great desire to inspect the volume for his own information, wrote to the Duke of Devonshire begging the loan of it for a short time, for the satisfaction of himself, Dr. Bodenstedt of Munich, and a few friends.

On the 26th, the book was placed in Sir Frederic's hands, and, at his request, a discretionary power was shortly after granted him by the noble owner, to exhibit the book to a more

---

* In a memorandum communicated to me by Sir Frederic Madden, he states—" I had a great wish to see the volume, after this second avowal of doubts expressed by Mr. Staunton and Dr. Ingleby, but my mind was so free from any bias, that I did not entertain the least suspicion of forgery, and in September, 1858, I eagerly availed myself of the opportunity afforded me by Mr. Collier (who had sent me a copy of the Hamlet of 1603, lithographed at the expense of the late Duke of Devonshire), to express to him *my wish to see the annotated folio,* but not having the honour to be acquainted with the now Duke of Devonshire, I asked Mr. Collier *if he could manage to gain me access to the volume.* To this request Mr. Collier never made any reply."

extended literary circle, in consequence of the numerous applications to see it, which had been sent in, as soon as it was known to be at the Museum. In accordance with this permission, a considerable number of persons interested in the matter did so examine the volume during the period it remained in the Museum, and no application to see it was declined, except during the brief period in which Mr. Frederick Netherclift was occupied in making from it the fac-similes prefixed to this volume.

Such were the circumstances under which the "Folio" came into the Museum; and it was not at first imagined that anything would result from its examination tending to invalidate the manuscript corrections on its margins.

A short inspection, however, of the ink corrections in the text and on the margins was sufficient to give rise to the gravest doubts as to their genuineness. In the first place, although evidently written by one hand throughout, yet the forms of the letters, especially of the capital letters, presented strange anomalies. On one page would be found a word or letter, characteristic rather of the writing of the 16th than of the 17th century; while in close juxtaposition, and sometimes on the same page, the identical letter or word would occur, bearing every appearance of having been written within the present century.

Then, again, many of the letters, although executed with evident care, were seen to be rather exaggerations of the style of the 17th century than examples of the style itself; while instances occur in almost every page, in which the operator, apparently not satisfied with his first attempt at an antique appearance, has subsequently retouched his work, in a manner greatly calculated to arouse suspicion, as the ink employed for the purpose is not uncommonly of a different shade, and the stroke of a different thickness from that in which the word or letter was originally written. Thus, on mere palæographic grounds, the authenticity of the corrections appeared questionable. But it was further discovered, and this, too, before the whole weight of these *literal* objections had been fully considered, that a series of partially-obliterated pencil corrections was visible throughout the margins of the Folio, *corresponding* with the corrections made in ink, and sometimes *actually underlying* them. The appearances presented by these pencil corrections merit exact description.

In the first place, they have none of the feigned antiquity about them of the ink corrections, either in form or spelling. They are in a bold, clear

handwriting of the present day, are evidently executed by one hand throughout, and have been placed
on the margins to direct the alterations afterwards
made in ink, and with which they invariably correspond. They are of various kinds. Amongst the
most common are crosses and ticks, apparently
used to call attention to words or letters requiring
correction. Some of them may, of course, be the
"crosses, ticks, or lines" which Mr. Collier acknow-
ledges he introduced himself; but as cases occur
where such pencil-ticks actually *underlie* corrections in ink, some of them at least must have been
placed on the margins before the "Old Corrector"
commenced his labours. The ordinary signs in
use to indicate *corrigenda* for the press are of
common occurrence in the margins, while the
corrections indicated thereby are made in the text
in the *quasi*-antique ink. Again, whole syllables
or words occur in pencil, partially rubbed out,
but still legible, and in which the character of the
modern handwriting is plainly visible; while in
near neighbourhood to them, the same syllable or
word is repeated in ink in the antique hand. In
some cases the ink word and the pencil word
occupy the same space in the margin, and are
written one upon the other; and in these instances
the naked eye readily detects the fact that the

E

pencil has been written prior to the ink.   As,
however, the most positive evidence on this head
was desirable, its decision forming one of the
turning-points of the inquiry, Mr. Maskelyne, by
permission of the Duke of Devonshire, undertook
to institute a series of microscopic and chemical
experiments on the subject.   The importance of
the point lay in this : that since the pencil alterations were undeniably recent (as a glance at the
fac-similes prefixed to this volume will show),
it followed that the ink corrections, if written
subsequently to these, must be modern likewise, however carefully an antique appearance
might have been simulated for them.   Mr. Maskelyne's experiments set this point completely at
rest, and at the same time elicited several particulars as to the chemical composition and spurious
character of the ink itself.   It was, in fact, proved
by scientific demonstration, that the antique-looking alterations in ink were not so venerable as
the modern pencilling ; that they were in reality
modern fabrications, although executed with such
dexterity as to deceive on a cursory glance even
an experienced eye. So important are these experiments, that I re-state them here in Mr. Maskelyne's
own words.   He says :—

" This simple test (the microscope) of the character of

these emendations, I brought to bear on them, and with the following results :—

"Firstly, as to any question that might be raised concerning the presence of the pencil-marks asserted to be so plentifully distributed down the margin, the answer is, they are there. The microscope reveals the particles of plumbago in the hollows of the paper, and in no case that I have yet examined does it fail to bring this fact forward into incontrovertible reality. Secondly, the ink presents a rather singular aspect under the microscope. Its appearance in many cases on, rather than in, the paper, suggested the idea of its being a water-colour paint rather than an ink; it has a remarkable lustre, and the distribution of particles of colouring matter in it seems unlike that in inks, ancient or modern, that I have yet examined.

"This view is somewhat confirmed by a taste, unlike the styptic taste of ordinary inks, which it imparts to the tongue, and by its substance evidently yielding to the action of damp. But on this point, as on another, to which attention will presently be drawn, it was not possible to arrive at a satisfactory conclusion in the absence of the Duke of Devonshire's permission to make a few experiments on the volume.

"His Grace visited the Museum yesterday, and was good enough to give me his consent to this. The result has been that the suspicions previously entertained regarding the ink were confirmed.

"It proves to be a paint removable, with the exception of a slight stain, by mere water, while, on the other hand, its colouring matter resists the action of chymical agents which rapidly change inks, ancient or modern, whose colour is due to iron. In some places, indeed, this paint seems to have become mixed, accidentally or otherwise, with ordinary ink, but its prevailing character is that of a paint formed perhaps of sepia, or of sepia mixed with a little Indian ink. This, however, is of secondary importance in comparison with the other point which has been alluded to. This point involves, indeed, the most important question that has arisen, and concerns the relative dates of the modern-looking pencil-marks and the old emendations of the text which are in ink. The pencil-marks are of different kinds. Some are *d's*, indicative of the deletion of stops or letters in the text, and to which alterations in ink, I believe, invariably respond. Others, again, belong to the various modes at present in use to indicate corrigenda for the press. Some may, perhaps, be the " crosses, ticks, or lines;" which Mr. Collier introduced himself. But there are others again in which whole syllables or words in pencil are not so effectually rubbed out as not to be still traceable and legible, and even the character of the handwriting discernible, while in near neighbourhood to them the same syllable or word is repeated in the paint-like ink before described. The pencil is in a modern-looking hand, the ink in a quaint antique-looking writing. In several cases, however, the ink word and the pencil word occupy the same ground in the margin, and are one over the other. The question that arises in these cases, of whether these two

writings are both ancient or both modern, or one ancient and the other modern, is a question for the antiquary or palæographist. The question of whether the
pencil is antecedent or subsequent to the ink is resolvable into a physical inquiry as to whether the ink overlies the pencil, or the pencil is superposed upon the ink.
The answer to this question is as follows :—

" I have nowhere been able to detect the pencil-marks
clearly overlying the ink, though in several places the
pencil stops abruptly at the ink, and in some seems to
be just traceable through its translucent substance,
while lacking there the generally metallic lustre of the
plumbago. But the question is set at rest by the removal by water of the ink in instances where the ink
and the pencil intersected each other. The first case I
chose for this was a *u* in *Richard II.*, p. 36. A pencil
tick crossed the *u*, intersecting each limb of that letter.
The pencil was barely visible through the first stroke,
and not at all visible under the second stroke of the *u*.
On damping off the ink in the first stroke, however, the
pencil-mark became much plainer than before, and even
when as much of the inkstain as possible was removed,
the pencil still runs through the ink line in unbroken
even continuity. Had the pencil been superposed on
the ink, it must have lain superficially upon its lustrous
surface, and have been removed in the washing. We
must, I think, be led by this to the inference that the
pencil underlies the ink—that is to say, was antecedent
to it in its date ; while, also, it is evident that the "old
commentator" had done his best to rub out the pencil

writing before he introduced its ink substitute."—*Times,
July* 16, 1859.

It seemed incomprehensible how these various
and irrefragable proofs of forgery could have
escaped Mr. Collier, considering the "most careful scrutiny" to which he states he committed
the folio.   But I now began to compare the
marginal corrections with Mr. Collier's Complete
List of them, published in 1856, and with very
singular results.   The *List* professes to give, in a
tabular form, the "entire body" of the emendations.   Nothing can be more clear than this.   It
is not only indicated by the title,* but asserted
in the strongest manner in the preface, as the
following extracts show.   Mr. Collier says :—

"These *Notes and Emendations* are before the world in
two separate editions; but as the whole of the alterations and corrections were not included, and as those
interested in such matters are anxious to see *the entire
body* in the shortest form, I have appended them to the
present volume in one column, while in the opposite
column I have placed the old, or the received text.
Thus a comparison may be made in an instant, as to the

---

* "A List of *every* MS. Note and Emendation in Mr. Collier's
copy of Shakespeare's Works, folio, 1632." (Appended to Coleridge's "Lectures on Shakespeare and Milton," ed. J. P. Collier.
London, 1856. Octavo.)

particular letters, syllables, words, or lines in which changes have been introduced."—*Preface to Coleridge's Seven Lectures,* p. 60.

Again, Mr. Collier says :—

" I have gone over *every* emendation in the folio 1632, recently, for the purpose of the last portion of my present volume ; and I am more and more convinced, that the great majority of the corrections were made, not from better manuscripts, still less from unknown printed copies of the plays, but from the recitation of old actors while the performance was proceeding."—*Preface to Seven Lectures,* p. 73.

And still further he adds :—

" Fault has been found with me, in other quarters, for not having at once seen everything in the way of MS. note in my folio 1632. I have often gone over the thousands of marks of all kinds in its margins ; but I will take this opportunity of pointing out two emendations of considerable importance, which, happening not to be in the margins, and being written with very pale ink, escaped my eye until some time after the appearance of my second edition, as well as of the one-volume Shakespeare. For the purpose of the later portion of my present work *I have recently re-examined every line and letter of the folio 1632, and I can safely assert that no other sin of omission on my part can be discovered.*"— *Preface to Seven Lectures,* p. 79.

And yet in spite of these reiterated assertions,

the *literal* fact is, that the Complete List does
not contain one *half* of the corrections, many of
the most significant being among those omitted.
That it may be seen this is no exaggerated statement, I subjoin a collation of the entire play
of *Hamlet*; the collations faithfully representing
the "emendations on the margins of the folio."
Such of them as Mr. Collier has inserted in his
Complete List being indicated by a capital C. I
have likewise, through the kind assistance of my
friend Mr. Howard Staunton, indicated the original sources, from which the principal corrections
have been derived. Many of my readers will
probably be surprised to see the number of them
which can be thus identified, and the small claims
to originality which the "Old Corrector" actually
possesses. Some of the readings not given in the
List are certainly to be met with in the one-
volume edition of Shakspere, published by Mr.
Collier in 1853; but the text of that volume,
although purporting to be "regulated by the
recently discovered folio of 1632," sometimes
follows the printed folios of the first and second
edition, sometimes the MS. corrections in the
folio 1632, and sometimes the quartos, and is
therefore, as a book of reference, utterly worthless, it being impossible for the reader to dis-

criminate from what source any given reading is derived. "The truth is," says a sound Shaksperian critic (Grant White), " that the text of the pernicious one-volume edition, professing to be ' regulated by the recently discovered folio of 1632, containing early MS. emendations,' is composed from the readings of the first folio, the uncorrected second folio, Mr. Collier's corrected second folio, and all other previous and subsequent editions; the changes from the first folio, or from any other edition, being in no way indicated. To the well-read, critical student of the text, the book is useless; to him who has but commenced his studies, indescribably confusing; to the general reader, a delusion and a snare. With all respect due from me to a gentleman who was a man when my father was a boy, I must say that the publication of that volume was a crime against the republic of letters."

F

" EMENDATIONS " IN THE PLAY OF " HAMLET," FROM THE
" CORRECTED FOLIO " 1632.

[The left-hand column contains the printed text of the folio 1632. The words, letters, &c.ˌ to the right placed between crotchets, refer to words, letters, &c. in italic, and placed between crotchets in the text, and exhibit the manuscript " *corrections* " found on the margins of Mr· J. P. Collier's " Corrected Folio," 1632 , such of these as have been published by Mr. Collier in the Complete List being distinguished by the letter C. The foot-notes show the sources from which the manuscript corrections to which they refer were originally derived.]

	Printed Text of Folio 1632.	*MS. Corrections.*
p. 272, col. 1.	ᴧ Enter BERNARDO *and* FRANCISCO.	[Act I.]
	BAR. Tis n[o]w struck twelve[,] get thee to bedᴧ Francisco.	[e][1] C.[:] [,]
	[MAR.] What, ha's this thing appear'd againe	[HOR.][2]
	Wh[o]n yond same Starreᴧ thats Westward	[e][3] [,]
col. 2.	The Bell then [beating] one	[tolling] this in a modern hand in ink, but afterwards partially obliterated.
	*Enter the Ghost*ᴧ.	[*armed*]
	BAR. Lookeᴧ it not like the King?	[s][4]
	HOR. Most like [:]	[ ] with pencil cross in margin.
	Whenᴧ th' Ambitious Norway combatted	[he][5] C.
	He smotᴧ the sledded Pollax	[e] with pencil mark.
	MAR. Thus twice before, and just at this [*same*] houre	[dead][6] afterwards part. oblit.
	HOR. In what particular [*thoughte to*] worke	[it] partially obliterated.

[1] Steevens.   [2] 4to 1604.   [3] 4tos and fol. 1623.   [4] 4tos.   [5] 4tos.   [6] Fol. 1623, and 1st and 2nd 4tos.

Printed Text of Folio 1632.	*MS. Corrections.*

MAR. Good now_ʌ sit downe, and tell me_ʌ he that   [, , ,] with pencil mark.
     knowes_ʌ

Do's not divide the Sunday from the weeke[,]   [?]¹ with pencil mark.

p. 273, Which he stood seiz'd [*o*]n,   [ı]
col. 1. Was gagea by our King : which had re[*turn'd*]   [maind] partially obliterated.

And carriage of the Article [*de*]sign'd   [then ?] afterwards oblit.

Shark'd up a List of L[*and*]lesse Resolutes   [aw]² C.

     ʌ *Enter Ghost againe.*   Entire line of Stage direction obliterated.

Which happily foreknow[*ing*] may avoyd   [ledge] partially obliterated.

Speake of it. Stay, and speake. Stop it, Marcellus.   [*Cock crowes*]³

The Cocke that is the Trumpet to the [*day*]   [morne]⁴ C.

Some saye[*s*], that ever 'gainst that season   crossed out.

And_ʌ (they say) no spirit can walke abroad   [then]⁵

No Faiery ta[*l*]kes   crossed out. C.

p. 273,[But looke, the Morne in Russet Mantle clad,   These two lines crossed through.
col. 2. Walkes o're the Dew of yon high Easterne hill.]   A pencil × in margin.

     OPHELIA, *Lords Attendants.* ʌ   [*King takes his seate*]

To [*beare*] our hearts in griefe   [bathe] C.

⌜With one Auspicious, and one Dropping eye,

With mirth in Funerall, & with Dirge in Marriage,   These lines crossed out.

In equall Scale weighing Delight and Dole]

Colleagued with the dreame of _ʌhis Advantage [;]   [t] partially obliterated. [,]

Of these dilated Articles allow [:]_ʌ   [.] [Give them]

p. 274,   [beg Laertes
col. 1.   *to*   Crossed out.

What wouldst thou have Laertes ?]

---

¹ Jennens. ² 4tos. ³ 4to 1604 ⁴ 4to 1605. ⁵ 4tos & folio 1623.

Printed Text of Folio 1632.	MS. Corrections.

HAM. A little more then kin, and lesse then kind.   [(*Aside*)][1]

QUEE. Good Hamlet cast thy nightl [*y*] colour off   [ike] C.

Doe not for ever, with thy v[*e*]yled lids   [a][2]

[It shewes a will most incorrect to Heaven

to   Crossed out.

As any the most vulgar thing to sence.]

[———————— Fye, tis a fault to heaven

to   Crossed out.

This must be so.]

p. 274, col. 2. And the King's Rou[*c*]e[,] the heavens, &c.   [s][3] [dele]

Manet HAMLET_Δ   [*Trumpets*]

Seeme[*s*] to me all the uses of this world   [dele][4]

Fye on't? Oh fie, [*fie*,] tis an unweeded Garden   [dele][5]

That he might not [*beteene*] the windes of heaven   [let e'en][6] but afterwards partially obliterated.

Visit her face too roughly. Heaven and Earth[,]   [!][7]

Must I remember [:] why_Λ she would hang on him   [?] [,][8]

Enter HORATIO, [BARNARD,] *and* MARCELLUS   [BARNARDO][9]

HAM. I am glad to see you [*well*]   [dele] C.

p. 275. col. 1. HAM. I would not [*have*] your enemy say so   [heare][10] C.

To [*take*] it truster of your owne report   [make][11]

HOR. Indeed my Lord, it [*followeth*] hard upon   [followed][12]

I [*should*] not looke upon his like againe   [shall][13]

HAM. Saw? Who?   [Saw whom.][14]

Within his Truncheon's length; whilst they [*bestill'd*] [bechill'd] C.

---

[1] Warburton.   [2] 4to 1604.   [3] 4tos.   [4] 4tos.   [5] 4tos.   [6] Theobald.   [7] Variorum.   [8] Variorum [9] 4to 1604.   [10] 4tos.   [11] 4tos & fol. 1623.   [12] 4tos & fol. 1623.   [13] 4to & fol. 1623.   [14] Johnson.

Printed Text of Folio 1632.	*MS. Corrections.*
It lifted up it⌃ head	[s][1]
HOR. As I doe live my [*honourable*] Lord 'tis true	[honoured][2]
col. 2. HAM. His Beard was [*grisly*]	[grisled][3] C.
Let it be [*trebble*] in your silence still	[tenable][4] C.
[*Froward*,] not permanent ; sweet not lasting	[Forward][5]
The suppliance of a minute ;⌃ No more	[but]
In thewes and Bulke : but as [*his*] Temple waxes	[the][6]
The vertue of his [*feare*:] but you must feare	[will][7] C.
p. 276. The [*sanctity*] and health of the whole state	[safety][8] C.
col. 1. As he in his peculiar [*sect*] and [*force*]	[act][9] C. [place][9] C.
If with [*two*] credent eare	[too][10]
And keepe [*within*] the reare of your affection	[you in][11] C.
The Canker galls the [*infant*] of the Spring	[infants][12]
Be wary th[*a*]n	[e]
As watchm[*e*]n to my heart	[a]
And re[*a*]kes not	[c]
Bear't that th' [*opposed*] may beware of thee	[opposer][13]
Are of a most select and generous [*cheff*] in that	[choise][14] C.
[*A*] borrowing duls, &c.	[And][15]
col. 2. [*Roaming*] it thus, you'l tender me a foole	[Running] C.
OPHE. And hath given countenance to⌃ his speech	[it in] afterwards part. oblit.
My Lord, with all the⌃ vowes of heaven	[holy][16]
You must not take for fire. [*For*] this time, Daughter	[From][17]
Not of the [*eye*,] &c.	[dye][18] C.
Breathing like sanctified and pious [*bonds*]	[bawds][19] C.
[Doe not beleeve his vowes ; for they are Broakers	
to	Crossed out
The better to beguile. This is for all]	

[1] 3rd 4to. [2] 4tos & fol. 1623. [3] 4tos. [4] 4tos. [5] 4tos. [6] Hanmer. [7] 4tos. [8] 4to 1604.
[9] 4tos. [10] 4tos and fol. 1623. [11] 4tos. [12] 4to, 1604, & fol. 1623. [13] 3rd 4to. [14] Steevens.
[15] 4tos & fol. 1623. [16] 4to 1604. [17] 4tos. [18] 4tos. [19] Theobald.

Printed Text of Folio 1632.	MS. Corrections.

Have you so [*slander*] any [*moment*] leisure

Look too't, I charge you ;ᴀ come your way

ᴧ
Enter HAMLET, HORATIO, MARCELLUS.

p. 277, What does this meane my Lord ?ᴀ
col. 1.
And as he dr[*e*]ines his draughts

*Enter Ghost.*ᴀ

Be thy e[*v*]ents wicked or charitable

King, Father, Royall Dane : Oh [*oh*] answer me

With thoughts beyond [*thee ; reaches*]

Or to the dreadfull S[*onnet*] of the Cliffe

Which might deprive your Soveraignty of Reason
                This line had been corrected into
[Which might deprive you of your Soveraign Reason]
        but the corr. afterwards partially obliterated.

HOR. Be rul'd, you shall not goe.ᴀ

col. 2.   HOR. Heavenᴀ will direct it.

And for the day confin'd to [*fast in*] fi[*er*]s

To eares of Flesh and Blood ; list Hamleᴀ, [*oh*] list

With witchraft of his wit[*s*], [*ha*]th traiterous gifts

p. 278, But soft, methinks I scent the Morning[*s*] Ayre
col. 1.
Of Life, of Crowne, and Queene at once [*dispatcht*]

Cut off even in the blossom[*es*]

And shall I couple hell ? Oh fie : hold [*my*] heart

MS. Corrections:

[squander] C. [moments][1] C.

[so now] C.

[Sc. 4][2]

[*Chambers*] Chambers also in pencil on outer margin.

[a][3]

[*armed as before*] [armed] oc-
curs also in pencil on the   [outer margin.

[nt][4] C.

[dele][5]

[the reaches][6]

[ummit][7] C.

[*They struggle*]

[s]

[lasting][8] C. [re] but after-
wards obliterated.
Opposite to the correction *lasting*
is the following pencil note :
"See LLL 133. This is in
Smith's . . . . 1765."

[t] [dele]

[dele] [wi][9] C.

[dele][10]

[despoiled] C.

[dele]

[dele] C.

---

[1] 3rd 4to. [2] Rowe. [3] 4to 1604. [4] 4tos. [5] 4tos. [6] 4tos. [7] Rowe. [8] Heath. [9] 4tos & var. [10] 4tos.

Printed Text of Folio 1632.	MS. Corrections.
Unmixt with baser matter ; [*yes*,] yes, by heaven :	[dele][1]
Oh most pernicious_∧ woman	[and perfidious] C. *perfidious* in pencil can be seen underneath the ink.
At least I'm sure it may be so in Denmarke_∧	[wri . .][2] afterwards oblit.
Enter HORATIO *and* MARCELLUS.	[*lower down*]
MAR. How ist't my Noble Lord ?	[*Enter*]
col. 2. HOR. These are but wilde & hur[*l*]ing words, my Lord.	[t]
HOR. What is't my Lord ?_∧ we will	[‖Mar.]
GHO. Sweare.	[*vnder*]
GHO. Sweare.	[*vnder*]
Than [*are*] dream't of in [*our*] Philosophy	The two *italic* words have been crossed through, the crossing afterwards obliterated.
With Armes encombred thus, or th[*u*]s, head shake	[i][3]
Or such ambiguous giving_∧ out to note	[s][4]
p. 279, GHOST. Sweare.	[*vnder*]
col. 1. With all my love_∧ commend me to you	[I doe][5] pencil underneath.
Actus Secundus ∧	[*Scœna prima*]
POLON. You shall doe marvel_∧s wisely.	[ou][6] also in pencil.
A[*nd*] thus, I know his father and his friends,	[s][7] C. *s* also in pencil.
[REYNOLD. As gaming my Lord *to*	These lines crossed through in ink, also marked in pencil.
Reynol. I my Lord, I would know that]	
[*Polon.*] Marry Sir, here's my drift	[dele]
col. 2 [*Reynol.*] At closes in the consequence, I marry,	[Pol.][8]

---

[1] 4to 1604.   [2] Rowe.   [3] 4tos, 1603, 1604-5.   [4] Warburton.   [5] 4tos & fol. 1623.   [6] 4to 1605.
[8] 4tos.   [9] 4to 1604 & fol. 1623.

Printed Text of Folio 1632.   *MS. Corrections.*

The[*ir*] falling out at Tennis   [re][1]

I saw him enter such a house of sa[*i*]le ;   [dele][2]

Your bait of falshood, takes this Ca[*p*]e of truth ; [rp][3] C.

He rais'd a sigh, so [*hid*]eous and profound   [pit][4]

p. 280, I am sorry that with better [*sp*]eed and judgement   [h][5] C
col. 1.
         I had not quoted him. I fear[*e*] he did but trifle   [d][6]

col. 2. My Newes shall be the [*Newes*] to that great Feast   [fruite][7] C.

         KING. Thyselfe doe grace to them, and bring them in.ₐ [*Exit Pol.*][8]

         KING. Well, we shall sift him. Welcomeₐ good [my][9]
             Friends

With an intreaty herein further shewneₐ   [(*letter*)]

Meane time we thanke you for your well-[*look't*]   [took][10]

         POL. This businesse is [*very*] well ended   [dele][11] C.

My Liege and Mad[*r*]m   [a][12]

p. 281, That we find out [*the*] the cause of this effect   [dele][13]
col. 1.
         Hath given me this : now gather, and surmiseₐ   [*reades*][14]

Thats an ill Phrase, a vil[*d*]e Phrase, beautified   [dele][15]

         is a vil[*d*]e   [dele][16]

And more above hath his soliciting ₐ,   [s][17]

Or my deere Majesty youₐ Queene   [r][18]

Into the Madnesse where[*o*]n   [i][19]

And [*all*|*we*] waile for   [2. 1.] C.

He walkes fo[*u*]r[*e*] houres together   [dele][20] C.

p. 281,   QUEE. So he [*has*] indeed   [doth][21]
col. 2.
         [*And*] keepe a Farme and Carters   [But][22] C.

One man pick'd out of [*two*] thousand   [ten][23] C.

---

[1] 4to 1604 & fol. 1623.   [2] 4to 1604.   [3] 4tos.   [4] 4tos & fol. 1623.   [5] 4tos.   [6] 4tos.
[7] 4tos.   [8] Rowe.   [9] 4tos.   [10] 4tos & fol. 1623.   [11] 4tos.   [12] 4tos & fol. 1623.   [13] 4tos.
[14] Variorum.   [15] 4tos.   [16] 4tos.   [17] 4tos   [18] 4tos & fol. 1623.   [19] 4tos.   [20] Hanmer.   [21] 4tos.
[22] 4tos.   [23] 4tos.

Printed Text of Folio 1632.   MS. Corrections.

HAM. [For if the Sun breed Magots in a dead
      dogge, being a good kissing Carrion]   [dele]
[POL. I have my Lord.]   [dele]
[HAM. Let her not walke i'th Sunne:
      Conception is a blessing, but not
      as your daughter may conceive.   [dele]
      Friend, looke too't.]
POL. How say you by that &c.ᴧ   [to himselfe]¹
      What doe you read my Lord?ᴧ   [to him]
POL. I meane the matter you [meane]   [reade]²
      purging thicke Amber, [or] Plum-Tree   [and]³
      l[o]cke of Wit,   [a]⁴
How pregnant (sometimes) his Replies areᴧ   [to himselfe]¹
My honorable Lord, I will most humbly   [him]

p. 282,   HAM.ᴧ These tedious old fooles   [Enter]
col. 1.   POLON. You goe to seeke my Lord Hamlet, there
he isᴧ   [Exit]⁵
      HAM. Nor the soales of her Shooeᴧ?   [s]
      [GUILD. Faith, her privates, we]   [dele]
      HAM. [In the secret parts of Fortune? Oh, most
true: she is a Strumpet.]   [dele]
      [GUILD. Which dreames indeed are ambition
                    to   [dele]
Heroes the Beggers Shadowes:]

col. 2.   prevent your discovery [of] your secrecy   [and]⁶
              it goes so heav[en]ly with my disposition [i] C.⁷
              this brave ore-hanging,ᴧ this Majesticall [firmamᵗ]⁸ C.
              golden fireᴧ; why, it appear[ed]   [s] [s]⁹
              though by your smiling,ᴧ   [Smile, R.]

---

¹ These *asides* are as old as Rowe.   ² 4tos.   ³ 4tos.   ⁴ 4tos.   ⁵ Rowe.   ⁶ 4tos.   ⁷ 4tos.
                                                        4tos.   ⁹ Var.

Printed Text of Folio 1632.	*MS. Corrections.*
[HAM. How chances it they travaile	
to	[dele]
if Philosophy could find it out.]	

p. 283, HAM. Then ca[*n*] each Actor on his Asse. [me][1] C.

col. 1. [POLO. The best Actors in the world, either for Tragedy [dele]

        to   *Pans* has however been made

    the [*Pans*] Chanson will shew you more] into [pious][2] C.

col. 2.   twas Cau[*t*]ary   [i][3]

      there was no [*Sallets*] in the lines   [Salt][4] C.

      but it was (as I [*re*]ceived it   [con] but partially obliterated.

One [*chiefe*] speech in it   [dele][5] C.

Blacke as h[*e*] purpose   [is][6]

When h[*is*] lay   [e][7]

p. 284, And lik'[*d*] a Newtrall   [e][8]

col. 1. Breake all the Spokes and F[*a*]llies   [e][9]

About her lanke and all ore-te[*a*]med Loynes [e][10]

And passion‸ [*in*] the Gods   [ate][11] C. [dele] C.

    according totheir des[*a*]rt   [e][12]

You are welcome to Elsonower‸   [*Exeunt Players*]

col. 2. Make mad the guilty, and apal[*e*] the free [l][13]

Like John a-d‸eames   [r][14]

To make [*Opp*]ression bitter   [transg] C.

Wh[*o*]? What an Asse am I? [*I sure*] [y][15] C. [dele]

Ile [*r*]ent him to the quicke   [t][16]

Wherein Ile catch the Conscience of the King

         ‸   [*Act* 3. *Scene* 1.]

p. 285, ROSIN. Niggard of question, but [*of*] our demands [to][17] C.

col. 1.

---

[1] 4tos. [2] 4to 1604-5. [3] 4tos & fol. 1623. [4] Pope. [5] 4tos. [6] 4tos & fol. 1623. [7] 4tos and fol. 1623. [8] 4tos & fol. 1623. [9] Variorum. [10] Variorum. [11] Hanmer & Capell read *passioned.* 4tos & fol. 1623. [12] 4to 1604. [13] Rowe. [14] 4tos and fol. 1623. [15] 4tos. [16] 4tos. [17] Made up from Hanmer and Warburton.

Printed Text of Folio 1632.   *MS. Corrections.*

[We are oft too blame in this

to

Oh heavy burthen !]

[dele] The passage has nevertheless been corrected, in two
instances.

And pious Action, we doe [*surge*] ore   [suger][1]

KING. Oh 'tis true.‸   [*Aside*][2]

[POL.] I heare him comming   [dele]

Enter HAMLET.‸

    [*Ophelia behinde reading*]

The Oppressors wrong, the [*poore*] mans Contumely   [proud][3] C.

col. 2. The pangs of [*disprized*] Love

first made into [misprized,]
the *m* afterwards obliterated,
and the word made [dis-
pized][4] C.

Who would [*these*] Fardles beare   [dele][5]

from whose Bo‸rne   [u][6]

OPH. Good my Lord, ‸   [*forward*]

OPHE. Could beauty my lord, have

better Comerce then [*your*] honesty ?   [with][7] C.

[For vertue cannot so inocculate our

old stocke, but we shall rellish of it.]   [dele]

With more offences at my b[*e*]cke   [a] C.

play the Foole no [*way*]   [where][8] C.

p. 286, [Goe, farewell, Or if thou wilt needs marry
col. 1.

to

    [dele]

the rest shall keepe as they are]

notwithstanding corrected as follows :—

HAM. I have heard of your [*pratl*]ing   [paint][9]

God has given you one [*p*]ace   [f]C.[10]

4tos.   [2] Pope.   [3] 4tos.   [4] 4tos 1604-5.   [5] 4tos.   [6] Pope.   [7] 4tos.   [8] 4tos.   [9] Theobald ; 4tos.
paintings.   [10] 4tos.

Printed Text of Folio 1632.	*MS. Corrections.*
[*gidge*]	[gigge][1] C.
all but one shall_ᴧ	[live][2] C.
That unmatch'd for[*tun*]e	[m][3]
Whereon his brain[*es*]	[brain] C.
ᴧ	[*Scene* 2]
Enter HAMLET & *two or three of the Players.*	[*unreadie*]
too much_ᴧ your hand thus	[with][4] C.
Su[*r*]e the Action to the word	[t][5]
That you ore-st[*o*]p not	[e][6] C.
[*or*] [Nor man]	[dele] [nor man][7] C.
*Exe*_ᴧ*nt Players*	[*u*][8]
HAM. Bid the Players make hast_ᴧ.	[e]
HAM. What hoa, Horatio_ᴧ.	[*Enter* Ho.][9]
As ere my Conv[*s*]er_ᴧation	[dele] [s][10]
[Why should the poore be flatterd	[dele] The line, however,
to	" corrected "
As I doe thee. Something too much of this.]	
And crooke the pregnant Hindges of the Knee	[begging] in pencil
Even with the_ᴧComment of [*my*] soule	[very][11] C. [thy][11] C.
As Vulcans Styth_ᴧ. Give him [*n*]eedful note	[y][12] C. [h][12] C.
And after we will both our judgement_ᴧ joyne	[s][13]
_ᴧ*Enter* KING, QUEENE, POLONIUS, &c.	[*Sennet*]
[*his*] Guard carrying Torches	[a][14]
Get you a place	
ᴧ	[*Enter*]
POLO. Oh ho, doe you marke that ?_ᴧ	[*Goes to O*φ*elia*]

p. 286, col. 2.

p. 287, col. 1.

---

[1] 4tos.   [2] 4tos & fol. 1623.   [3] 4tos & fol. 1632.   [4] 4tos.   [5] 4tos & fol. 1623.   [6] 4tos.   [7] 4tos.
[8] This direction is first found in 4to 1603.   [9] 4to 1604.   [10] 4tos & fol. 1623.   [11] 4tos & fol.
1623.   [12] 4tos.   [13] 4tos & fol. 1623.   [14] Jennens.

Printed Text of Folio 1632.	MS. Corrections.
[HAM. Lady, shall I lye in your Lap	
to	[dele]
HAM. Nothing]	
OPHE. I my Lord‸	[Lie downe neare her]
col. 2. HAM. Let the Divell weare blacke	
for Ile have [a] suite of Sables	[no]
[OPHE. Will they tell us what this shew meant	
to	[dele]
Ile ma‸ke the Play.]	[r][1]
Enter ‸ KING, and his QUEENE.	[Player][2]
Phœbus Car[t]	[r] C.[3]
World have time‸ twelve	[s][4]
p. 288, And as my love is [siz,] my feare is so.	Apparently first corrected into
col. 1.	[fix'd].afterwards obliterated
	and made [siz'd][5] C.
The violence of [o]ther Griefe or joy	[ei][6]
Directly [seasons] him his Enemy	[p . . .s] but obliterated
HAM. If she should breake [it now]	[her vow] C.
col. 2. [HAM. I could interpret betweene you and your love	
to	[dele]
HAM. So you [mis]take husbands]	[must][7]
HAM. Why let the str[u]cken Deere goe weepe	[i][8]
[Would not this Sir, and a Forrest of Feathers	
to	[dele]
HORA. You might have Rim'd]	
Provinciall Roses on my ra[c]'d shoes	[ais][9] C.
[Ham.] Oh good Horatio	[dele]

4tos & fol. 1623.   [2] Pope.   [3] Rowe.   [4] 4tos & fol. 1623.   [5] fol. 1623.   3rd and 4th folios
have fix'd. So Rowe and Pope.   [6] 4tos.   [7] Theobald.   [8] 4to 1603.   [9] Steevens.

Printed Text of Folio 1632.	*MS. Corrections.*
p. 289, So wildly from [*my*] affaire	[the] C.
col. 1. You doe [*freely*] barre the doore of your owne	[surely][1] C.
col. 2. In this little Organe, yet cannot you make it‸	[speake][2] C.
Polon. By th' M[*i*]sse.	[a][3]
Tis now the very witching time of night,‸	[*Exeunt*]
How in my words so[*m*]ever she be shent	[dele][4]
‸	[Scene 3]

Enter King, Rosincross, & Guilderstar.

To keepe those‸ many bodies safe	[verie] C.
[the cease of Majesty	
to	[dele]
Did the King sighe, but with a general grone]	
Fixt on the Som[*ne*]t of the highest Mount	[mi][5]
Are mortiz'd and adjo‸n'd	[i][6]
p. 290, In the corrupted curr[*a*]nts of this world	[e][7]
col. 1. And oft tis seene, the wicked p[*rize*] it selfe	[urse] C.
All may be well.‸	[*Kneeles*]

Enter Hamlet.‸   ‸ [(*behind*) *his sword drawen*]

col. 2. my thoughts remaine below.‸	[*rising*]
S[*o*]ree'nd	[c][8]
Ile [*sile*]nce me [*en'e*] heere	[sco][9] C. [even][9] C.
Withdraw, I heare him comming.‸	[*Exit Pol. behind the arras*]
Ham. Goe, goe, you question with an [*idle*] tongue	[wicked][10] C.
Quee. Nay, then Ile se[*t*] those to you	[nd] C.
You goe not till I set‸ up a glasse	[you][11]

---

[1] 4tos ; *surely but*, variorum.   [2] 4tos.   [3] 4tos.   [4] 4th 4to.   [5] Rowe, &c.   [6] 4tos & fol. 1623.
[7] 4tos.   [8] 4tos & fol. 1623.   [9] Hanmer and Warburton.   [10] 4tos.   [11] 4tos & fol. 1623.

Printed Text of Folio 1632.	*MS. Corrections.*
Pol. What hoa, helpe, helpe, helpe.ᴧ	[*within*]
Pol. Oh I am slaine.　　　*Killes Polonius.*	[*at the backe and then comes forward*]
Quee. As kill[*d*] a King?	[dele][1]
Ham. I Lady, twas my word	[*Seeing Polonius*]
Leave wringing of your hands, peace, sit you downe	[(*to her*)]
p. 291, col. 1. See what a graceᴧ seated on his Brow	[was][2]
N[*o*]w lighted on a	[e][3]
Heere is your husband, like a Mildew'd [*d*]eare	[dele][4]
Blasting his wholesome br[*eath*]	[other][5] C.
Would st[*e*]p from this	[oo] C.
When the compulsive Ard[*u*]r[*e*]	[o][6]
A[*s*] Reason panders Will	[nd][7] C.
Enter Ghostᴧ	[*unarmed*]
That laps't in [*Ti*]me and Passion.	[fu] C.
col. 2. And with [*the*] corporall ayre	[th' in][8] C.
Startᴧ up and standᴧ an end	[s] [s][9]
Looke where he goes even now out at the Portall. *Exit*ᴧ	[*Ghost*][10]
And doe not spred the Compost o[*r*] the Weedes	[n][11]
Thus bad begins, and worse remaines behindᴧ	[*to himself*] but almost oblit.
p. 292, col. 1. And breath of life : I have no life to breathᴧ	[e][12]
ᴧ	[*Exit Queene*]
Exit Hamlet *tugging in* Polonius.	[*IIII Act* 4. *Sc.* 1.][13]
There's matter[*s*]	[dele]
Ore whom his very madnesse, like some O[*a*]re	[dele][14] nearly obliterated.
But we will ship him hence, and this vil[*d*]e deed	[dele][15]

---

[1] 4tos.　[2] 4tos & fol. 1623.　[3] 4tos & fol. 1623.　[4] 4tos & fol. 1623.　[5] 4tos.　[6] Rowe, &c.　[7] 4tos.
[8] 4tos.　[9] 3rd & 4th 4tos.　[10] 4to 1604.　[11] 4tos.　[12] Rowe, &c.　[13] Rowe.　[14] 4tos & fol. 1623.　[15] 4tos.

Printed Text of Folio 1632.	MS. Corrections.

<table>
<tr><td>p. 292,
col. 2.</td><td>Enter ^Λ King.</td><td>[Scene 2.]</td></tr>
</table>

p. 292,
col. 2.

Enter ^King.

Who like not in their judgement_Λ, but their eyes :   [s]

But ne[*ar*]er   [v]¹ C.

HAM.   a certaine convocation

of_Λ wormes are ene at him   [palated] C.

[KING. What dost thou meane by this ?]   [dele]

p. 293,
col. 1.

[HAM. Nothing but to shew you —— gut of a   [dele]

Begger]

HAM. He will stay till ye come _Λ   [*Exeunt*]²

HAM. [I see a Cherube that sees him   [dele]

but,] [*c*]ome   [C]

Payes homage to us; thou maist not coldly se[*t*]   [e]

How ere my h[*a*]p_Λs,   [o] [e]³ C.

[Scene 3.]

[*Enter* FORTINBRAS *with an Army.*

to   [dele]

FOR. Goe safely on.]

[Scene 4 3.]

Enter QUEENE and HORATIO.

col. 2. At his head a [*grass*|-*greene*] Turfe   [2. 1.] C.

Let in the Maid, [*let in*] a Maid, never departed more   [that out]⁴

p. 294,
col. 1.

[*Keep*]es on his wonder, keepes himselfe in cloudes   This has been crossed through, but the margin on which the correction is made has been carefully torn away.*

---

¹ 4tos. ² Variorum. ³ Johnson suggested *hopes*, and that the passage should rhyme; and the folio, 1623, has—*were ne'er begun*. ⁴ 4tos & fol. 1623.

* In the *Complete List* we are told by Mr. Collier that the " corrected " Folio has "*Feeds* for *Keepes ;*" *Feeds* being the reading of the 4tos. Consequently the margin must have been intentionally mutilated *since* 1856, when the *List* was published, in order to get rid of the reading of the 4tos ! Similar instances of recent mutilation occur throughout the " Folio."

Printed Text of Folio 1632.	*MS. Corrections.*
*Enter a Messenger*₄	[*Enter*]
Let them guard the door. What is the matter?	[*in haste*]
Ore-beares your officers[,] the rabble call him [*Lord*]	[:] [King] C.
The Ratifiers & props of every wor[*d*]	Altered but obliterated.
KING. The doores are broke.	[*Sword out*]
Even here betweene the chaste unsmi[*t*]ched brow	[r]¹
[KING. Good Laertes	
to	[dele] but the following correc-
Repast them with my blood]	tions nevertheless made.
Of your deare fathers death, [*if*] writ in yʳ revenge	[is't]² C.
That S₄oop-stake	[w]
KING. Why now? [*what noyse is that?*]	[you speake]
Enter OPHELIA₄.	[*still distraught*]
[Nature is fine in Love	
to	[dele]
After the thing it loves.]	
And on his grave raine[*s*] many a teare	[dele]
No, no, he is dead, go₄e to [*thy*] Death-bed	[n] C. [his] C.
His Beard ₄as white as Snow	[w] C.³
And o[*f*] all Christian Soules, I pray God	[n]⁴
God buy ye. *Exit* OPHELIA₄.	[*dauncing distracted*]
Be you content to lend your pa₄ience	[t]⁵
₄	[*Scene* 3, 4.]
Enter HORATIO, *with an Attendant.*	
SAY. God bless you[*r*] Sir	[dele]⁶
[*Stood*] Challenger on mount of all the Age	[Sole] C.
KING. Laertes you shall₄them	[heare]⁷

p. 294.
col. 2.

p. 295,
col. 1.

col. 2.

¹ 4tos & fol. 1623.   ² 4tos.   ³ 4tos.   ⁴ Johnson.   ⁵ 4tos & fol. 1623.   ⁶ 4tos & fol. 1623.
⁷ 4tos & fol. 1623.

H

Printed Text of Folio 1632.	*MS. Corrections.*
Or is it some abuse? [*Or*] no such thing	[and][1] C.
And for his death no wind of blame	
shall breath_Λ.	[e][2]

p. 296, col. 1.

Had witchcraft in't; he grew [*i*]nto his Seat	[u][3]
And Iemme of all [*our*] Nation	[that][4]
If one could match you [*Sir.*] This report of his	[dele][5]
Did Hamlet so envenom with hi[*s*] Envy	[r]
Your sodaine comming [*over*] to play with him	[o'er][6]
LAER. Wh[*y*] out of this, my Lord	[at][7] C.
A Sword unba[*i*]ted	[dele][8]
Requit_Λ him for your Father	[e][9]
And for that purpose I'll annoi[*o*]t my Sword	[n][10]
So mortall, [*I*] but dip[*t*] a knife in it	[that][11] C. [dele][11] C.
Wee'l make a solemne wager on your co[*mm*]ings	[n n][12] C.

col. 2.

As make your bowts more violent to th[*e*] end	[at][13]
Or like a creature Native, and [*d*]educed	[r] *r* also in pencil at side. C.
Pull'd the poore wretch from her melodious [*b*]y	[la][14] C
	[V. *Act 5, Scene 1.*][15]

               Λ

Enter two Clownes _Λ	[*with Spades & tooles.*]
and an Act hath three branches :	
It is [*an*] Act	[to][16] C.
OTHER. Nay but he_Λre you, Goodman Delver	[a][17]

p. 297, col. 1.

[OTHER. Was he a Gentleman	
to	[dele]
OTHER. Goe to.]	

---

[1] 4tos. [2] Rowe, and all after. [3] 4tos.   In the Complete List *the* is given as the reading: *the* is also the reading of the quartos. [5] 4tos & fol. 1623. [6] 4tos & fol. 1623. [7] 4tos. [8] 4tos. [9] 4tos & fol. 1623. [10] 4tos & fol. 1623. [11] 4tos. [12] 4tos [13] 4tos [14] 4tos. [15] Rowe. [16] 4tos. [17] 4tos & fol. 1623.

Printed Text of Folio 1632.	*MS. Corrections.*
Get thee to [*Yaugan,*] fetch me a	[You']¹
sto[*a*] pe Liquor	[o]²
Sings [and digges.] ˄	[*Exit other Clo.*]³
Clowne sings ˄	[(*Skull*)]
But age, &c.	

col. 2.

Clowne sings ˄	[(*Skull*)]
A Picke-axe, &c.	
HAM. or equivocation will	
[*follow*] us	[undoe]⁴
[How long hast thou been a Grave-maker ?	
to	[dele]
Its no great matter there.]	

p. 298,
col. 1.

[HAM. Why	
to	[dele]
Man and Boy thirty yeeres.]	
A Tanner will last you nine yeere[*s*]	[dele]⁵
Alexander returne[*th*] into dust	[d]
Should patch a Wall, ˄expell the Winter's flaw	[t']⁶
with˄ *Lords attendant*	[*Priest and*]⁷

col. 2.

Foredoe it˄ owne life ; [*t*]was some Estate	[s]⁸ [it]⁸
Couch we a while, and marke,	[*At one side*]
To sing sa[*ge*] Requiem	[d] C.
QUEEN. Sweets, to the sweet farewell ˄	[*Flowers*]
LAER. Oh, t[*er*]r[*i*]ble wooe[*r*]	[dele] [e] C. [dele]⁹ C.

---

¹ Yon *Complete List.*   ² fol. 1623, and subsequent editions read *stoup* or *stoop.*   ³ Rowe.
⁴ 4tos & fol. 1623.   ⁵ 4tos & fol. 1623.   ⁶ 4tos & fol. 1623.   ⁷ *Priest* in all modern editions.
⁸ 4th 4to.   ⁹ 4tos.

Printed Text of Folio 1632.	*MS. Corrections.*
HAM. What is he, whose griefes ᴀ	[*Forward*]
LAER. The Divell take thy soule ᴀ	[*Seize him*][1]
Sir though I am not spleen[*ative*] and rash	[eticke]
Which let thy wisenesse feare. Away thy hand ᴀ	[*Strive*]
Woo't weepe ? woo't fight ? woo't ᴀ teare thy selfe ?	[storme or] C.
p. 299, Ile doo't ᴀ. Dost thou come here to whine	[Ile doo't] C.
col. 1. ᴀ Anon as patient as the female Dove	[QUEENE][2]
The Cat will mew, [*and*] Dog will have his day	[the][3] C.
Strengthen you ᴀ patience in our last nights speech	[r][4] [*Exit*]
Wee'l put the matter to the present push ᴀ	[*To Laertes*]
ᴀ	*Scene* 2.[5]
Enter HAMLET *and* HORATIO.	
[me thought I lay	[dele] corrected however as follows.
to	
HOR. That is most certaine.]	
(And praise [*be*] rashnesse for it) let us [*know*]	[to] oblit. [owne] C.
When our de[*are*] plots do [*paule*]	[epe][6] C. [faile][7] C.
[HAM.] Up from my Cabin.	[dele]
(My [*t*]eares forgetting manners)	[f][8]
No not to stay the grin[*g*]ding of the Axe	[dele][9]
But wilt thou heare, how I did proceed ? ᴀ	[*Giving it*]
The effect[*s*] of what I wrote	[dele][10]
And many such like Ass[*i*]s of great charge	[e][11]
col. 2. Subscrib'd it, gau' ᴀ th' Impression	[e][12]
Was our Sea-fight, and what to this was se[*ment*]	[quell] C.[13]
They are not neere my conscience ; their de[*b*]ate	[fe][14] C.
Tis dangerous when ᴀ baser nature comes	[a]

---

[1] Rowe. [2] 4tos. [3] Theobald. [4] 4tos. [5] Rowe. [6] 4tos. [7] Pope. [8] 4tos & fol. 1623.
[9] 4tos & fol. 1623. [10] 4tos. [11] The suggested quibble of *asses* is Johnson's. [12] 3rd and 4th folios.
[13] 4tos read *sequent*. [14] 4tos.

Printed Text o Folio 1632.	*MS. Corrections.*
HAM. Does it not, think'st th[*ee*]	[ou][1]
Throwne out │his Angle for my proper life	[2] C.
[dost know this waterfly	
to	[dele]
spacious in the possession of dirt.]	
OSR. Swe⌃t Lord, if your [*friend*]ship	[e][2] [lord][2] C.
were at leasure	
He hath on[*e*] twelve for mine	[dele][3]
[*Ile*] gaine nothing but my shame	[I]
[he does well to	
commend it himselfe	[dele]
to	the line however corrected.
the Bubbles are out.]	
there are no tongues else for's [*tongue*]	[turne][4] C.
but thou wouldest not thinke	
how⌃ all heere	[ill is][5] C.
HOR. If your mind dislike any thing, obey⌃	[it][6]
HAM. Give me your pardon, Sir, I've	
done you wrong⌃	[*To Laertes*]
[Was't *Hamlet* wrong'd *Laertes*? Never, *Hamlet*.	
to	[dele]
His Madnesse is poore *Hamlets* enemy]	
And hurt my [*M*]other	[Br][7] C.
LAER. Come one for me⌃	[*Bring foiles*]
KING. Set me the Sto⌃pes of Wine upon that Table	[o][8]
And in the Cup an union shall [*h*]e throw⌃	[b] [ne] but obliterated.
The Cannons to the Heavens, the Heaven⌃ to Earth	[s][9]

p. 300, col. 1.

col. 2.

p. 301, col. 1.

[1] Rowe. [2] 4tos. [3] 4tos. [4] 4tos. [5] 4tos. [6] 4tos. [7] 4tos. [8] 4tos.
[9] 3rd 4to.

Printed Text of Folio 1632.	*MS. Corrections.*
HAM. Ile play this bout first ; set⌄ by a while	[it]¹ C.
Here'[*s*] a Napkin, rub thy browes⌄	[is] C. [my sonne] C.
QU. I will my Lord.⌄	[*She drinkes*]²
KING. Part them ; they are incens'd.⌄	[*Both wounded*]
HOR. They bleed on both sides. How is'[*t*] my Lord.	[it]³
To my⌄ Sprindge, Osricke	[owne]⁴ C.
I am poyson'd.⌄	[*dies*]⁵

p. 301, col. 2.

(*as this fell Sergeant death*	[dele] obliterated.
Is strick't in this Arrest) oh I could tell you⌄	[all] obliterated.
HOR. Never beleeve it.	[*takes the Cup.*]
Let go, by heaven I'le have't.	[*Struggling, Hamlet gets it.*] The word *struggling* afterwards in part obliterated.
Good night [*sweet Prience*]	[be blest] [Finis.]
[Why do's the Drumme come hither	
to	[dele] a line however corrected.
To tell him his command'ment is fulfill'd]	
[*His*] quarry cries on Havocke	[This]⁶ C.

p. 302, cols. 1 & 2.

These two columns crossed through [dele], but nevertheless the following alterations [made.

col. 1. I have some Ri⌄t[*e*]s of memory in this Kingdome	[gh] [dele]⁷
col. 2. Which [*are*] to claime, my vantage doth	[now]⁸ C.
HOR. Of that I shall [*alwayes*] cause to speake	[have also]⁹
But let this s[*ame*] be presently perform'd	[cene] C.
	[While I remaine behind to tell a tale
	That shall hereafter turne the hearers pale.]

---

¹ 4tos. ² Capell. ³ Variorum. ⁴ 4tos. ⁵ All modern editions from Rowe. ⁶ 4tos.
⁷ 4tos. ⁸ 4tos. ⁹ 4tos.

Collation of a page taken from Henry VI. Part II.

Corrected folio, p. 142. Collier, 1856, p. 223, col. 2.

MS. Corrections.

col. 1.
What say ye, Countrimen? will ye [*relent*]
Or let a [*rabble*]
Shake he his weapon at us, and passe by.

[repent] C.
[rebell]
[As he doth passe us let his weapon shake.] partially obliterated.

col. 2.
given [*out*] these arms
Henry hath mony[,] you are strong and [*manly*]
God on our side, [*we*] doubt not [*of*] Victorie
Follow me souldiers wee'l devise a [*meane*]
Was ever king that [*joy'd*] an earthly Throne
[*in*]fortunate
And with a puissant and [*a mighty*] power
Like to a Ship, that having scap'd a Tempest
Is straightway [*claim'd*] and boorded with a Pyrate.
Of gallow-glasses and stout ₄ Kernes
I pray thee, Buckingham, go ₄ and meet him*
Come wife, let's in and learne to [*governe better*]

[up] obliterated.
[;] [crye]
[dele] obliterated.
[thing] obliterated.
[filled] obliterated.
[unfortunate] obliterated.
[united] C.

[calm'd]
[Irish] C.
[thou] C.
[rule againe] obliterated.

---

* In *Complete List*, Mr. Collier incorrectly printed—

I pray thee, Buckingham, then go and meet him.

Mr. Collier will perhaps be able to explain how so small a proportion of the marginal corrections of the " Folio " is recorded in his *List,* in which he informs us he can " safely assert that no sin of omission can be discovered."

I now proceed to examine the only other ground put forward by Mr. Collier in proof of the authority of his "Folio," viz., *that it, with all its corrections, had been in the possession of Mr. Parry some half-century ago.* This assertion he first made in the Preface to the second edition of *Notes and Emendations,* 1853, and confirmed by the affidavit of 1856.

Had such been actually the case, it would of course have relieved the present generation from the suspicion of having perpetrated this " most discreditable fraud."   But, as we shall presently see, Mr. Parry altogether denies having ever possessed this volume, and states that *he had not even seen it* until the thirteenth of July in the last year (1859.)

Mr. Collier, however, asserts that the book was identified by Mr. Parry, and he gives two distinct narratives, not only of the fact but of the manner of the identification.   These two narratives differ materially, if they are not actually contradictory.   I subjoin both for the purpose of comparison. The first occurs in the Preface to the second edition of *Notes and Emendations*, 1853, where "the important discovery regarding the ownership and history of my corrected folio 1632" is thus related :—

"John Carrick Moore, Esq., of Hyde Park Gate, Kensington * * * was kind enough to address a note to me, in which he stated that a friend of his, a gentleman of the name of Parry, had been at one time in possession of the very folio upon which I founded my recent volume of " Notes and Emendations," that Mr. Parry had been well acquainted with the fact that its margins were filled throughout by manuscript notes, and that he accurately remembered the handwriting in which they were made On being shewn the facsimile, which accompanied my first edition, and which is repeated in the present, he declared his instant conviction that it had been copied from what had once been his folio 1632. How, or precisely when, it escaped from his custody he knew not, but the description of it in my " Introduction," exactly corresponded with his recollection.

" I lost no time in thanking Mr. Moore for these tidings, and in writing to Mr. Parry for all the particulars within his knowledge. Unfortunately the latter gentleman, just before he received my note, had met with a serious injury, which confined him to his bed, so that he was unable to send me any reply,

" For about ten days I remained in suspense, but at last I determined to wait upon Mr. Moore, to inquire

I

whether he was aware of any reason why I had not received an answer from Mr. Parry. He accounted for
the silence of that gentleman on the ground of his
recent accident; and as Mr. Moore was confident that
Mr. Parry was correct in the conclusion that my folio
1632 had formerly belonged to him, he advised me to
call upon him, being sure that he would be glad to satisfy me upon every point. I accordingly hastened to
St. John's Wood, and had the pleasure of an interview
with Mr. Parry, who, without the slightest reserve, gave
me such an account of the book as made it certain that
it was the same which, some fifty years ago, had been
presented to him by a connexion of his family, Mr.
George Gray. Mr. Parry described both the exterior
and interior of the volume, with its innumerable corrections and its missing leaves, with so much minuteness, that no room was left for doubt."

" On the question from whence Mr. Gray, who resided
at Newbury, had procured the book, Mr. Parry was not
so clear and positive; he was not in a condition to state
any distinct evidence to show out of what library it had
come; but he had always understood and believed that
it had been obtained, with some other old works (to the
collection of which Mr. Gray was partial), from Upton
Court, Berkshire,—formerly and for many years before
the dispersion of the library, the residence of a Roman
Catholic family of the name of Perkins, one member of
which, Francis Perkins, who died in 1736, was the husband of Arabella Farmer, the heroine of the 'Rape of
the Lock.'

" This information has been communicated to me so recently, that I have not yet been able to ascertain at what date, and in what way, the books at Upton Court were disposed of. Mr. Parry is strongly of opinion that Mr. Gray became the owner of this copy of the folio 1632, considerably before the end of the last century; and Mr. Parry was himself at Upton Court about fifty years since, when a Roman Catholic clergyman, eighty years of age, who had remembered the books there all his life, showed him the then empty shelves upon which they had been placed in the library.

" A Mr. Francis Perkins died at Upton Court three years after the publication of the folio 1632; and if Mr. Parry's belief be correct, that the copy which Mr. Gray gave to him had once been deposited there, it is not impossible that Francis Perkins was the first purchaser of it. If so, we might be led to the inference, that either he, or one of his immediate descendants, was the writer of the emendations ; but as has been mentioned elsewhere, the present rough calf binding was not the original coat of the volume ; and as far as my imperfect researches have yet gone, I do not find any Thomas Perkins recorded as of Upton Court.

" The Christian name of the great actor of the reign of Charles I. was Richard ; and a Richard Perkins, called Esquire in Ashmole's Collections, at a date not stated, married Lady Mervin, a benefactress of that parish. Why should we deem it impossible that Richard Perkins having attained eminence on the stage, subsequently married a lady of title and property ?

" However, this and other points, dependent chiefly upon dates, remain to be investigated, and upon any of them I shall be most thankful for information.

" The only facts that I am yet able to establish are, that my folio 1632, with its elaborate corrections, about half a century since, came into the possession of Mr. Parry, from Mr. George Gray, who, it is probable, obtained it from Upton Court (about eight miles from his residence), where it is unquestionable that at an early date there was a library, likely to have contained such a book, which library was afterwards dispersed. The name of ' Tho. Perkins' on the cover, is a strong confirmation of the opinion that it once formed part of that library; and as to the identity of the volume, and handwriting of the marginal notes, Mr. Parry feels absolutely certain.

" Having thus made, very unexpectedly, the first step (decidedly a long one), towards the history of this copy, &c., &c., it remains for me to advert to objections, &c."— (*Preface to Second Edition of " Notes and Emendations,"* 1853.)

Now I think the expressions " Mr. Parry gave me such an *account* of the book, as made it certain that it was the same which, some fifty years ago, had been presented to him by a connexion of his family ;" and " Mr. Parry *described* both the exterior and interior of the volume, with its innumerable corrections and its missing leaves, with so much minuteness that no room was left for doubt," lead inevitably to the conclusion that *the book* itself was not shown to Mr. Parry. Indeed had it been, Mr. Collier would certainly have stated that fact in his narrative, as being much more conclusive as to its identification than the most minute *description* could possibly be.

In regard to Mr. Parry's account of "the exterior and interior of the volume," that gentleman and Mr. Collier are at issue. Mr. Parry asserts that he certainly recollects his volume sufficiently well to describe its appearance accurately; but that then the description could not possibly have led Mr. Collier to suppose it was the same as his corrected copy of 1632; on the contrary, it must at once have proved to him that it was wholly different, since Mr. Parry states that his volume was of the first edition, 1623, and was bound in smooth dark leather, that it had been supplied with a new back which was lettered, that there was no name of any former possessor written on the cover, and that the margins had been partially ploughed off in binding. On the other hand, Mr. Collier's folio is of the edition of 1632, is bound in rough light-coloured sheep, is neither re-backed nor lettered, the words "Tho. Perkins his Booke," are written in a bold recent hand on the upper cover, and the margins are

not mutilated.   How then, we may ask, could
Mr. Collier have possibly identified his Folio with
that formerly in the possession of Mr. Parry,
when every word of that gentleman's description
must have proved to him that the two volumes
were wholly different?

But on the 19th of July, in the present year
(1859), Mr. Collier published a second version of
the identification of the Folio, differing from, and
as seems to me, at variance with his former
narrative.   It proves at least that his memory
is treacherous, since his recollection of the facts
now are inconsistent with his statement of
them some years ago.   In the first instance,
he informed the reader that he had himself
been enabled to identify the volume by means
of Mr. Parry's *description* of it; in the second account he shifts the responsibility upon Mr. Parry,
by stating that that gentleman identified the
volume himself, by *personal inspection* of it; and
he even recounts the exact words of a conversation
which according to him took place on the occasion.
Mr. Parry however asserts that, to the best of his
belief, the circumstance thus recorded of the
volume having been shown to him never occurred;
and he further stated, in conversation with the
writer, that the incidents of his *taking* and

handing back the Folio were simply impossible, inasmuch as on the occasion alluded to he was, in consequence of an accident, halting along the road on two crutches, the management of which occupied both his hands, and must certainly have totally prevented his handling a folio volume.

Subjoined is Mr. Collier's second narrative, followed by Mr. Parry's reply to it :—

" *To the Editor of the Times.*

" Sir,—I feel most unwillingly compelled to say one other word respecting the corrected folio of Shakespeare's works in 1632, which came into my hands in 1849.

" According to Mr. Hamilton's letter, inserted in your paper of the 16th inst., Mr. Parry states that the book which he owned, and which was given to him by his relative, Mr. George Gray, about fifty years ago, was an edition different from the folio of 1632, with different corrections.

" I saw Mr. Parry twice upon the subject in the year 1853,—first at his house in St. John's Wood, when he told me (as he had previously told a common friend) that he had recognized the corrections instantly, from the fac-simile which accompanied the earliest edition of my *Notes and Emendations*, 8vo, 1852. Very soon afterwards, for greater satisfaction, I brought the corrected folio of 1632 from Maidenhead to London, and took it to St. John's Wood, but I failed to meet with Mr. Parry at home. I therefore paid a third visit to that gentleman, again carrying the book with me. I met him coming from his house, and I informed him that I had the corrected folio of 1632 under my arm, and that I was sorry he could not then examine it, as I wished. He replied,—' If you will let me see it now, I shall be able to state at once whether it was ever my book.' I therefore showed it to him on the spot, and, after looking at it in several places, he gave it back to me with these words :—' That was my book, it is the same, but it has been much ill-used since it was in my possession.'

" I took Mr. Parry's word without hesitation ; and it certainly gave me increased faith in the emendations, to which I never applied a microscope or magnifying glass beyond my own spectacles. I was then living in the house of my brother-in-law ; and, almost from day to day, I showed him such of the emendations of Shakespeare's text in the corrected folio of 1632 as seemed most striking or important.

" If there be upon the volume any pencillings by me, beyond crosses, ticks, and lines, they will speak for themselves ; they have escaped my recollection, and, as I stated in my former letter, I have not seen the book for several years. Perhaps the microscope used by Mr. Hamilton might discover that the plumbago of my pencil was the same as that of other marks, said to be in connexion with some of the emendations.

"J. PAYNE COLLIER.

" *Maidenhead, July* 16."

" My dear Sir,—In reply to your application I have only to make the following statement, in which you will see that Mr. Collier's memory and mine are in question.

" In Mr. Collier's letter to *The Times,* printed July 19, 1859, he states that he was coming to call on me in 1853 with ' the corrected folio of 1632 under his arm,' and that he showed it to me on the road, and that I gave it back to him with these words, ' that was my book—it is the same; but it has been much ill-used since it was in my possession.'

" Now, I believe Mr. Collier to be utterly incapable of making any statement which is not strictly in accordance with his belief. I remember well meeting him, as he says, in the road, and as I was then very lame, from having hurt my knee by a fall, and was using sticks to assist me in walking, he kindly did not allow me to turn back, but walked with me in the direction I was going. I well remember some of the conversation we had during our walk; but I have not the slightest recollection that the volume of *Shakspere* was then under his arm, or of my having asserted that ' it was my book.'

" Previously to this interview with Mr. Collier he had shown me the fac-simile which he mentions in his letter, when I immediately said, on seeing it, that it was from my book. I now believe that I was mistaken, and that I was too hasty in so identifying *the volume* from a *fac-simile* of a part of a page of it. At that time Mr. Collier knew that there were several corrected folios of

K

Shakspere in existence, but he did not tell me that there were. At that time I did not know that there was any other corrected folio in existence, and I therefore supposed that Mr. Collier's fac-simile could only have been taken from my book. It was not till the 14th of this month that I learnt from Sir Frederic Madden that there are five or six corrected folios now in being, but he (Sir Frederic) did not tell me so till he had laid on the table Mr. Collier's corrected folio, and then he seemed surprised that I did not recognise it.

" Again I repeat, that having frequently since the 14th of this month, when I saw Sir Frederic Madden, tried to recollect everything about the book, I cannot remember that Mr. Collier ever showed me the book, but I well remember his showing me the fac-simile. I may be wrong, and Mr. Collier may be right.

" I have a very strong impression that *my* book was a copy of the edition of 1623, and was rather surprised when I saw Mr. Collier's ' Supplemental volume ' (1853) to find that *his* book was of the edition of 1632.

" I may also add that I certainly did not tell, and could not have told Mr. Collier, that Mr. Gray ' was partial to the collection of old books,' for I believe he set no value at all on them.

" Believe me to be, my dear Sir, yours very truly,

" F. C. PARRY.

" *Mr. N. E. Hamilton, British Museum, W.C.*"

A third narrative is contained in a letter from
Mr. Collier to the *Athenæum*, June 4th, 1853.*
This presents some points of difference of its own,

---

* " Your readers, who have taken so lively an interest in the
emendations and alterations of the text of Shakspeare contained
in my copy of the folio 1632, will be glad to hear that I have
just advanced an important step towards tracing the ownership
and history of that remarkable book. The proof that it was in
existence, in its annotated state, 50 years ago, is clear and positive ; and upon the foundation of strong probability I am able
to carry it back almost to the period when the volume was
published. The facts are these :—

" John Carrick Moore, Esq., of Hyde Park Gate (nephew to Sir
John Moore, who fell at Corunna, in Jan. 1809), being in possession of a copy of the ' *Notes and Emendations* ' founded upon my
folio 1632, happened to show it to a friend of the name of Parry,
residing at St. John's Wood. Mr. Parry remarked that he had
once been the owner of a folio 1632, the margins of which were
much occupied by manuscript notes in an old hand-writing ; and
having read my description of the book, both externally and
internally, and having looked at the fac-simile which accompanied that description, he declared, without a moment's hesitation, that this very copy of the folio 1632, had been given to
him about 50 years since, by Mr. George Gray, a connexion of
his family, who, he believed, had procured it some years before,
from the library of a Roman Catholic family of the name of
Perkins, of Upton Court, Berkshire, one member of which had
married Arabella Farmer, the heroine of ' The Rape of the
Lock.'

" Those particulars were, as kindly as promptly, communicated
to me by Mr. Moore, with whom I was not personally acquainted ; and he urged Mr. Parry also to write to me on the
subject ; but that gentleman was prevented from doing so by a

but in the main agrees with that quoted from
the *Notes and Emendations;* and it will be observed that neither of these narratives, published

---

serious fall, which confined him to his bed. Being, of course,
much interested in the question, I soon afterwards took an
opportunity of introducing myself to Mr. Moore, who, satisfied
that Mr. Parry had formerly been the proprietor of my copy of
the folio 1632, advised me to call upon that gentleman at his
house, Hill Road, St. John's Wood, assuring me that he would
be glad to give me all the information in his power.

"I was, I think, the first person whom Mr. Parry saw after
his accident ; and in a long interview he repeated to me the
statement which he had previously made to Mr. Moore, respecting the gift of Mr. Gray half a century ago, and his conviction
of the identity of the volume. He could not prove the fact, but
he had always understood and believed, that Mr. Gray had
become possessed of it on the dispersion of the library of the
Perkins family at Upton Court, and that it had been in his
hands some years before the conclusion of the last century.
Mr. Parry had himself had the curiosity to visit Upton Court
about 1803 or 1804 ; when a Roman Catholic priest, not less
than 80 years old, showed him the library and the then empty
shelves, from which the books had been removed.

" On referring subsequently to the 'Magna Britannia' of
Lysons, under the head of 'Berkshire,' I found various parti-
culars regarding the Perkins family at Upton Court, between
1635 and 1738 ; but I did not meet with any mention of Thomas
Perkins, whose name, it will be remembered, is on the cover of
the folio 1632, in question. The name of the distinguished
actor of the reigns of James the First and Charles the First, was
Richard Perkins ; and Ashmole's Collections, according to
Lysons, speak of a Richard Perkins as the husband of Lady
Mervin, of Upton Court. It is just possible that this Richard

at the time when the occurrence actually took place, countenance in the slightest degree Mr. Collier's subsequent belief that he had exhibited the volume itself to the examination of Mr. Parry.

Perkins was the actor; for, although the 'Historia Histrionica' tells us that he was buried at Clerkenwell, that authority is by no means final: just before it notices the death of Perkins, it speaks of Lowin as having expired in great poverty at Brentford, when we know that this 'player' (so designated in the register) was buried at St. Clement Danes, Strand, on the 24th of August, 1653. However, it is a mere speculation that the Richard Perkins who married Lady Mervin may have been the actor, and I am not yet in possession of any other dates or circumstances to guide me.

"Having put in writing the particulars with which Mr. Parry had so unreservedly favoured me, I took the liberty of forwarding them to Mr. Moore; and he returned the manuscript with his full approbation as regarded what had originally passed between himself and Mr. Parry. After it was in type, I again waited upon Mr. Parry, only three days ago, in order that I might read the proof to him, and introduce such additions and corrections as he wished to be made. They were few, but not unimportant; and among them was the fact (confirming the probability that Mr. Gray had obtained this copy of the folio 1632, from the Perkins library) that Mr. Gray resided at Newbury, not far from Upton Court—a circumstance which Mr. Parry had previously omitted. The connecting link between the book and this library is, therefore, not complete; and we have still to ascertain, if we can, who was Thomas Perkins, and by whom the notes and emendations were introduced into the folio 1632. A Francis Perkins died at Upton Court in 1635, and he may have been the first purchaser and owner of this second folio of the works of Shakespeare.   ["At

Here the *extrinsic* evidences against the authenticity of the corrected folio of 1632 may be brought to a close : nor is it to be forgotten that the *internal* proofs of its spurious character are no less powerful, and have long since been independently urged against it by Singer, Dyce, Knight, Staunton, Halliwell, Ingleby, Grant White, and the whole phalanx of Shaksperian Commentators. That anyone, using due consideration, can still maintain the authority of the volume, seems not possible.

" At all events, however, it is certain that this very volume was for many years in the possession of Mr. Parry (how he lost it he knows not), who obtained it from his connexion, Mr. George Gray, of Newbury. Mr. Parry was well acquainted with the fact that various leaves were wanting ; and he so perfectly recollects its state and condition, the frequent erasures of passages, as well as the handwriting of the numerous marginal and other corrections, that when I asked him, just before I wished him good morning, whether he had any doubt on the point of his previous ownership, he answered me most emphatically in these words—' I have no more doubt about it, than that you are sitting there.'

" J. PAYNE COLLIER.

" *Maidenhead, May* 28."

" P.S.—I ought not to omit the expression of my warmest acknowledgments to both Mr. Moore and Mr. Parry, for the zealous and ready assistance which they have afforded me. I hope that if any of the readers of the *Athenæum* are in possession of information that may tend to the further elucidation of the subject, they will communicate it with equal alacrity."

But the facts I am now about to advert to are far graver than the question of the authenticity of that or any other particular volume. They have reference to a *series* of systematic forgeries which have been perpetrated, apparently within the last half century, and are in connection generally with the history of Shakspere and Shaksperian literature, although other subjects have occasionally been introduced.

The first instance I shall bring forward, as being more nearly related than any other to the question of the annotated edition of 1632, is that of Lord Ellesmere's first edition of Shakspere's Plays, 1623. This folio his Lordship submitted to my scrutiny, subsequently to the publication in *The Times* of my remarks on the folio belonging to the Duke of Devonshire. Like it, Lord Ellesmere's folio has also received marginal annotations. In both instances the corrections have been made first in pencil and afterwards in ink, the mode of obliteration is characteristic and similar, and on examination I recognise *the same hand-writing in both*.

Beyond the fact that Lord Ellesmere's volume was supposed to be the finest copy of the first folio in existence, little seems to have been known

about it, until the year 1842, when the late Lord
Ellesmere, then Lord Francis Egerton, lent the
volume to Mr. Collier. How long it remained in
that gentleman's custody I am not aware. But subsequently, Mr. Collier published a letter addressed
by him to the Rev. Joseph Hunter, in which he
mentions the loan of the volume, and states that
he has discovered in its pages some important marginal emendations, examples of which he proceeds
to cite. The alterations in this first folio are
not numerous, but they are frequently identical
with those afterwards discovered by Mr. Collier
in the folio of 1632; the identity in one or
two instances being strikingly significant. Prior
to their discovery by Mr. Collier, it does not
seem, so far as I can learn, that any alterations
were known to exist on the margins at all. He
is certainly wrong in attributing them to the time
of the Commonwealth; they are not only modern,
but, decidedly, *by the same hand* as those in
his more famous copy of the second edition.
I subjoin Mr. Collier's account of the discovery;
also a list of the whole of the corrections found in
the edition of 1623, in which I have been careful
to distinguish such as likewise occur in the
" Folio " 1632.

"Reasons for a New Edition of Shakespeare's Works. 1842.
By Mr. John Payne Collier, p. 13."

" Lord Francis Egerton was also kind enough to add
to the obligation, by lending me his folios of 1623
and 1632 ; the first being more than ordinarily interesting on account of certain early manuscript corrections in
a few of the plays, which will put an end to doubts on
some passages of the original text, and will most satisfactorily illustrate and explain others not hitherto well understood.   *   *   *   These corrections in the
margin of the printed portion of the folio, are probably
as old as the reign of Charles I.   Whether they were
merely conjectural, or were made from original MSS. of
the plays to which the individual might have had access,
it is not perhaps possible to ascertain ; it has been stated,
these verbal, and sometimes literal, annotations, are only
found in a few of the plays in the commencement of the
volume, and from what follows, it will be a matter of
deep regret that the corrector of the text carried his
labours no further."

L

Manuscript Corrections in the Bridgewater folio, 1623.

Printed Text of Folio 1623.	MS. Corrections.
As You Like It, p. 191, c. 2.	
[*Wearing*] thy hearer in thy mistris praise	[Wearying] but afterwards obliterated. This is the printed reading in 1632.
Do., p. 204, c. 1.	
I will ore-run thee with polic[*e*]	[y] obliterated. The printed reading of 1632.
All's Well, p. 234, c. 1.	
The mistrie of yon lo[*u*]elinesse, and finded	[n] [v] in ed. 1632.
Do., p. 236, c. 1.	
Where hope is coldest, and despair most [*shifts*]	[ffits] fits 1632.
Measure for Measure, p. 63, col. 2.	
(The needful bits and curbes to headstrong [*weedes*])	[steedes] The same cor. has been made in the folio 1632, but afterwards obliterated.
Do., p. 70, c. 1.	
Owe, and succeed [*thy*] weaknesse	[this] *with a trace of pencil.* The same cor. in the folio of 1632.
Love's Labour Lost, p. 133, c. 1.	
Disfigure not his [*Shop.*]	[shape] slop 1632.
As You Like It, p. 189, c. 2.	
After my flight: now goe [*in we*] content	[we in] *we in* printed in 1632.
Do., p. 190, c. 2.	
˄ Why, what's the matter?	[ORL.] in print in 1632.
All's Well, &c., p. 240, c. 1.	
[*A*]nd ere I do begin	[E] The same correction is made in folio 1632.
Do., &c., p. 125. c. 1.	
LAF. You begge more than˅ word then	[a] with a trace of pencil underneath. [one] 1632, but blotted, a pencil distinct underneath the ink.

Printed Text of Folio 1623.	*MS. Corrections.*
All's Well, &c., p. 252, c. 2.	
KING. I wonder, Sir, [*Sir,*]	[for]
I wonder, [*Sir,*] wives are such monsters to you	[since] in ed. 1632, but almost wholly obliterated.
Winter's Tale, p. 279, c. 1.	
Of my Boyes face, m[*e*] thoughts I did me requoyle	[y] y 1632
Do., p. 280, c. 1.	
My Wife's a Ho[*l*]y-Horse	[b] b 1632
Do., p. 285, c. 2.	
So sure as th[*is*] Beard's gray	[y] your 1632
Do., p. 294, c. 1.	
And hand͙ ed love, as you do ; I was wont	[l] pencil traceable. [l] 1632.
Do., p. 299, c. 1.	
Above a better, gone ; so must thy gra[*v*]e	[c] pencil distinct.
Do., p. 299, c. 2.	
Give you all greetings, that a king (a[*t*] friend)	[s] *as* printed in 1632.

But besides the marginal corrections in Lord
Ellesmere's folio, Mr. Collier likewise discovered in
the library of Bridgewater House, a series of remarkable documents of the highest interest, supposing
them genuine, in regard to the life of Shakspere.
The particulars of the discovery were made public
in a letter addressed to Mr. George Amyot in
the year 1835. In this letter Mr. Collier dwells
at considerable length upon the importance of the
documents in question, but does not hint at anything in the appearance of the handwriting calculated to throw doubts upon their genuineness;
while the particulars stated respecting their being
contained in bundles of manuscript, probably un-
opened since the days of Chancellor Ellesmere,
would tell strongly in their favour. Some of
these particulars I transcribe from Mr. Collier's
letter.

However assuring and satisfactory the particulars respecting the discovery of these MSS. as
thus stated by Mr. Collier, the contents of the
documents themselves, when carefully considered,
were of a nature not merely to raise suspicion, but
to shake belief in them altogether, as I shall
presently show.

In addition to this it was understood that two
skilled palæographists, the Rev. Joseph Hunter,

and Mr. Black (both of the Public Record Office), having had an opportunity of examining the originals, had privately expressed an opinion adverse to their pretensions as authentic documents, judging from the handwriting. But to Mr. Halliwell is the real merit due of having stated distinctly the whole case against these remarkable documents. This he did in a pamphlet printed "for private circulation only," in 1853, the pamphlet being accompanied by a *fac-simile* of one of the documents in question. His argument is so forcible, that I prefer to quote his own words.

" When I came to make a personal inspection of these interesting papers, facilities for which were kindly granted by their noble owner, grave doubts were at once created as to their authenticity. The most important of all, the certificate from the players of the Blackfriars' Theatre to the Privy Council in 1589, instead of being either an original or a contemporary copy, is evidently at best merely a late transcript, if it be not altogether a recent fabrication. The question naturally arises, for what purpose could a document of this description have been copied in the seventeenth century, presuming it to belong to so early a period ? It is comparatively of recent times that the slightest literary interest has been taken in the history of our early theatres, or even in the biography of Shakespeare ; and, unless it was apparent that papers of this kind were transcribed for some legal or other special

purpose, there should be great hesitation in accepting the
evidence of any other but contemporary authority. The
suspicious appearance of this certificate is of itself sufficient to justify great difficulties in its reception; but
the doubt thus induced as to the integrity of the collection was considerably increased by an examination of a
paper in the same volume purporting to be a warrant
appointing Daborne, Shakespeare, Field, and Kirkham,
instructors of the children of the Queen's Revels, which
unquestionably appears to be a modern forgery. This
document is styled by Mr. Collier, " a draft either for a
Patent or a Privy Seal." It is not a draft, for the lines
are written bookwise, and it is also dated; neither is it a
copy of a patent, as appears from the direction, " Right
trustie & well-beloved ;" but, if genuine, it must be
considered an abridged transcript of a warrant, under the
sign-manual and signet, for a patent to be issued. Now
if it be shewn that the letters patent to " Daborne
& others " were granted on the same day on which Lord
Ellesmere's paper is dated, and, if it be further proved
that the contents of the latter are altogether inconsistent
with the circumstances detailed in the real patent, it
will, I think, be conceded that no genuine draft or transcript of the nature of that printed by Mr. Collier, can
possibly exist.

"It appears that the following note occurs in an entry-
book of patents that passed the Great Seal while it was
in the hands of Lord Ellesmere, in 7 James I. :—" A
Warrant for Robert Daborne and others, the Queene's
Servants, to bring up and practice children in places by

the name of the Children of the Queen's Revells, for the
pleasure of her Majestie, 4° Januarii, anno septimo
Jacobi." This entry may have suggested the fabrication, the date of the questionable MS. corresponding
with that here given ; though it is capable of proof that
if it were authentic, it must have been dated previously,
for the books of the Signet Office show that the authority for Daborne's warrant was obtained by the influence
of Sir Thomas Munson in the previous December, and
they also inform us that it was granted "to Robert
Daborne, and other Servauntes to the Queen, from time
to time, to provide and bring up a convenient number
of children to practize in the quality of playing, by the
name of the Children of the Revells to the Queene, *in
the White Fryers, London,* or any other convenient place
where he shall thinke fit." The enrolment of the instrument, which was issued in the form of letters patent
under the Great Seal, recites, " Whereas the Queen, our
dearest wyfe, hathe for hir pleasure and recreacion,
when shee shall thinke it fitt to have any playes or
shewes, appoynted hir servantes Robert Daborne, Phil-
lipe Rosseter, John Tarbock, Richard Jones, and Robert Browne, to provide and bring upp a convenient
nomber of Children, whoe shalbe called Children of hir
Revelles, Know yee that wee have appoynted and
authorised, and by theis presentes do authorize and
appoynte the saide Robert Daborne, &c. from tyme to
tyme, to provide, keepe and bring upp a convenient
nomber of children, and them to practice and exercise
in the quality of playing, by the name of Children of

the Revells to the Queene, within the White Fryers in
the suburbs of our Citty of London, or in any other
convenyent place where they shall thinke fitt for that
purpose." This patent is dated January 4th, 7 Jac. I.,
1609-10, so that any draft, or projected warrant, exhibiting other names than the above, could not possibly
have had this exact date. It will be observed that the
names, with the exception of that of Daborne, are entirely different in the two documents, and this company
of children was to play at the Whitefriars, not at the
Blackfriars. The fabricator seems to have relied on the
supposition that the entry relative to Daborne and
others referred to the latter theatre ; and consequently
inserted the name of Edward Kirkham, who is known
to have been one of the instructors of the children of
the Revels at the Blackfriars in the year 1604. There
is, in fact, no reasonable supposition on which the
Ellesmere paper can be regarded as authentic. Had no
date been attached to it, it might have been said that
the whole related merely to some contemplated arrangement which was afterwards altered ; although even in
that case, the form of the copy would alone have been a
serious reason against its reception. In its present
state, it is clearly impossible to reconcile it with the
contents of the enrolment just quoted. Fortunately for
the interests of truth, indications of forgery are detected
in trifling circumstances, that are almost invariably neglected by the inventor, however ingeniously the deception be contrived. Were it not for this, the search for
historical truth would yield results sufficiently uncertain

to deter the most enthusiastic enquirer from pursuing the investigation.

" The remaining Shakesperian MSS. in the possession of the Earl of Ellesmere, consist of a letter of Daniel the poet, mentioning the great dramatist as a candidate for the Mastership of the Queen's Revels; accounts in which a performance of *Othello* is stated to have taken place in the year 1602 ; a remarkable paper detailing the value of the shares held by Shakespeare and others in the Blackfriars Theatre ; and the presumed early copy of a letter signed " H. S.," supposed to have been written by Lord Southampton, and containing singular notices of Burbage and Shakespeare. The first two of them I have not seen, the volume including only a recent transcript of Daniel's letter ; but the other two, which have been carefully inspected, present an appearance by no means satisfactory. Although the caligraphy is of a highly skilful character, and, judging solely from a fac-simile of the letter, I should certainly have accepted it as genuine, yet an examination of the original leads to a different judgment ; the paper and ink not appearing to belong to so early a date. It is a suspicious circumstance that both these documents are written in an unusually large character on folio leaves of paper, by *the same hand*, and are evidently not contemporaneous copies. Again may the question be asked, Why should transcripts of such papers have been made after the period to which the originals are supposed to refer ? It is also curious that copies only of these important records should be preserved ; and the whole

M

matter is surrounded by the gravest suspicions and difficulties.

"Only one record-reader, as far as I know, viz., the
Rev. Joseph Hunter, has made a personal examination
of these MSS. He has not yet expressed any opinion
publicly, but I have reason to think that his views on
the subject coincide with my own. It is clearly Mr.
Collier's duty, as a lover of truth, to have the originals
carefully scrutinized by the best judges of the day."

On the 17th of November, 1859, I had an
opportunity of carefully examining these Bridgewater MSS. for myself, in company with Sir
Frederic Madden and Dr. Kingsley. How it was
Mr. Collier deceived himself as to their real
character I will not attempt to speculate.
With one exception, which manifests some dexterity of execution, these documents display their
spurious character at a glance; whilst two of the
number (the Daborne warrant and Daniel's letter), are such manifest forgeries, that it seems
incredible how they could have cheated Mr.
Collier's observation, even under the circumstances
of excitement described by him as consequent
upon their discovery.*

---

* "When first I obtained permission to look through the
Bridgewater MSS. in detail, I conjectured that it would be nearly
impossible to turn over so many state papers and such a bulk of
correspondence, private and official, without meeting with

Right trustie and welbeloved &c James &c To all Mayors Shireffs
Justices of the peace &c Wheras the Queene our dearst wife hath for
her pleasure and recreation appointed her servannts Robert Dabourne &c
to provide and bring upp a convenient nomber of Children who shalbe
called the Children of her Mate Revells Knowe yee that We have appointed
and authorizd and by these presents doe appoint and authorize the saide
Robert Dabourne Willm Shakespeare Nathaniel ffield & Edward Kirkham from
tyme to tyme to provide and bring upp a convenient number of Children and
them to instruct and exercise in the qualitie of playing Tragedies Comedies &c
by the name of the Children of the Revells to the Queene within the Black-
ffryers in our Cittie of London or els where within our realme of England.
Wherefore we will and commannd you and everie of you to permitte her
saide servannts to keepe a convenient number of Children of the
Revells to the Queene and them to exercise in the qualitie of
playing according to our Royall pleasure Provided allwayes that noe playes &c
shalbe by them presented but such playes &c as have receaved the approbacion
and allowance of our Maister of the Revells for the tyme being And
theise our Lres shalbe yor sufficient warrant in this behalfe In Witnesse
whereof &c 4° die Janẏ 1609

Bl ffru and globe
Wh ffront parishe garden] All m Encore
Curlon and fortune] London
Hope and Swanne

Rondo ponorohi
Widdowes mite
Antonio kinfmen
Triumph of truly
Tonyftone
Mirror of life
Gruffell
Engl tragedic
ffalfe ffriendes
gate and loue
Taming of S
b. Edw 2

Shayes

Facsimile of a Warrant of James I preserved at Bridgwater House.

F.G.Netherclift Fasim. lith.

Annexed is a fac-simile of the spurious Daborne warrant. Independently of every other evidence of its fictitious character, the form alone in which it is drawn, is sufficient to make one

---

something illustrative of the subject to which I have devoted so many years; but I certainly never anticipated being so fortunate as to obtain particulars so new, curious, and important, regarding a poet who, above all others, ancient or modern, native or foreign, has been the object of admiration. When I took up the copy of Lord Southampton's letter and glanced over it hastily, I could scarcely believe my eyes to see such names as Shakespeare and Burbage in connection in a manuscript of the time. There was a remarkable coincidence also in the discovery, for it happened on the anniversary of Shakespeare's birth and death. I will not attempt to describe my joy and surprise, and I can only liken it to the unexpected gratification I experienced two or three years ago, when I turned out, from some ancient depositories of the Duke of Devonshire, the original designs of Inigo Jones, not only for the scenery, but for the dresses and characters of the different masques by Ben Jonson, Campion, Townsend, &c., presented at Court in the reigns of our first James and Charles. The sketches were sometimes accompanied by explanations in the handwriting of the great artist, a few of which incidentally illustrate Shakespeare, who, however, was never employed for any of these royal entertainments. Annexed to one of the drawings was the following written description, from whence we learn how the actor of the part of Falstaff was usually habited in the time of Shakespeare.

"'Like a Sir Jon Falstaff: in a roabe of russet, quite low, with a great belley, like a swolen man, long moustacheos, the sheows [shoes] shorte, and out of them great toes like naked feete: buskins to sheaw a great swolen leg. A cupp coming

look upon it with the greatest doubt, the style of the Sovereign being placed after the opening words of the body of the warrant; a position inconceivable in any authentic instrument. A minute of the genuine document, which differs wholly from the above, was discovered by Mr. Halliwell, in an entry-book of Patents that passed the Great Seal while it was in the hands of Lord Ellesmere in 7 James I;* and which is entirely confirmed by an entry made by the Chancellor's riding-clerk in the "Book of Warrants which have passed the Great Seal," amongst the Bridgewater MSS.; thus affording another proof of the spurious nature of the warrant published by Mr. Collier.

Much as these five documents† vary in manner and style of execution, no one, I think, who

---

fourth like a beake—a great head and balde, and a little cap *alla Venetiane* greay—a rodd and a scroule of parchment.' "— *New Facts regarding the Life of Shakespeare, in a Letter to Thomas Amyot, from J. Payne Collier*, 1835.

It is somewhat remarkable that neither this drawing nor the description of Falstaff are to be found in the Shakspere Society's volume, edited by J. R. Planché, Esq., from the Duke of Devonshire's Library. The language of the "description" is, to say the least, suspicious.—[H.]

* See Observations on the Shaksperian Forgeries, by James O. Halliwell, Esq., 1853, p. 5.

† These documents are given in Appendix I.

examines them carefully (tracing through the whole of them similarities in the forms of certain letters, and even identity of mistakes), can doubt but that they are all the work of one pen. Nor can I too pointedly reiterate my belief *that the whole of the forgeries treated of in this volume have been executed by one hand.* The same exaggerations, the same blunders, and even the same excellencies in performance being observable in Mr. Collier's corrected folio, 1632, in Lord Ellesmere's folio, 1623, in the Bridgewater Manuscripts under discussion, and in the Dulwich forgeries, and the document in the State Paper Office described further on. In regard to the two former, indeed, this fact is pretty well indicated, not only by the handwriting itself, but by the similar use of pencil marks to direct the ink corrections, and by a precisely similar mode of erasure.

I pass from the Bridgewater Papers to an examination of the manuscripts in Dulwich College; and I commence by stating certain facts relative to the *misinterpretation* of a letter to which I have already alluded in the Preface, and where the question is not of a spurious document, but of a *mis-read* copy of one that is genuine.

In 1841 Mr. Collier edited for the Shakspere

Society a volume, entitled " Memoirs of Edward Alleyn." Amongst the Documents published by Mr. Collier in this volume is one correctly stated to be an original letter from Mrs. Alleyn, wife of the founder of Dulwich College, and addressed to her husband. The letter in itself is interesting; but the point upon which Mr. Collier mainly insists, as constituting its peculiar value, is a paragraph he prints as contained in it, relative to " Mr. Shakespeare of the Globe," and from which he proceeds to draw various deductions. On collating this letter with the original, it appears to have been entirely misread by Mr. Collier, *as there is not the smallest trace of authority for any allusion to Shakspere, or to any of the words concerning him found there by Mr. Collier, and printed by him as forming part of the original document.* I subjoin the whole of Mr. Collier's remarks and comments upon the letter, because his description of the physical appearance of its lower margin defaced by damp, and the passage in the letter at which the leaf turns over, are sufficient to identify the actual paper which he had before him, proving it to be the same as I have myself since examined, and not, as might possibly be suggested, another

Facsimile of a portion of a letter of Mrs. Alleyn, preserved at Dulwich College.

F. G. Netherclift. Facsim: lith: 17 Mill St. Conduit St.

copy in which the contents were altered; and, in addition, because his account of the difficulties attendant on deciphering it, lead one to the conclusion that he had himself minutely examined it.

"Of this date we have a very interesting letter from Mrs. Alleyn to her husband, written and subscribed by the person ordinarily employed : it is remarkable, because it contains a mention of Shakespeare, who is spoken of as 'of the Globe ;' and though it throws no new light upon our great dramatist's character, excepting as it shows that he was on good terms with Alleyn's family, any document containing merely his name must be considered valuable. The paper on which the letter was written is in a most decayed state, especially at the bottom, where it breaks and drops away in dust and fragments at the slightest touch. The notice of Shakespeare is near the commencement of a postscript on the lower part of the page, where the paper is most rotten, and several deficiencies occur, which it is impossible to supply : all that remains is extremely difficult to be deciphered.* We will insert it, and defer further remarks until afterwards, only premising that the address

* This description, both as to the decayed state of the paper, as well as to the difficulty of deciphering the handwriting, seems to me a very exaggerated one. On the latter point, the accompanying fac-simile will enable the reader to form an independent judgment.—[H.]

has completely disappeared, so that we cannot tell where Alleyn was at the time ; nor, indeed, excepting from internal evidence, can we decide that it was sent to him. Upon this point, however, there can be no doubt."—*Memoirs of Alleyn*, ed. Collier, p. 62.

I contrast on opposite pages two versions of this document ; the first is a copy made by myself, and containing a true reading of the original, the second is that published by Mr. Collier in the *Memoirs of Alleyn*, p. 62. I have broken the lines, both in my version of the document and in that of Mr. Collier, in exact accordance with the written document, so that the reader may see at a glance the average number of words contained in a line, and be thereby enabled to judge for himself of the actual impossibility of the paragraph in question having ever been contained in the original document where Mr. Collier avers that he found it. At the same time it will be observed that portions of three damaged lines are still legible, which are incompatible with the *Shakspere paragraph*, and in regard to which Mr. Collier is wholly silent. I need not remark that a case of misreading, and miscopying, however gross, is not to be confounded with the innumerable forgeries, (by whomsoever perpetrated,) which it is the object of this volume to bring to light; but it is for the literary world to estimate the magnitude and the character of the wrong done to literature by announcements of such a nature and of so deliberate a kind.

The *thirty-two* minor blunders, literal and verbal, which occur in Mr. Collier's professedly *verbatim* and *literatim* copy of this letter of Mrs. Alleyn, are of less importance, although not undeserving of reprehension. The Rev. A. Dyce, in his "Strictures on Mr. Collier's New Edition of Shakespeare, 1858," has published a series of alleged misstatements and inaccuracies committed by Mr. Collier, which would be incredible, were they not vouched for by the name of a scholar of Mr. Dyce's unimpeachable truth and accuracy.

N

Copy of Mrs. Alleyn's Letter, preserved at Dulwich College,
verbatim, literatim, and line for line.

JHESUS.

My intyre and welbeloved sweete harte still it joyes me and longe I
pray god maye I joye to heare of your healthe and welfare as you of ours.
Allmighty God be thancked my owne selfe your selfe and my mother and
whole house are in good healthe and about us the sycknes doth cease
and likely more and more by godes healpe to cease. All the companyes
be come hoame and well for ought we knowe, but that Browne of
the Boares head is dead and dyed very pore. He went not into the
owne   countrye at all, and all of your ᴧ company ar well at theyr owne houses.
My father is at the corte, but wheare the court ys I know not.
I am of your owne mynde that it is needles to meete my fathere
at Basynge, the Incertayntye beinge as it ys, I commend your
discreation. It were a sore journey to loase your labour besyd expenses
and change of ayre might hurte you, therfore you are resolved upon
the best course. For your cominge hoame I am not to advyse you,
neither will I ; use your owne discretion, yet I longe and am very
desyrous to see you, and my poore and symple opinion is, yf it shall please
you, you maye safely come hoame. Heare is none now sycke neare
us : yet let it not be as I wyll but at your owne best lykynge. I am
glad to heare you take delight in hauckinge and thoughe you
have   ᴧ worne your appayrell to rags, the best ys you knowe
wheare to have better, and as wellcome to me shall you be with
your rags as yf you were in cloathe of gold or velvet. Trye
and see. I have payd fyfty shillings for your rent for the warfe,
not in towne   the Lordes rent. Mr. Woodward, my Lordes bayly was ᴧ but poynted
his deputy who receaved all the rentes. I had witnesses with
me at the payment of the money and have his quittance, but
the quyttance cost me a groat, they sayd it was the baylives
fee. You know best whether you were wont to paye it : yf not,
they made a symple woman of me. You shall receave a letter
from the Joyner hym selfe and a prynted bill, and so with my

*Mrs. Alleyn's Letter, as printed in the "*Memoirs of Alleyn," *p.* 62,
ed. J. P. Collier, 1841.

"JHESUS.

" My intyre and welbeloved sweete harte, still it joyes me and longe, I
pray god, may I joye to heare of your healthe and welfare, *as of* ours.
Allmighty god be *thanked,* my *own* selfe, your selfe and my mother, and
whole house are in good healthe, and about us the sycknes dothe cease
and likely more and more by *gods* healpe to cease. All the companyes
be come *home* and well for ought we knowe, but that Browne of
the Boares head is dead, and dyed very pore. He went not into the
countrye at all, and all of your owne company ar well at *there* owne houses.
My father is at the corte, but wheare the *corte* ys I know not.
I am of your owne mynde, that it is needles to meete my *father*
at Basynge : the *entertaynment* beinge as it *is,* I *comend* your
discreation. It *weare* a sore journey to loase your labour, *besyde* expenses,
and change of ayre *mighte* hurte you ; therfore you are resolved upon
the best course. For your cominge hoame I am not to advyse you,
neither will I : use your owne discreation, yet I longe and am very
desyrous to see you ; and my poore and *simple* opinion is, yf it shall please
you, you maye safely come hoame. Heare is none now sycke neare
us ; yet let it not be as I wyll, but at your owne best lykynge. I am
glad to heare you take delight in hauckinge, and thoughe you
have worne your appayrell to rags, the best ys you knowe
where to have better, and as wellcome to me shall you be with
your rags, as yf you were in cloathe of gold or velvet. Trye
and see. I have payd fyfty shillings for your rent for the warfe,
the Lordes rent. Mr. Woodward, my Lordes bayly, was not in towne but poynted
his deputy who received all the rentes. I had witnesses with
me at the payment of the money, and have his quittance, but
the quyttance cost me a groat : they sayd it was the baylives
fee. You *knowe* best whether you were wont to paye it ; yf not,
they made a symple woman of me. You shall receave a letter
from the Joyner hym selfe, and a prynted bill ; and so with my

*

Mrs. Alleyn's Letter—continued.

humble and harty comendations to your owne selfe, Mr. Chaloners
and his wyfe, with thanckes for your kynde usage, with my good
mothers kyndest commendations with the rest of your houshould
God   . . . dle is well but can not speake, I ende prayenge allmighty͵
his   still to blesse us for͵ mercyes sake, and so sweete harte
once more farwell till we meete, which I hope shall not
be longe. This xxth of October 1603.

Aboute a weeke agoe there [cam]e a youthe who said he was
Mr. Frauncis Chalo[ner]s man . . . . ld have borrow[e]d xˢ to
bought have͵ things for [h]is Mr. . . . . t hym
Cominge without . . . token . . . . d
I would have . . . .
& I bene su . . . .
and inquire after the fellow and said he had lent hym a horse. I
us   feare me he gulled hym, thoughe he gulled not͵. The youthe
what   was a prety youthe and hansom in appayrell, we know not͵ became
of hym. Mr. Bromffeild commendes hym : he was heare yesterdaye. Nicke
and Jeames be well, and commend them, so dothe Mr. Cooke and his weife
in the kyndest sorte, and so once more in the hartiest manner
farwelle

Your faithfull and lovinge weife
JOANE ALLEYNE.

Mrs. Alleyn's Letter (ed. J. P. Collier)—continued.

humble and harty comendations to your owne selfe, Mr. Chaloners
and his wyfe, with *thankes* for your kynde usage, with my good
mothers kyndest *comendations* with the rest of your *houschould*
*   *   *he* is well but can not speake, I ende *prayinge* allmighty god
to blesse *you* for his mercyes sake, and so sweete harte
*   *   *noe more.*   *Farwell* till we meete, which I hope shall not
be longe.   This xxth of October 1603.

  " Aboute a weeke a goe there came a youthe who said he was
Mr. Frauncis Chaloner who would have borrowed x^{li} to
have bought things for   *   *   *   and said he was known
unto you, and Mr. Shakespeare of the globe, who came
*   *   *   said he knewe hym not, only he herde of hym that he was
a roge   *   *   *   so he was glade we did not lend him
the monney   *   *   *   Richard Johnes [went] to seeke
and inquire after the fellow, and said he had lent hym a horse.   I
feare me he gulled hym, thoughe he gulled not us.   The youthe
was a prety youthe, and hansom in appayrell : we *knowe* not what became
of hym.   Mr. *Benfield* commendes hym ; he was heare yesterdaye.   Nicke
and Jeames be well, and *comend* them : so *doth* Mr. Cooke and his *wiefe*
in the kyndest sorte, and so once more in the hartiest manner
farwell.

" Your faithfull and lovinge *wiefe,*

"JOANE ALLEYNE."

Dulwich College, however, is not without its forgeries. Of these I shall cite three examples, all of them first printed by Mr. Collier, in the same volume as that from which the inaccurate copy of Mrs. Alleyn's letter is already quoted, and all of them (as he states in the body of that work) discovered by him.

The first of these which I shall notice is a letter of John Marston, printed in the *Memoirs of Alleyn*, p. 154, and which will be found in the Appendix to this volume.

In its general aspect the writing of this letter certainly resembles Marston's genuine hand, and has no doubt been executed by some one to whom that hand was familiar ; but I soon noticed the existence of numerous modern pencil-marks underlying the ink, and on looking closely into the document, detected that *the whole of the letter had been first traced out in pencil, after the same fashion as the pencilling in the annotated folio of Shakspere's Plays*, 1632 ; and I may here remark that the existence of this system of pencilling in this letter at Dulwich College, as well as in Mr. Collier's and Lord Ellesmere's folios, seems of much importance in tracing these various fictitious documents up to one source, although other forgeries exist in the same libraries in which pencil-marks cannot be discovered, but which nevertheless there is reason for believing were perpetrated by the same hand. Of such forgeries I proceed to mention two : both of them in the library at Dulwich, both relating to Shakspere, and both, as before said, first published in the *Memoirs of Alleyn*, (p. 13.)

The first of these, the verses commencing,—

"Sweet Nedde, nowe wynne an other wager,"

is a forgery from beginning to end, although executed with singular dexterity. In the second the document itself is genuine, and is noticed in his "Inquiry" by Malone, but the "List of Players" added to it, in which Shakspere's name occurs, is a modern addition. Mr. Collier was the first to notice and publish this "List of Players;" but although he draws attention to the circumstance that Malone, while mentioning the letter, is altogether silent as to the remarkable "List" appended to it, he does not appear to regard this as a ground for suspecting the authenticity of the List, but seems to think that a satisfactory explanation may be found by supposing that Malone had "reserved" it for his Life of Shakspere : the true explanation, doubtless, being, that when Malone examined the document, the "List" in question was not there,

but has been added since his time. Any one
who will compare the character of the hand in
which the "List" is written, with the letter
signed H. S. in the Bridgewater library, will
probably arrive at the conclusion I have done,
that they are by the same hand.

But of the various documents which I believe
to be spurious, the most remarkable is the following :—

To the right honorable the Ll of her Maties most
honorable priuie Counsell

The humble petition of Thomas Pope Richard Burbadge John Hemings Augustine Phillips Willm Shakespeare Willm Kempe Willm Slye Nicholas Tooley and
others seruauntes to the right honorable the L. Cham-
berlaine to her Matie—Sheweth most humbly that yor
petitioners are owners and players of the priuate
house or theater in the precinct and libertie of the
Blackfriers wch hath beene for manie yeares vsed and
occupied for the playing of tragedies commedies histories enterludes and playes.   That the same by reason
of having beene soe long built hath falne into great decaye
and that besides the reparation thereof it hath beene
found necessarie to make the same more conuenient for
the entertaineme of auditories comming thereto
That to this end yor petitioners haue all and eche of them
putt down sommes of money according to their shares in

the saide theater and wch they haue iustly and honestlie
gained by the exercise of their qualitie of Stage players
but that certaine persons (some of them of honour)
inhabitantes of the precinct and libertie of the Black-
friers haue as yor petitioners are enfourmed besought yor
honorable Lps not to permitt the saide priuate house anie
longer to remaine open but hereafter to be shutt vpp
and closed to the manifest and great iniurie of yor petitioners who haue no other meanes whereby to mainteine
their wiues and families but by the exersise of their
qualitie as they haue heretofore done.   Furthermore
that in the summer season yor petitioners are able to
playe at their newe built house on the Bankside callde
the Globe but that in the winter they are compelled to
come to the Blackfriers and if yor honorable Lps give
consent vnto that wch is prayde against yor petitioners
they will not onely while the winter endureth loose the
meanes whereby they nowe support them selues and
their families but be vnable to practise them selues in
anie playes or enterluds when calde vpon to performe
for the recreation and solace of her Matie and her
honorable Court as they haue beene hertofore accustomed.
The humble prayer of yor petitioners therefore is that
yor hon^{ble} Lps will graunt permission to finishe the reparations and alterations they haue begunne and as yor
petitioners haue hitherto beene well ordred in their
behauiour and iust in their dealinges that yor honorable
Lps will not inhibit them from acting at their aboue
named priuate house in the precinct and libertie of the
Blackfriers and yor petitioners as in dutie most bounden

O

will euer praye for the encreasing honour and happinesse of your honorable Lps.*

Up to this point, the value of any addition, however slight, to the knowledge we possess regarding Shakspere's history, has alone given importance to the inquiry whether the documents from which such additional facts were taken, were genuine, as they professed to be. But the document above printed, claims, at the present moment, the dignity and credit of a Public Record. It is preserved in Her Majesty's State Paper Office, bears upon it the official stamp of that office, and forms one of a collection of public papers of undoubted genuineness. Yet there can be little question that it belongs to the same set of *forgeries* as those already investigated : that by some means, yet to be traced, it has been surreptitiously introduced among the Records where it is now found ; and in the course of official routine has received with the rest the stamp of authenticity.

A fac-simile of it is given by Mr. Halliwell, in his folio Shakspere, 1853, (vol. i. p. 137), who states that it was discovered by Mr. Collier in the State Paper Office ; and Mr. Collier prints it in

---

* Document preserved in H.M.'s State Paper Office, Domestic Series,—Elizabeth, 1596, Bundle 222.

his Annals of the Stage (1831), with the following notice:—"This remarkable paper has, perhaps, never seen the light from the moment it was presented, until it was very recently discovered. It is seven years anterior to the date of any other authentic record which contains the name of our great dramatist."*

---

* The following is the entire passage in which Mr. Collier states the discovery of the record. "The Blackfriars Theatre, built in 1576, seems, after the lapse of twenty years, to have required extensive repairs, if, indeed, it were not at the end of that period entirely rebuilt. This undertaking, in 1596, seems to have alarmed some of the inhabitants of the Liberty; and not a few of them, 'some of honour,' petitioned the Privy Council, in order that the players might not be allowed to complete it, and that their further performances in that precinct might be prevented. A copy of the document containing this request, is preserved in the State Paper Office, and to it is appended a much more curious paper—a counter petition by the Lord Chamberlain's players, entreating that they might be permitted to continue their work upon the theatre, in order to render it more commodious, and that their performances there might not be interrupted. It does not appear to be the original, but a copy without the signatures, and it contains at the commencement, an enumeration of the principal actors who were parties to it. They occur in the following order, and it will be instantly remarked, not only that the name of Shakespeare is found among them, but that he comes fifth in the enumeration:—

> Thomas Pope,
> Richard Burbage,
> John Hemings,

This petition bears no date, and is written on half a sheet of foolscap paper, without water-mark, and which, from the appearance of the edges, I should think had probably once formed the fly-leaf of some folio volume. A supposed date of 1596 has been placed upon it in pencil by one of the gentlemen in the State Paper Office. Its execution is very neat, and with any one not minutely acquainted with the fictitious hand of these Shakspere forgeries it might readily pass as genuine. But an examination of the handwriting

---

Augustine Phillips,
William Shakespeare,
William Kempe,
William Slye,
Nicholas Tooley.

" This remarkable paper has, perhaps, never seen the light from the moment it was presented, until it was very recently disco-vered. It is seven years anterior to the date of any other au-thentic record, which contains the name of our great dramatist, and it may warrant various conjectures as to the rank he held in the company in 1596, as a poet and as a player."—COLLIER, *Annals of the Stage*, vol. i. p. 207.

I endeavoured but unsuccessfully to see this " petition of the inhabitants," mentioned at the commencement of the above quo-tation. In reply to an official request for the production of the document, Charles Lechmere, Esq., Assistant Keeper of State Papers, writes, " I have referred to the Calendar of 1596, but I do not find any entry of the Petition from the inhabitants of the Blackfriars." Thus of these two documents, *one is an undoubted forgery—the very existence of the other seems problematical!*—[H.]

generally, the forms of some of the letters in particular, and the spurious appearance of the ink, led me to the belief not only that the paper was not authentic, but that it had been executed *by the same hand* as the fictitious documents already discussed. This conviction I made known to the Right Hon. the Master of the Rolls, who was good enough to direct an official inquiry into the authenticity of the document.

In accordance with this direction, on the 30th of January, Sir Francis Palgrave, Deputy Keeper of Public Records, T. Duffus Hardy, Esq., Assistant Keeper of Public Records, and Professor Brewer, Reader at the Rolls, met Sir Frederic Madden and myself for the purpose of investigation, and after a minute and careful examination *the following unanimous decision was arrived at as to the fact of its undoubtedly spurious character.*

" We, the undersigned, at the desire of the Master of the Rolls, have carefully examined the document hereunto annexed, purporting to be a petition to the Lords of Her Majesty's Privy Council, from Thomas Pope, Richard Burbadge, John Hemings, Augustine Phillips, William Shakespeare, William Kempe, William Slye, Nicholas Tooley, and others, in answer to a petition from the Inhabitants of the Liberty of the Blackfriars ; and we are of opinion, that the document in question is spurious.

"30th January, 1860.

> "FRA. PALGRAVE, K.H., Deputy-Keeper of H. M. Public Records.
> "FREDERIC MADDEN, K.H., Keeper of the MSS., British Museum.
> "J. S. BREWER, M.A., Reader at the Rolls.
> "T. DUFFUS HARDY, Assistant-Keeper of Records.
> "N. E. S. A. HAMILTON, Assistant, Dep : of MSS., British Museum."

"I direct this paper to be appended to the undated document now last in the Bundle, marked 222, Eliz. 1596.

"2 February, 1860.
> "JOHN ROMILLY, Master of the Rolls."

So far, then, as relates to this document, the question must be considered as set at rest : and it is almost unnecessary to point out the weight of the decision, not alone in regard to this *condemned forgery*, but in respect of its bearing upon the other writings here treated of. Before a new edition of Shakspere is issued, or a new life of Shakspere written, it will be necessary that the whole of the hitherto supposed *basis* of the Poet's history should be rigorously examined, and no effort spared to discover the perpetrator of that treason against the Majesty of English literature, which it has been my object to denounce.

I here bring this list of fabrications to a close. It exhausts neither the whole of the documents which actual examination convinces me are fictitious, nor yet of those which I have only reason to suspect. But before concluding I wish to offer an observation respecting a volume in the possession of Mr. Collier, to which he has frequently drawn the attention of the public, but the authenticity of which has never, I believe, been sufficiently inquired into. I allude to a manuscript volume of Ballads, stated by its owner to have been written about the time of the Protectorate, and from which he has at various times published extracts. The most noticeable of these, which I have seen, is a ballad entitled "The Inchanted Island," the plot of which bears some resemblance to *The Tempest*; and which was published by Mr. Collier in a letter to the Rev. Joseph Hunter, in the year 1839. Far am I from hinting that Mr. Collier has any unreadiness to submit it to the most searching scrutiny. It is, indeed, through a fac-simile furnished by that gentleman to Mr. Halliwell, that I am enabled to form any opinion on the subject. But no one, I think, experienced in ancient handwritings can

look at that fac-simile,* without feeling the
gravest doubts in regard to its authenticity, which
the intrinsic character of the verses themselves by
no means serves to allay.   Mr. Collier would
certainly be doing good service to the cause of
truth and literature, by bringing the volume in
question before a competent tribunal; while at
the same time he might satisfy literary curiosity,
by producing a remarkable document in connection with the history of Shakspere, various particulars in regard to which were minutely stated by
him in a letter to the Athenæum Dec. 6th, 1856,†

---

* Published by Mr. Halliwell in the first volume of his *Folio
Shakspere*, p. 312.

† "SHAKESPEARE AND HIS "RICHARD THE SECOND."
"Maidenhead, Dec. 3.

"I am afraid that I shall still further exasperate my Shakespearian adversaries (I wish I could say with Henry the Sixth,
'Let me embrace these sour adversaries') when I inform your
readers that I have recently found another document, very
curiously and importantly illustrating what Coleridge used to
call 'Shakespeare's greatest historical play'—'Richard the
Second.'

"All authorities mention that shortly before the 'insurrection'
of the Earls of Essex, Southampton, &c.,—early in 1601—Sir
Gilly Merrick, Cuff, and some others of their friends, negotiated
with the Company of Actors usually playing at the Blackfriars
and Globe Theatres, in order to procure the representation of
'Richard the Second' on the evening anterior to the rising.   It
was this circumstance which made Queen Elizabeth afterwards
say to Lambard, when he presented to her his Pandects of
Records in the Tower, 'I am Richard the Second; know you

in which he places its discovery on record, (although he does not mention *where* he found it,) but which I believe he has never yet published, and which, so far as I am aware, no one has yet seen.

---

not that?' Certain it is, that a tragedy entitled 'Richard the Second' was acted by the players of the Lord Chamberlain, of whom Shakespeare was one, on Saturday, the 7th of February, the evening before the defeat of the insane enterprise headed by the disappointed and irritated Earl of Essex. It had been the intention of the company to have acted some other more popular play on that night; but friends of the Earl of Essex had an interview with some of the leaders of the association; and at the instance of those friends the tragedy of 'Richard the Second,' (then considered 'an old play' and not likely to be attractive,) was substituted. To compensate the actors for their trouble, and for the probable loss they should sustain by the revival of an old drama, the exhibition of which, it was supposed, would advance the purposes of the insurgents, Sir Gilly Merrick and others, as was sworn upon their trial, agreed to give the performers 40s. beyond the money that might be taken at the doors.

"The document I have recovered is the account given by Augustine Phillipps, 'Servant unto the Lord Chamberlain, and one of his Players,' of what passed at the interview between the friends of the Earl of Essex and the members of the company, when the former consented to pay, and the latter to accept, 40s. on condition that they should substitute 'Richard the Second' for the play it had been their intention to perform on Saturday, the 7th of February, 1601. The date of the paper is the '18th of February, 1600;' but at that time the new year did not commence until the 26th of March, so that the '18th of February, 1600,' was, in fact, the 18th of February, 1601.

" It appears that, on the failure of the 'insurrection,' certain persons were appointed by the Crown to take the preliminary

P

I think the above is sufficient to satisfy the
reader that a series of skilful forgeries has
been practised at some late period, and apparently by some one person, on the literary

---

examinations of the different witnesses against the offenders,
and as Shakespeare was still an actor among the Lord Chamberlain's servants, as well as an author solely employed by them,
it might have happened that he would be the witness, or one of
the witnesses, to prove the agreement. We do not even know
that he was present when it was entered into ; for Phillipps tells
us that the friends of the Earl of Essex—viz., Sir Charles Pryce,
Jostlyne Pryce, and the Lord Monteagle (he does not mention
Merrick nor Cuff)—'spake with *some of the Players* in the presence of this examinant,'—but he does not give the names of the
other players, and it is very possible that Phillipps was the sole
witness to the fact on the arraignment and trial of the prisoners.
He distinctly gives the title of the play, calling it ' The Deposing
and killing King Richard the Second,' but he does not inform
us what newer and more attractive drama it was to displace, at
the instance of the two Pryces and Lord Monteagle.

" This examination is signed by Augustine Phillipps in his own
firm hand, and with both his names at length, and not merely
' A. Phillips,' as it appears at the close of his will, dated the
4th of May, 1605, and proved by his widow on the 13th of the
same month. He survived his examination, therefore, only
about four years, and died at his country residence at Mortlake.
(' Memoirs of the Actors in Shakespeare's Plays,' 8vo. 1846,
p. 83.)

" His prominence in the company in the spring of 1601, no
doubt, led to the selection of him as the person chiefly to be
negotiated with by the Pryces and Lord Monteagle, and afterwards as the witness in Court to the agreement for the representation of ' Richard the Second ' His name comes third in
the list of actors prefixed to the folio of Shakespeare's Works in

world.   Corrections of Shakspere's text, pretending to be of the seventeenth, have been proved
to be of the nineteenth century.   Documents
professedly original, relating important facts
concerning him, have been shown to have no
older or more venerable date than this or the
last generation.   I cannot disguise from myself
or my readers, that these discoveries are far
from rejoicing me.   On the contrary they seem
more suited to give a feeling of sadness.   How
far has the subtle poison, of which I have by
accident succeeded in tracking a few traces,
circulated " unknown to men" throughout the
body of our literature.   Many of the records of
the past, on which we are wont to rely, exist
only in print, and any test of their truth

1632, being only postponed to those of Heminge, the acknowledged head of the association, and of Burbadge, the great
tragedian.

" The title and the whole body of this interesting document is
in the not-easily-legible handwriting of Lord Chief Justice
Popham, and it is counter-signed by him, Mr. Justice Anderson,
and Edw. Fenner, who was, I believe, at that date one of the
Queen's Serjeants.   It may be recollected that Popham was one
of the Judges who went with Sir Thomas Egerton, then Keeper
of the Great Seal, to Essex House, in order, if possible, to
reason with the Earl upon the madness as well as treasonable-
ness of his proceedings."

                                        " J. PAYNE COLLIER."

beyond the doubtful one of internal evidence cannot now be brought to bear. What if " Old Correctors " were abroad then, and prudently destroyed the means of discovering their *youth!* In any case, without pushing suspicion beyond the soberest limits, the sight of successful deception is painful and unsettling. A distressing habit of doubt is apt to fasten on the mind, and a sense of helpless insecurity to overpower all other feelings.

But the history of past or present literary forgeries, does not warrant any excessive scepticism. The skill, dishonesty and knowledge, requisite for their successful perpetration, do not often meet in one individual ; neither are the commercial advantages sufficiently tempting to call forth many or frequent attempts.

We cannot always penetrate the motives of crime, nor, indeed, is it always necessary that we should do this ; but the good practical moral derivable from the present case, is, that greater caution in the reception of new discoveries should be practised than has been usual of late ; and that no amount of incompetent laudation, however sincere or boisterous, can guarantee to the public the authenticity of recently announced Manuscript Documents.

APPENDIX I.

THE BRIDGEWATER SHAKSPERE FORGERIES.

In the Library at Bridgewater House, is a large folio containing six documents. These are all forgeries, excepting the 4th, which is genuine, and is headed, " The opinions of the two Chief Justices of either bench concerning the jurisdiccōn authoritie and liberties claymed by the Cittizens of London within the precincte of the late dissolved howses of the white and black Fryers of London delivered the xxvijth of Januarie, 1579."

A fac-simile of the fifth document in the series, executed by Mr. Netherclift, will be found at p. 83. The resemblance between the character and forms of the letters in this document and in the marginal corrections in the Duke of Devonshire's " folio," is very striking.

The text shows the exact reading of the Bridgewater MSS. Numerous verbal and literal inaccuracies exist in the professedly *verbatim et litteratim copies* printed by Mr. Collier in his *New Facts*, 1835.

No. I.

For avoiding of the playhouse in the Blacke Friers.

Impr. Richard Burbidge owith the Fee, and is alsoe a sharer therein. His interest he rateth at the grosse summe of 1000 li for the Fee, and for his foure Shares the summe of 933 li 6s 8d

1933 li 6s 8d

Item Laz Fletcher owith three shares wch he rateth at 700 li, that is at 7 years purchase for eche share, or 33 li 6s 8d one yeare with an other.

700 li

Item W. Shakspeare asketh for the Wardrobe and properties of the same playhouse 500 li, and for his 4 shares, the same as his fellowes Burbidge and Fletcher, viz. 933 li 6s 8d.

1433 li 6s 8d

Item Heminges and Condell eche 2 shares	933 li	6s 8d
Item Joseph Taylor one share and an halfe	350 li	
Item Lowing one share and an halfe	350 li	
Item Foure more playeres with one halfe share vnto eche of them	466 li 13s 4d	

Sum^a totalis   6166 13 4

Moreover, the hired men of the companie demaund some recompence for their greate losse, and the Widowes and Orphanes of players, who are paide by the sharers at divers rates and proporcōns, soe as in the whole it will coste the Lo. Mayor and Citizens at the least 7000 li.

No II.

*To the Right honorable Sir Thomas Egerton, Knight,
Lord Keeper of the great Seale of England.*

I will not indeavour, Right honorable, to thanke you in
wordes for this new great and vnlookt for favor showne vnto
me, whereby I am bound to you for ever, and hope one day
with true harte and simple skill to prove that I am not
vnmindfull.

Most earnestly doe I wishe I could praise as your
Honour has knowne to deserue, for then should I, like
my maister Spencer, whose memorie your Honor cherish-
eth, leave behinde me some worthie worke, to be treasured
by posteritie; What my pore muse could performe in
haste is here set downe, and though it be farre below what
other poets and better pennes have written it commeth from
a gratefull harte and therefore maye be accepted. I shall
now be able to liue free from those cares and troubles that
hetherto haue been my continuall and wearisome companions. But a little time is paste since I was called vpon to
thanke yo' honor for my brothers advancement and nowe I
thanke you for my owne wch double kindnes will alwaies receive double gratefullnes at both our handes.

I cannot but knowe that I am lesse deseruing then some
that sued by other of the nobilitie vnto her Matie for this
roome, if M. Drayton my good friend had bene chosen I
should not have murmured for sure I am he wold have filled
it most excellentlie; but it seemeth to myne humble iudge-
ment that one which is the authour of playes now daylie
presented on the publick stages of London and the possessor
of no small gaines, and moreover himself an actor in the

kinges companie of Commedias, could not with reason pretend to be m¹ of the Queenes Matie Reuelles for asmuchas
he wold sometimes be asked to approue and allowe of his
owne writinge.   Therfore he and more of like qualitie can
not iustly be disappointed because through yor Honors gracious interposition the chance was haply myne.   I owe this
and all else to yor Honors and if euer I haue time and
abilitie to finishe anie noble vndertaking as god graunt one
daye I shall, the worke will rather be yor Honors then
myne.   God maketh a poet but his creation wold be in
vaine if patrones did not make him to liue.   Yo' Honor hath
euer showne yor selfe the friend of desert, and pitty it were
if this should be the first exception to the rule.   It shall not
be whiles my poore witt and strength doe remaine to me,
though the verses wch I nowe sende be indeede noe proofe of
myne abilitie I onely intreat yor Honor to accept the same
the rather as an earnest of my good will then as an example
of my good deede.   In all thinges I am yor Honors

Most bounden in dutie and

obseruance,

S. DANYELL.

No. III.

These are to sertifie yor right honorable Ll that her Ma^{tes} poore playeres, James Burbidge, Richard Burbidge, John Laneham, Thomas Greene, Robert Wilson, John Taylor, Anth. Wadeson, Thomas Pope, George Peele, Augustine Phillippes, Nicholas Towley, William Shakespeare, William Kempe, William Johnson, Baptiste Goodale, and Robert Armyn, being all of them sharers in the blacke Fryers playehouse, have neuer giuen cause of displeasure, in that they haue brought into their playes maters of state and Religion, vnfitt to be handled by them or to be presented before lewde spectators; neither hath anie complainte in that kinde ever beene preferred against them or anie of them. Wherefore they truste moste humblie in yor Ll consideracōn of their former good behauiour, beinge at all tymes readie and willing to yeelde obedience to anie commaund whatsoever your Ll in your wisedome maye thinke in such case meete, &c.

Novr., 1589.

No. IV.—GENUINE.

Q

No. V.

Right trustie and wellbeloved &c. James &c. To all
Mayors, Sheriffes, Justices of the peace &c. Whereas the
Queene our dearest wife hath for her pleasure and recreacōn
appointed her servauntes Robert Daborne &c. to prouide and
bring uppe a convenient nomber of children who shalbe
called the children of her Ma*ies* revelles, Knowe yee that
We have appointed and authorized and by these presentes doe
appoint and authorize the saide Robert Daborne, Willm̄
Shakespeare, Nathaniel Field, and Edward Kirkham from
time to time to prouide and bring vpp a convenient nomber
of children, and them to instruct and exercise in the qualitie
of playing Tragedies Comedies &c. by the name of the
children of the reuelles to the Queene, within the blacke
Fryers in our Cittie of London and els where within our realme
of England. Wherefore we will and commaund you and
everie of you to permitte her said servauntes to keepe a convenient nomber of children by the name of the children of
the reuelles to the Queene, and them to exercise in the
qualitie of playing acording to our Royall pleasure. Provided allwayes that noe playes &c. shalbe by them presented,
but such playes &c. as haue receiued the aprobacōn and allowance of our Maıster of the Reuelles for the tyme being.

And these our lr̃es shalbe yoͬ sufficient warraunt in this
behalfe.   In Witnesse whereof &c. 4° die Janii. 1609.

Bl Fr and globe	
Wh Fr and parishe garden	All in
Curten and fortune	& neere
Hope and Swanne	London

Proude pouertie
Widdowes mite
Antonio kinsmen
Triumph of truth
Touchstone
Mirror of life
Grissell
Engl tragedie
False Friendes
Hate and loue
Taming of S
K. Edw. 2

Stayed.

No. VI.

My verie honored Lo. the manie good offices I haue receiued at yor Lps handes wh^h ought to make me backward in asking further favors onely imbouldeneth me to require more in the same kinde.   Yo^t Lp. wilbe warned howe hereafter you graunt anie sute seeing it draweth on more and greater demaundes : this wch now presseth is to request yor Lp. in all you can to be good to the poore players of the blacke Fryers who call them selues by authoritie the Servantes of his Matie and aske for the proteccōn of their most gracious maister and Soueraigne in this the tyme of there troble. They are threatened by the Lo. Maior and Aldermen of London never friendly to their calling wth the distruccōn of their meanes of liuelihood by the pulling downe of their plaiehouse wch is a priuate theatre and hath never giuen ocasion of anger by anie disorders.   These bearers are two of the chiefe of the companie, one of them by name Richard Burbidge who humblie sueth for yor Lps kinde helpe for that he is a man famous as our english Roscius one who fitteth the action to the worde and the word to the action most admira[b]ly.   By the exercise of his qualitie industry and good behaviour he hath become possessed of the Blacke Fryers playhouse wch hath bene imployed for playes sithence it was builded by his Father now nere 50 yeres agone.   The other is a man no whitt lesse deseruing fauor and my especial friende till of late an actor of good account in the cumpanie, now a sharer in the same, and writer of some of our best english playes wch as your Lp. knoweth were most singulerly liked of Quene Elizabeth when the cumpanie was called vppon to performe before her Matie at Court at Christmas and Shrove tide. His most gracious Matie King James alsoe since his coming to the crowne hath extended his Royall favour to the companie in diuers waies and at sundrie tymes. This other hath to name William Shakespeare and they are both of one countie and indeede allmost of one towne, both are right famous in their qualities though it longeth not of yor Lo. grauitie and wisdome to resort vnto the places where they are wont to delight the publique eare. Their trust and sute nowe is not to bee molested in their waye of life whereby they maintaine themselues and their wiues and families (being both maried and of good reputacōn) as well as the widowes and orphanes of some of their dead fellows. Yo^{r} Lo. most bounden at com̃. H. S.

Copia vera.

APPENDIX II.

Forgeries among the Documents at Dulwich College: with Extracts from Mr. J. P. Collier's Remarks upon them.

No. I.

"But there is another paper of a very similar kind, apparently referring to the preceding, or to some other like contest, but containing several remarkable allusions, which Malone did not notice. Perhaps it never met his eye, or perhaps he reserved it for his Life of Shakespeare, and was unwilling to forestall that production by inserting it elsewhere. It seems to be of a later date, and it mentions not only Tarlton, Knell, and Bentley, but Kempe, Phillips, and Pope, while Alleyn's rival Burbage is sneered at as "Roscius Richard," and Shakespeare introduced under the name of Will, by which we have Thomas Heywood's authoritie (in his "Hierarchie of the blessed Angels," 1635, p. 206) for saying he was known among his companions. The paper is in verse, and runs precisely as follows :

"Sweet Nedde, nowe wynne an other wager
For thine old friende and Fellow stager;
Tarlton himself thou dost excell,
And Bentley beate, and conquer Knell,
And nowe shall Kempe orecome aswell.

The moneys downe, the place the Hope,
Phillipes shall hide his head and Pope.
Fear not, the victorie is thyne ;
Thou still as macheles Ned shall shyne.
If Roscius Richard foames and fumes,
The globe shall have but emptie roomes;
If thou doest act; and Willes newe playe
Shall be rehearst some other daye.
Consent, then, Nedde ; doe us this grace :
Thou cannot faile in anie case ;
For in the triall, come what maye,
All sides shall brave Ned Allin saye."

Memoirs of Alleyn, p. 13, ed. J. P. Collier, 1841.

No. II.

" Malone also appears to have reserved another circumtance, of very considerable importance in relation to Shakespeare, for his life of the poet. To the last-quoted document, but in a different hand and in different ink, is appended a list of the king's players. The name of Shakespeare there occurs second, and as it could not be written at the bottom of the letter of the Council to the Lord Mayor, &c. prior to the date of that letter, it proves that up to 9th April, 1604, our great dramatist continued to be numbered among the *actors* of the company. Hitherto the last trace we have had of Shakespeare as actually on the stage, has been as one of the performers in Ben Jonson's ' *Sejanus*,' which was produced in 1603. We will insert the list as it stands at the foot of the Council's letter to the Lord Mayor, &c.

" Ks Comp.
Burbidge
Shakespeare
Fletcher
Phillips
Condle
Hemminges
Armyn
Slye
Cowley
Hostler
Day."

Memoirs of Alleyn, p. 68.

No. III.

" The following undated note from Marston to Henslowe may not be unfitly introduced here : it refers to a play by Marston on the subject of Columbus, of which we hear on no other authority. It is one of the scraps of correspondence between Henslowe and the poets in his employ, existing at Dulwich College, of the major part of which Malone has given copies, but omitting the subsequent, which is certainly one of the most interesting of the whole collection.

" Mr. Hensloe, at the rose on the Bankside.

" If you like my play of Columbus, it is verie well and you shall give me no more than twentie poundes for it, but If nott, lett mee have it by this Bearer againe, as I knowe the kinges men will freelie give mee as much for it, and the profitts of the third daye moreover.

" Soe I rest yours

" JOHN MARSTON."

Memoirs of Alleyn, p. 154.

R

APPENDIX. III.

THE INCHANTED ISLAND.

The following is the ballad alluded to p. 102, and printed by Mr. J. P. Collier, in " FARTHER PARTICULARS REGARD- ING SHAKESPEARE AND HIS WORKS. In a letter to the Rev. Joseph Hunter, F.S.A., from J. Payne Collier, F.S.A. London. Thomas Rodd, Great Newport Street, Long Acre, 1839."

" I will now," (says Mr. Collier) " introduce to your notice a production *in verse*, in my opinion written subsequently to *The Tempest*, and adopting all or most of its principal inci- dents. I once thought it possible that this ballad (for such it is) might have preceded the play, but I now am satisfied that it is a later production, and that the writer was ac- quainted with *The Tempest*, though he does not employ a single name found in it. My conjecture is that it was pub- lished (if published at all, of which we have no evidence but probability) during the period when the theatres were closed (viz. from about 1642 to 1660), in order, by putting the stories of discontinued dramas into easy rhyme, to give the public some species of amusement founded upon old plays, although the severity of the Puritans in those times would not allow the performance of theatrical entertainments. Hence Jordan's ballads, derived from *The Merchant of Venice*,

The Winter's Tale, Much ado about Nothing, &c. quoted in
my letter to the Rev. A. Dyce. I also mentioned to him on
that occasion the ballad to which I am now adverting, and,
having since gone over it with him, I believe he concurs with
me in thinking that it is posterior to Shakespeare's *Tempest*.
The late Mr. Douce, who also had several opportunities of
reading it, at first hoped that it was the long-sought original
of that wonderful drama; and when I last saw him and
spoke of it, he was disposed to think that the play and the
ballad were derived from one common source; but though
the copying of particular expressions cannot be detected,
there are such strong general resemblances, that I feel assured that the writer of the ballad must have known, if he
did not in part use, the play. The initials at the end of the
MS. led me, when first I saw it, to conjecture that Robert
Greene, who died in 1592, might be the author of it, but it
is decidedly of too modern a cast and structure for him, and,
as I before observed, my conjecture is that it was written
about the period of the Protectorate.

I have never met with nor heard of any printed copy of it;
but it is inserted in the MS. volume I have had for years in
my possession, the particular contents of which may be seen
in my letter to the Rev. A. Dyce. The ballads appear to
be of all ages during the century between the opening of the
reign of Elizabeth and the time of the Restoration.

Mr. Douce called it " one of the most beautiful ballads he
had ever read," and shook his venerable head (as was his
wont) with admiring energy and antiquarian enthusiasm at
different passages in it; but I am by no means prepared to
give it so high a character. It is certainly vastly better,
both in style and sentiment, than any thing of the sort Jordan has written, and to whom the initials R. G. at the end

can apply, it would be vain to conjecture. Robert Gomersall was a poet of no mean eminence, about that period or a little earlier (he died in 1646); but it was not at all in the manner of any thing he has left behind him. It runs thus : —

THE INCHANTED ISLAND.

In Arragon there livde a king,
Who had a daughter sweete as Spring,
 A little playful childe.
He lovde his studie and his booke ;
The toyles of state he could not brooke,
 Of temper still and milde.

He left them to his Brother's care,
Who soone usurped the throne unware,
 And turnd his Brother forth.
The studious king Geraldo hight,
His daughter Ida, deare as sight
 To him who knew her worth.

The Brother who usurped the throne
Was by the name Benormo knowne,
 Of cruell harte and bolde.
He turned his niece and Brother forth
To wander east, west, north, or south,*
 All in the winter colde.

Long time he journeyd up and downe,
The head all bare that wore a crowne,
 And Ida in his hand,

---

* For the rhyme we should read " south or north," and for the sense it answers equally well. The transcriber was not a very accurate penman.—[C.]

Till that they reachd the broad sea side
Where marchant ships at anchor ride
       From many a distant land.

Imbarking ther, in one of these,
They were by force of windes and seas
       Driven wide for many a mile ;
Till at the last they shelter found,
The maister and his men all drownd,
       In the inchanted Isle.

Geraldo and his daughter faire,
The onelie two that landed there,
       Were savde by myracle ;
And, sooth to say, in dangerous houre
He had some more than human powre,
       As seemeth by what befell.

He brought with him a magicke booke,
Whereon his eye did oft times looke,
       That wrought him wonders great.
A magicke staffe he had alsoe,
That angrie fiendes compelld to goe
       To doe his bidding straight.

The spirites of the earth and aire,
Unseene, yet fleeting every where,
       To crosse him could not chuse.
All this by studie he had gaind
While he in Arragon remaind,
       But never thought to use.

When landed on thinchanted Isle
His little Ida's morning smile
       Made him forgett his woe :

And thus within a cavern dreare
They livde for many a yeare ifere,
    For heaven had will'd it soe.

His blacke lockes turnd all silver gray,
But ever time he wore away,
    To teach his childe intent;
And as she into beautie grew
In knowledge she advanced to [o]
    As wise as innocent.

Most lovlie was she to beholde ;
Her haire was like to sunn litt golde,
    And blue as heaven her eye.
When she was in her fifteenth yeere
Her daintie forme was like the deere *
    Sportfull with majestie.

The Demons who the land had held
By might of magicke he expelld,
    Save such as he did neede ;
And servaunts of the ayre he kept
To watch o'er Ida when she slept,
    Or on swift message speede.

And all this while in Arragon
Benormo raignde, who had a son
    Now growne to mans estate :
His sire in all things most unlike
Of courage tried, yet slow to strike,
    Not turning love to hate.

* This couplet is transposed in the MSS. with the figures 1 and
2 against the lines, to indicate the order in which they were to
be read.—[C.]

Alfonso was the Princes name,
It chancd posthaste a message came
    Just then to Arragon
From Sicilie to son and sire,
Which did their presence soone desire
To see Sicilia's son

Fast tyed in the nuptiall band
To Naples daughters lovelie hand,
    And they to go consent.
So in a galley on a day
To Sicilie they tooke their way,
    Thither to saile intent.

Geraldo by his magicke art
Knew even the hour of their depart
    For distant Sicilie :
He knew alsoe that they must passe
Neare to the isle whereon he was,
    And that revenge was nie.

He callde his spirites of the aire
Commanding them a storme prepare
    To cast them on that shore.
The gallant barke came sailing on
With silken sailes from Arragon
    And manie a guilded ore.

But gilded ore and silken saile
Might not against the storm prevaile :
    The windes blew hie aud loude.
The sailes were rent, the ores were broke
The ship was split by lightning stroke
    That burste from angrie cloude.

But such Geraldoe's powre that day
That though the ship was cast away,
    Of all the crue not one,
Not even the shipboy, then was drowned,
And old Benormo on drie ground
    Imbracde his dearest son.

About the isle they wandered long
For still some spirite led them wrong
    Till they were wearie growne ;
Then came to olde Geraldoe's cell,
Where he and lovelie Ida dwell ;
    Though seene they were not knowne.

Much marvelled they in such a place
To see an Eremit's wringled face,.
    More at the maid they start :
And soone as did Alfonso see
Ida so beautifull but hee
    Felt love within his hart.

Benormo heard with griefe and shame
Geraldo call him by his name,
    His brothers voyce well knowne.
Upon his aged knees he fell,
And wept that he did ere rebell
    Against his brother's throne.

Brother, he cried, forgive my crime !
I sweare, since that u[n]happie time
    I have not tasted peace.
Returne and take againe your crowne,
Which at your feete I will lay downe,
    And soe our jarres surcease.

Never, Giraldo said, will I
Ascend that seat of soverainty ;
     But I all wrongs forgett.
I have a daughter, you a son,
And they shall raigne ore Arragon,
     And on my throne be sett.

My head is all too olde to bear
The weight of crownes and kingdomes care,
     Peace in my bookes I find.
Gold crownes beseeme not silver lockes,
Like sunbeames upon whitend rockes,
     They mocke the tranquill minde.

Benormo, worne with cares of state,
Which worldlie sorrowes aye create,
     Sawe the advice was good.
The tide of love betwixt the paire,
Alfonso young and Ida faire,
     Had suddaine reacht the flood.

A galley, too, that was sent out
From Sicilie in feare and doubt,
     As having heard the wracke,
Arrived at the inchanted Isle,
And took them all in little while
     Unto Messina backe.

But ere his leave Geraldo tooke
Of the strange isle, he burnt his booke
     And broke his magicke wand.
His arte forbid he aye forswore,
Never to deale in magicke more
     The while the earth shuld stand.

S

From that daie forth the Isle has beene
By wandering sailors never seene.
  Some say 'tis buryed deepe
Beneath the sea, which breakes and rores
Above its savage rockie shores,
  Nor ere is knowne to sleepe.

In Sicilie the paire was wed,
To Arragon there after sped,
  With fathers who them blessed.*
Alfonso rulde for many a yeare,
His people lovde him farre and neare,
  But Ida lovde him best.

    FINIS.   R. G.

---

* In the MS it stands " blesse," but the rhyme clearly requires " blessed," no doubt an error of transcription.—[C.]

APPENDIX IV.

CORRESPONDENCE IN *THE TIMES* FROM JULY 2, TO AUGUST 1, 1859.*

LETTER I.

To the Editor of The Times.

Sir,—Perhaps amid the press and distraction of politics which are now agitating the great world, you can find room for the account of a most extraordinary deception which has been practised in the republic of letters, some details of which I now beg to lay before you.

In 1852 Mr. John Payne Collier published a volume containing numerous and important *Notes and Emendations* of the text of Shakspere, made, as he stated, on the faith of a copy of the folio edition of 1632, purchased by him of Mr. Thomas Rodd in 1849, and exhibiting a vast number of marginal corrections and alterations in a handwriting asserted by Mr. Collier to be, to the best of his belief, contemporary, or nearly so, with the date of the edition.

Such has been the effect of that publication throughout

---

* It has been thought advisable to reprint in a consecutive form the whole of the Correspondence which appeared in *The Times* on *The Shaksperian Discovery*, notwithstanding that portions of it have been already quoted in the preceding pages.

Europe that since the date of its issue the text of Shakspere has been extensively changed, and this, notwithstanding the strongest remonstrance and opposition from various quarters. I need not go over this ground, familiar as it is to all who know anything of the literary history of the last ten years.

In 1853 Mr. Collier published a second edition of his work, together with an edition of Shakspere founded on the corrected folio ; and in 1856 what professed to be a complete list of all the readings.

" I have," says he, in his preface to this last work (p. lxxix.), " often gone over the thousands of marks of all kinds in its margins ; but I will take this opportunity of pointing out two emendations of considerable importance, which happening not to be in the margins, and being written with very pale ink, escaped my eye until some time after the appearance of my second edition, as well as of the one-volume *Shakespeare*. For the purpose of the later portion of my present work I have recently re-examined every line and letter of the folio 1632, and I can safely assert that no other sin of omission on my part can be discovered."

These publications were accompanied by what professed to be a minute account of the appearance and history of the recently-discovered folio. It is, however, notorious. that by a considerable number of persons interested in the subject, the descriptions thus given were never deemed sufficient or satisfactory in a matter of such deep literary importance.

In common with others, I had often desired to see the volume, which meanwhile had become the property of the Duke of Devonshire. This wish has at length been gratified. Some two months ago his Grace, the present Duke, liberally placed the folio in the hands of Sir Frederic Madden,

Keeper of the MSS. in the British Museum, with the understanding that, while it should be kept by Sir Frederic Madden in the strictest custody, it might yet be examined, under proper restrictions, by any and all literary persons who were anxious to do so. I at once seized the opportunity, and determined, avoiding all Shaksperian criticism, to attempt an accurate and unbiased description of the volume from the literary point of view alone. Discoveries soon occurred, to which it seems advisable immediate publicity should be given, and which I now send you in as clear a manner as the narrow scope of a letter will permit.

The volume is bound in rough calf (probably about the middle of George II.'s reign), the water-mark of the leaves pasted inside the cover being a crown surmounting the letters " G. R." (*Georgius Rex*), and the Dutch lion within a paling, with the legend *pro patriâ ;** and there is evidence to show that the corrections, though intended to resemble a hand of the middle of the 17th century, could not have been written on the margins of the volume until after it was bound, and consequently not at the earliest, until towards the middle of the 18th.

I should enter more minutely into this feature of the case, did not the corrections themselves, when closely examined, furnish facts so precise and so startling in their character that all collateral and constructive evidence seems unnecessary and insignificant.

---

* I have recently investigated this point minutely, and am of opinion that the binding is even later than I had at first imagined. Paper of the same texture, and with the same watermark, was in common use from 1760 to 1780. See Haldimand Correspondence, in the British Museum. I have seen a watermark almost identical in Dutch foolscap of the present day.—[H.]

They at first sight seem to be of two kinds,—those, namely, which have been allowed to remain, and those which have been obliterated with more or less success, sometimes by erasure with a penknife or the employment of chemical agency, and sometimes by tearing and cutting away parts of the margin. The corrections thus variously obliterated are probably almost as numerous as those suffered to remain, and in importance equal to them. Whole lines, entire words, and stage directions have been attempted to be got rid of, though in many instances without success, as a glance at the various readings of a first portion of *Hamlet*, which I sub-join, will show.

Of the corrections allowed to stand, some, on a hasty glance, might, so far as the handwriting is concerned, pass as genuine, while others have been strangely tampered with, touched up, or painted over, a modern character being dexterously altered by touches of the pen into a more antique form. There is, moreover, a kind of exaggeration in the shape of the letters throughout, difficult, if not im-possible, to reconcile with a belief in the genuineness of the hand; not to mention the frequent and strange juxtaposi-tion of stiff Chancery capital letters of the form in use two centuries ago with others of a quite modern appearance : and it is well here to state that all the corrections are evidently by one hand; and that, consequently, whatever invalidates or destroys the credit of a part, must be considered equally damaging and fatal to the whole.

At times the correction first put in the margin has been obliterated, and a second emendation substituted in its stead, of which I will mention two examples which occur in *Cym-beline* (fol. 1632, p. 400, col. 1) :—

" With Oakes unshakeable and roaring Waters,"

where *Oakes* has first been made into *Cliffes*, and subsequently into *Rockes*. Again (p. 401, col. 2) :—

" Whose Roof's as low as ours : Sleepe Boyes, this gate,"

on the margin (a pencil cross having been made in the first instance) *Sleepe* is corrected into *Sweete*, afterwards *Sweete* has been crossed out, and *Stoope* written above.

There is scarcely a single page throughout the volume in which these obliterations do not occur. At the time they were effected it is possible the obliteration may have appeared complete ; but the action of the atmosphere in the course of some years seems in the majority of instances to have so far negatived the chemical agency as to enable the corrections to be readily deciphered. Examples of these accompany this letter, and I shall be surprised if in the hands of Shaksperian critics they do not furnish a clue to the real history of the corrector and his corrections.

I now come to the most astounding result of these investigations, in comparison with which all other facts concerning the corrected folio become insignificant. On a close examination of the margins they are found to be covered with an infinite number of faint pencil-marks and corrections, in obedience to which the supposed old corrector has made his emendations. These pencil corrections have not even the pretence of antiquity in character or spelling, but are written in a bold hand of the present century. A remarkable instance occurs in *Richard III.* (fol. 1632, p. 181, col. 2), where the stage direction, " with the body," is written in pencil in a clear modern hand, while over this the ink corrector writes in the antique and smaller character " with the dead bodie," the word " dead " being seemingly inserted to cover over the entire space occupied by the larger pencil writing, and ' bodie " instead of " body " to

give the requisite appearance of antiquity. Further on, in
the tragedy of *Hamlet* (fol. 1632, p. 187, col. 1) :—

    " And crooke the pregnant Hindges of the knee,"

" begging " occurs in pencil in the opposite margin, in the
same modern hand, evidently with the intention of super-
seding "pregnant" in the text. The entire passage from,
" Why should the poore be flatter'd ?" to " As I doe thee.
Something too much of this" was afterwards struck out.
The ink corrector, probably thrown off his guard by this,
neglected to copy over and afterwards rub out the pencil
alteration, according to his usual plan, and by this oversight
we seem to obtain as clear a view of the *modus operandi* as if
we had looked over the corrector's shoulder and seen the
entire work in process of fabrication. I give several further
instances where the modern pencil-writing can be distinctly
seen underneath the old ink correction ; and I should add
that in parts of the volume, page after page occurs in which
commas, notes of admiration and interrogation, &c., are
deleted or inserted in obedience to pencil indications of
precisely the same modern character and appearance as those
employed in correcting the press at the present day. *Twelfth
Night* (fol. 1632, p. 258, col. 1) :—" I take these wise men,
that crow so at these set kind of fooles, no better than the
fooles Zanies." The corrector makes it "*to be* no better
than," &c. Here the antique "to be " is written over a
modern pencil " to be " still clearly legible. A few lines
further down the letter *l* is added in the margin over a
pencil *l*.

    In *Hamlet* (fol. 1632, p. 278, col. 1) :—

        " Oh, most pernicious woman !"

is made into—

        " Oh, most pernicious and perfidious woman !

But here, again, the "perfidious" of the corrector can be seen to be above a pencil "perfidious" written in a perfectly modern hand.

In *Hamlet* (fol. 1632, p. 276, col. 2) the line

"Looke too't, I charge you ; come your way,"

has been altered by the corrector into

"Looke too't, I charge you ; *so ncw* come your way"

in the inner margin. The words "so now," in faint pencil and in a modern hand, on the outer margin, are distinctly visible. Immediately below this, and before

"*Enter* Hamlet, Horatio, Marcellus,"

the corrector has inserted "Sc. 4." This would seem to have been done in obedience to a pencil "IV." in the margin.

In *King John* (fol. 1632, p. 6, col. 2),

"Austria and France shoot in each other's mouth.

The corrector adds, as a direction, at this line "aside;" the same word "aside" occurs likewise in pencil in a modern hand on the outer margin.

I have thus endeavoured to give, in a dispassionate manner, and as clearly as the limited scope of a letter will admit, the grounds upon which I conceive it positively established that the emendations, as they are called, of this folio copy of *Shakspere*, have been made in the margins within the present century. What further deductions may be drawn from the large mass of hitherto unpublished alterations which the folio contains I leave others to determine. They may or may not be the means of identifying particular persons or particular dates, but in the main issue are comparatively unimportant.

T

While I am personally responsible for the conclusions I have been driven to by the discovery of the above-mentioned facts, the accuracy of the facts themselves and the fidelity of my statement of them have been carefully and scrupulously examined by men having greater ability and experience in such matters than I can lay claim to. Moreover, these are points which may be tested by any persons interested in the subject, and who will be at the pains of verifying for themselves the truth of what I have here advanced. I have only to add that I hope shortly to lay before the public, in another form and in fuller detail, other particulars relating to this remarkable volume.

I am, &c.,

N. E. S. A. HAMILTON.

Department of MSS.,
  British Museum, June 22.

———

LETTER II.

To the Editor of the Times.

Sir,—I trust to your sense of justice, to say nothing of my ancient connection with your establishment (see especially the *Times* of the summer of 1819), for the insertion of this letter with as much prominence as you gave to that of Mr. Hamilton in your paper of July 2. As I live entirely in the country, and take in only a weekly publication, I did not see your paper containing that letter until an hour ago. I shall reply to it briefly and positively.

First, as to the pencillings in the corrected folio, 1632, which I accidentally discovered. I never made a single pencil-mark on the pages of the book, excepting crosses,

ticks, or lines, to direct my attention to particular emendations.* I have not seen it for four or five years, but I
remember that on the board at the end (there was no fly-
leaf there) I wrote various words, and made several notes,
which I never attempted to erase. There they probably
remain ; and if the pencilings of which Mr. Hamilton speaks,
in the body of the volume, were made by me, they may be
compared with my writing on the last board, and by that
writing I may be convicted, unless somebody, which I do
not believe, have taken the pains to imitate my hand.
What is clearly meant, though somewhat darkly expressed,
is that I am the author both of the pencillings and of the
notes in ink.

I have asserted the contrary on oath in an affidavit
sworn and filed in the Queen's Bench, on Jan. 8, 1856. I
assert the contrary now, and if any person will give me
the opportunity, I am ready to confirm it by my *vivâ voce*
testimony, and to encounter the most minute, the most
searching, and the most hostile examination.

I have shown and sworn that this very book was in the
possession of a gentleman named Parry about half a century
ago, given to him by a relation named George Gray. Mr.
Parry recognized it instantly, annotated as it is now ; and
since it came into my hands, in 1849, I have not made the
slightest addition to the notes in pencil or in ink.

Then, as to the binding. I contend that it is considerably older than the reign of George II., and that the

---

* I ought to add, that I drew pencil lines round 18 additional
fac-similes from the volume, admirably executed by Mr. Netherclift, copies of which I furnished to my friends, to enable them
the better to judge of the general mass of emendations.—[C.]

date of the fly-leaf affords no criterion as to the date when
the leather covering was put on, and for this reason, that
fly-leaves are often added at a subsequent period for the pro-
tection of the title page, because the original ones have been
torn or destroyed. Upon my own shelves I have several
distinct proofs of this fact, but I will only mention one. It
is a copy of Samuel Daniel's *Panegyricke Congratulatory*, folio
(1603), which the poet presented to the Countess of Pembroke; Daniel wrote her name on the gilt vellum cover,
and she put her signature on the title-page. It is likely
that Daniel also placed an inscription on the fly-leaf, which
has disappeared, perhaps to gratify the cupidity of some
autograph collector. A comparatively modern substitute
has been inserted; it has no water-mark, but a moment's
inspection is enough to show that it was much posterior to
the time when the book was printed.

The rough calf binding of the corrected folio, 1632, I
contend is old; it is the same as Lord Ellesmere's copy of
the same edition; the fly-leaf described by Mr. Hamilton is
comparatively new; but I have all along admitted, privately
and in print, that the rough calf binding of the corrected
folio, 1632, was the second or third coat the book had worn.

In the same way, as to imperfect erasures and alterations of emendations, denoting changes of mind or better
information on the part of the maker of the old marginal
notes, I have been as distinct and emphatic as anybody, in
both the editions of my volume of *Notes and Emendations* in
1852 and 1853. Mr. Hamilton can, I think, point out
nothing that I have not anticipated.

Soon after I discovered the volume, and before I had
written more than a letter or two in the *Athenæum* upon it,
produced it before the Council of the Shakspeare Society—

at the general meeting of that body—at two or three evening assemblies of the Society of Antiquaries; and in order that it might not escape the severest scrutiny by daylight, I advertised that it would be left for a whole morning in the library of that society for the inspection of anybody who wished to examine it. I did not see Mr. Hamilton there, but no one who inspected it discovered, or at least pointed out, any of the pencil-marks which it seems are now visible.

I shall say nothing of the indisputable character of many of the emendations. The Rev. Mr. Dyce has declared, in his own handwriting, that 'some of them are so admirable that they can hardly be conjectural,' and in the course of his recent impressions of the works of Shakspeare, he has pronounced such as he unavoidably adopted, irresistible, indubitable, infallible, &c. All this I might have appropriated to myself; and, having burnt the corrected folio, 1632, I might have established for myself a brighter Shakspearian reputation than all the commentators put together. If, therefore, I have committed a fraud, it has been merely gratuitous. I certainly preferred a different course, in spite of the warning given me by a friend in the outset, that my enemies would never forgive my discovery, and that their hostility would outlive my existence.

I am determined not to make the poor remainder of my life miserable by further irritating contests; this is the last word I shall ever submit to say upon the subject in print, but if the matter be brought before a proper legal tribunal, I shall be prepared in every way to vindicate my integrity.

May I be allowed to add a word in answer to certain paragraphs stating that the late Duke of Devonshire gave me a large sum for my corrected folio, 1632? It was a free gift on my part, frankly accepted by his Grace, although he afterwards (knowing of my family bereavements and consequent expenses) unsuccessfully endeavoured to persuade me to accept £250 for the volume. The Duke was at Chatsworth when I sent my letter to him, stating that the book was a poor return for the many essential and substantial favours I had received at his hands during a period of thirty years, and on June 20, 1853, his Grace wrote me a letter containing the following words :—

"It is impossible for me to express how much I am gratified by your present, on which I shall place great value, not only for the merits and interest that accompany it, but as a proof of your enduring friendship and approbation."

It is clear, therefore, that if without motive I imposed upon the public, I did not without conscience victimise the man to whom I was already so deeply indebted.

I am, &c., J. PAYNE COLLIER.

Riverside, Maidenhead, July 5.

LETTER III.

To the Editor of the Times.

SIR,—As it has been suggested to me that I should put on record some observations regarding the singular Shaksperian discovery recently made in the MSS. department here, I hope this letter will be sufficient explanation for my appearance on the scene in the discussion now going on regarding it.

There are three kinds of evidence that may be brought to bear on a literary forgery. The intrinsic literary character of the document is one of these. Another is of a palæological kind, and its value is to be estimated by the amount of experience and antiquarian erudition and skill of the critic. There is a third to which I would more particularly invite attention in this letter, and that rests on the physical scrutiny of the document, by the aids which science has placed in our hands.

There is, indeed, another direction in which such an inquiry may be pursued, and which has to deal in circumstantial evidence—such as individual handwriting, or the tracing of analogous documents into a single channel, or in other details highly interesting to the literary " detective," but not congenial to an officer of the British Museum. The officers, indeed, of a great national establishment like the Museum owe a duty to the public, and, in a certain sense occupy a judicial position in questions like this under discussion. Thus, while our object is not to trace the hand in a forgery, it is our duty to denounce the forgery itself. It is in this spirit that I have approached the subject, and it is with the physical aspects of it alone that I have to deal.

Mr. Hamilton, a gentleman at the time only slightly known to me as an officer of this establishment, informed me some days since that the Duke of Devonshire had intrusted the far-famed Collier's *Shakspere* to the hands of my colleague, Sir Frederic Madden, for the inspection of literary men ; and Mr. Hamilton further informed me of the doubts which, after a careful scrutiny of the volume, had arisen in his mind regarding its genuineness. His reasons for these doubts he has since made public by his letter in *The Times*. On his mentioning the existence of a vast number of partially obliterated pencil-marks, which seemed anticipatory of the ink " emendations " of " the old commentator," I suggested the use of an instrument which has already done

good service in an analogous case (that of the Simonides'
Uranius)—the microscope. This simple test of the character
of these emendations I brought to bear on them, and with
the following results. Firstly, as to any question that
might be raised concerning the presence of the pencil-marks,
asserted to be so plentifully distributed down the margin,
the answer is, they are there. The microscope reveals the
particles of plumbago in the hollows of the paper, and in no
case that I have yet examined does it fail to bring this fact
forward into incontrovertible reality. Secondly, the ink
presents a rather singular aspect under the microscope. Its
appearance in many cases on, rather than in, the paper,
suggested the idea of its being a water-colour paint rather
than an ink ; it has a remarkable lustre, and the distribution
of particles of colouring matter in it seem unlike that in
inks, ancient or modern, that I have yet examined.

This view is somewhat confirmed by a taste, unlike the
styptic taste of ordinary inks, which it imparts to the tongue,
and by its substance evidently yielding to the action of
damp. But on this point, as on another, to which attention
will presently be drawn, it was not possible to arrive at a
satisfactory conclusion in the absence of the Duke of Devonshire's permission to make a few experiments on the volume.

His Grace visited the Museum yesterday, and was good
enough to give me his consent to this. The result has been
that the suspicions previously entertained regarding the ink
were confirmed.

It proves to be a paint removable, with the exception of a
slight stain, by mere water, while, on the other hand, its
colouring matter resists the action of chymical agents which
rapidly change inks, ancient or modern, whose colour is due
to iron. In some places, indeed, this paint seems to have

become mixed, accidentally or otherwise, with ordinary ink, but its prevailing character is that of a paint formed perhaps of sepia, or of sepia mixed with a little Indian ink. This, however, is of secondary importance in comparison with the other point which has been alluded to. This point involves, indeed, the most important question that has arisen, and concerns the relative dates of the modern-looking pencil-marks and the old emendations of the text which are in ink. The pencil-marks are of different kinds. Some are *d's*, indicative of the deletion of stops or letters in the text, and to which alterations in ink, I believe, invariably respond. Others, again, belong to the various modes at present in use to indicate corrigenda for the press. Some may, perhaps, be the "crosses, ticks, or lines," which Mr. Collier introduced himself. But there are others again in which whole syllables or words in pencil are not so effectually rubbed out as not to be still traceable and legible, and even the character of the handwriting discernible, while in near neighbourhood to them the same syllable or word is repeated in the paint-like ink before described. The pencil is in a modern-looking hand, the ink in a quaint, antique-looking writing. In several cases, however, the ink word and the pencil word occupy the same ground in the margin, and are one over the other. The question that arises in these cases, of whether these two writings are both ancient or both modern, or one ancient and the other modern, is a question for the antiquary or palæographist. The question of whether the pencil is antecedent or subsequent to the ink, is resolvable into a physical inquiry as to whether the ink overlies the pencil, or the pencil is superposed upon the ink. The answer to this question is as follows :—

I have nowhere been able to detect the pencil-mark clearly overlying the ink, though in several places the pencil

U

stops abruptly at the ink, and in some seems to be just
traceable through its translucent substance, while lacking
there the general metallic lustre of the plumbago.   But the
question is set at rest by the removal by water of the ink,
in instances where the ink and the pencil intersected each
other.   The first case I chose for this was a *u* in *Richard II.*,
p. 36.   A pencil tick crossed the *u*, intersecting each limb of
that letter.   The pencil was barely visible through the first
stroke, and not at all visible under the second stroke of the
u.   On damping off the ink in the first stroke, however, the
pencil-mark became much plainer than before, and even when
as much of the ink-stain as possible was removed, the pencil
still runs through the ink line in unbroken, even continuity.
Had the pencil been superposed on the ink, it must have
lain superficially upon its lustrous surface and have been
removed in the washing.   We must, I think, be led by this
to the inference that the pencil underlies the ink—that is to
say, was antecedent to it in its date; while, also, it is
evident that the "old commentator" had done his best to
rub out the pencil writing before he introduced its ink
substitute.

Now, it is clear that evidence of this kind cannot by itself
establish a forgery.   It is on palæographical grounds alone
that the modern character of the pencillings can be established; but, this point once determined in the affirmative,
the result of the physical inquiry certainly will be to make
this "old commentator" far less venerable.

I am, Sir, your obedient servant,

NEVIL STORY MASKELYNE,

Keeper of the Mineral Department.

Mineral Department,
   British Museum, July 13.

LETTER IV.

To the Editor of the Times.

Sir,—When bringing before your notice, in my letter of
the 22nd of June, various reasons which induced me to
question the genuineness of Mr. Collier's annotated folio of
1632, I stated that my main ground, for repudiating the
authenticity of the supposed ancient corrections, lay in the
fact that, while they were made in an antique handwriting
and spelling, having some resemblance to that used in the 17th
century, they could be shown in numerous instances to be
written sometimes by the side of and sometimes actually
upon the same space as similar pencil emendations made on
the margins in a modern hand, in a modern spelling, and to
the best of my belief within the present century. Since
writing that letter to you I have deemed it my duty to go
over a further portion of the volume with the greatest
possible scrupulousness. The results at which I arrive are
the same; and I am now prepared to say that what I then
considered highly probable as to the spurious nature of the
corrections, is now, to my mind, absolutely certain. That in
the great majority of instances the crosses, ticks, and the
literal and verbal emendations occurring in pencil throughout the volume are intended to direct the ink corrections, is
evident to every one who has examined the book with
reference to that point. The instances in which I miss almost
entirely the presence of pencil indications are where a whole
line of text or a stage direction is inserted; but here, from
the obvious difficulty of rubbing out entire sentences, the
annotator would naturally have avoided making his emendations first in pencil. In several cases, where whole words are

written in pencil, it is a suspicious circumstance that the
pencil spelling is modern, while that of the ink is old—for
instance, "body," "offals," in pencil; "bodie," "offalls," in
ink. The pencil-marks, which occur by hundreds, though
naturally faint from having been partially rubbed out, are,
nevertheless, visible and distinct; in some cases, indeed,
have not been rubbed out at all. It is impossible to convey
to the reader, without the aid of *fac-similes*, an exact idea of
their perfectly current and modern form. I can only state
that they appear to me clearly of this century, and, in fact,
as if written but yesterday. Yet, that they were placed on
the margins previously to the antique-looking ink corrections,
which in many instances they actually underlie, has been
proved by Mr. Maskelyne, keeper of the mineral department. Whatever, therefore, be the intrinsic worth we may
attach to such of the suggestions as are not found elsewhere,
they must strictly be regarded as coming before us in a hand
not of the 17th, but of the 19th century, and judged of from
that point of view alone.

In regard to the ink corrections it should be stated that,
although at first sight they bear considerable resemblance
to the set Chancery hand of the 17th century, yet on a
minute examination they will not readily support that
character, their genuineness on palæographic grounds alone
being very suspicious, not to say impossible; while the
spurious character of the ink itself has been proved by Mr.
Maskelyne.

One point alone remained, which it seemed absolutely
impossible to reconcile with the belief that the corrections
were of quite recent date; namely, the statement made in
various publications by Mr. Collier, and also in his letter
published in *The Times* on the 5th of the present month,

that the volume and its corrections had been identified by its former possessor, Mr. Parry, as being in the same state as when in his hands half a century ago. "I have shown and sworn," * Mr. Collier says, in the letter above referred to, "that this very book was in the possession of a gentleman named Parry about half a century ago, given to him by a relation named George Gray. Mr. Parry recognised it instantly, annotated as it is now." Here, apparently, was positive evidence. But not so. A common friend of Mr. Collier and Mr. Parry, anxious to clear away the aspersions cast upon the folio, and to offer to the world a guarantee that the volume was in the same condition as to corrections, at the present moment, as when first in Mr. Parry's hands, requested that gentleman to go to the Museum and identify the volume. With this object Mr. Parry called upon Sir Frederic Madden on the morning of to-day (July 13th). His surprise was hardly less than our own to find, on the volume being shown to him, that it differed in edition, in binding, in corrections—in fact, in every particular in which a book can differ—from the folio *Shakspere* formerly in his possession, and which he expected to have placed before him.

Thus has the last testimony to the authenticity of this volume failed as completely and more remarkably than any of the preceding. If any one still thinks to maintain its integrity, it must clearly be on different or rather on oppo-site evidence to that hitherto adduced in its behalf. I forbear to comment on facts which I cannot elucidate, but

---

* On referring to Mr. Collier's affidavit made in the Queen's Bench, January 8, 1856, I do not find that he actually swore to the identification of the volume by Mr. Parry.—H.

the world will no doubt anxiously wish for explanations which the interests of literature seem imperatively to demand.

As it has been objected that my opinion in regard to the modern character of the cover and binding is incorrect, I think it right to state that I have since made inquiries on the subject, both of men intimately acquainted with large libraries, and also of practical bookbinders. The reply I obtain from both entirely confirms my original statement. Rough sheep (not rough calf), such as this volume is bound in, is of late introduction, hardly reaching back to the first Georges, while the brown Bristol millboard which stiffens the cover is still more recent, a gray and softer kind of board having been employed till within the last hundred years.*

Regarding the main question, I have nothing further to add; but before concluding I deem it my duty to notice two points in Mr. Collier's letter. In the first place, he says, "I never made a single pencil-mark on the pages of the book, excepting crosses, ticks, or lines to direct my attention to particular emendations," whereas sentences and notes occur in Mr. Collier's handwriting throughout the margins. I build nothing on this beyond the reflection that a gentleman may in perfect good faith make statements contrary to fact, and which he would probably not have put forth if his recollection were more exact.

The second is the following assertion made by Mr. Collier in regard to my letter. He says,—" What is clearly meant, though somewhat darkly expressed, is that I am the author both of the pencillings and of the notes in ink."

* See note p. 133.

Now, I wish to say that I never "clearly meant" or "darkly expressed" anything of the kind. My statement was that I considered a literary deception had been practised—a belief which I still maintain to be borne out by facts, and which I see no reason to modify or abandon. There I am well content to leave a subject which I entered into, not in the spirit of a controversialist, still less as a personal accuser.

I am, Sir, your obedient servant,

N. E. S. A. HAMILTON.

Department of MSS.,
British Museum, July 13.

LETTER V.

To the Editor of the Times.

Sir,—I feel most unwillingly compelled to say one other word respecting the corrected folio of Shakspeare's works in 1632, which came into my hands in 1849.

According to Mr. Hamilton's letter, inserted in your paper of the 16th inst., Mr. Parry states that the book which he owned, and which was given to him by his relative, Mr. George Gray, about 50 years ago, was an edition different from the folio of 1632, with different corrections.

I saw Mr. Parry twice upon the subject in the year 1853 —first at his house in St. John's Wood, when he told me (as he had previously told a common friend), that he had recognized the corrections instantly, from the fac-simile which accompanied the earliest edition of my *Notes and Emendations*, 8vo, 1852. Very soon afterwards, for greater satisfaction, I brought the corrected folio of 1632 from Maidenhead to London, and took it to St. John's Wood, but I failed to meet with Mr. Parry at home. I therefore paid a third visit to that gentleman, again carrying the book with me. I met him coming from his house, and I informed him that I had the corrected folio of 1632 under my arm, and that I was sorry he could not then examine it, as I wished. He replied—" If you will let me see it now, I shall be able to state at once whether it was ever my book." I therefore showed it to him on the spot, and, after looking at it in several places, he gave it back to me with these words:— " That was my book, it is the same, but it has been much ill-used since it was in my possession."

I took Mr. Parry's word without hesitation; and it certainly gave me increased faith in the emendations, to which I never applied a microscope or magnifying glass beyond my own spectacles. I was then living in the house of my brother-in-law; and, almost from day to day, I showed him such of the emendations of Shakspeare's text in the corrected folio of 1632 as seemed most striking or important.

If there be upon the volume any pencillings by me, beyond crosses, ticks, and lines, they will speak for themselves; they have escaped my recollection, and, as I stated in my former letter, I have not seen the book for several years. Perhaps the microscope used by Mr. Hamilton might discover that the plumbago of my pencil was the same as that of other marks, said to be in connection with some of the emendations.

J. PAYNE COLLIER.

Maidenhead, July 16.

LETTER VI.

To the Editor of the Times.

Sir,—I beg to forward you the following communication, which I have just received from Mr. Parry in reference to Mr. Collier's letter of the 16th inst.

I may add, that Mr. Parry states, in conversation, that his *Shakspere* was bound in smooth dark leather, with a new back, which was lettered, that there was no name of any former possessor written on the cover; and that part of the margins containing the emendations had been ploughed off by the carelessness of the binder.

On the other hand, Mr. Collier's folio is of the edition of 1632; it is bound in rough light-coloured sheep, not re-backed nor lettered at all; has on the upper cover, written in a bold recent hand, "Tho. Perkins his Booke :" and the corrections have not been injured by the binding.

I am, Sir, your obedient servant,

N. E. S. A. HAMILTON.

Department of MSS.,
  British Museum, July 29.

"*July* 28, 1859.

" My dear Sir,—In reply to your application I have only to make the following statement, in which you will see that Mr. Collier's memory and mine are in question.

" In Mr. Collier's letter to *The Times,* printed July 19, 1859, he states that he was coming to call on me in 1853 with ' the corrected folio of 1632 under his arm,' and that he showed it to me on the road, and that I gave it back to

X

him with these words, ' That was my book—it is the
same ; but it has been much ill-used since it was in my
possession."

" Now, I believe Mr. Collier to be utterly incapable of
making any statement which is not strictly in accordance
with his belief. I remember well meeting him, as he says,
in the road, and as I was then very lame, from having hurt
my knee by a fall, and was using sticks to assist me in
walking, he kindly did not allow me to turn back, but walked
with me in the direction I was going. I well remember
some of the conversation we had during our walk; but I
have not the slightest recollection that the volume of
Shakspere was then under his arm, or of my having asserted
that ' it was my book.'

" Previously to this interview with Mr. Collier he had
shown me the *fac-simile* which he mentions in his letter, when
I immediately said, on seeing it, that it was from my book.
I now believe that I was mistaken, and that I was too hasty
in so identifying *the volume* from a fac-simile of a part of a
page of it. At that time Mr. Collier knew that there were
several corrected folios of *Shakspere* in existence, but he
did not tell me that there were. At that time I did not
know that there was any other corrected folio in existence,
and I therefore supposed that Mr. Collier's fac-simile could
only have been taken from my book. It was not till the
14th of this month that I learnt from Sir Frederic Madden
that there are five or six corrected folios now in being, but
he (Sir Frederic) did not tell me so till he had laid on the
table Mr. Collier's corrected folio, and then he seemed surprised that I did not recognise it.

" Again I repeat, that having frequently since the 14th
of this month, when I saw Sir Frederic Madden, tried to

recollect everything about the book, I cannot remember that Mr. Collier ever showed me the book, but I well remember his showing me the fac-simile. I may be wrong, and Mr. Collier may be right.

" I have a very strong impression that *my* book was a copy of the edition of 1623, and was rather surprised when I saw Mr. Collier's ' Supplemental volume ' (1853) to find that *his* book was of the edition of 1632.

" I may also add that I certainly did not tell, and could not have told Mr. Collier, that Mr. Gray ' was partial to the collection of old books,' for I believe he set no value at all on them.

" Believe me to be, my dear Sir, yours very truly,

" F. C. PARRY.

" *Mr. N. E. Hamilton,*
    British Museum, W.C."

LONDON:
PRINTED BY WILLIAM CLOWES AND SONS, STAMFORD STREET
AND CHARING CROSS.

MR. COLLIER'S REPLY

MR. HAMILTON'S "INQUIRY."

LONDON:
Printed by G. BARCLAY, Castle St. Leicester Sq.

MR. J. PAYNE COLLIER'S REPLY

To MR. N. E. S. A. HAMILTON'S

"INQUIRY" INTO THE

IMPUTED SHAKESPEARE FORGERIES.

LONDON:

BELL AND DALDY, 186 FLEET STREET.

1860.

My Letter in the *Athenæum* of the 18th Feb. last was necessarily written on the spur of the moment, and it will not surprise the reader that it should have stood in some need of correction : the corrections, with additional matter, chiefly in the shape of documents, are supplied in the following pages. Here and there a few new circumstances have since occurred to my memory ; and these I have also inserted, as well as enlarged others. It ought to be borne in mind that the most recent transaction referred to is now more than ten years old, and that others go back to the distance of twenty, thirty, and thirty-five years : it will not be surprising, therefore, if I have accidentally omitted even particulars which might be important.

REPLY,

&c.

THE substance of what here appears in more detail was published in the *Athenæum* of the 18th ult.; but the charges against me have been got up with such elaborate pomp and circumstance by the Manuscript Department of the British Museum, of which Mr. N. E. S. A. Hamilton is the mouthpiece, and have been printed in so imposing a shape, that I have thought it necessary to give my "Reply" in something like a corresponding form of permanence and prominence, in order, as the question must unavoidably survive the mere interest of the day, that one publication may accompany the other, and that the bane and the antidote may be taken together.

I can have no right to complain that, if there be fair and reasonable ground for believing that a fraud and imposture has been attempted or committed, one department, or even all the departments, of our great national institution should step forward to guard the public against the delusion. I look upon it, in fact, as part of their duty; but they are bound to discharge that duty with as much expedition as is compatible with a proper sifting of the case; and they are bound, moreover, not only to limit themselves, in the execution of their task, to what necessity may require, but to proceed with due regard to the character and dignity of their own position. A dispassionate sobriety ought to be observed, if merely for the sake of the effect to be produced; and the whole inquiry ought to be conducted with the utmost temper and moderation. Above all, no personal animosity or individual antipathy ought to be indulged, much less to be apparent. A spirit of judicial impartiality ought to pervade the proceedings of those who take upon themselves at once to accuse, to investigate, to give evidence, and to decide.

This is a truism so obvious that I shall not endeavour so much to enforce it, as to contrast it with the course the Manuscript Department of the British Museum have adopted in reference to the charges they have brought against me.

In the very beginning of July last, they opened their attacks by the boldest accusations of forgery, confessedly long before they were in possession of evidence to support them: all was then mere assertion; but they promised, without more delay than could not be avoided, to produce their authorities: they should, they said, "shortly lay before the public" all the particulars they could collect. What was the result? They have occupied nearly eight months in their inquiries: in the meantime, if they were believed, I have had to sustain all the odium produced by their preliminary denunciation; and yet, when their matured imputations are brought forward in the shape of an ambitious pamphlet of 155 quarto pages, they are not found to contain even as much as their original statement.*

In the interval, however, they have been far from idle in other ways; they have carried back their researches not merely to the year 1849, when I bought the corrected folio, 1632, of Shakespeare's Works (which, for brevity's sake, I shall call the Perkins folio) of Rodd the bookseller, but even to the year 1823, when, in fact, my avowed career of authorship was only in its commencement. They have hunted in every dirty hole and obscure corner for information; and if they happened to light upon anything that, in their opinion, at all contributed to the end of blackening my character, individual and literary, they have not failed, during the whole of the last seven or eight months, to make it public, not only by paragraphs and articles in newspapers,† but by

---

* Independently of documents and other reprinted matter, there are not 50 pages of the 155 that are new. The composition of these 50 pages occupied more than 220 days, or at the rate of considerably less than a quarter of a page per day—this, too, supposing only one hand to have been employed upon the work ; whereas it is notorious that the Manuscript Department not only brought all their resources to bear on the subject, but called in the aid of the Mineral Department also. We do not here take into account the separate labours of the lithographer. Is this, I may ask, to be taken as a test of the rate at which business is conducted in the Department ? I always thought, and had some reason to think, that it was one of the most industrious and well-conducted departments in the British Museum.

† I wish to avoid giving personal offence, and therefore mention no names ; but it is generally stated that the Manuscript Authorities of the British Museum specially invited gentlemen to see the book, and to listen to their criticisms upon it, who were engaged in various departments of the public press. The name of one gentleman in particular, for whom otherwise I enter-

laboured attacks upon me in magazines and reviews carefully forwarded to me anonymously. No chance was neglected of discovering something to confirm the impression which the Manuscript Department hoped they had produced by their earliest onslaught in *The Times* of the 2nd of July last.*

Surely it will not be said that such a course is creditable to the Manuscript Department of the British Museum, which ought only to be interested in the discovery of truth, for the sake of truth itself, and not for the purpose of injuring private reputation; yet its junior officers, it is said, have from time to time employed themselves in stimulating the public appetite, and in whetting the edge of public curiosity, for the sake, not only of directing

---

tain a high respect in his own branch of knowledge, has almost invariably been coupled in paragraphs directed against me and my literary labours. While I had any influences of the same kind, as all my friends and relations knew, I studiously kept my own name from thus attracting public attention.

* It is to be observed that at that date they had had the Perkins folio, by consent of his Grace the Duke of Devonshire, for nearly two months in their hands. I have always striven to make myself as unobjectionable as I could, but even my small reputation in an inferior department of letters seems to have excited envy; and I foresaw that, when Lord Campbell, as a kind compliment to that reputation rather than to my merits, addressed to me his letter *On the Legal Acquirements of Shakespeare*, it would materially tend to exasperate my enemies. It had not long been published before Sir F. Madden (who, in September, had intimated to me his wish to see the book) wrote to the Duke of Devonshire in order to borrow the Perkins folio ; and having procured it, Mr. N. E. S. A. Hamilton "seized the opportunity," as he himself expressed it, of subjecting it, with the aid of Sir F. Madden and others, to the most rigorous examination.

renewed attention to Mr. N. E. S. A. Hamilton's promised pamphlet, but for the purpose of increasing the prejudice against me.*

The whole of this inquiry and discussion has arisen out of my purchase in 1849 of the Perkins folio, from the late Thomas Rodd, a bookseller whom I had known for at least forty years, and who during the whole of that time carried on a most respectable business in Newport Street, Leicester Square. I have told the story of my acquisition of it so often that, as I am weary of it, and perhaps as the particulars are contained in both editions of my *Notes and Emendations,* and are more than touched upon in my Shakespeare, 6 vols. 8vo. 1858, it may not be necessary to say more on the present occasion than

* Let me here, with the utmost brevity, advert to Mr. T. J. Arnold's articles, two dozen pages long, in *Fraser's Magazine* for January and February, so well-timed as just to precede Mr. N. E. S. A. Hamilton's work. Mr. T. J. Arnold does not, it is true, belong to the MS. Department of the British Museum, but he takes the very same line of argument, uses almost the same expressions as Mr. N. E. S. A. Hamilton, and affords internal evidence of the closest connexion. The reader may remark also the most unfair manner in which an attempt is there made to connect me with a disreputable paper called *The Freebooter,* not merely as a correspondent, but actually as the editor of the publication in which an improper use was once made of my name, and for which the real editor afterwards endeavoured to make amends. I was no more editor than Sir F. Madden, or indeed than Mr. N. E. S. A. Hamilton, who was probably not then born. The transaction occurred so long ago, 1823, that it had quite escaped my memory; but I think I can say with certainty that I never saw more than one number of *The Freebooter.* The whole matter was explained to the late Sir H. Nicolas, and to Mr. Pickering, his publisher. If Mr. T. J. Arnold be the son of the late S. J. Arnold the dramatist, perhaps I can understand part of the cause of his undeserved animosity towards me. It may be an entirely different, but not an indifferent person.

that the Perkins folio came out of a parcel of books
from the country.; that I was in Rodd's shop when
the parcel arrived ; that I bought it for thirty
shillings (neither Rodd nor myself being aware of
the existence of any manuscript notes in it); and
that I left it for a time in the shop.* The truth of
this statement has been impugned ; and if it have
not been openly and broadly asserted, it has been
more than insinuated that the volume had no notes
whatever when it came into my hands ; that I subsequently added them, and that having so inserted
them in an old handwriting, or in what was meant
to look like it, I palmed upon the world my own
alterations and emendations of the text of Shakespeare, as the work of some person who had lived
about the middle of the seventeenth century.

Now, the first answer (besides my own direct
and flat contradiction) I shall make to this charge is
the following note to me from the distinguished
Principal of New Inn Hall, Oxford.

* An unworthy cavil has been raised because in the Preface
to my *Notes and Emendations* I said I " took the book home,"
and in my letter in the *Athenæum* that I " left the volume to be
sent home." The fact, I believe, is that I did *take* the Perkins
folio home, and that it was not *sent* home, but that I left it for a
short time in the shop. My frequent course was to call at Rodd's
on my way from Kensington, to see what he might have that was
new and interesting to me, and if the book or books I had bought
were of any size, to go on towards the City, and on my return to
carry away my purchase by an omnibus. I did not ordinarily
give Rodd the trouble of sending all the way to my house. Such
I feel pretty sure was the case with the Perkins folio : I left it in
the shop until my return, and then I " took it home" with another
folio. My enemies must be hard pressed to rely on such a paltry
quibble as this, or indeed to put it forward at all, as a reason for
doubting the veracity of my statement. I did not sufficiently
speak " by the card."

Dr. Henry Wellesley happened to hear (as who could avoid hearing ?) in July last the imputations cast upon me and my conduct by Mr. Hamilton, and feeling certain that he had seen the Perkins folio, *in its annotated state*, in Rodd's shop, before the volume arrived at my house, he said so to a mutual friend, who communicated the fact to me. Dr. Wellesley must have entered the shop just after I quitted it, and there saw the book in question. He examined it more than Rodd, or I had done,* saw, to use his own words, " an abundance of manuscript notes in the margins," and wished to become the purchaser of the volume; but Rodd told Dr. Wellesley that it was already sold to a customer (probably naming me), and the Principal therefore looked at it no farther. Learning that Dr. Wellesley had so spoken of the transaction, I took the liberty of writing to him, although personally unknown, and of requesting such particulars as he could readily furnish, impressing upon him their importance to me, in order to repel the calumnies with which I had been assailed. I was very soon favoured with the following reply, which in every respect tallied,.not merely with what I had heard, but with what I had myself seen :—

" Woodmancote Rectory, Hurstpierpoint,
" August 13th, 1859.

" Sir,

" Although I do not recollect the precise date, I remember some years ago being in the shop of Thomas Rodd on one occasion when *a case of books from the country had just been opened.* One of those books was *an imperfect folio*

---

* Perhaps by a better light. The front shop, where the parcel had been opened by Rodd, was dark from the books in the window, but the back shop was lighted by a large sky-light.

Shakspeare, with an abundance of manuscript notes in the mar-gins. He observed to me that it was of little value to col-lectors as a copy, *and that the price was thirty shillings.* I should have taken it myself; but, as he stated that he had put it by for another customer, I did not continue to examine it; nor did I think any more about it, until I heard afterwards that it had been found to possess *great literary curiosity and value.* In all probability, Mr. Rodd named you to me; but whether he or others did so, the affair was generally spoken of at the time, and I never heard it doubted that you had become the possessor of the book.

> " I am, Sir,
>   " Your faithful and obedient Servant,
>   " H. Wellesley."

"To J. P. Collier, Esq,"

Dr. Wellesley, therefore, saw the Perkins folio, with " an abundance of manuscript notes in the margins," in 1849, for Rodd died in that year; and it remained long in my possession before I became acquainted with its " great literary curiosity and value." As soon as I knew it, I proclaimed it with-out reserve everywhere. I wrote several letters on the subject in the *Athenæum:* I laid it before a Council of the Shakespeare Society, specially sum-moned for the purpose, which was attended by nearly all the members: I also produced it at the general meeting of the Society. Besides showing it at two, if not three, evening meetings of the Society of An-tiquaries, I published a letter stating that it would be upon their library-table for four hours by daylight, when everybody interested was invited to inspect it.*

---

* Preface to Collier's Shakespeare, 1858, p. xi. It was not perhaps convenient to Mr. Hamilton to notice this *daylight* ex-hibition at all, as there mentioned; nor does he say that the Perkins folio was shown first at a Council of the Shakespeare Society, and afterwards at the general meeting of the members.

I did not see there any of the officers of the Manuscript Department of the British Museum ; but I do not know what more I could have done to secure their attention to the book, unless I had carried it to them and begged them to look at it, and to afford it the sanction of their judgment. I have been told, but I do not believe it, that Sir F. Madden and his colleagues were irritated by this piece of supposed neglect ; and that they also took it ill that I presented the Perkins folio to the kindest, most condescending, and most liberal of noblemen,* instead of giving it to their institution. When I placed it in the hands of the Duke of Devonshire, I knew that, for any literary purpose, it would be just as accessible, and just as safe, in his Grace's library, as in that of the British Museum.

I shall make no other remarks in connexion with the preceding note from Dr. Wellesley than that, notwithstanding the lapse of more than ten years since the transaction, it agrees most precisely with my narrative in the Prefaces to the two impressions of my *Notes and Emendations* in 1853 : "the case of books from the country," the "abundance of manuscript notes in the margins," the very price of "thirty shillings" which I had paid for it, and the fact that, according to the Principal's belief, the book

---

* The Duke of Devonshire had the highest reverence for any degree of literary merit, and he was never tired of depreciating his own rank, and elevating that of men of learning and talents. He would not hesitate to show me infinitely more kind attention, than on any score I could lay claim to : as a trifling instance, I may be allowed to mention that, when I was at work in the library at the time he took lunch, he never failed to bring me, with his own hands, a glass of sherry and a biscuit from the ante-room where he sat. Neither was there in this condescension the slightest ostentation of humility.

had devolved into my hands : all these facts show that it could have been no other than the Perkins folio. I consider myself most fortunate to have thus secured such unimpeachable testimony : Dr. Wellesley might have died in the interval between 1849 and 1859 ; or I might myself have expired, and left my memory to be blotted by such unscrupulous adversaries as have recently assailed me. I can never enough thank Dr. Wellesley for the manner in which he has come forward, in the face of all the denunciations of the British Museum against me.

Thus I am warranted in asserting, as I do in the most unqualified manner, that when the volume came into my house it contained all the manuscript alterations for which credit has been given to it by me. Their real date and origin is another question ; and not long after the publication of the first edition of my *Notes and Emendations*, I was led firmly to believe that I could establish that they were in existence early in the present, if not late in the last, century. My book had been out only a short time before I was favoured by the receipt of the following letter by post :—

" Hyde Park Gate, Kensington,
"25th April, 1853.

" SIR,

" You will, I trust, forgive one who has not the honour of knowing you, for intruding on your leisure, when I state that the subject on which I am about to trouble you is the copy of the folio 1632 of *Shakespeare*, with the MS. emendations, which you have lately given to the world, and for which every lover of Shakspeare is so deeply indebted to you.

" The information which I wish to give you may, if followed up, enable you to trace the ownership of that copy for at least a century back.

" A friend of mine, Mr. Parry, with whom I was lately conversing on your extraordinary and interesting discovery, told me *he many years ago possessed a copy of* THE FOLIO 1632 *which had marginal notes in manuscript,* and which, being in bad order, he never consulted. This copy he lost, he did not know how, and gave himself no concern about it.

" When I showed him the fac-simile of the page out of *Henry VI.,* which forms the frontispiece to your work, Mr. Parry told me *he had no doubt that the copy was the same* as that which he lost, *as he remembered very well the hand-writing, and the state of preservation.* I pressed him to give me all particulars about the work, and how it came into his possession. He told me that *it was given him, with many old books, by an uncle of the name of Grey,* WHO WAS A LITERARY MAN, AND FOND OF CURIOUS WORKS. Mr. Parry believes that Mr. Grey got the copy at the sale of the Perkins library; and all I could learn of these Perkins's is, that they were related to Pope's Arabella Fermor, and that all the family were dead when the sale of their library took place. I urged Mr. Parry to inform you of these circumstances, thinking that they might interest you greatly, and hoping that if you could once trace the copy into the hands of one of the name of Perkins upwards, it might be a clue to further discovery. Whether from indolence or from modesty, Mr. Parry, I find, has not communicated with you; and I therefore told him that I assuredly would, as every fragment of information on such a subject had its value.

" Trusting to your indulgence, and your zeal for our great poet, to excuse the liberty I have taken, believe me to be, sir,

" Your faithful and obedient Servant,
" JOHN CARRICK MOORE.

" J. Payne Collier, Esq."

I knew that Mr. J. Carrick Moore was the nephew of the gallant General, Sir John Moore, who fell before Corunna in 1809, and I need not say how strong a feeling of interest and expectation his zealous note excited in me. I wrote to Mr. Parry, Mr. J. C. Moore having favoured me with his address, but received no answer, owing to a fall Mr. Parry had just suffered. I waited for about ten days, when I ventured to call upon Mr. Moore, who told me of Mr. Parry's accident, and advised me to see him at his residence at St. John's Wood. I did so ; and, without repeating what I printed and reprinted in my Prefaces, I may observe that Mr. Parry entirely confirmed every part of Mr. J. C. Moore's communication. He described his uncle, Mr. Grey, *as a man fond of old books, and as having a turn for literature,** and perfectly recollected the appearance of the folio 1632, both inside and outside, *especially dwelling on its rough calf-binding.* He was strong in his belief that the book had come out of the library of a Roman Catholic family of the name of Perkins, residing at Ufton Court, Berkshire; and he added, that an old priest had there shown him, some fifty years before, the empty shelves that had once been filled with the books.

Mr. Parry was so distinct and positive, and so sure as to the identity of the hand-writing in the notes, &c., that I returned home quite convinced that I had certain information as to the existence of those notes in the Perkins folio, at the end of the last or in the beginning of the present century. I was then living in the house of my brother-in-law, about three miles from Maidenhead, and I made an

---

* Such, it will be observed, was Mr. Parry's statement to Mr. J. C. Moore and to myself ; yet in a letter from him, published by Mr. Hamilton in *The Times* of August 1, 1859, Mr. Parry observes, "I may also add, that I certainly did not tell, and could not have told, Mr. Collier, that *Mr. Gray was partial to the collection of old books,* for I believe he set no value at all upon them." Mr. Parry's memory is obviously here defective, for he had told Mr. J. C. Moore that his, Mr. Parry's, "*uncle was a literary man and fond of curious works.*"

expedition to Reading, in order to institute some inquiries regarding Ufton Court and the Perkins family. I did not succeed in obtaining any additional information of the slightest importance; but I was fortunate enough to meet with some old books, which had very possibly come out of the Perkins library, two being imperfect tracts by Robert Greene, the celebrated Elizabethan pamphleteer, and the other a copy of Spenser, dated 1611, which had once been the property of Michael Drayton.*

My Preface to the second edition of *Notes and Emendations* was nearly completed when I first heard of Mr. Parry's ancient ownership of the Perkins folio. I finished it upon the strength of Mr. Parry's personal assurances ; and although the press was kept waiting, I carried that Preface with me to St. John's Wood, in order to be quite sure that what I said accorded entirely with Mr. Parry's recollection and statement. I feel no doubt whatever that I then added in that preface the parenthesis

---

* The conduct of the Museum authorities on this question would make people almost afraid of owning that they have on their shelves any books of value with contemporaneous notes ; but I have been all my long life collecting such relics, and I could with ease enumerate several that belong to me, for some of which, in my sanguine days, I gave high prices. I have Chapman's *Twelve Books of Homer's Iliad,* with his autograph inscription at the back of the title to Sir Henry Crofts, and manuscript emendations in various places. I have also the same old poet's *Hymns of Homer,* with a long autograph dedication ; I have Ben Jonson's copy of B. Yong's translation from *Montemayor,* 1598 ; Daniel's copy of his *Poems,* 1602, inscribed to Lady Pembroke ; the Earl of Essex's copy of Drayton's *Pastorals,* 1593, with many valuable corrections, &c. Drayton's copy of Spenser's *Poems,* folio 1611, has also corrections, but whether by Drayton, I have not yet been able absolutely to decide. I have made use of them in the edition of Spenser I am now printing.

that his uncle, Mr. George Grey, "*was partial to the collection of old books,*" at Mr. Parry's express instance; and I remember the words the better, because they tallied so precisely with what was stated in Mr. J. Carrick Moore's letter, and, above all, rendered it so probable, that Mr. Grey had once been the owner of the Perkins folio.

I was in haste to get my Preface to the printer, and I did not, on that occasion, carry the volume itself to St. John's Wood with me; but I afterwards did so, and met Mr. Parry a short distance from his house, walking lame, and aided by a stick. Mr. Parry has since said that he was "using *sticks;*" but this is a slight mistake, which Mr. Hamilton has, possibly only by error, exaggerated into *crutches*, —a word employed by nobody. Mr. Parry was walking with *a* stick; and after expressing my regret at his recent accident, and stating that I had the Perkins folio under my arm, I said that, under the circumstances, I could not think of asking him to return home in order to examine it: he replied, "If you will let me see it now, I shall be able to state at once, whether it was ever my book." I therefore produced it to him on the spot, and held his stick while he looked at the book in several places, including the cover: he then returned it to me with these words, "That was my book; it is the same, but it has been much ill-used since it was in my possession." I then gave him back his stick, and, thanking him for his most satisfactory assurance, I wished him good morning.

Very soon after reaching home, that is to say, within a day or two, it occurred to me that I ought to record Mr. Parry's expressions, and I did so with a pencil at the foot of page iv. of my Preface to the second edition of *Notes and Emendations*, in these words, which, it will be observed, differ from those above used, by having " This " for *That*, and " misused " for *ill-used*, but the meaning is of course exactly the same.

"I afterwards showed him [*i. e.* Mr. Parry] the book itself, and having looked at it in several places, he said, ' *This was my book : it is the same; but it has been much misused since it was in my possession.'* "

Therefore, I can be more certain of nothing than that I exhibited the Perkins folio to Mr. Parry, and that he employed the words regarding it I have imputed to him. In his letter in *The Times* of August 1, 1859, he observes, "I cannot remember that Mr. Collier ever showed me the book, but I well remember his showing me the fac-simile." Here are at once two mistakes of memory. I most assuredly did show him the book, and as assuredly I did not show him the fac-simile; for Mr. J. Carrick Moore, as he himself states in his letter to me, " showed him the fac-simile of the page out of Henry VI.," when Mr. Parry had "*no doubt that the copy was the same*" as the volume he had owned many years before. Mr. Parry, in his letter in *The Times*, only says that he "*cannot remember :*" he does not say positively that I did not show the book to him, merely that his memory does not serve him upon the point ; mine does serve me most distinctly, that he not only saw the book, but that he turned over several of its leaves, looked at the outside, and then replaced it in my hands. I put the fact on record very soon after the transaction. My evidence is clear and

C

affirmative, while that of Mr. Parry is indistinct and negative.

I do not impute the slightest blame to Mr. Parry. I am confident that he does not mean to deceive or misstate: I merely assert that his memory is defective on this point. I only wish that it were as good as mine; and then I should have no difficulty in establishing that *the Perkins folio of 1632*, with its emendations (the peculiar hand-writing of which Mr. Parry told Mr. J. C. Moore he at once recognised) had been the property of Mr. Parry early in the commencement of the present century.

I have no personal acquaintance with Mr. Parry beyond what I have seen of him in connexion with the book in question; but I believe him to be a man of honour and probity, and he is known to individuals for whom I have the highest respect and esteem. He is, like myself, advanced in years, and certainly little able to compete with the imposing authorities at the British Museum. When he went there on 14th July last, for the purpose of inspecting the Perkins folio, in the presence of Sir F. Madden, Mr. Hamilton, Mr. Maskelyne, and others, he may easily have been confused by the rapid passing and re-passing of the folios of 1623 and 1632 before his eyes; and at last he may not have been able to remember which edition had really been his own book, although he had first told Mr. J. C. Moore, and afterwards myself repeatedly, that *his corrected copy had been the edition of* 1632. The figures 1623 and 1632 are precisely the same, only with an inversion, which may have added to Mr. Parry's confusion;* but I should not be disposed to criticise too

* This is the more probable, because, in one of Mr. T. J.

nicely what may have passed on the occasion at the Museum, because I am sure, whatever he said, that Mr. Parry had no intention to state what was untrue. He spoke to the best of his memory, but his memory was bad ; and he may have been, as it were, cajoled out of his own conviction.

Without Mr. Parry's evidence, which, however, under all the circumstances, I am far from relinquishing (and without having since attempted to see him and to reconvert him to his old opinion, that the Perkins folio of 1632, *and no other*, had been his long before I bought it) I am able to prove conclusively by the Rev. Dr. Wellesley's ready and welcome assistance, that when I purchased the book of Rodd for thirty shillings, out of a parcel just received from the country, it contained "an abundance of manuscript notes in the margins."

These manuscript notes I never altered, added to, nor diminished. How much they may have been altered or diminished, while the Perkins folio was in the hands of the officers of the British Museum, it is impossible for me to judge ; but, I apprehend, on the showing of my antagonists, that something has been obliterated, with or without the consent of the present noble owner of the book. Mr. Maskelyne, before the Duke of Devonshire was applied to for permission, talks of having tested the ink by his tongue, which ink "evidently yielded to the action of damp :" therefore, a portion of the writing may have been thus removed, which was valuable as an

Arnold's papers in *Fraser's Magazine*, he makes a similar blunder, viz., 1853 for 1835 : he represents me as having published my *New Facts* only as long since as 1853, whereas they came out nearly twenty years earlier, in 1835.

emendation, or with reference even to the question of authenticity. How many pages or parts of pages may have been licked over, and licked out, by the tongues of the officers and under-officers of the Manuscript Department, it is impossible for me now to ascertain. Those who may make the same experiment with the book in future will not have a very agreeable duty.

Mr. Maskelyne also cannot deny that some of the writing, which he charges as artificial, has been made with "ordinary ink," or with "a mixture containing ordinary ink;" and who shall say, in the course of the many years that this book must have been more or less under the hands of the corrector, (perhaps in circumstances of difficulty with which we are not at all acquainted,) what inks he may, so long ago, have been under the accidental compulsion of employing? I know that such has not unfrequently been the case with notes I have from time to time made in my own books, especially in a copy of *England's Parnassus*, 1600, on which I have been engaged for the last twenty-five years in supplying the names of authors and their works. I have even sometimes resorted in the first instance to pencil, and when next I had a pen and ink at hand, I have written in ink over my own pencillings. Such a course is surely not unnatural, and therefore, I apprehend, not unusual.

That I did so in the case of the Perkins folio I utterly and absolutely deny; yet that is the impression which has been endeavoured to be produced against me. But, if it be true that pencils of plumbago were at that time in common use, as I believe they were, the old corrector may himself have now and then adopted this mode of *recording on the spot* changes which, in his judgment, ought hereafter permanently to be made in Shakespeare's text. Mr. Hamilton speaks of the bold modern character of the words still to be traced in pencil ; but for how much of this boldness and modernness (which for my own part I do not perceive) may we not be indebted to the unconscious lithographer who, under such watchful instructions, made the single fac-simile with which we are favoured.* In his letter in *The Times* of July 2d, 1859, Mr. Hamilton told us that there are an " infinite number " of these pencil-marks; yet his lithograph presents us with *only fifteen* of that " infinite number," and those fifteen relate to the most trifling and insignificant matters. Such specks and atoms as he has construed into letters, and even into words, might have been made in thousands, even during the time the Perkins folio was in the custody of the Manuscript Department. I certainly do not mean to say that this unworthy trick has been played : I am bound here to acquit my adversaries of such paltry and discreditable frauds : what I mean to say is, that if such specks and spots of plumbago be made, there is no word in our

---

* Without meaning at all to imply that it was so, is it not possible that even in giving these instructions, and pointing out to the lithographer the real, or supposed, course of the old pencil-marks, especially if it were done with the point of a pencil, some atoms of *new plumbago* may have found their way to the paper of the Perkins folio, and have been, on all hands, innocently mistaken for *old plumbago?* If the real or supposed course were pointed out with a dry pen, may we not imagine that the dry pen itself might easily make some suspicious indentation on the soft paper of the old book ? I am told that both pencil and dry pen were at times used for the purpose ; and that where plumbago was not to be found in the Perkins folio, indentation was relied upon.

language to which, with the smallest ingenuity, they may not be adapted.* Supposing, however, that such a word as "begging" (one of Mr. Hamilton's illustrations) were ever so plain in the Perkins folio, what is gained by it? There is actually no corresponding emendation of the old printed copy, so that "begging" must have been written in the margin, not as a suggestion for a change of language, but merely as an explanation, and a bad explanation too, if it refer to "pregnant" in the poet's text. No man who pretends to understand Shakespeare would

---

* On this point and some others I may be allowed to borrow the following note from the *Athenæum* of the 25th Feb. It comes from the most trustworthy and experienced lithographer in Europe, whose opinion is constantly sought and relied upon in our courts of justice :—

"113 St. Martin's Lane, February 22.

"Seeing in the *Athenæum* of last Saturday that my name has been used both by Mr. Collier, and also in your critique on Mr. Hamilton's 'Inquiry,' &c., and, as the general reader may suppose I have been engaged by both parties, permit me to state, that not myself, but my son, F. G. Netherclift, who is separated from me and in business alone, was employed by the party at the British Museum on the fac-similes in Mr. Hamilton's pamphlet. I had no knowledge of it or part in it, nor, under the circumstances, would I have attempted to show pencil-marks over or under any ink writing by any mode of printing; whilst, from my knowledge of facts, and my high respect for the character of Mr. Collier, for whom I have made very numerous fac-similes in the course of the last thirty years, I could not have joined in any way to aid this causeless and cruel persecution against him. As I am continually *subpœnaed* in the Law Courts to give evidence in matters relating to handwriting, and some kind cross-examining counsel may make a 'mare's nest' of the above circumstance, may I request the favour of your inserting this letter in the *Athenæum*?

"I remain, &c.,
"JOSEPH NETHERCLIFT, Sen."

think of placing "begging" in the margin as the true sense of "pregnant."

Is it not strange, if pencil-marks can be pointed out, as supposed instructions for such words, and fragments of words, as Mr. Hamilton has given us, that not the smallest trace of pencil is to be found in connexion with the entire lines, sentences, and parts of sentences, which abound in the Perkins folio ? There the old corrector has left *ex confesso* no vestige of a mark. Mr. Hamilton does not pretend to have found one atom of plumbago there, and, if it had been to be found, the powerful microscope which he and his coadjutors employed could not have failed to detect it.* Supposing for an instant, — I only suppose it — that anybody had maliciously and surreptitiously introduced these specks and

---

* In my letter in the *Athenæum* of the 18th Feb., I committed an error when I applied the terms *Simonides Uranius* to a microscope. I have no pretensions to science of any kind, and I misunderstood Mr. Maskelyne's parenthesis. I correct my own blunder here (which no doubt many others have already set right), because, irrelevant as it is, even that might in some way, for aught I know, be tortured into proof of fraud. It is just as much so as the twenty odd pages Mr. N. E. S. A. Hamilton has filled with real or supposed omissions in *Hamlet*, many of which I never dreamed at any time of including. How does it prove forgery if it could be shown that I had carelessly left out of my emendations all the proposed changes in *Hamlet?* The authorities of the Manuscript Department are no great logicians, or they would have been sensible that the emphasis they lay on the emendations in *Hamlet* is an unwilling tribute to their importance, if not to their excellence. The same remark will apply to Mr. Hamilton's ostentatious display of the few manuscript emendations in the Bridgewater folio, 1623, of which, by the way, *he himself omits two*. The fact is that few things are more difficult than to be utterly faultless in such extracts. I spared no pains to be accurate, but how often may the eye be deceived in turning over 900 folio pages in double columns, full of minor, as well as of major alterations.

spots for the purpose of discrediting the ink emendations, it would have been very easy to have applied
them as hints for a lithographer in forming such
short words as " wall," " now," or " over" (which
Mr. Hamilton has relied upon), but impossible to
have annexed them to whole lines and sentences
without their being observed in an instant, and followed by the naked eye. For instance, if the two
substituted lines in *Hamlet*, Act V., had been first
entirely written in pencil, and then inserted in ink,
the pencil could have been traced, more or less,
through the whole course of the couplet; it would not
have been a mere dot or touch, and nothing besides.

I declare most positively, in the face of the whole
world, that, while the Perkins folio was in my hands,
I never saw a pencil-mark in it that I had not made
myself, either as a note of reference to some other
book, or as a point of observation connected with the
book itself. If I wanted to be sure not to forget to
look at a particular passage in *Malone*, or in any
other commentator, or if I wished to note something
that required again to be examined in the folio, I
took the ordinary method with a pencil that I always
kept at hand ; but that I thus added the slightest
hint with reference to any projected alteration of the
language of the poet I deny in the strongest form in
which it is possible to clothe a denial. If a fancy
should ever cross the mind of any one who has ever
seen me write, that such and such a word or letter
in Mr. Hamilton's lithograph is not unlike my hand,
I can only say that for the last fifty years my handwriting must have been familiar to many in the
British Museum; and that if the likeness have been
more than merely accidental, the fact has an origin

not much to the credit of our national establishment.
I do not impute it:* I only assert that no letter,
syllable, or word of *so-called* bold and modern writing in Mr. Hamilton's fac-simile was placed in the
Perkins folio by me. I never saw Mr. Hamilton's
writing, but he must, from his position, often have
have seen mine, and I will venture to say, that his
lithograph of supposed pencil-words is quite as like
his hand as mine.

It may be urged that my eyes are bad, even when
aided by spectacles; that the late Duke of Devonshire's eyes (though about two years younger than
my own) were also bad; but it is a fact that, neither
together nor separately, did we ever discover a single
pencil-mark. I exhibited the Perkins folio by candle-
light and by day-light, and it was turned about in
every possible direction by those who inspected it,
and I never yet heard of an individual who saw pencil-
marks, until after the volume had been deposited in

* Other people, however, may not be so charitable. I lent the
book for a week to a very intimate and most intelligent Shakespearian friend in my own neighbourhood, who writes me a note
containing the following supposed address to Mr. Hamilton and
his coadjutors :—" Gentlemen of the Manuscript Department, who
impute fraud and forgery to Mr. Collier, what could you reply
to any one who declared his suspicion, that, to serve your turn,
you had fabricated the pencillings on the side of the old corrector's
notes and emendations?" My friend goes on to assert that, "in
the whole week that the Perkins folio was every day under his
eyes, when *he examined every page of it, he never saw a single
pencil-mark,* nor any indication which would lead him to doubt
the *bona fides* of the whole body of the emendations." He doubted
many of them as a matter of criticism, but never doubted that they
were genuine. Surely, if pencil-marks were required, as instructions for the subsequent insertion of trifling expletives, they would
be doubly necessary for long, new passages, so confessedly Shakespearian.

the Manuscript Department of the British Museum :
there, according to Mr. Hamilton, an " infinite number" were discovered. Even now I defy him to show
any such "infinite number ;" and it is not immaterial
to mention that the able and most pains-taking lithographer I employed never saw one of them. Mr.
Netherclift, senior, had the book in his hands, while
it was still mine, several times, and for an indefinite
period ; for he and his assistants not only executed
the fac-simile which accompanied both editions of
my *Notes and Emendations*, but *eighteen other fac-
similes from as many different parts of the volume*,
which were privately made for me, as the severest
tests of the genuineness and importance of the emendations. Yet he assures me, in a letter now before
me, that he and his assistants never once discovered
a pencil-mark from the first page to the last, excepting my avowed pencillings and lines round the passages I wished to be imitated. I placed my book
unreservedly in his hands, with no other charge than
to take care of it : he might show it to whom he
pleased ; and, if he had doubted, he would have done
me a favour to have asked any competent authority.

All I maintain is that the pencil-marks are so
few, so small, and so indistinct, that it is only by the
exercise of the most tortuous ingenuity that they can
be transformed into words and letters ; and that if
they were brought before any intelligent and well-
educated jury, as proofs, not merely of mine, but
of Mr. Hamilton's, or of any other man's hand-writing,
the case would at once be scouted out of every court
of justice in the empire.

I am tired of this subject of pencillings : but
there is one observation upon them, growing out of

Mr. Maskelyne's Letter in *The Times*, dated 13th July, 1859, which I must be allowed to make. He is mysteriously great upon the question, whether in some places the pencil overlies the ink, or the ink the pencil, apparently forgetting that if the pencil-mark overlies the ink, the pencil-mark must have been made last: he admits, however, without reserve, that *"in several places the pencil stops abruptly at the ink."* Is not this decisive? Why does it "stop abruptly at the ink," but because the ink had been previously written, and the person who made the pencil-mark went no farther than the ink would allow him? Truly, all this discussion about "the lustre of the plumbago," and about the plumbago "just traceable under the ink," is too paltry and puerile for a man of Mr. Maskelyne's scientific attainments; and it almost makes one smile to read his grave and authoritative denunciation of the *u* in *Richard II.*, and of the "tick" which "intersects each limb of that letter." If, as he tells us, the pencil sometimes *stops at the ink*, there is an end of the question, as far as every word so circumstanced is concerned.

And now let me ask, what has become of the wonderful binding-discovery which Mr. Hamilton declared in his Letter in *The Times* of 2d July, 1859, that he had made? He says not one syllable about it in the body of his pamphlet, but in his appendix (p. 133) he has thrust in a note, which does not at all explain away his original contradiction, when he first called the binding, as I myself had done in my Prefaces, "rough calf;" and afterwards, "rough sheep." Besides, a mighty fuss was made in his first letter regarding the water-mark on the fly-leaf. I dispute neither the "rough sheep" nor the water-

mark.   It is no part of my case to do so; for I expressly said in my Prefaces to *Notes and Emendations*, 1853, that it was not even the second coat the
Pérkins folio had worn.   The fly-leaf, with its " G. R.
and Dutch Lion," so exultingly dwelt upon by Mr.
Hamilton, may easily have been inserted even later;
but, later or earlier, *it has been abstracted from the
book;* and when it came from the Manuscript Department, no fly-leaf was found in it.   I do not deny
the " G. R." nor the " Dutch Lion ;" but, for aught
that appears, all this was a pure invention by Mr.
Hamilton.   He, or somebody else, has deprived us of
the means of testing his assertion: as his " calf" has
been metamorphosed into a " sheep," so his " G. R."
may by this time have been turned into C. R., and
his " Dutch Lion" into an English one.   Hence,
possibly, the present absence of the fly-leaf.

How and why the Manuscript authorities of the
British Museum have been heated into such animosity towards me I cannot pretend to explain.   I
was always upon good terms with Sir F. Madden,
whom I have known for more than a quarter of a
century, and upon two occasions I was of some service to him.   Of one of them I can say no more;
but of the other I may remark that it occurred within
the last two or three years, and it was when he had
involved himself in an awkward scrape by purchasing
manuscripts, which he ought to have known had
been dishonestly come by.   They had in some way
escaped from Lord Ellesmere's Collection, and the
most obvious and important of them had actually
been printed in a volume, with which Sir F. Madden
ought to have been well acquainted.   The late
Earl Ellesmere heard of the strange circumstance,

put the matter into the hands of his solicitor, and asked me to inquire of Sir F. Madden as to the facts. I did so; and finding, as I of course expected, that Sir F. Madden had innocently, though ignorantly and most incautiously, become possessed of the documents, they were restored to the noble owner, and the matter was dropped. Sir F. Madden showed me some of the manuscripts he had thus purchased, possibly all. One of them was an entire volume relating to the Mint in the reign of Elizabeth, with the handwriting of Sir Thomas Egerton (afterwards Lord Chancellor and Baron Ellesmere) on nearly every page, which Sir F. Madden, with his great skill and experience in palæography, might have recognised; and the other was a very remarkable document on parchment— so remarkable, that it is astonishing how Sir F. Madden could have become possessed of it without suspicion. It was an Address from all the Members of Lincoln's Inn to the Queen in 1584, declaring that they would defend her to the last against Spain, and against all her open or concealed enemies; and the very first name at the bottom of the instrument (and it contained very many) was that of Sir Thomas Egerton, then Solicitor-General. This document was printed at full length in the *Egerton Papers* by the Camden Society in 1840, and when it was printed it attracted much attention. Nevertheless, Sir F. Madden had bought the original; and the late Earl of Ellesmere wished the matter to be investigated, though, as far as I am aware, it was never his design to prosecute. Really and truly, if Sir F. Madden had then been indicted for receiving stolen goods, knowing them to have been stolen, it might have gone hard with him. I should willingly have been one of his witnesses to character.

Some men can forget an injury who never can forgive an obligation ; but I assure Sir F. Madden that he was not in the slightest degree indebted to me on the occasion : all along the Earl of Ellesmere was convinced that the Keeper of the Manuscripts had only acted carelessly, not criminally. The crime indeed lay elsewhere. Therefore I cannot for a moment suppose that Sir F. Madden and the younger officers of his department have taken any antipathy to me on this score. If the late Earl of Ellesmere, and my always kind and bountiful patron, and I may call him friend, the late Duke of Devonshire, had any ultimate design of placing me in a distinguished, but invidious position in the British Museum, which design secured me enemies there, I can only say that I never heard of it from either. They wished me well, I am certain ; but whether they attempted and failed in doing well for me in this respect, I cannot decide. I heard of it, it is true, but not from them. When the highest office in that great national establishment was, not very long since, vacant, I was urged to send in my name as a candidate for the place ; but I was not only well acquainted with the feebleness of my own claims, but with the strength of the interest, and the greatness of the abilities, that were opposed to me.

If the Duke and Earl had succeeded in any such project, I could hardly have experienced more bitter hostility than has been displayed towards me in my merely private capacity, as a writer of many productions tending to the illustration of our native language, and of the great authors who have em-

ployed it. The earliest work I published on the
subject was in 1820, but I had previously written
various anonymous essays and articles; and I was
called to the Bar too late in life to have a chance
of success against younger competitors. I therefore devoted myself mainly to letters, occupying
all my spare time in a way that was sufficiently
remunerative, but extremely fatiguing, generally
keeping me up so late at night that I seldom got
to bed until others were rising. My time and pen
were thus fully occupied; and I never had the
leisure, even if I had possessed the inclination, to
devote myself to the writing and acquisition of
feigned hands of any period, much less to the extremely difficult task of imitating the writing of two
or three centuries ago. The general reader must
here take my word for it, but I have not a relation
or friend who does not know that in every way I was
incapable of it. Here the charge is, not only that I
acquired one, but many ancient hands — that I
manufactured public and private documents at will;
and, beyond all, that I filled the Perkins folio with
thousands of emendations and corrections, besides
altering the old and incorrect punctuation in an
incalculable number of instances.

There is one point that my antagonists, in their
eagerness to convict me, have entirely forgotten:
indeed I apprehend that they are hardly qualified
to form a judgment upon the literary excellence
of not a few of the alterations suggested in the
margins of the Perkins folio. Their vision is
only not microscopic when they look back ten,
twenty, thirty, and even forty years into the incidents of my long life, and fancy that with telescopic

power they behold me sitting with manufactured
inks in a close and obscure study, and hard at work
upon old-seeming fabrications. They have left no
stone unturned, in the hope of finding a poisonous
toad under it—no place unsearched for some dirty
and neglected imputation; but as to the faculty of
judging of what is good or bad in criticism — of
what is excellent or mistaken in illustration, or of
what is valuable or worthless as a wide question
of composition and poetry—they prudently do not
pretend to it. These are points to which the manuscript authorities do not affect to be competent; but
whatever can be done by microscope, and even by a
more powerful moral magnifier, they eagerly " seize
the opportunity" to undertake; or if upon such
matters they hesitate, they call for the aid of other
departments. Then, indeed, the distorted monstro-
sities in an atom of plumbago are equalled only by
the magnified horrors of a drop of Thames water.

These gentlemen forget, therefore, that the indisputable emendations of the Perkins folio, which have
called forth the admiration even of the most bigoted
and antiquated editors, must be assigned to somebody. If I forged them, the least they can do is
to give me credit for them; and I can only say that
I would fain accept them upon any other terms
than that of having been their fabricator. Only
make out for me a legal and legitimate paternity,
and I will adopt the numerous and well-looking
family with joy and gratitude.

The fact, however, is, as almost everybody who
knows me can bear witness, that I have never
enjoyed facilities absolutely necessary to such elaborate trickery. I have not only wanted time and

skill, but place and means. I was married forty-four years ago, and in five out of the eight houses I have since occupied I never had a study to myself: my dwellings were too small and my family too large to allow of it. The common eating-room was therefore my common writing-room, liable to all sorts of interruptions, through which, by long habit, I continued my occupations; and if it were possible to accumulate into one point of view all that my pen then produced, by day and by night, people would be astonished at the mass of writing which, by the exercise of unwonted mental energy and power of abstraction, I was able to accomplish. I was always a hard-working man, and often was called upon to perform tasks I would fain have avoided. When I have had a study, I defy the world to show that I ever turned the key to prevent intrusion: everybody was admitted, and at all hours. Such impositions as are charged against me could not be attempted without seclusion and secresy; yet I had no secrets: my wife opened every letter I received; and in my study was always kept a chest of drawers to which every member of the family had access for some of the most ordinary requirements.*

Therefore upon nobody could this charge of fraud and forgery against me have come with greater astonishment than upon my children: if my wife had lived, I believe, it would have killed her to have known that such a base accusation had been

---

* I cannot forbear quoting here a brief passage from the letter of an old friend of eighty-four, now residing in the west of England, who, many years since, called upon me for a literary purpose. He is speaking of my " Reply," as it appeared in the *Athenæum* of 18th Feb. : — " The paragraph in your letter

kept hanging over her husband's head for eight
months, when she was well aware that it could be
refuted in about as many minutes.

I really have not patience, and, well as I can
usually command my feelings, I fear not temper, to
enter in detail into a discussion of Mr. Hamilton's
supplemental and subsidiary imputations, all of them
trumped up with the view to giving some appearance
of plausibility to the accusation, that I am myself the
author of the pen and pencil emendations in the
Perkins folio.

I admit, without reserve, that the weakest part of
my case relates to the finding of Shakespeare documents among the late Earl of Ellesmere's MSS. at
Bridgewater House. And why is it the weakest part
of my case ? For this sole reason, that I never could
have had any direct corroboration of my own testimony as to the discovery of them : nobody was with
me at the precise moment, although the noble owner
of the papers had been in the room only a few
minutes before. Mr. Hamilton, boldly begging the
whole question, styles them " the Bridgewater Shakespeare Forgeries." They may be " forgeries," but
at that time it never entered my head that they could
be so ; and at that time I had never heard the fact,
since mentioned, that Steevens had formerly been
admitted into the rooms which held both the books
and manuscripts. I do not believe that he had

---

alluding to your study and your private mode of life affected
me much, recollecting, as I perfectly do, the room in which you
kindly received me, when I called upon you about *Robin Hood
Ballads.* I well remember that one of your daughters was in the
front part of your parlour, while you retired into the back part to
examine your book-shelves."

any more hand in the "forgeries" than the Rev. H. J. Todd, with whom I once conversed about the papers,* and who had, as I understood, for some years filled the office of Librarian.

I never suspected the papers to be anything but what they purported to be, and the moment I discovered them and had hastily read them over, I carried them to the Earl of Ellesmere (then Lord Francis Leveson Gower) and read them to him. At his Lordship's instance I copied them, and left both originals and copies with his Lordship. Going again to Bridgewater House (I think it must have been on the very next day, for I was all eagerness to pursue my search) I overtook his Lordship about to enter the door, having just alighted from his horse. He told me that he had seen Mr. Murray, the publisher, who offered to give me £50 or £100 (I believe the smaller to have been the sum) if I would put the documents into shape and write an introduction to them. I declined the proposal at once, saying that I could not consent to make money out of his Lordship's property. Lord Ellesmere appeared a little surprised at my hyper-squeamishness, and replied, with his habitual generosity, that the documents were as much mine as his, for though I had found them in his house, but for me, they might never have been discovered till doomsday.

This circumstantiality may surprise some of my

---

* My object was to gain from him some information respecting the MS. where the performance of "Othello" before the Queen at Sir Thomas Egerton's was mentioned. Mr. Todd was very deaf, and I could learn no more from him than that he knew that such a circumstance was mentioned in some MS. In fact, part of the direction of a letter to the Rev. Mr. Todd remained between the leaves to keep the place, when I saw the book.

antagonists, and they may (like Mr. T. J. Arnold
in *Fraser's Magazine*) endeavour to turn it against
me with a *more suo*, &c. ; but, although twenty-five
years have since elapsed, I have the clearest recollection of the main facts, and I give them as they
occurred. From Bridgewater House I took all the
papers, originals and transcripts, to Rodd's, the
bookseller, where we examined them carefully ;
and, although I at first agreed that he should
sell some copies of them when printed, I afterwards (upon my own principle, as stated to Lord
Ellesmere) altered my resolution, and only a few
New Facts were passed over Rodd's counter to his
customers.

New Facts was therefore privately printed in
1835 at my own expense, and the same was the case
with *New Particulars* and *Farther Particulars;* if
any copies of these three tracts were sold, it was
without my knowledge, and without my advantage : I do not believe it, as Rodd was a very
conscientious and scrupulous man of business. Indeed, until the appearance of the first edition of
my Shakespeare in 1843, I had never received
one farthing for anything I had written regarding
Shakespeare or his works. Of course, I do not
include the few scattered points relating to him
and his plays in my *History of English Dramatic
Poetry and the Stage.* My *Memoirs of Alleyn*, the
Alleyn Papers, Gosson's *School of Abuse*, Nash's
Pierce Penniless, and perhaps other works, were
edited for the Shakespeare Society (of which I
happened to be Director) before 1843, and it was
the principle of that association that nobody should
be paid for trouble of that kind. I am confident

that I place it much below the amount, when I say that I was £100 positively out of pocket for printing, paper, &c., in illustration of my favourite pursuits.

After the discovery of the Perkins folio, and after I had laid it on the table of the Council of the Shakespeare Society, for the inspection of about twenty gentlemen and scholars, I told them, in all sincerity, that far from wishing to make money by it, I hoped that they would accept from me, as a free gift, a volume of *Notes and Emendations* founded upon it, then in rapid preparation. Time was taken to consider of the matter, and I was afterwards informed that, as the book would certainly secure a considerable sale, the Council were of opinion that it would neither be fair to me, nor to the trade, that the Shakespeare Society should first print it. I yielded (as everybody knows who was present) with some reluctance, and *Notes and Emendations* was afterwards published by Messrs. Whittaker and Co. as a supplemental volume to my Shakespeare of 1843. Part of this information is in some sort necessary to my case, but I should not have said so much about it, if I had not seen a few of the facts detailed in print by the literary newspaper called the *Critic*. It really has only done me justice in the matter; and I thank it, in perfect ignorance, as far as my own knowledge is concerned, of what it may have said about me at other times and on other subjects. Literary newspapers must usually take opposite sides upon questions of the day; and if the *Critic* have been, as I am informed, strongly opposed to me, it is partly, perhaps, because others have been energetic in my favour.

I am not of a money-getting, or of a money-saving turn, as all my friends and relations can witness; and I am sure that the Duke of Devonshire and the Earl of Ellesmere never thought me unprincipled or mercenary.

For the first I have often laid out large sums, once £1400 in a single month; and for the last I have frequently bought very expensive books: his Lordship allowed me always to lay out a certain sum per annum for the gradual formation of a Shakespeare Library; and neither the Duke nor the Earl ever expected from me receipt or memorandum.

My brochure, *New Facts regarding the Life of Shakespeare*, was in the form of a letter addressed to my old and constant friend Thomas Amyot, Esq. (not George Amyot, as Mr. Hamilton calls him) for above twenty years Treasurer of the Society of Antiquaries; who, had he now been living, could have afforded me most essential aid in my defence against the calumnies so industriously got up. My enemies have waited (I do not at all mean purposely) until, as might be expected in a series of scarcely less than forty years, I have been deprived by death of nearly all the witnesses I could have adduced in support of my own testimony. I say nothing of the Duke of Devonshire, because he knew little that was important of his own knowledge; but the late Earl of Ellesmere could have given most valuable testimony on many points: so with the late Sir Harris Nicolas; my old contemporary Mr. Barron Field; John Allen, Esq., Master of Dulwich College; the Rev. H. J. Todd; James Boswell, the nephew of Mr. Malone; Mr. Lemon, senior; Mr. Frederick Devon, formerly of the Chapter House; the Right Hon. J. W. Croker; Mr. Hallam; Mr. Thorpe; and Mr.

Rodd. My late wife and my eldest daughter were always willing helpmates, especially in the collation of proofs, and knew more or less of almost everything of a literary nature that proceeded from my pen. These are all no more, and yet all could have rendered me some degree of assistance in repelling an attack like the present : I am now left almost alone, and write in the country, without the opportunity of even consulting a friend. In the case of the two last, my wife and my eldest daughter, I can hardly regret that they did not survive to witness the suffering and irritation that, even in my innocence from all just imputation, I have been compelled for many months to endure. The losses I have sustained in friends and relations must in some measure account for any noticeable deficiencies in my narrative.

Besides the manuscripts found at Bridgewater House, which formed the main substance of my *New Facts*, another document (at what date I am uncertain) subsequently turned up in the same collection, which rendered it most probable that the account of the claims of the Players and Proprietors of the Blackfriars' Theatre, on their proposed removal from that precinct, was authentic : Lord Ellesmere insisted that I should keep it, as it was no necessary part of the other documents. It was a sort of summary of the account of the claims, in an Italian hand of the period, and underneath, in the hand-writing of Sir George Buck, the Master of the Revels to James I. was his memorandum that the Players and Proprietors demanded more than their interest was worth by £1500 : he first wrote £2000, but subsequently altered the sum to £1500. We know that the

Blackfriars' Theatre was in use as a private place of dramatic entertainment long afterwards; and it is to be concluded that the treaty for the purchase of it, either by the Crown or by the City of London, was broken off.

The copy of a letter signed H. S. (supposed to represent the initials of Henry Earl of Southampton) has attracted more attention than, perhaps, any of the other documents discovered in the same depository. It introduced, or has been supposed to have introduced, Shakespeare and Burbadge to the first Lord Ellesmere, then Lord Chancellor; but it is not necessary that I should further describe a paper, which has been at least thrice printed by myself, and which has been inserted in every recent Life of our great Dramatist. As it was in my possession, and had been so for some years, I produced it at a meeting of the Council of the Shakespeare Society about the year 1843 or 1844. I forget what individual members were present, but the authenticity of it seemed generally admitted, and I afterwards had a 'facsimile of it made by Mr. Netherclift, senior.

I put him under no restriction as to showing " the H. S. Letter " to anybody ; and when he re-delivered it to me, I asked him his opinion of it, knowing that he had paid great attention to the modes of writing at the period of its supposed date : his answer was in these words, —" If at any time you happen to want a witness that it is a genuine document, I will be that witness." He subsequently (I cannot fix the precise date) lithographed in fac-simile the other documents I discovered at Bridge-water House. A few weeks since I replaced the whole of them in his hands, and, after looking over them, he acknowledged the fac-similes as his own work, and reiterated his opinion that the originals, to the best of his belief, were authentic. A separate sheet of the water-marks of the paper on which they were written was added by Mr. Netherclift, in order that no information on a point, which, from time to time, has led to the exposure of much fraud, might in this case be wanting.

If I had manufactured the " Bridgewater House Shakespeare Forgeries," as Mr. Hamilton is pleased to call them, surely it is not likely that I should have placed them, without the slightest scruple or caution, in such skilful and knowing hands.

Let us see how these fac-similes were received by very capable judges. I sent copies of them to the Rev. Alexander Dyce (then my intimate friend in spite of his self-regretted attack upon me, as an editor of Shakespeare, in his *Remarks*, &c., 1844) but in the first instance only of " the H. S. Letter," for that was lithographed some time before the rest. What was his answer, not sent in haste, but after considerable delay and deliberation ? It was in these very words, which I copy from a note in his own hand-writing : —

" *The fac-simile has certainly removed from my mind all doubts about the genuineness of the letter.*"

This opinion, be it observed, was given while the Rev. A. Dyce was printing his " Beaumont and Fletcher," and before he entertained any immediate project of publishing a Shakespeare. Although I had known him very intimately from the year 1828 to the time I quitted London in 1850, it is remarkable that he never, on a single occasion, intimated to me a doubt as to the authenticity of any of " the Bridgewater House Shakespeare Forgeries." In his Shakespeare of 1857 I learned, for the first time, that he reiterated the suspicions some had expressed ; and it was then, be it remembered, that he was actually engaged on an edition of Shakespeare intended to rival mine; and it was then that he, for the first time, threw all sorts of discredit on my discoveries. As he had formerly given a decided opinion in favour of the genuineness of "the H. S. Letter," surely, when he subsequently, in his Shakespeare, expressed his doubts, and quoted the doubts of others, he might have added, that at one time he had misled Mr. Collier on the subject, by strengthening his belief that "the H. S. Letter" was a genuine manuscript of the period. The Rev. A. Dyce did not pursue this obvious course for his own reasons, but I doubt how far they are at present satisfactory even to himself.

If Mr. Halliwell have seen ground to alter his decision on the same question, I can have no right to complain : all I know is, that with regard to "the H.S. Letter," up to the year 1848, he gave it as his positive conviction, not merely that it was a genuine manuscript of the period, but that it could hardly (for a reason he assigned, and which at least convinced himself) be a forgery. In his *Life of Shakespeare*, 8vo. 1848, after giving a fac-simile of the conclusion of "the H.S. Letter," p. 225, he observes :— "The fac-simile of that portion of it relating to Shakespeare, which the reader will find at the commencement of this volume, will suffice *to convince any one acquainted with such matters that it is a genuine manuscript of the period.* No forgery of so long a document *could present so perfect a continuity of design;* yet it is right to state that grave doubts have been thrown on its authenticity. A portion of the fac-simile will exhibit on examination a peculiarity few suppositious documents would afford, part of the imperfectly formed letter *h,* in the word *Shakespeare,* appearing by a slip of the pen in the letter *f* immediately beneath it."

Mr. Halliwell then refers to Mr. Wright, who also had seen the original, as a highly competent judge of such matters, a point few will dispute; and he subjoins in a note, " In the library of the Society of Antiquaries, No. 201, Art. 3, is preserved 'a copye of the commyssion of Sewers in the countye of Kent,' marked as *vera copia,* and singularly enough, written apparently by the same hand that copied the letter of H.S." As I have never seen this "copy of a commission," I can offer no opinion upon the identity of handwriting, but it is a matter upon which no man can be better qualified to give final judgment than Mr. Halliwell.

Upon opinions such as those I have acted in uniformly attaching the weight and value of authenticity to the documents in question. I may be wrong, or others may be in error; but all the facts within my knowledge are before the world. The documents themselves, after I had printed them, remained for many years in my possession,—at least from 1836 to about 1845 : Lord Ellesmere never asked for them, nor inquired regarding them ; but one day, after 1845, Lord Ellesmere either told me, or wrote to me, that Mr. J. Wilson Croker had questioned their genuineness. His Lordship, therefore, desired me to send the original papers to his house : I did so instantly, and expressed my satisfaction that he had resumed possession of what was his own property, though he had kindly permitted it to remain so long in my custody. When I saw Lord Ellesmere next, some weeks had elapsed, and he informed me that in the interval the documents had been "tested:" he did not say by whom, nor in what way; but he added that he was perfectly satisfied. Afterwards Mr. Croker learned that I had, among my other manuscripts, an original poem by Pope, as the fact certainly was: he applied to me for it for his new edition, and I sent it to him, and he returned it to me with thanks, adding, that there was no doubt as to Pope's hand-writing. This introduced the topic of the Ellesmere Shakespeare manuscripts, and he informed me that he was now a believer in them, after having inspected them. The late Mr. Hallam at a dinner, while I filled the office either of Treasurer, or of one of the Vice-presidents of the Society of Antiquaries, gave me similar information.* While, therefore, I freely acknowledge the finding of those documents, the forging of them I as firmly deny.

I do not think that the Earl of Ellesmere would, in 1847, have appointed me Secretary to the Royal Commission on the British Museum (an office that, of itself, raised up against me some enemies in that institution), if his Lordship had not entertained a sufficiently good opinion of my integrity.

Before I quit Bridgewater House, my adver-

---

* Mr. Hallam, as I always understood, though I never had the good fortune to hear him say so, was a maintainer of the excellence (and of their genuineness from their excellence) of the notes and emendations in the Perkins folio. On this point others may easily be more capable of speaking than I can profess to be.

saries have made it necessary for me to notice the copy of the folio of Shakespeare's Works in 1623, there preserved : it contains a few manuscript emendations, which I inserted in my first edition, and have transferred to my second. It is made a question, or rather I should say it is broadly asserted, that they are in the same hand-writing as that of the " Bridgewater House Shakespeare Forgeries," and as that of the Perkins folio. I have not seen them for many years ; but my memory strangely fails me if such is the fact : and I think I do not ask too much when I request that Mr. Hamilton's interested testimony should not be implicitly received, while the present Earl's evidence is entirely suppressed. The noble Lord, in a letter to an acquaintance of mine, gives an opinion on the point, of which, he expressly says, I am at liberty to make use : it is in the following words, and I thank his Lordship heartily for the permission :—

" There is *no pretence, whatever*, for saying that the emendations in the Perkins Shakespeare are in the same handwriting as those in my first folio : on the contrary, except as they are (or profess to be) of the same period, *they are quite different*."

If I were to see all three together, *i.e.* the Perkins folio, Lord Ellesmere's folio, 1623, and the Bridgewater House documents, on the same table, and by the same light, considering the general, and even particular, resemblances of hand-writing at that date, I might have much difficulty in deciding whether this letter or that letter were sufficiently like others in form and manner, as to warrant a positive conclusion. I more than doubt Mr. Hamilton's opportunities for forming any decision. Nothing could well be more uncertain, even under the most favourable circumstances for forming a judgment; but as it never occurred to me to compare any of them, I must let the matter rest on my general and distinct asseveration, that, if it be meant that I had a concern in writing all, any, or either of them, nothing can be more false and unfounded.

I now come to speak of the Manuscripts at Dulwich College, and how they have been most unfairly thrown into the scale, in order that they may weigh against me with the rest of Mr. N. E. S. A. Hamilton's accumulation of trash and trumpery.

First of all, it will be expedient for me to quote a passage from Malone's *Inquiry*, published in 1796; it is from p. 215.

We see from hence that Shakspeare had no motive to reside in the Blackfriars before this period [March 1604–5]. The truth, indeed, I believe, is that he never resided in the Blackfriars at all. From a paper *now before me, which formerly belonged to Edward Alleyn, the player, our poet appears to have lived in Southwark, near the Bear-Garden, in* 1596. Another curious document *in my possession,* which will be produced in the History of his Life, affords the strongest presumptive evidence *that he continued to reside in Southwark to the year* 1608."

Let it be borne in mind that the documents, which Malone here and elsewhere refers to, were, in fact, the property of the Master, Warden and Fellows of Dulwich College — that Malone had quietly taken possession of them — that they remained in his hands for several years — that he did exactly what he liked with them — that he cut off signatures of old dramatists and players to place them on the title-pages of his own books — and that he or others mutilated *Henslowe's Diary* in such a

way, that some of the most valuable portions are now
entirely lost. Even the books, the title-pages of which
he decorated with the old autographs, had belonged to
Dulwich College; for he contrived to persuade the
Master, Warden and Fellows, of that day, that Old
Plays and Old Poetry did not half so well become
their shelves, as the musty divinity, dull chronicles,
and other volumes of the same sort, which he substituted. Hence the bulk of his collection; and he
must have chuckled amazingly at his success in
persuading unsuspecting people to make an exchange of works, which would sell for hundreds
of pounds, for others not worth as many shillings.
So of the Manuscripts: they seem to have allowed
Malone to carry away such as he pleased, to
keep them as long as he pleased, and to return
such as he pleased, in the state which he pleased.
Some that he did not return found their way
again to their old home after his death; and it is
not very long since the College, most properly,
bought back a bundle of papers that must have
originally come out of its archives.

It was to all that remained, that I had, by the
kindness and confidence of the authorities, between
about the year 1825 and 1830, access in the first
instance, when I was completing my materials for
*The History of English Dramatic Poetry and the
Stage.* I cannot call to mind the precise date, but I
can well recollect the politeness and readiness of the
then Master to aid my researches. I had been introduced to him personally by my learned and excellent friend Mr. Amyot.

One of the first documents I looked at was, I
think, a letter from Mrs. Alleyn to her husband,

dated 3rd Oct., 1603, upon which has now been founded the charge that I interpolated a passage not met with in the original. It was in one place in so decayed and crumbling a condition from the effects of damp and time, that I was obliged to handle it with the utmost caution. I did not read it nor examine it closely until afterwards, how long I do not pretend to say, but a friend, now unfortunately dead, was with me, and we then read as follows, in the latter part of the letter.

"Aboute a weeke a goe came a youthe, who said he was Mr. Frauncis Chaloner, who would have borrowed x^{li} to have bought things for * * *, and said he was known unto you, and Mr. Shakespeare of the globe, who came * * * said he knewe hym not, onely he herde of hym that he was a roge, * * * so he was glade we did not lend him the monney * * *. Richard Johnes [went] to seeke and inquire after the fellow, and said he had lent hym a horse. I feare me he gulled hym, thoughe he gulled not us." *Memoirs of Edward Alleyn*, 8vo. 1841, p. 63.

Now the question is, and the only question of the slightest importance (though that is in truth of little moment) whether the name of " Mr. Shakespeare of the globe " occurred in the most rotten and fragmentary part of the letter at the time when I copied it. Whether it did or did not is not of the smallest interest, as regards the biography of our poet, especially as there were two, if not three, other Shakespeares " of the Globe " Theatre, then resident in Southwark.* However, the charge is that from the

---

* One of these was an Edward Shakespeare, of whom nobody had ever heard till I published his name in 1846 (*Lives of Shakespeare's Actors*, Introd. p. xv.) from the Registers of Cripplegate

mere love of deception (for I could have no other motive) I imagined the part of the letter in which the name of Shakespeare occurs, and corrupted the immediately adjoining portions for the purpose of giving my invention support.

It is indisputable that since I first saw and copied the letter at Dulwich, portions of it have crumbled away and entirely disappeared; so that Mr. Hamilton's account of the contents differs from mine : he accuses me not only of inaccuracy, but of fraud and wilful misrepresentation. I do not deny that it is possible I misread some utterly unimportant letters or words : the paper was in such a state of demolition that it was extremely difficult to make any sense out of the latter part of it ; but I did my best to give a faithful transcript, and I am absolutely certain that " Mr. Shakespeare of the globe" was spoken of in it, and in the way I stated. Mr. Hamilton asserts that " there is not the smallest trace of authority for any allusion to Shakespeare :" this may be very true ; he is speaking of Mrs. Alleyn's letter in its present condition, but that is not the question : the question is, whether, when I saw the letter, some thirty, or even more years ago, the name of " Mr. Shakespeare of the globe" was not to be traced. I maintain that it was ; and had an intimate and excellent friend been still alive, I could have substantiated it by his evidence as well as by my own. Mr. Hamilton insists that the name of Shakespeare never was to be seen on any part of the paper which is now

Parish. I may here express my wonder that the MS. Department of the British Museum has not contended that I invented and forged most of the particulars I derived especially from the Southwark, Cripplegate, and Shoreditch parochial records.

rotted away; but how can he tell whether it did or did not exist there, when he cannot deny that much of what was originally written on that part of the paper has been utterly annihilated? Excepting as it impeaches me, the whole is really a *lana caprina* matter, valuable, perhaps, to Mr. Hamilton and to his coadjutors in the distress of their case, but utterly worthless to anybody else.

Here allow me to ask this question: If I had purposely misstated the import and contents of the letter, adding that it was in a state of ruinous decay, what would have been the natural course for me to have pursued? would it not have been to have left the letter as it was, in the hope that when it was next seen and consulted, as much of it might have disappeared as possible? Instead of doing so—instead of leaving it still exposed to the action of air and accident, I carefully inclosed it in paper, and either I or my friend wrote on the outside, that within was a document of value, which should not be roughly handled. I have also a faint recollection that I especially directed the attention of the Master of the College, or of the Librarian, to it: at all events, I diligently wrapped it up, as if to make sure that the next person who opened the paper should see that I had been guilty of fraud. If, indeed, I had so misrepresented the contents of the crumbling relic, what was to prevent my rubbing away a little more of the old paper, and who then would have been able to detect the trick I had played? I have never, I think, seen the letter from the day I copied it until this moment; but I understand that the envelope, on which my caution was written, is still in existence, though it did not suit the purpose of my adversaries to mention the care I had taken, if I were guilty, to preserve the evidence of my guilt.*

Such is the way in which these accusations have been prepared; I will not say manufactured. The passage I have quoted from Malone's *Inquiry*, shows that he knew from the documents before him, that is to say, from documents derived from Dulwich College, that Shakespeare was in all human probability living in Southwark during twelve successive years.

Mrs. Alleyn's letter proves that "Mr. Shakespeare of the globe" was seen in Southwark in October, 1603, and this was doubtless one of Malone's reasons for concluding that our great dramatist had a residence in Southwark from 1596 to 1608.

Malone, nevertheless, was unquestionably in error as to the latter year; for it is certain that it should be 1609; because the assessment to the poor for the liberty of the Clink, in which the names of Shakespeare, Henslowe and Alleyn appear, as giving a weekly contribution of 6*d.*, is dated 8th April, 1609: 1608 ended on 25th March, so that the year 1609

---

* See the *Athenæum* of 25th Feb. last, p. 269. The Editor seems to have been incredulous upon the point whether I did actually leave Mrs. Alleyn's letter so carefully inclosed, but he found it in an envelope inscribed thus: " Important document —not to be handled until bound, and repaired, the lower part being rotten." " Would any man in his senses (asks the Editor) sedulously guard from harm a document which he had consciously misread? Would any rogue guilty of foisting in a paragraph into a public paper, take pains to call instant and incessant attention to the very document which would witness to his crime? No one out of Bedlam." How happens it, I may be allowed to ask, that Mr. N. E. S. A. Hamilton says not one syllable of the pains I had volunteered to take that the letter should not receive farther injury? Does not this trifling fact tend to prove the *animus* with which I am pursued?

had then commenced exactly a fortnight, for which
Malone did not allow. In my letter in the *Athenæum,*
of 18th Feb., 1859, I hastily supposed (writing in a
hurry for immediate publication) that Mr. Hamilton
referred to this assessment: I was mistaken.* There
is no doubt that it was in existence when Malone
published his *Inquiry* in 1796, and that he had seen
it. I was then only seven years old, and of course
merely a probationer in " pothooks and hangers," so
that Mr. Hamilton will hardly contend that at that
early age I could be a proficient in forgery.

The " list of players," which Mr. Hamilton
charges as a modern addition to a genuine document,
I saw and quoted with the other papers; and if the
names were forged, I can only say that they must
have been upon the instrument when it was seen by
Malone before 1796, although he did not extract it,
reserving it, perhaps, (as I said in my *Memoirs of
Edward Alleyn*) for his *Life of Shakespeare.* My
materials for those *Memoirs* were in great part collected while I was engaged on my *History of English
Dramatic Poetry and the Stage;* and I can most
distinctly aver that the " list of players " was then
extant, and that it was seen by Mr. Amyot, who
accompanied me in one of my earlier expeditions to
Dulwich. I myself state (*Mem. of Alleyn*, p. 67)
that the " list " itself is " in a different hand and in
different ink," which I need not have mentioned,
if I had not wished to produce all the circumstances

---

* The reader will be so good as to observe that I emphatically
acknowledge my error. I call attention to it, lest Mr. Hamilton
should be disposed to argue that I purposely drew attention to one
document, that I might lead people's minds away from another.
My case as to that other is still stronger.

regarding it, that would enable a correct judgment to be formed of its authenticity. Moreover, to set this matter completely at rest, I have now before me Malone's copy of his *Inquiry* (8vo, 1796), as annotated by him for a second edition : it is full of scribbled scraps and notes with information, not contained in the first edition, and on the back of a letter addressed to " Mr. Malone, Queen Anne Street, East," is the very list of players in question. Therefore, whether it were or were not an addition subsequent to the date of the original document to which it is appended, it is certain that it was seen by Malone very many years before I was at Dulwich.*

If any of the documents returned to Dulwich College after Malone's death appear to have been tampered with, I most distinctly acquit him of any such misconduct. Whatever I may be, in the opinion of my adversaries, I feel sure that he was a man of honour and principle ; and supposing, only for a moment, that we were on a par in that respect, it must be admitted that Malone, with all the documents in his private room for years, had infinitely

---

* This book I bought some years after I had printed my *Memoirs of Alleyn* in 1841. As a bibliographical note, and as it may serve hereafter as a means of identifying the book (though Malone's writing, print-like or current, is to be found in hundreds of places in it), I quote the following particulars from the fly-leaf: Mr. Hamilton is fond of fly-leaves and their water-marks, and he may like to know that " 1795 " is distinctly to be seen in the substance of the paper. Malone's note is this :—" *For a second edition.* Begun to be written about the 10th of January. Begun to be printed about the 20th of January; finished at the press, Monday, March 28: published March 31st, 1796.—500 copies sold on that day and the next." So that it took Malone less than *three months* to write and print an 8vo. vol. of 424 pages.

the advantage over me, as far as the commission of fraud and forgery is concerned. At Dulwich I was never, at that period, anywhere but in a public library-room, always open, not only to the fellows and the servants of the College, but to individuals in the neighbourhood, who were well known. What opportunity I had for committing any of these elaborate offences, my antagonists have not attempted to show : I do not mean to say that I was not often alone, and for some time, but never without the constant danger of being interrupted and detected in my imputed practices.

With reference to the *Player's Challenge*, beginning, "Sweete Nedde, nowe wynne an other wager," which Mr. Hamilton declares a "forgery from beginning to end, although executed with singular dexterity," I may remark that Mr. Halliwell quotes it in his *Life of Shakespeare*, 8vo. 1848, p. 329, after having "collated it with the original ;" and he does not drop the remotest hint that he thought it a forgery. I have no particular recollection of the manner in which it is written, but, contrary to what Mr. Hamilton says, that it is "executed with singular dexterity," it now seems to me that the reduplication of consonants, and other points of orthography in it, might possibly raise suspicion.

What surprises me, in reference to the Dulwich Manuscripts, is that Mr. Hamilton should have confined his objections to such paltry points, when in the course of the *Memoirs of Alleyn*, I have for the first time printed so many papers of importance that are passed by without a word of notice. What does he say, for instance, to Ben Jonson's translation from Martial, to Sir W. Alexander's copy of verses, to Dekker's and Field's Letters, and to nearly the whole of Alleyn's part in R. Greene's *Orlando Furioso*, 1594, with various other curious original documents? All these receive no comment—and with very good reason, I can well believe.

I do not perceive in his *Inquiry* that Mr. Hamilton speaks, as he did in his letters in *The Times* of July last, of paint, pigment, and manufactured inks;* but I know, and he knows, that any ink, however old, may be removed if proper methods be applied; and the scientific department of the British Museum cannot be wanting in skill in this particular. The late Thomas Rodd, the bookseller, undertook for me, and accomplished it, to abolish the slightest appearance of ink-stain from scribbled title-pages; and I myself have taken envelopes sent from different hemispheres, east and west, and have obliterated the addresses by the simplest application. In truth, as most people are aware, no test of the genuine or the spurious can be more uncertain; and if the Trustees of the British Museum would give me leave, I could promise, with no other means, to expunge every vestige of the famous signature, " Willm Shakspere," in the Montaigne's *Essays* by Florio, 1603, for which alone Sir F. Madden paid out of the public purse no less a sum than £130. I am sure that he would not let it stand the test even of a sponge and

---

* In my Prefaces to *Notes and Emendations* I have myself not omitted to state that " the ink in the Perkins folio was of various shades, differing sometimes on the same page," and in the body of the book I have in several places, and with reference to particular emendations, pointed out the same peculiarity. I did so in order to enable people to form a just estimate upon the question of authenticity, as applied to the whole volume; and if I omitted any information of the kind, it was quite unintentionally.

water; and yet Mr. Maskelyne and Mr. Hamilton licked over the Perkins folio *ad libitum*, and were delighted to find that they could manage to get off some of the supposed colouring matter. They do not tell us how much of the soft surface of the old paper they destroyed in this process.

I am now glad to arrive at the last count in the indictment against me; it amounts to the very grave charge, that I was guilty of manufacturing and forging a State paper — a document deposited in the National Archives, and still existing there.

Many years were employed by me in collecting materials for my *History of English Dramatic Poetry and the Stage:* it was published twenty-nine years ago, and I think it took more than a year to print it, for it was a work requiring more accuracy than despatch: it was certainly not ready for press until 1829 or 1830, and it bears date in 1831. I cannot speak positively upon the point, but I think it must be about thirty-three or thirty-four years ago, that I first obtained admission into the State Paper Office that I might copy documents that bore upon my subject.

That always willing and zealous friend, Mr. Amyot, then Treasurer of the Society of Antiquaries, gave me a personal introduction to Mr. Lemon, the father of the gentleman who is now so deservedly high in the Department. Mr. Lemon, senior, was at that date in a post of great trust and confidence, and at my earnest request he promised to look out for me certain muniments relating to plays and theatres. I believe that, as he took a lively interest in my pursuits, he bestowed a good deal of pains on searching out relics that would contribute to my purpose—and calling in Great George Street, where the State Papers were then kept before their removal to their present abode, I found, much to my satisfaction, that he had instituted so active an inquiry, that he had discovered for me five or six papers of great novelty and curiosity.

My belief is that the office hours did not extend beyond three in the day; and as it was late before I arrived, I expressed my fears that I should not be able to copy all the documents that morning. One of them, I well remember, was a Memorial from some of the principal inhabitants of the precinct of Blackfriars against the continuance of a theatre there, on the ground that it was a nuisance,—that it attracted disorderly crowds, and that, as it was about to be repaired and enlarged by the players, the annoyance would be increased. Another document was in the form of a Petition from the players against that Memorial; and this last Mr. Lemon very kindly undertook either to copy, or to get copied for me: he took it away for the purpose, and by the time I had made some extracts from the Memorial, he returned into the room where I was sitting, with the Petition and the transcript of it in his hand. He was good enough to aid me in the collation of the two, and when we had finished, he took away the Petition itself (which I never saw again, but the authenticity of which I never for a moment doubted) and left me the copy, which I used for my book, sending the very same sheet to the printer of my *History*.

My notion was that Mr. Lemon's son, the present head of the family, had copied the paper for me; but I have since understood that such was not the case.

Even now, after the lapse of so many years, if it had been of any consequence, I might have been able to decide the point, had I not, when I quitted London in the spring of 1850, for the sake of putting everything into as small a compass as I could, sent away or destroyed all my proof-sheets, and the manuscript belonging to them. Until then it had been my constant habit to tie in bundles the proofs and " copy" of every separate work in which I had been concerned from 1820 to 1850. A large parcel of old, useless letters, shared the same fate, as I could not carry them with me into the country, and as the Pantechnicon would have charged heavily for the space they would have occupied.

That this Petition existed in the State Paper Office before I knew where that office was, is quite clear. It was found for, and pointed out to me, by Mr. Lemon, senior. Mr. Lemon, junior, still in that department, bears witness that *it was known, both to himself and to his father*, before I had been admitted into the State Paper Office : of this fact there exists the best possible evidence ; for the Editor of the *Athenæum*, having learned that such was the case, very recently wrote the subsequent note to Mr. Lemon, making the inquiry whether what he had heard were true :—

"Athenæum Office, Feb. 13, 1860.

" The Editor of the *Athenæum* presents his compliments to Mr. Lemon, and referring to the Petition of the Players— contained in the bundle of papers in the State Paper Office marked ' Bundle No. 222, Elizabeth, 1596,' a copy of which has been printed in text by Mr. Collier, and in fac-simile by Mr. Halliwell, takes the liberty of inquiring whether, within Mr. Lemon's knowledge, that Petition of the Players was in the State Paper Office before Mr. Collier began his researches in that office? An early answer will oblige."

The inquiry was, of course, very material; not merely with reference to the authenticity of the Petition, but with reference to the impossibility of my being concerned in "the surreptitious introduction of it," to use Mr. Hamilton's words. The answer, forwarded by return of post, was entirely satisfactory, and in these terms :—

        "State Paper Office, Feb. 14, 1860.
" DEAR SIR,
    " In reply to your question, I beg to state that the Petition of the Players of the Blackfriars Theatre, alluded to in your note, was well known to my father and myself, before Mr. Payne Collier began his researches in this office. I am pretty confident that my father himself brought it under the notice of Mr. Collier, in whose researches he took great interest.
      " I am very faithfully yours,
          " R. LEMON.
" The Editor of the Athenæum."

I am not aware, therefore, that it is necessary for me to say more upon this part of the subject. Mr. Lemon, senior, undoubtedly did bring the Players' Petition under my notice, and very much obliged to him I was, that he took so much trouble to assist me in my literary investigations. The genuineness of the Memorial, to which the Petition is obviously an answer, has, I believe, not been questioned; and as it is dated 1596, it may be said to ascertain that the Petition, which has no date, was of the same period. The following quotation from the *Loseley Manuscripts* (edited by the late A. J. Kempe, Esq.), 8vo., 1835, p. 496, proves in what way the Players at the

Blackfriars, at about this period, intended to enlarge their theatre, viz. by taking in part of the house of Sir William More.

" Lord Hunsdon to Sir William More. Wishes to take a house of him in the Blackfriars. Hears he has already parted with a portion of his own house to some that mean to make a playhouse of it. Somerset House, Jan. 9, 1595."

At that time, " Jan. 9, 1595," was in fact Jan. 9, 1596, which tallies with the date of the Memorial and consequent Petition. We know besides, that, in May, 1596, it was directed that the Players should not be disturbed. These, however, are only points of history, rendering it probable that the Players did present such a Petition; for it cannot now be disputed that I was not the discoverer of the document, but that having been found by the late Mr. Lemon, he brought it to my knowledge, and kindly procured it to be copied for me, in order to expedite me in my undertaking.

I consider myself much more than fortunate to be able to procure this important and indisputable piece of evidence; for, had the present Mr. Lemon died between about 1828 and 1860, how might not my enemies have triumphed in their imputation, that I had first forged the Petition, and then smuggled it into the State Paper Office!

Of the investigation instituted by the Master of the Rolls, from which Mr. Lemon was apparently excluded, and in which Mr. Hamilton was certainly included (though absolutely an interested party), all I shall say is, that there might be very sufficient reasons for not inviting Mr. Lemon to assist, seeing that *he knew perfectly well that the document in question was in the State Paper Office before I commenced my researches* in that department. Unless I "surreptitiously introduced it" before I knew where the State Paper Office was, even Mr. Hamilton and the Manuscript Department of the British Museum must acquit me of any concern in the supposed fabrication of it.

Have we not here, let me ask, another proof of the sort of spirit by which my adversaries seem to be influenced? While they most indelicately select Mr. N. E. S. A. Hamilton as a coadjutor in the inquiry respecting this Players' Petition, they, as it seems, carefully shut out from that inquiry the very man who could have given them conclusive information. That information, however, would have been fatal to their accusation.

As to Mr. Hamilton's sort of challenge " to produce a remarkable document," so "minutely stated by me " in the *Athenæum*, 6th Dec., 1856, and printed for the first time in my last edition of *Shakespeare*, iii., p. 214, I merely have to remark that it would become Mr. Hamilton, as an officer of the Manuscript Department of the British Museum, to be better informed about our public muniments before he scatters imputations in his usual fashion of *inuendo*. Why does he not say honestly, and at once, that he does not believe in the existence of any " Examination " of Augustine Phillipps, the fellow-actor with Shakespeare?* Perhaps he may be

---

* Let me take this opportunity of correcting a misprint in my copy of that very curious document: for " Sir Charles Pryce" and "Jostlyne Pryce" we must of course read *Sir Charles Percye* and *Jostlyne Percye*. The body of the paper is in Chief Justice Popham's infamously illegible scrawl.

equally incredulous respecting the " Examination " of Sir Gilly Meyricke, which I published in my new *Life of Shakespeare*, 1858, p. 154. These are documents that I found and printed ; but if we were to stay until such interesting papers are discovered by the Manuscript Department of the British Museum, we might wait, I fear, as many years as we have waited months for the recent pamphlet.*

It may even be doubted whether those officers do not owe me some ill-will for finding them work. Only a year or two ago I procured, for a comparative trifle, three large cases of Bentinck manuscripts from Germany, belonging to the period treated by Lord Macaulay in his recent History. How far they illustrate our annals of that time I know not, as I never looked at them ; but being asked by a friend in Oldenburg whither they ought to be sent, I at once recommended the British Museum. These manuscripts may, for aught I know, be yet uncatalogued ; I presume not ; and. such industrious workmen as Mr. N. E. S. A. Hamilton may have suffered in point of labour, from the occupation I was thus the innocent means of procuring for them.

I humbly and earnestly hope that all but my

---

* It is astonishing how little the Keepers and Assistant Keepers in our national depository appear to know of anything that is not immediately under their own eyes. One night, at the Society of Antiquaries, I produced copies of two letters from the famous Richard Hakluyt ; and one of the Museum Assistant Keepers, printing something about them afterwards, was obliged to confess his ignorance as to where the originals were deposited. I also stated that I knew of a copy (now before me while I am writing) of Hakluyt's *Divers Voyages touching America*, 4to. 1582, *with both the maps*. It did not gain credence from the Museum authority, who spoke of the " *supposed* possessor."

impenetrable enemies will be of opinion that I have cleared myself reasonably well — I put it in no stronger form — from all fair suspicion of guilt; and especially from any discreditable connexion with the emendations in the Perkins folio. The Rev. Dr. Wellesley knows that they were in it when I bought the book in 1849. It is all very well for certain people to decry them : those rival editors who do decry them, have often been compelled, by the especial excellence of the proposed changes, to adopt them. To have only suggested them would have made the fortune of any man ; and, if I were the real author of them, what could have induced me *to foist them into an old folio and to give anybody else the credit of them?* The charge is so ridiculous that it carries its own contradiction. Mr. Singer inserted many with very grudging acknowledgment, and adopted others, as if they were his own improvements : Mr. Knight behaved in a more straightforward way, but availed himself of them. The Rev. Mr. Dyce has been driven to the hard necessity of doing nearly the same, with this salvo, that in order to discredit the Perkins folio he has asserted, unknowingly I believe, that some of the best changes of text were contained in Mr. Singer's corrected folio, when Mr. Singer never had a corrected folio that presented them, or anything like them. Important as were other coincidences, it is remarkable that there never was the smallest outcry for the production of Mr. Singer's folio, and for the best of all reasons, — that the production of it would have directly contradicted those who disparaged the Perkins folio.*

* I do not think that Mr. Singer ever pretended that the

I know well what it must have cost the Rev. Alexander Dyce to insert such emendations as "diseases" for *degrees*, of "mirror'd" for *married*, of "bollen" for *woollen*, of "bisson multitude" for

emendations in his folio 1632 had any claim to consideration on the score of antiquity : on the contrary, I believe that some minor points, which concurred with those in the Perkins folio, were at one time not to be found in Mr. Singer's folio. I however entirely acquit him of introducing them. I never saw the work by Mr. Singer, called *Shakespeare Vindicated*, but I heard that he spoke hardly of me in it, and I took no notice of his attack : at last he seems to have been won over by his own convictions (for late in life he admitted that he had pursued a wrong system of commentation, if I may use the word) and by my patience, and in 1854 he presented me with a small translation, containing this inscription : "To J. P. Collier, Esq.—with Mr. Singer's compliments — *a peace-offering*." I at once accepted the amicable gift, and wrote him a letter of thanks in the following terms : —

"Maidenhead, 3d March, 1854.
" MY DEAR SIR,
        " I am much obliged to you for your interesting little volume (which reached me yesterday) but more for the inscription it contains. I gladly receive it in the spirit in which, I presume, it is intended.
    " I know not how far you have advanced in your new edition of Shakespeare, but I heartily wish you success in your endeavours to free his text from corruptions, and to render his meaning intelligible. Such has been the labour of my life, and I shall rejoice if it be the triumph of yours. Allow me to subscribe myself,

" Yours very sincerely,
" J. PAYNE COLLIER.
" S. W. Singer, Esq."

For some reason or other I never received the slightest recognition of my note, unless the series of imputations cast upon me in the course of Mr. Singer's Shakespeare, 12mo. 1856, are to be so considered. What had occurred to counteract his repentant and . pacific disposition of the spring of 1854, I never inquired. My earnest wish was to keep on good terms with everybody.

bosom multiplied, and many others ;* but he did insert them after he became an editor of Shakespeare; having before that, while he was yet friendly with me, written under his own hand that not a few of the emendations in the Perkins folio were "*so admirable that they can hardly be conjectural.*" This, too, when my volume of *Notes and Emendations* had been some weeks in his hands, so that he cannot say that he gave a hasty and unconsidered opinion. He must pardon me for once more reminding him of his very words, for they so forcibly

* The two first of these changes of text the Rev. A. Dyce vindicates on the ground that *they are supported by corrections in Mr. Singer's folio,* as well as in the Perkins folio, when the fact is that Mr. Singer's folio has neither of them : indeed, as to the first, Mr. Singer in his *Shakespeare,* v. 179, justifies *degrees* instead of "diseases," and blames those who, with the Perkins folio, have substituted " diseases," not pretending that he has any corrected folio that reads " diseases." As to the second, "mirror'd" for *married* (Singer's *Shakesp.* vii. 242), precisely the same remark will apply, excepting that Mr. Singer had the boldness to print "mirror'd," as if it were his own unprompted emendation, omitting to mention the Perkins folio, and not for an instant urging that he had any authority but his own conjecture for the alteration. Yet both these important changes the Rev. Mr. Dyce assigns to Mr. Singer's corrected folio, as if he wished to deprive the Perkins folio of the sole merit of such great improvements of the text. This, to say the least of it, is very unfair, and I willingly believe that Mr. Dyce unconsciously fell into an error in both cases. As to verbal objections to the Perkins folio, on the ground that modern words are found in its MS. notes, all that it is necessary to say is, that *wheedling,* though used by Butler just after the Restoration, was *pointed out by myself;* and that *cheer* was in use as a word of encouragement and approbation early in the reign of Elizabeth, and that the expression *three cheers* is found in *Teonge's Diary,* from 1675 to 1679. Yet we are told by the enemies of the Perkins folio that the earliest use of *three cheers* was about 1806! Those who make such unfounded objections come very ill provided to maintain them.

F

express my own convictions, and indeed almost go beyond them, that I cannot refuse myself the satisfaction of quoting them, whenever an occasion fairly presents itself.

As I stated in the Preface to my *Shakespeare*, 6 vols. 8vo. 1858, I am unable to guess what had operated so hostilely on the mind of the Rev. A. Dyce, beyond the fact, that in 1843 I had anticipated him in his project of publishing an edition of the poet's works. I have never seen even a quotation from his recent attack on my latest labours; but I hear that his anger scarcely knows bounds. I had occasion, in my Preface, to animadvert upon his animosity to me, and upon the mode in which he had treated my labours in 1844, when his adverse *Remarks* almost instantly followed the appearance of my first impression; and in his *Few Notes*, which, in 1853, were specially directed against my volume of *Notes and Emendations*. I heard, incidentally and accidentally, that he was offended at what I had written; and I immediately addressed a mutual friend, stating that my least object was to do injustice to a gentleman and a scholar whom I had known intimately for thirty years: I therefore offered to retract every syllable that was injurious, *if it could be shown to be unjust*, and to make my retractation public in every possible way. Subsequently I found that the Rev. Mr. Dyce was serious in his intention to publish an answer to my Preface; and thinking that a knowledge of my offer to our mutual friend might not have reached him, I wrote to him precisely to the same effect. This note he passed by with entire silence; but I never since have uttered, or written one word in the disparagement

of my sometime friend, that was not absolutely required for my own justification.* I still say of
him, as the great Saint said of the greater Sectary,
" I loved thee once ; I almost love thee still."

I have thus been, most unintentionally, involved
in the quarrels of authors; and strange it must seem,
that ever since the art of criticism was applied to
the works of " the gentle Shakespeare," the most
amiable of human beings, those works have been the
cause and source of relentless animosities among
his commentators. How grandly does the benevo-
lence and generosity of the great poet rise above the
petty bickerings of us would-be illustrators of his

---

* As my note was very short, perhaps I may be allowed to
subjoin a copy of it: it establishes how seriously anxious I was
to make amends, if I had done any wrong.

"Maidenhead, 5th Feb. 1859.
" SIR,
        " I heard some time ago, and I have just seen it in
print, that you are preparing an answer to the Preface to my
Shakespeare, 6 vols. 8vo. 1858.
    " If this report be true, it may be right that you should be
informed, that some months since, in consequence of what Mr. ——
said, I wrote to him, stating that if in that Preface you could
show that I had done you any injustice, however slight, I would
eagerly seize the occasion of acknowledging it, and would make
the acknowledgment public in the most effectual manner.
    " With the most vivid and painful recollection of our former
and long-enduring friendship,
                        " I am, yours,
                            " J. PAYNE COLLIER."

I cannot blame the Rev. Mr. Dyce for not accepting my offer :
he might have good reasons for wishing to pursue his own course;
but surely no sufficient reason for not taking any notice of what I
wrote. He might fancy that it arose, to use Tom Nash's words,
with which the Rev. Mr. Dyce must be familiar, " out of a base-
hearted fear" of another Harvey. Not so, I can assure him.

text! For myself, I never knew that I had an enemy until I undertook to edit Shakespeare.

Of the gentleman who seems, in a manner, to have been put forward by the British Museum, to represent them in this encounter, I knew nothing until I saw his accusatory letter in *The Times* of the 2nd of July last : he, I suppose, is the literary detective of the national establishment; but I doubt how far the whole body rely upon his skill and intelligence. Perhaps, from living so entirely in the country, I never heard of him; but he has been allowed to stir up a little the stagnation of a department, where the younger men seem eager " to seize opportunities" of gaining notoriety, while the older officers have necessarily been content with the fame acquired by publication of an old chronicle, or of a venerable household - book. When first I heard that I was attacked by Mr. N. E. S. A. Hamilton, I expressed my surprise that the enterprise was entrusted to such obscure hands; and I, not very courteously perhaps, added a couplet from a satirist, which I will not repeat here, because I am anxious to avoid anything like mere personality.

From Sir Frederick Madden I was unreasonable enough to expect rather different treatment, than from a subordinate to whom I was unknown. I have been acquainted with Sir Frederick nearly ever since he was introduced into the British Museum : we have not unfrequently corresponded, we have exchanged books, and have always observed at least the ordinary civilities of life. Mr. Hamilton, somewhere in his *Inquiry*, strangely, yet strongly, reproaches me with not having lent my assistance in the investigations respecting the au-

thenticity of the Perkins folio. I saw from the
newspapers that it had reached the Manuscript Department, and I saw that consultations were held
over it, not only by various officers of the establishment, but by many literary gentlemen, and
especially by editors of Shakespeare, some of whose
labours on the poet's works I had only heard of. I
thought, not unnaturally, that if any information
from me were wished, I should also have been
invited to the meeting ; but not having been so invited, I apprehended that it would be the height of
indelicacy, if not of presumption, in me to proffer my
services, or to thrust myself into a company where
my presence was not desired.

It seemed the more likely that I should have
been asked to attend, because Sir F. Madden, in the
preceding month of September, had written me a
note, in which he expressed a wish, *propriis oculis*,
to inspect the Perkins folio. The chief business of
his note, I remember, was to thank me for fac-similes
of the *Hamlets* of 1603 and 1604, with the distribution
of which the late and the present Duke of Devonshire had entrusted me ; and to inquire whether I
had seen a signature of Shakespeare on a map of some
county of England, and whether I looked upon it as
genuine. I answered the two last parts of Sir F.
Madden's note, but I postponed that incidental portion which related to the Perkins Shakespeare, because the present Duke of Devonshire was then in
Lancashire, and because I hoped that when his Grace
returned to London, he would, as his noble predecessor had done, entrust me with the book, in order
that I might carry it to Sir Frederick Madden at the
Museum.

In the meantime, his Grace had confided to my care the very responsible task of preparing a facsimile of the *Hamlet* of 1604; and the wish, only expressed *obiter* by the head of the Manuscript Department, I am sorry to say, escaped my memory. Sir F. Madden might surely without derogation have reminded me of his former request regarding the Perkins folio ; and I never dreamed that he would take, nor do I believe now that he has taken, offence at so trifling a piece of neglect on my part, counterbalanced as it is by the fact, that of the forty copies of the fac-similes of 1603 and 1604 (for no more were struck off for each distribution) I sent two, in the Duke of Devonshire's name, to Sir F. Madden himself, and two others to the Department of Printed Books in the British Museum. His Grace had given me only general instructions upon the subject, and it was of my own free will that I addressed these rare books to Sir F. Madden, whom I had known for so many years; and who, it should seem, at that date was aiding the case against me founded upon the Perkins folio.

If, therefore, as an act of courtesy, I was not to be asked to be present, it would appear only an act of justice that I should have been required, in the very first instance, almost before the Perkins folio had been opened in the Manuscript Department, to inspect it, in order that I might be sure that it was *precisely in the same condition* as when I had presented it to the late Duke of Devonshire. Instead of that, it seems as if it had been at once handed over to the tender mercies of Mr. Hamilton, as a literary detective; and he certainly claims to have been the person who first made the discovery of the pencil-marks. He tells us that "the correspondence between certain pencil-marks in the margins, with corrections in ink [was] *first noticed by myself.*" He does not add when he " first noticed" them, whether anybody else was by at the time, nor how long the book had been in his possession before he communicated his discovery of the pencil-marks. All may have been meant to be conducted with perfect fairness : I will presume so ; but would it not have occurred to any impartial person, on the discovery of the mysterious pencil-marks, to have requested me at once to look at them, and to say whether I had ever observed them while the volume was mine, or while the book had been in the library of the late Duke of Devonshire? Such a course would certainly have saved an infinite deal of trouble.

However, I will not fritter away the substantial features of the case by these comparatively insignificant topics : those substantial features beyond all cavil or dispute, are, 1. That the manuscript notes were in the Perkins folio when I bought it in 1849, if not fifty years before that date;—2. That I discovered the Bridgewater House manuscripts precisely under the circumstances stated, and that the authenticity of some of them was maintained by the best judges of our day, both literary and artistic ;— 3. That the Dulwich manuscripts were in the condition I have described them at least as far back as the year 1796, as is evidenced, among other proofs, by Malone's *Inquiry* of that date;—and 4. That with regard to the Players' Petition of 1596, if it be a forgery at all, it was a forgery before I set foot inside the State Paper Office, before I commenced my researches there, and before I even knew where the Office was situated.

I ought to apologise to the reader for occupying so much of his time, but I was anxious, once for all, to go into the case as fully as my materials, after the lapse of so many years, would enable me.   *Hic arma repono.*

J. PAYNE COLLIER.

Maidenhead, 12 March, 1860.

ADDITIONAL NOTES.

Page 1.   I did not see Mr. Hamilton's Letter of the 7th inst. in the *Athenæum* until some days after my earlier sheets were at press, or I would have made some alterations in them.   I am glad to observe that he now denies the participation of his colleagues in office.   I only used the word "mouthpiece" as it is defined by Johnson, — "one who delivers the sentiments of others associated in the same design."

Page 50.   Having written to the Rev. J. Lindsay on the subject of Mrs. Alleyn's Letter, he has promptly replied that he does not remember the circumstance.   He, like me, regrets the death of John Allen, Esq., then Master of Dulwich College, who may have been the person to whom I mentioned the decayed state of the document.

Printed by G. Barclay, Castle St. Leicester Sq.

A REVIEW

OF THE

PRESENT STATE

OF THE

SHAKESPEARIAN CONTROVERSY.

BY THOMAS DUFFUS HARDY,

ASSISTANT KEEPER OF THE PUBLIC RECORDS.

LONDON:

LONGMAN, GREEN, LONGMAN, AND ROBERTS.

1860.

LONDON :
Printed by G. E. EYRE and WILLIAM SPOTTISWOODE,
Printers to the Queen's most Excellent Majesty.

"I can have no right," says Mr. Collier in his reply to Mr. Hamilton's "Inquiry," "to complain that " if there be fair and reasonable ground for believing " that a fraud and imposture has been attempted " or committed, one department, or even all the " departments of our great national institution, " should step forward to guard the public against " the delusion. I look upon it, in fact, as part " of their duty; but they are bound to discharge " that duty with as much expedition as is com- " patible with a proper sifting of the case; and they " are bound, moreover, not only to limit themselves " in the execution of their task to what necessity " may require, but to proceed with due regard " to the character and dignity of their own position. " A dispassionate sobriety ought to be observed, " if merely for the sake of the effect to be " produced, and the whole inquiry ought to " be conducted with the utmost temper and " moderation."

If Mr. Collier had followed the precepts he has thus laid down, an important question, which to a certain extent may be said to concern the whole literature of England, would have been dispassionately discussed, and his opponents, if opponents they must be called, would have no reason to object to the ungenerous insinuations with which his statements abound. Should Mr. Collier complain of the tone which has been adopted by those who differ from him in this matter, he has no one to blame but himself. It was the injudicious answer he sent to the "Times" newspaper, in reply to Mr. Hamilton's letter, that has caused him the annoyance, by making it a personal, rather than a literary, question.

Public Record Office,
July 1860.

these gentlemen, they were not what they professed to be; the " Old Corrector" (as Mr. Collier termed their author) had no authority for his corrections; on the contrary, the greater part of them were adopted from recent annotators; those of which the original could not be traced were violent and inconsiderate changes for the worse; the larger number were frivolous and unnecessary.—Such was the gist of the allegations made in reference to these readings.

The scholars who thus impugned the genuineness of these emendations, arrived at their conclusions wholly from their knowledge of Shakespeare's text, and of what had been done for it by Commentators during the present century and the last. They had never examined Mr. Collier's folio, though more than one had endeavoured to obtain an opportunity of doing so. As early as 1853 Mr. Charles Knight pointed out, in a temperate but forcible manner, the propriety of having the folio deposited in the custody of some public body, who would allow access to it, under proper regulations, and a full and satisfactory examination of its contents. Disregarding, however, the adverse opinions thus expressed, Mr. Collier, in 1853, issued a Second Edition of the Notes and Emendations; and, shortly after, the folio became the property of the Duke of Devonshire. All further chance of a critical examination of the volume had now become ap·parently hopeless; and it was after a considerable lapse of time, that Mr. Howard Staunton determined, if possible, to have the handwriting in which these emendations were made examined. "Having myself," he remarks,[*] "from the first publication of the Notes and Emendations, felt assured, by the internal evidence, that they were for the most part plagiarized from the chief Shakespearian editors and critics, and the rest of quite modern fabrication, I earnestly longed to have the writing tested. That which was a desire before, when the present work was undertaken, became a necessity; and during the year 1858 I more than once communicated to Sir Frederick Madden, as the most eminent palæographer of the age, my motives for wishing that the volume should undergo inspection by persons skilled in ancient handwriting." Sir F. Madden's official engagements at that time prevented his giving the subject the attention it deserved; but in consequence of Mr. Staunton's

---

[*] Preface to his Edition of Shakespeare.

A REVIEW

OF THE

PRESENT STATE OF THE SHAKESPEARIAN CONTROVERSY.

A MOST important literary question has engaged public attention since last July. Not that it is new to those who take an interest in dramatic, and more especially Shakespearian, literature; for it has been before the world since January 1852, when Mr. Collier first announced, in the *Athenæum* that he had discovered in a copy of the second folio edition of Shakespeare's Plays, published in 1632, a large body of Notes and Emendations, amounting to nearly 20,000, in a hand not much later than the time when this edition emanated from the press, and that in his belief the Annotator had made these emendations from better authority than that of the Editors of the first folio.

This announcement naturally created a great desire on the part of Shakespearian critics, and other literary men, for a detailed account of these Notes and Emendations; and in order that any person interested in the subject might have an opportunity of inspecting them, Mr. Collier, as he states, exhibited the book before the Shakespearian Society, and, on three occasions, before the Society of Antiquaries. Further to gratify the curiosity that had then been raised, in the year 1852 Mr. Collier published a volume professing to contain the greater part, but not all, of these manuscript alterations, with a fac-simile of a portion of one page. No sooner had Mr. Collier made public some of the emendations of this annotated folio, than the most lively interest was excited, not only in England, but on the Continent as well. The new readings were, however, violently assailed by critics of every denomination; one alone (Professor Mommsen) accepting them as genuine. In England, Mr. Singer, Mr. Dyce, Mr. Staunton, Mr. Hunter, and Mr. C. Knight repudiated them in no very measured terms. According to solicitations, Sir Frederick applied to Mr. Collier for his good services in obtaining access to the volume. To this application Mr. Collier made no reply; whereupon, Sir F. Madden requested of the Duke of Devonshire himself the loan of the volume for a short time, in order to afford Professor Bodenstedt, Mr. Staunton, and others an opportunity of inspecting it. These gentlemen, and others, who seem to have been perfectly familiar with the handwritings of the period in question, after careful examination were unanimously of opinion that the manuscript notes and emendations were modern fabrications, although written in imitation of hands of the seventeenth century. This opinion was communicated by Mr. N. E. S. A. Hamilton to the *Times* newspaper in a letter of the 22d June 1859 ; when he also pointed out the remarkable fact, that an infinite number of faint pencil-marks and corrections, written in a hand of the present century, could be seen on the margins of the book, and that some of these pencil-marks could be distinctly traced underneath the ink of many of the emendations.

Mr. Collier, in his reply, also published in the *Times*, denied these assertions; and courted " the most minute, the most searching, and the most hostile examination of Mr. Hamilton's allegations."

We purpose, therefore, taking Mr. Collier at his word, to enter upon such an examination as he courts.—Not, however, in any hostile spirit, but with a sincere desire to ascertain the truth. The subject is too important and too grave to require or admit of personal recriminations.

As Mr. Collier rests the authority of his folio upon the antiquity of the handwriting in which those emendations are made, we purpose examining this claim to authority under the following heads:—

I. Is the writing, in which the Notes and Emendations occur, of the period of which Mr. Collier alleges it to be?

II. Are there any pencillings in the margin, as Mr. Hamilton professes to have discovered?

III. Do the Notes and Emendations carry upon their face proofs of their genuineness?

IV. What is the history of the folio in which these Notes and Emendations are found?

and lastly, on collateral grounds : —

> V. Are certain Letters and Papers relating to Shake-
> speare which Mr. Collier has printed, or referred
> to, genuine or not?

I. Is the writing, in which the notes and emendations
occur, of the period of which Mr Collier alleges it to be?

It is almost impossible to convey to the mind of the
uninitiated a correct notion of the shades of difference in the
handwritings of the sixteenth and seventeenth centuries ; and
yet a practised eye distinguishes at a glance one from
another, as easily as a man who, finding half a dozen letters
from intimate friends upon his table, can tell who are the
writers without looking at the signatures, and yet would be
at a loss to describe the different characteristics which enabled
him to form his conclusion.

The handwriting of the notes and alterations in the
Devonshire folio is of a mixed character, varying, even
in the same page, from the stiff laboured Gothic hand of the
sixteenth century to the round text-hand of the nineteenth,
a fact most perceptible in the capital letters.   It bears
unequivocal marks also of laborious imitation throughout.

In their broader characteristics the features of the handwriting of this country, from the time of the Reformation,
may be arranged under four epochs, sufficiently distinct to
elucidate our argument : —

1. The stiff upright Gothic of Henry VIII. and Edward VI.

2. The same, inclining, and less stiff, as a greater amount of
correspondence demanded an easier style of writing, under
Elizabeth.

3. The cursive, based on an Italian model (the Gothic
becoming more flexible and now rapidly disappearing), in the
reign of James I., and continuing in use for about a century.

4. The round hand of the schoolmaster, under the House
of Hanover, degenerating into the careless half-formed hands
of the present day.

Now, it is perfectly possible, that any two of these hands in succession, may have been practised by the same person ; although hand-writings, with all their modifications, are far more stationary in their essential characteristics, than an inexperienced inquirer would generally suppose. That the first and third, or the second and fourth should be co-existent is very improbable. That all, or that the first, second, and fourth should be found together, as belonging to one and the same era, we hold to be utterly impossible.

Yet this is a difficulty that Mr. Collier has to explain ; as the hand-writings of the MS. corrections in the Devonshire folio, including those in pencil, vary, as already said, from the stiff, upright, laboured, and earlier Gothic to the round text-hand of the nineteenth century.

" But," says the *Edinburgh* Reviewer,* with considerable caution though he betrays the uncertainty of the ground on which he is venturing, " in many an instrument of the seventeenth century, engrossed in the Gothic, names of places and persons, and other words to which it was wished to attract special attention, were inserted in a cursive hand, very like modern handwriting in general appearance. Such a cursive an old Corrector may have used in his freer pencil jottings, to be replaced by elaborate half-printing in penmanship."

Now, the truth is, that the cursive hand of the seventeenth century is utterly unlike the cursive hand of these pencillings. It is so far from being like, that no practised eye could be deceived by it. The cursive hand of these Gothic instruments is of the most perfect and graceful kind. It was derived from the Italian scholars, and based on the type now named ' italic.' If the reader will refer to any works printed in italics in the 17th century, *e. g.* to Bacon's " Novum Organum," or his " De Augmentis," or, still better, to his MSS. preserved in the British Museum, he will be able to form a tolerably accurate conception of the nature of cursive writing in the 17th century ; a hand as distinct from the slovenly round text-hand of these pencillings as it is from the Gothic of an earlier period.

---

* No. 226, pp. 452–486.

The Reviewer might as well confound Norman with Pointed Architecture, or Batty Langley with Cinque Cento.

But the reason assigned by the Reviewer for the prevalence of the stiffer Gothic hand in the Shakespeare emendations is really extraordinary.   The folio in which they are made appeared in 1632.   We must allow some years to have elapsed before the Corrector had completed his labours. Mr. Collier assigns them to the Commonwealth.   Assume the period to be 1650.   The corrections, then, ought to have appeared in the prevalent writing of that era; that is, in the ordinary cursive hand of the period, or, it may be, in a hand a little more antiquated, supposing they were the work of a provincial; for handwriting, like manners, was in those times somewhat less in advance in the provinces than in the metropolis.   Fac-similes of this hand are too common for any one to be at a loss to understand its general character. But, on turning to the corrections in the Devonshire folio, they are ostensibly in the hand of a much earlier date, *i.e.* of Queen Elizabeth or the earlier period of James I., while the pencillings are in a cursive hand of the 19th century. Supposing, however, for a moment that these pencillings had really been (what they are not) in a cursive hand with all the undeniable characteristics of the middle of the 17th century, what conceivable motive could the "old Corrector" have had in deliberately transforming them into a hand which had long gone out of fashion ?   It can hardly be supposed that it could be for his own convenience or pleasure that he undertook such an amount of unprofitable labour, for what was to be gained by it ?   Could it, then, be for the printer's use?   Certainly not ; though the corrections are made in the style of adapting a book for the press.

It is possible to conceive a reason for inverting the process, that is, for transforming Gothic pencil writing into ink cursive; but none whatever for the reverse.   Had the pencil writing been in Gothic, and had the majority of the written corrections been in the prevalent hand of 1650, we could then have conceived that the writer, for the sake of clearness, had been transferring the less legible Gothic into the more legible cursive ; but why he should undertake the task of replacing the distinct and modern by the indistinct and antiquated, passes our comprehension.

There is another consideration which, slight as it may appear, will not fail to have weight with those who have been accustomed to the study of handwriting in general. Mr. Collier avows his belief that all these corrections are by one and the same hand. Perhaps he is right; but, if so, how does he account for the extraordinary variations in the letters ? In the commonest capitals there are to be found as many as half a dozen different forms of the same letter; several of which appear to have been written at first in an ordinary modern character, and afterwards altered and retouched with the evident design of creating a more antique appearance. Let Mr. Collier, from the British Museum, or from the State Paper Office, furnish a single instance of one writer at any period who, in writing according to the usage of that period, has thus luxuriated in varying the form of his capitals.

We shall say only a few words on the subject of the material in which the corrections are made, as Mr. Maskelyne has given clear evidence that it is not what is commonly called the "black ink" in use at any period.

The pigment, or whatever else it may be, is of different shades, often varying on the same page from a yellow brown to a light Indian ink; a fact that seems to show that the corrections were made at different times. This may have given rise to the supposition that they were made by different persons at long intervals of time; but it appears to us, from the peculiarities in the writing and the different shades of ink, that they were made by the same hand, though undoubtedly at different periods. Believing, as we do, that they have no claims to antiquity, but are in reality recent fabrications, our opinion is simply this : that whenever the " Old Corrector" has come across any reading suggested, or error corrected, by any of the Shakespearian scholars of the last century or the present that has at all taken his fancy, he has seized upon them and inserted them in the folio; and that thus are the various shades of the ink to be accounted for. Chemical tests, if they were allowed to be tried, would at once determine what are the component parts of the liquid in which the corrections are written.

II. Are there any pencillings in the margin, as Mr. Hamilton professes to have discovered?

It has been already stated that Mr. Hamilton, on examining the emendations, discovered in the margins a number of faint pencil-marks and corrections, written in a hand of the present century, and that some of these pencil-marks could be dis· tinctly traced underneath the ink. This fact and other circumstances, singly of little importance, tend collectively to establish the charge of fabrication. On this point, too, there is other evidence than palæography ; and Mr. Maskelyne's testimony,* resting on independent grounds, cannot be lightly set aside.—" This simple test (the microscope) of the character of these emendations, I brought to bear on them, and with the following results :—

" Firstly. As to any question that might be raised concerning the presence of the pencil-marks asserted to be so plentifully distributed down the margin, the answer is, they are there. The microscope reveals the particles of plumbago in the hollows of the paper; and in no case that I have yet examined, does it fail to bring this fact forward into incontrovertible reality.

" Secondly, the ink presents a rather singular aspect under the microscope. Its appearance in many cases on or rather in the paper suggested the idea of its being a water-colour paint rather than an ink; it has a remarkable lustre, and the distribution of the particles of colouring matter in it seems unlike that in inks, ancient or modern, that I have yet examined.

" This view is somewhat confirmed by a taste, unlike the styptic taste of ordinary inks, which it imparts to the tongue, and by its substance evidently yielding to the action of damp. But on this point, as on another, to which attention will be presently drawn, it was not possible to arrive at a satisfactory conclusion in the absence of the Duke of Devonshire's permission to make a few experiments on the volume.

" His Grace visited the Museum yesterday, and was good enough to give me his consent to this. The result has been, that the suspicions previously entertained regarding the ink were confirmed.

---

* Printed in Mr. Hamilton's *Inquiry*, p. 27–29.

" It proves to be a paint removable, with the exception of a slight stain, by mere water, while, on the other hand, its colouring matter resists the action of chymical agents which rapidly change inks, ancient or modern, whose colour is due to iron. In some places, indeed, this paint seems to have become mixed, accidentally or otherwise, with ordinary ink ; but its prevailing character is that of a paint formed perhaps of sepia, or of sepia mixed with a little Indian ink. This, however, is of secondary importance in comparison with the other point which has been alluded to. This point involves, indeed, the most important question that has arisen, and concerns the relative dates of the modern-looking pencil marks, and the old emendations of the text which are in ink. The pencil marks are of different kinds. Some are d's, indicative of the deletion of stops or letters in the text, and to which alterations in ink, I believe, invariably respond. Others, again, belong to the various modes at present in use to indicate corrigenda for the press. Some may, perhaps, be the ' crosses, ticks, or lines ' which Mr. Collier introduced himself. But there are others, again, in which whole syllables or words in pencil are not so effectually rubbed out as not to be still traceable and legible, and even the character of the handwriting discernible, while in near neighbourhood to them the same syllable or word is repeated in the paint-like ink before described. The pencil is in a modern-looking hand; the ink in a quaint antique-looking writing. In several cases, however, the ink word and the pencil word occupy the same ground in the margin, and are one over the other. The question that arises in these cases, of whether these two writings are both ancient or both modern, is a question for the antiquary or palæographist. The question of whether the pencil is antecedent or subsequent to the ink, is resolvable into a physical inquiry as to whether the ink overlies the pencil or the pencil is superposed upon the ink. The answer to this question is as follows :—

" I have nowhere been able to detect the pencil-marks clearly overlying the ink, though in several places the pencil stops abruptly at the ink, and in some seems to be just traceable through its translucent substance, while lacking there the general metallic lustre of the plumbago. But the question is set at rest by the removal by water of the ink in instances where the ink and the pencil intersected each other. The first case I chose for this was an *u* in *Richard II.*, p. 36.

A pencil tick crossed the *u*, intersecting each limb of the letter. The pencil was barely visible through the first stroke, and not at all visible under the second stroke of the *u*. On damping off the ink in the first stroke, however, the pencil-mark became much plainer than before, and even when as much of the ink stain as possible was removed, and the pencil still runs through the ink in unbroken continuity. Had the pencil been superposed on the ink, it must have lain superficially upon its lustrous surface, and have been removed in the washing. We must, I think, be led by this inference that the pencil underlies the ink, that is to say, was antecedent to it in its date; while also, it is evident that the ' old commentator' had done his best to rub out the pencil writing before he introduced its ink substitute."

To this evidence other considerations must be added: the appearance of white spots in the paper, as if acids had been used to delete the ink; and the frequency of erasures by penknife or wet cloth. All these cannot but be startling facts to persons acquainted with ancient MSS., and would at once raise a doubt of the genuineness of any document where they occurred, more especially one alleged to belong to the 17th century. If this statement be questioned, let the believers in the genuineness of these emendations produce instances of such usages prevailing in the middle of the 17th century; MSS. of that period are numerous enough. No one can undertake to prove an universal negative; but until some positive proof has been given of the prevalence of such practices as these, unusual and suspicious as they undoubtedly are, we cannot do otherwise than refuse our assent to the arguments adduced in favour of the antiquity of the emendations in the Devonshire folio.

Attempts have been made, and indeed very unjustly, from the inadequacy of the fac-simile in Mr. Hamilton's volume to imply the non-existence in reality of these pencil-marks. Mr. Netherclift, senior, has taken upon himself the superfluous task of informing the public that he did not execute them. What inference he would have us to deduce from this, it is difficult, perhaps impossible, to say; but it would have been more to the point if he could have shown that these pencil-marks did not exist. On this point, however, we have the evidence of the " Old Corrector's" own advocate, the *Edinburgh* Reviewer :—

" There they are (the pencil marks) most undoubtedly, and in very great number too. The natural surprise that they were not earlier detected, is somewhat diminished on inspection. Some say they have ' come out' more in the course of years; whether this is possible we know not. But even now they are hard to discover, until the eye has become used to the search. But when it has—especially with the aid of a glass at first—they become perceptible enough; words, ticks, points, and all. In many places even the most sceptical observer can hardly doubt that the mode of correction was, as alleged for the prosecution, by pencil first, and ink afterwards. And in others, where no pencilling can be read, there is an appearance as if it had been rubbed out. Are these pencillings in a modern hand? That, after all, is the real issue of this complicated case. And it is one which me must leave to better eyes and more experienced judges, whenever this unfortunate volume shall be honestly examined. For the vehement assertions of partisans we care nothing. All we can say is, that to our eyes the faint and feeble ghosts of words and letters which are here and there to be made out, do wear the appearance of a hand more like that now in use, than the stiff gothic ink writing. But then we must observe on the other hand, that even in Elizabeth's reign the mixture of cursive with Gothic was very common. In many an instrument of the seventeenth century engrossed in the Gothic, names of places and persons, and other words to which it was wished to attract special attention, were inserted in a cursive hand very like modern hand-writing in general appearance. Such a cursive an old corrector may have used in his freer pencil jottings, to be replaced by elaborate half-printing in penmanship. This, however, we can but give as conjecture. We must, at all events, utterly disclaim and repudiate Mr. Netherclift's fac-similes in Mr. Hamilton's volume, if they are intended to be verified by the naked eye or by an ordinary glass. They are to our view infinitely too distinct, and we have carefully compared each of them with the original. In particular we must caution our readers against the very modern-looking ' r ' in armed (cited as from Hamlet, p. 277, col. 1.) Our sight, at least, failed altogether to discover its counterpart in the Perkins volume."

The tortuous ingenuity displayed in this extract is worth observing. The Reviewer having inveighed, in the earlier portion of his remarks, against the current maxim, *Cuilibet in arte sua credendum,* now requires his readers to yield their judgment at discretion to his own notions upon palæography and his unsupported surmise. True, he has the modesty to say that he offers the explanation as his own conjecture; not the less, however, intending to have it accepted as all-sufficient in reference to these pencil-marks; an issue which he has the very moment before " left to better eyes and more experienced judges."

Again, a recent writer in the *Athenæum* (N° 1686) dismisses the question of the pencil-marks, because Mr. Netherclift's fac-simile represents them as more legible than they really are: a fault, in fact, which could hardly have been avoided. Had he exaggerated the forms of the letters, or drawn them more nearly resembling modern handwriting than they really do, the objection might have been to some purpose. But, in reality, the only question is the fact of their being there, not of their being more or less legible. Indeed the more distinct and legible they were, the more would they tell in favour of the volume; the less studied intention would they betray of having been obliterated to serve the purposes of conceal-ment.* The *Athenæum* states that no pencil-marks existed; and Mr. Collier has improved this apparent advantage by asserting that there were no such pencil-marks in the book while it was in his possession; apparently intending to imply that if there now are, they must have been inserted by the British Museum authorities, who are well acquainted with his handwriting. We will not insult the common sense or candour of the reader by comment on such a defence as this; but we must again call attention to the contradictory argu-ments employed by Mr. Collier's supporters in upholding his views and statements as to this volume. What Mr. Col-lier and the *Athenæum* deny to exist at all†,—what the Editor of *Notes and Queries* " cannot see,"— is perceptible enough to the *Edinburgh* Reviewer.

---

* Whatever may have been the origin or purpose of these pencil-marks, it is clear that some one has deemed it advisable that their traces and evidence should be destroyed as far as possible, and that great efforts had been made to obliterate them by rubbing out.

† Mr. Collier states that neither he nor the Duke of Devonshire ever dis-covered a single pencil-mark, and that another friend of his had the folio under his eyes for one week and examined every page of it, and never saw a single pencil-mark.

"There they are," he states, "most undoubtedly, and in very great number too." "In many places (he subjoins), the most sceptical observer can hardly doubt that the mode of correction was by pencil first and ink afterwards. And in others, where no pencilling can be read, there is an appearance as if it had been rubbed out.'

Whatever the public may think of this admission Mr. Collier can hardly thank the writer for making it. The Reviewer continues: "All we can say is, that to our eyes, the faint and feeble ghosts of words and letters which are here and there to be made out, do wear the appearance of a hand more like that now in use than the stiff Gothic ink writing." The method by which he escapes the fatal conclusion is, at all events, novel. These pencillings do occur; "but then we must observe, on the other hand, that even in Elizabeth's reign the mixture of cursive with Gothic was very common."

What "experts" were at the elbow of the Reviewer when he put forth this novel discovery in palæography? It exhibits all the pomp and pretentiousness of sciolism, and, like most novelties, is equally false and flimsy. What have instruments *engrossed*, or *legal* documents, of the seventeenth century to do with annotations scribbled in the margin of a book, first in pencil, in a modern hand, and afterwards in ink, in a hand of a much earlier period? Because Gothic engrossing is to be found in legal documents of 1650, therefore he concludes that such hand was the ordinary hand of the Commonwealth. But what, it may be further asked, has the mixture of cursive and Gothic in the time of Elizabeth to do with the handwriting of 1650? and even if it had, what has it to do with pencillings which wear all the appearance of a hand of the present century? The juxtaposition of the Reviewer's sentences looks very much like a studied attempt to mislead the unwary. Without any logical connexion, they carry the appearance of such connexion to the mind of the inexperienced reader. The Reviewer wishes to show that engrossing and cursive hands were commonly intermixed to a very late period. Gothic and cursive, he tells us, are found together in the common hands of the age of Elizabeth; what then? To have gained any real support to his cause he ought to have shown that the same admixture of hands prevailed in the middle of the seventeenth century.

III. Do the Notes and Emendations carry upon their face proofs of their genuineness?

The corrections and conjectural emendations which occur in the Devonshire folio are, so far as we have been made acquainted with them, of four descriptions :—

1. Typographical errors that are self-evident, and which could be corrected by the merest tyro in Shakespearian reading.

2. Typographical errors that require some critical acumen, or perhaps fancy, to amend.

3. Errors, the corrections of which have been made by other Commentators.

4. Errors that are corrected for the first time in the Devonshire folio.

Upon each of these divisions a few words are necessary. Unfortunately, however, this part of the case hardly admits of that complete examination which it demands, as Mr. Collier has failed to furnish us with all the necessary means for dealing with it. He has given to the world only those emendations which might seem to carry with them some air of probability; while three-fourths, at least, of their less fortunate brethren lie still unrevealed in the margins of this folio, there to remain until some future Editor shall deem them worth ushering into the light of day. But to proceed :—

1. The typographical errors that are self-evident, and which the merest tyro might correct, are such as ſight for fight, ſaith for faith, ſail, for fail, &c., and reversing topsy-turvy letters, such as Mr. Collier describes.

2. Typographical errors that require some critical acumen or fancy to amend; such as " When *it* was out—let me not " live quoth he ;" which is amended by Mr. Staunton thus, "When *wit* was out—let me not live quoth he."·

It may be remarked, that corrections of this kind may be arrived at by three different processes :—(1.) By writing the suspected word in the hand of the 16th century, or by imitating the writing of Shakespeare, as far as possible, from the little that is known of it, and seeing how it would look in that writing; thus *ℓₐₑ* which might be read either 'haste' or 'halter,' especially if it were carelessly written, or where the long *s* has been used by mistake for *f*, and *vice versâ.* (2.) By writing down the consonants or principal letters* of the doubted word, and guessing what the word ought to be, for at that period words were abbreviated by the omission of many of the vowels, as in *prnz*, which, being extended, might be read 'prinzie' or 'princely.' (3). By pronouncing the line or phrase rapidly, and catching the sense by the sound, as "I should not have thought it," which, when rapidly and not clearly pronounced, would sound like "I should not *of* thought it." "'Tis not alone my inky cloak, good mother," which was misprinted in the edition of 1611, evidently from faulty pronunciation, "'Tis not alone my incky cloake *could smother.*" Again, there are several instances where one word is mistaken for another by being pronounced more broadly, or slenderly, than usual, as in w*o*nder and w*a*nder—b*o*tcher and b*u*tcher—be*tt*er and b*i*tter —p*i*n and p*e*n.

There is no doubt that a person resorting to any of these methods would frequently be able to correct corrupt readings, or at any rate produce clever suggestions. This seems to have been the mode adopted by the "Old Corrector;" and if he had confined himself to the exposure of such errors as he had by such means discovered, he would have been entitled to much praise for his ingenuity. But where he has allowed his unrestrained fancy or his ignorance to prevail, he has committed the most egregious blunders and absurdities.

---

* Shorthand may possibly have been employed in writing down from the mouths of the players those plays which were surreptitiously printed. Mr. Collier cites a passage from Heywood ("Life of Shakespeare," p. 142) in reference to the errors in plays thus procured and hastily printed, which proves that it was employed on some occasions:

> "that some by stenography drew
> The plot, put it in print scarce one word true."

But it is not at all probable that the manuscript which was supplied by the author or editor to the printer was ever in shorthand. It was doubtless occasionally written with the contractions in common use; as ℘ for *pro*, p for *per*, *par, por,* ꝩ for *ter* or *tre,* ꝓ for *pre,* tꝭ for *tis* or *tes,* wᵗ for *what,* wᵗʰ for *with,* yᵗ for *that,* yᵉ for *the,* etc, and the compositors in extending such words frequently made mistakes.

B

On a rough calculation from the data furnished by Mr. Collier, the number of alterations in the Devonshire folio amounts to about 12,000, though he himself says near 20,000, which of course must include palpable mis-spellings and instances of incorrect punctuation. Taking the German Professor, Mommsem, for our authority, through the medium of the *Edinburgh Review*, there are 52 instances in which the initial letter of a word is altered, 7 in which it is added, 11 in which it is erased, 34 of initial double consonants altered, 95 of initials altered, together with other letters, 266 (if we count rightly) of final letters variously altered, and a proportional number of changes in letters between the first and the last. Mr. Collier has published about 2,700 of these alterations, leaving all others that occur in the folio un-noticed. Of the 2,700 so noticed, about 270 have been made by Malone, Theobald, Johnson, and others; the remainder being, almost entirely, worthless as blunders, or mere corrections of typographical errors. Judging from those which Mr. Collier has thus published, we are able to form some opinion of the value of those which he has declined to publish.

3. Errors, the corrections of which have been made by other Commentators.

A few of these, which have been taken at random from the various plays, will show to what extent his pilferings have been carried on by the " Old Corrector :"—

MEASURE FOR MEASURE.

Old or received text.	*" Old Corrector's" text.**
ACT I. Sc. 5.	
Sir, make me not your story.	Sir, make me not your *scorn.—Davenant.*
ACT II. Sc. 4.	
Proclaim an en-shield beauty.	Proclaim an *inshell'd* beauty.—*Tyrwhitt.*
ACT V. Sc. 1.	
Make rash remonstrance.	Make rash *demonstrance.—Malone.*

---

* The alterations by the "Old Corrector" are printed in Italics: at the end of each line is given the name of the Commentator from whom the "Old Corrector" is supposed to have borrowed the alteration.

COMEDY OF ERRORS.

Old or received text.	*" Old Corrector's" text.*

ACT V. Sc. 1.

The place of depth, and sorrie execution.	The place of *death* (¹) and *solemn* execution.—(¹) *Rowe.*

MIDSUMMER NIGHT'S DREAM.

ACT V. Sc. 1.

A lion fell, nor else no lion's dam.	A *lion's* fell, nor else no lion's dam.—*Baron Field.*

AS YOU LIKE IT.

ACT I. Sc. 1.

Bequeathed me by will.	*He* bequeathed me by will.—*Blackstone.*

ACT I. Sc. 3.

Some of it for my child's father.	Some of it for my *father's child.*—*Rowe.*

LOVE'S LABOUR LOST.

ACT I. Sc. 1.

A dangerous law against gentility.	A dangerous law against *garrulity.*—*Warburton* and *Theobald.*

ACT III. Sc. 1.

By my penne of observation.	By my *paine* of observation.—*Theobald.*

TAMING OF THE SHREW.

ACT I. Sc. 1.

Or so devote to Aristotle's checks.	Or so devote to Aristotle's *Ethics.*—*Blackstone.*

ACT I. Sc. 2.

My mind presumes, for his own good and yours.	My mind presumes, for his own good and *ours.**—*Theobald.*

ACT V. Sc. 2.

Hath cost me five hundred crowns since supper-time.	Cost me *one* hundred crowns since supper-time.—*Pope.*

MERRY WIVES OF WINDSOR.

ACT I. Sc. 3.

She carves, she gives the leer of invitation.	She *craves,* she gives the leer of invitation.—*Zach. Jackson.*

---

* This is omitted in the edition of the *Notes, Emendations,* etc. of 1856.

ALL'S WELL THAT ENDS WELL.

Old or received text.   *" Old Corrector's" text.*

Act II. Sc. 1.

Where hope is coldest and despair most shifts.	Where hope is coldest and despair most *fits.—Theobald.*

Act II. Sc. 3.

My honour's at the stake, which to defeat.	My honour's at the stake, which to *defend.—Theobald.*

Act II. Sc. 3.

To the dark house and the detected wife.	To the dark house and the *detested* wife.—*Rowe.*

Act III. Sc. 2.

Fly with false aim; move the still-peering air.	Fly with false aim; *wound* the still-*piecing* (¹) air.—(¹) *Malone.*

Act IV. Sc. 2.

I see that men make ropes in such a scarre.	I see that men make *hopes* in such a *suit.—Rowe.*

Act IV. Sc. 4.

And time revives us.	And time *reviles* us.—*Stevens.*

Act IV. Sc. 5.

Faith, Sir, a' has an English maine.	Faith, Sir, a' has an English *name.—Rowe.*

Act IV. Sc. 5.

And, indeed, he has no pace.	And, indeed, he has no *place.— Tyrwhitt.*

Act V. Sc. 3.

Done i' the blade of youth.	Done i' the *blaze* of youth.—*Theobald.*

Act V. Sc. 3.

Her insuit coming, with her modern grace.	Her *infinit cunning*, with her modern grace.—*Sidney Walker.*

TWELFTH NIGHT.

Act I. Sc. 1.

O! it came o'er my ear like the sweet sound.	O! it came o'er my ear like the sweet *south.—Pope.*

Old or received text.   *" Old Corrector's" text.*

Act II. Sc. 5.

And with what wing the stallion checks at it.

And with what wing the *falcon** checks at it.

Act IV. Sc. 1.

Adieu, goodman divel.

Adieu, goodman *drivel.—Farmer* and *Stevens.*

KING JOHN.

Act II. Sc. 1.

His own determin'd aid.

His own determin'd *aim.—Mason.*

Act III. Sc. 2.

Some airy devil hovers in the sky.

Some *fiery* devil hovers in the sky.—*Warburton.*

Act V. Sc. 4.

Unthread the rude eye of rebellion.

Untread the *road-way* of rebellion.—*Theobald.*

FIRST PART OF HENRY IV.

Act I. Sc. 1.

A conquest for a prince to boast of.

Faith 'tis a conquest for a prince to boast of.—*Pope.*

Act I. Sc. 3.

Shall we buy treason, and indent with fears?

Shall we buy treason, and indent with *foes?* —*Hanmer.*

Act I. Sc. 3.

I'll steal to Glendower, and loe Mortimer.

I'll steal to Glendower, and *lord* Mortimer. —*All Editions* for upwards of a century.

Act V. Sc. 2.

Supposition all our lives.

Suspicion all our lives.—*Pope.*

SECOND PART OF HENRY IV.

Act I. Sc. 1.

The ragged'st hour.

The *rugged'st* hour.—*Theobald.*

Act IV. Sc. 1.

Turning your books to graves.

Turning your books to *glaives.—Warburton.* (Stevens suggested *greaves.*)

---

  * This alteration is one of the emendations pointed out by the *Edinburgh* Reviewer as a proof of the authenticity of the " Old Corrector." Now the word *stannyel* for *stallion* was happily suggested by Hanmer; and the Old Corrector for *stannyel* substitutes *falcon*, " which means nearly the same thing."

Old or received text.   *" Old Corrector's" text.*

HENRY V.

Act II. Sc. 1.

There shall be smiles.   There shall be *smites.—Farmer.*

Act II. Sc. 4.

Whiles that his mountain sire on moun-   Whiles that his *mighty* sire on mountain
tain standing.   standing.—*Tollet.*

Act III. Sc. 3.

Desire the locks.   *Defile* the locks.—*Pope.*

FIRST PART OF HENRY VI.

Act II. Sc. 4.

I scorn thee and thy fashion.   I scorn thee and thy *faction.—Theobald.*

Act III. Sc. 3.

On her lowly babe.   On her *lovely* babe.—*Warburton.*

Act V. Sc. 4.

The hollow passage of my poison'd voice. The hollow passage of my *prison'd* voice.--
                                                                                    Pope.

SECOND PART OF HENRY VI.

Act I. Sc. 3.

She'll gallop far enough.   She'll gallop *fast* enough.—*Pope.*

Act III. Sc. 2.

And to drain upon his face.   And to *rain* upon his face.—*Stevens.*

Act IV. Sc. 1.

The lives of those which we have lost in   *Can* lives of those which we have lost in
fight.   fight.—*Stevens.*

Act V. Sc. 3.

And all brush of time.   And all *bruise* of time.—*Warburton.*

THIRD PART OF HENRY VI.

Act I. Sc. 1.

Hear but one word.   Hear *me* but one word.—3d Folio, *Mason;
Singer,* 1826.

Act II. Sc. 2.

And this soft courage.   And this soft *carriage.—Mason.*

Act V. Sc. 6.

To wit, an indigested deformed lump.   To wit, an *indigest* deformed lump.—*Malone*

RICHARD III.

Old or received text.   *" Old Corrector's" text.*

Act V. Sc. 3.

To desperate adventures.

To desperate *ventures.—Stevens.*

Act V. Sc. 3.

They would restrain the one, distain the other.

They would *distrain* the one, distain the other.—*Warburton.*

HENRY VIII.

Act I. Sc. 2.

There is no primer baseness.

There is no primer *business.—Warburton.*

Act I. Sc. 2.

Whom after, under the commission's seal.

Whom after, under the *confession's* seal.—*Theobald.*

Act I. Sc. 2.

Things that are known alike.

Things that are known, *belike.—Theobald.*

Act II. Sc. 3.

I shall not fail t'approve the fair conceit.

I shall not fail *t'improve* the fair conceit.—*Knight.*

Act V. Sc. 1.

The good I stand on is my truth and honesty.

The *ground* I stand on is my truth and honesty.—*Johnson.*

Act. V. Sc. 2.

In our own natures frail and capable.

In our own natures frail and *culpable.—Theobald; Mason.*

TROILUS AND CRESSIDA.

Act I. Sc. 1.

So traitor, then she comes!

So traitor, *when* she comes!—*Rowe.*

Act I. Sc. 1.

As when the sun doth light a scorn.

As when the sun doth light a *storm.—Rowe.*

Act I. Sc. 2.

Achievement is command.

Achiev'd men(1) *still*(2) command.—(1)*Harness* ; (2) *Collier's own emendation in a previous edition of Shakespeare.*

Act I. Sc. 3.

Retires to chiding fortune.

Replies to chiding fortune.--*Hanmer.*

Act II. Sc. 3.

His pettish lines, his ebbs, his flows.

His pettish *lunes,* his ebbs, his flows.—*Hanmer.*

Act III. Sc. 3.

Keeps place with thought.

Keeps *pace* with thought.—*Hanmer.*

CORIOLANUS.

Old or received text.	*"Old Corrector's" text.*

Act II. Sc. 1.

| His soaring insolence shall teach the people. | His soaring insolence shall *touch* the people. —*Knight.* |

Act II. Sc. 3.

See Singer's remark in "The text of Shakespeare Vindicated," *p.* 216, about the "Old Corrector" and Pope's line respecting Censorinus.

Act IV. Sc. 3.

| But your favour is well appear'd by your tongue. | But your favour is well *approv'd* by your tongue.—*Stevens.* |

Act IV. Sc. 4.

| My birth place have I. | My birth place *hate* I.—*Stevens.* |

ROMEO AND JULIET.

Act II. Sc. 2.

| Lady, by yonder moon I vow. | Lady, by yonder *blessed* (¹) moon I *swear* (²). (¹) wanting only in the 1st Folio.   (²) in the 4to. of 1597. |

Act III. Sc. 5.

| Tis but the pale reflex of Cynthia's brow. | 'Tis but the pale reflex of Cynthia's *bow.*— *Singer.* |

TIMON OF ATHENS.

Act I. Sc. 1.

| Our poesy is a gown which uses. | Our poesy is a *gum* which *issues.*—*Pope.* |

Act IV. Sc. 3.

| It is the pastor lords the brother's sides. | It is the *pasture lards* the *rother's* sides.— *Singer.* |

Act V. Sc. 2.

| To stop afflction, let him take his haste. | To stop affliction, let him take his *halter.** |

---

* This example does not properly come under this head, but we have drawn attention to it because the *Edinburgh* Reviewer selects this alteration as proof of the genuineness of the emendations of the " Old Corrector," and remarks that " let *him take his haste* " is sheer nonsense, and yet it is so near sense that every Editor has passed it by without remark, as not worth touching.   The Corrector reads it " take his halter," and the Reviewer asks, " Why should a forger have gone out of his way to meddle with a text which no man had disturbed before ? "   It is not necessary to point out the illogical inference drawn by the Reviewer, but the error, it should be remarked, does not lie in *haste* but in *take.* " Let him *make* his haste " is very good sense; but the " Old Corrector," not understanding the passage, thought the error was in *haste*, and

brought back the word to the writing of the sixteenth century; thus, *lost*, which he thought would read either " halter " or " haste ;" and then " boldly " (we use the Reviewer's own word) amends the text, and substitutes *halter* for *haste.*

Old or received text.   *" Old Corrector's" text.*

Act V. Sc. 4.

Some beast read this; there does not live a man.

Some beast *rear'd* this; there does not live a man. — *Warburton.* See Staunton's restoration of this passage.

MACBETH.

Act I. Sc. 4.

The swiftest $\left\{ \begin{matrix} wine\ (1632) \\ wing\ (1623) \end{matrix} \right\}$ of recompense is slow.

The swiftest *wind* of recompence is slow. —*Pope.*

Here are upwards of 70 emendations taken from 23 plays at hazard, in which the " Old Corrector " has anticipated the conjectures of Tyrwhitt, Rowe, Baron Field, Blackstone, Davenant, Knight, Singer, Theobald, Malone, Stevens, Sidney Walker, Pope, Hanmer, Jackson, Capell, Farmer, Mason, Warburton, Tollet, Johnson, and even Mr. Collier himself!

Upon the value of these emendations there is no necessity for comment * (beyond observing that many of the rejected readings of Malone and Hanmer have been adopted by the annotator of the Devonshire folio), because a question of far more importance to the present inquiry will occur to the reader. How came the " Old Corrector " to anticipate the conjectures of minds so various as these? Asmodeus, in Le Sage's story, sees, though certainly through brick walls, the deeds of existing men; but the " Old Corrector " performs a feat far more astonishing--he sees at a glance, and in embryo, all these, both probable and improbable, conjectures, which shall enter the fertile brains of Shakespearian critics and correctors, a century or more before those brains are yet in existence.

It might be said, and it cannot be denied, that, amid the thousands of suggestions made by Shakespearian critics of the last century and a half for amendment of the text, the probabilities are, in many instances, owing to a happy surmise, the correct reading would be restored,—such readings, in fact, as might have been within the personal knowledge of a scholar living in 1652; but if there are many instances in which the Old Corrector agrees with the suggesters of these happy emendations, the instances unfortunately are tenfold more numerous where he agrees with

---

* Perhaps the best test of the value of these emendations is the number of them which have been adopted by the last two Editors of Shakespeare, Messrs. Dyce and Staunton.

none of them, and where his alterations are not tenable for a moment. The only conclusion, then, that we can arrive at is, that for nearly all his emendations of the slightest value, this "Old Corrector" has been indebted, not to his personal acquaintance with the early actors of Shakespeare's plays, but to the whole body of Shakespearian critics since the time of Queen Anne; and that for the rest of his corrections, which from their utter worthlessness are self-condemned, he has been indebted, not to the early actors of Shakespeare's plays, but, as already suggested, to his own misdirected fancy. Mr. Collier ("*Notes and Emendations*," p. xxi.,) asks "was he (the " Old Corrector ") indebted to his own sagacity and ingenuity, and did he merely guess at arbitrary emendations? I am inclined to think that the last must have been the fact as regards some of the changes." With this opinion we readily concur; only instead of *some changes*, we should suggest *most of the changes*.

4. Errors that are corrected for the first time in the Devonshire Folio.

The number of these emendations, as printed by Mr. Collier in his last Edition of them, amounts as already mentioned to about 2,400, which the *Edinburgh* Reviewer states is not one-fourth of all these readings. In "Hamlet" there are 463 MS. alterations in the Devonshire folio; though Mr. Collier has noticed only 126 of them. The whole of them may be seen, however, in Mr. Hamilton's "*Inquiry, &c.*" pp. 34–54. Now of some 2,000 guesses, it would be strange indeed if some few were not to the purpose. The dullest commentator that ever lived must have had a surprising faculty for perverseness if he could not sometimes blunder into the right reading, after so many years' practice as this unknown commentator must have enjoyed, and such continuous toil.

Dr. Delius, the well-known German Shakespearian critic, says Mr. R. Grant White,* after a careful consideration and examination of the Notes and Emendations printed by Mr. Collier, admits only 17 new readings as corrections worthy of adoption. Mr. Grant White likewise informs us, from the data supplied to him by Mr. Collier's "*Notes and Emendations*," that the " Old Corrector " has made

---

* *Shakespeare's Scholar* (1854), p. 75.

thirteen hundred and three modifications of the text of the second folio. Of these thirteen hundred and three, at least two hundred and forty-nine are old; that is, either restorations of the text of the original folio, adoptions of readings from the old quartos, or identical with the conjectural emendations of editors and commentators during the last hundred and fifty years. Of these 249 old readings, 29 have long ago been rejected by common consent, as unworthy of the least attention; 47 have been rejected from the text, but are allowed to have a certain plausibility; and 173 are found in the received text.* Mr. White further states that Mr. Collier's emendations from the Devonshire folio contain 1,013 inadmissible alterations; a total which would have been wonderfully increased had he counted the numbers in the folio itself. This, however, is no fault on the part of Mr. White; he could only take his data from Mr. Collier's publications.

But what would twenty, or thirty, or even fifty, ingenious guesses be worth in determining the question of the authenticity of the "Old Corrector's" copy, if the remainder exhibited absurdities and misapprehensions of Shakespeare's meaning, as well as tawdry sentiments unworthy of the pen of Shakespeare's humbler contemporaries even?

To make this plain, it will be necessary to place before the reader some of the emendations which Mr. Collier has printed, in which it is clear that the "Old Corrector" has exhibited his utter incapacity to appreciate the poetic genius of the man whose works he undertook to amend, and that he must have gone into the highways and byeways to collect his materials, taking them indiscriminately as he found them. He cared not for quality; quantity was evidently his great object.

In addition to the many other liberties which the "Old Corrector" has taken with Shakespeare's works, he has presumed to add entire lines, and to alter the ends of others over and over again for the mere purpose of supplying a tag or rhyme, in the worst possible taste, and wholly destroying the sense of the passage which he professes to improve. These

---

* *Shakespeare's Scholar* (1854), p. 67.

are neither amendments nor corrections of existing errors; they supply no deficiency, but are mere useless additions. In fact, he has done that which was never intended to be done; he has washed pure gold with a lackering of brass.

It can hardly be denied, we should think, that a man's ear must have been greatly corrupted by dabbling in doggrel imitations of the ballad literature of the sixteenth and seventeenth centuries before he could venture to insert such lines* as these, for no apparent purpose beyond the gratification of a morbid taste for jingling rhymes:—

> " Inspire me that I may this treason finde,
> My lord, looke heere, looke heere Lavinia."
>
> *Altered to*
>
> " Inspire me that *this treason finde I may*,
> My lord, looke heere, looke heere Lavinia."

> " And madam, if my uncle Marcus goe,
> I will most willingly attend your ladyship."
>
> *Altered to*
>
> " And madam, if my uncle Marcus goe,
> I will most willingly attend *you so*."

> " May run into that sinke, and soaking in,
> Drowne the lamenting foole in sea-salt-teares."
>
> *Altered to*
>
> " May run into that sinke, and soaking in,
> Drowne the lamenting foole *in sea-salt-brine*."

> " No funerall Rite, nor man in mournfull weeds;
> No mournfull Bell shall ring her Buriall."
>
> *Altered to*
>
> " No funerall Rite, nor man in mournfull *pall*;
> No mournfull Bell shall ring her Buriall."

> " For two and twenty sonnes I never wept,
> Because they died in honours lofty bed."
>
> *Altered to*
>
> " For two and twenty sonnes I never wept,
> Because in honours lofty bed they *slept*."

> " And keep eternall spring-time on thy face,
> So thou refuse to drinke my deare sonnes blood."
>
> *Altered to*
>
> " And keep eternall spring-time in the *flood*,
> So thou refuse to drinke my deare sonnes blood."

---

* The Devonshire folio abounds in alterations of this description. With the exception of two (the last quoted in the next page), the instances here given have not been inserted by Mr. Collier in any of his editions. Nothing would so well show the utter worthlessness of these alterations as by printing all those which Mr. Collier has omitted.

"Oh, be to me, though thy hard heart say no,
Nothing so kind, but something pittiful."

Altered to

"Oh, be to me, though thy hard heart say no,
Nothing so kind, but *still some pity show*."*

"That hath expres't himselfe in all his deeds,
A Father and a friend to thee and Rome."

Altered to

"That hath expres't himselfe *abroad at home*,
A Father and a friend to thee and Rome."

Queen.—"I see no reason, why a king of yeares
Should be to be protected like a child;
God and King Henry governe England's Realme:
Give up your staffe, Sir, and the King his Realme.
Glost.—My staffe? Here, noble Henry, is my staffe,
As willingly doe I the same resigne."

Altered to

Queen.—"I see no reason, why a king of yeeres
Should be to be protected like a child; *by peeres*,
God and King Henry governe England's *helm*,
Give up your staffe, Sir, and the King his Realme.
Glost.—My staffe? Here, noble Henry, is my staffe,
To think I fain would keep it makes me laugh,
As willingly doe I the same resigne."

"While I remaine behind to tell a tale,
That shall hereafter turne the hearers pale."†

"Fight for your King, your Country, and your Lives;
And so farewell, for I must hence again."

Altered to

"Fight for your King, your Country, and your Lives:
And so farewell: *rebellion never thrives*."‡

Instances in which the "Old Corrector" has entirely
misunderstood the sense :—

In "As You Like It," Act IV. Sc. 1.:

Orland.—"Who could be out, being before his beloved mistress?
Rosal.—Marry, that should you, if I were your mistress, or I should think
my honesty ranker than my wit."

Rosalind's speech has been altered by the "Old Corrector"
thus—

"Marry, that should you, if I were your mistress, or I should
thank my honesty *rather* than my wit."

What Shakespeare meant is clearly expressed. The "Old
Corrector" by his amendment makes it sheer nonsense.
For what should Rosalind thank her honesty?

---

* So altered, but afterwards struck out.
† These two lines are additions; but they are not published by Mr. Collier.
‡ The reader will remember the verse from which this "tag" was evidently
derived :—

"Treason can never prosper—for this reason :
That if it prospers, none dare call it treason."

In "Henry the Fifth," Act II. Sc. 3., the Hostess, describing the death of Falstaff, says—

"'A parted eve'n just between twelve and one, e'en at the turning o' the tide; for after I saw him fumble with the sheets, and play with flowers, and smile upon his finger's ends, I knew there was but one way; *for his nose was as sharp as a pen,** and 'a babbled † of green fields.*"

But the " Old Corrector " gives the passage in italics, thus—

" For his nose was as sharp as a pen *on a table of green frieze.*"

There is something exquisitely touching, as well as truthful, in Shakespeare's description of the dying old man, whose thoughts reverted to the innocence of his childhood, and to its "green fields;" and it is almost lamentable to think how the passage has thus been misunderstood and vulgarized by the " Old Corrector," who must have sadly taxed his ingenuity for the purpose of distorting the poet's meaning.

In "Henry the Fifth," Act IV. Sc. 1., Henry speaks of—

"   ·   ·   ·   ·   the wretched slave,
Who, with a body fill'd, and vacant mind,
Gets him to rest, cramm'd with distressful bread."

The " Old Corrector " amends the third line thus—

"Gets him to rest, cramm'd with *distasteful* bread."

Thus robbing the figure of its poetical drapery, and dressing it in a patchwork robe. Shakespeare's image is touching and beautiful. We can picture the poor slave eating the bread of sorrow—distressful to his spirit—not as the " Old Corrector " suggests, distasteful to his stomach.

In " Cymbeline," Act III. Sc. 2., Imogen, eager to meet Posthumus, calls for horses, and when Pisanio submits that they can go no farther than twenty miles a day, she exclaims—

"   ·   ·   ·   ·   I have heard of riding-wagers,
Where horses have been nimbler than the sands
That run 'i the clock's behalf."

This simile is perfect —meaning that the horses are nimbler than the sands that run in the hour-glass—substituted for a clock. The " Old Corrector " makes Imogen speak thus—

"   .   ·   :   ·   Nimbler than the sands,
That run 'i the clocks, *by half.*"

---

* This is probably a misprint for *pin*.
† In the folio editions of Shakespeare, the above final words are incorrectly printed, "and *a table* of green fields," which Theobald most happily restored as given above.

An emendation that is ridiculous. In addition to misapprehending Shakespeare, the " Old Corrector " has made an egregious blunder, by making the sands a portion of the works of a clock; the horses are nimbler by half than the sands that run in a clock ! !

In " The Tempest," Act I. Sc. 2., Prospero says—

> "One,
> Who having, unto truth, by telling of it,
> Made such a sinner of his memory,
> To credit his own lie."

The text of this passage is certainly obscure; but the " Old Corrector " has made it no less so. He gives it thus :-

> "One,
> Who having *to untruth*, by telling of it,
> Made such a sinner of his memory,
> To credit his own lie."

There is something eminently absurd in the following alteration. In the Induction of "The Taming of the Shrew," Sc. 2. Christopher Sly says,—" If she say I am not fourteen pence on the score for sheer ale, score me up for the lyingest knave in Christendom."

The meaning is clear enough, and yet the " Old Corrector," out of sheer wantonness, one might almost think, alters the passage thus : " If she say I am not fourteen pence on the score for *Warwickshire* ale, score me up, etc." And Mr. Collier gives some equally baseless justification of the alteration ; whereas " *sheer* " here signifies nothing more or less than *pure* or *unmixed* (equivalent to the Latin *merus*), an expression still in common use. Johnson even selects his example of the use of this word from the drunken Tinker's speech; but the " Old Corrector," perhaps, wished to improve on what Malone had suggested on the subject, who thought that it meant *shearing* or reaping ale.

---

* We would, however, suggest the following reading—
> " One,
> Who *adding* unto truth by telling of it,
> Made such a sinner of his memory,
> To credit his own lie."

That is, he had exaggerated truth so often, that at last he believed his own exaggeration.

A few words are called for in reference to the numerous passages which are struck out in the Devonshire folio. The principal purpose of these mutilations seems to have been to shorten the Scenes, for they occur in the plays that were most frequently performed. Some few passages, however, may have been struck out because the audience did not understand them, and some, though not many, as Mr. Collier suggests, on account of their indecency. It has been asked, if these corrections are really forged, what motive could any modern forger have in eliminating a number of magnificent passages from the folio? Would he have ventured to incur the odium of such imprudence? So far, however, from there being any intrinsic value in this suggestion, the friends of the folio have far from mended their case by inviting attention to the fact; one in itself most strange and most unaccountable, on the supposition of the genuineness of the corrections in the folio.

There are throughout the book a number of the finest passages scored out, as is common in prompters' copies. (A copy of the same edition in fact is now lying open before us, in which some of the most poetical passages are similarly struck out.) It is assumed that these elisions in the Devonshire folio must have been made by the "Old Corrector," in conformity with some original from which he derived his emendations. Now the overwhelming probability seems to be, that the passages in question were *not* struck out by the person who wrote the Notes and Emendations, but were expunged at a much *earlier* period, and that solely for theatrical, and not critical, purposes; the ink in which the corrections are made being evidently different from that in which these deletions or elisions occur. This fact too seems the more clear, as these scored passages are accompanied by exactly the same sort of amended readings in the margin as the rest of the book. If they were scored out by the "Old Corrector" with the view of being omitted, how came they, equally with the unscored passages, to exhibit these various readings?

A word or two also on the punctuation and stage directions which have been added throughout the Devonshire volume; a point of some importance, although little attention seems to have been directed to it throughout this controversy. On this subject Mr. Collier writes:—" The changes in punctuation alone, always made with nicety and patience, must have required a long period, considering their number; the other alterations, sometimes most minute, extending even to turned letters and typographical trifles of that kind, from their very nature could not have been introduced with rapidity."

Now it is greatly to be doubted whether Mr. Collier, with all his experience in such matters, can show any other instance, in dramas of the first half of the seventeenth century, either manuscript or printed, where such minutiæ are to be found. Every one must know, who has given the slightest attention to the subject, that the punctuation introduced into this folio is not the punctuation of the seventeenth century, nor even of the eighteenth. It is too elaborate to be genuine. Indeed, it may be doubted whether an editor, in preparing an edition for press in the present century, could have been more exact. The volume has all the appearance in fact of having been actually punctuated for press;* and, singular to say, minute as this punctuation is, and savouring so strongly of the present century, it unquestionably was inserted in pencil before it was written in ink, as in many instances it underlies the ink.

In reference also to the stage directions,—they are much too abundant to be genuine. In fact, Mr. Collier has remarked that the written additions of this kind seem even more frequent and more explicit than might be thought necessary. It may be observed, that many of the stage directions prove that the corrections were not made at the time to which they professedly belong; for painted or moveable scenery (especially of such a character as trees into which a person might climb) was not in use

---

* No one, we feel persuaded, who has carefully examined the volume, can come to any other conclusion than that this folio was corrected with the full intention of printing it; why that intention was abandoned, it is not for us to surmise. In this respect, we perfectly agree with the writer in the *Edinburgh Review*, who states, that " not only are words and sentences altered, lines added, omitted, or transposed, but the orthography and punctuation are set right with the minutest and most fastidious care."

at that period.*   When, therefore, we find in " Love's
Labours Lost," Act IV. Sc. 3., where the original direction
" *He stands aside* " is obliterated, and " *He gets him in a
tree* " is written in its place in manuscript ; when, too, Biron
interposes some remark to himself, and it is added, " He
is *in the tree*," and when upon his descending to detect
his companions " *Come down*" is inscribed in the margin,—
these alterations are more than suspicious; indeed, they
are fatal to the antiquity of the directions.   A similar remark applies also to the alteration in " Much Ado About
Nothing," Act II. Sc. 3., where Benedick says " I will hide
me in the arbour," the " Old Corrector " having added,
"*Retires behind the trees*." In some instances the printed stage
directions have been obliterated ; in others, again, the stage
instructions of undoubtedly a succeeding century have been
anticipated.   No one knows better than Mr. Collier that
there is a dearth of them in all early printed dramas, and he
admits that in the old printed copies there is but one note
of *aside* in the whole of Shakespeare's thirty-six plays.
Surely, then, these facts must afford some ground at least
for the suspicion that these additions were not inserted until
long after the time at which the emendations are alleged to
have been made.

So far, too, from it being probable that any person at all
conversant with the usages of the stage would commit to
paper minutiæ of this description, it is the fact that many
of the stage directions are traditional, and handed down

---

* Painted scenery was not in use at public theatres until after the Restoration, though it was undoubtedly introduced into Masques at Court and a few
private exhibitions at an earlier period. The advocates for the genuineness of
the Notes and Emendations in the Devonshire folio may possibly contend
that these stage-directions were inserted after the Restoration. This position,
however, is not tenable, as the writing in which they occur is a hand professedly of earlier date. Indeed, Mr. Collier himself evidently admits that they
are of earlier date, for he says that " these stage-directions are of the highest
importance in illustrating the wonderful judgment and skill of Shakespeare
in conducting the business of the scenes ;"—implying that they must have
come immediately from Shakespeare himself. Also, in his affidavit of the
8th January 1856, he says that he has not inserted a single word, stop, sign,
note, correction, alteration, or emendation, which is not a faithful copy of the
original manuscript, and which he believes *to have been written not long after
the publication of the folio copy of the year* 1632. The reader who is interested
in this portion of the history of our Drama may consult " An Historical
Account of the English Stage," vol. iii., pp. 79–109 in the *Variorum* edition
of Shakespeare, 1813 ; as also the *Historia Histrionica* by Wright, published
in 1699; and Collier's *Annals of the Stage*, vol. iii., p. 365, *et seq.*

from actor to actor; consequently, there would be no need either to print or to write them for the information of persons who would as a matter of course learn their bye-play from the oral communications of their stage-managers, who, in their turn, learned them in a similar manner from their predecessors belonging to the theatre.

Another suspicious circumstance in connexion with these emendations is the liberty taken by the " Old Corrector " in modernizing words. He has not stopped, as the *Edinburgh* Reviewer remarks, at his own supposed day, but has absolutely brought his modernizings down to the present century.

At the close of this branch of the inquiry, it may be not irrelevant to remark that whatever else may have been accomplished by the researches of the non-believers in the Notes and Emendations of the Devonshire folio, this at least has been done :—they have been the means of bringing forward evidence utterly destructive of the authority of the " Old Corrector." Even the most ardent supporters of the " Old Corrector " must now hesitate before they accept his emendations as valid authority *per se* of any reading ; and that, after all, is the more important branch of the question. Who the interpolator may have been is a matter of comparative indifference.

IV. What is the history of the folio in which these notes and emendations are found?

At the risk of seeming tedious, it will be necessary to recapitulate under this head many details with which most readers of these pages will in all probability be familiar. Viewed as a matter of feeling, the *Edinburgh* Reviewer is fully justified, no doubt, in his remark that the subject is a painful one to approach ; but justice alike to the impugners of the Devonshire folio and to Mr. Collier himself demands that it should not be passed over in silence.

As already stated, from the very moment that Mr. Collier gave to the world a sample of the Notes and Emendations in his folio, grave doubts were entertained of their genuineness ; and no long period elapsed before he was assailed on all sides by Shakespearian critics, who asserted that an attempt had been made upon their credulity, notwithstanding the statement given in his Preface relative to the volume. Having, however, been more directly attacked in an anonymous pamphlet, entitled "Literary Cookery," Mr. Collier thought it necessary to make an affidavit on the subject in the Court of Queen's Bench, in which he swore to the truth of the facts stated in his Preface, and made some further disclosures respecting the history of his obtaining possession of the volume in question.

As some new materials have been recently imported into this part of the case, which are at variance with Mr. Collier's statement, it will be necessary to give his own version of the story;* which is as follows:—

"In the history of the volume to which I have been thus indebted, I can offer little that may serve to give it authenticity. It is very certain that the manuscript notes in its margins were made before it was subjected to all the ill-usage it experienced. When it first came into my hands, and indeed for some time afterwards, I imagined that the binding was the original rough calf in which many books of about the same date were clothed; but more recent examination has convinced me, that this was at least the second coat it had worn. It is, nevertheless, in a very shabby condition, quite consistent with the state of the interior, where, besides the loss of some leaves, as already mentioned, and the loosening of others, many stains of wine, beer, and other liquids are observable; here and there holes have been burned in the paper, either by the falling of the lighted snuff of a candle, or by the ashes of tobacco. In several places it is torn and disfigured by blots and dirt, and every margin bears evidence to frequent and careless perusal. In short, to a choice collector, no book could well present a more forbidding appearance.

"I was tempted only by its cheapness to buy it, under the following circumstances:—In the spring of 1849 I happened to be in the shop of the late Mr. Rodd, of Great Newport Street, at the time when a package of books arrived from the country; my impression is that they came from Bedfordshire; but I am not at all certain upon

---

* *Notes and Emendations* (1852)—Introduction, p v.

a point which I looked upon as a matter of no importance. He opened the parcel in my presence, as he had often done before in the course of my thirty or forty years' acquaintance with him; and, looking at the backs and title pages of several volumes, I saw that they were chiefly works of little interest to me. Two folios, however, attracted my attention; one of them gilt on the sides, and the other in rough calf. The first was an excellent copy of Florio's " New World of Words," 1611, with the name of Henry Osborn (whom I mistook at the moment for his celebrated namesake, Francis,) upon the first leaf; and the other a copy of the second folio of Shakespeare's Plays, much cropped, the covers old and greasy, and as I saw at a glance on opening them, imperfect at the beginning and end. Concluding hastily that the latter would complete another poor copy of the second folio, which I had bought of the same bookseller, and which I had for some years in my possession, and wanting the former for my use, I bought them both, the Florio for twelve, and the Shakespeare for thirty shillings."

Mr. Collier goes on to state, " As it turned out, I at first repented of my bargain as regarded the Shakespeare, because, when I took it home it appeared that two leaves which I wanted were unfit for my purpose, not merely by being too short, but damaged and defaced; thus disappointed I threw it by, and did not see it again until I made a selection of books I would take with me on quitting London. In the mean time, finding that I could not readily remedy the deficiencies in my other copy of the folio 1632, I had parted with it; and when I removed into the country with my family in the spring of 1850, in order that I might not be without some copy of the second folio, for the purpose of reference, I took with me that which is the foundation of the present work.

" It was while putting my books together for removal, that I first observed some marks in the margin of this folio; but it was subsequently placed upon an upper shelf, and I did not take it down until I had occasion to consult it."

" It then struck me that Thomas Perkins, whose name, with the addition " his book," was upon the cover, might be the old actor, who had performed in Marlowe's " Jew of

Malta," on its revival shortly before 1633. At this time I fancied that the binding was of about that date, and that the volume might have been his; but in the first place I found that his name was Richard Perkins, and in the next I became satisfied that the rough calf was not the original binding. Still, Thomas Perkins might have been a descendant of Richard; and this circumstance, and others, induced me to examine the volume more particularly. I then discovered, to my surprise, that there was hardly a page which did not present, in a handwriting of the time, some emendation in the pointing or in the text, while on most of them they were frequent and on many numerous."

Further examination led to more important discoveries.— " Of course I now submitted the folio to a most careful scrutiny; and as it occupied a considerable time to complete the inspection, how much more must it have consumed to make the alterations? The ink was of various shades, differing sometimes on the same page, and I was once disposed to think that two distinct hands had been employed upon them. This notion I have since abandoned; and I am now decidedly of opinion that the same writing prevails from beginning to end, but that the amendments must have been introduced from time to time, during perhaps the course of several years. The changes in punctuation alone, always made with nicety and patience, must have required a long period, considering their number; the other alterations, sometimes most minute, extending even to turned letters, and typographical trifles of that kind, from their very nature could not have been introduced with rapidity, while many of the errata must have severely tasked the industry of the Old Corrector."

Such is Mr. Collier's statement in the year 1852, when he first printed some of these emendations in an 8vo. volume, before any suspicions had been raised as to their genuineness.

The statement thus put forth at leisure eight years ago, when the circumstances were more recent in his memory, was repeated by him in the following year, when he brought out a second edition; but, with an extraordinary reticence and inconceivable self-restraint, for which there is no satisfactory or assignable motive, instead of publishing these corrections at once, he dribbled them out piecemeal; first in the volume of 1852, "containing some, but not all the said MS. Emendations, &c.;" then in a second edition of the volume, which was published in 1853; and next in a one-volume Shakespeare,* published also in 1853, where such of them were given as "did not seem to require distinct and separate mention among the *Notes and Emendations* recently published." A professedly Complete List appeared only in 1856, at the end of Mr. Collier's edition of Coleridge's *Seven Lectures on Shakespeare and Milton;* and now it is in evidence that this professedly Complete List does not comprise one half of the manuscript emendations that exist in this folio; while, on the other hand, many that had appeared in the above-mentioned publications of 1852 and 1853, are not to be found in the List of 1856.†

Now such a mode of proceeding as this, really seems irreconcileable with the ordinary motives which actuate mankind; indeed, the writer in the *Edinburgh Review* himself, favourable as he is to Mr. Collier and the claims of the folio, cannot disguise his annoyance, when speaking of it.

"In possession of the mysterious volume," says the Reviewer, "Mr. Collier proceeded, however, to deal with it in so strangely inconsistent and inadequate a manner as to rouse, not unnaturally, the suspicions of his many ill-wishers. True to the instinct of his former literary career, always fumbling with the text of Shakespeare, advancing new conjectures and new discoveries by piecemeal, and never taking counsel of time and silence to ripen his own convictions, he first brought out, in 1853, his volume called 'Notes and Emendations from early MS. Corrections,' but which comprised a great deal of conjectural matter besides these corrections, and gave only fragments of the corrections themselves. Then followed his one volume edition of Shakespeare, professing to incorporate the corrections, but really incorporating only some of them, and without the slightest attempt to enable the reader to find out where the correc tions are; respecting which, we are half inclined to echo the sentiments of the infuriated Mr. Grant White:—'With all

---

* *The Plays of Shakespeare;* the text regulated by the Old Copies, and by the recently discovered Folio of 1632, containing early MS. emendations.
† See Note, page 40.

respect due from me to a gentleman, who was a man when my father was a boy, I must say that the publication of that volume was a crime against the republic of letters.' And, lastly, to omit other intermediate fidgettings with the subject, he published in 1856 his ' Seven Lectures on Shakespeare and Milton ' (a compilation from alleged original Notes, in which some hostile eyes have seen another forgery), and for some inscrutable reason, added, in an Appendix to this volume, what he terms ' A List of every Note and Emendation in Mr. Collier's copy of Shakespeare's works,' but which really contains, says Mr. Hamilton, not above half the emendations, we should have fancied, hardly a third or a fourth."

How, it may here be parenthetically inquired, can the writer of this article reconcile these statements of his own with his avowed belief in the alleged history of this unhappy folio since the year 1849 ?

Mr. Collier says, in his affidavit sworn in the Court of Queen's Bench, in 1856 :—

" And I say, that all the statements in the said preface and introduction, relative to the discovery, contents, and authenticity of the said folio copy, and the manuscript notes, corrections, alterations, and emendations thereof, are true; and that every note, correction, alteration, and emendation in each of the said two editions, and every word, figure, and sign therein purporting or professing to be a note, correction, alteration, or emendation of the text, is, to the best of my knowledge and belief, a true and accurate copy of the original manuscript in the said folio copy of 1632 ; and that I have not, in either of the said editions, to the best of my knowledge and belief, inserted a single word, stop, sign, note, correction, alteration, or emendation of the said original text of Shakespeare, which is not a faithful copy of the said original manuscript, and which I do not believe to have been written, as aforesaid, not long after the publication of the said folio copy of the year 1632."

According to Mr. Collier's reiterated statements,* *all* the emendations contained in the " Old Corrector " are

---

* Preface to *Coleridge's Lectures*, pp. 60, 73, and 79.

printed in his List of 1856, whereas it is now admitted that scarcely one-fourth is to be found therein; while again it is not a little singular that many of the emendations contained in the before-mentioned publications of 1853 are left out in the List of 1856.*

Again, in his *Reply* to Mr. Hamilton's letter, Mr. Collier refers to his affidavit sworn and filed in the Queen's Bench, January 8th, 1856; and he further states,—" I have shown and sworn that this very book was in the possession of a gentleman named Parry about half a century ago, given to him by a relation named George Gray."

On no point has Mr. Collier laboured more than to prove that the Devonshire folio belonged to Mr. Parry ; yet he

---

* The reader is not required to accept this fact upon assertion only. He is referred to Mr. Collier's three versions; they are the evidence in the matter.

Two or three instances, however, may be subjoined of the omission of emendations in the " *Complete List* " of 1856, which had appeared in the earlier editions. At page 222 of the edition of 1853, Mr. Collier states, " The folio of 1632 misprints the following line :—

" Give sorrow leave a while to tutor me,"

by absurdly putting *return* for 'tutor.' This blunder is *set right by the Old Corrector;* but it seems as if he had previously substituted some other word, and had erased it. *Such may have been the case in several other places* where he himself blundered." These are Mr. Collier's words, italics and all, upon which Mr. Singer remarks :—

" This is hardly candid on the part of Mr. Collier, for who would not think that 'this blunder was set right' by the sagacity of the corrector; whereas it is only the reading of the first folio, where the word is *tuture,* and the misprint had been corrected in all editions! Do not the frequent *erasures* in this corrected volume excite any suspicion in Mr. Collier's mind that it has been extensively tampered with."

After Mr. Singer's allegation, in these terms, of Mr. Collier's want of candour, Mr. Collier has thought proper to leave out the emendation in his " *Complete List* " of 1856.

In 1853 Mr. Collier writes, " The Corrector has ' as *surely* as I live,' of the quarto of 1597, instead of ' as sure as I live,' which is the reading of some of the folios and some of the quartos." Mr. Singer points out this emendation as a remarkable coincidence with Mr. Collier's adoption of it from the quarto of 1597. After Mr. Singer's remark, Mr. Collier forbears to insert this emendation in his List of 1856.

Again, in reference to the line which appeared for the first time in the Devonshire folio:—

" To brook control without the use of anger,"—(*Coriolanus,* Act iii. Sc. 2.)

Mr. Collier has adopted the line in his edition of Shakespeare of 1858, but has changed the word *control* to *reproof,* with this remark, " This line is from the corrected folio of 1632, and is clearly wanted, since the sense is incomplete without it." Mr. Collier, however, makes no allusion to the fact that he had three times previously (in 1852, 1853, and 1856,) printed the line in the form given above.

appears (undoubtedly, in the first instance, and, according to
Mr. Parry's statement, throughout the whole transaction,) to
have neglected the means which above all others would
have enabled him to obtain his desired end; viz., the exhibiting of the volume to Mr. Parry. Mr. Collier admits
that he did not exhibit it to him until after his Preface to
his edition of 1853 was finished, though he had talked to
him about the volume more than once; while Mr. Parry,
on the other hand, has publicly denied every particular that
Mr. Collier has asserted; and his truthfulness and memory,
it may be presumed, although Mr. Collier's senior by some
years, are as much to be relied upon as Mr. Collier's.
Mr. Parry can gain nothing by denying that the Devonshire
folio ever was his property, while Mr. Collier would be no
loser if he could prove it was.

In addition to this denial on the part of Mr. Parry, it
now appears that, while searching among his books and
papers, he has discovered the fly-leaf of his folio copy (which
had come loose while it was in his possession), and it has
been compared with the Devonshire folio. The result is, that
it does not fit this copy at all, being a quarter of an inch too
short, and a quarter of an inch too broad; a fact which goes
far towards substantiating Mr. Parry's declaration, when
he first saw the Devonshire folio at the British Museum,
and from which he has never deviated, that the margins of
his copy were wider than those of the (Devonshire) folio.

Mr. Collier, failing in his endeavour to prove that his folio
had belonged to Mr. Parry, and feeling it necessary to adduce
evidence that he bought the volume of Rodd in 1849, made
application to Dr. Wellesley by letter, a copy of which surely
ought to have been given, in addition to the Doctor's answer.
That answer, which Mr. Collier kept to himself for six months
before he thought proper to publish it, is as follows:—

"Woodmancote Rectory, Hurstpierpoint,
August 13th, 1859.

"Sir,

"Although I do not recollect the precise date, I remember
some years ago being in the shop of Thomas Rodd on one
occasion when a case of books from the country had just been
opened. One of those books was an imperfect folio
Shakespeare, with an abundance of manuscript notes in the

margins. He observed to me that it was of little value to collectors as a copy, and that the price was thirty shillings, I should have taken it myself; but, as he stated that he had put it by for another customer, I did not continue to examine it; nor did I think any more about it, until I heard afterwards that it had been found to possess great literary curiosity and value. In all probability, Mr. Rodd named you to me; but whether he or others did so, the affair was generally spoken of at the time, and I never heard it doubted that you had become the possessor of the book.

" I am, Sir,

" Your faithful and obedient servant,

" To J. P. Collier, Esq."　　　" H. WELLESLEY."

What was *generally* spoken of?—that Mr. Collier had purchased an imperfect folio of the second edition of Shakespeare, which (as he himself says) Mr. Rodd considered of no value? Was there anything remarkable in a man buying such a book? Even at this time that edition is by no means unattainable, and even less so was it then. But if the affair was *generally* spoken of, how is it that Mr. Collier was wholly ignorant of the reputation which he had thus gained? How, in fact, is this statement of Dr. Wellesley reconcileable with Mr. Collier's assertion of his indifference for, and neglect of, his new acquisition for a considerable period of time, a whole year, at the very least?* It seems altogether impossible to bring these conflicting statements into anything like consistency.

We do not at all impeach Dr. Wellesley's veracity, and readily admit that he has stated his impression of the facts; a statement quite reconcileable with the hypothesis that Mr. Collier did purchase a folio Shakespeare of Mr. Rodd in a very imperfect condition, scribbled over with marginal annotations of no value, as such copies often are; but it is our belief that the copy which Dr. Wellesley saw, and which Rodd described to him as of *little value to collectors,*

---

* " It remained *long in my possession before* I became acquainted with its great literary curiosity and value." (Collier's *Reply,* p. 10.) See the particulars as to the intervening lapse of time, in pages 36, 37, *ante.*

was not the copy which Mr. Collier calls the "Perkins Folio."*

Mr. Rodd, we are told, asserted that the copy he sold for 30s. was of little value to collectors. Would he have asserted this of a folio of 1632, enriched with marginal notes and emendations, and those apparently in the hand-writing of that period? Certainly not, or he would have acted in a manner that no other dealer in old books in this kingdom would.

Mr. Rodd was in the habit of buying and disposing of MSS., and books with MS. emendations, to the British Museum; which would have given him, probably, many times as many pounds, and would have been eager to possess the volume. He, too, was at that time the London Agent for the Shakespearian Society's publications. If there was one subject which he thoroughly understood, and one in which he took a commendable pride, it was in the matter of Shakespearian literature and Shakespearian emendations; and his great sagacity in such matters, equally with his interest, would prompt him to examine, with more than usual attention, all the MS. notes and names in works of this description.

Mr. Collier states, that neither Mr. Rodd nor himself was aware of the existence of any manuscript notes in the volume which he bought for thirty shillings; if so, Mr. Rodd must have known nothing about the inside of the volume. On what grounds, then, did Mr. Rodd fix the price? He knew that the true value depended entirely on the condition of the volume. Is it at all likely then that he would have fixed the price and sold the book without having first examined it, to ascertain its precise condition? Mr. Rodd was not the man to have been guilty of such an unbusiness-like proceeding. Moreover, it has been already shown, from Dr. Wellesley's letter, that Mr. Rodd *had* examined the volume, and

---

* "It may not be necessary to say more on the present occasion than that the Perkins folio came out of a parcel of books from the country; that I was in Rodd's shop when the parcel arrived; that I bought it for thirty shillings (neither Rodd nor myself being aware of any manuscript notes in it)." *Reply,* pp. 7, 8.

pronounced it "of little value ;" a thing that he certainly could never have said of the Devonshire folio, unless he had previously examined it, and had come to the conclusion that the emendations were worthless. In fact, the only inference that can fairly be drawn from Dr. Wellesley's letter is this, that if the volume he saw had been the Devonshire folio, Mr. Rodd's attention (supposing for a moment that it had not been previously given to it) would at that time, and from the very nature of Dr. Wellesley's inquiry, have infallibly been drawn to it; he would at once have seen that it was no ordinary volume, and would have lost no time in apprizing Mr. Collier of the lucky purchase which (to his own loss) he had made. Instead of which, Mr. Rodd, we are left to presume, let Mr. Collier take away his precious acquisition without one word more on the subject, to repose for at least twelve months on the shelves of one of the most indefatigable Shakespearian inquirers of the day, without being examined!

But Mr. Collier, we are told, purchased the volume in order to supply some missing leaves in a poor copy of that edition which he had already bought of the same bookseller. He would, therefore, naturally look into it to see whether or not it contained the leaves he wanted. On looking into it, could he possibly have failed to see that it was positively studded with marginal emendations thoughout?

How was it that he did not discover them at once? Did he by instinct open the volume at the very places where the pages he wanted ought to have been? And did he studiously avoid opening it anywhere else?

Let the reader take any copy of Shakespeare, the one even that he has in common use, and let him see whether he can hit, at two successive openings, on two given pages, in two plays, without making a search for them. Mr. Collier must either have done this, or he must have gone over the leaves to see if the volume contained those which he required; in doing the latter of which, it would seem to be wholly impossible that he could escape seeing the emendations which he himself tells us " were on most of the pages frequent, and on many numerous."

Taking all these points into consideration, it is impossible to avoid coming to the conclusion that Mr. Collier's account of the whole of this branch of the question is anything but satisfactory.

V. We proceed to the fifth division of this inquiry, viz., whether certain Letters and Papers relating to matters of Shakespearian interest, which Mr. Collier has printed or referred to, are genuine or not.

To begin with. " The Players' Petition," a document at present in the State Paper Branch of the Public Record Office.—It is without date, but purports to be a Petition to the Lords of Queen Elizabeth's Council, from certain Players (eight of whom are therein named, one of them being " William Shakespeare,") praying their Lordships' permission that they may finish the reparations and alterations in their Theatre in the precinct of the Blackfriars, and that their performances there may not be interrupted. Mr. Collier calls it " a Counter Petition by the Lord Chamberlain's Players," and he was the first to direct public attention to it, by printing it in his " *Annals of the Stage* " (1831). He there announces his belief that it is not the original Petition, but merely a copy without the signatures.

Now, if the paper thus printed by Mr. Collier be only a copy of the Petition, it is at least a very unaccountable circumstance that the *copy* should have been preserved in the public archives, and the *original* not be found there as well.

We can quite understand why a fabricator (not aware that it was unusual for petitioners, during the reigns of Elizabeth and James I., to subscribe their names to Petitions) should prefer that a document fabricated by him should be considered as a *copy*, rather than as an *original*, seeing that the former could be much more easily manufactured than the other He may have thought that in a document of this nature, if professing to be an original, it would be necessary to forge the signatures of eight persons,—a puzzling and awkward process; for though he might know how to imitate the signatures of some, yet he might not be acquainted with the signatures of all, and the failure of one would be the condemnation of the whole.

Mr. Collier, however, in one instance, says, "This remarkable paper has, perhaps, never seen the light, from the moment it was first presented, until it was recently discovered." Here he would seem to treat the document as an *original*, though in another place he has distinctly called it a *copy*. If it is not a contemporary copy,* the original would surely have been among the State Papers when the copy was made; and if it is a contemporary copy, why was it made? Surely not for the purpose of being preserved as a State Paper in lieu of the original.

Mr. Lemon, of the State Paper Branch Record Office, might possibly be able to throw some light on the subject; at any rate, as he is pretty confident of the fact of his father bringing the document in question under the notice of Mr. Collier, he ought to be able to say, with something like an equal degree of confidence, whether it was the *original* or the *copy* that his father placed before Mr. Collier, or both. And here, even at the risk of giving pain to Mr. Lemon, we must say, that in penning his hasty letter to the *Athenæum* (No. 1686), he has cast at least a shadow of a reproach upon his father's memory, by implying that he produced this "Petition" to Mr. Collier as a genuine document. If Mr. Lemon, Senior, really did produce this Petition, and pronounce it genuine, his judgment was marvellously at fault: but of the two alternatives, we should be inclined rather to doubt the accuracy of the son's memory than the father's skill as a palæographer; for we say, and say advisedly, that any one who could pronounce the "Players' Petition" to be genuine, would be totally unfit to hold the office that Mr. Lemon, Senior, held.

But supposing for a moment that the "Players' Petition" was a genuine document, and that the fact of its existence

---

* Although slightly anticipating what will be more fully discussed hereafter, this most curious coincidence here calls for some notice, that several of the spurious documents that have been noticed or printed by Mr. Collier are termed by him *copies*, instead of originals; viz., The Players' Petition; The Memorial attached to the Players' Petition; The Certificate from the Players of the Blackfriars Theatre to the Privy Council in 1859; The Letter signed H. S., and other papers in which Shakespeare's name occurs. Is it not "strange, passing strange," that copies of all these papers should have been religiously preserved, the *originals* being nowhere to be found?

had been discovered by Mr. Lemon, his first duty, on such discovery, would be to communicate the fact to Mr. Hobhouse, the head of his office, and to make an entry of the purport of the document in the official Repertory. There is no evidence that he did either; on the contrary, the Petition was never heard of by the public until Mr. Collier printed it in 1831. Viewing the matter, too, as one of feeling, and laying aside all considerations of duty, if Mr. Lemon, Senior, had indeed discovered this precious document, and been convinced of its genuineness, no reasonable doubt can be entertained that he would have been too eager to announce the fact to the public, and that the whole of literary England would have rung with the intelligence of his good fortune. He, of all men, was not the person to conceal it from the chief of his office, from his colleagues, from his personal friends, and from the whole body of Shakespearian scholars. He was much too alive to the pleasure of congratulation to have kept such a discovery secret for a period of four years (1825 to 1829), and then to have communicated it to Mr. Collier, at that time an unknown individual, and recently introduced to him by a mere acquaintance. Such, however, is Mr. Collier's statement. But how comes it that he never thought of this before? One would certainly suppose that Mr. Collier would have made some mention (as he has done in instances where Mr. Lemon* had introduced a document to his notice) of Mr. Lemon's kindness in placing a document of such surpassing interest as this before him; but, on the contrary, not the slightest allusion is there made to him in connexion with the "Players' Petition," although Mr. Collier states that it had been very recently discovered in the State Paper Office. Why should he *then* have concealed the fact that he *now* vouchsafes to tell us? Nay, more than this, Mr. Halliwell, in giving a printed fac-simile of the document in question, announced to the public that it was *discovered by* Mr. Collier; a statement which Mr. Collier has never contradicted until the moment when public attention is critically drawn to the subject.

---

* "The Minute in the Registers of the Privy Council (pointed out to us by Mr. Lemon) is this," &c. Again, "This new and valuable piece of information was pointed out to us by Mr. Lemon,"

There is another point, too, in Mr. Lemon's Letter that calls for notice, as tending somewhat to impugn the accuracy of his memory in reference to these transactions. He is only "pretty confident," he says, that his father first brought this document under the notice of Mr. Collier; but he speaks positively, or at all events seems to do so, as to the fact that this document "was well known to his father and himself *before* Mr. Collier began his researches in the office." Now it seems no more than reasonable to suppose that if he is only "pretty confident" in the one case, he can hardly be *more* than "pretty confident" in the other, which is more distant in point of time, and dating from a period prior to the alleged commencement of Mr. Collier's researches at the State Paper Office in 1829; a period at which, if we are not much mistaken, Mr. Lemon had nothing whatever to do with the State Paper Office in an official capacity, he having resigned his situation there in 1825, at the direction of the Under Secretary of State, "in order that he might devote his time exclusively to the Commission for printing and publishing State Papers," to which he had been appointed Assistant Secretary. This office he held until 1835, in which year he was appointed Second Clerk in the State Paper Office.

Under these circumstances, without meaning the slightest offence to Mr. Lemon, we cannot but be of opinion that he has spoken somewhat too hastily upon subjects which could hardly have come within his knowledge; viz., the existence of one document in particular, out of very many thousands, at a certain period of time, upwards of thirty years ago, the period of Mr. Collier's first admission into the State Paper Office; if indeed his letter can be construed to speak positively as to the latter point, which, after all, seems somewhat uncertain. Mr. Lemon, doubtless, is speaking the truth to the best of his belief; but not one iota beyond this can we admit.

To revert once more to the *Edinburgh* Reviewer, and *his* opinions on the "Players' Petition." Somewhat to our surprise, he boldly asserts (p. 484) that "the authenticity of the paper (the Players' Petition) is still maintained by the best authorities in the State Paper Office to be equal to that of any other document in the collection; and this opinion is curiously confirmed by the fact, that there are spots of corrosion by rust in the paper, which have eaten away not only the paper, *but the ink,* showing that the *writing,* as well as the paper, *is old.* The handwriting is not only not the handwriting of the Corrector, but it is of an essentially different character and period."

In the space of ninety words it is hardly possible to string together so many inaccuracies. In the first place, there is abundant reason for denying that " the authenticity of the paper˙is still maintained by the best authorities in the State Paper Office." Of the three Assistant Keepers of Public Records at the State Paper Branch Office, Mr. Lechmere, the chief, has hitherto declined to offer any opinion at all upon the subject; Mr. Lemon himself can at most be said to have expressed only by *implication* his belief in its genuineness; while the remaining Assistant Keeper, Mr. Hans Claude Hamilton, has stated his conviction that the so-called "Players' Petition " is an indubitable forgery.

Again, it is not the fact that " there are spots of corrosion by rust in the paper, which have eaten away not only the paper but the ink "; though, if there were such, it would point to an exactly opposite conclusion, as we could convince the Reviewer in two minutes, by affording him ocular demonstration. Further than this, our belief is, that the liquid with which the document was written was not what is commonly called 'ink,' or, at all events, the ink in use at that period. We admit that the paper is old, a century, perhaps, older than the writing; and as to the writing, if it is not that of the " Old Corrector," it is a very happy imitation of it, and bears a strong resemblance to that of some of the papers at Bridgewater House.

In the last place, the Reviewer commits an egregious error in reference to this subject (one that he might have avoided if he had only consulted so common a book as the "Royal Calendar " for 1859), in alleging, when making mention of the State Paper Office at Westminster, and the Record Office at the Rolls House, that, although under one head, " each department has its own staff of superior and subordinate officers, and its own distinct class of archives." This is not the fact; they are not distinct. The State Paper Office is only a branch of the Public Record Office, and the Deputy Keeper of the Public Records is the chief officer of the State Paper Branch, the whole being under his direction and management. He is, in fact, the responsible *Custos* of all the documents in the State Paper Branch, as well as in the Public Record Office itself. The Assistant Keepers located at the Public Record Office, are equally Assistant Keepers of the Branch at the State Paper Office, and *vice versâ*. Even more than this, the two offices have not their distinct archives. Both contain State Papers; though the Public Record Office contains, probably, the larger number of the two.

It is therefore a fallacy for the Reviewer to assert as he does that the officers of the State Paper Office were excluded from the official inquiry as to the Players' Petition; in addition to which, as already stated, Mr. Lechmere has, from the very first, declined to give an opinion as to the genuineness of this document. Mr. Lemon, too, had the opportunity, when he wrote his letter to the *Athenæum*, of distinctly stating his opinion as to the genuineness of the paper, but he forbore to do so.

As Mr. Collier and his supporters, however (notwithstanding the contradiction previously noticed), seem to hesitate at maintaining that the Players' Petition is genuine, it would be little better than a work of supererogation to prove that it is spurious. We therefore content ourselves with asserting that, be it original or copy, it was not written in the reign of Elizabeth or of James the First,—reigns which, of course, we particularly mention, because the handwriting is ostensibly an imitation of the handwriting of that period, and the context is intended to bear reference to the first of them. The orthography of the petition, the ink or pigment in which it is written, are not of those reigns, and the writing itself is tainted with clerical anachronisms; while the paper is, to all appearance, the fly-leaf cut out of a book, and certainly would never have been used either for an original Petition to the Council, or for an official copy of one. These assertions the officers of the State Paper Office, it is believed, will not be disposed to contradict. As yet they have shown no inclination to do so— (for even supposing Mr. Lemon's memory to be accurate in every respect, his evidence goes no way whatever towards establishing the genuineness* of the document),—though, on the other hand, the reserve shown by them on this point (with the exception of Mr. H. C. Hamilton), is not unlikely to be misconstrued as seeming to give countenance to the statements circulated in reference to the great literary value of this spurious production. That they entertain such an opinion in reference to it, it would really be an ill compliment to suppose; but if so, why did they not, immediately upon reading the certificate impugning the genuineness of the document, send to the Master of the Rolls a counter-certificate, declaring their own belief in its genuineness, and protesting against such a certificate being appended until further consideration had been given to the subject? Why, in such case, have they allowed Mr. Collier's assertions to be called in question, 'and himself defrauded of that testimony, whatever its value, to which he has a right at their hands, if they believe in its genuineness? This, if ever there was one, is a matter in which the semblance even of a mistake should not be allowed to exist.

This subject leads us incidentally to the consideration of another matter that has grown out of the question of the genuineness of this document; the graceless and improper insinuations that have been recently put forth by one or two Reviewers, to the effect that the Master of the Rolls has made himself a party, in appearance or by implication, in a personal attack upon a private individual.

What are the simple facts of the case? A complaint was made to the Master of the Rolls that one of the Public Records in his charge was of a suspicious character. He directed an inquiry to be made into the matter. He did no more than this; and he certainly could do no less; indeed the country had a right to demand that, in virtue of his office, he should institute such an inquiry. Had he acted otherwise than he did, we do not hesitate to say that he would singularly have failed in the performance of his duty as Keeper of the Public Records.

---

* The *Edinburgh Review* (p. 455) thinks proper to say of this document, in reference, we presume, to Mr. Lemon's Letter, "Its *authenticity* has since been confirmed by evidence which appears to us to be irresistible." Either the Reviewer must be a man very easily satisfied in point of evidence, or he must be totally ignorant what the word "*authenticity*" means.

Of course, it did not lie within his own province to act as judge in a matter of this description.   He therefore appointed a committee for the purpose, consisting of gentlemen whose daily study, for more than half their lives, has been the handwriting of the last six or eight centuries. These gentlemen came to the conclusion that the document was spurious, and gave their certificate accordingly ; this the Master of the Rolls directed to be appended thereto, in order that the present inquiry might not be lost to memory, should the same question ever arise in future This certificate did not charge, nor was it intended that it should charge, Mr. Collier, or any other person, either with fabricating the document or with inserting it among the Public Records.   It merely stated that, in the opinion of the persons there named, the writing was spurious,—a dictum that neither Mr. Collier nor Mr. Lemon has since attempted to repudiate.

On this point, however, it is quite unnecessary to enlarge; and we should be loth to bear the semblance even of obtruding ourselves upon the reader as defending one whose high and unassailable character needs no defence.   Even the little that has been said is based solely upon a determination that the truth shall be spoken, and that the public shall not be hoodwinked by insinuation or misled by a distortion of facts.

There yet remains to be noticed another fact connected with the Players' Petition,—we mean the loss of the Memorial which, Mr. Collier states, was appended to it when he last saw it.   We do not require Mr. Collier to explain this loss ; but we certainly do think that the officers of the State Paper Branch Office should do so.   Mr. Collier says that the authenticity of this Memorial has never been questioned ; perhaps not; but until it is produced and subjected to examination, it will be as well perhaps to withhold implicit confidence in its genuineness.

While on the subject of documents belonging to, or said to belong, to the State Paper Office, we would direct public attention to the disappearance of two other documents to which Mr. Collier has referred.—(1.) The Petition to the Privy Council from James Burbage and others in 1576, printed by Mr. Collier in his " *Annals of the Stage*,"

i. 227. (2.) Lord Pembroke's Letter, dated 27th August 1624. In reference to this last document, we have a Calendar made by Mr. Kempe, some twenty years since, of the papers of that period then in the State Paper Office. This Calendar has been lately printed by Mrs. Everett Green, and it makes no mention of this document; so that the paper must have been lost or removed more than twenty years ago, and apparently we have no memorial of its existence since it was used by Mr. Collier.

So much, then, for four documents made use of by Mr. Collier which he asserts were in the State Paper Office when he published his volume. One is positively declared, on no slight authority, to be spurious, and three others are now not forthcoming,—a curious coincidence, to say the least of it, and one that demands inquiry.

We now proceed to some examination of the papers alleged to have been discovered by Mr. Collier among the MSS. of the Earl of Ellesmere, in the Library at Bridgewater-house. They consist of the seven following documents, bearing reference to the life and times of Shakespeare :—

1. A paper " For the avoiding of the Play-house in the Blacke Friers."
2. A Letter of the poet Daniell.
3. A Certificate of the Players of the Blackfriars Theatre in reply to certain complaints.
4. The opinions of the two Chief Justices of either Bench concerning the jurisdiccōn, authoritie, and liberties claymed by the cittizens of London, within the precincte of the late dissolved howses of the White and Black Fryers of London, delivered the xxviith of Januarie 1579.
5. An Order to Robert Daborne and others to provide children for Her Majesty's Revels (dated 4th January 1609).
6. A copy of a letter from H. S. in favour " of the poore Players of the Black fryers."
7. Mainwaring's Account.

" The moment I discovered them," says Mr. Collier, speaking of these papers, " I carried them to the Earl of Ellesmere (then Lord Francis Leveson Gower), and read them to him.

At his lordship's instance I copied them, and left both originals and copies with his lordship."

The particulars of his discovery Mr. Collier afterwards communicated to his friend, Mr. Thomas Amyot, in the following words:—" When first I obtained permission to look through the Bridgewater MSS. in detail, I conjectured that it would be nearly impossible to turn over so many State Papers and such a bulk of correspondence, private and official, without meeting with something illus- trative of the subject to which I have devoted so many years; but I certainly never anticipated being so fortunate as to obtain particulars so new, curious, and important, regarding a poet who, above all others, ancient or modern, native or foreign, has been the object of admiration. When I took up the copy of Lord Southampton's Letter, and glanced over it hastily, I could scarcely believe my eyes to see such names as Shakespeare and Burbage in connection in a manuscript of the time. There was a remarkable coincidence also in the discovery, for it happened on the anniversary of Shakespeare's birth and death. I will not attempt to describe my joy and surprise; and I can only liken it to the unexpected gratification I experienced two or three years ago, when I turned out, from some ancient depositories of the Duke of Devonshire, the original designs of Inigo Jones, not only for the scenery, but for the dresses and characters of the different masques by Ben Jonson, Campion, Townsend, &c. presented at court in the reigns of our First James and Charles. The sketches were sometimes accompanied by explanations in the handwriting of the great artist, a few of which incidentally illustrate Shakespeare, who, however, was never employed for any of these royal entertainments. Annexed to one of the drawings was the following written description, from whence we learn how the actor of the part of Falstaff was usually habited in the time of Shakespeare:— ' Like a Sir Jon Falstaff: in a roabe of russet, quite low, with a great belley, like a swolen man, long moustacheos, the sheows [shoes] shorte, and out of them great toes like naked feete: buskins to sheaw a great swolen leg. A cupp coming fourth like a beake—a great head and balde, and a little cap alla Venetiane greay—a rodd and a scroule of parchment.*' "

---

* "New Facts regarding the Life of Shakspeare," in a Letter to Thomas Amyot, from J. Payne Collier, 1835.

" It is somewhat remarkable," says Mr. Hamilton, " that neither this drawing, nor the description of Falstaff, is to be found in the Shakespeare Society's volume, edited by J. R. Planché, Esq., from the Duke of Devonshire's Library.* The language of this ' description ' is, to say the least, suspicious." The orthography, Mr. Hamilton might have added, is conclusive against its authenticity.

Mr. Collier in this letter, it will be observed, dwells emphatically on the value of these documents ; but makes no observation on the handwriting that could raise a suspicion as to their genuineness, while he enters into all the particulars of their being found in bundles of MSS. which had probably never been examined since the days of Chancellor Ellesmere ; —a circumstance, he considers, which tells strongly in their favour.

To proceed, however, to an examination of the above-mentioned documents individually.

1. " For the avoiding of the Play-house in the Blacke Friers."†

---

* Mr. Hamilton, in his " Inquiry," p. 103, has called marked attention to the spurious character of a MS. volume of Ballads stated by Mr. Collier to be in his possession, and in a handwriting of the time of the Commonwealth, but which, from the internal evidence of the ballads published, as well as from a fac-simile of the handwriting of a portion of one of them, he pronounces to be unmistakeable modern forgeries. Mr. Collier has silently passed over Mr. Hamilton's challenge to him to produce the book, even though his supporter, the *Edinburgh* Reviewer, declares that in this particular instance Mr. Collier must be either deceiver or deceived.

" Mr. Collier," says the Reviewer, " published in 1839, as an extract from an alleged manuscript volume in his possession, a trashy ballad called *The Inchanted Island*, the plot of which is similar to that of *The Tempest*. Mr. Douce, he says, shook his venerable head, and called it one of the most beautiful ballads he had ever read ; which must have been in some strange fit of after-dinner enthusiasm. Mr. Collier conjectures that it was written between 1642 and 1660. It has been fac-similed for Mr. Halliwell. Mr. Hamilton says that the writing is suspicious ; of which we say nothing. But we fully agree with him that the intrinsic character of the verses themselves by no means serves to allay these suspicions. It would take a good deal to persuade us that lines in which it is said of a magician that—

> Sooth to say, in dangerous hour
> He had some more than human power ;'

in which a lady's hair is described as ' like to sunlit gold ;' and in which it is said of a father that ' his little Ida's morning smile made him forget his woe '—were by any very ancient ballad-monger. But we know not whether Mr. Collier in this particular instance is either deceived or deceiver." (*Edinb*- *Review*, No. 226, p. 483.)

† Printed in Mr. Hamilton's " *Inquiry*," p. 110.

This paper is cleverly executed, and might at first sight pass for a copy of a genuine document; but certainly neither for an original nor for a contemporaneous copy. The more, however, it is examined, the more suspicious it appears. The ink is not what the ink of that period was, and the paper has been evidently the fly-leaf of a book.

No one, probably, will contend that this piece is the original; and if it is not the original, it becomes of interest to know where the original is, and how a copy of this document should have been found among papers having no connexion whatever with those belonging to the Egerton family.

This circumstance not improbably influenced the late Lord Ellesmere, when he insisted on Mr. Collier keeping the document he had found, as it was no necessary part of the Egerton family documents.

> 2. A Letter * " To the Right Honorable Sir Thomas Egerton, Knight, Lord Keeper of the Great Seale of England, from S. Daniell." *

The statement that this is an original letter sent by Daniell to Sir Thomas Egerton is preposterous, and, to say the least, must have been made in utter ignorance; for neither in the handwriting, the ink, nor in any other particular does it bear any characteristic of the reign of Elizabeth.

If, on the other hand, it is asserted that it is a copy, how comes it that the copy of a letter addressed to the founder of this noble house should have been preserved, and neither the original preserved nor the fact of its having existed in any way recorded ?

> 3. A Certificate † of the Poore Playeres, being sharers in the Blacke Fryers Playhouse in November 1589.

This is written on a slip of paper, evidently taken from a book. Mr. Collier suggests that it passed into the hands

---

* Printed in Mr. Hamilton's " *Inquiry,*" p. 111.
† Printed in Mr. Hamilton's "*Inquiry*," p. 113.

of Lord Ellesmere, then Attorney General, and that it has
been preserved among his papers ever since. This, however,
must be an error, for Popham was Attorney General at that
time, and not Sir Thomas Egerton.

The document itself is of a most suspicious character;
and it is impossible not to agree with Mr. Collier that "it
seems strange that this testimonial should have come from
the players themselves. We should rather have expected
that they would have procured a certificate from some
disinterested parties."

The fabricator of the document, however, must have had
some reason of his own for making it in this form, which, of
course, it is not for others to pretend to divine. Be this,
however, as it may, no one who has the slightest pretensions
to a knowledge of the handwriting of the reign of Elizabeth, would hesitate for an instant in condemning the paper
from the writing alone; and we canot forbear expressing
our surprise that any person should venture to call this
document an original of the 16th century.

> 5. The opinions of the two Chief Justices of either Bench
> concerning the jurisdiccōn, authoritie, and liberties
> claymed by the cittizens of London, within the
> precincte of the late dissolved howses of the White
> and Black Fryers of London, delivered the xxvii[th] of
> Januarie 1579.

This piece is written in the Gothic hand of the 16th
century, and is supposed by gentlemen of acknowledged
skill in such matters to be a genuine document. Still, after
a close examination, to us its genuineness seems questionable
at least. Be this the case or not, it certainly is not an
original, but only a copy.

> 5. An Order * to Robert Daborne and others, to provide
> children for Her Majesty's Revels (dated 4th January
> 1609).

This document is perhaps the most transparent fabrication
of any that has been put forth as an original. As a fac-simile

---

* Printed in Hamilton's "*Inquiry*," p. 114.

of it has been published in Mr. Hamilton's "*Inquiry*," the reader has the opportunity of forming his own opinion ; and, if he has any knowledge of the handwriting of the reign of James I. he cannot fail to condemn it at once.

> 6. *Copia vera* of a Letter* from H. S. in favour of the poore Players of the Black fryers.

This piece professes to be only a true copy (*copia vera*, and has excited considerable attention.   It has no date, and is not addressed to any one,— a somewhat extraordinary circumstance, seeing that it is attested as *copia vera*.   For how can it be "*copia vera*" unless the name of the person addressed is also given ?   The fabricator of the paper must have felt this difficulty, but was at a loss how to remedy it.   He needed some such document probably to supply a link in a certain chain that he was weaving, and he knew that the less definite the document should be, the smaller the chance of detection.   He knew, in fact, that there would have been considerable risk in affixing either the date, the name of the writer, or the name of the person addressed.   Mr. Collier, however, when publishing the document, thus gets over the difficulty : " We may conclude," he says, " that the original was not addressed to Lord Ellesmere, or it would have been found in the depository of his papers, and not merely a transcript of it."   This argument, however, would seem hardly tenable, for how is it that the Lord Keeper did not preserve the original of the letter from the poet Daniell, which was addressed to him ?   Why should he have preserved the copy among his family papers, and not the original ?

" But," continues Mr. Collier, " a copy of it may have been furnished to the Lord Chancellor, in order to give him some information respecting the characters of the parties upon whose cause he was called upon to adjudicate." What cause ?—certainly none in the Chancery ; of that we have very good evidence.   But why should a letter addressed to some nameless person by an anonymous writer, signing himself H. S., be sent to the Lord Keeper ?   Mr. Collier supposes, though without a shadow of support, that the letter was written by the Earl of Southampton, and was sent by

---

* Printed in Hamilton's "*Inquiry*," p. 116.

the nameless person to the Lord Keeper merely to enlighten him as to the deserts of Shakespeare and Burbage! The idea cannot be entertained, for a moment even.

> 7. Rewardes to the vaulters, players, and dauncers. Of this x^{li} to Burbadge's players: for Othello, lxiii^{li}, xviii^s, x^d. Rewarde to Mr. Lillye's man, which brought the lotterye box to Harefield, x^{li}.

This document professes to be an account of the expenditure of the Lord Keeper of the Great Seal (signed by Arthur Mainwaring, who appears to have been his auditor) for the reception of Queen Elizabeth, on her visit to him at Harefield, in the beginning of August 1602. It furnishes a fact which, if it could be relied upon, would to a certain extent settle the question as to the date of the first appearance of the Tragedy of "Othello,"—a disputed point; some critics assigning it to 1604, others to 1611.

Mr. Collier produces this Account to prove that Burbadge's Players received from the Lord Keeper 63*l*. 18*s*. 10*d*. for playing Othello before the Queen, on Her Majesty's visit to Harefield, in August 1602; consequently, that the play must have been written and performed in London before that date.* Unfortunately, however, the paper upon which Mr. Collier rests his proof must be condemned as spurious. The difference between it and the others in the same volume of manuscripts, signed by Arthur Mainwaring, which are unquestionably genuine, is striking; and, although it is written on paper similar to the others, the writing, the ink, and the signature equally condemn it at once.

Speaking of these documents, Mr. Collier says,† " I admit, without reserve, that the weakest part of my case relates to the finding of Shakespeare documents among the late Earl of Ellesmere's MSS., at Bridgewater-house; and why is it the weakest part of my case? For this sole reason, that I never could have had any direct corroboration of my own testimony as to the discovery of them. Nobody was with

---

* *See* Mr. Collier's "*Introduction to Othello,*" vii. 493.
† "Reply to Mr. Hamilton's ' *Inquiry,*' " p. 34.

me at the precise moment, although the noble owner of the papers had been in the room only a few minutes before."

We agree with Mr. Collier, that it is unfortunate that no other person was present when he found these papers; and even more unfortunate is it that he never is able to cite the testimony of any living person as being present at the moment of any one of his discoveries.

But to follow Mr. Collier a step further.—" Mr. Hamilton," he says, " boldly begging the whole question, styles them ' the Bridgewater Shakespeare forgeries.' They may be ' forgeries,' but at that time it never entered my head that they could be so; and at that time I had never heard the fact, since mentioned, that Stevens had formerly been admitted into the rooms which held both the books and the manuscripts. I do not believe that he had any more hand in the forgeries than the Rev. H. J. Todd, with whom I once conversed about the papers, and who had, as I understood, for some years filled the office of librarian."

To say the least of it, this is a most unworthy insinuation. To remove suspicion from himself, Mr. Collier, by a sort of negative pregnant, would impugn the honour of two gentlemen long since deceased, and unable therefore to speak for themselves.

Every one who knows anything of the world, knows full well that the man who forges a document produces and makes it public in order that he himself may reap the benefit of his forgery; that it is " *sic vos non vobis* " least of all with a person of such crooked tendencies as these. Had either Stevens or Todd forged them, he would most assuredly have drawn the attention of the public to them, and would not have allowed another person to reap the benefit of his labours. Mr. Collier was both the discoverer of these documents and the editor of them as genuine; while, from his own admission, it would seem that he would not be very reluctant now to admit them to be forgeries.

But why is Mr. Collier indignant with Mr. Hamilton for calling these documents forgeries? He exhibited no such indignation in 1853 against Mr. Halliwell, who not only denounced them as such, but gave a fac-simile of one of the documents in question, with the view of substantiating his position.

" Fortunately for the interests of truth," says Mr. Halliwell, "indications of forgery are detected in trifling circumstances, that are almost invariably neglected by the inventor, however ingeniously the deception be contrived. Were it not for this, the search for historical truth would yield results sufficiently uncertain to deter the most enthusiastic inquirer from pursuing the investigation." To which he adds: " It is clearly Mr. Collier's duty, as a lover of truth, to have the originals carefully scrutinized by the best judges of the day."

An ordinarily sensitive man would surely, upon a challenge like this, have adopted such a course, rather than that a shadow of suspicion should rest upon his name. Mr. Collier forbore to do so; on the contrary, he has remained silent and inactive until now, when he assumes an air of indignation, and rises, armed at all points with insinuations, sneers, and insults, directed against every person who ventures to come forward to investigate, in the name of truth and learning, a great literary question. Mr. Collier, if conscious of being above all blame, ought to have been thankful to Mr. Hamilton for affording him, in whatever spirit, the opportunity of dispelling any suspicion that might lurk in the minds of Shakespearian scholars that he had brought before the literary world numberless supposititious emendations of the text of Shakespeare, and some equally supposititious facts connected with his life.

Having thus cursorily noticed the spurious Shakespearian papers in the Ellesmere Collection, we now come to the Dulwich documents of a like character, to which Mr. Collier has called the attention of the literary world. They consist of four papers, three of which are undoubtedly anything but genuine; and the fourth, known as " Mrs. Alleyn's Letter " to her husband, has been treated by Mr. Collier in a most extraordinary manner in the use which he has made of it. We take Mrs. Alleyn's Letter first.

Mr. Collier professes* to give the world a correct copy of this letter; but, on examination, his copy has been found

---

* *Memoirs of Alleyn*, p. 62.

to differ, in by far its most material points, from the original. In his version not only have words been left out and others inserted (we do not here allude to several inaccuracies of minor importance), but one entire passage—a most important one, containing a mention of William Shakespeare—has been introduced!

Subjoined is a correct copy of that portion of the letter to which we allude, accompanied by Mr. Collier's version of it. In italics are given the words, and fragments of words, which Mr. Collier has omitted, and in small capitals those which appear in their place. It will thus be seen at a glance, that there can be no mistake about the matter, but that in reality the passage in question does not exist, and never could have existed.

```
           "Aboute a weeke agoe there [cam]e a youthe who said he was
           Mr. Frauncis Chalo[ner]s man . . . . ld have borrow[e]d xs to
bought     have things for [h]is Mr. . . . . . . . . . . . . . t hym
           Cominge without . . . token . . . . . . . . . . d
           I would have . . . . . . . . . . . . . .
           & I bene sit . . . . . . . . . . . . .
           and inquire after the fellow and said he had lent hym a horse.  I
    us     feare me he gulled hym, thoughe he gulled not.  The youthe
   what    was a pretty youthe and handsom in appayrell, we know not became
           of him Mr. Bromffeild commends hym:  he was heare yesterdaye.  Nicke
           and Jeames be well, and commend them, so dothe Mr. Cooke and his weife
           in the kyndest sorte, and so once more in the hartiest manner
           farwelle
                        "Your faithfull and lovinge weife
                                        "JOANE ALLEYNE."
```

```
  "Aboute a weeke a goe there came a youthe who said he was
Mr. Frauncis Chaloner who would have borrowed xll to
have bought things for  *  *  *  AND SAID HE WAS KNOWN
UNTO YOU, AND MR. SHAKESPEARE OF THE GLOBE, WHO CAME
 *  *  *  SAID HE KNEWE HYM NOT, ONLY HE HEARDE OF HYM THAT HE WAS
A ROGE  *  *  *  SO HE WAS GLADE WE DID NOT LEND HIM
THE MONNEY  *  *  *  RICHARD JOHNES [WENT] TO SEEKE
and inquire after the fellow, and said he had lent hym a horse.  I
feare me he gulled hym, thoughe he gulled not us.  The youthe
was a pretty youthe, and hansom in appayrell:  we knowe not what became
of hym.  Mr. Benfield commendes hym;  he was heare yesterdaye.  Nicke
and Jeames be well, and comend them:  so doth Mr. Cooke and his wiefe
in the kyndest sorte, and so once more in the hartiest manner
farwell.
                "Your faithfull and lovinge wiefe.
                                "JOANE ALLEYNE."
```

It is not our intention to notice all the inaccuracies of Mr. Collier's version, but a few only of the most striking. The reader who is desirous of seeing them in their totality may consult Mr. Hamilton's "*Inquiry,*" pp. 91-93, where all the variations between Mr. Collier's text and the original letter at Dulwich College are printed in italics.

In the second line, 10s. has been misread as 10l., a thing that certainly betrays no little ignorance, as 10l. in those days would have equalled about 60l. of our present money

A strange youth calls on Mrs. Alleyn, and asks the loan of 10*l.* as coolly as he would have asked for as many pence!

But the really unpardonable discrepancy in this case is the introduction of the following words,—words which are not, and never by any possibility could have been, in the original :—" *and said he was known unto you, and Mr. Shakespeare of the Globe, who came . . . said he knewe hym not, only he hearde of hym that he was a roge . . . . so he was glade we did not lend him the monney . . . . Richard Johnes* [*went*] *to seeke ;*" while not one of the ten words in this place, which really do exist and are plainly visible in the original document, is to be found in Mr. Collier's version.

The fact is indisputable that he has put fourteen lines in the space that in reality is occupied by thirteen only in the original ; while the terminations of the third and fourth lines in the above extract are wholly changed, and nine words, which are distinctly legible at the beginning of the fourth, fifth, and sixth lines, are suppressed.

In defending himself against the charges brought against him in reference to this letter, Mr. Collier, it seems hardly too much to say, is at once evasive and illogical. He says :* " Now the question is, and the only question of the slightest importance (though that is in truth of little moment), whether the name of ' Mr. Shakespeare, of the Globe,' occurred in the most rotten and fragmentary part of the letter at the time when I copied it. Whether it did or did not, is not of the smallest interest as regards the biography of our poet."

Mr. Collier is correct, no doubt, in saying that the question is not of the smallest interest as regards the biography of our poet ; but, in reference to the trustworthiness and accuracy of Mr. Collier, it cannot but be of the greatest importance that the words should be where he has alleged that he had seen them to be.

He further states :—" I do not deny that it is possible I misread some utterly unimportant letters and words."

* " *Reply,*" p. 48.

Unfortunately, however, not only has Mr. Collier misread what he thinks proper to call " unimportant " words, but he has omitted several which are evident to even an unskilled eye, and has inserted words, indeed whole sentences, where they never could have occurred. But to proceed with his statement. He says : " I am absolutely certain that ' Mr. Shakespeare, of the Globe,' was spoken of in it in the way I stated. Mr. Hamilton asserts that ' there is not the smallest trace of authority for any allusion to Shakespeare.' This may be very true ; he is speaking of Mrs. Alleyn's letter in its present condition, but that is not the question. The question is, whether, when I saw the letter, some thirty or even more years ago, the name of ' Mr. Shakespeare, of the Globe,' was not to be traced."

Now, in answer to this, we maintain with Mr. Hamilton, and so must every other person who is possessed of eye-sight and common understanding, that not only is it not there now, but that it never could by any possibility have been in the place where Mr. Collier asserts it was ; any more than that those words could have been added to the document since Mr. Collier saw it which have been omitted by him. Under these circumstances, if Mr. Collier could call twenty dead friends, in addition to the one he invokes,* it would make no difference in his favour ; facts speak for themselves, and neither dead nor living can gainsay them.

Another link—one of circumstantial evidence—may be added to the argument already adduced. Malone, that careful Shakespearian critic and indefatigable inquirer, had the box of papers which contained this letter to look over and examine at his leisure. Surely, if he had discovered any allusion to William Shakespeare, whose very name would in his estimation have hallowed the paper whereon it was written, he would have made some note or mention of it ; but we turn to him in vain for corroborative evidence of Mr. Collier's assertion.

A few more words in reference to Mrs. Alleyn's letter. Mr. Collier states† that he carefully enclosed the letter in

* " *Reply*," p. 49.
† " *Reply*," p. 50.

E

paper after he had copied it, and that either he or his now deceased friend wrote on the outside of the paper, that within was a document of value, which should not be roughly handled; and he asks whether it is likely he would have done so had he purposely misstated the import and contents of a letter that was in a state of ruinous decay? Would not the natural course for him to pursue have been to have left the letter as it was, in the hope that when it was next seen and consulted, as much of it might have disappeared as possible? He further asks,—If he had misrepresented the contents of the crumbling relic, what was to prevent his rubbing away a little more of the old paper, and who then would have been able to detect the trick he had played?* Now, the only answer to this is, that true it is, there is in the tin box at Dulwich College a sheet of paper enclosing this identical document, with a memorandum written in pencil to the above effect; but, singular to relate, this memorandum is not in the handwriting of Mr. Collier, nor yet of his friend Mr. Amyot, as the writer of the article in *Notes and Queries* has inconsiderately asserted.

A fac-simile of that portion of the letter which is the subject of the present discussion was made by that careful and expert artist, Mr. Fairholt; and which agrees *verbatim et literatim* with the fac-simile made by Mr. Nethercliffe, Junior, as given in Mr. Hamilton's " Inquiry."

Too much, it may possibly be thought, has been said upon this branch of our subject; but it is one of so much importance in the enquiry, that it could hardly have been dismissed in fewer words.

To proceed, however, with the other documents at Dulwich College.

The next document that calls for notice is a paper in verse, consisting of seventeen lines, called by Mr. Collier

---

* It is somewhat strange that, in his earlier answer to Mr. Hamilton, which appeared in the *Athenæum*, Mr. Collier makes no allusion to the circumstances of his having placed the " crumbling relic " in a sheet of paper and indorsed it with the caution we have here mentioned. The Editor of the *Athenæum* was the first to assert in print that the indorsement is in Mr. Collier's handwriting.

" The Players' Challenge," and commencing "Sweet Nedde, now wynne an other wager." It was printed by him in 1841, in his " *Memoirs of Alleyn*," p. 13.

A cursory examination of this paper must convince most persons at all acquainted with handwriting of the sixteenth and seventeenth centuries that it is spurious. It is, however, neatly written, and would not improbably deceive a person inexperienced in palæography. Mr. Collier says :* " I have no particular recollection of the manner in which it is written ; but, contrary to what Mr. Hamilton says, that it is ' executed with singular dexterity,' it now seems to me that the re-duplication of consonants, and other points of orthography in it, might possibly raise suspicion." Mr. Collier is right. The facts that he mentions do raise suspicion,—a suspicion which we are surprised did not cross his mind when he published the document, and which is not confined to the orthography alone.

The Letter from Marston, the dramatist, to Hensloe, also printed by Mr. Collier in his " *Memoirs of Alleyn*," p. 154, is another of these Dulwich documents. " It refers," says Mr. Collier, " to a play by Marston, on the subject of Columbus, of which we have no other authority." In this letter, pencil-marks are visible, faintly indeed, for the most part, though in one or two instances they are pretty distinct; and not so very faint are they but that in them nearly every word of the letter can be distinctly traced. As to the letter itself, written in ink, it is evidently penned in imitation of Marston's hand. To a practised eye, however, the difference between the genuine handwriting of Marston and this imitation is quite perceptible; and there cannot be the slightest doubt that the document is a fabrication.

The next paper at Dulwich which calls for notice, is a " List of Players," in which Shakespeare's name occurs. It is printed in the " *Memoirs of Alleyn*," p. 68, and Mr. Collier himself admits that it is in a different ink from that used in the document to which it is appended. The document to which the List of Players is attached is genuine, no doubt, and is noticed by Malone in his " *Inquiry*" (1796); but he

---

* " *Reply*," p. 54.

makes no allusion whatever to any List of Players being thereto annexed. However, Mr. Collier, when in 1841 he published the List in question, suggested that Malone's reason for passing it over was, that he intended to use the information contained in it in his Life of Shakespeare which he did not live to publish.

Mr. Collier's suggestion is by no means satisfactory. It seems little short of incredible that Malone should have passed over such a remarkable paper without some notice of it, if he really had seen it. His was no hurried inspection of the Dulwich papers, for they remained in his hands for several years. It is more than probable, then, that he saw this document many a time, and if so, he could not have overlooked the List of Players attached to it. Be this, however, as it may, the handwriting proclaims the " List of Players " to be spurious.

We cannot dismiss the name of Malone without calling attention to another subject; one that certainly seems to demand some explanation at Mr. Collier's hands, if he would prevent the literary world from judging him by his own apparent estimate of honour and morality. In pp. 46, 47, of his *" Reply"* to Mr. Hamilton, we find the following passage— (the italics are our own) :—

" Let it be borne in mind that the documents which Malone here and elsewhere refers to were, in fact, the property of the Master, Warden, and Fellows of Dulwich College ; that Malone had *quietly* taken possession of them ; that they remained in his hands for several years ; that *he did exactly what he liked with them ;* that he *cut off signatures* of old dramatists and players, to place them on the title-pages of his own books; and that *he or others mutilated* ' *Henslowe's Diary,*' in such a way that some of the most valuable portions are entirely lost. Even the books the title-pages of which he decorated with the old autographs, had belonged to Dulwich College ; for *he contrived to persuade* the Master, Warden, and Fellowes of that day that old plays and old poetry did not half so well become their shelves as the musty divinity, dull chronicles, and other volumes of the same sort, which he substituted ; hence the bulk of his collection. And he must have *chuckled amazingly at his success in persuading unsuspecting people to make an exchange of*

*works, which would sell for hundreds of pounds, for others not
worth as many shillings.* So of the manuscripts ; they seem
to have allowed Malone to carry away such as he pleased,
to keep them as long as he pleased, *and to return such as he
pleased, in the state which he pleased.* Some that *he did not
return* found their way again to their old home, after his
death ; and it is not very long since the College, most
properly, bought back a bundle of papers that must have
originally come out of its archives."

Now, if we know anything as to the force and meaning of
the English language, this is a circumstantial description
of the thoughts and actions of none other than a violator
of the ordinary ties of honour, friendship, and integrity ; in
other words, a swindler and a rogue. But be this as it may,
it is Mr. Collier's deliberate description of the doings and
dealings—so far as Dulwich College was concerned—of
Edward Malone.

We next turn to page 53 of Mr. Collier's " *Reply,*"—the
italics again our own.

" If any of the documents returned to Dulwich College
after Malone's death appear to have been tampered with, I
most distinctly acquit him of any such misconduct. Whatever I may be in the opinion of my adversaries, I feel sure
that he was *a man of honour and principle.*"

How does Mr. Collier reconcile this passage with the
distinct statements and the downright assertions as to
Edward Malone made by him in the passages that have
been previously quoted ? If the conduct there imputed
to him is in any way reconcileable with Mr. Collier's code
of " honour and principle," all that we have to add is, that
we are far from surprised at the phase this most unhappy
controversy has now assumed.

It is necessary, before concluding these remarks, to bestow
some notice upon an argument, if, indeed, an argument it
can properly be called, which is prominently put forward by
Mr. Collier in his " *Reply,*" and, indeed, repeated by him
again and again.

This is the gist of his charge; that his opponents, and more particularly what he calls the MS. Department of the British Museum, of which he styles Mr. Hamilton " the mouthpiece," entertain certain feelings of personal enmity against himself. As to the motive for making this charge, it is obvious. All persons, particularly the English public, have an instinctive love of fair play ; and if it could be shown that a man, entertaining feelings of personal animosity against another, had taken advantage of a plausible opportunity for gratifying his malignity and resentment, the feelings of the community would assuredly be strongly enlisted in favour of the object of the attack. Still stronger would that feeling be, if the person attacked were an aged man of literary acquirements and unblemished reputation; and least of all would such a violation of propriety be tolerated, if committed by one literary man against another.

It is not too much to say that such assailants, and under such circumstances, would find disfavour from all ; their arguments would be unwillingly listened to, and their conclusions reluctantly admitted; while any plausible answer in excuse would be eagerly accepted, nor would the public be very eager to inquire into the exact balance of merits in such a contest as this.

Still, however, in reference to such a case as the present, the public would, in equal justice, deem itself bound to distinguish between the hostility which is the result of the indignation natural to honourable men, who, after a fair and impartial investigation, have had the suspicion forced upon them that a series of literary deceptions had been committed, and *that* hostility, which, springing from a previously existing enmity, has seized a favourable occasion to inflict an injury upon a literary colleague.

In the former case a certain amount of hostility—not unmixed, perhaps, with different feelings—might be fairly supposed to be the natural and inevitable consequence of a suspicion, amounting to reasonable belief, that so grave an offence had been committed. For what graver offence could possibly be committed against the republic of letters than the forgery of documents and annotations connected with the name of a deceased writer, for every fact connected with whom the last century and a half have been athirst ?

proving a source of error and confusion to the literary world, and this, merely to gratify the fabricator's literary ambition, or to conduce to his profit.

An offence of this description unsettles literary questions, introduces distrust into the assertions of authors, compels the reader to test for himself the truth of everything he reads, and above all tends to lower the standard of English literary honesty in the eyes of the enlightened men of other nations. Well, then, might the literary men of England, and especially those connected with a department so peculiarly interested in such questions as is the MS. Department of the British Museum, feel indignant, if such a case, in their belief, were made out ; and as readily would the public excuse any one who had advocated the cause of what he sincerely believed to be the truth, with more than ordinary warmth.

Now, in reference to the language of his " Reply," Mr. Collier evidently had this distinction present to his mind; for he labours to persuade his readers, not so much that the articles recently written in reference to his Shakespearian discoveries contain marks of hostility, as that those articles are the result of a previously existing enmity. He feels that it is not sufficient for him to show that such a relation *now* exists between himself and those who impugn his statements, but that, in order to enlist the public in his favour, he must establish the fact that he is the object of a previously existing hostility, and that this is an occasion taken for its display.

And how does Mr. Collier prove this? Assuming its existence, and reasoning from it as from a fact that is undoubted and undeniable, he would evidently ascribe it to the literary reputation which he has acquired.

In his " Reply "* to Mr. Hamilton, he says : " I have always striven to make myself as unobjectionable as I could, but even my small reputation, in an inferior department of letters, seems to excite envy ; and I foresaw, that when Lord Campbell, as a kind compliment to that reputation rather than to my merits, addressed to me his letter ' On the Legal Acquirements of Shakespeare,' it would materially tend to exasperate

---

* Page 6.

my enemies. It had not long been published before
Sir F. Madden, &c. wrote to the Duke of Devonshire, in
order to borrow the Perkins folio; and having procured it,
Mr. N. E. S. A. Hamilton 'seized the opportunity,' as he
himself expresses it, of subjecting it, with the aid of Sir
F. Madden and others, to the most rigorous examination."
He further ascribes the hostility of Sir F. Madden, as will be
seen, to other unintentional causes of offence,—supposed
neglect (pp. 11, 70), and services rendered on two occasions
(pp. 28, 29). Mr. Arnold also he assumes to be his personal enemy, and vaguely suggests that it is to something
that had passed between him and the father of that most
estimable and enlightened magistrate,* that he is indebted
for this enmity.

Occasionally, however, Mr. Collier seems to profess
himself at a loss to account for this unmerited hostility. At
one time he suggests that the cause of the enmity of the
Museum officials may have arisen from his not having
especially invited them to see the folio when he publicly
exhibited it; and then, in a similar spirit, he proceeds to say:
" I have been told, but I do not believe it, that Sir
F. Madden and his colleagues were irritated by this piece of
supposed neglect, and that they also took it ill that I presented the Perkins folio to the kindest, most condescending,
and most liberal of noblemen, instead of giving it to their
institution. When I placed it in the hands of the Duke of
Devonshire, I knew that for any literary purpose it would
be just as accessible,† and just as safe in his Grace's library
as in that of the British Museum." In another place‡ he
evidently seems inclined to ascribe their hostility to his
having been recommended to the Queen to fill the office of
Principal Librarian of the Museum. Again, he suggests that

---

* " If Mr. T. J. Arnold be the son of the late S. J. Arnold, the dramatist,
perhaps I can understand part of the cause of his undeserved animosity towards
me. It may be an entirely different, but not an indifferent person."—*Reply*,
page 7.
† This is a fallacy, seeing that as the Duke of Devonshire's Library was not
open to the public, while that of the British Museum was, the former could
not, for literary or any other purposes, be deemed as accessible as the latter.
Indeed, to place it in the Duke's Library was the very way to hide it from the
public view; for the Duke might with justice have refused the applications of
the literary public, a thing that neither Mr. Collier nor the Museum could
have done.
‡ " *Reply*," p. 30.

the officers of the Museum may possibly owe him * some ill-will for finding them work, in procuring three large cases of Bentinck MSS. from Germany; he thus having been "the innocent means of procuring for them occupation." In another place,† he says: "How and why the MS. authorities of the British Museum have been heated into such animosity towards me, I cannot pretend to explain. I was always on good terms with Sir F. Madden, whom I have known for more than a quarter of a century, and upon two occasions I was of service to him. Of one of them I can say no more; but of the other I may remark that it occurred within the last two or three years, and it was when he had involved himself in an awkward scrape, by purchasing MSS. which he ought to have known had been dishonestly come by. * * * *." "Some men can forget an injury, who never can forgive an obligation;" but still, he‡ "cannot for a moment suppose that Sir F. Madden and the younger officers of the Museum have taken any antipathy to him on that score."

The public, no doubt, will, equally with Mr. Collier, be unable from such causes as these to account for such hostility as he imputes to those gentlemen who have done no more than exert themselves to solve the question as to the genuineness of the annotations in the Devonshire folio,‖ and to prove the existence of certain forgeries in the shape of documents professing to contain the poet's name.

Should it be urged by Mr. Collier, in reference to these charges of preconceived hostility, that he requires nothing beyond what is contained in the publications against him to prove the truth of his assertion, this will not answer his purpose. It is a mere begging of the question, and in reality leaves the question wholly untouched. Is all this mere animosity? or is it the result of an enforced conviction that

---

* "*Reply*," p. 62.   † "*Reply*," p. 28.   ‡ "*Reply*," p. 30.
‖ So great an offence is this in Mr. Collier's eyes, that his insinuations as to unfair motives extend beyond the British shores. Speaking of the criticisms which appeared on the publication of "*Notes and Emendations*," he says :— "In Germany both it and I have been violently assailed by critics of every grade ; in some instances with a degree of personal rancour, for which I can only account on the supposition that I have unwarily, unwittingly, and sometimes unavoidably, neglected publications which have been sent to me as presents from their authors."

F

the writings and documents in question are forgeries? If the latter, which, for our own part, we are convinced really is the case, Mr. Collier's charges of hostility are a mere fallacy, and of course the question is left exactly where it was. That question is this: Does the evidence establish, first, that these documents are forged, these annotations modern? And, next: Is Mr. Collier, according to the existing evidence, so connected with them as to justify something more than mere doubt and hesitation on the part of careful and impartial investigators?

If we look abroad into the world, we shall find that the charge of hostility, derived in reality from the matter in question itself, but ascribed to preconceived enmity, is one of common occurrence. It is a matter of almost every-day experience for the losing party in a suit to say that some of the jurors were his enemies. The defendant in a Chancery suit is not uncommonly heard to express his surprise that the judge has shown such remarkable animosity towards him, and to profess himself at a loss to know what he could have possibly done to deserve or occasion it. A pertinent illustration of this will be familiar to the recollection of all who are well acquainted with the writings of the late Rev. Sydney Smith, who, having severely castigated certain of the States of the North American Union for the repudiation of their public debts,— their refusal, in fact, to pay either principal or interest of monies received by them, and of which the inhabitants of the State had received the advantage—was met by various answers; in most of which, however, was prominently put forward, by way of exordium, an expression of surprise as to what could be the cause or origin of all this hatred of our American brethren. Sydney Smith's reply is so very germane to a controversy of this description that we cannot but commend it to the notice of the reader.*

Possibly, however, too much may have been said on this point. Still, as Mr. Collier repeats it so often, and makes it so leading, indeed, so offensive a feature of his defence, a more elaborate notice of it may be justified than in reality would have been due to any real claims to notice that it possesses.

---

* *Miscellaneous Works of the Rev. Sydney Smith* (1859), vol. ii., p. 330.

For ourselves personally (and, indeed, for all those who have arrived at conclusions in this investigation similar to our own, so far as the opportunity has been afforded us of penetrating into their thoughts or motives,) we can honestly say that we disown any species of personal animosity against Mr. Collier.   Indeed, so far as we ourselves are concerned, we entertain more of another feeling than of the indignation which, as already observed, might naturally spring from a reasonable belief in the truthfulness of the charges made by Mr. Collier's opponents: but still, we feel ourselves bound to say that, convinced as we are that the documents in question are spurious, and the annotations in the folio of modern fabrication, and that Mr. Collier has by no means satisfactorily explained his connexion with them, our sorrow and our indignation are not unmingled with a sense of humiliation for the discredit that this controversy, under its present aspect, must of necessity throw on the character of English literary men.   It has been no agreeable task for us to take the course we have done; but we cannot but deem it the bounden duty of every man (and more especially of one who by avocation is devoted to the promotion of literature and the establishing of historic truth), at whatever sacrifice, to do his utmost towards setting in their true light a series of demands upon the public credulity, by which, connected as they are with a name of world-wide renown, the unenquiring portion of the literary world might possibly be most seriously misled.

LONDON :

Printed by GEORGE E. EYRE and WILLIAM SPOTTISWOODE,
Printers to the Queen's most Excellent Majesty.

Lightning Source UK Ltd.
Milton Keynes UK
UKOW042229040413

208697UK00001B/65/P